REVITALIZING THE WORLD TRADING SYSTEM

In recent years, the world trading system has been confronted by a range of new and developing challenges: the risk of climate change, the rapid growth of the digital economy, and the ongoing impacts of COVID-19 and the threat of future pandemics, to name but a few. In this book, veteran trade negotiator Ambassador Alan Wm. Wolff draws from his years of experience at the World Trade Organization to consider the history of trade, the current trading system, and how it should be reformed in the future. Offering a rare insight into the inner workings of the WTO, Wolff is uniquely placed to identify deficiencies in the current system and suggest actionable solutions. This essential guidebook to the WTO equips readers with the tools and knowledge required to tackle emerging and emergent challenges of a global trading system.

Ambassador Alan Wm. Wolff is a Distinguished Visiting Fellow at the Peterson Institute for International Economics, and was co-Acting Director General (2020–21) and Deputy Director-General of the World Trade Organization (2017–21). He is a leader in the field of international trade, with over five decades of experience as a trade lawyer and trade negotiator. He is a member of the Council on Foreign Relations (CFR) and the Friends of Multilateralism Group (FMG).

Revitalizing the World Trading System

ALAN WM. WOLFF
Peterson Institute for International Economics

CAMBRIDGE
UNIVERSITY PRESS

CAMBRIDGE
UNIVERSITY PRESS

Shaftesbury Road, Cambridge CB2 8EA, United Kingdom

One Liberty Plaza, 20th Floor, New York, NY 10006, USA

477 Williamstown Road, Port Melbourne, VIC 3207, Australia

314–321, 3rd Floor, Plot 3, Splendor Forum, Jasola District Centre, New Delhi – 110025, India

103 Penang Road, #05–06/07, Visioncrest Commercial, Singapore 238467

Cambridge University Press is part of Cambridge University Press & Assessment, a department of the University of Cambridge.

We share the University's mission to contribute to society through the pursuit of education, learning and research at the highest international levels of excellence.

www.cambridge.org
Information on this title: www.cambridge.org/9781009289313

DOI: 10.1017/9781009289290

First published 2023

A catalogue record for this publication is available from the British Library.

Library of Congress Cataloging-in-Publication Data
NAMES: Wolff, Alan Wm. (Alan William), author.
TITLE: Revitalizing the world trading system / Alan Wm. Wolff, Peterson Institute for International Economics (PIIE).
DESCRIPTION: Cambridge, United Kingdom ; New York, NY : Cambridge University Press, 2023. | Includes bibliographical references and index.
IDENTIFIERS: LCCN 2022050936 (print) | LCCN 2022050937 (ebook) | ISBN 9781009289313 (hardback) | ISBN 9781009289320 (paperback) | ISBN 9781009289290 (epub)
SUBJECTS: LCSH: Foreign trade regulation. | World Trade Organization.
CLASSIFICATION: LCC K4600 .W65 2023 (print) | LCC K4600 (ebook) | DDC 343.08/7–dc23/eng/20230105
LC record available at https://lccn.loc.gov/2022050936
LC ebook record available at https://lccn.loc.gov/2022050937

ISBN 978-1-009-28931-3 Hardback
ISBN 978-1-009-28932-0 Paperback

For Hélène
Without whom none of this would have been possible for me

Contents

Foreword

The European Union and the United States were two main players during the formative years of the WTO. Both Alan Wolff and I were active in various roles with respect to the evolution of the two trading partners' trade policies and global trade arrangements over an extended period: We both served at the WTO at different times and in different capacities. I was Director-General of the organization during the financial crisis and during the attempted last great round of trade negotiations, the Doha Development Agenda. Alan was Deputy Director-General serving at the WTO at the beginning of the important innovation consisting of open plurilateral negotiations called "Joint Statement Initiatives" and through the onset and brunt of the COVID-19 pandemic. We both had had long careers in international trade, I was a senior official in the French government and then with the European Commission as Trade Commissioner. He served in the US government, first at the US Treasury and later as Deputy US Trade Representative, before entering private trade law practice in Washington and becoming chairman of the Board of the National Foreign Trade Council.

We share a commitment to the premise that the WTO has continuing great potential as a force for good in the world. The recent Twelfth WTO Ministerial Conference demonstrated that finding common ground is possible. It showed what could be done with new leadership at the WTO, with a change in administration in Washington, with renewed dedication to multilateralism in Brussels, and with a Chinese government quietly assuming a positive role in reaching widely supported negotiated outcomes. People matter, leadership matters.

The progress in Geneva at the Ministerial Conference is praiseworthy but it is mainly an installment that provides much-needed breathing space. This race is not a sprint, but a marathon, a hardship I happen to be familiar with. One cannot say that the risks to an open multilateral trading system are over, far from it. The challenges are very great. The COVID pandemic is still causing both continuing damage to human health and to the world economy. The effects of climate change and of biodiversity loss are growing. The digital economy does not have a set of common rules that would help avoid its fragmentation. Agricultural and industrial subsidies are growing, not declining. Inflation is back. War has returned to the European continent, and the trade upon which food security depends has been disrupted. The hardest problems have not been solved and whereas the risks of deglobalization are overstated in my view, they exist. I have thought for a long time that globalization was efficient while often painful for the weakest. I now believe that deglobalization would be inefficient and painful for all.

The leaders of the G20 and the G7 have repeatedly called for WTO reform. The WTO trade ministers have now promised to deliver. They have a very large task before them. This guidebook to the WTO – past, present, and future – could not be more timely. Reform of the WTO cannot substitute for leadership from the largest trading members, but it can provide them with better institutional tools to accomplish what needs to be done to improve the multilateral trading system.

To most of the world, although its rules are vitally important to the world economy, the WTO is something of a mystery. How does it work? What are the values it incorporates? What are its challenges? How can they be met? This thoughtful guidebook provides a very readable brief history of trade and the current trading system. It takes the reader for a rare behind-the-scenes look at the workings of the institution. It shows where there are deficiencies to be remedied and suggests ways in which this can occur. A better future is attainable, but it is far from assured. Washington did not roll back its national security tariffs on its allies without agreed trade restrictions being established in their place. American senior officials talk of "friend-shoring," the antithesis of nondiscrimination. Brussels is putting in place review mechanisms for trade and foreign investment, heightened "precautionism." Beijing objects to the concept that the international trading rules are based on a "market-oriented" unbiased approach to trade. This is not to say that these three major players are not responding to some valid concerns. The question is whether they will give at least equal weight to seeking international cooperation to address common problems. Or will a domestic political focus cause them to underinvest in the multilateral trading system, in the WTO?

The author acknowledges these centrifugal forces. He cites the dangers of fragmentation, and points to the need to find ways to make the WTO more fit for purpose, as the place for making global trade rules, as it was intended to be: the place for monitoring their implementation, the place for settling trade disputes, and an institution that with an enhanced role given to the WTO Secretariat and its chief, the Director-General, can improve the workings of the system. An institution that is more than an organization. During the financial crisis, I led the WTO in providing much greater transparency regarding WTO members' trade measures with the help of the G20. This is a start, not the end of what is needed, with respect to providing trade intelligence to policy makers. Vulnerabilities need to be identified in advance, whether the cause is geopolitical, natural disasters, or damage to the environment. This takes engaging in strategic foresight. Governments of major countries, businesses, or civil society organizations engage in this practice of anticipating problems, and the WTO can do so as well. Policy planning is then needed. This is not a function of a committee of the whole WTO membership, it is an executive function. As Wolff points out, the Director-General and committee chairs should be neutral with respect to favoring members, but not neutral as to whether new agreements are crafted to meet the needs of the planet.

The future is about providing for sustainability. The future is about allowing new technologies to serve all the peoples of the world. The future is about equality of opportunity, for women, for small enterprises, for individual entrepreneurs, for workers. It is also for people living in conflict-affected countries. The subjects of trade and peace have been close to my heart and my thinking for a long time. I became President of the then newly created Paris Peace Forum in 2018, designed to bring thinking about global governance to the cause of peace. Alan spoke at our November 2018 session of the Paris Peace Conference, describing the WTO's newly launched trade for peace (T4P) initiative. He quoted a former US Secretary of State, Cordell Hull, who said in 1938, on the eve of the cataclysm that was to befall Europe and Asia: "Our nation, and every nation, can enjoy sustained prosperity only in a world which is at peace; a peaceful world is possible only when there exists for it a solid economic foundation, an indispensable part of which is active and mutually beneficial trade among the nations." This would seem like ancient history to most observers today, but it is not about the distant past for a group of conflict-affected countries, many of which were in the process of acceding to the WTO. They came together in December 2017 at the WTO Ministerial Meeting in Buenos Aires to form a "g7+ group for accessions" dedicated to assisting these fragile economies in their WTO accession effort.

The linkage of trade and peace has returned with the EU deciding to accept Ukraine as a candidate to become integrated in the European single market as a member state. Trade was vitally important to deal with the pandemic, and it is vitally important to maintaining food security. As I am writing these words, several nations are negotiating to try to remove the blockage of desperately needed grain and allow its shipment from Odessa to people in Africa who are moving from hunger to starvation. Trade is essential. Peace, where it can be obtained, is an essential condition for trade. Trade also promotes peace.

Trade cannot cure all the world's ills, but it can contribute to a better future for its peoples. The WTO, the multilateral trading system, is an essential tool for international cooperation. I commend this guidebook to those who want to understand the possibilities for international cooperation, and hope that it will aid them in working to meet the challenges the world faces where trade can be an important part of the answer.

Pascal Lamy
Paris, July 25, 2022

Acknowledgments

When I reflect upon the influences that enabled me to write this book, I find that the list is extensive. Pride of place goes to my wife, Hélène Novick Wolff, patient editor and critic of my writings for over half a century, without whom I could not have made this journey.

There are four phases of my life that are relevant to this book and form a foundation for it – formative experiences in early life and formal education, twelve years of service in the US government, thirty-nine years in private law practice, and my time at the WTO (2017–21).

This book would never have been written, with the content and point of view that it has, without a lifelong appreciation for trade. I grew up in a family in which international trade was integral to our lives. My father, Louis K. Wolff, set out to be and became a "merchant." Growing up in the opening days of the twentieth century, he was referring to the occupation in which a person who understands how something sourced in one place that would have greater value in another (with or without further transformation), by meeting the needs and desires of customers, goes about making trade happen. This is, in fact, a major basis for all trade since the beginning of time. He could not have succeeded without the active support and participation of my mother, Etta B. Wolff. I ran errands for the company business to the warehouses on the docks of East Boston bordering on the Atlantic Ocean. Goods flowed in from Europe and Hong Kong. There was a romance to trade. I must have subconsciously absorbed my father's insatiable curiosity about how goods were made, where they were produced, and where they would be consumed, knowing why trade takes place. Most importantly, my parents instilled in me, as parents should, my set of values.

At Harvard College, I gravitated toward the study of government due to courses in foreign policy formulation, thanks to Professor Richard Ullman, and the theory and practice of international relations, thanks to Henry

Kissinger and Ernest May. I learned about the working of the legislative branch in my senior dissertation, under the tutoring of Dr. Bruce Smith. I sought an understanding of the cultures of India, Japan, and China, with the able teaching of Professors Lloyd and Susanne Rudolph, Benjamin Schwartz, and Howard Hibbett, an interest that has remained with me. As president of the Harvard Radcliffe International Relations Council, I grew accustomed to hosting foreign and American policy makers and analysts, particularly Zbigniew Brzezinski and journalist Theodore H. White, and others whose role in history I only faintly understood. Columbia Law School provided me with an additional framework to understand how laws are to be applied, with Judge Marvin Frankel and Professors Wolfgang Friedmann, Louis Henkin, and E. Alan Farnsworth.

The path to the present became more clearly defined when I joined the US Treasury Department in the International Affairs Section of the Office of General Counsel, headed by Michael Bradfield, a place that prized excellence, and required more preparation than I had, necessitating evening classes at the George Washington University in economics (with Prof. Robert Dunn), more international law, and becoming acquainted with the GATT and the European Communities (with Lester Nurick, Walter Surrey, and Peter Ehrenhaft). John Jackson brought me into the Executive Office of the President, as his Deputy General Counsel in the Office of the Special Representative for Trade Negotiations (now USTR), where I worked on drafting the fundamental law for much of America's participation in the trading system. This necessitated living with the US Congress for two years, an invaluable experience in the politics of law-making. I succeeded Jackson as USTR General Counsel, and represented the United States for an interim period during the GATT Tokyo Round as acting head of delegation, thanks to Harald Malmgren (who was retiring as Deputy STR at that point). With a change in administration, I was appointed by President Jimmy Carter to be Deputy Trade Representative, serving under Robert S. Strauss, another mentor. Much of my twelve years in the US government were spent commuting to Geneva, Brussels, and Tokyo, increasingly moving from legal matters into negotiating trade issues.

There followed nearly four decades in the private practice of international trade law, assembling an extraordinary team of highly skilled lawyers, economists, and analysts, who had an unparalleled ability to take core samples of international commerce to make clear what caused or obstructed trade. With that knowledge, we could work to affect trade and trade policy. At its peak, our Dewey Ballantine trade group numbered over fifty highly talented professionals. Serving with me for most of those years were Dr. William Noellert,

Thomas R. Howell, Michael H. Stein, and W. Clark McFadden and included many others who continue to contribute to the world trading system. We represented major clients in major matters. The representations ranged from my working with the presidents of the Industrial Unions of the AFL-CIO and an equal number of CEOs of Fortune 100 major US exporting companies, to being trade counsel to the US Semiconductor Industry Association (SIA) almost from its inception. I had the opportunity to work with the founders and their successors in this great industry from 1980 to 2017, an invaluable experience with a world-class industry engaged in global competition. Several of my law firm colleagues and I published three books with Westview Press, on trade in steel, semiconductors, and trade policy more generally.

For a few decades, I was also active with the US National Academies, serving on the Science, Technology and Economic Policy Board, and chairing the Board's Committee on Comparative Innovation. I am indebted to Dr. Charles Wesner, for making that experience very rewarding. The National Academies and the work with the SIA provided multiple opportunities to be involved in international negotiations, as did my law practice.

During the last six years in private law practice, I also served as chairman of the Board of the National Foreign Trade Council, a venerable organization championing open world trade, and writing often for Fortune.com with an online commentary on international trade issues. I am indebted to my colleagues and clients for an invaluable education in why and how trade takes place.

An unexpected turn came with the offer of the position of Deputy Director-General of the World Trade Organization. I was reluctant to uproot my wife and myself from our Washington lives. Robert Lighthizer, US Trade Representative, persuaded me to take the job. He advised me that if I did not like it, I could always leave after a year. As it turned out, it gave me a marvelous opportunity to see this international organization from the inside, and when the then Director-General left before his term expired, to be one of four Deputies to act in his place during the last six months of our time in Geneva. I give my thanks to the ambassadorial corps accredited to the WTO, to their staff, and to the 700 members of the WTO Secretariat for the warm friendships and support throughout. In particular, I wish to single out my very thoughtful fellow Deputy Director-General, Karl Brauner, and division Directors with whom I worked most closely, Maika Oshikawa (Accessions), Edwini Kessie (Agriculture), Aik Hoe Lim (Standards and Environment), Fabrice Boudou (Information Technology Support), as well as Bob Koopman (Chief Economist) and those who knew the history and workings of the organization intimately, Victor do Prado (Council Division) and Keith

Rockwell (External Relations), for the training wheels they provided to me early on. I could not have succeeded at the WTO without the steady support and friendship of the marvelous Maria Verastegui, who continues in her accustomed role with a successor Deputy Director-General.

It gave me hope for the future that so many talented people, even with their differing priorities, were dedicated to making this experiment in international cooperation succeed. I could say what I wished to say, a bit diplomatically, in a series of well over 100 speeches, and had the rare opportunity to give lectures at many universities in far-flung places. It was an extraordinarily rewarding experience.

There is another category of persons to thank for my continuing education – some of the leading members of the international economy commentariat – the reporters and columnists at the *FT* (Martin Wolf, Alan Beattie, Ed Luce, and Gillian Tett), at the *Economist* (Soumaya Keynes), at Bloomberg (Bryce Baschuk), Politico (Doug Palmer), and Inside US Trade (Hannah Monicken) to name a few (without intending to slight others).

This has been an incomparable odyssey – in the 1970s representing the United States in Abidjan, Côte d'Ivoire, for the drafting of the Articles of Agreement of the African Development Fund, sitting at the cabinet tables in the White House and at Number 10 Downing Street (to draft a G7 Summit Communiqué), negotiating through the night at various ministries in Tokyo, seeing where organized labor and Fortune 100 CEOs could come together on at least some trade policy issues, in the 1980s and thereafter, working with the co-inventor of the integrated circuit, Robert Noyce, CEO of Intel, and his colleagues on public policy for the industry and the country, litigating major trade cases with decent results, and, most recently, as acting WTO DG, meeting with the heads of international economic organizations and Chinese Premier Li Keqiang in the "1 + 6" meetings, and participating in the meetings of the G20 agricultural ministers and leaders.

I recommend future generations who care about policy formulation and the good that it can do, to work for their governments, for NGOs, for international economic institutions, and in the private sector to devote themselves to continue to improve the international trading system.

In the preparation of this book, my special thanks to the Peterson Institute for International Economics (PIIE) for its support, to its President, Adam Posen, Steven Weisman, and Institute staff, and to the Trade Team (Jeff Schott, Gary Hufbauer, Mary Lovely, Nicolas Véron, Chad Bown, Fred Bergsten, Doug Irwin, Robert Lawrence, Sherman Robinson, and others) for inviting my participation in their lively continuing dialogue on current trade matters and for their specific contributions, and Sean Hagan for sharing his knowledge on comparative organizational structure. I am also, for similar reasons, indebted to the Friends of Multilateralism Group (FMG) for their insights into current challenges to the trading system, and to Professor Simon Evenett for his suggestions on the monitoring of trade measures. My research assistant (virtually at PIIE), Angela Min Yi Hou, was invaluable and unflagging in her support for this project. In the editing process, my thanks go to Marianne Nield, Rachel Imrie, Becky Jackaman, Joan Dale Lace, and others affiliated with the Cambridge University Press process.

Last, my thanks to the members of the WTO Secretariat past and present for their invaluable service to the world trading system and to many of them for their unflagging help to me to better understand the system and its contribution to the well-being of all.

Abbreviations

AB	Appellate Body
ACCTS	Agreement on Climate Change, Trade and Sustainability
ACP	African, Caribbean, and Pacific Group of States
AD	Anti-Dumping Duties
AfCFTA	African Continental Free Trade Agreement
AGI	Artificial General Intelligence
AI	Artificial Intelligence
AMIS	Agricultural Market Information System
AMS	Aggregate Measure of Support
AoA	Agreement on Agriculture
APEC	Asia-Pacific Economic Cooperation
ASDEA	Australia–Singapore Digital Economy Agreement
ASEAN	Association of Southeast Asian Nations
AVMSD	Audiovisual Media Services Directive
BTAMS	Bound Total Aggregate Measure of Support
CAI	Comprehensive Agreement on Investment
CAP	Common Agricultural Policy
CBAM	Carbon Border Adjustment Measures
CBPR	Cross-Border Privacy Rules
CEPA	Comprehensive Economic Partnership Agreement
CETA	Comprehensive Economic and Trade Agreement
CG	Consultative Group
CIFIUS	Committee on Foreign Investment in the United States
COVAX	COVID-19 Vaccines Global Access
COVID-19	Coronavirus Disease 2019
CPTPP	Comprehensive and Progressive Agreement for Trans-Pacific Partnership

CTD	Committee on Trade and Development
CTD-SS	Committee on Trade and Development in Special Session
CTE	Committee on Trade and Environment
CTS	Council for Trade in Services
CVD	Countervailing Duties
DDA	Doha Development Agenda
DDG	Deputy Director-General
DEPA	Digital Economy Partnership Agreement
DFFT	Data Free Flow with Trust
DG	Director-General
DISC	Domestic International Sales Corporation
DMA	Digital Markets Act (EU)
DSB	Dispute Settlement Body
DST	Digital Services Tax(ation)
DSU	Dispute Settlement Understanding
EC	European Communities
ECIPE	European Centre for International Political Economy
ECOSOC	Economic and Social Council of the United Nations
ECOWAS	Economic Commission of West African States
ED(s)	Executive Director(s)
EEA	European Economic Area
EEC	European Economic Community
EFTA	European Free Trade Association
EGA	Environmental Goods Agreement
EIF	Enhanced Integrated Framework
ELKS	Emergency Lane Keeping System
EPA	Economic Partnership Agreement
ERSD	Economic Research and Statistics Division
EU	European Union
FAO	Food and Agriculture Organization of the United Nations
FDI	Foreign Direct Investment
FSB	Financial Stability Board
FTA	Free Trade Agreement
G20	Group of Twenty
GAMS	Government and Authorities Meeting on Semiconductors
GATS	General Agreement on Trade in Services
GATT	General Agreement on Tariffs and Trade
GDP	Gross Domestic Product
GDPR	General Data Protection Regulation
GFFA	Global Forum for Food and Agriculture

GHG	Greenhouse Gas
GMO	Genetically Modified Organisms
GPA	Government Procurement Agreement
GPS	Global Positioning System
GSP	Generalized System of Preferences
GTA	Global Trade Alert
HoDs	Heads of Delegation
HS	Harmonized (Commodity Description and Coding) System
IAEA	International Atomic Energy Agency
IBRD	International Bank for Reconstruction and Development
ICC	International Chamber of Commerce
ICT	Information and Communications Technology
ICTSD	International Centre for Trade and Sustainable Development
IEA	International Energy Agency
IFRI	Institut Français des Relations Internationales
IISD	International Institute for Sustainable Development
ILO	International Labour Organization
IMF	International Monetary Fund
IP(R)	Intellectual Property (Rights)
IPEF	Indo-Pacific Economic Framework
ISA	International Seabed Authority
ITA	Information Technology Agreement
ITC	International Trade Centre
ITO	International Trade Organization
ITTC	Institute for Training and Technical Cooperation
ITU	International Telecommunication Union
IUU	Illegal, Unreported and Unregulated Fishing
JITAP	Joint Integrated Technical Assistance Program
JSI	Joint Statement Initiative
KMD	Division for Knowledge and Information Management, Academic Outreach and the WTO Chairs Program
Lao PDR	Lao People's Democratic Republic
LCIA	London Court of International Arbitration
LDC(s)	Least Developed Countries
LNG	Liquified Natural Gas
MAGA	Make America Great Again
MC	Ministerial Conference
MD	Managing Director
MFN	Most-Favored-Nation
MFTR	Memorandum of Foreign Trade Regime

MPIA	Multiparty Interim Appeal Arbitration Arrangement
MSME	Micro, Small and Medium-Sized Enterprises
MTN	Multilateral Trade Negotiations
MTS	Multilateral Trading System
NAFTA	North American Free Trade Agreement
NAMA	Non-Agricultural Market Access
NB	Notified Bodies
NFIDC	Net Food-Importing Developing Countries
NMPIA	New Multiparty Interim Appeal Arbitration Arrangement
NQI	National Quality Infrastructure
NTB	Non-Tariff Barrier
NTE	National Trade Estimate
ODA	Official Development Assistance
OECD	Organisation for Economic Co-operation and Development
OLC	Office of Legal Counsel
OPA	Open Plurilateral Agreement
OPEC	Organization of Petroleum Exporting Countries
PIIE	Peterson Institute for International Economics
PSH	Public Stockholding for Food Security Purposes
RCEP	Regional Comprehensive Economic Partnership
RTA	Regional Trade Arrangements
SAFTA	Singapore–Australia Free Trade Agreement
SCM	Agreement on Subsidies and Countervailing Measures
SD	Structured Discussions
S(&)DT	Special and Differential Treatment
SIDS	Small Island Developing States
SME	Small and Medium-Sized Enterprise
SOE	State-Owned Enterprise
SPS	Sanitary and Phytosanitary
SSG	Special Agricultural Safeguards
SSM	Special Safeguard Mechanism
STC	Specific Trade Concern
STDF	Standards and Trade Development Facility
STE	State-Trading Enterprise
TBT	Technical Barriers to Trade
TFA	Trade Facilitation Agreement
THAAD	Terminal High Altitude Area Defense
TISA	Trade in Services Agreement
TNC	Trade Negotiations Committee
TPP	Trans-Pacific Partnership Agreement

TPR(M)	Trade Policy Review (Mechanism)
TRIMs	Agreement on Trade-Related Investment Measures
TRIPS	Agreement on Trade-Related Aspects of Intellectual Property Rights
TRQ	Tariff-Rate Quota
TTIP	Transatlantic Trade and Investment Partnership
UAE	United Arab Emirates
UK	United Kingdom
UN	United Nations
UNCED	United Nations Conference on Environment and Development
UNCITRAL	United Nations Commission on International Trade Law
UNCTAD	United Nations Conference on Trade and Development
UNDP	United Nations Development Program
UNHRC	United Nations Human Rights Council
US	United States
USMCA	United States–Mexico–Canada Agreement
USSR	Union of Soviet Socialist Republics
USTR	United States Trade Representative
VAT	Value-Added Tax
VCLT	Vienna Convention of the Law of Treaties
WEF	World Economic Forum
WFP	World Food Programme
WHO	World Health Organization
WIPO	World Intellectual Property Organization
WOAH	World Organisation for Animal Health
WSC	World Semiconductor Council
WTO	World Trade Organization
WWI	World War I
WWII	World War II

Introduction

Saving the World Trading System

This book is designed as a guide to the multilateral trading system, its past, its present, and a look toward its potential future. It includes taking the reader on a virtual walk through the corridors of the World Trade Organization (WTO), the Italianate Centre William Rappard, and, after hearing of the history of trade and trade negotiations, to sit in on some of the working sessions of delegates. The book's objective is to convey an understanding of the value of the WTO, as well as the values that it promotes, to have a first-hand feel for what the WTO is all about, to understand its importance and its shortcomings, and to join with it in celebrating its successes. The look to the future in these pages includes some ideas upon which to start a discussion of how to obtain the oft-pledged "WTO reform."

The United States, at the apogee of its power, working with its allies, created a multilateral trading system of rules and greater liberalization for trade on a global scale, the likes of which had never been seen before in human history. It was built upon the unshakable belief of the American Secretary of State Cordell Hull and his President, Franklin Delano Roosevelt, that open markets and nondiscrimination would be, if not a guarantor of peace, the means to underwrite a more durable peace.

Their generation, the founding generation, had been scarred by the First World War. They had experienced the Great Depression interposed between the two wars. A full third of a century, from 1914 to 1945, the years in which the postwar leadership matured, was filled with hardship and international conflict. Their mission was driven, in part, by their disappointment at America failing to take up the mantle of world leadership a quarter-century earlier when Woodrow Wilson, shortsighted in other ways, had sought to build a better world in relations among sovereign nations. It was also because these founders felt a deep obligation to, in current parlance, build back better.

The International Trade Organization (ITO) that these Americans and their allies created on paper was destined never to come into being. It was a bridge too far even for a Congress that had become more outward-looking than ever before during the presidency of Franklin Roosevelt. His successor, Harry Truman, sought to carry the cause of multilateralism forward but for Congress and the American business community, the ITO proved too intrusive for the United States to join. Instead, a code of rules and tariff schedules that accompanied them, embodied in the GATT (General Agreement on Tariffs and Trade), survived.

The world envisioned by the creators of the GATT did not come into being overnight. There was nothing like free trade at the outset. Quantitative restrictions had to be dispensed with, and tariff walls, at least among the industrialized countries, were gradually dismantled brick by brick over the course of four decades. The new order of rules-based freer trade was patiently constructed through eight rounds of multilateral negotiations, each one having more participants than the prior one. In the seventh round, the Tokyo Round, which turned out to be the penultimate one, new rules were crafted for subsidies, product standards, antidumping, government procurement, and customs valuation – nontariff barriers as well as tariffs.

In the last great negotiating round, the Uruguay Round, 134 nations decided to create a global institution, the World Trade Organization – to fill the role envisioned by the founding generation as part of a troika of global economic institutions. It, along with the International Monetary Fund and the World Bank, was designed to foster the well-being of all peoples. This time, it was not the United States that pressed for the creation of the institution. Rather it was in large part a reaction by Canada, the European Union, and others to what were seen as problems of the day, arguably the largest being American unilateralism, using trade measures as leverage to obtain concessions from its trading partners.

Astrophysicists measure the rate of expansion of the universe and extrapolate their findings backwards to assess a single point of origin, when all matter was concentrated at a hypothetical center, before becoming the universe that can be observed today.[1] For those of us who are interested in the multilateral trading system, the origins are relatively clear and are described in this book. What is unknown is whether what we are observing, the WTO's *acquis* of rules and the current degree of openness to trade, is going to continue to

[1] In 1927, an astronomer named Georges Lemaitre theorized that a very long time ago, the universe started as just a single point. He said the universe stretched and expanded to get as big as it is now, and that it could keep on stretching.

expand. Here the laws of physics are inapplicable. We leave the realm of natural science behind and deal with political science. Continued progress depends on the strength of the community of supporters of the system, transcending national borders, as well as differences in culture, geography, and political beliefs.[2] The experiment of the multilateral trading system was not aimed at creating a global government with independent powers to regulate international commerce, to supersede the nation-state. It was and is about whether there will be a system of global rules for international trade that nations will uphold and live by, for mutual benefit.

This book addresses the value of the multilateral trading system, how it is currently threatened, and why it must be preserved and strengthened. What is absolutely certain is that it will not endure in any meaningful sense absent a level of effort from its members not witnessed for at least the last two decades. The book is also about what must be done to save the system for the benefit of all the world's peoples. It is clear that world peace, having existed among major powers for the last three-quarters of a century, is not a natural state for humanity, given Russia's invasion of Ukraine, and tensions between the United States (and to a degree its allies) and China. Nor for that matter is engaging in effective international cooperation necessarily a natural condition for sovereign nations. One suspects not. Just as the founding generation was faced with catastrophe and met the challenge of that era, the world's peoples are faced with current tests of pandemics, climate change, and famine. We do not know if the nations constituting the WTO will rise to meet the current challenges collectively or whether the liberal international economic order is a natural equilibrium that will persist. The jury is out.

In studying the world trading system, the first hurdle is the lack of an accurate picture of how and why trade is taking place. As a result, we lack perspective. In architecture, this is analogous to a problem faced by Filippo Brunelleschi, the Italian architect who built the duomo of the cathedral in Florence. He is credited with discovering linear perspective in the year 1415. Linear perspective is an approximate representation, generally on a flat surface, of an image as it is seen by the eye. In any writing on the world trading system, one is looking at a flat surface, a description of the complex world of trade, trading rules, their implementation and nonimplementation, in a narrative that will always be based upon an insufficiency of accurate

[2] Were this a reference to a religious community of Islam, the area occupied by believers would be called the Ummah. For trade, there is no estimate of the number of believers. All 164 members of the WTO and 24 who seek to join claim deep dedication to the multilateral trading system. As with Islam, there are divisions, however.

information, because there are serious limits as to what is known. No present system of monitoring trade reveals more than the surface of what is taking place. This is true both in the case of what the WTO is able to report, as well as for private sources, such as the Global Trade Alert, which is able to discern more due to its being freed from member-imposed restrictions on reporting. These sources constantly seek to make improvements in their coverage.

Beyond the fact that those interested in saving the WTO are operating on the basis of a finite body of knowledge with respect to the forces that shape trade, there is one more element for the reader to be aware of, and that is the perspectives of those offering interpretations of trade realities and prescriptions for improving the system. Points of view are likely to differ if the commentator is situated in Brussels, Beijing, or Washington, or, for that matter, Pretoria or New Delhi. It will also sometimes differ by individual, and over time. We are all shaped by our personal experiences. I have set out to provide my own narrative of what I have witnessed of the trading system, as a believer in the Washington Consensus, updated to take into account current concerns, and supplemented by additional research for this volume. Parts of this book are a journey of personal exploration. To the extent possible I draw upon contemporaneous sources, including my own observations contained in several hundred speeches and writings delivered as a US government trade negotiator and lawyer, as a trade law practitioner, as chairman of a pro-trade group of multinational companies, as an international civil servant at the WTO, and now affiliated with a distinguished group of international economists in a Washington think tank.

My objective is to give the reader a sense of both the possibilities and the limitations of nearly 200 nations interacting in one location, either in-person, or since the pandemic also virtually, on the shores of Lake Geneva. In these pages, I have tried to place the reader onsite as much as possible, to witness the evolution of the multilateral trading system, the values it represents, and the cooperation and conflicts that take place. The attempt is to provide a guidebook, to convey an accurate feeling to the armchair traveler, to prepare any who are to enter the fray, as well as to be a resource for those in one part of the arena as to what has been taking place in another part. I have, where I could, let the combatants, the negotiators, speak for themselves. Attaining international cooperation among so many nations is a daunting task, and not for the fainthearted.

I have also tried to report on the perspectives of those who created and managed the trading system, taken from the record that they created. What did they intend this system to be? Has it fulfilled its promise? Is any course correction necessary? We and they are most often the captives of our times, so a comparison is warranted to adjust, if necessary, the lens through which we view the system today.

Studying impressionist paintings helps inform the eye when looking outside at nature itself – to appreciate to a greater extent light and shadows, colors and shapes. It is my hope that readers will emerge from sharing my experiences and observations, to see trade policies and measures and international trade agreements, differently to some extent than they did before, sometimes in agreement with what they have read here and sometimes in reaction to it, but with greater clarity.

My objective in writing this volume is to help assure that the WTO does not, in the words of the great novelist, Carlos Ruiz Zafón, become "a relic of a vanished civilization."

PART I

Why Trade?

1

The Origins of Trade

Trade has been with humankind for over 100,000 years. It is a vital part of all civilizations. The motivations for trade have included a full range of possibilities, from dire necessity to improving the quality of life.

Winston Churchill famously advised, "Study history, study history. In history lies all the secrets of statecraft." This chapter traces in brief the origins of trade and how it developed from the very beginnings of human time through the ensuing millennia. As the ultimate purpose of this book is to address how best to manage the world trading system and how it can be improved, viewing the role of trade in succeeding epochs that preceded our own can provide insights into the primary objectives of trade and how they can best be served now. Why did trade happen? What was the relationship of trade to the spread of civilization? When can we see evidence of the beginnings of the role of government in trade? What effects did commerce have on technology and economic growth?

Ur-trade. Trade has existed for a very long time, driven by both necessity and its utility. Paleoanthropologists believe that long-distance trade networks existed some 300,000 years ago. This was perhaps 100,000 years before *Homo sapiens*, our species, first walked the Earth. Our remote ancestors needed to obtain better tool-making materials than could be found locally. They particularly prized obsidian.[1] In this distant prehistory, the beginnings of trade have been surmised through the fact that where early tools are found is often not where deposits of obsidian exist.

[1] Lorraine Boissoneault. 2018. "Colored Pigments and Complex Tools Suggest Humans Were Trading 100,000 Years Earlier Than Previously Believed." *Smithsonian Magazine*. March 15. www.smithsonianmag.com/science-nature/colored-pigments-and-complex-tools-suggest-human-trade-100000-years-earlier-previously-believed-180968499/; Joshua D. Englehardt and Michael D. Carrasco eds. 2019. *Interregional Interaction in Ancient Mesoamerica*. Louisville: University Press of Colorado.

Over 5,000 years ago, bitumen, the thickest of petroleum products, was carried over substantial distances. It was used, for example, to seal reed boats and in building construction. Bitumen, like obsidian, can be traced to its source from where it was found, indicating where early trade routes existed.[2] Similarly, nearly 2,000 years later, geology helps explain another major instance when trade was essential. The Bronze Age dates to around 3300 BC. Bronze was prized because it was harder and more durable than copper. Bronze is made by alloying copper with tin. Tin deposits are relatively rare and not evenly distributed around the world.[3] Compared with iron ore deposits, ores bearing tin occur in a ratio of about 1 to 25,000. There are known sources of tin in Yunnan, the Malay Peninsula, Devon and Cornwall, Brittany, Germany, the Czech Republic, Spain, Portugal, and some parts of Africa.[4] While this variety of sources makes tin appear readily available, demand was present everywhere in the societies of that age while sources were dispersed. Tin had to be traded widely for bronze objects to be made.[5]

A clear example of trade in essential goods consists of ingredients for medicines, in early times largely derived from plants. The Ebers Papyrus, dating from around 1550 BC, lists some 850 plant medicines.[6] So do earlier Sumerian tablets, especially the Nagpur tablet dating from around 5000 BC.[7] It comprised 12 recipes for drug preparation referring to over 250 various plants, some of them alkaloids such as poppy, henbane, and mandrake. The Chinese book on roots and grasses *Pen T'Sao*, written by Emperor Shen Nung

[2] I am indebted for my interest in this subject to a conversation with Raymond Westbrook, who was Professor of Ancient Near Eastern Law at Johns Hopkins University. Mark Schwartz and David Hollander. 2016. "The Uruk Expansion as Dynamic Process: A Reconstruction of Middle to Late Uruk Exchange Patterns from Bulk Stable Isotope Analyses of Bitumen Artifacts." *Journal of Archaeological Science: Reports* 7: 884–899; K. Kris Hirst. 2019. "The Archaeology and History of Bitumen." ThoughtCo. January 30. www.thoughtco.com/bitumen-history-of-black-goo-170085

[3] Daniel Berge et al. 2019. "Isotope Systematics and Chemical Composition of Tin Ingots from Mochlos (Crete) and Other Late Bronze Age Sites in the Eastern Mediterranean Sea: An Ultimate Key to Tin Provenance?" *PLoS ONE* 14(6): e0218326, 1–46.

[4] Pam J. Crabtree and Peter I. Bogucki eds. 2003. *Ancient Europe, 8000 B.C. to A.D. 1000: An Encyclopedia of the Barbarian World.* New York: Charles Scribner & Sons.

[5] R. D. Penhallurick. 1986. "Tin in Antiquity: Its Mining and Trade throughout the Ancient World with Particular Reference to Cornwall." London: The Institute of Metals. *Antiquaries Journal* 67(1): 134. https://doi.org/10.1017/S0003581500026378

[6] Aleksandra Hallmann-Mikołajczak. 2004. "Ebers Papyrus. The Book of Medical Knowledge of the 16th Century B.C. Egyptians." *Archives of the History and Philosophy of Medicine* 67(1): 5–14.

[7] Biljana Bauer Petrovska. 2012. "Historical Review of Medicinal Plants' Usage." *Pharmacognosy Reviews* 6(11): 1–5; Kate Kelly. 2009. *The Middle Ages: 500–1450 (History of Medicine).* New York: Infobase Publishing.

circa 2500 BC, treats 365 drugs (dried parts of medicinal plants), many of which are used even today.[8] We can deduce from this ancient knowledge of plant remedies that trade took place, making medicines available far from the source of the plants from which they were made.

While tin was a necessity for the Bronze Age, and medicinal plants have been deemed essential throughout history, another good, amber, was widely prized for its beauty and extensively traded. In some ancient societies, wearing it was thought to have medicinal qualities, such as warding off tonsillitis in damp, cold climates.[9] Heinrich Schliemann, the most famous of the fathers of modern archeology, in excavating grave sites at Mycenae, found amber objects. During the Bronze Age there was an amber trade route stretching from modern St. Petersburg to Sicily, linking deposits of the material in the ground with the places where it was made into jewelry. In ancient Egypt, the pharaoh Tutankhamen wore an amber bead in his necklace. It might have come from Ethiopia or the coast of what is now Italy.

The trade imperative was a major factor in the spread of civilization. The first city in the world is said to have been Uruk in ancient Sumer in the southern part of Mesopotamia. Uruk was located some 300 km SSE from modern Baghdad and was founded some seven millennia ago. Indications of trade dating back six millennia can be found at this site. Around 5,000 years ago, cuneiform characters began to be impressed onto small clay tablets. Once deciphered, the messages that were originally considered by some as mere decoration revealed something about the commerce of that era. No small number of tablets recorded commercial contracts. Some of the tablets, it was thought, were intended for long-distance communication designed to facilitate trade. Some scholars have seen trade as one reason why writing on clay tablets was invented.

Some of these early records of trade have survived. A great library of clay tablets dating back to 3500 BC was found largely intact in the ancient city of Ebla, in what is today Syria. Some tablets that were fresh were fired by the blaze that destroyed the building in which they were housed but ironically preserved them for us to see thousands of years later. The library documents the commerce of the time at this trading center, referring repeatedly to the role of "long-distance traders." They also tell us that the rulers of Ebla were concerned with having too many petty kings exacting tolls on the Euphrates River trade. Diplomatic and other political solutions were needed to assure the seamless

8 Petrovska, "Historical Review of Medicinal Plants' Usage."

9 "Amber Medicine, Amber Amulets." Getty. www.getty.edu/publications/ambers/intro/13/

movement of goods.[10] This has to be one of the first records in history of the existence of tariffs or their equivalent and the need to do something about them.

Trade over distance required rules. Within a few hundred years of the earliest tablets that have been found, the first indications of law were recorded on tablets.[11] The Code of Eshnunna, dating to the eighteenth century BC and found at a site near present-day Baghdad, seems to be confined to criminal matters. It preceded a far more famous code, now located in the Louvre, which does address trade. Around 1780 BC, the Babylonian king Hammurabi had incised on a black basalt stele a code of laws that may contain the first surviving rule applicable to trade. It provides:

> 104. *If a merchant give[s] an agent corn, wool, oil, or any other goods to transport, the agent shall give a receipt for the amount, and compensate the merchant therefor. Then he shall obtain a receipt from the merchant for the money that he gives the merchant.*

This is perhaps the earliest reference being recorded of a requirement for documentation to accompany traded goods. With this rule, another step was taken in the evolution of the trading system.

Trade, as it was scaled up and became more sophisticated, also required a bureaucracy. Perhaps the first ministry of trade anywhere was established by the pharaohs in the First Dynasty (c. 3150–c. 2890 BCE) at the capital at that time, Memphis. Governments became more deeply involved in trade the more important it became to their peoples. The grain trade was so important to Ancient Egypt that state trading was introduced, and quality control officials were appointed to monitor traded products.[12]

The exchange of goods required the setting of standards and compliance with them. Around 1340 BC, Burna-Buriash II, the king of Babylon, sent a letter to the Egyptian Pharaoh Akhenaton (Amenhotep IV).[13] Having exchanged a substantial amount of lapis lazuli, which was at the time mined in the mountains of Afghanistan, and horses for gold from Egypt, the Babylonian

[10] Ryan D. Winters. 2019. "Negotiating Exchange: Ebla and the International System of the Early Bronze Age." Doctoral Dissertation, Harvard University Graduate School of Arts & Sciences. https://dash.harvard.edu/handle/1/41121311

[11] Raymond Westbrook ed. 2003. *A History of Ancient Near Eastern Law*. Leiden: Brill. https://brill.com/view/book/edcoll/9789047402091/B9789047402091-s001.xml

[12] Mark Cartwright. 2018. "Trade in Ancient Greece," *World History Encyclopedia*. May 22. www.worldhistory.org/article/115/trade-in-ancient-greece/; Benjamin R. Foster. 1970. "Agoranomos and Muhtasib." *Journal of the Economic and Social History of the Orient* 13(2): 128–144.

[13] We remember Amenhotep today primarily for being an early monotheist among polytheists, and for having as his wife Nefertiti, whose famous image is dated to 1341 BC and survives in the Berlin Neues Museum as a portrait in the form of an alabaster bust.

king politely asked the pharaoh to personally inspect and seal future shipments of gold sent in exchange. He informed the pharaoh that the last shipment of gold received, when melted down, came up seriously short.[14] It is likely among the earliest examples of a written record discussing adherence to standards for trade and the need for an assessment of conformity with an agreed standard.

The security of trade routes was of vital importance, true then and true thereafter. In the late fourteenth century BC, the Babylonian kings built a series of fortresses to protect trade routes into northern Iran that supplied Babylon with chariots, horses, and lapis lazuli.[15] Ancient Egypt provided an umbrella of security for the flow of trade in the Eastern Mediterranean. Later, the Athenians would protect the grain trade from the region of the Black Sea. The Han Dynasty emperors built the Great Wall (220–202 BC) in part to protect the trade along the Silk Road.[16] The Romans would likewise guard the trade routes for grain from Egypt.

Trade was instrumental in fostering the growth of centers of civilization. The peoples that engaged in trade continued to expand their reach. In very early times, trading colonies in what are now Turkey, Syria, and Iran were founded to supply bitumen and other products, including copper, stone, timber, and pottery. The Phoenicians, Carthaginians, and Greeks, successively, established trading settlements along the eastern and southern coast of what is now Spain for both primary products and simple manufactures. The first Greek colonies were founded along the northeast coast of Spain in the ninth century BC, leaving the south coast to the Phoenicians.[17] Marseille was founded by the Ionian Greek city-state Phocaea (in modern-day Turkey) around 600 BC, to serve new markets with luxury goods such as wine, moving their cargoes from the Mediterranean up the Rhone valley to Central Europe.[18] Economists have examined the growth of settlements during the first millennium BC and see a correlation with trade (connectedness).[19]

[14] Aaron Irvin. 2007. "Regional Foundations for Internationalism in the Ancient Near East: The Case of Canaan." UC Berkeley: UC World History Workshop: 1–18.

[15] Ibid.

[16] Raluca-Maria Nicoara. 2013. "The Han Empire at the Origin of Modern Chinese Diplomacy." *Research and Science Today* 1(5): 28–38.

[17] Luminiţa Preoteasa. 2019. "Morphological Changes in the Proximity of the Greek Colonies Founded along the Western (Romanian) Black Sea Coast: Orgame, Histria, Tomis, and Kallatis." *Revista de Geomorfologie* 21: 15–28.

[18] Richard Stillwell et al. "Phokaia (Foça) Turkey." *The Princeton Encyclopedia of Classical Sites*. 1976. www.perseus.tufts.edu/hopper/text?doc=Perseus%3Atext%3A1999.04.0006%3Aid%3Dphokaia&redirect=true

[19] Jan Bakker et al. 2018. "Trade and Growth in the Iron Age." VoxEU & CEPR. August 23. www.voxeu.org/article/trade-and-growth-iron-age

Trade drove the development of industry. Greece was known throughout the ancient world for its pottery. Splendid vases, particularly during the period from 550 to 450 BC, with images of the gods and scenes from myths and everyday life, were much prized then and now.[20] The painted vases from Greece during this period, each an original work of art, were produced in vast quantities. Examples of these great pieces of ceramic art have been found throughout the known world of that time, and fill rooms of today's museums.

Trade facilitated technological progress. As noted, one theory holds that trade was one of the motivations for writing. We know that trade facilitated great shifts in the advancement of human society such as the creation of the Bronze Age. In the following Iron Age, the role of trade in iron products, given that iron ore was relatively plentiful, is given less emphasis by scholars, in part because geology does not identify trade routes. What is sure is that the spread of ideas, namely the global diffusion of technology to make iron objects, particularly weapons, was relatively rapid. Throughout history, there were myriad smaller but still important advances brought about by trade. Trade, for example, enabled the ancient Egyptians to replace reed boats with those made with cedar from Lebanon.[21]

Trade grew beyond a few major products. While the Ancient Greeks exported olives and olive oil and imported grain, a map of trade routes of around 300 BC would show horses sourced from North Africa and the steppes of Central Asia, silver from the Black Sea, sulfur and tin from the Italian peninsula, incense from Oman, gold, pearls, and coral from the Arabian peninsula, papyrus, linen, beer, and glass from Egypt, myrrh, slaves, elephants, and ivory from continental Africa, timber and wheat from the Black Sea region, wool and wine from Greece, and silk from China.

Trade became far more elaborate and well-developed during the time of the Roman Empire. Roads were established as well as a common currency. Imports included beef, corn, glassware, iron, lead, leather, marble, olive oil, perfumes, purple dye, silk, silver, spices, timber, tin, and wine. The main trading partners were in regions located today in Spain, France, the Middle East, and North Africa.[22]

[20] Laura Hayward. 2020. "7 Incredible Ancient Greek Vase Paintings to Marvel At." The Collector. October 23. www.thecollector.com/greek-vase-paintings-from-ancient-greece/

[21] Joshua J. Mark. 2017. "Trade in Ancient Egypt." *World History Encyclopedia*. June 15. www.worldhistory.org/article/1079/trade-in-ancient-egypt/; William F. Edgerton. 1923. "Ancient Egyptian Ships and Shipping." *American Journal of Semitic Languages and Literatures* 39(2): 109–135.

[22] Mark Cartwright. 2018. "Trade in the Roman World." *World History Encyclopedia*. April 12. www.worldhistory.org/article/638/trade-in-the-roman-world/

There were at least eight major routes: moving spices from east to west, incense from south to north, plus trading routes for trade in cloth, salt, tea, amber beads, gold, jade, and tin to make bronze – and also, regrettably, slaves. The most famous of all routes, of course, was the Silk Road, formally founded in the Han Dynasty around 207 BC. It began in west-central China in Xi'an and crossed overland for 6,400 kilometers to reach the Mediterranean. It created cities along the way. Samarkand (in what is now Uzbekistan), a remarkable place, was a major trading center in Central Asia. It owes its existence to the Silk Road.[23]

Wherever trade thrived, so did exploration. A major source of trade was driven by demand for spices, carried from Oman to India. The historian and political scientist Robert Kaplan wrote in his book *Monsoon*:

> *The Arabs are known in the West as a desert people … But they have also been a great seafaring race, as the frankincense trade and the historical experience of Oman demonstrate, the very harbingers of cosmopolitanism, who have been sailing these waters [of the Indian Ocean] for thousands of years before Vasco da Gama.*

Some historians have called this route a Maritime Silk Road – stretching from the west coast of Japan, through the islands of Indonesia, around India, to the lands of the Middle East – and from there, across the Mediterranean to Europe. Traded were cinnamon from Sri Lanka and cassia cinnamon from China.[24]

Frankincense has been traded on the Arabian peninsula for more than 5,000 years and was written about in antiquity. It was brought back to Western Europe by the crusaders and reached China. It was widely valued by the ancient Egyptians for mummification. Many peoples used it in religious observances. It is mentioned in the Old and New Testaments of the Bible, and valued for its medicinal purposes in China.[25]

New advances in transportation drove trading relationships further and faster. Sailing ships enabled trade to expand. For Northern Europe, this gave rise to the Hanseatic League, dating from 1267. German cities combined their

[23] A few months before the COVID-19 pandemic made travel impossible, my wife and I visited Samarkand, which still has signs of its preeminent early glory.

[24] "What Are the Spice Routes?" United Nations Educational, Scientific and Cultural Organization – Silk Roads Programme. https://en.unesco.org/silkroad/content/what-are-spice-routes#:~:text=The%20Spice%20Routes%2C%20also%20known,across%20the%20Mediterranean%20to%20Europe.

[25] Ralph Kauz ed. 2010. *Aspects of the Maritime Silk Road: From the Persian Gulf to the East China Sea.* Wiesbaden: Harrassowitz Verlag, p. 130.

efforts to secure their trade, bringing raw materials to centers of manufacturing and sending finished products to large markets.

Grain, timber and pitch, tar, potash and charcoal, wax, honey, hemp and flax all were drawn from the south and east of the Baltic (modern-day Russia and Poland) and shipped to the industrial west (Flanders and England), which in turn sent cloth and other manufactured goods eastward.[26] Swedish copper and iron ore were traded westward, and herring caught off the southern tip of Sweden was traded throughout Germany and southward to the Alps. The members of the League extended their reach from trade to the sources of production, creating a monopoly over the Norwegian production of whale and cod.[27]

Trade gave rise to the first mass production in history. In Asia, Chinese exports of pottery beginning in the ninth century were sent in quantity to other destinations in Asia and to Africa.[28] In the sixteenth century, trade enabled the producers to move upscale, driven by demand in Europe for much-prized porcelain, which China exported in copious quantities.[29]

Throughout history, trade has been a major positive force for humanity, but there have been some stark exceptions (as seen from our current vantage point). Trade in the sixteenth century drove exploration, but also exploitation. The Dutch East India Company reached out into the Pacific. The British East India Company reached into South Asia. Each engaged in conquest and colonization. Slavers reached into Africa. Spanish treasure ships returned laden with precious metals from the Americas. A moral low point in the history of trade was marked by the Opium Wars with China. Colonization was not confined to the European powers. In the twentieth century, Japan annexed Manchuria and sought raw materials through conquest in Southeast Asia.

Why trade? It would be an overreach to suggest that trade was an exclusive driver of human progress. It was not. Nevertheless, trade continually emerges to a surprising extent in the rich tapestry of that story, and we can learn from

[26] "The League at Its Outset." *Encyclopedia Britannica*. www.britannica.com/topic/Hanseatic-League/The-League-at-its-outset

[27] "Hanseatic League." *Encyclopedia Britannica*. www.britannica.com/topic/Hanseatic-League

[28] John Miksic. 2017. "Chinese Ceramic Production and Trade." Oxford Research Encyclopedias – Asian History. www.oxfordre.com/asianhistory/view/10.1093/acrefore/9780190277727.001.0001/acrefore-9780190277727-e-218

[29] Suzanne G. Valenstein. 1975. *A Handbook of Chinese Ceramics*. New York: The Metropolitan Museum of Art. https://books.google.com/books?id=wnVwuJvo4YgC&printsec=frontcover#v=onepage&q&f=false; Jan-Erik Nilsson. "Armorial Porcelain." Gotheborg. www.gotheborg.com/glossary/armorial.shtml#G

this record. From the above narrative, reflected in current experience, there are at least five dominant reasons that become apparent as to why trade has taken place and continues to grow. Each has a continuing strong influence today. These are:

Necessity: Of the first order of importance is the movement of food in long-distance trade. Grain trade was central to the interests of Ancient Greece and Rome. In a time of climate change, the movement of food across borders will assume a growing importance. In this century, during the pandemic, all came to understand the absolute necessity of moving vaccines and essential medical supplies across borders through trade. The ingredients for medicines, the more sophisticated they became, always had to be supplied over distances from their source to where they were needed.[30] From earliest times, trade in intermediates – not just end products – was essential, from tin for the Bronze Age, to oil for the age of the internal combustion engine, to rare earths and semiconductors today.

Utility is a second motive for trade. Bitumen for reed boats and construction was an early example. Trade must supply the components for medicines, chemicals of all kinds. In earlier times tall pine trees were sought after for the masts for the Royal Navy. Currently imported rebars are needed for construction in modern Addis Ababa and syringes from India are needed to make injections of vaccines available everywhere.

Efficiency, a third motive, closely related to utility, drove trade from early times. The first producers of goods for trade often found inputs from distant places. They did, we may be sure, infer benefits from trade that David Ricardo articulated much later, having specialized for the same reason that Adam Smith found to be so logical – efficiency. Trade will take place when the usefulness (the value) of a good at a point of consumption rises to a level that exceeds that of the value it has in the place of production plus the costs of transporting the good. Factored into the costs would be the ships lost in storms, piracy, and other harms. If the costs of shipping did not exceed local acquisition costs, trade would take place – as it did in copious quantities in the nineteenth century for guano (nitrate) from the rookeries of Chile as fertilizer destined for the farms of Europe.

Giving life color – luxury goods and consumer choice. The examples are myriad: amber and gold for jewelry (found in burial mounds at Mycenae), and diamonds from Africa. Ice was cut in northern climes and shipped south to

[30] Biljana Bauer Petrovska. 2012. "Historical Review of Medicinal Plants' Usage." *Pharmacognosy Reviews* 6(11): 1–5.

population centers before mechanical refrigeration existed;[31] fruit was shipped to be available out of season. There was and still is an attraction to acquire from abroad that which is therefore more exotic than something produced locally. Marble from Italy graces building lobbies everywhere, as also do tropical hardwoods. Trade has enriched life on this planet since the dawn of human time. In time, environmental concerns would also be factored in, with a focus on making trade sustainable.

Profit: Commerce also generated returns on investment, for individuals in terms of income, and for government through revenues – whether through state trading or levying imposts on imports.

Necessity, utility, color, and economic forces created the trade imperative. From the earliest times, assurance of supplies and of markets were of keen interest to those engaged in commerce and therefore to their governments. The latter needed to supply order, and this they did through international agreements. The next chapter describes how governments came together to do so on a global scale.

[31] Eric H. Cline. 2015. *1177 B.C.: The Year Civilization Collapsed*. Princeton, NJ: Princeton University Press.

PART II

The Multilateral Trading System

2

The Founding of the Multilateral Trading System

The attempt to underwrite peace was initially made through trade by creating the International Trade Organization (ITO), followed by an international contract for rules-based trade under the General Agreement on Tariffs and Trade (GATT), and then the World Trade Organization (WTO).

TRADE REPURPOSED: THE ITO

The eternal verities of trade – that it will take place because of necessity, utility, adding variety to life, or to gain profit – were still valid in the 1940s. But these objectives were not foremost in the minds of the leaders and planners of the Allies as they decided on how the world economy should be shaped once victory was achieved. They had three overriding objectives, none solely domestic – to have trade support a more durable peace, to restore the world's productive capabilities, and to assure that their economies could reach full employment.

Postwar planning. The Allies' thinking was formed in the crucible of two catastrophic world wars largely separated by a global economic depression of a magnitude never before witnessed. That generation of leading politicians and thinkers in the United States had before them the specter of what might have been if only the idealism of Woodrow Wilson had been translated into agreed policy following the First World War. Wilson had offered a blueprint for restoring prosperity and world peace in the form of Fourteen Points, which included as Point III: "The removal, so far as possible, of all economic barriers and the establishment of an equality of trade conditions among all the nations consenting to the peace and associating themselves for its maintenance."[1]

[1] "President Woodrow Wilson's 14 Points." National Archives. January 8, 1918. www.archives.gov/milestone-documents/president-woodrow-wilsons-14-points

This proposition much impressed a young economist, John Maynard Keynes, who was advising the British during the Peace Conference. In his book *The Economic Consequences of the Peace*, published in 1919, he warned that the Versailles Treaty had created a Carthaginian peace designed to crush the defeated Central Powers, especially Germany. The results of errors in policy by the victors toward the vanquished had been horrific.

Franklin Roosevelt and Winston Churchill were of the same opinion. Meeting at Argentia Bay, Newfoundland, they foreshadowed what was to become the liberal international economic order by stating their postwar aims. The two leaders pledged in an *Atlantic Charter* that "they will endeavor, with due respect for their existing obligations, to further the enjoyment by all states, great or small, victor or vanquished, of access, on equal terms, to the trade and to the raw materials of the world which are needed for their economic prosperity."

This joint declaration was issued on August 14, 1941, four months before the United States was drawn into becoming a combatant in the war. Roosevelt's thinking was remarkable in its prescience in stating postwar aims for a war the USA was not formally a part of. It was not until December 8, after Pearl Harbor, that the United States declared that a state of war existed between it and Japan. Three days later, on December 11, Germany and Italy made their own declarations of war on the United States.

During the war, three British economists, Keynes, James Meade, and Lionel Robbins, pursued the idea of an international organization for trade, to parallel an international economic organization for international monetary matters. Keynes was an official at the Treasury, Robbins was the Director of the Economic Section of the War Cabinet Secretariat, and Meade served as a negotiator for the Ministry of Foreign Trade.[2] Talks between the US Department of State and representatives of the United Kingdom ensued. Political leaders would shortly move to fulfill a vision voiced by US Secretary of State Cordell Hull during the 1930s and contained in the Atlantic Charter, of using open markets to support the peace and a restoration of economic growth.

As the war was coming to a close, on March 26, 1945, President Roosevelt sent a message to Congress urging the renewal of his trade negotiating authority. He began by telling Congress that: "The coming victory of the United Nations [the Allies] means that they, and not their enemies, have

2 Claude Schwob. 2007. "Keynes, Meade, Robbins and the International Trade Organization." *L'Actualité Économique* 83(2): 255–283.

power to establish the foundations of the future."[3] He welcomed the establishment of the Fund, the Bank, and the FAO, and turning to trade, ended his statement by quoting his Bretton Woods Address delivered a month earlier: "We have a chance, we citizens of the United States, to use our influence in favor of a more united and cooperating world. Whether we do so will determine, as far as it is in our power, the kind of lives our grandchildren can live."[4]

Franklin Roosevelt did not live to see the end of the war, dying on April 12, 1945. Allied victory was declared in the European war on May 8, 1945, and with respect to Japan on September 2, 1945. Roosevelt had converted the United States from isolationism, propelling it to world leadership, with, at this time, strong bipartisan support from Congress.

The planners' concerns. In November 1945, the US Department of State issued a pamphlet entitled "Proposals for World Trade and Employment."[5] It began with a preface by President Truman's Secretary of State James F. Byrnes, stating that "nations are now determining the policies which they will apply to trade in the post-war world. It is urgently necessary that these policies should be agreed upon, in order that the world may not separate into economic blocs." The proposals were the responsibility of William (Will) Clayton, Assistant Secretary of State, who was to be a key actor in the launch of the world trading system. In his report, he informed Secretary Byrnes that if nations "do act together, there is every possibility that the peoples of the world may enjoy, in our lifetime, a higher degree of prosperity and welfare than they have ever had before."[6] This prophesy was to prove accurate beyond imagination.

Will Clayton stood at an extraordinary juncture of world history, and he knew it. He wrote that:

> *The main prize of the victory of the United Nations is a limited and temporary power to establish the kind of world we want to live in.*
>
> *That power is limited by what exists and by what can be agreed on. Human institutions are conservative; only within limits can they be moved by conscious*

3 *Journal of the House of Representatives of the United States* 79(1).

4 "Message to Congress on the Trade Agreements Act." The American Presidency Project. www.presidency.ucsb.edu/documents/message-congress-the-trade-agreements-act

5 "Proposals for Expansion of World Trade and Employment." Department of State. November 1945. https://fraser.stlouisfed.org/files/docs/historical/eccles/036_04_0003.pdf

6 William L. Clayton. "Analysis of the Proposals." The Department of State Bulletin Volume 13, No. 314. July 1, 1945. p. 914.

choice. But after a great war some power of choice exists; it is important that the United Nations use it wisely.

The fundamental choice is whether countries will struggle against each other for wealth and power, or work together for security and mutual advantage.

At the time that this report was written, it was not at all clear to US postwar planners that a slide toward an economic depression would not resume with the end of enormous wartime demand driven by military procurement and with the demobilization of the troops. US military personnel in 1945 numbered over 12 million compared with a civilian work force of 54 million. The fear that the postwar economy would fail to provide sufficient numbers of jobs was a dominant theme of the American founders of the trading system.

Mass unemployment was the scourge of the interwar period. It overshadowed all other issues and concerns, affected the lives of millions of people and was the social problem that finally destroyed the last remaining vestiges of legitimacy of the gold standard and laissez-faire free trade.[7]

The founders of the multilateral trading system sought to ensure prosperity through the creation of a new international order for trade.

Every country will seek so to manage its own affairs that its business life will be free from violent depressions. The object of international action should be to ensure that these national efforts reinforce each other and do not cancel out.

When industry in any country slows down and its purchases of foreign materials are cut, the effects are felt in every corner of the globe. Full and regular production at home with increased participation in world trade is the greatest boon which any people can confer upon producers throughout the world.[8]

The American proposals were based on the deeply imbedded belief of the founders that:

World trade is not only the device through which useful goods produced in one country are made available to consumers in another; it is also the means

[7] Daniel Drache. 2000. "The Short but Significant Life of the International Trade Organization: Lessons for Our Time." Centre for the Study of Globalisation and Regionalisation Working Paper No. 62/00, University of Warwick, Coventry. http://wrap.warwick.ac.uk/2063/1/WRAP_Drache_wp6200.pdf

[8] "Preparatory Committee of the International Conference on Trade and Employment, Memorandum on the Objectives of the International Trade Organization in Respect to Employment." United Nations Economic and Social Council. October 19, 1946. https://docs.wto.org/gattdocs/q/UN/EPCT/CI-5.PDF

> *through which the needs of people in one country are translated into orders and therefore into jobs in another. Trade connects employment, production and consumption and facilitates all three. Its increase means more jobs, more wealth produced, more goods to be enjoyed.*[9]

The persistent theme repeatedly articulated was that opening world trade was essential to providing more employment. It was the worker-centered policy of its time, a theme that would return to be emphasized by American officials three-quarters of a century later.

Institution-building. To make their conception operational, the trading nations of the world were to be convened to address creating a structure for world trade:

> *What is needed is a broad and yet detailed agreement, among many nations, dealing at one time with many different sorts of governmental restrictions on trade, reducing all of them at once on a balanced and equitable basis, and stating rules and principles within which the restrictions permitted to remain should be administered. To prepare such an agreement should be one of the main tasks of an international conference on trade and employment.*

Although focused on thinking about how to bring about a better future, the interwar period was not a time of inactivity for the US State Department's trade negotiators. Twenty-one bilateral agreements were entered into by the United States from the enactment of the President's trade agreement authority in 1934 to the fall of 1940.[10] Many of the provisions of these agreements would be incorporated later into the global trade regime. The most prominent of these provisions was most-favored-nation treatment, providing the benefits to all nations on a nondiscriminatory basis of each concession negotiated bilaterally. Avoiding conferring too many benefits on non-signatories was of necessity a limiting aspect of these bilateral agreements.

[9] William L. Clayton. "Analysis of the Proposals." The Department of State Bulletin Volume 13, No. 314. July 1, 1945. p. 915.

[10] These countries (in chronological order of their effective dates) were: Cuba, Belgium, Haiti, Sweden, Brazil, Canada, the Netherlands, Switzerland, Honduras, Colombia, France, Guatemala, Nicaragua, Finland, El Salvador, Costa Rica, Czechoslovakia, Ecuador, the United Kingdom, Turkey, and Venezuela. Through 1945, thirty-two agreements were negotiated. "Chapter 3: US Trade Policy Since 1934." In *The Economic Effects of Significant US Import Restraints: Sixth Update 2009 Investigation No. 332-325*. United States International Trade Commission. August 2009. www.usitc.gov/publications/332/us_trade_policy_since1934_ir6_pub4094.pdf; John H. Jackson. 1969. *World Trade and the Law of GATT: A Legal Analysis of the General Agreement on Tariffs and Trade*. Indianapolis, IN: Bobbs-Merrill Company.

For the post-Second World War period, the US government saw a need for more than a series of additional two-party trade agreements. Will Clayton proposed that a new multilateral institution be created:

> *Arrangements on this scale clearly require, for their successful operation, both an international forum where they may be discussed and improved and an international staff to assist in their administration.*
>
> *The Proposals therefore suggest that an International Trade Organization be created, to stand beside the existing international agencies dealing with currency, investment, agriculture, labor, and civil aviation.*

By February 1, 1946, the Food and Agriculture Organization, the International Monetary Fund, and the World Bank had already been founded.[11] On that day, the US delegation to the newly created Economic and Social Council of the United Nations introduced a resolution that called for the Council to convene a conference with an agenda aimed at achieving and maintaining high and stable levels of employment and economic activity, reaching agreement on regulations, restrictions, and discrimination affecting international trade, addressing restrictive business practices, providing for intergovernmental commodity agreements, and for the establishment of an international trade organization. "Effective action in regard to employment and to trade barriers and discriminations must ... be taken or the whole program of international Economic Cooperation will fail and an economic environment conducive to the maintenance of peaceful international relations will not be created."

The organization the United States had in mind was to be robust. It was to collect, analyze, and publish information relating to general commercial policy, provide technical assistance to members requiring it, make recommendations to members regarding relaxing and removing trade restrictions, interpret the agreement's provisions, and provide for settlements of disputes growing out of application of the new rules. The conference of all members would make decisions by majority vote, each member having one vote. Between meetings of the membership, the institution was to be governed provisionally by an eighteen-country Executive Board, with large countries serving as permanent members. The Secretariat was to be headed by a Director-General, aided by three or more Deputy Directors-General. Contrary to the current operation of the WTO, the Director-General, and the Deputy Directors-General, the proposal was explicit that these

[11] Known during that period as the International Bank for Reconstruction and Development (IBRD).

international officials were to "have the authority to initiate proposals for the consideration of any organ of the Organization."

The United States proposed that a preparatory committee be established to elaborate an agenda and create a draft convention for consideration at a conference for the creation of the new institution. The Committee, as proposed, would have fifteen members: Australia, Belgium-Luxembourg, Brazil, Canada, China, Cuba, Czechoslovakia, France, India, the Netherlands, New Zealand, South Africa, the USSR, the United Kingdom, and the United States.

In September 1946, Will Clayton presented a draft proposed charter for the creation of an international trade organization. The Preparatory Committee met from the fall of 1946 to the late fall of 1947. On March 24, 1948, the *Havana Charter for the Creation of the International Trade Organization* was signed by fifty-three countries. The Charter begins:

> *For the Purpose of* REALIZING ... *the attainment of the higher standards of living, full employment and conditions of economic and social progress and development ...*
>
> TO THIS END *they pledge themselves, individually and collectively, to promote national and international action designed to attain the following objectives:*
>
> 1. *To assure a large and steadily growing volume of real income and effective demand, to increase the production, consumption and exchange of goods, and thus to contribute to a balanced and expanding world economy.*
> 2. *To foster and assist industrial and general economic development, particularly of those countries which are still in the early stages of industrial development, and to encourage the international flow of capital for productive investment.*
> 3. *To further the enjoyment by all countries, on equal terms, of access to the markets, products and productive facilities which are needed for their economic prosperity and development.*
> 4. *To promote on a reciprocal and mutually advantageous basis the reduction of tariffs and other barriers to trade and the elimination of discriminatory treatment in international commerce.*
> 5. *To enable countries, by increasing the opportunities for their trade and economic development, to abstain from measures which would disrupt world commerce, reduce productive employment or retard economic progress.*
> 6. *To facilitate through the promotion of mutual understanding, consultation and co-operation the solution of problems relating to international trade in the fields of employment, economic development, commercial policy, business practices and commodity policy.*

For several years, the Truman administration sought to have Congress accept and approve the ITO, but that could not be achieved. Fortunately, in parallel, the General Agreement on Tariffs and Trade (GATT) was negotiated. The GATT text was the product of a companion negotiation moving alongside the creation of the ITO. It concerned itself with the less lofty but more practical job of limiting tariffs imposed by signatories, together with a set of rules that banned most quantitative restrictions. It included other key conditions, such as requiring that most-favored-nation treatment be extended to the goods of all contracting parties, as well as national treatment for imported goods with respect to taxes and regulations. The GATT was a trade negotiators' document. It was a commercial contract among sovereign nations. It did not contain institutional provisions because those were contained in the Havana Charter for the ITO.

There appears at the time to have been more concern that the tough tariff negotiations for the GATT might undermine the realization of the Havana Charter for an ITO coming into force than that the adoption of the Charter might itself fail. The chief Australian negotiator, pressing his colleagues to conclude the tariff negotiations, said:

> *The Charter cannot stand by itself. The Charter and the proposed multilateral trade agreement are integral parts of the general plan to expand trade. The success or failure of the whole plan now depends on a similar degree of understanding being reached in the trade negotiations.*

The trade negotiators understood the importance of what they were doing. They laid the foundation for further trade-liberalizing negotiations throughout the rest of the twentieth century. Their chair, the Belgian trade negotiator and diplomat Max Suetens, summed up their effort when he spoke at the Final Session of the Preparatory Committee on October 30, 1947:

> *We are here witnessing the birth of the first fruits of post war international action towards reorientating international trade on constructive and productive lines, towards more copious production of the products needed by mankind, towards increasing employment of the men and women producing them, and towards a steadily rising standard of living.*[12] …
>
> *The signing of the Final Act today marks the completion of the most comprehensive, the most significant and the most far-reaching negotiations ever*

[12] "Second Session of the Preparatory Committee of the United Nations Conference on Trade and Employment: Speech to be Delivered by M. Max Suetens at Final Session of Preparatory Committee, October 30, 1947." World Trade Organization. October 29, 1947. https://docs.wto.org/gattdocs/q/GG/PRESSRELEASE/475.pdf

undertaken in the history of world trade. Twenty-three countries or territories, sharing amongst them approximately seventy percent or a little less than three quarters of the trade of the world, have worked together, cordially and in the best traditions of fair give and take, to complete over one hundred [bilateral] negotiations, involving literally thousands of items. The results of these negotiations have been incorporated in a General Agreement on Tariffs and Trade, a multilateral trade agreement unique in its character, both in scope and in application.

The rules of the GATT, with the support of a "temporary" Secretariat informally assigned to it, were to shape world trade for the next half-century.

IN THE SERVICE OF COMMERCE: THE ADVENT OF THE WTO

The United States was not an initial proponent of the creation of the WTO. Academics had championed the idea of a world trade institution – from the proposal of economists Keynes, Meade, and Robbins in the 1940s for the ITO to a University of Michigan law professor, John H. Jackson,[13] in the 1990s. Jackson was serving as a consultant to the Canadian government. Ottawa welcomed the idea of creating a formal international trade institution, a concept which was then embraced by the European Communities. The United States was skeptical at first but went along with the idea. As proposed, it was at first called the Multilateral Trade Organization, but the chief US trade negotiator, Mickey Kantor, suggested that it be called what it is today, the World Trade Organization– a name that had more of a political ring to it. The WTO was a major step forward in consolidating and improving the multilateral trading system, building on what had been started with the ITO and GATT experiments.

The contracting parties to the GATT concluded eight rounds of multilateral trade negotiations from 1947 to 1993.[14] Import quotas were substantially

[13] John Jackson was perhaps the world's leading expert on the GATT, having written the definitive work, *World Trade and the Law of GATT*, in 1969. I hired him as a consultant during 1970–71 when I had the trade law portfolio at the Office of General Counsel, at the US Treasury.

[14] "GATT Bilateral Negotiating Material by Round." World Trade Organization. www.wto.org/english/docs_e/gattbilaterals_e/indexbyround_e.htm. The Uruguay Round of negotiations ended in 1993 but cleanup work continued into 1994. The WTO began operations on January 1, 1995. "During the GATT (General Agreement on Tariffs and Trade) years, eight rounds of tariff negotiations were held between 1947 and 1994: Geneva (1947), Annecy (1949), Torquay (1950–51), Geneva (1956), Geneva (1960–61) – also known as the Dillon Round, the Kennedy Round (1964–67), the Tokyo Round (1973–79) and the Uruguay Round (1986–94)."

eliminated (at least for industrial goods) early on and industrialized countries' tariffs were cut dramatically through this process. The eighth and last GATT round, the Uruguay Round, provided for the creation of the WTO.

The Uruguay Round results. In 1995, 128 parties to the GATT became the original members of the new World Trade Organization. The world economy and political situation were much sunnier during the negotiation of the eighth round of multilateral trade negotiations, the Uruguay Round, which created the WTO, as compared with the years preceding the negotiation of the Havana Charter for the ITO.

Between September 1939 and August 1945, an average of 27,000 persons perished every day as a consequence of the Second World War. Much of the world lay in ruins. In the West, in Europe, from the Atlantic and deep into Russia, and in the East, Japan and China, were devastated. A total of 20 to 25 million combatants were killed in battle. An estimated 50 to 55 million civilian deaths, half from disease and famine, were caused by the war. In addition, there were some 20 million displaced persons in Europe alone. There could not have been a sunnier time by comparison during the Uruguay Round. The world economy had been steadily expanding year after year. The Soviet Union had dissolved, and the world was at peace, at least insofar as the major powers were concerned. US unemployment was around 5.5 percent in 1995, far below the 1930s range of up to 25 percent. Japan was booming.[15] Perhaps because the next step in the creation of the world economic order, remaking the GATT into the WTO, occurred in a time of less stress, less worry over potential unemployment, there was nothing like the excitement at the end of the Uruguay Round over the creation of the WTO that attended the creation of the Bretton Woods institutions, the ITO or the GATT. In the period 1986–93, the negotiators were free to think mainly about commercial interests, not world peace, economic reconstruction, or massive unemployment.

[15] John Schmidt. 2015. "How We Created the WTO: A Memoir." *The Wilson Quarterly*. Summer. www.wilsonquarterly.com/quarterly/summer-2015-an-age-of-connectivity/a-world-of-hopes-and-a-world-of-fears-how-we-created-the-wto/. A US trade negotiator attributed the creation of the WTO in substantial part to this period of economic expansion and political relaxation:

> *For the talks, the "Big Three" great economic powers were the United States, the EU, and Japan. In 1993, each was in a period of prosperity and growth. The United States was emerging from recession into the economic boom of the 1990s. Europe was, if anything, even more optimistic: the Cold War was finally over, Germany was reunified, the EU had expanded eastward, … in 1993 Japan was still very much an emerging economic powerhouse, looked to by many nations as a model for economic success.*

I was in Geneva for the conclusion of the Uruguay Round negotiations in 1993,[16] meeting with senior negotiators from major participating countries, including US Trade Representative (USTR) Mickey Kantor and his senior associates, through to the last night of the negotiations. The focus of the negotiators that I met with was on tariff reductions and new substantive trade disciplines. They were not focused on institution building, with the sole exception of making dispute settlement binding which had largely been agreed upon years earlier. Binding dispute settlement, from the European and Japanese perspective, meant American unilateralism would be curbed. For the United States, it was the long-sought objective of bringing international discipline to the Common Agricultural Policy (CAP). It was the important new agreements on intellectual property, agriculture, and services that got the headlines.[17] In the *New York Times* coverage at the time, the focus was on a GATT round coming to an end, not the introduction of major change in the way that international trade relations were to be managed.[18] The negotiated results were presented as being evolutionary rather than revolutionary.

While the WTO was the product of trade lawyers and trade negotiators rather than world leaders and foreign ministers, it was still aspirational. The Marrakesh Agreement Creating the WTO opened by stating the objectives of the signatories:[19]

- *that their relations in the field of trade and economic endeavour should be conducted with a view to raising standards of living, ensuring full employment and a large and steadily growing volume of real income and effective demand, and expanding the production of and trade in goods and services, while allowing for the optimal use of the world's resources in accordance with the objective of sustainable development, seeking both to protect and preserve the environment and to enhance the means for doing so in a manner consistent with their respective needs and concerns at different levels of economic development,*

16 Similarly, I had been present in Brussels for what was supposed to have been the conclusion of the Uruguay Round in 1990. Had that ministerial meeting been "successful," one wonders if there would have been a WTO at all.

17 A new provision for peer review of national trade policies and measures – the trade policy review mechanism – had already been put into place earlier, before the conclusion of the Round.

18 "The World Trade Agreement: The Overview; GATT Talks End in Joy and Relief." *New York Times*. December 16, 1993. www.nytimes.com/1993/12/16/business/the-world-trade-agreement-the-overview-gatt-talks-end-in-joy-and-relief.html

19 "Marrakesh Agreement Establishing the World Trade Organization." World Trade Organization. www.wto.org/english/docs_e/legal_e/04-wto_e.htm

- *that there is need for positive efforts designed to ensure that developing countries, and especially the least developed among them, secure a share in the growth in international trade commensurate with the needs of their economic development,*

Being desirous of contributing to these objectives by entering into reciprocal and mutually advantageous arrangements directed to the substantial reduction of tariffs and other barriers to trade and to the elimination of discriminatory treatment in international trade relations,

Resolved, therefore, to develop an integrated, more viable and durable multilateral trading system encompassing the General Agreement on Tariffs and Trade, the results of past trade liberalization efforts, and all of the results of the Uruguay Round of Multilateral Trade Negotiations.

The trade ministers stated in a separate declaration that what had been achieved they "believe will strengthen the world economy and lead to more trade, investment, employment and income growth throughout the world" due to the creation of:[20]

- *the stronger and clearer legal framework they have adopted for the conduct of international trade, including a more effective and reliable dispute settlement mechanism,*
- *the global reduction by 40 percent of tariffs and wider market-opening agreements on goods, and the increased predictability and security represented by a major expansion in the scope of tariff commitments, and*
- *the establishment of a multilateral framework of disciplines for trade in services and for the protection of trade-related intellectual property rights, as well as the reinforced multilateral trade provisions in agriculture and in textiles and clothing.*

These were major accomplishments.

An emphasis on continuity. The drama of the creation of a new international institution appeared to be soft-pedaled. Care needed to be exercised to avoid the creation of the WTO meeting the same fate as the ITO. The chairman of the Senate Finance Committee, Senator Daniel Patrick Moynihan, was well-versed in the history of the ITO and what motivated the United States to lead in the failed effort to create that institution:

Mr. MOYNIHAN. Mr. President, on July 8, 1916, in a speech on the House floor, Cordell Hull, then a Democratic Congressman from Tennessee, called

[20] "Marrakesh Declaration of 15 April 1994." World Trade Organization. www.wto.org/english/docs_e/legal_e/marrakesh_decl_e.htm

for a "permanent international trade congress" to formulate agreements to dismantle destructive trade practices. Today, over 78 years later, it is with great honor that I, as chairman of the Committee on Finance, bring to the floor of the Senate legislation that will finally realize that vision.[21]

He stressed that the WTO was not revolutionary, distinguishing the new WTO from the ITO that grew from Hull's vision: "This World Trade Organization is no more than a rather pale image of the International Trade Organization which was contemplated at the end of World War II."

He reassured the Senate that US sovereignty was not at risk, that binding dispute settlement would be on balance positive for the United States, and that voting would be as unlikely in the WTO as it had been in the GATT where consensus prevailed for decisions. The United States would not be outvoted in a system relying on a majority of votes cast. He said that it was estimated that the WTO Secretariat would require only fifteen additional staff positions as compared with the GATT.

The bottom line was that the WTO was presented as being about continuity, improvement of an existing institutional arrangement, with economic benefits, not radical change. This is how Senate Majority Leader George Mitchell put it: "A global trading system is not a new and untested concept: It has been an integral factor of our economic policy, working for our producers and exporters for almost five decades."

Senator Bill Bradley made the economic case for the package of agreements:

The Uruguay Round Agreement will bring direct dollars-and-cents benefits to the American economy. The numbers bear repeating. For example, the 1994 Economic Report of the President estimates that the aggregate increase in US annual income after 10 years will be about $100 and $200 billion, the equivalent of 1.5 or 3 percent of the whole income of the economy ... The Treasury Department estimates that the agreement will lead to 300,000 to 700,000 net new jobs after 10 years. These will be high-paying jobs, since the jobs in the export sector pay over 10 percent more than average.

As opposed to the ITO, which Congress refused to consider, the Uruguay Round Agreements Act, authorizing the United States to participate in the WTO, passed the House by 288 to 121 and the Senate by 76 to 24.

The WTO provided a formal organization in which members could administer the multilateral trading system with the support of a professional Secretariat.

[21] "Congressional Record Volume 140, Number 148 (Wednesday, November 30, 1994) Uruguay Round Agreements Act." Govinfo.gov | US Government Publishing Office. November 30, 1994. www.govinfo.gov/content/pkg/CREC-1994-11-30/html/CREC-1994-11-30-pt1-PgS15.htm

The organization came out of the shadows of being an interim arrangement, which it had been during the GATT years. For the first three decades of the GATT's existence, it operated out of two small villas, le Bocage and la Fenêtre, on the hillside overlooking Lake Geneva, begging the occasional larger conference room from the UN. In 1977, it moved into the old ILO building on the shores of the lake, and in 2007 it added a new conference center and a modern office building attached to the original Centre William Rappard.

The GATT's institutional permanence, however, was testified to, less by masonry than by the creation of the WTO, and by the fact that since the WTO began its existence on January 1, 1995, another 36 countries have joined and 24 countries are in the process of applying to accede. With its 164 members (the EU as one, and its member states counted in addition), the WTO currently covers 98 percent of world trade and is headed toward universality.

Lessons. What can be learned from comparing the foundering of the ITO with the founding of the WTO? In the United States and possibly in other countries, there must be solid domestic support to enter into and implement trade agreements. They will be judged primarily by their commercial value offset by their negative impact on sovereignty (the freedom to freely pursue commercial objectives in the future, relatively unconstrained by the agreement). In rare exceptions, the motivation to conclude an agreement may include or be driven by foreign policy considerations. At some point in the future, were the United States to seek to rejoin the Trans-Pacific Partnership (now the Comprehensive and Progressive Agreement for Trans-Pacific Partnership – CPTPP), geopolitics may play a dominant role.

The ITO was a State Department project with strong White House support. The negotiators failed to obtain sufficient backing from business and failed to bring along Congress. The ITO was not even given a hearing. Commercial considerations largely dominate negotiations, with a few exceptions, for example, the US–Israel and US–Jordan Free Trade Agreements were driven by foreign policy, not commercial interests. For the European Union, its creation and expansion have had a strong foreign policy element as well as commercial interests, but in its agreements with more distant partners – with Mercosur for a free trade agreement and with China for a Comprehensive Agreement on Investment (CAI) – the motivations were primarily commercial and in fact, in the case of the latter, geopolitical aspects have been a complication.

In ancient Greek mythology, the giant Antaeus, son of the god Poseidon, could not be defeated unless he lost contact with the ground, his earth goddess mother, Gaea. The same is true of trade negotiators. In a democracy, if they lose touch with their domestic constituencies, their ability to deliver on their trade agreements is destroyed.

3

Core Elements of the World Trading System

At the heart of the multilateral trading system is the commitment to nondiscrimination, the most-favored-nation (MFN) principle, mandating that all nations participate on equal terms. Added to this are a series of obligations to limit government interventions in trade. To give assurance that the system will deliver what it promises, transparency is required, making clear to all the measures that affect trade. Reality diverges from the ideal.

Attending a meeting of all members in the large auditorium-style Council Room of the WTO, delegation after delegation takes the floor. While often expressing disparate views on various agenda topics, they give voice to one common theme: each strongly supports the "multilateral trading system." What is it that they are in fact supporting?

In its literal sense, "multilateral" simply means many-sided. A "multilateral agreement" has more parties than does a bilateral or regional trade agreement. Current examples of multiparty agreements include the Regional Comprehensive Economic Partnership (RCEP) with fifteen parties and the Comprehensive and Progressive Agreement for Trans-Pacific Partnership (CPTPP) with eleven parties. When hearing the term "multilateral trading system," however, there is no confusion in international meetings. No one considers that this is a reference to regional multiparty agreements. The speakers are referring solely to the WTO as an institution and the set of agreements that it administers. This is their multilateral trading system, designed for universal membership and applying to global trade.

A sense of the scope of the global system can be gotten by referring to the European Union's *acquis communitaire* which EU member states agree to support. That *acquis* consists of the EU's objectives, decisions, substantive rules, and the outcomes in disputes. The same kinds of features exist for the WTO *acquis*. World trade is to be governed by rules centered on the WTO. This multilateral trading system was initially created by the GATT's contracting parties in 1948 with just 23 nations. The Uruguay Round transformed it into the WTO forty-seven years later on January 1, 1995, with 128 original members. Today there are 164 members and 24 nations as observers.

THE FOUNDATIONAL PRINCIPLES OF THE MULTILATERAL TRADING SYSTEM

The multilateral trading system was founded upon three basic precepts – nondiscrimination, binding levels of tariffs together with commitments limiting the use of other trade-restrictive measures (thus providing market access), and transparency. To this foundation, the WTO added enforceability. These four elements cannot be found operating together outside of the global trading system. They constitute the bedrock of the international trading order.

Nondiscrimination, also called most-favored-nation treatment (MFN), is the hallmark of multilateralism, because it is believed to be the best arrangement for all trade. Nondiscrimination cannot readily exist outside of a global platform. Sub-multilateral agreements can have some of these elements, and they often bind tariff levels. They can include a dispute-settlement mechanism. But they can never be completely nondiscriminatory in their application; quite the reverse, they are almost always based on discrimination, and they are unlikely to provide transparency as complete as that provided by the WTO.

At the Extraordinary G20 Leaders' Summit on March 26, 2020, the leaders of the world's largest economies affirmed that their common objective for the world trading system was "to realize a free, fair, non-discriminatory, transparent, predictable and stable trade and investment environment, and to keep our markets open."[1] The countries of the G20 account for more than 80 percent of world GDP, 75 percent of global trade, and 60 percent of the population of the world. Under the Saudi presidency during the fall of 2020, G20 members participated in what was called the *Riyadh Initiative on the Future of the WTO*. An important part of that exercise was to identify the principles to which all G20 members subscribe. The leaders agreed without dissent that among the key principles of the WTO under the heading "Rule of Law" were nondiscrimination and transparency.

[1] "DDG Wolff Urges G20 Leaders to Back WTO Action to Support Economic Rebound, Pandemic Response and WTO Reform." World Trade Organization. November 21, 2020. www.wto.org/english/news_e/news20_e/ddgaw_21nov20_e.htm. At this G20 Summit Meeting, I urged the leaders "to utilize trade to help underwrite the economic recovery, to facilitate trade in essential medical products to treat the pandemic, and to reform the institutional framework for world trade."

NONDISCRIMINATION

Clearly the heart and soul of the world trading system is nondiscrimination.[2] Both a benefit and a burden, it is the central feature of the system distinguishing it from all other trade agreements. The most visible form of nondiscrimination is that the same tariff must be applied to all merchandise from whatever source. In addition, internal taxes and regulations are to be applied based on "national treatment," meaning that imported goods (and services supplied by foreign entities, to the extent the services are covered in schedules filed with the WTO) are to be treated no less favorably than domestic products (and services) once they enter domestic commerce. For example, there cannot be a VAT levied differentially on imported as compared with domestic products. The same rule applies to other internal taxes and domestic regulations.

Discrimination. The passion of American leaders for the principle of nondiscrimination and for making it the cornerstone of the multilateral trading system stemmed from the fact that the United States had experienced a history of American products suffering from discrimination. In 1932, during the Great Depression, the nine members of the British Commonwealth met in Ottawa for a Commonwealth Conference on Economic Consultation and Co-operation. While the conference was positive in terms of fostering Keynesian macroeconomic policies, from an American point of view the conference's positive effect was offset by the decision of those attending to give preferential tariff treatment to "home producers first, empire producers second, and foreign producers last."[3]

The advent of Cordell Hull. The conference took place the summer before Cordell Hull became Franklin Roosevelt's Secretary of State. Hull had been serving in the House of Representatives and had hotly opposed the Smoot–Hawley Tariff Act in 1930 which raised America's tariff wall against imports. He saw the conference which formalized Great Britain's Imperial Preference scheme as a damaging foreign reaction to the increase in US trade protection.[4]

[2] Gerard Curzon. 1965. *Multilateral Commercial Diplomacy: The General Agreement on Tariffs and Trade and Its Impact on National Commercial Policies and Techniques.* London: Michael Joseph. One of the great scholars of the GATT, Gerard Curzon, put this as follows: "non-discrimination is probably the most important single concept that informs General Agreement."

[3] "Imperial Preference." *Encyclopedia Britannica.* www.britannica.com/topic/imperial-preference

[4] Kenneth W. Dam. 2004. "Cordell Hull, The Reciprocal Trade Agreement Act, and the WTO." The Brookings Institution. www.brookings.edu/wp-content/uploads/2016/06/20041010dam.pdf

Beginning in 1934, with the passage of the Reciprocal Trade Agreements Act, Hull was able to begin his attack on Smoot–Hawley with more than rhetoric. The Reciprocal Trade Agreements Act authorized the President to negotiate the reduction of tariffs at home and abroad. Hull became an apostle of nondiscrimination – but it took over a decade to accomplish the demise of the Imperial scheme.

Nondiscriminatory bilateral agreements. It was under Hull in the 1930s that the US State Department concluded a series of bilateral agreements that applied tariff concessions on an MFN basis – meaning non-signatories could benefit. This approach had some obvious practical limitations. Since MFN concessions applied to all imports from whatever source, it was important that the parties to each bilateral agreement be the principal supplier of the article on which a tariff concession was made. Where there were multiple important suppliers, bilateral agreements would be required with each of them to prevent non-signatories from being substantial free riders (non-signatory countries which did not provide reciprocal concessions in return for those from which they would benefit).

War aims. Hull wanted equal treatment to be the cornerstone of the postwar global economy. In August 1941, Franklin Roosevelt pressed Winston Churchill to join him in this vision, but Churchill felt himself unable to do so. Despite the United Kingdom being the closest of allies, Churchill, a free trader, sought to preserve the Imperial Preference System by hedging the goal for trade that was included in the Atlantic Charter. The two leaders called for equal access to trade and raw materials but qualified this objective with the caveat: "with due respect for existing obligations." The issue of preferential trade remained contentious between the United Kingdom and the United States throughout the Second World War and the negotiation of the postwar economic agreements. After the war, with the relative economic positions of the two nations diverging further, the US view was to prevail. MFN, nondiscrimination, was adopted as the basis for the world trading system. Imperial preferences ceased to exist.

On the eve of war. How important nondiscrimination (equality of treatment) was to Hull is dramatically demonstrated by his repeatedly inserting the principle in negotiations with the government of Japan. His note of November 26 can be viewed as one of the most consequential documents in human history. It was a last-ditch attempt to avert war. Had it opened a path to good faith negotiations, Japan might not have attacked the United States thirteen days later at Pearl Harbor on December 7, 1941. And if Japan and the United States were not at war, Germany and Italy would not have declared war on the United States – not then anyway.

For our purposes, here are the relevant sections of Hull's note which he dictated on the eve of the Second World War:

Strictly Confidential

November 26, 1941.

The representatives of the Government of the United States and of the Government of Japan have been carrying on during the past several months informal and exploratory conversations for the purpose of arriving at a settlement, if possible, of questions relating to the entire Pacific area based upon the principles of peace, law and order and fair dealing among nations. These principles include the principle of equality, including equality of commercial opportunity and treatment . . . (Emphasis added).

Hull then included a draft of elements of an agreement:

Strictly Confidential, tentative and without commitment

November 26, 1941.

Outline of proposed basis for agreement between the United States and Japan.

Section 1

Draft mutual declaration of policy

The Government of the United States and the Government of Japan . . . affirm . . . that . . . in their national policies they will actively support and give practical application to the following fundamental principles upon which their relations with each other and with all other governments are based: . . .

(3) *The principle of equality, including equality of commercial opportunity and treatment. . . .*

The Government of Japan and the Government of the United States have agreed that toward eliminating chronic political instability, preventing recurrent economic collapse, and providing a basis for peace, they will actively support and practically apply the following principles in their economic relations with each other and with other nations and peoples:

(1) *The principle of non-discrimination in international commercial relations.*

The General Agreement on Tariffs and Trade. Hull's dedication to nondiscrimination survived the war to become a principal means to govern international economic relations. It became the template for a new world order for trade and is included as Article I of the GATT.

With respect to customs duties and charges of any kind imposed on or in connection with importation or exportation or imposed on the international transfer of payments for imports or exports, and with respect to the method of levying such duties and charges, and with respect to all rules and formalities in connection with importation and exportation, and with respect to all matters

> *referred to in paragraphs 2 and 4 of Article III, any advantage, favour, privilege or immunity granted by any contracting party to any product originating in or destined for any other country shall be accorded immediately and unconditionally to the like product originating in or destined for the territories of all other contracting parties.*

National treatment. Article III standing by itself confers "national treatment," another key form of nondiscrimination, on products that have cleared customs. Its opening paragraph reads:

1. *The contracting parties recognize that internal taxes and other internal charges, and laws, regulations and requirements affecting the internal sale, offering for sale, purchase, transportation, distribution or use of products, and internal quantitative regulations requiring the mixture, processing or use of products in specified amounts or proportions, should not be applied to imported or domestic products so as to afford protection to domestic production.*
2. *The products of the territory of any contracting party imported into the territory of any other contracting party shall not be subject, directly or indirectly, to internal taxes or other internal charges of any kind in excess of those applied, directly or indirectly, to like domestic products . . .*
4. *The products of the territory of any contracting party imported into the territory of any other contracting party shall be accorded treatment no less favourable than that accorded to like products of national origin in respect of all laws, regulations and requirements affecting their internal sale, offering for sale, purchase, transportation, distribution or use.*

Aspiration and reality, fracking of the bedrock. Of course, there are exceptions to MFN. Preferential trade agreements, including bilateral free trade agreements (FTAs) and regional trade agreements, that eliminate substantially all tariffs on trade among signatories, are allowed to limit the benefits of tariff elimination or other preferential market access to signatories. It is not credible to believe that the drafters of the GATT, through Article XXIV (the free trade agreement provision), thought that they were sabotaging the nondiscrimination principle contained in GATT Article I. The theory behind the free trade area exception is that there would be more trade creation than trade diversion.[5] In

[5] Jagdish Bhagwati and Arvind Panagariya. 1996. "The Theory of Preferential Trade Agreements: Historical Evolution and Current Trends." *American Economic Review* 86(2): 82–87. The debate over whether there can be more trade creation than trade diversion from preferential trade agreements continues.

other words, the world of non-signatories would benefit from the preferential trade agreements despite the discrimination inherent in them.

What happened would have exceeded the expectations of the 1940s negotiators of the GATT. WTO members have reported 562 preferential agreements which are still in force.[6] The largest preferential arrangement consists of the European Union, which is a customs union. The EU in turn has negotiated nearly 100 such arrangements with third countries, as close as Switzerland and Norway, most recently with the United Kingdom after Brexit, and as far away as the South Pacific. The United States has twenty free trade agreements, the largest of which consists of the United States–Mexico–Canada Agreement (USMCA) which entered into force on July 1, 2020. In November 2020, China and fourteen other countries signed the Regional Comprehensive Economic Partnership. The Comprehensive and Progressive Agreement for Trans-Pacific Partnership is a free trade agreement among Canada and ten other countries in the Asia-Pacific region (not including the United States as of the second day of the Trump administration). The African Continental Free Trade Agreement will link fifty-four countries on the African continent.

Had Cordell Hull lived to witness this development, it would probably have killed him. But possibly he would have seen merit in some of the departures from his beloved principle of nondiscrimination. Regional integration – the formation of the European Economic Community (EEC) for example – was greeted as a move toward freer trade, one of Hull's central goals. It would have been consistent with the Hull doctrine to welcome not only the EEC but also NAFTA (now USMCA), the African Continental Free Trade Agreement and possibly CPTPP if they were seen as stepping stones back to Geneva, to an improved, more comprehensive WTO.

Hull might also take some cold comfort in that the proliferation of preferential trade agreements entered into promiscuously for reasons that Alan Beattie of the *Financial Times* has labeled "standard, off-the-shelf mercantilism" do not dominate world trade. The impression that the principle of nondiscrimination exists in theory but has been shredded in fact is not accurate. According to the WTO's Economic Research and Statistics Division, 75 percent to 80 percent of world trade flows at MFN, WTO-pledged rates. The reason is a practical one: for those engaged in making things and selling them internationally, qualifying a product for preferential tariffs can be onerous. It may just be too much trouble to trace the origins of parts in, for example, a computer, and more efficient to pay whatever tariff

6 "Regional Trade Agreements – Facts and Figures." World Trade Organization. www.wto.org/english/tratop_e/region_e/region_e.htm#facts

might be applicable at an MFN rate than to qualify an article for the preferential tariff. For smaller companies, qualifying products for preferential treatment may be prohibitively expensive. Companies generally aspire to sell their products worldwide. Seeking to meet what has been described as a spaghetti bowl of origin requirements under numerous bilateral agreements is often simply not worth the effort.

There is also a more fundamental reason to take heart. All sub-multilateral agreements rest on the foundation of the WTO, which guarantees a negotiated level of openness, and a baseline of rules. In addition, while one can be justifiably skeptical about the discrimination inherent in bilateral free trade and regional trade agreements, they can be laboratories for provisions that might in the future fit into the multilateral system. For example, many preferential trade agreements had provisions specifically addressing aspects of electronic commerce, while the WTO did not. The negotiators at the WTO looked to these examples in seeking to write global rules. Preferential trade agreements can also be entered into for reasons of foreign policy, to assist a particular country or forge a closer relationship, and not primarily for the enjoyment of mutual discriminatory advantage. The US–Israel and US–Jordon Agreements fit into this latter category, and the expansion of the EU into Eastern Europe was at least in part a foreign policy-driven process.

There is also a limit to the utility of sub-multilateral negotiations. Some issues, such as disciplines on agricultural and industrial subsidies, or dealing with climate change or a pandemic, do not lend themselves to resolution other than on the multilateral level. To be effective certain rules must be global.

Plurilaterals within the WTO. Before leaving the subject of nondiscrimination, it is necessary to look at plurilaterals negotiated within the WTO. There are a few agreements that are plurilateral rather than multilateral, although they are accepted as part of the WTO *acquis*. There have been two instances of sectoral negotiations resulting in tariff elimination: the Information Technology Agreement and the Pharmaceutical Agreement which are not adhered to by all WTO members. In each case, the agreements covered at their inception over 90 percent of world trade in products listed, short of all members producing the goods in question but deemed sufficient for the zero tariffs called for under these agreements to be applied on an MFN basis. These agreements benefit the trade of all WTO members, not just that of signatories.[7]

[7] This is no longer the case for the Pharmaceutical Agreement, as China and India are not parties, and they now account for significant production and trade in pharmaceuticals.

There have also been plurilateral agreements within the WTO *acquis* under which benefits are not extended to non-signatories. A prime example is the Government Procurement Agreement, with twenty-one parties covering forty-eight WTO members (counting the European Union and its twenty-seven member states as one party). It is part of the WTO body of agreements because members have decided that it would be. Any member willing to schedule concessions sufficient to be accepted by existing signatories can join the agreement. Open plurilateral agreements, not MFN at present but only prospectively, can be a path forward for the current negotiations of Joint Statement Initiatives (JSIs). These negotiations have addressed e-commerce, domestic regulation of services, improvements in the trading system for micro, small, and medium-sized enterprises, and investment facilitation for development. These are designed to lead to open agreements, openly arrived at. Two of these JSIs have been concluded and will be nondiscriminatory in application (Domestic Regulation of Services and Micro, Medium and Small Enterprises – MSMEs). The Investment Facilitation for Development negotiation and the e-commerce negotiation have not been completed. If the participants choose to do so, they may seek to make them non-MFN in their application. It is an open question whether they will become part of the WTO *acquis*.

TRANSPARENCY

Why it is important. In order for governments and businesses to plan, there needs to be current information on what trade measures have been introduced by other members in order to understand how their trade interests might be affected. To provide this level of transparency, the WTO has numerous requirements. These include obligations for the publication of measures, notification of changes, and the provision of enquiry points to permit those engaged in trade and their governments to better understand how the measure is to be applied.

Notifications received special emphasis during the pandemic. The Secretariat created a cross-divisional task force to gather information on trade measures imposed by countries related to containing the spread of the virus that could have an effect on international trade, both trade-facilitating and trade-restrictive. This extraordinary effort resulted in current information being made available to national authorities to enable them to make more informed decisions. In addition, providing data to members on the anticipated levels of production of world agricultural crops and stocks played a role in the pullback from the imposition of export controls on food. The same effect was demonstrated with respect to measures affecting trade flows of essential goods, pharmaceuticals, critical personal protective equipment, and medical equipment. The WTO Secretariat provided notes to members on critical information such as the nature of global supply chains for these products. Lack of information can easily cause governments to err on the side of imposing unnecessary trade restrictions as a precaution. Indeed, Pascal Lamy, former Director-General of the WTO, has flagged "precautionism" as a new and insidious form of protectionism.

Enhanced data collection also helped the WTO estimate the range of negative impact on global trade when it issued its trade forecast assessing the anticipated depth of the COVID-related downturn of trade and the timing of the recovery.

An abundance of notification requirements. As noted at the outset of this chapter, the transparency requirements of the WTO are not set forth neatly in a few articles of the WTO/GATT, as occurs with nondiscrimination. A WTO lawyer setting out to brief representatives of countries which acceded to the WTO after its founding as well as of those seeking to accede by providing an overview of transparency provisions, took 33 detailed PowerPoint slides to do so.[8] She catalogued nearly 300 separate notification commitments required of members. The WTO's search for transparency is so detailed that the WTO published in April 2021 a "Technical Cooperation Handbook on Notification Requirements" that runs to 244 pages and covers 23 separate substantive areas of WTO agreements.[9]

A prime example of the value of notifications in the normal work of the WTO is found in the area of national product standards. In an extraordinary example of international cooperation, members notify proposed standards voluntarily while the measures are still in draft, giving other members the opportunity to review and comment on their likely trade impact in the Technical Barriers to Trade (TBT) Committee. A practice in the WTO that has received considerable positive attention is the regular discussion in the TBT Committee on specific trade concerns (STCs). This process drives the detailed, technical deliberations on specific measures that have (mostly) not yet entered into force and therefore may not yet be entrenched in domestic law. WTO notifications receive members' attention, and if members consider them to be of concern, they are scrutinized in the Committee. The degree of transparency embodied in the process is remarkable. All WTO members and

8 Anna Varyanik. 2019. "Transparency and Notification Requirements." World Trade Organization. February 12. www.wto.org/english/thewto_e/acc_e/transparency_anna_varyanik_12_feb_2019.pdf

9 "Technical Cooperation Handbook on Notification Requirements." World Trade Organization. www.wto.org/english/tratop_e/handbook_on_notifications_complete_e.pdf

observers are party to the discussion and the minutes are available to the public. This is an example that many hope other WTO agreements will emulate. To date, under the TBT, there have been almost 40,000 notifications with over 600 targeted for discussion in the Committee. The process is a model that contributes to lessening trade friction, reducing the need for costly and time-consuming WTO litigation.

During the pandemic, efficiency was greatly enhanced by automating the process of notifications, the filing of concerns, and access to them. There had already been a new online access system known as ePing developed over the last several years.[10] The service allows users, whether officials or those engaged in commerce, to register to receive standards notifications of particular interest to them, whether pertaining to agricultural or industrial goods. It fosters communications between those who may have their trade subject to the standards and the regulators who promulgate them. Since notifications top 5,000 per year, this online service transforms transparency from a theoretical possibility into something real, practical, and timely.

Shortcomings and proposed remedies. Many WTO members believe that compliance with the WTO's notification requirements needs to be improved. In mid-2021, thirty-seven members, including the USA, the EU, and Japan, proposed a decision for adoption by the entire membership flagging a problem, namely "the chronic low level of compliance with existing notification requirements under many WTO agreements, and the difficulties that some Members are facing to comply fully with the notification requirements due to capacity limitations." Listing fourteen separate WTO agreements with notification requirements, including the Agreement on Agriculture and the Agreement on Subsidies and Countervailing Measures (SCM), the proponents recommitted to filing their own notifications promptly. They also suggested a series of procedural improvements along with very mild sanctions for a continued record of noncompliance. The member would be shamed, and to some extent shunned: it would still be permitted to pose questions during trade policy reviews, but members would not be obliged to respond; and its representatives would not be eligible for nomination to preside over WTO bodies.

Four of the members proposing the above-described reforms – Canada, USA, EU, and Japan – on July 21, 2021, tabled a separate more detailed draft Ministerial Decision to make improvements to transparency requirements just for agriculture.[11]

[10] "ePing SPS and TBT Platform." ePing SPS and TBT Platform. www.epingalert.org/en/

[11] "Committee on Agriculture – Special Session – Proposal for a Ministerial Decision on Transparency Improvements in Agriculture – Communication from Canada, the European

The TPRM. Another prime example of the WTO providing transparency consists of the process of peer reviews of each member's trade policies. The Trade Policy Review Mechanism (TPRM) is an important innovation of the Uruguay Round negotiations and was put into place in 1988, years before the Round was concluded. The reviews cover goods, services, and intellectual property. The review mechanism is considered one of the best innovations of the multilateral trading system. The objectives are:

- *to increase the transparency and understanding of countries' trade policies and practices, through regular monitoring,*
- *to improve the quality of public and intergovernmental debate on the issues, and*
- *to enable a multilateral assessment of the effects of policies on the world trading system.*[12]

A combination of factors makes the TPRM successful. The preparation is a collaborative effort of the Secretariat and the member focused on the member's trade policies and practices. The Secretariat provides an independent report. An ambassadorial-level Head of Delegation of one of the other WTO members takes on the assignment of chairing the meetings for a particular member whose practices are the subject of the review. The chair presents a summary at the end of the session and this summary is published promptly after the proceedings.

A sample of the outcome of the December 2018 review of US trade policies included the following observations:

> *the trade and investment regime of the United States remained overall open and liberal, but raised concerns over the increasingly active recourse to anti-dumping and countervailing measures by the United States, global safeguard measures on solar cell products and large residential washing machines, action taken related to US national security, in the form of additional tariffs on imports of steel and aluminium products, the introduction of new "Buy American" provisions with respect to government procurement legislation, the low uptake of international standards in the United States, which may result in unnecessary trade barriers, limited market access for sugar, dairy and cotton, high tariffs, and the continued use of trade distorting support.*
>
> *... it was noted that a shift had occurred in US trade policy in the period under review,*[13] *with a distinct new emphasis on national security considerations in*

Union, Japan and the United States JOB/AG/213." World Trade Organization. July 26, 2021. The Ministerial Conference did not adopt the Decision.

12 "Trade Policy Reviews: Ensuring Transparency." World Trade Organization. www.wto.org/english/thewto_e/whatis_e/tif_e/agrm11_e.htm

13 This period covers the beginning of the Trump administration.

> *the pursuit of free, fair and reciprocal trade relations ... [and that] ... increasing trade tensions were clouds gathering on the horizon. It was in this context that the continued support and commitment of the United States to a predictable, rules based multilateral trading system took on a critical dimension, not only for its trading partners near and far, but also for the long-term economic well-being of the United States itself.*[14]

The United States received more than 1,700 written questions prior to this Trade Policy Review, and it has already responded to most of them.

For the Trade Policy Review of the European Union in February 2020, the chair summed up the review by noting that the EU remains the largest market in the world and is the most important trading partner for some eighty economies. The chair also noted that many members looked to the EU to help resolve the situation with respect to the Appellate Body (its work having been suspended for blockage of the appointment process), lead reform efforts, help relaunch the negotiating function, and propel the WTO to a successful outcome at MC12 (the planned November/December 2021 Ministerial Conference which took place in June 2022). The chair remarked that the EU had led by example in many areas, including by complying with WTO notification requirements and incorporating gender equality in its trade agreements and policies. The chair went on to state:

> *While many Members recognised the importance of trade with the EU under the multilateral trading system, they noted with appreciation the advantageous trade regimes in place between them and the EU to further liberalize trade, such as Free Trade Agreements and Economic Partnership Agreements and other regional arrangements.*[15]

This reference to bilaterals indicates that they coexist with the global system, praised by their signatories even if a source of potential concern to others.

The EU received more than 1,600 written questions prior to this trade policy review, and it had already responded to most of them. The chair noted that many members posed questions and raised concerns regarding certain EU sanitary and phytosanitary measures which in their view were not based on science or international standards and did not provide adequate opportunity to take into account the views of third countries: measures regarding the setting

[14] "Concluding Remarks by the Chairperson – Trade Policy Review: United States." World Trade Organization. December 17–19, 2018. www.wto.org/english/tratop_e/tpr_e/tp482_crc_e.htm

[15] "Concluding Remarks by the Chairperson – Trade Policy Review: European Union (Formerly EC)." World Trade Organization. February 18–20, 2020. www.wto.org/english/tratop_e/tpr_e/tp495_crc_e.htm

of maximum residue levels under EU technical regulations and standards, for example with respect to chemicals; rules on medical devices; high agricultural tariffs; high levels of domestic support; maintaining fisheries subsidies; and the continued application of the safeguard measure on steel.

In short, the TPRM shines a non-adversarial light on issues raised by a member's trading partners. Its purpose is to provide transparency and not to pose legal challenges.

The chair's summary of the 2018 Trade Policy Review of China stated that:

> *Members generally expressed appreciation for China's active role in the WTO. China being the world's biggest merchandise trader and one of the largest recipients of FDI, its policies have a direct impact on the global economy. Hence, Members called upon China to assume the increased responsibility linked with being a major player in the multilateral trading system.*

The chair continued:

> *[M]any Members expressed serious concerns about the preponderant role of the State in general, and of state-owned enterprises in particular. Some Members felt that State influence in China's economy has increased in various sectors. Members also raised questions about China's support and subsidy policies and local content requirements; continuing issues in China's IPR regime; they encouraged continued IPR protection and enforcement, called for more predictability regarding market price support and public stockpiling measures used for certain agricultural products, administrative licensing and approval process, inconsistency in certain sanitary and phytosanitary measures, restrictions on certain agricultural products; [they expressed concerns with respect to] cross-border data restriction and data localization requirements, the scope and impact of China's cybersecurity legislation and restriction of Virtual Private Network services; restrictive measures in certain services sectors such as tourism, and industrial policies in certain manufacturing sectors, including the production of new energy vehicles. Several Members also referred to what they perceived to be market-distorting policies resulting in excess capacity in some sectors, such as steel and semi-conductors. China was called upon to help address global overcapacity in these sectors.* (This section has been edited to be a summary of points made by the chair.)

As in the previous review, China was encouraged to increase the transparency of its trade policy regime. Members highlighted the importance of fulfilling all WTO commitments, in particular the notification obligations concerning, for example, subsidies (including those on fisheries), agricultural support, and state-trading enterprises. Members encouraged China to publish all laws, regulations, and other measures related to trade, and to make them available in one of the WTO official languages. China had received more than 1,900 written questions and had already responded to most of them.

The bottom line. It is fair to ask what impact trade policy reviews have. Those most deeply involved in the process confess that with respect to the largest trading countries, it is difficult to connect comments made with changes in policies. Transparency is, after all, not a cure-all. Smaller countries, it is said, utilize the reviews to work for positive change. To be sure, there needs to be more effect on larger members. Making the chair's summary available in a video message online might stir domestic forces for change. Greater compliance with WTO obligations by all members should be obtained, including by the largest.

REASONS FOR HAVING THE MULTILATERAL TRADING SYSTEM

Why multilateralism? A common set of rules with no country left behind makes both practical and economic sense, especially as digital technologies and improvements in logistics continue to shrink the world. Moreover, some matters are not susceptible to negotiation through less than a multilateral approach. This is true when it comes to seeking disciplines on subsidies, whether the area is industrial or agricultural. For some to agree to forgo subsidies, but with less than a critical mass of members participating, opens the possibility of adherents to new disciplines being at a competitive disadvantage vis-à-vis countries that do not accept enhanced subsidy disciplines. An exception to this general statement with respect to a sub-multilateral agreement is the EU's single market. Its state-aids code, regulating member state spending, can preempt measures that would potentially distort internal trade between member states.

Learning from Brexit. An instance in which there has been scope for regulation of domestic subsidies in a preferential trade agreement occurred with the United Kingdom opting out of the EU in Brexit.[16] Brussels was concerned that at some time in the future, with its products facing fewer EU barriers to entry, Britain might subsidize to achieve competitive advantage.

Brexit also illustrated dramatically that the global trading system is a safety net. Without being in the single market and had there been no Brexit Agreement, the United Kingdom would still have had the benefit of

[16] "EU State Aid Rules and WTO Subsidies Agreement." UK Parliament – House of Commons Library. August 4, 2021. https://commonslibrary.parliament.uk/research-briefings/sn06775/

nondiscriminatory treatment from nearly all of the world. It would have the transparency the WTO provides, it would have access to WTO dispute settlement, and it would have an equal voice in setting the trade rules and the benefit of those rules. Its exports would have the assurance of tariff treatment within established limits and national treatment within foreign markets. It would have the flexibility to defend its interests through permitted trade remedies to avoid injury to domestic industries. It would maintain its sovereignty, as compliance with WTO obligations is voluntary. A member may face retaliation for not living up to its obligations, but the WTO is not a supranational government. The WTO cannot compel any member to take any action.

CONCLUSION

Businesses are now global, actually or potentially. This is true for the world's largest multinational companies and for the single-person businesses selling designs or apps over the web. Their needs for nondiscriminatory market access and transparency are or will be global, not regional or bilateral. What they require is predictability, certainty. To the extent that these can be constructed, they can only be fully supplied by a global forum.

All those involved in trade require rules, whether they are buyers, sellers, brokers, transportation companies, or those who regulate trade or set trade policies. Often, the rules need to be of broader applicability than any bilateral or regional agreement could provide. Exporters rarely wish to have only a single foreign market to sell to. Importers rarely wish to obtain all their goods from one foreign source. A former US Trade Representative in an administration that was openly hostile to multilateralism said, "if the WTO did not exist, it would have to be created." There are no second-best options. Global trade requires a global organization and global rules.

The concept of a community of nations is an extension of Cicero's concept of *civitas*.[17] The members are united by law, with consequent rights and responsibilities. The WTO is more than a body of members and the WTO Secretariat. It is the contract, the order, and the rules that the members created. Consensual international governance can bring about order, stability, peace, and economic growth. These precepts, embedded in major traditions, found their way through Dutch lawyer, Hugo Grotius, to the political theorists creating the liberal international order following the Second World War. The

[17] William Smith. 1875. *A Dictionary of Greek and Roman Antiquities*. London: John Murray.

philosophical foundation upon which the multilateral trading system rests, the difference between world government and collective world governance, channeling Grotius, has been expressed as follows:

> *While rejecting the idea that there are common interests among states sufficient to underpin a supranational authority, the Grotian system identifies a "solidarity" of interests around basic principles of order (such as mutual independence, adherence to promises, the limitation of war) that enables sovereign states to constitute their relations as a (limited) community rather than as a contest governed by the dynamics of power alone.*[18]

This is the vision that the founders had. They were neither naïve nor shortsighted. It is the mission the WTO members and Secretariat are to serve.

A flame of multilateralism for trade was lit three-quarters of a century ago. It has burned ever brighter for most of the ensuing years, but its incandescence is not what it was, and can diminish further, or it can reach a much-needed increased luminosity. The outcome is in the hands of its members.

The essence of the world trading system is creating a world order acceptable to and supported by its members, who retain in the extreme full sovereignty over their trade but have lent some of this precious commodity to a common endeavor for the benefit of all.

[18] "Hugo Grotius (1583–1645)." *The Internet Encyclopedia of Philosophy*. www.iep.utm.edu/grotius/#H4. – Among international law theorists during the period leading up to and following the Second World War, none was more influential than the Oxford Professor Sir Hersch Lauterpacht. He held that compulsory adjudication is essential to promote the rule of law within the international community. This element of the trading system was not contained in the GATT and was not added to the trading system until 1995 with the founding of the WTO.

4

Twenty Values of the Multilateral Trading System

In creating the WTO and the GATT before it, the world's trading nations did more than enter into a contract. They also created a compact that is imbued with a series of values. No understanding of the WTO would be complete without understanding this qualitative aspect, often explicit, but sometimes only to be derived from the operation of the WTO and its agreements.

The G20 leaders at their summit in Buenos Aires on December 1, 2018, declared that "the system is currently falling short of its objectives and there is room for improvement. We therefore support the necessary reform of the WTO to improve its functioning." A year later, in Osaka, the leaders reaffirmed their "support for the necessary reform of the World Trade Organization (WTO) to improve its functions," adding, "we agree that action is necessary regarding the functioning of the dispute settlement system consistent with the rules as negotiated by WTO Members."[1]

The reason most often cited for the need to reform was the seizing up of the dispute settlement system. The United States blocked new appointments to the WTO Appellate Body (AB). As three AB members are needed to hear a case, on December 10, 2019, when the terms of two out of its three remaining members came to an end, the AB ceased to operate. This deprived the WTO of one of its core functions: to deliver, upon a complaint being filed, authoritative decisions on whether the actions of a member were consistent with its obligations. While dispute settlement panels would still continue to meet and render their decisions, these would be deemed preliminary on matters of law.

[1] They added, interestingly, in their statement: "Furthermore, we recognize the complementary roles of bilateral and regional free trade agreements that are WTO-consistent." "G20 Osaka Leaders Declaration." G20 2019 Japan – Ministry of Foreign Affairs of Japan. June 29, 2019. www.mofa.go.jp/policy/economy/g20_summit/osaka19/en/documents/final_g20_osaka_leaders_declaration.html

Because the AB ceased to exist except on paper, all too often major country litigants, rather than accepting a panel report as final or making an alternative arrangement to conclude a case, chose to "appeal into the void," to a chimera, in effect freezing the prospect of reaching a final outcome in the matter being litigated.

A second, equally important and related concern was that the WTO had become barren of any new accords and there was little prospect that any negotiated agreements would be reached any time soon. The last attempt at a comprehensive multilateral negotiation providing for both trade liberalization and establishing new rules for trade was the ill-fated Doha Development Agenda effort that foundered in 2008. In terms of multilateral agreements, the only prospect was a single negotiation to control fisheries subsidies, important in its own right but not sweeping in scope, nothing like the eight major rounds of multilateral negotiations under the GATT. And, sad to say, even the fish negotiations were not making much progress until partial agreement was reached at MC12 in June 2022. If the members could not meet to forge new agreements, they were even less likely to be able to give effective review to any decisions of the Appellate Body which they might feel added to the rights and obligations of WTO members, which the AB was, under the agreement establishing it, expressly forbidden to do.

Despite the repeated calls for reform by leaders and trade ministers, there was insufficient activity within the WTO to examine what reform meant, to identify what changes would be needed. In this vacuum, the Kingdom of Saudi Arabia, having the presidency of the G20 for a year, decided to ask the G20 trade ministers to make a beginning by at least identifying principles of the WTO to which they could all agree without dissent. The Saudi effort was given the name "The Riyadh Initiative on the Future of the WTO."

Consulted by representatives of the Saudi government as to what I thought should be on the list, I considered it necessary, before addressing what changes should be made in the Organization, to first understand what values the multilateral trading system stands for and promotes. On May 27, 2020, in a discussion hosted by the Korean International Trade Association (KITA), I provided an initial list of sixteen underlying values of the WTO. I headed the list with promoting peace and stability, because those were the two values that dominated the thinking of the founders of the trading system in 1948. The two were not, however, thought about very much during the Uruguay Round negotiations when the WTO was being conceived. The times were very different. The Cold War had just ended and there were no conflicts among the major powers. Nevertheless, these values remain critical as central objectives of conflict-affected and fragile acceding countries today.

Looked at from an institutional point of view, the foundational values of the WTO are nondiscrimination and transparency, addressed in the prior chapter. We begin in this chapter to address the third value of overriding importance to the trading system – the rule of law. Other values are more nuanced and emerge only upon reflection. They include: reciprocity, equality, sovereignty, market forces, convergence, universality, well-being, development, international cooperation, morality, and sustainability. When I spoke to a working session of the Riyadh Initiative hosted by the Saudi government on June 25, 2020, I identified three additional values: openness, balance, and trust. In this chapter, I would add still another value, deliberation.

I have consciously chosen to address "values" rather than "principles" to avoid sifting through a taxonomy to determine which qualities of the WTO should be designated principles and which should be seen as values or objectives, as they largely amount to the same thing, with differences more in degree than substance.

THE RULE OF LAW

On September 28, 2020, at a virtual meeting of the G20 trade ministers, the Saudi chair, in his summing up of its Riyadh Initiative, stated that all members agreed to a list of the principles of the WTO. The first in the list was "Rule of Law."[2]

At the heart of the multilateral trading system are the rules as agreed to by the WTO's members, including those inherited from the GATT years. It is by virtue of their existence that world commerce flows as freely as it does. In the absence of WTO rules, there would either be at worst anarchy or at best a patchwork of bilateral and regional arrangements and lower global economic growth. Taken for granted by most of those who engage in international commerce, the rules are, in fact, essential.

It is the rule of law that provides the basis for several other qualities of the multilateral trading system, each interrelated with the others. Under a rule of law well-administered, nations are better able to *trust* each other. Trust among sovereigns provides a higher degree of certainty, essential if trade is to move unimpeded across borders. Businesses, even those consisting of one person or

[2] The others were "Transparency, Non-discrimination, Inclusiveness, Fair competition, Market openness, Resistance to protectionism and Reciprocal and mutually advantageous arrangements, . . . [which] provide for differential and more favorable treatment for developing economies, including special attention to . . . least developed countries." "G20 Trade and Investment Ministerial Meeting: Communiqué." G20 Information Centre. September 22, 2020. www.g20.utoronto.ca/2020/2020-g20-trade-0922.html

just a few, require the rules to be clear and predictable before they decide to ship a good or provide a service to a foreign market. For major international companies wherever there is uncertainty trade and investment slow, and in extreme cases, stop. For consumers, importers, exporters, and producers alike, in short for most of the world's inhabitants who engage in trade, the predictability upon which world commerce relies is underpinned by WTO rules. The result is increased *stability*, a condition in which economic growth can occur and positive political relationships can be developed.

Civilization is necessarily based on the rule of law. Evidence for this truth exists almost wherever one looks throughout history. The famous Chinese emperor Qin Shi Huang, founder of the Qin Dynasty and known to us primarily for his grand parade of terra cotta warriors unearthed in Xi'an, issued an early Imperial Chinese legal code.[3] Examples of rules to govern conduct are found in all cultures and times, including the Code of Hammurabi, the Dharmasutras, the Bible, the Quran, the teachings of Solon, the Pax Romana, the US Constitution, the Code of Napoleon, and the Treaty of Rome of the European Union. Whether the form of government is autocracy or democracy, whether laws are created and employed through the application of force or freely determined by consensus, legal systems are created to guide human conduct. Where there is society, there are rules.

For global trade, the rules are contained in the WTO. There is no effective substitute. For international commerce to thrive, the rule of law is a necessary precondition.

The presence of law does not mean that there will be no conflicts. To the contrary, law exists because there will always be differences that are not automatically reconcilable. This is as true for the rules needed for traffic entering a roundabout as it is for international commerce. Interests, and perceived interests, clash. In the world of geopolitics as well as of trade, given that there will always be conflicts, the question is how they will be managed. At the global level, where sovereign nations interact, governance needs to be achieved and maintained without creating an overarching world government, which is not only unattainable but is not desired by any of the WTO's 164 members.

Hundreds of conflicts have been managed successfully in the GATT and in the WTO over the course of nearly eight decades. In 1965, the United States and the European Communities (EC) engaged in a "Chicken War," which at the time did feel like a trade war – although by today's standards it seems as if it

[3] Qin Dynasty (221–206 BC).

were only a skirmish. The facts are these: the formation of the European Common Market resulted in the curtailing of US chicken exports to its six original member states, a diminution of the market access that had been committed to the United States. Under GATT rules, the United States was allowed to counter this loss of market access by imposing additional duties on products coming from the EC, in this case: brandy, dextrose, potato starch, and light trucks.

The United States and the EC acted within their rights and lived up to their obligations, rebalancing their trade commitments. This has been broadly true in general throughout most of the history of the GATT and WTO. Countries largely live up to their obligations, and should in most cases have been aware that there would be consequences for failure to do so. Eventually the retaliation was largely removed in subsequent trade negotiations.

Most disputes do not result in retaliation. In most instances, the offending measure is withdrawn. As of May 2022, 612 disputes had been brought to the WTO and over 350 rulings were issued. Compliance with the rules may be achieved before a panel is composed following one or more rounds of consultations. This occurred in the first WTO case brought against China. In 2004, the United States, joined by the EU and Japan, sought formal consultations with China. China had imposed a 24 percent VAT on domestic and foreign-produced semiconductors but rebated 17 percentage points of the tax to domestic producers. This was a clear violation of China's national treatment obligation. China withdrew the subsidy shortly after the consultation.

The very existence of the rules has a salutary effect. Countries usually act in accordance with their obligations voluntarily without being compelled to do so. International agreements are generally observed. (*Pacta sunt servanda.* Agreements are to be honored.) When I served in the US government during the late 1970s, I chaired an interagency committee that formulated US trade policy (the Trade Policy Review Group). A new GATT code was about to be adopted, a plurilateral agreement covering government procurement. A question arose with respect to the treatment of fourteen small countries with which the United States had nondiscrimination obligations under pre-existing treaties. These fourteen countries were not planning to sign up to the new code. Under the procurement agreement, only signatories were required to be accorded the benefits. The question being debated was whether the United States would honor its bilateral treaty obligations, extending the benefits of the new code to these countries and getting nothing additional in return. While there were strong voices against extending the benefits of the code on a nonreciprocal basis, it was clear that if the decision were referred to the President at the time, Jimmy Carter, he would without doubt decide that America would keep its word.

There were other instances like this during the GATT years, even though dispute settlement at the time was not binding – that is, panel results could be blocked by the losing party. A panel found that the US Domestic International Sales Corporation, a program under which the tax burden on exporting companies would be alleviated, violated US obligations. The measure was repealed. During the WTO era, when a WTO panel found against the United States, holding a 2002 safeguard action on steel imports inconsistent with the rules, the George W. Bush administration terminated the measure.

This may also have been what happened after the US brought a case against Japan to obtain market access for photographic film. Thereafter, Japan engaged in a series of domestic economic reforms, favoring a more market-oriented economy. Was there a cause and effect? That would be hard to prove. During that era, Japanese government officials from time to time welcomed *gaiatsu*, foreign pressure, to bring about change desirable from Japan's own point of view. The two countries adjusted their trading relationship toward greater openness, and eventually the trade frictions disappeared.

There have been and always will be cases in which the rules do not appear to cover all forms of conduct complained of. The chief problems cited with respect to trade with Japan during that era often involved Japanese companies acting, with government support, in ways that did not allow market forces to determine competitive outcomes. The problems resulted from failures of competition policy to a greater extent than violations of the GATT rules. The frictions between China and its trading partners at present are not all clearly covered by existing rules. In these cases, conflicts will continue until new rules are agreed, or conduct that is of concern is modified.

As addressed in Chapter 3, a peaceful and positive global environment for world commerce can best be created through multilateral agreements. No set of unilateral actions can create a world trading system. The same holds true for a plethora of bilateral commercial deals between governments or the negotiation of regional arrangements. There is no substitute for an overarching set of rules to govern world commerce.

This does not mean that regional arrangements cannot advance the rule of law, even if selectively. Bilateral and regional trade agreements, for example, include provisions dealing with digital commerce among signatories. They are often potential building blocks for wider future reforms at the multilateral level. However, all ad hoc deals seeking to fix a trade problem and discriminatory trading arrangements should be closely scrutinized. They may be of commercial benefit for the participants through trade diversion but may do little or nothing positive for world commerce. Rule-making on a multilateral level must be restored if the relevance of the WTO to new challenges is not to be greatly diminished.

The rule of law provides benefits beyond the pursuit of narrow commercial self-interest expressed solely in terms of swapping reciprocal concessions – that is, country A lowering its tariff on product X in return for country B lowering a tariff on product Y. Were this the sole content of trade negotiations, there would not be a world trading system, just a collection of thousands of limited deals. Some additional elements must be added for creating and maintaining institutional arrangements for the good of all. For over seventy years, nations chose to act beyond their narrow commercial self-interest to make a net contribution to the structure of the system itself. As a result, the world economy grew much faster than would otherwise have been the case, and the overall level of worldwide poverty declined dramatically.

RECIPROCITY

Reciprocity is the touchstone of negotiators. Not much mentioned in public pronouncements, it is a necessary value of the WTO, looming large as a practical matter. It is less a high-minded ideal than a practical political necessity. No trade negotiator wishes to go home from a negotiation and have to counter a charge from domestic legislators and their constituents that more was given than was received.

Reciprocity will always be a litmus test of whether a negotiation was a success, whether the subject is trade or foreign policy. John Jay negotiated a treaty with England in 1794 bringing about peace after the American Revolution. The result was controversial. No negotiator wishes to be burned in effigy upon returning from the negotiating table, as Jay was. In Washington, DC, the downtown area is a grid, with numbered streets running north–south and streets designated by the letters of the alphabet running east–west. There is still no "J" street.

Reciprocity was the selling point that allowed Cordell Hull to get tariff negotiating authority from Congress, in the aptly named Reciprocal Trade Agreements Act of 1934. The law made possible the process of using more open trade as an antidote to the Great Depression. The heart of the Act was a delegation of tariff authority to the President:

> *The President, whenever he finds as a fact that any existing duties or other import restrictions of the United States or of any foreign country are unduly*

> *burdening and restricting the foreign trade of the United States ... is authorized ... To enter in foreign trade agreements with foreign governments ... and to proclaim such modifications of existing duties and other import restrictions ... as are required to carry out any foreign trade agreement that the President has entered into hereunder.*[4]

Without those words, that Act, and its subsequent extensions, the GATT could not have come into existence, and we would not have a multilateral trading system or the WTO today.

The acceptability of trade concessions granted is judged by weighing concessions gained against concessions granted. While strict reciprocity has practical limits, as a political matter, all participating countries should have a general sense that a negotiation has reached balanced results.

This of course is not the only reason to make trade policy decisions. Countries often remove tariffs on inputs of needed raw materials and food. They may not care very much whether what they have done out of self-interest is matched by others. This was the case with respect to the many unilateral (and temporary) trade-liberalizing measures countries applied to imports of essential medical supplies in response to COVID-19.

Judging whether there is reciprocity is to some extent always a subjective exercise. In any complicated negotiation, as all multilateral negotiations are – even when conducted on a sectoral basis, such as for duty-free treatment for pharmaceuticals,[5] or information technology products,[6] or with respect to the opening to a degree of government procurement[7] – one has entered the realm of uncertain estimates. For a great negotiating round – the Tokyo Round or the Uruguay Round – at its conclusion there would be a variety of highly subjective tests given to justify results to domestic constituencies.

Acceding to the WTO also involves negotiation. The acceding country will consider what benefits it will receive compared with the notional freedom of action (also known as "policy space") it may have to give up when it existed in a state of nature. Likewise, members voting to admit a major country, such as

4 "Reciprocal Tariff Act of 1934." Fraser – Federal Reserve Bank of St. Louis. June 12, 1934. https://fraser.stlouisfed.org/title/reciprocal-tariff-act-1934-5876

5 "The WTO's Pharma Agreement." World Trade Organization. www.wto.org/english/tratop_e/pharma_ag_e/pharma_agreement_e.htm

6 "Information Technology Agreement." World Trade Organization. www.wto.org/english/tratop_e/inftec_e/inftec_e.htm

7 "Agreement on Government Procurement." World Trade Organization. www.wto.org/english/tratop_e/gproc_e/gp_gpa_e.htm

China in 2001, will consider whether the benefits received are worth the extension by them of the benefits from their existing WTO to the new entrant. In the case of China's accession, the balance of benefits remains a subject of current debate in some quarters in the United States, even though China entered the WTO two decades ago. When a very small country seeks to accede, while there may be modest haggling over a few specific trade items, the central focus will be on whether the government has put into place the institutions and domestic laws and processes that all members of the WTO should be expected to have.

As noted in the discussion of the rule of law, WTO members also can and should make a net positive contribution, giving more than they directly receive – for example, making their notifications as complete as possible even if some other members do not. The surplus beyond strict reciprocity is a contribution to making the trading system work for all, the creation of a common good. This leads to greater global economic growth and more certainty for trade, which is very much in each member's own self-interest.

Even the poorest least developed nation can make a net positive contribution. Providing good ideas for the system, innovations, is not the sole province of the most industrialized and largest trading nations. The least developed are certainly experts on many of their own needs. Practical suggestions for positive measures are worth more than rhetoric – this is true for all members. During my service as Deputy Director-General of the WTO, I chaired the Consultative Forum for Cotton Development Assistance. Chad, Burkina Faso, Benin, and Mali are very poor countries, but they made the effort to present workable ideas on how to assist their productivity in growing cotton and increasing income from cotton by-products, a major interest for each of the four. In doing so, they served the trading system.

The system will function best with net positive contributions received from all. Collectively, the whole is greater than the sum of its parts. Trade is a multiplier of economic benefits, just as the capital in banks creates more financial support for the community in which it is located than the amount of capital itself.

SOVEREIGNTY

Every international agreement that includes obligations requires a participant to give up, to a limited degree, some element of sovereignty. The party to the agreement must make a judgment that any narrowing of complete freedom of action is at least offset by the gains from the restraints imposed on the actions of others. In practice, there is a net gain for each signatory.

Sovereignty is a subject not discussed at the WTO, but it is very much present. For some, it is referenced obliquely as the desire for "policy space," meaning maintaining freedom of action unconstrained by additional WTO obligations. For others, policy space is found under the existing provisions of the WTO Agreements when they assert either that a given rule was inapplicable due to an exception to the rules to a measure they wish to put into place or that an exception to the rules applies. due to an exception to the rules. Policy space is most expansively provided, in the views of some members, including prominently the United States, when national security is seen to be at risk.

Sovereignty is respected by the multilateral trading system in many ways. That which is not regulated or prohibited by the WTO rules is, by implication, permitted. These extensive areas of unconstrained freedom of action have often been advanced as a selling point for the trading system. A common example consists of wide freedom to impose measures for protection of the environment. There is a plethora of other examples of unregulated conduct. Governments are free to impose measures taken to preserve an endangered species or preserve domestic stocks of agricultural or industrial products deemed to be in short supply. The guiding principle is that such measures are consistent with a country's WTO obligations (for example, not constituting camouflaged trade protection) and that the measure does not unnecessarily discriminate against foreign goods.

Policy space is not an unalloyed positive. At times, the actions of one country in an area where global trade rules do not apply can cause adverse consequences to the interests of others. An example is the granting of domestic industrial subsidies: only very lightly regulated by the WTO rules but nevertheless potentially trade-distorting.

Policy space is also damaging where collective action is needed, such as when confronting a pandemic or climate change. Policy space can result in too many uncoordinated national actions being put into place which have an adverse impact on others. This happened in 2020 during the global health crisis. While policy space invoked by large trading countries has more of an impact globally than when it is being claimed by smaller countries, policy space for some may well mean not only potential harm to the interests of others, but a net loss for global commerce and impairing the growth of new areas of endeavor – for example, maintaining policy space to adopt national regulations for e-commerce that will inevitably fragment world trade.

Sovereignty is also largely unimpaired as a legal matter because unless a country so chooses, a WTO obligation has no direct effect within a member's territory. In the United States, as is the case with most WTO members, WTO rules have not been incorporated into domestic law. An infraction of a rule, or receipt of an adverse finding by a panel, changes nothing automatically. The government receiving an adverse finding by a panel, that its measure was inconsistent with its obligations, is obligated to take positive steps to comply with the ruling. The WTO has no enforcement arm. The WTO, like the Pope, does not have an army.[8] It can, however, authorize retaliation if a noncomplying member does not remove or amend the offending practice. A government can act contrary to its commitments, but it may pay a price for doing so.

Owing a debt of compensation for the breach of the rules is an ancient practice. This is a concept with which the Babylonian king Hammurabi, ruling 4,000 years ago, was fully familiar with and which he included repeatedly in the 282 laws that he had inscribed on a basalt stele. These distant forebears were familiar with the payment of compensation as an appropriate response to an offending measure not being removed. Countries winning a case at the WTO may have the right to restrike the balance of concessions with the losing party if the value of what they bargained for is diminished by actions found to be WTO-inconsistent. In some provisions of the WTO, such as with respect to safeguards, offsetting action is permitted without resorting to dispute settlement. The EU sought to employ this Babylonian concept when it placed sanctions on American exports in response to the US restrictions on imports of steel and aluminum.[9]

There is another way in which WTO practice respects national sovereignty, some would say to too great a degree. Members are protected against an erosion of their sovereignty as the WTO has, during its quarter-century of existence, operated exclusively by consensus. For example, no multilateral agreement can be put into place without the support of a substantial number of members and at least acquiescence from *all* of the rest. Consensus has

[8] The Papal Army was disbanded in 1870.

[9] See Law no. 200 of the Code of Hammurabi: "If a man knock out the teeth of his equal, his teeth shall be knocked out" [A tooth for a tooth]. "The Code of Hammurabi." Yale Law School – Lillian Goldman Law Library. 2008. https://avalon.law.yale.edu/ancient/hamframe.asp. The EU was seeking to shoehorn its retaliatory measure into the WTO Agreement on Safeguards, which provides:

> 2. *If no agreement is reached within 30 days in the consultations under paragraph 3 of Article 12, then the affected exporting Members shall be free, not later than 90 days after the measure is applied, to suspend, upon the expiration of 30 days from the day on which written notice of such suspension is received by the Council for Trade in Goods, the application of substantially equivalent concessions or other obligations under GATT 1994, to the trade of the Member applying the safeguard measure, the suspension of which the Council for Trade in Goods does not disapprove.*

come close to being defined as unanimity. Operationally, consensus should be seen as similar to the ability of passengers traveling on a train to stop the train, where there is an emergency brake handle on each car. This brake, the ability of any member to prevent a consensus from being reached, is a guarantee of not only sovereignty, but a form of super-sovereignty. One member can even block a meeting agenda from being adopted. In effect, one member is delegated the sovereignty of all 164 members to stop an action. Forward motion is possible only to the extent that no member exercises its option to reach for the emergency brake except in the case of an emergency that threatens all. Again, as with any society or organization, self-restraint is fundamental. It is a precondition for any social interaction, and for any collaboration, to operate successfully.

At the opposite extreme, a "negative consensus" is a concept that is applicable to the adoption of panel and Appellate Body reports by the WTO's Dispute Settlement Body. A decision is adopted unless all, including the prevailing country, decide to reject it – a null set. This process, to which all have agreed, completely deprives members of their sovereignty in this one respect. For in WTO dispute settlement as it was designed, all members have donated their sovereignty into a pool from which no withdrawals are permitted insofar as they cannot block an outcome with which they disagree. As noted, however, these findings by themselves have no direct effect on the losing party. The great irony of the two extremes of super-sovereignty – from complete sovereignty with respect to stopping agreements from being reached to none at all in the case of dispute outcomes – is that the rule of positive consensus has allowed one member (the United States) to end the operation of the negative consensus rule with respect to operations of the Appellate Body, by dismantling that institution.

Clearly there are serious flaws to be examined and remedied with respect to the application of a rule either of positive or negative consensus, reaching some agreement as to their limits. The result of not facing this question, which no member has suggested be faced, is that the multilateral trading system has ceased to function fully, either for rule-making or for dispute settlement. To this extent, sovereignty has prevailed over international cooperation.

Freedom of action has natural limits. With no WTO, there might be the illusion of greater sovereignty, that is, no constraints whatsoever on a country's trade actions. But given that all other countries would be likewise totally free of agreed constraints, the individual nation's sovereignty would in reality be seriously compromised. Being completely free in the middle of a jungle can be a dangerous position in which to find oneself.

EQUALITY

In the Atlantic Charter, the document that Franklin Roosevelt and Winston Churchill issued to state their aims for the world that they envisaged as emerging following the Second World War, they stated that they would "endeavor, with due respect for their existing obligations, to further the enjoyment by all states, great or small, victor or vanquished, of access, on equal terms, to the trade and to the raw materials of the world which are needed for their economic prosperity."

The ideal of equality has a distinguished, if relatively modern, pedigree. The first founding principle of the United States, enshrined in the most famous of its documents of origination, the Declaration of Independence, is that "all men are created equal." This is a statement that has echoed across the ensuing centuries and around the world. Similarly, equality is a founding principle of France, adopted by Maximilien Robespierre, stated as one of three central objectives of the French Republic – *liberté, égalité, fraternité*. It is a powerful organizing mandate.

Equality is an unstated principle of the WTO. All WTO members have an equal right to speak, table proposals, and vote (although operating by consensus has eliminated voting, and instead gives each the unspecified right to join, abstain, or block a consensus). (For example, one of the smallest African countries blocked African unity and therefore adoption of a proposal that had the strong support of all the industrialized countries and most of the developing world.) All countries regardless of size have a right to demand support from the Secretariat for activities that they wish to pursue at the WTO. Moreover, the principle of equality conveys with it the concept of inclusiveness, often cited as one of the hallmarks of the Organization.

Of course, equality is an aim, not an instant result. Within a domestic economy and among nations, there is little actual equality. In the WTO, as often elsewhere, the levels of capacity of members differ. In physical terms, for example, a few delegations to the WTO are nonresident, not being able to afford maintaining a permanent mission in Geneva. Some are resident but do not have enough officers to cover all meetings of all UN organizations based in Geneva, while still others have large numbers of staff. Many country representatives have multiple responsibilities within Geneva, covering not just the WTO but also a number of other international organizations. Some have responsibilities to represent their country in Bern or in more than one capital. Capacity is a limit on enjoying equality.

How well the principle of equality works depends on whether those WTO members with greater capacity take on proportionally greater responsibilities for the success of the common endeavor – the functioning of the Organization, its maintenance and growth. Fortunately, a number of the small and medium-sized members do take on a higher-than-average level of responsibilities, and occasionally so do the largest members. Equality would lack meaning if there were not meaningful benefits of participation to be shared. Fortunately, there is not only a stock of benefits to share but they are also being added to, from time to time, such as greater transparency during the pandemic, available equally to all members.

MARKET FORCES

The fundamental underlying assumption of the WTO is that market forces will dictate competitive outcomes. Few if any of the WTO's rules would have their intended positive effect if commercial considerations – price, quality, delivery, and the like – were overcome by political considerations, such as the implementation of buy-national policies through government influence. This value is also a basic principle of the WTO. It is not stated in the WTO articles themselves, because presumably it was so obvious as a principle that it was assumed. In the Declaration accompanying the WTO Agreement, on April 15, 1994, ministers declared that they were: "determined to build upon the success of the Uruguay Round through the participation of their economies in the world trading system, based upon open, market-oriented policies and the commitments set out in the Uruguay Round Agreements and Decisions."[10] The principle is fundamental to the WTO. Its rules, the commitments with respect to both border and internal measures, become inoperable if market forces are not allowed by members to determine competitive outcomes in general.

The existence of this principle does not mean that there is no place for legitimate regulation by the state. There is room for governments to pursue public policies that do not constitute hidden protection. All governments, however free-market-oriented their economies are, intervene for public purposes to varying degrees. They have antitrust laws, prevent harmful substances from being traded, and regulate domestic commerce for public safety, among tens of thousands of other measures.

The WTO does not dictate the organization of economies. It has not ruled out state ownership, and the unwritten requirement of market orientation should not be conflated with a question of government ownership. All

[10] "Marrakesh Declaration of 15 April 1994." World Trade Organization. www.wto.org/english/docs_e/legal_e/marrakesh_decl_e.htm

governments have a public sector – whether for public works, health, postal services, or some other purpose deemed to require direct government ownership. This does not detract from the WTO principle. Even a state-owned enterprise (SOE) is to conduct its activities in accordance with commercial considerations. It is also understood that market forces determining competitive outcomes could have undesirable effects in extreme circumstances, such as the bidding up of prices of scarce medical supplies during the pandemic to the disadvantage of those in need. Governments are expected to react and do so, but the fundamental principle of market orientation remains essential.

CONVERGENCE

A corollary of the value that market forces will determine competitive outcomes is that where this is not the case – such as in Soviet Socialist states (when they joined the GATT) and, in a different manner, the economy of Japan during part of the last third of the twentieth century – the assumption was made that these economies would evolve toward operating like all others, allowing market forces to determine competitive outcomes. The WTO, the multilateral trading system would, without the assumption of convergence, need to wall off economies functioning on a different basis, with what GATT legal expert John Jackson referred to as "interface mechanisms." These would, and did for Eastern European countries joining the WTO, for example, require import-purchasing quotas, and more informally export restraint agreements in the case of Japan. Either the market will over time begin to become increasingly determinative of the flow of commerce or more direct management of trade would be required. Without doubt, the WTO is about convergence, not coexistence of incompatible domestic economies.

UNIVERSALITY

Multilateralism, by definition, must be all-inclusive, bringing in all countries which are willing to assume the obligations of the system. This harks back to the notion of equality. For Cordell Hull, Churchill, and Roosevelt, it was logical that the multilateral system had to be global. Open to all. WTO members of all stripes, but particularly the smaller economies, call for "inclusiveness." It is not set out in this book as a separate value, because it is already part of other values, particularly that of equality. Nevertheless, it is a value of the WTO so long as it does not suggest that unanimity is needed for any progress to be made. As far as non-members are concerned, inclusiveness should not be a value that can logically be confined to members. The WTO cannot by definition be a closed club. It must bring in any countries that qualify for membership. If there is reciprocity, if all are willing to contribute, the best system of governance for world trade is one that is universal, for much the same reason as in physics, an optimal shape to contain a fluid is a sphere. It is inefficient to utilize any other form. While there are other values to be fostered beyond efficiency, the burden should be on those who advance those values to demonstrate that there are sufficient benefits to eschewing efficiency.

STABILITY

For hundreds of thousands of years *homo sapiens* apparently invented nothing. There was no clear physiological reason for this, no limits imposed insofar as anthropologists know due to human brain size. One answer to this paradox may be that inventiveness requires at least a modicum of a stable environment.

This is also true of entrepreneurial activity, of engaging in commerce. It is an axiom of business that it needs a degree of certainty, of predictability, in order to plan, in order to take risks. The word "stability" figures in the opening line of the ITO Charter, which states at the outset that the countries creating the ITO recognized "the determination of the United Nations to create conditions of stability."

The entirety of the GATT and the WTO rule book, including the accompanying procedures, are designed to impose a degree of order for the conduct of global commerce. Tariffs are not to exceed contractually committed levels other than in certain limited and usually temporary circumstances. This obligation is one of the cornerstone commitments of the GATT Articles and is set forth in WTO/GATT Article II. Proposed standards are to be notified in draft for comment by other WTO members. Transparency is required throughout the two dozen agreements that constitute the WTO's rulebook. The grand design of the entire sweep of WTO rules and procedures is to provide greater certainty for world commerce, to create a degree of stability that enables trade to take place and entrepreneurs to plan.

None of this is perfection. The degree of transparency can be improved. But what exists is nevertheless remarkable. It was the result of a common effort, spanning just over seven decades, to provide order. The result, the WTO, provides conditions governing almost all of world trade. Even with shortcomings in coverage or shortfalls in compliance, this is an outstanding achievement, providing greater harmony for the governments and the peoples of the planet.

WELL-BEING

In the opening words of the Havana Charter for the ITO, the second value enumerated, following stability, was "well-being." The United Nations, it read, was determined "to create conditions of stability and well-being."

Stability by itself does not produce well-being. Stability can as readily promote stagnation as economic growth. Stability is a precondition, not a guarantee of improvement in the economic lot of trading nations and their peoples. Nor does trade guarantee economic growth. It is a multiplier, an accelerant of possibilities. As theorized by Adam Smith and elaborated upon by David Ricardo, specialization within an economy and then internationally allows for a higher level of income on average. It does not address the distribution of benefits, but relies on the proposition that there are far more economic benefits to share if there is trade than without trade. The major determinants of trade flows are macroeconomic forces, but liberalized trade taking place within a context of agreed rules can have a strong positive effect, while trade restrictions will almost always have a negative effect.

That there have been major benefits from trade in the post-Second World War period should be beyond dispute. Trade is a large multiple of what it was in 1947,[11] and from what it was when the WTO was founded in 1995.[12] So are the levels of national and global income. In addition, the reduction in the levels of global poverty has been dramatic.

Overall well-being can be enhanced by economic efficiency, but it is not an end in itself. The WTO charter in the Marrakesh Agreement Establishing the WTO states that the purpose of this endeavor is to achieve "full employment and a large and steadily growing volume of real income and effective demand, and expanding the production of and trade in goods and services."

Trade is to have broad societal benefits. The mosaic on the wall of the main hall at the entrance to the Centre William Rappard in which the WTO makes its home – a home inherited from the International Labor Organization – reminds any visitors who pause to read it: "[U]niversal and lasting peace can be established only if it is based upon social justice." The tiles continue by

[11] According to World Bank data, the volume of world trade in merchandise exports grew from US$122.993 billion in 1960 to US$17.692 trillion in 2020. Measured in nominal terms (current US$), world trade multiplied by more than 140 times between 1960 and 2020. The figure of world trade volume peaked in 2018 at US$19.672 trillion, which is approximately 160 times higher than 1960 levels.

[12] According to World Bank data, trade as a percentage of GDP increased by 40% between 1995 and 2019. During this period, world GDP doubled, and world trade volume of goods and services tripled.

calling for "the protection of the worker against sickness, disease and injury arising out of his employment."

The plain meaning of the term "well-being" must include health. Aside from international security, which is the province of the United Nations and nation-states, well-being rests on both global health and positive economic circumstances. The hard lesson of the pandemic is that a global health crisis gives rise unavoidably to a global economic crisis. Both inevitably involve trade policy. How countries react to a pandemic matters, not just with respect to the availability of medical supplies and vaccines but also in terms of the damage that is caused to the economy.

A fundamental measure of the value of the WTO, and the multilateral trading system it embodies, is how well it serves the well-being of the world's peoples. While WTO members might be excused by the suddenness of the arrival of COVID-19 for not having immediately formulated a collective response, this justification lost any force which it might have had as the coronavirus returned as predicted with subsequent waves. There will be no excuses at all for a lack of preparedness for future pandemics. What will be remembered from this challenging time for the world trading system will be less the initial concerns over export restrictions on essential goods but the differentiation among nations with regard to access to effective vaccines.

The multilateral trading system, as with other international organizations, should be judged ultimately by the good that it does for people. The system of rules under which trade flows globally is most often a remote public good, generally unseen. Current generations have not witnessed the alternative, the prior world of war and trading blocs. But some observers are already warning of deglobalization, of a world divided, characterized to a great extent by discriminatory trading arrangements. The negative impact on global well-being would be felt.

DEVELOPMENT

In a liberal international trading order that has among its precepts equality and universality, development – that is, bringing all members to a level at which they can enjoy the full benefits and undertake the full obligations of membership – of necessity must be a primary objective and value of the system.

It is an article of faith on the part of some and perhaps many representatives of developing country members of the WTO that a primary purpose of the Organization is development. This is articulated in numerous statements made in WTO General Council meetings. It is also translated into a belief that special and differential treatment is a right. This position has elicited statements from some developed countries that there must be differentiation among self-designated developing countries depending on the capacity of each. This clash of views has given rise to spirited verbal exchanges with no resolution in sight.

It has been said by some representatives of industrialized countries that the WTO is not a development institution. This argument goes beyond the parameters of the differentiation debate. The WTO clearly is a development institution in some respects. A basic purpose of the WTO is to facilitate economic growth – that is, economic development for all. Countries have differing capacities to take advantage of what is offered by the WTO Agreements and the degree to which they can fulfill WTO obligations. It is in the interests of all WTO members that continuing progress be made by all members to achieve the twin objectives of receiving the benefits offered and living up to the obligations required by membership. For this reason, technical assistance is made available to all developing countries, including through WTO internships for future officials from developing countries. In addition, the WTO offers onsite and in-country training sessions on a wide variety of subjects, from the requirements of the Government Procurement Agreement to those of intellectual property protection.

The multilateral trading system supports the specialization of production which in turn raises income levels in countries moving into more advanced stages of economic activity. For the cotton farmers of West Africa, being helped to take advantage of the value of what is often now wasted in underutilized by-products can make a positive difference. This is also a benefit for world trade in general. Specialization fosters the economic progress of advanced industrialized countries through the trading system making global value chains possible, very often including developing countries.

Development must be a continuing WTO value applicable to all. It is in aid of economic development for the benefit of all that members seek to put into place rules to serve the emerging global digital economy. It is imperative that all countries, including the least developed, be able to participate in the rapidly evolving world of digital commerce. Not allowing the free flow of data, or burdening e-commerce with forced localization of servers, can only slow economic development. It is the opposite of inclusiveness that the same developing country representatives call for.

If a country does not accept, despite all evidence, that trade is good, and good for development, membership in the WTO may not be appropriate for that country.

MORALITY

Morality, as with other matters from the realm of philosophy, does not figure much in exchanges between trade negotiators. But as the multilateral trading system is the product of human beings and morality is part of their individual and collective composition, morality underlies the multilateral trading system, even if it is implicit. All actions taken could be explained solely in utilitarian terms, but there is more to the WTO's agreements than that. Were there no moral element present, there would not be a special provision related to intellectual property rights governing the availability of pharmaceuticals in cases of urgent need.

It is worth a separate discussion whether government trade policy, or for that matter companies' public policies, should include moral obligations. Should governments adopt trade policies that improve the environment or avoid harm to the health of other countries' citizens? It has not been a traditional subject for trade negotiators, but that is likely changing. WTO Agreements to date have mostly been about what countries commit to do for commercial reasons and not about moral obligations. But in a number of instances the WTO Agreements do support greater moral rectitude, most clearly, for example, in the government procurement agreement, which seeks to prevent corruption. Transparency requirements can have a positive effect in this regard as well. The negotiations on fisheries subsidies and the Trade and Environmental Sustainability Structured Discussions which are underway provide venues for discussion on the moral issues involved in the stewardship of the planet.

SUSTAINABILITY

In the mid-1940s, the priorities of the founders of the multilateral trading system were reconstruction and development, aiding in recovery from the ravages of war. For this reason, the original structure of the multilateral trading system was centered on rules to facilitate trade through removal of quantitative restrictions and lowering of tariff levels. Environmental concerns were largely dealt with by avoiding the rules of the trading system interfering with national measures designed for the protection of the environment, as long as they did not result in unnecessary protection or in discrimination.

The interests of WTO members have evolved and continue to evolve. In 2015, all WTO members as member states of the United Nations adopted a 2030 Agenda which includes seventeen goals for sustainability. These goals reflect UN member priorities and are reflected in their work in the WTO. At the 2017 Buenos Aires Ministerial Conference (MC11), ministers decided on a work program to conclude negotiations on establishing disciplines on fisheries subsidies, which would deliver on Sustainable Development Goal 14. Goal 14 is to conserve and sustainably use the oceans, seas, and marine resources for sustainable development. Goal 14.6 calls on signatories to:

> *by 2020, prohibit certain forms of fisheries subsidies which contribute to overcapacity and overfishing, and eliminate subsidies that contribute to IUU [illegal, unreported and unregulated] fishing, and refrain from introducing new such subsidies, recognizing that appropriate and effective special and differential treatment for developing and least developed countries should be an integral part of the WTO fisheries subsidies negotiation.*

In addition to seeking to address the fisheries subsidies objective, Groups of WTO members are expressing interest in bringing into the WTO potential initiatives for promoting the circular economy (to reduce waste), curbing plastics pollution in the oceans, assisting in slowing climate change, and disciplining fossil fuel subsidies.

OPENNESS

It should not be necessary to state what may be taken as a self-evident proposition, that the multilateral trading system is about a progressive opening of markets to international trade. The entire structure of the WTO and the GATT, the multilateral trading system itself, rests upon the principle that to the extent provided within the bounds of the WTO Agreements, markets will be open to international trade and that trade is to be as free from distortions as possible. Examples abound – tariffs are bound at maximum levels, quantitative restrictions are largely forbidden, and product standards are not to be a disguised restriction on international trade.

The 1994 Marrakesh Declaration states that the WTO was being created to reflect "the widespread desire to operate in a fairer and more open multilateral trading system." In addition, it states that the ministers express their determination to resist protectionist pressures of all kinds and are desirous of contributing to these objectives by entering into reciprocal and mutually advantageous arrangements directed to the substantial reduction of tariffs and other barriers to trade and the elimination of discriminatory treatment in international trade relations.

The seventy-five-year history of the multilateral trading system is one of progressive opening of markets, although progress slowed once tariffs of industrialized countries on average reached low levels. Still, duty-free treatment was achieved for pharmaceuticals and information technology products for a high proportion of world trade in these products. Movement of goods across borders also received a substantial prospective boost from the entry into force of the Trade Facilitation Agreement. An attempt was made to achieve duty-free treatment for environmental goods, which came very close to conclusion and negotiations may well be revived. The last intended great round of negotiations would have been the Doha Round, but that negotiation ran out of track in 2008. One notable place where continuing opening takes place at present is through the negotiations undertaken by acceding countries as a precondition for their entry into the WTO.

A caveat to the principle of openness and lack of distortions of trade is that openness is required of WTO members only insofar as members undertake contractual commitments to be open. As an illustration, a representation was once made to a state legislature by the US State Department that adopting a buy-local preference "would be contrary to the spirit of the Government Procurement Agreement." While there is an animating spirit inherent in the creation of the WTO toward greater openness, it is as a legal and practical matter achieved only through negotiations and the undertaking of binding commitments, not through an invocation of spirits. Where it has made no commitment, a member is not constrained from acting based on its own decision as to what is in its best interests. In the case cited, the judgment would largely be made on whether a buy-local preference made economic sense to that jurisdiction, and whether the extra budgetary cost incurred by a buy-local preference was worth the support provided to the local or national economy. Recent manifestations of moving toward greater openness can be found in the unilateral tariff reductions on imports of essential goods during the pandemic, even if these reductions were intended to be temporary. Likewise, the Canada-led initiative to renounce resorting to export restrictions on food during the pandemic was a contribution to open trade.

BALANCE

Balance in the world trading system, as seen through the eyes of WTO members, is provided in a variety of ways:

- through the member's judgment of the costs and benefits of the rights it enjoys and the obligations it has undertaken;
- through its view of how its costs and benefits compare with those of other members; and
- through its judgment of whether it has sufficient freedom to act to temper its commitments for trade liberalization (*openness*) with measures designed to deal with any harms caused thereby.

To date, 164 current members of the WTO and twenty-four countries that seek to join have made the judgment that there is a more than sufficient positive balance for those in to remain in and for those countries on the outside to accede. But there are some evident strains. Individual members are often not convinced that the balance is perfect on one or more of the criteria just cited, at least in some respects.

The impact of obligations will more often than not on occasion be seen by governments and their constituents as more measurable than benefits received. The obligations undertaken by other members are not always seen as equivalent to those that they have undertaken.[13] The current or future freedom of action for a member (what some call "policy space"), the flexibility to restrict trade and temper trade liberalization (*openness*), is sometimes seen as being inadequate. Each instance, each test of faith in the system, can lead to disaffection.

This is an epoch marked by the publication in 2013 of Thomas Piketty's book *Capital*, which provided a renewed focus on income inequality. The book became a bestseller, coinciding with a rise in populism around the world. Alongside this movement, there is a growing minority view in the economics profession that following the path illuminated by David Ricardo and trod by Cordell Hull is not always the best national policy.[14] The July–August 2020 issue of *Foreign Affairs* contained an article by the then-US Trade Representative calling for the United States to have an employment-based trade policy, and the subsequent Biden administration has made this central to its policies. The rise of dissatisfaction in public sentiment with other countries' trade practices poses a serious threat to the post-Second World War liberal international order.

Reading the WTO Agreements and examining the way in which they have been applied in the light of an employment and real income objective is an increasingly necessary exercise. The WTO was founded, according to the opening words of the Marrakesh Agreement creating the Organization, with the objectives of "raising standards of living, ensuring full employment and a large and steadily growing volume of real income and effective demand."

Rising global GDP, to which trade is an important contributor, has meant that on average all are better off. A rising tide lifts all boats – on average. The

[13] Article XII members, those that joined after the WTO was created, often state that their obligations are more extensive than those of the original members. This is the case because joining the WTO requires negotiations with current members whose trade interests have expanded to additional subjects since the organization was founded in 1995.

[14] For example, this includes scholars such as Dani Rodrik and Joe Stiglitz.

trading system's contribution to global economic growth and the raising of hundreds of millions out of poverty is worthy of solid praise. That said, more attention should be paid to the relationship of the multilateral trading system to employment, the level and nature of which are a substantial determinant of income inequality. This is a political question, not just an economic abstraction. Getting the answer right can affect the degree of support that the WTO and the multilateral trading system receive.

It should be acknowledged at the outset that trade policy is not the only or the best lever to accomplish a reduction in income inequality or economic insecurity. Income distribution and assurance of employment are very largely, almost entirely, best addressed by domestic policies. For example, during the pandemic, in a number of countries, emergency financial aid to businesses was conditioned on business recipients' maintenance of jobs. Trade policy can, however, contribute to softening the effects of the ultimately ineluctable movement toward increasing globalization.

Economic forces and continued technological advances mandate the direction of change. Globalization may pause, it may even temporarily retreat, but it will continue. On September 7, 1424, the Hongxi Emperor terminated the voyages of exploration by the great Chinese Admiral Zheng He, but six centuries later, China is now perhaps the foremost trading country. Economic forces ultimately triumph. It was not foreign black ships in the tradition of the West's prying open of Japan that caused Deng Xiaoping to begin the opening of the Chinese economy in 1978. It was a domestic policy choice.

In the current era of ease of global communication, travel, and movement of goods and services, it can take just a few months to return to trend – steadily increasing globalization. No substantial reduction in international commerce will prove sustainable over time. The laws of economics governing the conduct of every business, whether for a giant multinational corporation or a single entrepreneur, drive toward this outcome.

US domestic laws and practice provide a number of means for dealing with severe declines in economic activity. Without the bankruptcy laws in the United States, many small businesses, and some large, would not survive the economic effects of the pandemic. When investor sentiment seeks to adjust to the daily news and creates extreme market volatility involving massive declines, the New York Stock Exchange relies on circuit-breakers, temporary suspensions of trading.

The circuit-breakers of the WTO can be found largely in the form of trade remedies – safeguard measures and tools to offset the effects of subsidies and dumping. Here there is another balance to be struck. The health of world trade cannot be sustained with overuse of trade remedies. On the other hand, if these temporary, limited departures from the overall movement in the direction of trade liberalization are unavailable, this will undermine support for the trading system. The system of rules is to be reinforcing. Sufficiently effective WTO rules mandating the general openness of borders can make it less likely that antidumping or anti-subsidy measures will be necessary. Dumping most often occurs from a protected home market.

Where the WTO disciplines are weakest, such as with respect to domestic subsidies, there will inevitably be trade friction. The situation can be compounded by shortcomings in WTO consultative processes caused in part by the shortfalls in the notifications of these measures. Differences in market structures and openness of borders can give rise to harms for which there are no clearly approved WTO remedies.

The experience of the last half-century shows that WTO-acknowledged trade remedies are most often invoked with respect to labor-intensive manufacturing industries, not coincidentally where international competition can create the greatest public discontent. Relief from trade distortions, when seen from an exporter's point of view, impairs market entry and is unpredictable. At the same time, from a domestic industry's point of view, relief from harmful imports when available is episodic and insufficiently effective. Domestic adjustment measures are rarely adequate and too often are not prescribed to accompany import-restricting trade measures. When the response mechanisms to dumping and subsidization are seen by exporters as being illegitimate and by importers as being ineffective, the trading system appears to be imbalanced from both perspectives.

The absence of appropriate buffering mechanisms can lead to a buildup of pressures that ultimately causes structural harm to the system.[15] Steam engines had governors to release excess pressure. For the WTO, either the means will be found to deal with trade frictions and transitional harm from international competition, or excess pressure can and will be vented through resort to measures taken outside of the WTO framework. If the capacity of the circuit-breakers of the WTO is inadequate to contain a surge in the perceived need for their use, there will be increased risk to the system itself.

Systemic risks are heightened if there is already a level of discontent due to a perceived imbalance of rights and obligations, and if it is a member's view that others have more benefits from the system than it has. The durability of the system depends on the conclusion being reached by most countries that

[15] As noted in the section above on convergence, John H. Jackson, a law professor who was one of the fathers of the idea of the WTO, referred to the need for interface mechanisms between countries whose domestic practices differ.

despite these comparisons, in fact the benefits of belonging far outweigh the costs.

There is no cause for complacency. Improvements are needed to reinforce support for the trading system. Support has been on the wane in general globally. Every member government of the WTO has at least an implicit social contract with its people to look after their employment. There is a similar collective commitment – a social contract of members – to be found in their membership in the World Trade Organization. This is contained in the employment objective cited in the Marrakesh Agreement Establishing the WTO. It is inherent in the commitment of the WTO to be an engine for economic development, to ensure that developing countries, and especially the least developed among them, secure a share in the growth in international trade commensurate with their needs.

Employment and development are subjects that will increasingly be used to define balance in the multilateral trading system. Nations will continue to search for balance in their participation in the international trading system.

INTERNATIONAL COOPERATION

International cooperation is part of the essence of multilateralism. Global cooperation has the potential to provide better results quantitatively and, in many instances, qualitatively than two nations working bilaterally or a few nations working together in a region. Indeed, some matters do not lend themselves to sub-multilateral outcomes. Regulation of subsidies, both for industrial goods and for agriculture, is one of these subjects. Leaving some free to subsidize while others demonstrate restraint will lead to unequal conditions of competition and will not be tolerated. A multilateral negotiation is needed.

There is no sub-multilateral arrangement that can equal the possibilities of global cooperation, difficult as achieving results on a global scale is. Governments are learning that for the largest challenges – dealing with the pandemic and climate change – there is no alternative to cooperation with others.

TRUST

The multilateral trading system depends almost entirely on members voluntarily living up to their commitments. It is true that the structure of the WTO provides a remedy through dispute settlement for failures to do so, but international trade would largely cease if trade-restrictive measures that were inconsistent with the rules were as a regular matter simply put into place and then only removed prospectively through lengthy litigation. Without voluntary compliance, the process for restoring a balance of rights and obligations where a breach has occurred would too often require that the breach be ruled to be inconsistent by a dispute settlement panel, followed by an appellate finding, followed by adoption of the decision by the WTO's dispute settlement body, followed by a ruling by a compliance panel, followed by threatened or actual retaliation. This is a painfully long process that caused discontent with the system. The members are now experiencing the opposite by living in most instances without binding dispute settlement. Voluntary compliance is diminishing when judged by adverse judgments of panels that, rather than being complied with, are notionally "appealed" when no commonly agreed appeal mechanism exists. Trust is necessarily diminished.

If there was a jewel in the crown of the WTO, it is the widespread willingness of members to live in accordance with the rules of the system. No negotiations would take place providing for either increased market access through trade liberalization or the formulation of new rules, if there were a low expectation that the resulting agreement would be lived up to by its signatories. Fortunately, most obligations are taken seriously by the WTO members and are fulfilled. Otherwise, the system would not work. Trust is a quality that comes only from an accretion of experience, that agreements will be lived up to, both in general, and on the part of any specific member.

Trust can also be damaged even where the coverage of the agreements is incomplete, where there is freedom of action. The WTO rules will never be sufficiently prescriptive to meet every contingency. While there can be a justifiable hope that trade will remain unrestricted and undistorted, there is no guarantee that this will be so. During the early days of the COVID-19 pandemic, export controls were imposed because of concerns over short supply of medical devices. Measures were taken, for example, by preemptive purchasing or preemptive investments in companies that did or could produce medical supplies. Whether the challenge is a global health or climate crisis, or geopolitical rivalry, there is a danger to trade as well as to amicable relations among nations if they are cast adrift in an ocean of policy space. Trust will then erode. Where there are no clear rules, trust, to the extent that it exists, must be based on an expectation of international cooperation.

Trust is a perishable commodity. If there is too much testing by members of the outer limits of existing rules or the taking of excursions outside of them, trust deteriorates, and the multilateral trading system becomes less reliable.

PEACE

At its most fundamental level, the trading system, like the European Union (*née* European Communities and European Economic Community), was founded to promote peace. It seems rather quaint to cite peace in the current context. Surely, some might say that it is an anachronism of remote historical interest at best. Something to be left to academic inquiries. But how relevant is it today?

The quest for peace has strong philosophical roots. In 1795, Immanuel Kant published an essay entitled "Perpetual Peace: A Philosophical Sketch." In his essay, Kant states:

> *There must be a league of a particular kind, which can be called a league of peace (foedus pacificum), and which would be distinguished from a treaty of peace (pactum pacis) by the fact that the latter terminates only one war, while the former seeks to make an end of all wars forever. This league does not tend to any dominion over the power of the state but only to the maintenance and security of the freedom of the state itself and of other states in league with it, without there being any need for them to submit to civil laws and their compulsion, as men in a state of nature must submit.*

Kant was setting out a fundamental purpose of humanity, to create a state of perpetual peace. To serve this end, in the aftermath of nearly a half-century of war, the liberal international order was constructed. It was based on four pillars – the multilateral trading system (ITO and GATT, and became eventually the successor, the WTO), the United Nations, the IMF, and the World Bank. Together, these institutions were intended to help build a better world than the one that preceded it. They were each part of an effort to underwrite the hope for perpetual peace. In this context, the WTO and the GATT are not simply contracts, but are a purposed construct for achieving a much more basic human aspiration.

You will not hear Immanuel Kant being quoted often by WTO members taking the floor. The idea of promoting peace seems very remote in most respects from subjects that daily engage the minds of the commercial diplomats who represent the members in the corridors and conference rooms of the WTO in Geneva. Yet sustaining peace was very much on the minds of the founders of the multilateral trading system. This is evidenced by the very first paragraph of the Havana Charter for the International Trade Organization, the intellectual forebear for the WTO, which states:

> *RECOGNIZING the determination of the United Nations to create conditions of stability and well-being which are necessary for peaceful and friendly relations among nations . . .*

> *... they hereby establish the INTERNATIONAL TRADE ORGANIZATION through which they shall co-operate a[s] Members to achieve the purpose and the objectives set forth in this Article.*

I have set out previously a short history of the role of peace in trading arrangements which led to that moment of creation of the multilateral trading system and of the disappearance of "peace" from our WTO lexicon – until its resurrection by conflict-affected countries which are in the process of acceding to the WTO.[16] These fragile economies are unexpectedly numerous. The list includes Afghanistan and Liberia, both of which joined a short time ago, and now Ethiopia, Somalia, Sudan, South Sudan, Timor-Leste, and Iraq among others. For these countries, and those who seek to help them accede to the WTO, the promotion of peace is a very real principle, a cause espoused as being fundamental to their rationale for becoming members of the WTO. The hopes for peace for most WTO members today are a distant echo of what US President Abraham Lincoln called the "mystic chords of memory," in this case a first founding principle of the multilateral trading system's striving for peace. These fragile economies seek to reform their economies, to expand their trade through integration into the world economy, thus stimulating their own economic growth, leading to increasing stability, and thereby improving the possibility of sustaining peace. This is not a fanciful theoretical exercise; it is a pragmatic policy at the core of their survival as nations.

Economic growth through trade does not guarantee peace. It did not for the nations that entered the First World War, which enjoyed robust trading relationships with each other before they began engaging in one of the bloodiest of human conflicts. Trade does, however, help increase the chances for peace to be achieved and maintained. Trade and peace can feed positively into each other. There is no peace where there is complete uncertainty in trade relations. Indeed, throughout history, cutting off trade has been a method of warfare. In its current manifestation this can take the form of imposing export restrictions or engaging in cyberattacks that disrupt the economies and commerce of others. It cannot be said that the WTO overregulates with regard to such measures.

DELIBERATION

One central quality that was to be attributed to the GATT and the WTO was deliberation. Legislative bodies are designed for long and careful consideration or discussion. It may not seem to be much in evidence at the

[16] "DDG Wolff: Trade and Peace are Intimately Related." World Trade Organization. June 16, 2020. www.wto.org/english/news_e/news20_e/ddgaw_16jun20_e.htm

WTO – more an aspiration than a reality. It does take place, however, in committee meetings, whether the members are addressing the WTO budget or a substantive matter. Among representatives of governments, it can easily descend into reading statements from capitals that are repetitive and have little effect on those within hearing distance. There are certainly sterile exchanges. Within the Trade Policy Review Mechanism, there are also elements of thoughtful consideration by the member being reviewed as well as the delegates asking questions. There is no acceding member that is waived into the WTO without undergoing more than bilateral negotiations but also deliberate consideration of its qualifications for membership. There is deliberation in every negotiating body if the participants are intent on making progress, as they have been in the Joint Statement Initiatives.

To the charge that there is insufficient deliberation, one would have to give the objective judgment that this is the case. There was during the first year of the pandemic only one council meeting dedicated entirely to the subject. What is needed in the WTO are more "dedicated discussions," as have been initiated for topics regarding trade and the environment. There need to be more workshops. There needs to be a greater ability to listen to other members' views, more sensitivity to understanding them, and finding areas of compromise. For this, greater trust must be earned and common purpose found.

One of the six candidates for Director-General of the WTO in 2020, Hamid Mamdouh of Egypt ran on a platform of restoring deliberation to the WTO. It is hard to disagree with his recommended cure for a central deficiency of the WTO, the shortfalls in deliberation. Any sensible and effective program of WTO reform must contain this basic element.

CONCLUSION: VALUES MATTER

As noted earlier in our discussion, on September 28, 2020, at a virtual meeting of the G20 Trade Ministers under Saudi Arabia's leadership, the chair, in his summing up of its Riyadh Initiative, stated that all members agreed to a list of the principles of the WTO. The full agreed list is as follows:

Rule of law
Transparency
Non-discrimination
Inclusiveness
Fair competition
Market openness
Resistance to protectionism

> *Reciprocal and mutually advantageous arrangements ... [which] provide for differential and more favorable treatment for developing economies, including special attention to ... least developed countries.*

As these are principles agreed to without dissent by the world's twenty largest economies, it ought to be possible to infuse the daily work of the WTO Secretariat and members with the mission to fulfill them.

The ensuing discussion in this book will delineate the shortfalls in living up to these agreed principles and the values listed above and suggest ways in which gaps in performance could and should be filled.

While economists would see the sum of all WTO values as being the promotion of economic efficiency, politicians would judge the WTO more by another standard: does the institution, the WTO, which is no more than the embodiment of the members' cooperation in the field of international trade, promote fairness? If this cannot be demonstrated, the future of the WTO will be in doubt. I have not set out fairness as a separate value, as it is the sum of all of the values, as white sunlight is a composite of the full spectrum of colors.

There is practical use to be made of listing values. In the notional rush to reform, inchoate as it is, it is best to understand the nature of the public good that the WTO does and is to embody. To promote useful change, first any approaching the task should understand the value and values of what already exists or was supposed to exist.

5

A Brief History of the WTO as Told to Us by Its Ministerial Conferences

The modern history of the World Trading System may be said to start with ministers gathering in Hakone, Japan, to launch the Tokyo Round of Multilateral Trade Negotiations, followed a decade later by the launch of the Uruguay Round Negotiations at Punta del Este, Uruguay. This chapter will trace the journey taken by the WTO, covering twelve WTO Ministerial Conferences from 1996 to 2022.

PRELUDE: THE TOKYO AND URUGUAY ROUNDS

A PERSONAL NOTE

The arc of history of the multilateral trading system, once it was founded, is recorded in its Ministerial Conferences, in what ministers representing the interests of their countries stated as their hopes, plans, and concerns in trying to shape the system. Over the span of five decades, I had a seat somewhere in the vicinity of the action, sometimes somewhere on stage, sometimes with a rather good seat, sometimes in the back of the hall and often only in the theater lobby.

I enter the picture in a remote role, in 1972 at the US Treasury Department, as the representative of the Treasury in interagency meetings called to craft the US negotiating mandate for what was going to become the Tokyo Round of multilateral trade negotiations (MTN), the next to last great GATT negotiating round. I moved a bit closer to the action, but still rather distant, by joining the Office of the Special Representative for Trade Negotiations as Deputy General Counsel, under the renowned GATT scholar, John H. Jackson, to continue to work on the US mandate for participation in the talks. In that era the United States was arguably still the most important player. So being on the most important team, although not playing a central position, did get me closer to the action. As a junior player, I did ask to be included in the delegation headed by Treasury Secretary George Shultz, going to Hakone for the launch of the Round in 1973, but they really did not need my legal skills for that endeavor and I was left at the home base organizationally at the White House in Washington,[1] to continue work with congressional staff, hammering out what the US negotiating mandate and the new trade laws would look like.

Later, in 1975, fate would make me for several months acting head of the US delegation to the Tokyo Round in Geneva. It could best be described as a time of painful inactivity for the Round, with occasional maneuverings among the actors to gain a more favorable position for when the negotiations would someday pick up momentum.[2] At the end of the Round, I was back in Geneva as US Deputy Trade Representative with the rank of Ambassador to handle aspects of the final negotiations between the United States and Japan, perhaps America's foremost trade adversary in the negotiations. It was not the most important role in the play, but it was not unimportant.

During the next chapter in this narrative, the Uruguay Round, I was out of government but seeking to shape elements of the negotiation from a gallery seat in the private sector, working on behalf of either a client or broader interests where I felt that the national interest as I saw it required some adjustment in the positions America was taking. That brought me to the Heysel conference center in Brussels in 1990 for a ministerial gathering for what was to have been the conclusion of the Uruguay Round. Three years later I was in Geneva for the actual formal substantive conclusion in 1993, when in those vital final moments of the Round, I could be found arguing with the US Trade Representative in the early hours of the morning for some important changes in the Round's results, one item successfully and one unsuccessfully.

Often, I was to be found in hotel and convention center lobbies, aiming to understand what was taking place among government delegations, and to be of assistance where help was required on subjects that were important to me. "Lobbying" is a term of opprobrium,[3] and a misidentification of an essential

[1] The STR office was located at 1800 G Street NW, a block away from where the Deputy Trade Representative had his office, in the Old Executive Office Building (Old EOB), as it was then called (later named the Eisenhower Executive Office Building). His was a fine office on the second floor of the Old EOB commanding a view to the Ellipse, parkland to the south of the White House. STR was part of the Executive Office of the President, and therefore located virtually, but not physically, in the White House.

[2] It proved to be more than two years later that serious negotiations resumed.

[3] Barack Obama, as President, banned those who had been lobbyists from service in his administration, depriving it of expertise that would have contributed to a more successful presidency. Ambassadorial posts continued to be filled with financial contributors to his campaign, regardless of level of competence.

part of the process of international trade negotiations. It is not the government that is engaged in trade, but private actors, individuals, and companies. It was my job to help staff the negotiators, to act as an intermediary of business interests that would benefit from trade concessions, or be harmed by them, to make sure that the negotiated results would have the effect that the negotiators intended. It was not in the lobby where negotiating positions were shaped, but in the kitchen of the trade negotiations.

A remark attributed to German Chancellor Otto von Bismarck is that "to retain respect for sausages and laws, one must not watch them in the making." The same is true of all phases of international negotiations. At various junctures, I was involved in the sausage making. For the causes I was involved in, this was an essential side of the process, and I still do see it that way. Policy making is messy, but it is far better to be in the fray, in the arena, than to heckle from a safe distance as an irrelevant spectator. On the most important aspects of policies that I sought to influence, I testified in public hearings before Congress in aid of my objectives.

As a private sector participant in attempts at trade policy formulation, I was onsite for three WTO "Ministerials" – Seattle, Cancún, and Hong Kong. I was either in the lobby or in the back-row seat in the balcony during these performances, and sometimes closer. My role changed with MC11, the eleventh conference of WTO ministers held in Buenos Aires. I had just joined the WTO Secretariat as a Deputy Director-General, formally on October 1, 2017,[4] and the Ministerial Conference was held only two months later, in December. Within the WTO there is a strong convention that individuals in the Secretariat have only a supporting role, not even allowed into the chorus, and certainly not on stage. That is probably accurate for at least the time that I served (October 2017 through March 2021). Not having eaten the lotus petals yet,[5] I was still trying, despite being a putative nonplayer, to influence the process, to try to ensure the Ministerial would have some positive results, by getting it to agree to a ministerial declaration. Besides assisting the conference chair, Susana Malcorra, Minister Advisor to the President of Argentina, I tried a carom shot[6] –

4 I arrived one month earlier at the WTO, on September 1, 2017, as a consultant to the Director-General.

5 In Greek mythology, the lotus-eaters were a race of people living on an island sustained by the lotus tree. The fruits and flowers of the tree caused lotus-eaters to sleep in peaceful apathy and blissful forgetfulness of their duties and previous communities.

6 "Pool Lessons & Billiards Instruction – How to do Carom Shots – Terry Bell Master Class #20." YouTube. www.youtube.com/watch?v=3LWkKly429c

I asked that Moscow make representations to Pretoria and New Delhi to try to get the major players on the same page, to unblock the negotiating process. It did not work.

The purpose of this introduction is to let the reader know of vantage points that I have occupied during the times covered by the narrative that will now unfold. I have attempted in this narrative to depend upon the words of the major players to tell their story. It is largely uncolored by my perspectives, other than in my selection of what I thought were the most important elements of what the participants had to say. My role in this chapter is to present this history as objectively as possible.

The ministerial meetings over the course of five decades give a broad overview of how the multilateral trading system struggled to evolve from the GATT to the WTO. Arguably, this narrative could have begun with the Kennedy Round that concluded in 1967, but due to lack of implementation of the two nontariff agreements reached (the Anti-dumping Code and the American Selling Price System of customs valuation), the Round stands as another in a series of six GATT tariff reduction rounds and as such has little other precedential value.[7] The course of history changed, as was often the case during that era (and up through the present), through an unorthodox move by the United States that shook the system. On August 15, 1971, the United States imposed a 10 percent surcharge on imports in a manner knowingly in technical violation of its GATT obligations not to raise tariffs.[8] It did this ostensibly to force reform of the international monetary system, a system characterized by fixed exchange rates backed by gold. The gold-backed fixed exchange rate system was unsustainable. The United States was running out of gold. There was a trade aspect to the surcharge as well. Worried about its balance of payments position beyond exchange rate relationships, the United States demanded unilateral concessions from the European Communities (EC), Japan, and Canada. Understandably, these trading partners refused to enter into one-way, nonreciprocal agreements in which they gave trade concessions and received none in return. What they offered instead was a more ambitious multilateral negotiation, going beyond tariffs, reaching into dealing with nontariff barriers.

7 "Operations of the Trade Agreements Program with a Special Chapter on the Kennedy Round – 19th Report." United States Tariff Commission. August 6, 1969. www.usitc.gov/publications/332/pub287.pdf

8 Douglas A. Irwin. 2012. "The Nixon Shock after Forty Years: The Import Surcharge Revisited." National Bureau of Economic Research. www.nber.org/system/files/working_papers/w17749/w17749.pdf

HAKONE, SEPTEMBER 1973, THE TOKYO ROUND

Two years after the US import surcharge had been imposed and twenty months after it had been removed,[9] on September 14, 1973, the United States and its major trading partners reached agreement to begin a new round of trade negotiations, to be known as "the Tokyo Round" after the capital of the country where it was launched. The heads of delegation were finance ministers, not trade ministers. Two conditions imposed by the European Communities (EC) for the talks moving forward were that there had to be an agreement on a new international monetary system with fixed bands within which currencies could fluctuate, and that the United States would arrive at the talks with an advance grant from Congress of "negotiating authority."[10] These conditions were expressed by Sir Christopher Soames, the EC Vice President for External Relations, and Valerie Giscard d'Estaing, the French Finance Minister.[11] US Treasury Secretary George Shultz agreed. The US mandate for trade negotiations was being negotiated by the administration with the Ways and Means Committee of the House of Representatives at that time. The result was ultimately to become the Trade Act of 1974 when signed into law by President Ford on January 3, 1975.[12]

Japan was reported to be prepared to propose that it would remove tariffs immediately and fully in return for assurances of uninterrupted food supplies (the Nixon administration had imposed export controls on soybeans).[13] This

9 As part of the Smithsonian Agreement of December 18, 1971.

10 A technical point: the US Constitution vests the sole negotiating role for the United States in the President. However, if he seeks to implement the results of a negotiation and it requires any change in US law, this must be obtained from Congress in the form of legislation. President Nixon sought to circumvent this constitutional arrangement, by giving Congress the possibility of a veto (by a vote of either house) over the President simply changing US law to carry out an agreement. The House of Representatives would have gone along with that scheme, but the Senate would not. Had the Senate adopted the position of the House, it is likely that the Supreme Court would have struck down the statute as being an unconstitutional arrangement. "The End of the Bretton Woods System (1972–81)." International Monetary Fund. www.imf.org/external/about/histend.htm; John S. Odell. 2009. "The US and the Emergence of Flexible Exchange Rates: An Analysis of Foreign Policy Change." *International Organization* 33(1): 57–81.

11 "MIN(73)SR/Add.1 Statements Delivered at the First Meeting – Wednesday, 12 September 1973, 9.30 a.m." General Agreement on Tariffs and Trade. October 3, 1973. www.wto.org/gatt_docs/English/SULPDF/91870247.pdf

12 "Trade Act of 1974 – Summary of the Provisions of H.R. 10710." United States Senate Committee on Finance. December 30, 1974. www.finance.senate.gov/imo/media/doc/trade9.pdf

13 "The Impact of Trade Agreements: Effect of the Tokyo Round, US–Israel FTA, US–Canada FTA, NAFTA, and the Uruguay Round, Investigation No. TA-2111-1." United States International Trade Commission. August 2003. www.usitc.gov/publications/332/pub3621.pdf

tradeoff was not adopted by the finance ministers. The ministers presumably did not think that tariffs alone would result in full market access, and it was unclear that the United States would give an agricultural supply commitment.

The Tokyo Round negotiations were initially scheduled to last two years.[14] They did not in fact conclude until the spring of 1979. The Round was begun during the Nixon administration, continued during the Ford administration and concluded during the Carter administration.[15] One of the remarkable aspects of the conduct of major trade negotiations is that for many of the participants, they stretch over several incumbent administrations – whether in Japan, the EC,[16] or elsewhere. As we shall see, this was true also of the Uruguay Round and the Doha Development Agenda.

The Tokyo Round, thus initiated, was to reduce tariffs and other barriers to trade, based on reciprocity, and there was, at least initially, to be a single undertaking (everything was to be agreed as one package), although it did not in the end mean that every participant had to agree to join all of the agreements.[17] For example, the government procurement code offered increased access to signatories and not others. While the primary purpose of the Round was to continue "ever greater liberalization of world trade and improvement in the standard of living and welfare of the people of the world," this was to be done in a manner that would produce "a better balance as between developed and developing countries in the sharing of the advantages resulting from this expansion."[18]

Ultimately 102 countries participated in the Round. It reduced average tariffs to 4.7 percent and created nontariff barrier (NTB) codes on customs valuation, product standards, and government procurement.[19] It accomplished far less for agricultural products.

[14] Richard Halloran. "GATT Begins Talks to Liberalize World Trade." *New York Times*. September 13, 1973. www.nytimes.com/1973/09/13/archives/gatt-begins-talks-to-liberalize-world-trade-the-origin-and-purpose.html

[15] Alfred E. Eckes ed. 2000. *Revisiting US Trade Policy: Decisions in Perspective*. Athens: Ohio University Press. Page 125.

[16] The European Community (EC) was the economic association formed by six European member countries in 1957, consisting of three communities (the European Coal and Steel Community, Euratom, and the European Economic Community) that eventually were replaced by the European Union (EU) on November 1, 1993.

[17] "Ministerial Meeting Tokyo, 12–14 September 193 Declaration, GATT/1134." General Agreement on Tariffs and Trade. September 14, 1973. https://docs.wto.org/gattdocs/q/GG/GATT/1134.PDF

[18] Ibid.

[19] "The Tokyo Round 'Codes'" in "The Multilateral Trading System: 50 Years of Achievement." World Trade Organization. www.wto.org/english/thewto_e/minist_e/min98_e/slide_e/tokyo.htm. The Tokyo Round codes include: 1) subsidies and countervailing measures – interpreting

PUNTA DEL ESTE, SEPTEMBER 1984, THE URUGUAY ROUND

The Uruguay Round of Multilateral Trade Negotiations was launched at Punta del Este during a ministerial conference of GATT contracting parties (September 16–20, 1986). This was the last and greatest of the GATT rounds. It was the most ambitious. It did not set out to create a new World Trade Organization. Ninety-five GATT contracting parties (as countries participating in the GATT were called[20]) met to launch negotiations that were to broaden the GATT dramatically, going beyond lowering tariffs on goods to establishing an international agreement governing services, bringing agriculture meaningfully under multilateral disciplines for the first time, and providing for trade-related protection of intellectual property.[21] To benefit the developing countries, the Round was to reduce duties on tropical products. Other important aims were to create a new and more effective dispute settlement system, and to bring about meaningful trade policy reviews, as well as fulfilling to a much greater extent the GATT promise of transparency of trade regulation.[22] The *Financial Times* praised the resulting declaration in an editorial headed "Kiss of Life for the GATT."[23] (At this juncture, it is worth keeping in mind that in multilateral trade negotiations, whether one is referring to the GATT or later the WTO, there have always been times when onlookers would be tempted to hold a mirror to the mouth of the recumbent institution to see whether it was still breathing. It always was.)

Bringing agriculture into the disciplines of the trading system was a major objective of the negotiations. While there was to be liberalization through market access, as importantly, there were also the first limits on the use of agricultural subsidies, and an attempt to minimize the adverse effects of sanitary and phytosanitary (SPS) regulations.[24] The multilateral trade

Articles 6, 16 and 23 of GATT, 2) technical barriers to trade – sometimes called the Standards Code, 3) import licensing procedures, 4) government procurement, 5) customs valuation – interpreting Article 7, 6) antidumping – interpreting Article 6, replacing the Kennedy Round code, 7) Bovine Meat Arrangement, 8) International Dairy Arrangement, and 9) Trade in Civil Aircraft.

20 The word "countries" is chosen for ease of expression but includes customs territories (such as Hong Kong and the European Union) and its various incarnations such as the European Communities.

21 "The Uruguay Round." World Trade Organization. www.wto.org/english/thewto_e/whatis_e/tif_e/fact5_e.htm

22 Ibid.

23 Earnest H. Preeg. 1995. *Traders in a Brave New World, The Uruguay Round and the Future of the International Trading System.* Chicago, IL: University of Chicago Press.

24 "The WTO Agreements Series – Agriculture." World Trade Organization. www.wto.org/english/res_e/booksp_e/agric_agreement_series_3_e.pdf; Robert Griffin. "History of the

negotiations were continuing to reach behind borders to address policies that were seen at home as being domestic but affected trade in very significant ways. There are hardly more sensitive political subjects than domestic support for agriculture and regulations governing food safety. Subsidies (in the WTO Agreement on Agriculture termed "domestic support") can readily cause a major distortion of trade (at times creating an EC wine lake and butter mountain) and standards, as opposed to tariffs, can block trade entirely. It was these measures that the Uruguay Round sought to deal with.

The negotiations were to end in Brussels in December 1990, but it was found at the ministerial meeting held at the Heysel conference center that the Round could not be concluded, as no final agreement could be reached. The negotiations then entered a period of dormancy followed by a period of intense activity. The participants finally concluded the Round successfully in Geneva on December 15, 1993, and the results were formally signed by most of the 123 participants at Marrakesh, Morocco, on April 15, 1994.

The American delegation to the Uruguay Round was focused primarily on three aspects of the negotiations, one to cover intellectual property protection, a second to expand the ambit of the trading system's rules to services, and a third to strengthen dispute settlement.[25] During the George H. W. Bush administration, the American negotiators viewed US interests in dispute settlement primarily as complainants, bringing cases to achieve conformity by others to the GATT rules – particularly with respect to gaining better discipline over the EC's Common Agricultural Policy (CAP).[26] The CAP both limited market access into Europe for American products and provided subsidized competition in world markets. The attitude was, if the United States also had to defend cases with respect to its own measures, so be it. It was worth the price to tackle the trade-distorting effects of the Common Agricultural Policy. That the United States would accept binding dispute settlement was itself very largely a settled issue during this Republican administration.

Development of the SPS Agreement." Food and Agriculture Organization. www.fao.org/3/x7354e/X7354e01.htm

[25] "General Agreement on Tariffs and Trade: Uruguay Round Final Act Should Produce Overall US Economic Gains (Volume 2)." US Government Accountability Office. July 29, 1994. www.govinfo.gov/content/pkg/GAOREPORTS-GGD-94-83B/html/GAOREPORTS-GGD-94-83B.htm

[26] Charan Devereaux, Robert Z. Lawrence, and Michael D. Watkins. 2006. "Introduction" in *Case Studies in US Trade Negotiation Vol. 2*. Peterson Institute for International Economics. www.piie.com/publications/chapters_preview/3632/00iie3632.pdf; Robert L. Paarlberg. 1992. "How Agriculture Blocked the Uruguay Round." *SAIS Review* 12(1): 27–42.

The Americans did not originate the idea of having a new institutional framework, a WTO instead of a GATT. At a technical level, there would be some attraction in having a formally recognized organization, as opposed to an ad hoc structure that the GATT had always been served by since its inception. When the ITO failed to come into existence, what was left behind was the GATT, with a Secretariat to the Interim Commission for the ITO to look after it. When it became apparent that there was not going to be an ITO, the GATT contracting parties took over the Secretariat and the Interim Commission for the ITO.

The GATT was an executive agreement, never ratified by the United States or approved by Congress. It took Congress decades after the GATT came into being to mention its existence in the laws it passed, although Congress always appropriated monies to pay US GATT dues.[27] Perhaps it was the recollection of the fate of the ITO, just another challenge to take on, but creating another international organization was not on the US agenda. The organizational aspect that was seen to merit the administration's attention was the creation of a binding dispute settlement, not so much its structure (adding an appellate level) but the fact that the outcomes would be binding.

To the extent that the US industries and Congress were focusing on any institutional aspect emerging from the Round, it was not the creation of the WTO itself but the binding nature of dispute settlement, though differing from the point of view of agricultural interests. Binding dispute settlement was seen accurately as an attempt by America's negotiating partners, led by the Europeans, to curb the use of section 301, the legal basis for America's hated unilateralism.[28]

The idea for creating a legitimate international trade organization can be traced to a seed planted by John H. Jackson, a consultant to the Canadian government. This story rings true. Jackson was seen as the world's leading scholar on the GATT. I had hired him as a consultant at the US Treasury in the early 1970s when the United States was contemplating an import surcharge and a tax measure to boost exports (the Domestic International Sales Corporation, or DISC). During the 1980s, he discussed with the Canadian government recreating an ITO of sorts. The Canadian government liked the idea of having a formal organization for the GATT and associated agreements.

[27] Richard N. Gardner. 1969. *Sterling–Dollar Diplomacy: The Origins and the Prospects of Our International Economic Order.* New York: McGraw-Hill Book Company. Page xxxiv.

[28] Jared R. Silverman. 1996. "Multilateral Resolution over Unilateral Retaliation: Adjudicating the Use of Section 301 before the WTO." *University of Pennsylvania Journal of International Law* (17)1: 233–294. https://scholarship.law.upenn.edu/cgi/viewcontent.cgi?article=1461&context=jil

The EU then joined in supporting the idea.[29] The US ultimately acquiesced, without much emotional attachment to the creation of a new institution. It did suggest that there be an executive board, like the World Bank and the IMF had, but this idea was not adopted.[30]

When it came time to obtain congressional approval of the outcome of the Uruguay Round, a crucial step for the multilateral trading system, the focus was not on whether or not there would be a WTO instead of a GATT. The primary question for Congress was whether US sovereignty would be impaired as a result of the Round. That dealt not with the WTO as an institution but with whether agreements reached in the WTO, through negotiation or dispute settlement, would have automatic binding effect within the United States as domestic law, without further action by the President or Congress. This concern was holding up congressional action to approve the results of the Round. On November 23, 1994, President Clinton reached an accord with key senators with the following assurance:

> *Today we have moved one step closer toward gaining broad bipartisan support for GATT. I'm pleased to announce that an understanding has been reached with Senator Dole to reaffirm our United States sovereignty and to make sure that the reaffirmation will be protected in the GATT process. That means that the WTO will be accountable and fair and will meet our expectations.*[31]

It is revealing that the President referred to gaining support for GATT. He did not emphasize the creation of a new international organization.[32] The central focus of the Congressional debate to implement the Uruguay Round agreements and therefore the WTO was on the potential for any impairment of US sovereignty. The proponents of the legislation and the US Trade Representative maintained that it would not be impaired. Here is what Senator Bill Bradley assured his fellow senators:

[29] Further and perhaps most importantly, the agreement to create a World Trade Organization to integrate all the outcomes of the Round and to provide a central forum for the management of the world's trading system, the product of close cooperation between Canada and the European Union, was a major result of the Uruguay Round from Canada's perspective. "C/RM/G/51 Trade Policy Review Mechanism – Canada, Report by the Government." General Agreement on Tariffs and Trade. October 25, 1994. https://docs.wto.org/gattdocs/q/GG/CRM/G51.PDF

[30] Debra P. Steger ed. 2010. *Redesigning the World Trade Organization for the Twenty-First Century*. Waterloo, ON: Centre for International Governance Innovation. Pages 139–140.

[31] "Remarks on the General Agreement on Tariffs and Trade." The American Presidency Project. November 23, 1994. www.presidency.ucsb.edu/documents/remarks-the-general-agreement-tariffs-and-trade

[32] Ibid.

Finally, rules need enforcement. You cannot have a rule-based multilateral trading system unless you have some way to enforce the rules. We need only look at our endless trade rows with Japan for proof. One of the most important features of this agreement is that it strengthens the dispute settlement system. For the first time, no single country can block a panel report. In the past, the losing party could deny us our rights. We could win and they could say, "I am sorry." Under the WTO procedure, that can no longer happen. Either the offending country will change its policy, or we can exact retaliation against other exports.

This does not mean, however, that we have given the WTO sovereignty over US law, as some have asserted. When we lose cases – and we will, although statistics show we lose less often than any other country – the result does not automatically change US law. I will quote from the legislation so we understand this. This is what it says:

"No provision of any of the Uruguay Round Agreements, nor the application of any such provision to any person or circumstance, that is inconsistent with any law of the United States shall have effect."

In other words, nothing that violates US law will have any effect. The decision made will have no effect. Only the Congress of the United States can change American Federal law.[33]

As it turned out, the key to moving forward was obtaining an additional assurance. The US Senate was able to support the creation of the WTO because Senators Dole and Moynihan proposed, and the administration accepted, review by American judges of decisions rendered by WTO dispute settlement panels, in a process that could notionally lead to US withdrawal from the WTO.[34]

I am emphasizing America's reactions to the formation of the WTO over that of other nations because at this time in world history, the participation of

[33] "General Agreement on Tariffs and Trade." C-SPAN. November 23, 1994. www.c-span.org/video/?61755-1/general-agreement-tariffs-trade

[34] "World Trade Organization (WTO) Dispute Settlement Review Commission Act, Hearings before the Senate Committee on Finance, Testimony of Alan Wolff." United States Senate Committee on Finance. May 10, 1995. www.finance.senate.gov/imo/media/doc/Hrg104-124.pdf. The idea was crafted by Robert Lighthizer and Alan Wolff, with Wolff uncomfortable with anything too automatic triggering US withdrawal from the Organization. It appears that there would not have been a WTO without first US unilateralism, powered by Section 301 (this according to Arthur Dunkel), and without the idea of the Dole–Moynihan Commission, which never in fact came into being. Oddities of sausage-making in US trade history. "3-Strikes Test for The WTO." *Washington Post*. May 8, 2000. www.washingtonpost.com/archive/opinions/2000/05/08/3-strikes-test-for-the-wto/cfd7d0ab-3b70-4caa-9207-b6cebb860865/

the United States was the single most important determinant in whether an international organization or other multilateral arrangement could come into being or endure. The United States had already compiled a steady record of failing to support broad international cooperative efforts – from the League of Nations to the ITO, to the two "non-tariff" agreements concluded in the Kennedy Round. They all died from US failure to gain enough domestic support to ratify its participation in the agreements reached.

The birth of the WTO was not revolutionary; it was not regime change. There was more continuity than a break with the past. Binding dispute settlement (with an appellate stage), an agreement on services, an agreement on trade-related intellectual property, the trade policy review mechanism, and monitoring of trade measures could have continued with a GATT Secretariat to an Interim Commission still in place. Moreover, the creation of the WTO in some respects lacked the full attributes of an international organization. The Director-General of the WTO was no more of an independent executive than was the Director-General of the GATT. There was no executive board of directors, just rule by a membership comprised of all. The WTO, like the GATT before it, would conduct its business by consensus. In short, but for very noteworthy expansions of coverage of new subject matter and binding dispute settlement, in essence the WTO was a continuation of the multilateral trading system with official recognition of an organizational identity and with a Secretariat, with no major additional functions.

To outward appearances, the WTO physically resembled the GATT. The GATT Secretariat had moved into the Centre William Rappard, an imposing Italianate building on the shores of Lake Geneva, in 1977 when the ILO vacated the building. The GATT contracting parties and WTO members occupied the same meeting rooms. Thus, the move to permanent quarters was complete eighteen years before the WTO came into being. What had changed besides the logo and name of the inhabitant was its status as a permanent legal entity. The multilateral trading system had evolved, but several basic attributes remained the same – both were a gathering place of sovereigns. They made rules. They brought cases to seek enforcement of the rules. There were no clear executive functions – other than relations with the host country and other international organizations and having administrative authority over staff. The GATT as an organization was not as it seems today, some part of prehistory, with the WTO era being markedly different. The WTO assumed the persona of an international trade organization, but this is what the GATT had for decades already been. The WTO had a broader scope for administration of agreements with a more extensive committee structure. But as it turned out, the GATT proved to have had a better record by far than the WTO of achieving broad multilateral trade-liberalizing agreements and new rules.

There are two other elements of the Uruguay Round worthy of mention – the built-in agenda and the single undertaking. The built-in agenda was the promise, for example in agriculture, that the landmark Agreement on Agriculture would continue to evolve to serve member needs as circumstances changed and to improve both disciplines and market access.[35] This wish has not been fulfilled.

The second element that stands out is the single undertaking. Not just that all matters would be negotiated in parallel but ultimately it came to mean that all members would have to join all agreements emerging from the Round, even if with differing speeds of implementation tied to their respective levels of development. That the WTO would supersede the earlier GATT was through the device of terminating GATT 1947 and folding it into the WTO *acquis* as GATT 1994.[36] For those who might not have wanted to come along, there was nothing left to belong to of the old GATT. A shotgun marriage had been arranged, which still forms the basis of grievance on the part of some WTO members.

This brings us to the beginning of the WTO, which came into being on January 1, 1995. The Uruguay Round provided the foundation of the current WTO. How the WTO evolved from that point forward can be traced through biannual WTO Ministerial Conferences (MCs).

The first three Ministerial Conferences of the WTO sketched a parabolic arc: the first in Singapore, full of plans for the future, the second in Geneva, a gathering of government luminaries never to be rivaled, and the third, resulting in deadlock and substantial destruction in the host city.

MINISTERIAL CONFERENCES 1–3

THE WTO MINISTERIALS

When in 2020 the atrium at the WTO headquarters building, the Centre William Rappard, was decorated with historical photographs to celebrate the

35 "The Uruguay Round," World Trade Organization. www.wto.org/english/thewto_e/whatis_e/tif_e/fact5_e.htm; "Built-In Agenda," World Trade Organization. www.wto.org/english/thewto_e/minist_e/min99_e/english/about_e/04agen_e.htm

36 "GATT 1947 and GATT 1994: What's the Difference?" World Trade Organization. www.wto.org/english/docs_e/legal_e/legalexplgatt1947_e.htm

twenty-fifth anniversary of the WTO, it struck me that all too many of the pictures of the eleven Ministerial Conferences were a pictorial record of failure as judged by contemporaries and the public. This was not true in every case. Seven of the eleven MCs did result in agreed declarations. But all too often, the absence of a declaration at the end of a Ministerial Conference indicated that no consensus could be reached, no multilateral agreements concluded.

THE FIRST WTO MINISTERIAL CONFERENCE, SINGAPORE, DECEMBER 1996 (MC1)

Singapore hosted a ministerial conference full of promise for the future of the WTO. At this first MC of the WTO era, convened in December 1996, there still seemed to be an afterglow from the official founding of the Organization a year earlier. There was more than a little momentum, an upwelling of liberal economic sentiment, a desire for further achievement still in the air from the conclusion of the Uruguay Round almost four years earlier, although also a recognition of some storm clouds gathering on the horizon.

In their agreed declaration, the ministers stated:

> *[W]e envisage a world where trade flows freely. To this end we renew our commitment to:*
>
> - *a fair, equitable and more open rule-based system;*
> - *progressive liberalization and elimination of tariff and non-tariff barriers to trade in goods;*
> - *progressive liberalization of trade in services;*
> - *rejection of all forms of protectionism;*
> - *elimination of discriminatory treatment in international trade relations;*
> - *integration of developing and least developed countries and economies in transition into the multilateral system; and*
> - *the maximum possible level of transparency.*[37]

It was a largely upbeat meeting. Sadly, it is not clear that half of these commitments, those relating to progressive liberalization and elimination of discriminatory treatment, could be reissued today in a current ministerial meeting. Populism and anti-globalization militate against sentiments of progressive liberalization and the existence of some 400–500 preferential trade

[37] "Singapore Ministerial Declaration." World Trade Organization. December 13, 1996. www.wto.org/english/thewto_e/minist_e/min96_e/wtodec_e.htm

agreements could readily be cited as evidence of massive deviation from the goal of eliminating discriminatory treatment.

The Singapore ministerial statement of the United States Trade Representative, Charlene Barshefsky, however, has elements that sound relatively current, calling for "disciplines against disguised subsidies and non-traditional forms of protection, such as the trade-restraining and non-transparent activities of state trading enterprises."[38] There was also in her statement an awareness of the pressures on the trading system and of the absolute need for domestic support for trade negotiations:

> *To remain viable, the WTO must reflect the needs of various constituencies involved in world trade. Each of our economies will be facing more pressure from globalization in the coming years, and we must help workers adjust to and benefit from an open trading system. We must do more to acknowledge that there is a mutually reinforcing relationship between an open trading system and respect for core labour standards.*
>
> *That is why we hope to have an agreement that the WTO should, in cooperation with the International Labour Organization, examine in greater detail the important nexus between trade and labour standards. We believe strongly that increased trade and the economic growth that it brings should also engender greater respect for the basic human rights which are the focus of our core labour standards proposal.*[39]

This kind of statement would be very much something a US Trade Representative might say during the Biden administration. There was to be no significant follow-up in the intervening years at the WTO with respect to labor and the trading system. At the Singapore Ministerial, the trade ministers declared that the International Labor Organization (ILO) was the competent body to negotiate labor standards. As a result, no work activities on labor were pursued in the committee work of the WTO. The two Secretariats keep trace of each other's activities, and that is about the extent of the interaction. There are several reasons for this reluctance by the WTO's members to have their trade organization explore the linkages of trade and labor. One reason is that the WTO is not a standards-making organization. Another is that enforcing labor standards or seeking equivalence of wage levels could simply prevent trade from being a means for economic development by countries not yet industrialized.

[38] "WT/MIN(96)/ST/5 Statement by the Honourable Charlene Barshefsky, Acting United States Trade Representative." World Trade Organization. December 9, 1996. https://docs.wto.org/dol2fe/Pages/SS/directdoc.aspx?filename=Q:/WT/MIN96/ST5.pdf&Open=True

[39] Ibid.

During the period when I was Co-Acting WTO Director-General, I reached out to ILO Director-General Guy Ryder to establish contacts between the ILO and the WTO for purposes of conducting joint economic research.

At Singapore, the US delegation sought more transparency in government procurement, but was open to commencing work that others wanted done. A spirit of cooperation was manifested that is not much found in subsequent ministerial meetings:

> *We are prepared to consider whether the WTO should begin careful examination of new issues some feel should be debated. Like others, we are concerned about finding the right balance of interests. That is why we have been willing to go along with others who wish to begin a modest work programme in the areas of investment and competition, as part of a balanced overall agenda for the WTO.*[40]

This is the language of trade negotiators, recognizing that each participant in a negotiation needs to be able to carry away something to take back home. The art of compromise is essential to reaching a result and the table should be set accordingly.

For its part, the representative for the European Communities (predecessor to the European Union), Sir Leon Brittan, called for immediate adoption of the Information Technology Agreement (ITA) and the outcome of telecommunications discussions, and foresaw the need over time to deal with data protection and privacy, foreshadowing issues that would arise again in the course of Joint Statement Initiatives launched two decades later.[41] He saw an urgent need for WTO expansion, particularly to include China, and called for resisting the marginalization of many least developed countries. He also cited the need to remember the highly political nature of trade:

> *Trade is now a domestic political issue for all of us, developing and developed. WTO excites worldwide attention and all too often suspicion. For me this means that concerns about environment, about labour standards and other apparently domestic political issues are now the legitimate concern of the WTO because they are concerns of our constituents. Only when WTO is seen to meet the aspirations of our constituents can we be sure of keeping the way open for continued trade liberalization.*[42]

His vision was for a WTO that developed fair trade rules and the pursuit of ever easier market access. It was the EC that led the effort to bring investment

[40] Ibid.

[41] "WT/MIN(96)/ST/2 Statement by Sir Leon Brittan Q.C., Vice-President of the European Commission." World Trade Organization, December 9, 1996. https://docs.wto.org/dol2fe/Pages/SS/directdoc.aspx?filename=Q:/WT/MIN96/ST2.pdf&Open=True

[42] Ibid.

and competition policy into the WTO's workstream. These are necessary adjuncts to an effective, open, rules-based trading system. The EC also called for attention to labor standards and environmental protection. Lastly, he envisaged a grand new round of negotiations, a Millennium Round, to be called into being in a few years' time.[43] This was a visionary program for multilateral cooperation. It would have brought the trading system to an entirely new and higher level.

A down-payment on that more open world was made at this ministerial conference. In Singapore, fourteen members (including the EU) agreed to the Information Technology Agreement (the ITA), eliminating tariffs on a wide range of IT products with tariff reductions phased in over a period of four years. Fourteen signatories may not sound like a lot, but the EU itself accounted for twenty-eight WTO members, and the forty-two WTO members participating accounted for 90 percent of world trade in covered products. The ITA was the WTO's first broad trade-liberalizing agreement. (The Pharmaceutical Agreement was negotiated in 1994, between the formal conclusion of the Uruguay Round and the WTO's first day, on January 1, 1995.[44]) The ITA was multilateral in the sense that it was open to all, but more – its benefits would be applied to all on an MFN basis, those that agreed to participate and those members that did not.

And, because we know how things worked out, we know that a work-stream was launched at Singapore that would much later add to the WTO *acquis* another agreement decades later. The WTO began work on trade facilitation, which reached agreement status seventeen years later in 2013 and entered into force in 2017. We also know that not every issue raised at this Ministerial Conference ended in an agreement. Work on trade and competition, one of three other Singapore issues, lingered for a while before being ended at Cancún. Trade and investment ceased to be a WTO issue for the next two decades. The fourth Singapore issue, transparency in government procurement was reflected in a new Government Procurement Agreement in 2012.

THE SECOND WTO MINISTERIAL CONFERENCE, GENEVA, 1998 (MC2)

The Second WTO Ministerial Conference was opened on an optimistic note by Director-General Renato Ruggiero. He cited the successful conclusion,

43 Ibid.

44 The signatories are Canada, the European Union, Japan, Macao (China), Norway, Switzerland, the United Kingdom, and the United States. India and China, which later became major pharmaceutical producers, did not join.

since Singapore, of agreements on basic telecommunications and financial services, and the implementation of the ITA, calling these accomplishments the equivalent of a finance and technology Round for the twenty-first century.[45] He noted that the new dispute settlement system was functioning well, and that the WTO had held successful seminars on trade and the environment and trade facilitation.

Still relevant today, the Canadian chair of the General Council, John Weekes, pointed to what was going to be an ambiguous relationship between the members and the Secretariat:

> *I would like to emphasize the importance of maintaining the right balance in the WTO between the role of permanent representatives and delegations on the one hand, and the role of the director general and the secretariat on the other. The WTO is a member driven organisation, housing a trade agreement setting out rights and obligations governing the trade relationships of the members. Active members are essential for the WTO's success, but the WTO members also look to the Director General and the Secretariat, to provide leadership, assistance and advice. The power of decision must always rest with the members, but the organisation needs a secretariat which offers ideas on how to create possible solutions to the many challenges we face.*[46]

The "right balance" he called for has never been found, but Weekes' prescription was as close as the WTO ever got to a positive description of the necessary relationship. This statement would be unlikely to be repeated in the present (2022) by a current chair of the General Council.

Based on reading the agreed declaration at the end of the conference, the meeting was unremarkable – it launched no new initiatives, and it achieved no breakthroughs, and yet of all the Ministerial Conferences, it sparkled with a firmament of world leaders, due to the fact that it marked the fiftieth anniversary of the founding of the multilateral trading system, the GATT. With court being paid by many of the leaders of that time, this was arguably in some respects the apogee of the WTO, or at least of its ministerial meetings.

Among the most eloquent speakers, as would be expected, was Nelson Mandela, attending as the President of South Africa. His remarks led off with an arresting turn of phrase: "Today's auspicious occasion is rich with the

[45] "Address by the Director-General Mr. Renato Ruggiero." World Trade Organization. May 18, 1998. www.wto.org/english/thewto_e/minist_e/min98_e/anniv_e/dg_e.htm

[46] "Notes for Statement by Chairman of the General Council Monday, May 18, 1998 – Ministerial Conference, Geneva." World Trade Organization. May 18, 1998. www.wto.org/english/thewto_e/minist_e/min98_e/anniv_e/weekes_e.htm

ironies of the latter half of the twentieth century."[47] What he was referring to was the construction of a new international trade order (the GATT) to overcome the devastation of a war fought for universal principles of freedom, but which had only two African signatories at its founding, with neither of those two countries' peoples being free at that time. Mandela proceeded to quote some of the opening words of the GATT charter, that "relations in the field of trade and economic endeavour should be conducted with a view to raising standards of living, ensuring full employment and a large and steadily growing volume of real income and effective demand, developing the full use of the resources of the world and expanding the production and exchange of goods," and reiterated the agreement of his government to work cooperatively with others to fulfill the promise of those words.[48]

The wider political context of the multilateral trading system that Nelson Mandela highlighted then deserves some reflection now. He said that over the five-decade span of the GATT's history, "the international community came to insist with increasing vigour that freedom is indivisible." He was articulating a moral purpose to nations coming together to regulate world commerce. He related freedom to taking "the chance to achieve a better life for all our people" through domestic economic reforms and "strengthening our engagement with the WTO because of its importance to our economy." He was not viewing the world through rose-colored glasses. He saw it as it was but said his country "chooses to look forward rather than deal with the imperfections of the past."

Mandela reflected on the fact that the world was still divided into nations that were industrialized and those that were largely not, between haves and have nots. He called upon members to engage in "wise work" to remedy structural inequalities and historical imbalances utilizing the new rules-based system. He said: "Where there are manifest inequalities when the rules are introduced then special and thoughtful measures have to be applied. This care at the beginning will promote the conditions that will sustain and nurture a rules-based system." It was a message that few could argue with. But it foretold a continuing problem for the trading system: how best to promote development. He did not believe that the correct balance had been struck. His view was that the Uruguay Round was shaped by the "preoccupations and problems of the advanced industrial economies" with the result that the

47 "South Africa, Statement by H. E. Mr. Nelson Mandela, President." World Trade Organization. May 19, 1998. www.wto.org/english/thewto_e/minist_e/min98_e/anniv_e/mandela_e.htm

48 Ibid.

"developing countries were not able to ensure that the rules accommodated their realities."[49]

This sentiment is still strong among developing countries at the WTO. In 2021, at a panel discussion at the Harvard JFK School, a former ambassador of India to the WTO said: "Equal treatment accorded to unequal participants does not yield equality." But there is more than one way to address inequalities, and who better on the face of the planet than Nelson Mandela to point the way. Mandela's message was strongly positive, and is worth keeping in mind:

> *We must start by a reaffirmation that the building of a multilateral rules-based system is fundamentally correct.*
>
> *Powerful economies must stop applying unilateral measures and the developing countries must negotiate their specific needs within this framework.*
>
> *Rules are respected when they are above expediency, in perception and in practice.*
>
> *The developing countries should now give leadership to the development of a positive agenda that fully addresses their needs.*[50]

Putting this credo into practice should have been inspiring enough to carry the world trading system to new heights.

UK Prime Minister Tony Blair took the floor to emphasize two points that still have resonance today. He talked of trade and peace, a linkage fresh in the minds of the founders of the multilateral trading system in the 1940s. For Blair, the Good Friday Agreement bringing peace to Northern Ireland was only a few months old. He chose the platform of the WTO meeting to make clear that the linkage still had force:

> *I hope that, when you return home, you will all encourage your companies to look at the new opportunities for trade and investment in Northern Ireland the agreement will bring. That you will help us bring the economic prosperity needed to underpin peace. We must not let pass by the best chance for many years for real peace in Northern Ireland.*[51]

But he spoke not just for Northern Ireland. He saw trade and investment as having broader applicability for the cause of peace. "Let that then be a signal

[49] Ibid.

[50] Ibid.

[51] "UNITED KINGDOM Statement by The Rt. Hon. Tony Blair, MP, Prime Minister." World Trade Organization. May 19, 1998. www.wto.org/english/thewto_e/minist_e/min98_e/anniv_e/blair_e.htm

for peace throughout the troubled parts of the world."[52] The interrelationship of trade and peace had been a strand in the history of the trading system at the outset that had later been forgotten by most major countries. For Blair, having dealt with the Troubles and terrorism, the cause of peace and the harnessing of trade to achieve it, to underwrite it, were both current and pressing.

Blair's second message that is still very relevant today was about the relationship between regional trade liberalization and the multilateral trading system:

> *The world is opening up with freer travel, common mass media, open communication systems. Free trade is a vital part of this movement. The emergence of Mercosur, NAFTA, ASEAN and of course the EU shows how strongly the tide is turning in favour of free trade.*
>
> *It may be regional for now, but it all strengthens the move to wider free trade – as long as we keep these trading areas open to the rest of the world, as the EU is and must remain.*[53]

Blair saw that regional trade agreements and the WTO could be complementary, not contradictory, but the benefits of trade had to be spread more widely: "So the question now is not so much whether there should be free trade, but how best to manage what I believe is an irreversible and irresistible trend so that all countries and all peoples can benefit. That is the millennium challenge – for us and for the WTO."[54] Blair's forebears, Cobden and Churchill, would have applauded this sentiment.

There was much additional wisdom relevant to us today in the former UK Prime Minister's speech: to foster development, to provide rules for digital commerce, to care for the environment, to press for universal application of the ILO's Core Labor Standards, to settle differences based on rules rather than power, to oppose damaging discrimination, and to respect agreements reached freely by consensus.

President William Jefferson Clinton in his remarks also harked back to the fundamental geopolitical purpose of the trading system:

> *Near the end of World War II, as leaders and ordinary citizens began to dream of a system that would prevent a return to war, President Franklin Roosevelt asked the people of the United States, and the world, to look ahead to peace.*

52 Ibid.
53 Ibid.
54 Ibid.

He said that "a basic essential to permanent peace is a decent standard of living for all individual men and women and children in all nations."[55]

President Clinton proceeded to list his administration's priorities:

- To pursue an ever-more-open global trading system.
- To lift living standards around the world, through environmental protections, consumer protections, and labor standards, with the WTO providing a forum where business, labor, environmental, and consumer groups can speak out and help guide the further evolution of the WTO.
- To increase the transparency of the workings of the WTO with an opportunity for stakeholders to convey their views, such as the ability to file "amicus briefs," to help inform the panels in their deliberations.
- To agree that no barriers will be erected to electronic commerce, with a standstill on any tariffs to electronic transmissions sent across borders, with a market-oriented private-sector-led approach to enhance privacy, protect intellectual property, and encourage the free flow of information and commerce on the internet.

None of these goals for the WTO would be fulfilled in the next quarter-century.

The list of specific areas of liberalization that followed in Clinton's remarks was extensive. He concluded with an invitation to hold the next WTO Ministerial in the United States.

There is a lesson from this gathering of leaders. First, it is incumbent on leaders to lead. They were showing the way forward, as no group of trade ministers could do. They had the authority to speak for their peoples. Never before and never again did as many leaders, fifteen of them, gather to press for the future of the multilateral trading system, and address the issues constructively with as much thoughtfulness. During the pandemic, speaking to an empty hall, but over a video link to all WTO members and the Secretariat, Guy Parmelin, Vice President of the Swiss Confederation, I, and others spoke of the importance of the WTO to the world, but nothing could match the eloquence of the endorsement of the luminaries who attended the 1996 ministerial meeting.

[55] "UNITED STATES Statement by H. E. Mr. William J. Clinton, President." World Trade Organization. May 18, 1998. www.wto.org/english/thewto_e/minist_e/min98_e/anniv_e/clinton_e.htm

THE THIRD WTO MINISTERIAL CONFERENCE, SEATTLE, 1999 (MC3)

If MC2 was celebratory, MC3 turned out to be literally embattled. It started off well enough. The American host at the conference, represented by US Secretary of Agriculture Dan Glickman, stated the American goals for the meeting. Ministerial meetings for the multilateral trading system set out to do what they had always done. The GATT had had eight rounds of multilateral trade negotiations – grand convocations in which all participated. So it was natural that the American chair of this conference call upon the WTO's members to launch a new multilateral round of trade negotiations. He suggested that a new round:

- *Aggressively reform agricultural trade by lowering trade barriers, substantially reducing trade-distorting subsidies and other measures;*
- *Further open world trade in services and industrial goods;*
- *Examine the basic questions of trade facilitation and customs;*
- *Meet the challenge of the twenty-first century, notably by ensuring that electronic commerce develops as freely and rapidly as it should, and by helping us to ensure that farmers and ranchers can use biotechnology products approved through transparent, science-based, and timely regulatory processes, and consumers enjoy the benefit of safe and beneficial products;*
- *Promote development world-wide, by opening markets more fully to products especially from the least developed countries and offering significantly expanded technical assistance to ensure that all Members can meet their commitments, use the WTO and its dispute settlement mechanism as appropriate, and take greater advantage of market access opportunities;*
- *Ensure sustainable development, by opening trade areas such as environmental goods and services that improve environmental protection; and eliminating environmentally damaging subsidies such as agricultural export subsidies and fishery subsidies that contribute to overcapacity;*
- *Create a Working Group on the links between trade and core labor standards; and*
- *Ensure that the WTO itself meets the test of a more open and democratic world, by improving transparency and accessibility to the public throughout the organization.*[56]

[56] "WT/MIN(99)/ST/12 UNITED STATES OF AMERICA Statement by the Honourable Daniel Glickman Secretary of Agriculture." World Trade Organization. December 1, 1999. www.wto.org/english/thewto_e/minist_e/min99_e/english/state_e/d5245e.pdf

The call for a new "development round" was supported in particular by Pascal Lamy, the EU Trade Commissioner, Rubens Ricupero, the Secretary-General of UNCTAD, and James Wolfensohn, President of the World Bank. Wolfensohn said:[57]

> *This new "Development Round" must move beyond the narrow negotiation of mutual concessions. We must seize the day, and work flexibly and creatively towards a world trading system that really makes a difference for developing countries. It makes no sense to urge poor countries to reform their economies, to urge them to compete and "pay their way in the world," while denying them the means to compete. But this is what we do in practice, by restricting their market access in areas like agriculture, construction and textiles. It is precisely these areas where developing countries have a comparative advantage. Granting access may be temporarily tough for protected industries in developed countries, but in the long run it will benefit us all. It will contribute to the peace and security we surely all seek. It is time we took those tough steps.*[58]

In the view of most of the developing countries participating in the meeting, pride of place in the new round was to be given to meeting the concerns of the developing countries. The work program of the WTO was to be "development-centric," a focus at odds with the views of those who see expanded trade, even without preferential treatment, as naturally benefiting development. Through this lens, e-commerce should be looked at with a view to finding ways in which it could play a role in development. In agriculture, the flexibilities of developed countries should be limited, but the need for protection of large rural agrarian economies should be respected. In this view, new issues such as environment and labor are beyond the competence of the WTO. National governments, not the WTO, should deal with civil society.

The Indian Minister of Commerce and Industry, Murazoli Maran, made clear that there was more than one way to look at the history of the trading system:

> *Our assessment has all along been that the Uruguay Round Agreements have not served all the membership well. There are critical gaps that need to be urgently addressed.*
>
> *Asymmetries and inequities in several of the agreements including those relating to anti-dumping, subsidies, intellectual property, TRIMs and the non-*

57 In the early days of the WTO, it was not unusual for James Wolfensohn as President of the World Bank to attend. "DDG Wolff Pays Tribute to James Wolfensohn." World Trade Organization. December 2, 2020. www.wto.org/english/news_e/news20_e/ddgaw_25dec20_e.htm

58 "WT/MIN(99)/ST/19 WORLD BANK Statement by Mr. James D. Wolfensohn, President." World Trade Organization. November 30, 1999. www.wto.org/english/thewto_e/minist_e/min99_e/english/state_e/d5200e.pdf

realization of expected benefits from agreements such as textiles and agriculture during implementation have been a matter of great concern. The special and differential treatment clauses have remained virtually inoperative. The textile sector has thus far witnessed a mere 4 percent of integration of the restrained items by the developed countries. Even in areas where developing countries began to acquire trade competitiveness, anti-dumping or subsidy investigations have been initiated in increasing numbers. The TRIPS Agreement places the rights of a patent holder on a higher pedestal than obligations. However, it does not confer corresponding rights to countries or indigenous communities whose bio-resources or traditional knowledge are put to use.[59]

The conference was by all measures a disaster. The streets of Seattle became a cauldron of protesters, by various counts numbering from 40,000 to 60,000, with a small group of anarchists joining peaceful protesters and engaging in rioting and looting, leaving stores boarded up after their windows were broken. What had given rise to mass demonstrations in the streets? Apparently, the fear, however unjustified, was widespread that this conference of the WTO members would agree to sweeping changes in the direction of liberalization, primarily for the benefit of multinational companies. The principal emotion in evidence was fear – fear shown by British Columbia nurses that their jobs might be at stake, fear by others that their food supply would be tainted through the use of GMOs in farm products, fear that fishing for shrimp would endanger sea turtles, fear of dumped steel imports manifested by steelworkers gathering by the harbor to symbolically dump steel into the water, the way they felt that foreign steel was being dumped into the US market. The only float in the parade addressed the closing of a GE lightbulb plant that relocated from Lynn, Massachusetts to Hungary.

There was a clear mismatch between these sentiments within the conference hall and those expressed by others in the street, where tear gas was being deployed and mass arrests were taking place, in what became popularly known as "The Battle of Seattle." The demonstrators were concerned not about inequality among nations but in disparities within national economies, and blamed trade for exacerbating them and causing dislocations. The demonstrators were to have nothing to be concerned about. As matters turned out, the meeting did not pose a threat to anyone's livelihood. It was inconclusive, ending without even issuing an agreed declaration.

[59] "INDIA Statement by H. E. Mr. Murasoli Maran Minister of Commerce and Industry." World Trade Organization. November 30, 1999. www.wto.org/english/thewto_e/minist_e/min99_e/english/state_e/d5194e.pdf

Discord replaced the fine sentiments expressed by world leaders just one year earlier. Ministers had met almost continuously for three days and could not narrow gaps. Mike Moore, the new Director-General, could take credit for inclusiveness, but it was including countries in a process in which the members could not reach a result. The talks were accordingly "suspended." Blame was apportioned depending on point of view. Some pointed to the lack of flexibility of some on agriculture, others to too much flexibility on the use of trade remedies. There were no apologies on the part of ministers for the shambles inside the conference venue. The city of Seattle later settled with a cash payment to demonstrators who had been arrested "without probable cause."

US Trade Representative Charlene Barshefsky said it was necessary to take a "time out," that the resources of many government delegations had been strained. Bizarrely, time ran out because the conference venue had been booked by a convention of optometrists, and the hall had to be cleared. Astoundingly, the world would have to wait for further progress being made in the trading system due in part to the use of the venue having expired. The WTO delegations simply had to leave the premises, outcome or no outcome. World leaders were shocked. Business interests expressed their dismay. Pascal Lamy, the European Union's top negotiator, told reporters that the WTO's membership had grown so large, and the range of issues it dealt with so broad, that it will have to be "reassessed and maybe rebuilt. The WTO does not have the institutional strength or the culture or the procedures to do this right."[60] It would be Lamy, coming back into this narrative, who would try to get the multilateral trading system back on track with an attempt at launching a ninth great negotiating round for the system, and the first for the WTO, but this lay two years in the future.

Suspension of talks, it was noted, had occurred before. Most notably, the Uruguay Round itself, which was to have concluded in Brussels in 1990, found no conclusion until most issues were resolved in Geneva in 1993. The difference was that in the case of the Uruguay Round, there were active negotiations on a number of key agreements and work simply continued thereafter. The "suspension" in Seattle related to an attempt to begin negotiations rather than conclude them. Suspension was something of a smallish fig leaf to mask the failure to achieve an outcome.

[60] Steven Pearlstein. "When Negotiators' Reach Far Exceeds Their Grasp Complexity, Diversity Humbled WTO." *Washington Post*. December 5, 1999. www.washingtonpost.com/wp-srv/WPcap/1999-12/05/073r-120599-idx.html

Objectively, the context for the meeting should have been better. World merchandise exports in constant dollars had grown from $58 billion in 1948 to $5.2 trillion in 1998. Prosperity, the gains from trade, had been widespread, but the WTO members were defensive. In a WTO pamphlet issued in connection with the Ministerial Conference, the problems as well as the benefits of trade were cited:

> *In some aspects, however, openness and interdependence can bring a sense of discomfort. Competition from foreign imports, and changes in export markets, demand an extra effort of adjustment, even beyond the constant and sometimes painful adjustments needed to meet domestic competition, technological advances and changing consumer tastes. Economic difficulties in one part of the world can affect exports and jobs in other countries.*[61]

The pamphlet quoted WTO Director-General Mike Moore as saying that increasing numbers of people "feel excluded, forgotten and angry, locked out and waiting for a promised train that may never arrive. They see globalization as a threat, the enemy, the reason for all their woes." The answer in large part would have been to move forward at Seattle to provide greater fairness through improvements in the rules, expansion of their coverage, but that did not happen.

While there was no agreement on a way to proceed in negotiations, no convergence on ways forward, there was an increase in disputes brought to the WTO to be settled. The Secretariat noted that "between January 1995 and August 1999, [in just over three and a half years since the WTO was founded] WTO Members invoked the settlement procedures 183 times over 142 distinct matters." This can be compared with the GATT, whose "dispute procedures were invoked only about 300 times in 48 years."[62] Was trade becoming more contentious, or was the dispute settlement process, now that the results were binding, even more attractive? That was unclear.

The pause in the attempt to agree on a negotiating agenda was not to be forever, and development as a goal was about to be given further prominence. But this would have to wait until the convening of the next Ministerial Conference.

MINISTERIAL CONFERENCES 4–7

Immediately after the attacks on the World Trade Center on September 11, 2001, in the face of concerns about a terrorist attack on attendees at the Ministerial Conference in Qatar, the Doha Development Agenda was launched with

61 "Seattle: What's at Stake? Resource Booklet for the Seattle Ministerial Meeting." World Trade Organization. 1999. www.wto.org/english/thewto_e/minist_e/min99_e/english/book_e/stake.pdf

62 Ibid.

follow-up at conferences in Cancún, Hong Kong, and Geneva, until it expired inconclusively in 2008.

"Better no deal than a good deal," was a tongue-in-cheek statement by a textile industry trade association executive opposed to trade liberalization, during the Tokyo Round.

Trade negotiators are primarily judged by a single criterion: whether they conclude agreements. There is an added layer of complexity when the subject that they are dealing with is the launch of a new major negotiation which will be concluded long after they have left the scene. The entirety of the negotiation, from launch to conclusion, is something like the flight of a new, highly complex, experimental aircraft. The designers are due some credit, as are those who pilot the craft and perhaps those who repair it if there is a problem, but special credit goes to those who land it successfully. If it crashes, those who come after begin a process of examining what went wrong. Was there a design flaw? Was the piloting at fault? And there is the added complexity that in fact there were well over 100 persons giving the pilot advice, some of whom take their hand at the controls, some just come forward into the flight deck and give the wheel an extra tug in an unfortunate direction, or perhaps cause the plane to stall. After a crash, there will be plenty of opinions as to what went wrong.

Whether the subject is a major negotiating round, or another key element of the WTO, a fully working dispute settlement system, there will be enough praise to share out if the journey is a success, and some disagreement over why it got off-course and who is to blame if it ends in disaster. Sometimes, if there is a tragic outcome, as with the Zeppelin Graf Hindenburg, the unsuccessful flight can mark the end of that type of aircraft, that form of endeavor.

Our narrative picks up in the first year of a new millennium with what may prove to be the last attempt at a great round of negotiations, where an omnibus package of negotiating subjects is assembled, as was successfully done in the case of the Tokyo and Uruguay Rounds and was attempted less successfully in the Kennedy Round.[63] The negotiating theory behind a grand round is, as described by a Texan trade negotiator,[64] like a poker game – to have enough in the pot so that no player can afford to leave the table. Of course, the greater the range of subjects, the greater the risk that instead of more trade-offs becoming available, more linkages are created, and if one segment does not move forward, others get bogged down as well. There is the added complexity

[63] The negotiation took place in Geneva, 1964–67.

[64] Robert S. Strauss, US Trade Representative during the Tokyo Round.

of trying to do everything at once. Does the negotiation become so complex and freighted with items that prove to be contentious that it is too ponderous, too difficult to move?

On July 22, 2001, the G8 leaders met in Genoa and "agreed to support the launch of an ambitious new Round of global trade negotiations with a balanced agenda."[65]

THE FOURTH WTO MINISTERIAL CONFERENCE, DOHA, QATAR, SEPTEMBER 2001 (MC4)

On September 11, 2001 (known forever after as 9/11), the World Trade Towers in New York City were attacked by terrorists and destroyed. The Pentagon suffered damage from a third aircraft, and a fourth aircraft thought to be headed for the White House or the Capitol was brought down in a field in Pennsylvania. On September 14, the US Trade Representative Robert Zoellick declared that "while we will take every possible step to ensure security, it is important that the World Trade Organization meeting in Doha proceed so that the world trading system can continue to promote international growth, development, and openness."[66] MC4 took place a scant two months after the attack.

Those attending MC3, the Ministerial Conference in Seattle, despite what was going on in the streets, were not in any personal danger. As long as one avoided the tear gas and obeyed the lockdown when anarchists roamed the streets, attacking Starbucks and other shops, it was completely safe. This was not clear with respect to any American planning travel to Doha for MC4. National delegations were kept very limited. US government intelligence officials advised that Al Qaeda (the terrorist group responsible for 9/11) was believed to have infiltrated the staff of the hotel where American private sector advisors were to be housed. Having no direct responsibility for the negotiations, I did not go to Doha, with some regret, but watching the WTO evolve did not seem to be worth the personal risk. In the event, so few went from the business community or civil society that the US government delegation made room for American advisors at its hotel, which was more secure.[67]

[65] "Communiqué – 2001 G8 Genoa Summit." G7 Information Centre. July 22, 2001. www.g8.utoronto.ca/summit/2001genoa/finalcommunique.html

[66] "USTR Zoellick Statement on World Trade Ministerial in Doha." Office of the United States Trade Representative. September 14, 2001. www.ustr.gov/archive/Document_Library/Press_Releases/2001/September/USTR_Zoellick_Statement_on_World_Trade_Ministerial_in_Doha.html

[67] *The Economist* newspaper reported: "It did nothing to soothe frayed nerves. On November 7th, a Qatari national was shot dead by security forces in the small Gulf state as he fired at an airbase

Pascal Lamy and Robert Zoellick, the chief trade negotiators for the EU and the USA respectively, were intent on getting a major round of negotiations launched. The Round was called the Doha Development Agenda (DDA). Indeed, in the fifty-two-paragraph Ministerial Declaration issued on September 14, 2001, the words "developing" or "development" were mentioned ninety-seven times. The essence of the policy of the Round was captured in the preamble of the Declaration:

> *The majority of WTO members are developing countries. We seek to place their needs and interests at the heart of the Work Programme adopted in this Declaration. Recalling the Preamble to the Marrakesh Agreement, we shall continue to make positive efforts designed to ensure that developing countries, and especially the least developed among them, secure a share in the growth of world trade commensurate with the needs of their economic development.*

That is the preamble. It is the operative part of the Declaration that is now most often cited, twenty years later, by developing countries, in almost every, perhaps every, WTO General Council meeting.[68] It provides:

> 44. *We reaffirm that provisions for special and differential treatment are an integral part of the WTO Agreements. We note the concerns expressed regarding their operation in addressing specific constraints faced by developing countries, particularly least developed countries ... We therefore agree that all special and differential treatment provisions shall be reviewed with a view to strengthening them and making them more precise, effective and operational. In this connection, we endorse the work programme on special and differential treatment set out in the Decision on Implementation-Related Issues and Concerns.*

Special and differential treatment is an exception to nondiscrimination. It is a carve-out from most-favored-nation treatment. It recognizes that the capacity to carry out obligations differs by members' level of development. It originated in November 1979 during the GATT era and is still in common use throughout the WTO Agreements today.[69] The enabling clause allowed the granting

which is used by American military aircraft. Security scares ahead of the ministerial meeting of the World Trade Organisation (WTO) in the Qatari capital, Doha, have already slimmed delegations and scared off hangers-on. Ministers and officials from 142 countries are attending the meeting which runs from November 9th–13th and which should see the launch of a new round of world trade negotiations." "Push Comes to Shove." *The Economist*. November 7, 2001. www.economist.com/unknown/2001/11/07/push-comes-to-shove

68 The highest-level regular meetings of the WTO, consisting of ambassadors/permanent representatives to the WTO, are open to all members.

69 "Differential and More Favourable Treatment Reciprocity and Fuller Participation of Developing Countries L/4903." World Trade Organization. November 28, 1979. www.wto.org/

of trade preferences to developing countries by GATT contracting parties and later WTO members, and in the multilateral trading system providing explicitly for better treatment for developing countries.[70] Special and differential treatment (SDT) has led notionally to there being three classes of WTO members: developed, developing, and least developed. Of these, only the third category is clearly defined, in this case by the United Nations.[71] However, which members are developing and which are developed is, in the view of many if not most developing country WTO members, a matter of choice, of self-designation.

According to a 1979 GATT Council decision, SDT is to consist of:

1. Developed countries generally granting preferential tariff treatment to products originating in developing countries in accordance with the Generalized System of Preferences;
2. Differential and more favorable treatment with respect to nontariff measures governed by the provisions of instruments multilaterally negotiated under the auspices of the GATT;
3. Regional or global arrangements entered into among less-developed contracting parties for the mutual reduction or elimination of trade barriers;
4. Even greater special treatment for the least developed countries.[72]

It was stipulated in the 1979 decision that providing SDT "shall not constitute an impediment to the reduction or elimination of tariffs and other restrictions

english/docs_e/legal_e/enabling1979_e.htm: "1. Notwithstanding the provisions of Article I of the General Agreement, contracting parties may accord differential and more favourable treatment to developing countries, without according such treatment to other contracting parties."

70 For a perceptive discussion of SDT by three very knowledgeable WTO experts, see: Patrick Low, Hamid Mamdouh, and Evan Rogerson. 2018. "Balancing Rights and Obligations in The WTO – A Shared Responsibility." Government Offices of Sweden, Stockholm. www.swedenabroad.se/globalassets/ambassader/fn-geneve/documents/balancing-rights-and-obligations-in-the-wto.pdf

71 The UN's Committee for Development Policy (CDP) Secretariat of the Department of Economic and Social Affairs/Department of Economic and Social Affairs (DPAD/DESA) creates a list of LDCs based on income, human assets, and economic vulnerability: income thresholds are $1,018, which is set at the three-year average of per capita gross national income (the graduation threshold is 20 percent higher at $1,222); human assets calculated using five indicators, grouped into a health and education subindex; and an economic vulnerability index which measures structural vulnerability to economic and environmental shocks, with a high level of vulnerability, indicating major structural impediments to sustainable development.

72 "Differential and More Favourable Treatment Reciprocity and Fuller Participation of Developing Countries L/4903." World Trade Organization. November 28, 1979. www.wto.org/english/docs_e/legal_e/enabling1979_e.htm

to trade on a most-favored-nation basis."[73] This reference is needed because those benefiting from preferential treatment have an interest in not seeing it diluted. MFN negotiations among developed countries lower the margin of preference.

Many developing country members consider special and differential treatment a right. This is a point of contention among members in general, as is the question of whether SDT is to be uniform or tailored to the needs of individual members.

The Doha Ministerial Declaration called upon the WTO's Trade and Development Committee to examine the operation of SDT that arises under the provisions of the WTO Agreements, including the GATT. According to the WTO Secretariat, the special provisions include:

- *longer time periods for implementing Agreements and commitments,*
- *measures to increase trading opportunities for developing countries,*
- *provisions requiring all WTO Members to safeguard the trade interests of developing countries,*
- *support to help developing countries build the capacity to carry out WTO work, handle disputes, and implement technical standards, and*
- *provisions related to least developed country (LDC) Members.*[74]

Unlike the names of the eight negotiating rounds concluded under the GATT – Geneva (1947), Annecy (1949), Torquay (1950), Geneva II (1956), Dillon (1960), Kennedy (1964), Tokyo (1973) and Uruguay (1986) – the designation "Doha Development Agenda" was not a neutral formulation. It was an "agenda" and, lest there be any doubt, it was to be about "development." The mission was clear, and it was to be woven into the fabric of all areas of negotiation. This can be seen in the statement of each of the Declaration's specific negotiating aims for key subjects.[75]

- **Agriculture**
  - *We commit ourselves to comprehensive negotiations aimed at: substantial improvements in market access; reductions of, with a view to phasing out, all forms of export subsidies; and substantial reductions in trade-distorting domestic support.*
  - *We agree that special and differential treatment for developing countries shall be an integral part of all elements of the negotiations and*

[73] Ibid.

[74] "Special and Differential Treatment Provisions." World Trade Organization. www.wto.org/english/tratop_e/devel_e/dev_special_differential_provisions_e.htm

[75] "Doha Declaration." World Trade Organization. www.wto.org/english/res_e/booksp_e/ddec_e.pdf

shall be embodied in the schedules of concessions and commitments and as appropriate in the rules and disciplines to be negotiated, so as to be operationally effective and to enable developing countries to effectively take account of their development needs, including food security and rural development.

- **Services**
  - *The negotiations on trade in services shall be conducted with a view to promoting the economic growth of all trading partners and the development of developing and least developed countries.*
- **Intellectual Property**
  - *The TRIPS Council shall take fully into account the development dimension … including the relationship to traditional knowledge and folklore.*
- **Market Access for Non-Agricultural Products**
  - *We agree to negotiations which shall aim, by modalities to be agreed, to reduce or as appropriate eliminate tariffs, including the reduction or elimination of tariff peaks, high tariffs, and tariff escalation, as well as non-tariff barriers, in particular on products of export interest to developing countries.*

The focus on developing country concerns was added with respect to addressing four "Singapore issues" beginning at the next Ministerial Conference, MC5, on the basis of an explicit requirement for consensus. These were:

- **Trade and Investment**
  - *Recognizing the case for a multilateral framework to secure transparent, stable and predictable conditions for long-term cross-border investment, particularly foreign direct investment, that will contribute to the expansion of trade, and the need for enhanced technical assistance and capacity-building in this area.*
- **Trade and Competition Policy**
  - *Recognizing the case for a multilateral framework to enhance the contribution of competition policy to international trade and development, and the need for enhanced technical assistance and capacity-building in this area.*
  - *Full account shall be taken of the needs of developing and least developed country participants and appropriate flexibility provided to address them.*
- **Transparency in Government Procurement**
  - *Negotiations shall be limited to the transparency aspects and therefore will not restrict the scope for countries to give preferences to domestic supplies and suppliers. We commit ourselves to ensuring adequate technical assistance and support for capacity building both during the negotiations and after their conclusion.*

- **Trade Facilitation**
    - *Recognizing the case for further expediting the movement, release and clearance of goods, including goods in transit, and the need for enhanced technical assistance and capacity building in this area.*

Other subjects listed for negotiation included:

- **Trade and Technology Transfer**
    - *We agree to an examination, in a Working Group under the auspices of the General Council, of the relationship between trade and transfer of technology, and of any possible recommendations on steps that might be taken within the mandate of the WTO to increase flows of technology to developing countries.*
- **Trade and Environment**
    - *We agree to negotiations, without prejudging their outcome, on the reduction or, as appropriate, elimination of tariff and non-tariff barriers to environmental goods and services.*
    - *We instruct the Committee on Trade and Environment, in pursuing work on all items on its agenda within its current terms of reference, to give particular attention to:*
        - *the effect of environmental measures on market access, especially in relation to developing countries.*
- **E-Commerce**
    - *Electronic commerce creates new challenges and opportunities for trade for members at all stages of development.*
    - *We instruct the General Council to consider the most appropriate institutional arrangements for handling the Work Programme on e-commerce and to report on further progress to the Fifth Session of the Ministerial Conference. We declare that members will maintain their current practice of not imposing customs duties on electronic transmissions until the Fifth Session.*
- **Disciplines for Trade Remedies and Subsidies**
    - *In the light of experience and of the increasing application of these instruments by members, we agree to negotiations aimed at clarifying and improving disciplines … while preserving the basic concepts, principles and effectiveness of these Agreements and their instruments and objectives, and taking into account the needs of developing and least developed participants.*

Comment: There should have been a red flag for the US delegation at this point. The Senate had mandated by resolution the non-implementation of the Kennedy Round's Anti-dumping Code. Improving the "disciplines" over trade remedy instruments could only mean curbing their use, although with a potential trade-off of getting additional disciplines over subsidies.

There was also a brief reference to obtaining a "clarifying and improving of disciplines on fisheries subsidies," a matter that was to loom large twenty years later as a central objective of MC12.[76] The fisheries negotiation had a development aspect as well, as it was developing countries that suffered most from the depletion of ocean fish stocks promoted by subsidies – Somalia, for example, in Africa, and the small vulnerable nations of the South Pacific. However, large developing countries were perhaps the largest subsidizers.

- **Trade, Debt and Finance**
  - *We agree to an examination, in a Working Group under the auspices of the General Council, of the relationship between trade, debt and finance, and of any possible recommendations on steps that might be taken within the mandate and competence of the WTO to enhance the capacity of the multilateral trading system to contribute to a durable solution to the problem of external indebtedness of developing and least developed countries.*
- **Trade and Technology Transfer**
  - *We agree to an examination, in a Working Group under the auspices of the General Council, of the relationship between trade and transfer of technology, and of any possible recommendations on steps that might be taken within the mandate of the WTO to increase flows of technology to developing countries.*
- **Technical Cooperation and Capacity-Building**
  - *We confirm that technical cooperation and capacity building are core elements of the development dimension of the multilateral trading system ... We instruct the Secretariat, in coordination with other relevant agencies, to support domestic efforts for mainstreaming trade into national plans for economic development and strategies for poverty reduction. The delivery of WTO technical assistance shall be designed to assist developing and least developed countries and low-income countries in transition to adjust to WTO rules and disciplines, implement obligations and exercise the rights of membership, including drawing on the benefits of an open, rules-based multilateral trading system.*

The most important, perhaps only, hard law decision reached at Doha was an understanding that IP protection was not to interfere with developing countries' combating serious outbreaks of communicable disease. The ministers at MC4 decided:

4. *We agree that the TRIPS Agreement does not and should not prevent members from taking measures to protect public health. Accordingly,*

[76] Ibid.

> *while reiterating our commitment to the TRIPS Agreement, we affirm that the Agreement can and should be interpreted and implemented in a manner supportive of WTO members' right to protect public health and, in particular, to promote access to medicines for all.*

In this connection, we reaffirm the right of WTO members to use, to the full, the provisions in the TRIPS Agreement, which provide flexibility for this purpose.

> 5. *Accordingly and in the light of paragraph 4 above, while maintaining our commitments in the TRIPS Agreement, we recognize that these flexibilities include: . . .*
>   - *Each member has the right to grant compulsory licences and the freedom to determine the grounds upon which such licences are granted.*
>   - *Each member has the right to determine what constitutes a national emergency or other circumstances of extreme urgency, it being understood that public health crises, including those relating to HIV/AIDS, tuberculosis, malaria and other epidemics, can represent a national emergency or other circumstances of extreme urgency.*
>   - *The effect of the provisions in the TRIPS Agreement that are relevant to the exhaustion of intellectual property rights is to leave each member free to establish its own regime for such exhaustion without challenge, subject to the MFN and national treatment provisions of Articles 3 and 4.*

A developing country could henceforth ask a country that had the necessary manufacturing capability to produce for it medicines to deal with a public health crisis, caused for example by HIV/AIDS, tuberculosis, malaria, and other epidemics constituting a national emergency or other circumstance of extreme urgency, under a compulsory license, overriding to a degree the exclusive rights of a patent holder. It was essential both for humanitarian and political reasons to be responsive to this need.

Evaluating Doha

The Doha Ministerial Conference was important for a variety of reasons. It brought China formally into the world trading system after a gap of just over four decades since China left the GATT in 1949. That accession marked one of the most important decisions that the WTO members were ever to make.[77] Second,

[77] When referring to the WTO, a shorthand may often be used that implies that the Organization has capabilities it does not in fact possess. While one can say that the WTO as an institution hired someone, or that the WTO published a text, it is never accurate to state that "the WTO

it dealt with an extremely sensitive issue of emergency access to medicines to fight epidemics despite rules for the protection of intellectual property, a subject that was to return with force two decades later during the COVID-19 pandemic. Third, it would put on the table an extensive list of items for negotiation, some of which eventually yielded negotiated results in later Ministerial Conferences, at Bali and Nairobi. Fourth, MC4 also signaled the launch of a negotiation for duty-free treatment of environmental goods. Less positively, and generating more heat than light, MC4 recorded positions for what would become battle lines over developing country status.

The noble and somewhat selfless objective of the DDA led by the chief negotiators of the European Union and the United States, concentrating to the extent that it did on development, may well have had two built-in defects. The GATT had been founded largely on the basis of tough bargaining for reciprocal concessions, with all being treated in most respects equally. There was always leeway for those countries unable to contribute as much as others, but this was a matter to be dealt with pragmatically, not rigidly institutionalized, with longer time periods for compliance where there were capacity limitations and pressing for less in the way of trade liberalization. This concept began to be modified by the grant of generalized preferences in connection with the Tokyo Round. But these preferences were voluntary on the part of the parties granting them. DDA was different. The Doha Agenda was building in a class structure, although with an expectation, at least on the part of some, of class mobility.

In looking at history, it is best not to indulge in the erroneous practice of imputing to those in the past knowledge of the future. Hindsight tells us where good beginnings were made, and hindsight lets us know what did not work at all. The creators of the DDA would not have known that China would grow as dramatically as it did, as quickly as it did, nor that it would not evolve as Japan did into a fully market-driven economy. The facts at the time of the Doha Ministerial when China was admitted to WTO membership were that its accession had involved a very lengthy negotiation, with substantial changes in its trade regime through literally thousands of changes in domestic law, and that special safeguards were included in the accession that were to last 12–15

decides or fails to decide a negotiating issue," or that "the WTO adopts a policy." It is the WTO members that agree or disagree, or that adopt a policy. The WTO does have a legal personality. It can be said to agree to work with a sister international organization. That is within its remit, although some WTO members might challenge that assertion. For almost all matters, making rules, coming to decisions, these are the exclusive preserve of the members. Anything more is only extremely rarely delegated to the Director-General or other staff.

years, all in the direction of preparation for further integration into a liberal international economic order.

The negotiators also would not have known that self-designation would be considered by some developing countries as a right that could not be challenged, claimed notionally by all, or that developing countries might consider that they should be treated the same in an undifferentiated preferential blanket fashion.

What the negotiators from the major developed members, the USA and the EU, should have known is that given they would ultimately have to satisfy domestic constituencies, there would be a need at the end of the negotiation to demonstrate that their domestic commercial interests would receive substantial reciprocity.[78] And perhaps they should have foreseen that the Declaration would be read as creating an expectation on the part of the more advanced developing countries that they need not contribute. Looking back, it appears that the Round overpromised and would therefore, of necessity, underperform.

The DDA stands out in WTO's quarter-century history because it is the only launch of a major multilateral round of negotiation during this segment – the WTO years – of the longer story of the multilateral trading system. If we do not understand the place of the DDA in the narrative, including its possible flaws, we cannot understand the WTO today or plan for the future of the multilateral trading system.

Sometimes it is fortunate that the future is not known, or there would be fewer attempts at progress. This applies to the events of 2001 at Doha and to the present. In what is deemed to be an apocryphal anecdote, US Secretary of State Henry Kissinger was said to have asked China's Foreign Minister, Zhou Enlai, what he thought the influence was of the French Revolution that had taken place almost two centuries earlier and received the reply "It is too early to say." The same may be said for the Doha Development Agenda. It lives on in the rhetoric and in the minds of some, but its story was not yet written when MC4 adjourned.

THE FIFTH WTO MINISTERIAL CONFERENCE, CANCÚN, SEPTEMBER 10–14, 2003 (MC5)

Cancún's failure goes deeper than miscalculations on timing. It happened because of intransigence and brinkmanship by both rich and poor countries;

[78] The interpretative note to GATT Article XXXVI:8 reads: "It is understood that the phrase 'do not expect reciprocity' means, in accordance with the objectives set forth in this Article, that the less-developed contracting parties should not be expected, in the course of trade negotiations, to make contributions which are inconsistent with their individual development, financial and trade needs, taking into consideration past trade developments."

because of irresponsible and inflammatory behaviour by NGOs; and because of the deeply flawed decision-making system of the WTO itself.

The Economist. September 20, 2003.[79]

The Mexican Trade Minister, who was the chair of the Ministerial Conference, and the then Director-General, Supachai Panitchpakdi, put forward a draft declaration on their own responsibility. It was not adopted. It contained specific ways to move the DDA forward on agriculture and non-agricultural market access and called for the tabling of offers for market access for services. Most of the other provisions consisted of noting progress made, without detail. With respect to development, the draft stated:

We particularly welcome the statement of support from the Executive Heads of the IMF and the World Bank, contained in their letter to the Director-General of 20 August 2003, to work with the WTO to address problems that some developing-country Members may encounter in adjusting to a more liberal trade environment, through preference erosion, loss of tariff revenue, or other factors.

This was recognition of the proviso on the enabling clause, that MFN liberalization was not to be blocked by preservation of tariff preferences. The joint draft also included a long and detailed annex to assure that there would be implementation of special and differential treatment. The four Singapore Issues were completely surrounded by brackets, distancing the authors from endorsing positive outcomes for these topics. Some members felt that a declaration could have been issued had the ministerial meeting been extended, but it was the chair's choice not to do so. *The Economist* laid the blame at the feet of the WTO's members: "It was that too many countries continued grandstanding at the Mexican resort, rather than seeking the compromises on which trade talks depend."

I was at Cancún as a private sector advisor to the US delegation, not as a negotiator. I gave a lecture on the side of the official meetings on the need to curb industrial subsidies. During one day, there were demonstrations that cut the single road running down the center of Cancún Island. As with all demonstrations to date, they had no effect on what went on inside the conference hall. The demonstrators in Cancún, as in Seattle, need not have worried. Within the venue, no consensus was emerging.

Whether it is called grand-standing or just restating existing positions, when it comes to broad movement forward, the WTO seemed to be becoming a talk

[79] "The WTO Under Fire." *The Economist*. September 18, 2003. www.economist.com/special-report/2003/09/18/the-wto-under-fire

shop. Deliberation is a necessary quality to achieve closure, negotiated results. Restatement of positions does not serve this purpose. A question that was emerging was whether country representatives were being sent as negotiators or as functionaries to read prepared statements for resonance back in capitals, not to change minds. If there were ministers who wished for results, they went away disappointed. There is a limit to having meetings with few negotiated outcomes before the damage becomes irreparable.

A total of 148 countries were present at the meeting at Cancún. There was a clear North–South divide, although the South was not homogeneous. Brazil wished to gain export markets for its agriculture. India was defensive when it came to farm commodities. Too many countries focused on what they wanted for themselves to the exclusion of looking more closely at what others might need and whether there were possibilities to accommodate some of those needs. Some took too much pride in walking away rather than looking for satisfaction in accomplishment. The world economy did not swoon with the failure of Cancún, which the chair warned could happen. The WTO did not sink into oblivion, as some others warned. The world of trade continued, but it was not improved by this Ministerial Conference.

Tempers were short. Pascal Lamy, the EU minister, described the WTO decision-making process as being "medieval," a position that he walked back a bit later.[80] Lamy had raised implicitly a fundamental point. Had all to agree for any to agree to anything? Was there always going to be a single undertaking, meaning not just a requirement that subjects be negotiated in parallel but that all must sign up to all results? It would be very hard for the Uruguay Round version of a single undertaking to be an acceptable procedure given the diversity of interests of WTO members. Was the Texan poker theory of negotiation correct – to put so much in the pot that no one could afford to leave the table? Here, that was not the problem, or the solution, as the pot was seemingly empty, with no participant moving to make contributions.

All was not lost, however. The EU did not give up on launching a new Round. Its diversion of negotiating energies into bilateral preferential trade agreements did not occur until a few years later. The lingering question after Cancún was whether the 148 WTO members could put aside their narrow interests to focus on getting something major underway on a broad front. Towards the end of the meeting, compromises were said to be emerging, but they would have to wait.

80 "Speech by Pascal Lamy European Commissioner for Trade – Speech at the Confederation of British Industries Confederation of British Industry London." European Commission. July 6, 2000. www.ec.europa.eu/commission/presscorner/detail/en/SPEECH_00_258

A side note: Cambodia and Nepal were brought into the WTO at the meeting. This was not, perhaps, momentous for world trade but it was vitally important for these two countries.

THE SIXTH WTO MINISTERIAL CONFERENCE, HONG KONG, DECEMBER 13–18, 2005 (MC6)

The Hong Kong Ministerial did find a degree of consensus. The trade ministers were able to agree to a Ministerial Declaration. The Australian Trade Department described the outcome as follows:

> *Key elements of the declaration include:*
>
> - *A reaffirmation of Members' commitment to the Doha mandate and July 2004 framework;*
> - *Commitment by Members to the elimination by 2013 of all forms of agricultural export subsidies;*
> - *A deadline of April 30, 2006 for modalities on agriculture and NAMA (industrials), with revised schedules to be submitted by July 31, 2006;*
> - *Agreement to use a "Swiss" tariff-cutting formula with the potential to produce an ambitious result on industrials (but still a long way to go to achieve that outcome);*[81]
> - *Maintenance of the basis for further work on services;*
> - *A significant Aid for Trade package;*
> - *An agreement on the difficult cotton issue;*
> - *A commitment by developed countries and those developing countries in a position to do so, to provide duty and quota-free access to most goods from LDCs.*

For domestic support (subsidies) for agricultural production, it was agreed that greater cuts would be made in higher levels of subsidies – sort of a Swiss formula notion. Accordingly, the EU was to embrace the highest cuts (top band), followed by the United States and Japan (middle band), and the rest of the members (bottom band). For cotton, export subsidies would be eliminated by 2006, and with respect to market access, developed countries would provide duty-free and quota-free access for cotton exports from least developed countries from the commencement of the implementation period.

Getting this far on agriculture had required the United States to take the lead, putting an offer on the table. It required the EU to come part of the way toward greater disciplines, and for developing countries to retreat from their

[81] Tariff peaks are cut to a greater extent than are lower tariffs.

demands for earlier progress. Regarding non-agricultural market access (NAMA), members adopted the Swiss formula mandating greater cuts in higher tariffs. Environmental issues did not occupy center stage in Hong Kong.

The date for the conclusion of the Doha Development Agenda was extended for a year, to the end of 2006.

The Conference was marked by street violence of protestors in the area surrounding the venue, with over 900 arrests made. The demonstrators were largely representatives of farming interests from the region, concerned about prospective competition from imports.

THE EFFORT TO KEEP ON SCHEDULE, 2006–2008

The Doha Round was declared to be near death on more than one occasion. *The Economist* provided the following report on July 27, 2006:

> *At last, it is official. After stumbling on for months, the Doha trade talks have collapsed. On July 24th, at the end of yet another futile gathering of trade ministers in Geneva, Pascal Lamy, the World Trade Organisation's director general, formally suspended the negotiations. He set no date for their resumption. As Kamal Nath, India's trade minister put it, the Doha round "is definitely between intensive care and the crematorium."*[82]

What had happened? On Sunday, July 23, 2006, ministers from Australia, Brazil, the European Union, India, Japan, and the United States met in Geneva to try to bridge gaps in how to move forward on agriculture, and on market access for industrial products. They could not come to an agreement on agricultural domestic support, market access, or non-agricultural market access (NAMA). The USA and the EU would not cut their flexibilities to provide farm subsidies without a contribution in the form of market access from the larger developing countries.

WTO Director-General Pascal Lamy announced that he would call a "time out" – a suspension of the Round – at a meeting of the General Council to be held on July 27. He did not suggest how long the talks would be suspended. He said that the talks could only resume when progress could be made, which in turn would require changes in entrenched positions. The least developed were concerned that this pause would delay the promised duty-free, quota-free

[82] "In the Twilight of Doha." *The Economist*. November 17, 2021. www.economist.com/special-report/2006/07/27/in-the-twilight-of-doha

access for their products. Negotiating sessions resumed in 2007, but no major breakthroughs occurred.

In July 2008, a series of intensive discussions utilized "Green Room" meetings.[83] These are meetings of relatively small groups called by the Director-General, with differing configurations of members in attendance depending on the negotiating topic to be addressed. At the time, this was a usual practice, designed to generate consensus by starting with those most interested or representing key constituencies and regions, plus the relevant WTO committee chairs and group coordinators (African, Latin American, etc.). Drafts were prepared and processed in the small groups before fanning out to larger groupings and finally the entire membership.

Today, and ever since the Doha Round was launched, the Director-General chairs a Trade Negotiating Committee of the whole membership. This TNC meets at the heads of delegation level (HODS). These acronyms are in common use at the WTO and helpful when delving into the records of past events to know which configuration of meetings is being referred to. Lamy was assembling a package of texts for this July meeting, trying to clear away potential sticking points. The key elements of the package were agriculture, industrial goods, services, rules (dispute settlement, industrial subsidies, and fish subsidies), and intellectual property. The Green Room, when the practice was employed, which was throughout much of WTO history until relatively recently, was where deals were to take shape. A number of negotiating groups were involved in the TNC for the Doha Round, including Non-Agricultural Market Access, Rules, Trade Facilitation, Agriculture, Services, Trade and Development, Trade-Related Intellectual Property, and Trade and Environment.[84]

Difficulties Encountered

Linkages. While moving the full membership of 153 countries (at that time) forward at the same speed would be challenging under any circumstances, an

[83] Wikipedia tells us that one of the oldest stories is that London's Blackfriars Theatre (1599) included a room behind the scenes where the actors waited to go on stage, which happened to be painted green and was called "the green room." Whether that is the origin or not, the term has been in use at the GATT and for years in the WTO for preparatory sessions to try to move negotiations forward. The Director-General's conference room in his/her suite of offices was for a time used for small meetings of delegations that were termed "green room" meetings.

[84] See the expanded version provided by the WTO Secretariat of this rundown: "How the Meeting Was Organized." World Trade Organization. www.wto.org/english/tratop_e/dda_e/meet08_org_e.htm

added layer of difficulty was to live with the "single undertaking" approach in which nothing was agreed until everything (in all subjects under negotiation) was agreed. This form of negotiation was required by cross-linkages that participants saw as necessary. For example, in the US law that provides the mandate for trade negotiations, agricultural issues were to be negotiated "in conjunction with" industrial issues.[85] The United States was not alone in needing linkages. The description of this process provided by the WTO is that it helps to engender a consensus by creating a more balanced package of agreements in which there will be something for everyone – in other words, the Texan poker game approach. When it works, it is brilliant. When it prevents progress, it produces a negotiating nightmare.

Irreconcilable differences. The chair of the Rules Committee put forward a text with respect to antidumping on his own responsibility. This meant that while not all would see in it what they wished, an attempt was being made to bridge differences.[86] Antidumping was at the time, and perhaps always will be, a very contentious area of the trading system. Members are allowed to assess duties on goods that were being "dumped," generally meaning sold at less than fair value. How administering authorities go about making their calculations greatly affects the level of the additional duties that will be imposed on imports. Hotly contested issues were "zeroing," "public interest," and introducing a "sunset clause." Zeroing was the practice where the United States (and from time to time others) in calculating the amount of antidumping duty would zero out the amounts by which other shipments were sold at more than fair value. This has the effect of increasing the protective effect of the remedy. Introducing a public interest test, on the other hand, would allow those who benefit from the dumping to make their case that the antidumping duty should not be fully applied because of offsetting considerations. A sunset provision would terminate the remedy after a stipulated period that the relief had been in place.

Countries with import-sensitive industries would wish for flexibility to impose more effective relief. Exporting countries would like to see protection eroded in foreign markets to which they were shipping goods.

The chairman's text contained the following on zeroing: "[**ZEROING: Delegations remain profoundly divided on this issue. Positions range from**

85 A formulation suggested by Hélène N. Wolff, my wife, and adopted by Congress and signed into law by the President.

86 "Draft Consolidated Chair Texts of the AD and SCM Agreements." World Trade Organization. November 3, 2007. www.wto.org/english/tratop_e/rulesneg_e/rules_chair_text_nov07_e.htm

insistence on a total prohibition of zeroing irrespective of the comparison methodology used and in respect of all proceedings to a demand that zeroing be specifically authorized in all contexts.]"[87] And on sunsetting:

> ***[SUNSET REVIEWS: Delegations have widely differing views regarding various aspects of the sunset issue. There is sharp disagreement as to whether there should be any automatic termination of measures after a given period of time and, if so, after how long. On the two extremes of this issue are those delegations that favour automatic termination after five years without any possibility of extension and those that reject the principle of automatic termination altogether.]***

On public interest:

> ***[PUBLIC INTEREST …: Participants are sharply divided on the desirability of a procedure to take account of the representations of domestic interested parties when deciding whether to impose a duty. Some consider that such a procedure would impinge on Members' sovereignty and would be costly and time-consuming, while others support inclusion of such a procedure.]***

The bold font and brackets are from the original. The gaps between negotiating parties' positions were too large to allow the chair to even try to offer compromise language.

On fisheries subsidies, even the issues were insufficiently clear:

> *On fisheries subsidies, as envisaged in my Report of July 2008, instead of a new draft text I am tabling a roadmap for our further discussions, as in this area the situation is of a different nature. The Group is mandated to strengthen disciplines on subsidies in the fisheries sector, including through the prohibition of certain forms of fisheries subsidies that contribute to overcapacity and over-fishing, while formulating appropriate and effective special and differential treatment that addresses the interests and concerns of developing Members. Yet, we have no pre-existing agreement to which to revert, and the differences among delegations go to the very concepts and structure of the rules.*

Economic interests at stake. Trade negotiations incorporate provisions that affect the futures of industries, and therefore are politically sensitive. Domestic support (subsidies) for farm production is as highly politically charged as antidumping is for all domestic industries. Fisheries subsidies disciplines would limit the possibilities for factory ships operating far from home waters, where

[87] "New Draft Consolidated Chair Texts of the AD and SCM Agreements TN/RL/W/236." World Trade Organization. December 19, 2008. https://docs.wto.org/dol2fe/Pages/SS/directdoc.aspx?filename=Q:/TN/RL/W236.pdf&Open=True

they deprive poor local fishermen of their livelihoods while depleting the ocean's fish stocks. Each of these negotiations involves large economic stakes for particular actors. Many economists have tended to disparage "special interests." However, all of commerce consists of special interests. Each change in trade regulation will result in some who gain and others who may suffer a loss. The idea behind trade as a common good is that, on the whole, the gains far outweigh the losses, and the global economy grows. Most economists tell us that the global gains have been enormous as a result of having the multilateral trading system and a continuing opening of national markets.

The Final Act

The efforts to bring negotiations forward in the Doha Round were gargantuan. Many very talented individuals were involved. The endeavor did not come together. Some could or would not act on agricultural market access, others on other subjects. Reaching a solution was not an imperative for all. The negotiations broke down. The failure was announced by Director-General Pascal Lamy at a General Council meeting on July 31, 2008, and the six-minute audio recording of his report as TNC chair is worth listening to, as he remains upbeat that much was done and that this was not to be the end – "no one is throwing in the towel."[88] Lamy thanked ministers for not engaging in a "blame game," but in fact they did. It was clear to the press that the talks broke down over developing countries, led by India, wanting more flexibility to protect their farmers from agricultural imports, which USTR Susan Schwab said was a rollback from current market access. The *New York Times* reported that "Mari Elka Pangestu, the Indonesian Trade Minister, said the failure of the talks reflected the inability of the rich industrial powers to deal with the growing influence of China, India and Brazil in the global economy." She blamed the United States, according to the *Times*, for not showing sufficient flexibility.[89]

THE SEVENTH WTO MINISTERIAL CONFERENCE, GENEVA, NOVEMBER 30–DECEMBER 3, 2009 (MC7)

Over 3,000 delegates from the 153 members and 59 observer delegations converged on Geneva in late 2009 to reiterate their dedication to moving

[88] "No One Is Throwing in the Towel: Audio Statement by Pascal Lamy." World Trade Organization. July 31, 2008. www.wto.org/audio/2008_07_31_gc_dgstat.mp3

[89] "After 7 Years, Talks Collapse on World Trade." *New York Times*. July 30, 2008. www.nytimes.com/2008/07/30/business/worldbusiness/30trade.html

the Doha Round forward. The ministers, according to the chair's summary, "reaffirmed the need to conclude the Round in 2010."[90] He noted: "Gaps remain on substance and there was wide acknowledgment of the need for leadership and engagement on the remaining specific issues over the coming weeks." The lack of progress could, perhaps, be excused, given the state of the world economy. The ministers were mostly concerned with holding the line against protectionism in the wake of the global financial crisis. On March 6, 2009, the Dow Jones industrial average had sunk to a new low of 6,469.95,[91] a stunning drop from a peak of 14,198.10 on October 11, 2007.[92] In this time of financial stress, according to the chair, members noted that finishing the Round was itself a stimulus package with limited fiscal cost, and "is vital in order to ensure that the WTO remains relevant."[93]

The trading system was not moving forward into new territory of liberalization, but nor was it retreating. In the face of economic calamity, the prescription that Franklin Roosevelt and Cordell Hull had chosen – the pursuit of trade liberalization through reciprocal trade negotiations – was not applied. But nor were the Americans, or the other participants, ready to give up, not officially in any event.

Broader concerns were also emerging. Many ministers raised climate change as an issue that needed to be addressed. The need to remove barriers to trade in environmental goods and services was widely endorsed. There were also warnings against "green protectionism."[94] There was in addition some recognition that the WTO was not the only venue for trade negotiations, that there was action taking place elsewhere. The chair noted that concerns were voiced over the growth of what were called "regional trading agreements" (RTAs) which are sub-multilateral and always discriminatory.

MINISTERIAL CONFERENCES 8–11

In the second decade of the twenty-first century, four Ministerial Conferences rather than five took place due to the advent of the COVID-19 pandemic. The meetings were held, respectively, in Geneva, Bali, Nairobi, and Buenos Aires.

90 "WT/MIN(09)/18 Seventh Ministerial Conference – Chairman's Summary." World Trade Organization. December 2, 2009.

91 "Dow Fights Back." CNN. March 6, 2009. www.money.cnn.com/2009/03/06/markets/markets_newyork/index.htm

92 "Dow Finishes at All-Time High, Smashes 2007's Record CSE." CNBC. March 5, 2013. www.cnbc.com/id/100522542

93 Ibid.

94 Ibid.

The Doha Development Agenda was not restarted. The members were seeking to find their footing and, in several respects, they succeeded with discrete deliverables and a way forward.

THE EIGHTH WTO MINISTERIAL CONFERENCE, GENEVA, DECEMBER 15–17, 2011 (MC8)

The Ambassador of Nigeria to the WTO, Yonov Fred Agah, serving as the chair of the General Council in 2011, must have known that after eight months of strenuous efforts to pull the membership together the chances of a fully agreed outcome in the form of a Ministerial Declaration at MC8 were slim. The central fact was that there was still an impasse over whether the Doha Development Agenda (DDA) could move forward. He foreshadowed the upcoming divisions among trade ministers by lowering expectations and pointing to the clear accomplishments that could be claimed:

> *Part of the challenge that our Organization faces is that our temporary setbacks are publicly magnified and our successes are unheralded. Nevertheless, what matters is that we continue to chalk up our gains and forge ahead collectively. I am therefore pleased to note that this year we will be welcoming four new Members – Vanuatu; Samoa; the Russian Federation; and Montenegro. This is testimony to the continued belief and faith in the value of the multilateral trading system. It is an important step in making the WTO a more global organization and shows that the WTO and multilateralism remain a priority for trade policy even during these challenging economic times.*[95]

Fred Agah pointed to the central problems of holding Ministerial Conferences. Half of them, five out of the first eleven, illuminated for all the world to see the differences among members by not concluding with an agreed Ministerial Declaration. As opposed to the annual meetings of the Bank, Fund, or OECD, as a trade negotiating forum, the WTO was expected to produce agreements, not just have a biennial meeting without clear deliverables. The problem extended beyond a public relations issue. Biennial Ministerial Conferences were unavoidably a report on the state of health of the world's trade organization. Each time the ministers met in this framework, a judgment would be rendered on what the members collectively could

95 "Statement by H. E. Mr. Yonov Frederick Agah – Chairman of the General Council." World Trade Organization. December 15, 2011. www.wto.org/english/thewto_e/minist_e/min11_e/stat_e/agah_opening_e.doc

produce, not on the value of the daily work of the WTO committees and the WTO Secretariat, which would largely escape public notice.

A key accomplishment of WTO Ministerial Conferences was the accession of additional WTO members, progressively making the WTO universal. While accessions over the years would cumulatively extend the coverage of the multilateral trading system, making it truly global, it was never by itself enough for contemporaries to deem a given Ministerial Conference a success. This was true even when the system welcomed the accession of China in 2001 and the Russian Federation in 2011. Fred Agah, while announcing that the Russian Federation, a country accounting for 11 percent of the world's land mass, after a decade and a half of effort, was being brought into the WTO, still sounded a defensive note: "We all know that there is no credible alternative to the rules-based multilateral trading system. We therefore require leadership of Ministers to demonstrate that our Organization is credible, relevant and can act decisively to deliver for all its Members."[96] What then did MC8 yield, beyond increasing the WTO's membership?

The Conference recorded the usual pledges to resist protectionism. The ministers called upon themselves to strengthen the multilateral trading system. They called for strengthening and improving the working of the regular bodies of the WTO. They adopted an extensive agreed "political guidance" text that reaffirmed that "development is a core element of the WTO's work."[97] A considerable number of ministers stressed "the centrality of development," worth recording here primarily because the US view as expressed at a later date by Trump administration officials was that "the WTO is not a development institution." The political guidance also reaffirmed the "integrality" of special and differential treatment provisions to the WTO Agreements and expressed support for other, more direct, aids to development.

While keeping the flame of hope alive for ultimate multilateral success for the DDA, the ministers took an important decision to move away from the single undertaking approach, stating that "it is unlikely that all elements of the Doha Development Round could be concluded simultaneously in the near future."[98] The ministers therefore committed themselves "to advance negotiations, where progress can be achieved, including focusing on the elements of

96 Ibid.

97 "Eighth Ministerial Conference – Chairman's Concluding Statement WT/MIN(11)/11." World Trade Organization. December 17, 2011. https://docs.wto.org/dol2fe/Pages/SS/directdoc.aspx?filename=Q:/WT/MIN11/11.pdf&Open=True

98 "Day 3: Samoa and Montenegro Join Russia with Membership Agreed, as Ministers Wrap Up Conference." World Trade Organization. December 17, 2011. www.wto.org/english/news_e/news11_e/mn11a_17dec11_e.htm

the Doha Declaration that allow members to reach provisional or definitive agreements based on consensus earlier than the full conclusion of the single undertaking."

In parallel to the Ministerial Conference, participating ministers marked the near conclusion of the renegotiated plurilateral Government Procurement Agreement (GPA), an update of the 1979 Code on Government Procurement. The Conference also granted a waiver for providing preferential treatment to services provided by LDCs.

The chair's closing statement recorded differences rather than consensus. While ministers highlighted the importance of keeping markets open, many wanted a stronger statement against protectionism, a firmer commitment, something with teeth. Other ministers countered that in the name of fostering development, it was necessary to use existing WTO-consistent policy space to achieve economic and development objectives and this policy space should not be curtailed.

Some ministers wanted to address emerging global challenges, such as climate change, energy, food security, exchange rates, competition, and investment. Others expressed reservations about taking on new matters, concerned about the dangers of "addressing issues selectively or shifting the focus away from unresolved issues in the DDA negotiations."[99] Some ministers expressed concern with the explosion of regional trade agreements (RTAs) and the implications for the multilateral trading system.

There was a division as well over the use of export restrictions for food that might adversely affect purchases for humanitarian reasons by the World Food Programme (WFP). Those who opposed these restrictions were met with an argument that it was more important to address the root causes of food security. This is worth noting here because it was still a subject being debated a full decade later, with a compromise agreement reached at MC12.

As opposed to the first year of the pandemic when crops were plentiful, the years following the 2007–8 global financial crisis were characterized by serious price volatility that particularly worried the least developed countries and net food-importing developing countries (NFIDCs). The members sought to agree by consensus to deal with the difficulties being experienced: "We direct the General Council to develop a comprehensive, fact-based, result-oriented and time-bound work program on the trade-related response to mitigate the

[99] "Eighth Ministerial Conference – Chairman's Concluding Statement WT/MIN(11)/11." World Trade Organization. December 17, 2011. https://docs.wto.org/dol2fe/Pages/SS/directdoc.aspx?filename=Q:/WT/MIN11/11.pdf&Open=True

impact of the food market prices and volatility on WTO LDCs and NFIDCs."[100]

Proponents sought a work program to explore exemptions from any food export restrictions for food destined for these food-import-dependent countries, and to explore additional financing for food purchases by them. As is still true today, the only answer for meeting a current crisis was to call for a report containing solutions that would be submitted to the next Ministerial Conference, notionally two years into the future. However, even this effort failed. No agreement could be reached, and the draft ministerial decision was not adopted.

The primary response to the food volatility crisis came not from the WTO but from a G20 meeting of agriculture ministers held in Cannes a month earlier. It established the Agricultural Market Information System (AMIS), a cooperative venture to provide food market transparency to aid in enhancing food security.[101] Major trading countries were to provide information on global supplies of agricultural commodities (focusing on wheat, maize, rice, and soybeans). The participants in AMIS are the G20 members plus Spain and seven additional major exporting and importing countries of agricultural commodities, accounting for some 80–90 percent of the crops being monitored. Better information might make it easier for individual food exporting and importing governments to make wiser decisions.

Another issue, beyond food security, discussed at MC8 and still the subject of debate ten years later, was an impasse over "the balance in contributions and responsibilities between emerging and advanced economies."[102]

One gets the impression, over a decade after MC8, that while there was nothing to show in the way of firm commitments at the WTO, that is, no new rules, no new multilateral trade liberalization (outside of that provided by the acceding countries), there was a positive atmosphere in which deliberation among ministers could and did take place, which Ambassador Agah called "a promising basis for renewing the political dimension of the WTO in a lasting way."[103] The countries

[100] "The WTO Response to the Impact of the Food Crisis on LDCs and NFIDCs WT/GC/140/Rev.1." World Trade Organization. November 25, 2011. https://docs.wto.org/dol2fe/Pages/SS/directdoc.aspx?filename=Q:/WT/GC/140R1.pdf&Open=True

[101] "About AMIS." Agricultural Market Information System. www.amis-outlook.org/amis-about/en/

[102] "Eighth Ministerial Conference – Chairman's Concluding Statement WT/MIN(11)/11." World Trade Organization. December 17, 2011. https://docs.wto.org/dol2fe/Pages/SS/directdoc.aspx?filename=Q:/WT/MIN11/11.pdf&Open=True

[103] "Summary Record of the Closing Session WT/MIN(11)/SR/7." World Trade Organization. April 20, 2012. docs.wto.org/dol2fe/Pages/FE_Search/FE_S_S009-DP.aspx?language=E&CatalogueIdList=65843,63217,79464,1149,352,1150,102&CurrentCatalogueIdIndex=6&FullTextHash=&HasEnglishRecord=True&HasFrenchRecord=True&HasSpanishRecord=True

participating at MC8 were not inert, but what they did accomplish, they accomplished in other fora, such as the G20, and exclusively plurilaterally, as with the GPA.

THE NINTH WTO MINISTERIAL CONFERENCE, BALI, DECEMBER 3–7, 2013 (MC9)

> *We are on the cusp of an accomplishment that has eluded us for 12 long years. We are closer than ever before to the first tangible results of the long-running Doha Round. We can see the finish line, and if we are able to cross it, our achievements here will restore the world's faith and confidence in the WTO and the multilateral trading system. Success in Bali is critical. Now is the time for us to demonstrate to the world that the WTO is still relevant.*[104]
>
> Chair's Report to the President of the Republic of Indonesia
> by Indonesian Trade Minister H. E. Mr. Gita Wirjawan, Chair of MC9

The headline from MC9 was that it delivered the WTO's first and to date (through 2021) only truly multilateral trade agreement – that is, an agreement with reciprocal rights and obligations, with all members approving – the Trade Facilitation Agreement.

The newly selected WTO Director-General, Roberto Azevêdo, in office for less than three months, expressed the euphoria he and others felt:

> *In recent weeks the WTO has come alive.*
> *We have seen this organization the way it should be.*
> *Negotiating.*
> *Dynamic.*
> *Working hard to get an agreement.*
> *Working through weekends (and through the weeks!)*
> *Working through the night.*
> *Seeking common ground, finding innovative solutions, making compromises.*
> *We have not seen such effort and engagement for a long, long time.*[105]

The reason for his rejoicing was that the WTO, in its nineteen years of existence up until that point, had not produced any other agreement that all subscribed to, in terms of both obligations and benefits, and now it had done so.

104 "Chair's Report to the President of the Republic of Indonesia at the Opening Session of the 9th WTO Ministerial Conference Bali, 3 December 2013, 15.05–15.20." World Trade Organization. December 3, 2013. www.wto.org/english/thewto_e/minist_e/mc9_e/stat_e/chair_report_wirjawan_e.pdf

105 "Azevêdo: 'The WTO Has Truly Delivered'." World Trade Organization. December 7, 2013. www.wto.org/english/news_e/spra_e/spra16_e.htm

The objective of the Trade Facilitation Agreement (TFA) was straightforward, although the commitments needed to attain it were many, and the complexity of implementation was great. When goods seek to cross a border, the tariff is only the most overt barrier. What is more daunting is red tape (differing from country to country) and lack of transparency. The mantra of those negotiating the agreement was "simplification, modernization and harmonization of export and import processes."[106] The economists at the WTO estimated that, on average, the cost of moving goods across a border was the equivalent of a 24 percent tariff. Worse, perishable commodities, food, rotted at borders while waiting to receive clearance. Expediting the movement, release, and clearance of goods, including goods in transit, they estimated, "could reduce trade costs by an average of 14.3 percent and boost global trade by up to $1 trillion per year, with the biggest gains in the poorest countries."[107]

A novel approach to reaching agreement was acknowledging that acceptance of obligations would take effect at different speeds linked to capacity, with developing and least developed members deciding for themselves how many of the obligations could be taken on board at once, and which required delay.[108] Developed members agreed to implement all provisions of the TFA from the date of its entry into force, which occurred on February 22, 2017.

[106] "Trade Facilitation." World Trade Organization. www.wto.org/english/tratop_e/tradfa_e/tradfa_e.htm

[107] "World Trade Report 2015 – Speeding Up Trade: Benefits and Challenges of Implementing the WTO Trade Facilitation Agreement." World Trade Organization. 2015. www.wto.org/english/res_e/publications_e/wtr15_e.htm

[108] "Agreement on Trade Facilitation." World Trade Organization. www.wto.org/english/docs_e/legal_e/tfa-nov14_e.htm

Under TFA Article 15, there are three categories of provisions:

> *(a) Category A contains provisions that a developing country Member or a least-developed country Member designates for implementation upon entry into force of this Agreement, or in the case of a least-developed country Member within one year after entry into force, as provided in Article 15.*
>
> *(b) Category B contains provisions that a developing country Member or a least-developed country Member designates for implementation on a date after a transitional period of time following the entry into force of this Agreement, [which date it is to specify].*
>
> *(c) Category C contains provisions that a developing country Member or a least-developed country Member designates for implementation on a date after a transitional period of time following the entry into force of this Agreement and requiring the acquisition of implementation capacity through the provision of assistance and support for capacity building, as provided for in Article 16.*

Each developing country and least developed country member is to self-designate, on an individual basis, the provisions it is including under each of the categories.

The first review of implementation was scheduled to take place in November 2021 and was held as scheduled despite the COVID-19 pandemic. The review concluded on the basis of members' notifications that implementation commitments were received by the members at a rate of just over 70 percent. The highest rates of commitments received were those relating to pre-shipment inspection, movement of goods from point of entry to customs point of clearance, transparency of post-clearance audits, provisions on the use of customs brokers, and temporary admission of goods. Fewer implementation commitments were received with respect to other obligations of the agreement, on risk management, border agency cooperation, test procedures, authorized operators, and the single window (enabling traders to submit documentation and/or data requirements for importation, exportation, or transit of goods through a single entry point to the participating authorities or agencies). The purpose of recapitulating this list here is to indicate the complexities faced by trade in crossing borders, and the herculean task of simplification, modernization, and harmonization of border measures, both for imports and exports.

Developing countries and least developed countries were to notify members of their needs. A Trade Facilitation Trust Fund was established. The November 2021 review noted that "85 Members had notified their need for technical assistance and capacity-building, and that the most cited request was for human resources and training; assistance in amending laws or regulations or implementation."[109] The European Union reported in October 2021 that in 2019, the EU and its member states provided €232 million for trade facilitation, which it said, accounted for 48 percent of the world's TF support.[110] Since the entry into force of the TFA in 2017, the EU and its member states "committed to mobilise at least EUR 400 million in trade facilitation assistance over a five-year period, including for projects improving developing countries' customs systems," having already committed €630 million for 2017 to 2019.[111] Making tangible, funded technical assistance available was key to making it possible to get agreement on the TFA as well as enabling its implementation.

The second substantial outcome of MC9, and likely part of the price for getting the TFA agreed, was to provide an interim solution for public stockholding (PSH) and commit to achieving a permanent solution by

[109] "Members Conclude Milestone Review of Trade Facilitation Agreement." World Trade Organization. November 26, 2021. www.wto.org/english/news_e/news21_e/fac_26nov21_e.htm

[110] "EU Aid for Trade." European Commission. October 29, 2021. www.ec.europa.eu/international-partnerships/system/files/eu-aid-for-trade-progress-report-2021_en.pdf

[111] "The EU Ratifies WTO Trade Facilitation Agreement." European Commission. October 5, 2015. www.trade.ec.europa.eu/doclib/press/index.cfm?id=1374

MC11. The interim solution provided that stocks of grains could be purchased without the fear of WTO complaints being brought against the country exercising this privilege for exceeding its subsidy limits – provided that there was transparency, and the support was within certain bounds. The member was to ensure that stocks procured under its programs did not distort trade or adversely affect the food security of other members, and that the flexibility granted "*not be used in a manner that results in an increase of the support subject to the Member's Bound Total AMS [aggregate measure of support] or the de minimis limits*" (both being the member's committed subsidy limits).[112] In addition, the decision was limited to existing stockholding arrangements that were compliant with certain provisions of the WTO Agreement on Agriculture, including that "food purchases by the government shall be made at current market prices and sales from food security stocks shall be made at no less than the current domestic market price for the product and quality in question."[113] The intent was to keep the disposition of public stocks from disrupting world markets.

This interim arrangement was to remain controversial. India subsequently withheld its approval well into 2014. It took President Obama meeting with Prime Minister Modi in the fall of 2014 for a breakthrough to be announced just short of a year after the adoption of the Bali Package. The two countries agreed that the peace clause (an inability to challenge food security measures as agreed at Bali) would remain in place until a permanent solution regarding the issue could be adopted, and they identified elements for an intensified work program to arrive at a permanent solution. The food security issue was clearly not a minor political issue for India and remained in play as an obstacle to multilateral progress even into 2021.

Two other decisions at the Ministerial Conference merit mention. One provided for preferential rules of origin for LDCs, with guidance that, "given the limited productive capacity in the LDCs, it is desirable to keep the level of value addition threshold as low as possible, while ensuring that it is the LDCs that receive the benefit of the preferential trade arrangements."[114] In another declaration, the ministers agreed to "undertake to ensure to the maximum extent possible that: The progress towards the parallel elimination of all forms

[112] "Public Stockholding for Food Security Purposes WT/MIN(13)/38 WT/L/913." World Trade Organization. December 11, 2013.

[113] "Agreement on Agriculture – Articles 8-21." World Trade Organization. www.wto.org/english/docs_e/legal_e/14-ag_02_e.htm

[114] "Preferential Rules of Origin for Least-Developed Countries Competition – Ministerial Decision of 7 December 2013 WT/MIN(13)/42, WT/L/917." World Trade Organization. December 11, 2013. www.wto.org/english/thewto_e/minist_e/mc9_e/desci42_e.htm

of export subsidies and disciplines on all export measures with equivalent effect will be maintained."[115] This was among the unfinished business left at the end of the Bali Ministerial that would be returned to later.

In the celebratory mood of the close of the Bali Ministerial, there was one somber note, but one placed in a positive context. The South African delegation noted that Nelson Mandela had just died on December 5, two days before MC9 was convened. The South African Minister, Rob Davies, said that Mandela had opted for South Africa to remain in the system, although President Mandela had said at the fiftieth anniversary celebration of the GATT in 1998 that the vast majority of South Africans had had "no vote" in South Africa being a founding contracting party to the GATT. He added that Mandela had "expressed the need for a strengthened multilateral trading system that was fair, balanced and inclusive, and that addressed the needs of the developing countries."[116] The South African delegation pledged "to continue to work with the membership of the WTO to prioritise this development mandate, including the implementation of agreements of importance to developing countries reached at this conference in Bali."

The bottom line for Bali, for MC9: DDA had not progressed as a whole, but the Trade Facilitation Agreement was a major deliverable that was in fact delivered. While clearly the agreement would benefit developing countries, it was of commercial interest to all WTO members. It was simply good for world trade, and LDCs in particular.

THE TENTH WTO MINISTERIAL CONFERENCE, NAIROBI, DECEMBER 15–19, 2015 (MC10)

Kenya hosted this Ministerial Conference on behalf of Africa. It marked the twentieth anniversary of the founding of the WTO. The chairperson of MC10, the formidable Kenyan Trade Minister Amina Mohamed, welcomed the ministers with a challenge – a challenge which was important then and whose relevance endures to the present, to find common ground among diverse interests:

> *Let's face up to it. The WTO is the principal forum for trade negotiations that delivers the public good of non-discriminatory trade rules, and much more. It is*

[115] "Export Competition – Ministerial Decision of 7 December 2013 WT/MIN(13)/40, WT/L/915." World Trade Organization. December 11, 2013. www.wto.org/english/thewto_e/minist_e/mc9_e/desci40_e.htm

[116] "The Actuarial Society of South Africa Convention Dinner." Department of Trade, Industry, and Competition. Republic of South Africa. 2013. www.thedtic.gov.za/publications.jsp/page/81/?year&subthemeid

a primary arena for international cooperation. Its credibility and capacity to deliver would be called into question, were we not to be successful in delivering "meaningful" outcomes in Nairobi.

The WTO, building on its GATT foundations, embodies the core values of openness, transparency, good governance and the rule of law. It is structured on the separation of powers: as in its legislative function through negotiations; its Executive Secretariat; and, in the judicial function pursuant to the Dispute Settlement Understanding (DSU). In other words, the WTO embodies modern democratic governance, in its structure, substance and, method of work. [Emphasis added][117]

Were we not to deliver, how would we, the champions of the WTO and the beneficiaries of the gains from trade, answer the sceptics and the opposition, frequently impervious to reason, who have always perceived the WTO negatively and wrongly, as a club where the agenda of the rich are set?[118]

The headline achievement of MC10 was an agreement to introduce a ban on agricultural export subsidies as part of a Nairobi Package. The subject heading was "export competition." Developed countries agreed that they would immediately eliminate export subsidies. Developing countries would be given three more years, until the end of 2018. Some additional leeway, allowing for assistance that would not breach overall commitments, was given to the developing and least developed countries and net food-importing countries. This permissible assistance was to terminate by the end of 2023 for developing countries generally and 2030 for the least developed. This flexibility pertained to support for costs such as freight and marketing.

The prohibition on agricultural export subsidies was a milestone, although it trailed rather than led member interests, as there had been a lessening of export subsidies before the agreement was entered into. It was the only major agreement to emerge on agriculture during the WTO years (at least through the time of the publication of this book).

The second achievement of Nairobi came in the form of a plurilateral agreement to update the product coverage of the Information Technology Agreement (ITA). The ITA was the first and only major tariff-cutting agreement of the WTO era. Eighty-two countries accounting for 97 percent of

[117] Amina Mohamed gives here as important a statement describing the structure of the trading system as has even been made.

[118] "Statement by H. E. Ambassador Amina Mohamed, Cabinet Secretary for Foreign Affairs and International Trade of the Republic of Kenya, MC10 Opening Session WT/MIN(15)/22." World Trade Organization. December 16, 2015. www.wto.org/english/thewto_e/minist_e/mc10_e/statements_e/mohamed_opening1_e.pdf

world trade in the covered products bound the tariffs and other charges on these products at zero. The annual trade in these products at the time of the conference was $1.3 trillion, accounting for approximately 7 percent of total global trade. The expansion list had actually been agreed to in July 2015. What made this a product of Nairobi was that participants agreed at the Ministerial Conference to the staging of reductions of any remaining tariffs on the list of covered products, eliminating most tariffs over a three-year period.

Two landmark accessions also were concluded at MC10, that of Afghanistan and Liberia, which became the 163rd and 164th members of the WTO, respectively.[119] These were countries that had known conflict and were seeking a better life for their peoples through integration into the world economy. As Mohammad Khan Rahmani, First Deputy Chief Executive of the Islamic Republic of Afghanistan, in his remarks to the Conference put it, "WTO membership has always been an integral part of our overall strategic objectives to achieve economic stability, improve regional security and cooperation, and achieve everlasting peace."[120] Liberia had known ten years of peace at the time of the conference, but its economy had been hard hit by Ebola as well as a drop in commodity prices. WTO accession was designed to support peace and improve the economic outlook of the country. Looking back in 2021 on Liberia's accession to the WTO, Mawine Diggs, the current Minister of Commerce and Industry, said:

> *Despite socio-economic and health challenges, the Liberian government seized WTO membership as an opportunity to carry out extensive reforms to address domestic insecurity and re-start and rebuild the economy for inclusive growth. … Building on our accession-related reforms, the government of Liberia has institutionalised our belief that economic growth, stability, and peace can be mutually supported through international cooperation.*[121]

Additional ministerial decisions were taken with respect to agriculture. These involved continuing the conversations on finding a permanent solution for public stockpiling (PSH) for food security and a Special Safeguard

[119] The accessions of the Republic of Yemen, the Republic of Seychelles, and the Republic of Kazakhstan had taken place in the period between MC9 and MC10.

[120] "Remarks by H. E. Mohammad Khan Rahmani, First Deputy Chief Executive, the Islamic Republic of Afghanistan at the WTO Tenth Ministerial Conference." World Trade Organization. December 17, 2015. www.wto.org/english/thewto_e/minist_e/mc10_e/statements_e/acc_afg_e.pdf

[121] "High-Level Political Forum Side Event – Trade for Peace: Addressing Fragility through Economic Integration and Shared Prosperity – The Case of WTO Membership for Liberia and Afghanistan." World Trade Organization. July 8, 2021. www.wto.org/english/news_e/news21_e/mawine_g_diggs_statement.pdf

Mechanism (SSM) for developing countries to have recourse to when facing a surge of imports. A somewhat soft commitment was made by developed countries to provide duty-free and quota-free access to cotton exporters from least developed countries from 2016, provided that this would be compatible with existing agreements and the granting country considered itself in a position to do so. Other decisions postponed the date when WTO members would feel free to impose duties on electronic transmissions (e-commerce) and postponed when they could bring Trade-Related Intellectual Property (TRIPS) cases that were not grounded in violation of a specific commitment but nevertheless impaired a member's benefits under the agreement.

There was continuing disagreement among ministers as to whether the Doha Development Agenda was alive and whether it needed to be concluded before new issues could be brought up for negotiation in the WTO. The Indian Cabinet ratified the agricultural outcomes a few months later, but there was some bitterness in developing countries and especially in Indian quarters. It was called a humiliating setback for the "South" by those who wished the DDA and only the DDA to be the focus of WTO negotiations. On the other hand, USTR Michael Froman had cheered the outcome because "WTO Members will be freed to consider new approaches to pressing unresolved issues and begin evaluating new issues for the organization to consider."[122] Whether Nairobi was an inflection point would remain a disputed matter.

What had happened? Doha issues could continue to be addressed, but without carrying on with the Doha Development Agenda as a *prix fixe* menu with no substitutions. It is illuminating to look at contemporary press reports to understand better what trade officials fought over in terms of subtleties of language in the final declaration. An article in the Indian press fills in some of the blanks when a WTO document is cast in terms of "some Members" were for something and "some Members were against." It conveys a sense of the line-up of WTO members with respect to the wording of one particular paragraph in the declaration:

> 30. *We recognize that many Members reaffirm the Doha Development Agenda, and the Declarations and Decisions at the Doha and at the Ministerial Conferences held since then, and reaffirm their full commitment to conclude the DDA on that basis [language proposed by China, India, South Africa, Ecuador, Venezuela, and the African Group of*

[122] "Statement by Ambassador Michael Froman at the Conclusion of the 10th World Trade Organization Ministerial Conference." Office of the United States Trade Representative. December 19, 2015. www.ustr.gov/about-us/policy-offices/press-office/press-releases/2015/december/statement-ambassador-michael

countries]. Other Members [the US, the EU, Japan, and a handful of other countries] do not reaffirm the Doha mandates, as they believe new approaches are necessary to achieve meaningful outcomes in multilateral negotiations. Members have different views on how to address the negotiations.[123]

The bottom line for the Nairobi Ministerial Conference is that the members of the WTO did reach agreements, and MC10 did deliver tangible results. It went into overtime, an extra day, in order to conclude the agreement on banning export subsidies for agriculture. One logistical/tactical lesson from Nairobi is to have the possibility to stay onsite until a deal can be reached (which was not possible to do in Seattle, as the convention center had been booked by another group following the planned end of that Ministerial Conference).[124] The divisions among members would continue – generally between North and South, with many calling for solidarity of all developing countries versus some that were willing to join in a consensus that implied differentiation.[125]

THE ELEVENTH WTO MINISTERIAL CONFERENCE, BUENOS AIRES, DECEMBER 2017 (MC11)

The Conference opened on December 10, 2017, with a joint declaration of five Latin American Presidents on behalf of the Governments of Argentina, Brazil, Colombia, Chile, Guyana, Mexico, Paraguay, Peru, Suriname, and Uruguay, seeking to build on the accomplishments of the seventy-year-old multilateral trading system. Their statement of objectives was muted. There were no promises of completed negotiations, no forecasting the beginning of new negotiations. They said that they would:

Undertake to coordinate actions in the WTO in order to pursue the process of reforming the rules of international trade in agricultural products, to work towards the prohibition of certain forms of fisheries subsidies, to make progress in domestic regulation in services, and to discuss topics of increasing relevance

[123] "Draft Nairobi Ministerial Declaration Part I WT/MIN(15)/W/33/Rev.3." World Trade Organization. December 19, 2015. https://docs.wto.org/dol2fe/Pages/SS/directdoc.aspx?filename=q:/WT/MIN15/W33R3.pdf&Open=True

[124] "WTO Officials Were Rushing to Clear Out to Make Way for a Convention of Optometrists." *Washington Post*. December 5, 1999. www.washingtonpost.com/wp-srv/WPcap/1999-12/05/073r-120599-idx.html

[125] "TWN Info Service on WTO and Trade Issues (Dec15/19)." Third World Network Berhad. December 23, 2015. www.twn.my/title2/wto.info/2015/ti151219.htm

> *to the trade agenda of the twenty-first century, including electronic commerce, micro, small and medium-sized enterprises (MSMEs), and investment facilitation.*[126]

The five Latin American governments invited other countries to join the declaration. There is no record that any did. Whether this was the result of lack of proselytizing, lack of interest on the part of others, or lack of preparation, the historical record does not indicate.

Work had begun in Geneva among delegations on a joint ministerial declaration that in principle would be endorsed by all. There was, however, a wide gulf between those developing countries that wished to emphasize that the central purpose of the WTO was development, and other members that hoped to move forward selectively on a range of subjects, some of which the Latin American declaration had highlighted.

The first year of the Trump administration was 2017. In March, Trump had said that he would ignore adverse trade rulings at the WTO "if they infringed on US sovereignty." He also indicated that US retaliation against what it considered the unfair trade practices of others would be the new normal for the United States.[127] For America, unilateralism was again in vogue. A national security investigation was begun on imports of steel and aluminum.

As MC11 preparations were underway, it was unclear whether the US Trade Representative, the US "Trade Minister" Robert Lighthizer, would even attend the Ministerial Conference. A key issue for all members was that the United States was blocking appointments to the WTO's Appellate Body, threatening the existence of that entity, spelling the end of binding dispute settlement. Foreign trade officials wondered aloud whether the global trading system would have to continue without the United States.[128] It was an inauspicious beginning for MC11.

Once the Conference convened, ministers each gave what were supposed to be three-minute speeches in their plenary meeting, each statement standing alone with no exchange of views, a sterile exercise. In parallel, work proceeded in smaller settings to try to see what could be agreed upon. Given the time limitation, the speeches do not usually contain negotiating proposals, but they

126 "Presidential Declaration – Opening Ceremony of the Eleventh WTO Ministerial Conference." World Trade Organization. December 1, 2017. www.wto.org/english/thewto_e/minist_e/mc11_e/declarationmc11_e.htm

127 "Trump Suggests Ignoring World Trade Organization in Major Policy Shift." *Washington Post*. March 1, 2017. www.washingtonpost.com/news/wonk/wp/2017/03/01/trump-may-ignore-wto-in-major-shift-of-u-s-trade-policy/

128 "WTO Faces an Identity Crisis as Trump Weighs Going It Alone." *Financial Times*. December 5, 2017. www.ft.com/content/38c56f52-d9a5-11e7-a039-c64b1c09b482

do provide some understanding of whether members were coming together. The EU Trade Commissioner, Cecilia Malmström, summed up the general feeling in the room:

> *The successes of our last two Ministerial Conferences brought some optimism that despite significant differences of views among its Members, the WTO is still capable of delivering important negotiated outcomes. One could also detect certain openness for more pragmatism going forward. Unfortunately, however, we start this year's Ministerial Conference with more questions than answers, and little sense of concrete progress over the past two years. The system is being challenged, Members show insufficient collective ownership and are divided on key questions such as what the WTO should be doing. And there are growing calls for conducting business outside the multilateral setting.*[129]

The Indian Trade Minister, Suresh Prabhakar Prabhu, stated that e-commerce should not be addressed as a matter for negotiation, calling on "the WTO membership to re-endorse the centrality of development in WTO negotiations without creating new sub-categories of countries" and urging that "this Ministerial Conference be an occasion for concluding the unfinished agenda of the Doha Work Programme."[130]

The Chinese Minister of Commerce, Zhang Shan, chose not to be contentious, stating that China was committed to the WTO, to multilateralism, to globalization, citing the Belt and Road Initiative, and Chinese contributions to the WTO for the benefit of least developed countries.

Attention focused perhaps most on what the US Trade Representative Robert Lighthizer would say, given the Trump administration's trade policy pronouncements, which were negative with respect to all prior trade agreements. In his remarks, there was no saber-rattling, but clear specific criticisms:

- *The WTO is losing its essential focus on negotiation and becoming a litigation-centered organization. Too often Members seem to believe they can gain concessions through lawsuits that they could never get at the negotiating table. We have to ask ourselves whether this is good for the institution and whether the current litigation structure makes sense.*
- *We need to clarify our understanding of development within the WTO. We cannot sustain a situation in which new rules can only apply to the*

[129] "Statement by EU Commissioner Cecilia Malmström – Plenary Session of the Eleventh Ministerial Conference of the World Trade Organization." World Trade Organization. December 11, 2017. www.wto.org/english/thewto_e/minist_e/mc11_e/statements_e/eec_e.pdf

[130] "Statement by H. E. Mr. Suresh Prabhakar Prabhu – Union Minister for Commerce and Industry of India." World Trade Organization. December 13, 2017. https://docs.wto.org/dol2fe/Pages/SS/directdoc.aspx?filename=q:/WT/MIN17/ST9.pdf&Open=True

few, and that others will be given a pass in the name of self-proclaimed development status.

- *It is impossible to negotiate new rules when many of the current ones are not being followed. This is why the United States is leading a discussion on the need to correct the sad performance of many Members in notifications and transparency.*[131]

The United States would follow up on the points it made about development status and transparency with specific proposals. It offered no specifics with respect to improvements that should be made in WTO dispute settlement.

The attempt to craft an agreed joint declaration was unsuccessful.[132] When there is no declaration, and there was an attempt to have one – as with black smoke issuing from St. Peter's Basilica in Rome when a new pope is to be chosen but has failed to be – at a WTO Ministerial Conference, the absence of a declaration is a clear indication of a lack of consensus. The members were divided over the centrality of development to the WTO as embodied in the DDA, as opposed to moving forward to negotiate new disciplines and trade liberalization. The differences proved to be irreconcilable. With intransigence on the part of several members to new undertakings blocking the multilateral path forward, a broad swath of members began what they called "Joint Statement Initiatives." These JSIs were gatherings of like-minded members that decided to come together to deliberate on a given topic and ultimately negotiate new understandings. This was as promising as green shoots appearing from the frozen earth in the early spring. The press, however, regarded the meeting as a disaster, with members riven by discontent and rancor:

WTO Meeting Ends in Discord, Ministers Urge Smaller-Scale Trade Talks

BUENOS AIRES/WASHINGTON (Reuters) – The World Trade Organization failed to reach any new agreements on Wednesday, ending a

[131] "Opening Plenary Statement of USTR Robert Lighthizer at the WTO Ministerial Conference." US Embassy in Argentina. December 11, 2017. https://ar.usembassy.gov/opening-plenary-statement-ustr-robert-lighthizer-wto-ministerial-conference/

[132] There were some decisions, urging work to go forward, preserving the status quo for certain suspended matters until MC12, agreeing not to impose duties on electronic transmissions, and bringing Trade-Related Intellectual Property (TRIPS) cases where there was impairment of trade concessions but no violations:

WT/MIN(17)/64 Ministerial Decision on Fisheries Subsidies
WT/MIN(17)/65 Work Programme on Electronic Commerce
WT/MIN(17)/66 TRIPS Non-Violation and Situation Complaints
WT/MIN(17)/63 Work Programme on Small Economies

"Ministerial Conferences – Documents." World Trade Organization. www.wto.org/english/thewto_e/minist_e/mc11_e/documents_e.htm

> *three-day ministerial conference in discord in the face of stinging US criticism of the group and vetoes from other countries.*
>
> *The stalemate dashed hopes for new deals on e-commerce and curbs to farm and fisheries subsidies and raised questions about the body's ability to govern increasingly disputed global trade.*
>
> *The frustrations led some ministers, including US Trade Representative Robert Lighthizer, to suggest that negotiations among smaller groups of "like-minded" WTO countries were a better approach going forward.*
>
> *"We have not achieved any multilateral outcomes," European Union Trade Commissioner Cecilia Malmstrom told a news conference. "The sad reality is that we did not even agree to stop subsidizing illegal fishing."*
>
> *She said the meeting laid bare one of the WTO's biggest deficiencies – that all agreements must have the unanimous consent of all 164 Member countries. She said the United States was partly to blame but that other countries also blocked progress.*
>
> *WTO Director-General Roberto Azevedo added that WTO Members needed to do some "real soul searching" about the way forward and realize they cannot get everything they want.*
>
> *"Progress was going to require a leap in Members' positions," Azevedo said at the event's closing ceremony. "We didn't see that."*
>
> *Malmstrom said "short-term plurilateral arrangements within the WTO framework" were the best way forward. Two such arrangements came together at the Buenos Aires conference …*
>
> *Driven by President Donald Trump's "America First" strategy and a preference for bilateral deals, the United States had pushed against ministers drafting a perfunctory ministerial [declaration] that included references to the centrality of the global trading system and to trade as a driver of development. The statement was ultimately blocked.*[133]

Well, that was one view of the outcome of MC11. Actually, intransigence is usually not one-sided in any stalled trade negotiation. Assigning fault is a subjective exercise. Neither side appeared to be sufficiently invested in achieving a positive outcome. None of the major players was sufficiently determined to reach a multilateral breakthrough. The status quo seemed to be fine with

[133] "WTO Meeting Ends in Discord, Ministers Urge Smaller-Scale Trade Talks." Reuters. December 12, 2017. www.reuters.com/article/us-trade-wto/wto-meeting-ends-in-discord-ministers-urge-smaller-scale-trade-talks-idUSKBN1E71IJ.

China, which was not pressing for specific multilateral progress. The Trump administration had set itself up for blame, given its blocking of the Appellate Body nomination process. The developing countries were dug in. The Doha Declaration, the Doha Development Agenda, was no longer what the EU or the USA could accept as the sole basis for negotiation. It promised development, impliedly not through further global trade liberalization, but through special and differential treatment and preferences.

China had emerged as the world's largest goods-exporting country but was not driving the multilateral process. The mood had soured in the United States with respect to globalization in general, and trade with China in particular. A populist government had been elected, committed to correcting imbalances. It was offended by the conduct of China at the WTO, as China had declared repeatedly that it was a developing country, by implication requiring better treatment than it would offer. Reciprocity, the touchstone along with nondiscrimination, it appeared, would thereby be discarded if there was to be no differentiation among self-declared developing countries.

The response from Brussels was to emphasize to its member states the conclusion of its trade agreement with Mercosur,[134] a continuation of its bilateral approach with specific, discriminatory trade benefits for itself and its counterparty. The United States for its part appeared to be choosing a path of unilateralism (which would shortly be an evidence-based conclusion). It was entirely predictable that the two largest trading countries – the United States and China – were poles apart in what language they could agree upon. If there was a middle ground, there was perhaps little appetite for finding it.

China had aligned itself with most developing countries, hotly opposed to any differentiation among developing countries. India's Trade Minister said that the members had to pledge themselves to development "without creating new sub-categories of countries."[135] There was no leadership to be found among the largest trading nations.

But was MC11 a failure? In terms of WTO history, Ministerial Conferences are best judged only after the passage of a considerable amount of time. The beginning of exploration of the issue of trade facilitation at MC1 in Singapore saw fruition only two decades later when the Trade Facilitation Agreement came into effect. By way of contrast, there was a good feeling at the end of

[134] Mercosur, founded in 1991, was to have been a common market of Argentina, Brazil, Paraguay, and Uruguay (Venezuela had been suspended).

[135] "Statement by H. E. Mr. Suresh Prabhakar Prabhu – Union Minister for Commerce and Industry of India." World Trade Organization. December 13, 2017. https://docs.wto.org/dol2fe/Pages/SS/directdoc.aspx?filename=q:/WT/MIN17/ST9.pdf&Open=True

MC4 with the launch of the Doha Development Agenda, only to see it fail in 2008. The fisheries negotiations have extended over two decades, and a partial answer was not delivered until MC12 in mid-2022.

As a participant in MC11 at Buenos Aires, I felt that it had been a great success. Enough time has now elapsed to judge it. Unnoticed, largely at the time, it turns out that this was the official US government view as well, probably dismissed when uttered by the US Trade Representative as *schadenfreude*. "MC11 will be remembered as the moment when the impasse at the WTO was broken. Many Members recognized that the WTO must pursue a fresh start in key areas so that like-minded WTO Members and their constituents are not held back by the few Members that are not ready to act."[136]

The key development at MC11 was the convening of Joint Statement Initiatives (JSIs). A beginning was made to reach open plurilateral agreements (OPAs), that is, like-minded members coming together to discuss and then negotiate outcomes. That they would be successful could not be foretold with certainty in 2017 in Buenos Aires. That was to be verified only when results were agreed upon after years of negotiations.

Four JSIs were launched in Buenos Aires – domestic regulation of services (joined in at the outset by 58 members including the EU of 28); investment facilitation for development (59 members, including the EU of 28);[137] e-commerce (72 including the EU and the USA);[138] and micro, small, and medium-sized enterprises (85 members including the EU and its member states).[139] Separately, 118 members issued a Joint Declaration on Trade and Women's Economic Empowerment.[140]

136 "USTR Robert Lighthizer Statement on the Conclusion of the WTO Ministerial Conference." Office of the United States Trade Representative. December 14, 2017. www.ustr.gov/about-us/policy-offices/press-office/press-releases/2017/december/ustr-robert-lighthizer-statement

137 "Joint Ministerial Statement on Services Domestic Regulation WT/MIN(17)/61." World Trade Organization. December 13, 2017. https://docs.wto.org/dol2fe/Pages/SS/directdoc.aspx?filename=q:/WT/MIN17/61.pdf&Open=True

138 "Joint Statement on Electronic Commerce WT/MIN(17)/60." World Trade Organization. December 13, 2017. https://docs.wto.org/dol2fe/Pages/SS/directdoc.aspx?filename=q:/WT/MIN17/60.pdf&Open=True

139 "Joint Ministerial Statement – Declaration on the Establishment of a WTO Informal Work Programme for MSMEs WT/MIN(17)/58." World Trade Organization. December 13, 2017. https://docs.wto.org/dol2fe/Pages/SS/directdoc.aspx?filename=q:/WT/MIN17/58.pdf&Open=True

140 "Joint Declaration on Trade and Women's Economic Empowerment on the Occasion of the WTO Ministerial Conference in Buenos Aires in December 2017." World Trade Organization. December 12, 2017. www.wto.org/english/thewto_e/minist_e/mc11_e/genderdeclarationmc11_e.pdf; "Buenos Aires Declaration on Women and Trade Outlines

This may have been an inflection point for the WTO. Why not just say it was one? Because that assessment has to await results. Was this a way around an overused hair-trigger veto that allowed any WTO member to block the making of new rules, even if they were only applicable to those who signed up to them? It clearly held some promise. The DDA-or-nothing proponents would continue a rearguard action to block JSI progress. They would fight against documents generated in the JSIs being circulated by the WTO Secretariat. They fought any formal Secretariat involvement as not being approved by all the members. They would later table a paper indicating that the JSIs could never become part of the WTO *acquis* without unanimous consent. In the face of this, in an organization not known for the prominent role of the Secretariat, the Director-General would not back down, saying that many groups were given assistance by the Secretariat in terms of meeting rooms and other physical support, including the African Group, the Group of Small and Vulnerable Economies. It turned out that the single-member veto could not be wielded against a Director-General willing to support the activities of a group of members over the opposition of other members, as long as the DG concluded that the activity was within the scope of appropriate WTO activities, an unreviewable decision.

There was more that was of interest in connection with this Ministerial, matters that did not make the headlines at the time. At Buenos Aires, just before the opening of MC11, a small group of countries, having similar concerns to those that motivated the founders of the multilateral trading system, to foster peace, met and formed the g7+ WTO Accessions Group, a new platform designed to help postconflict and fragile economies through WTO membership.[141] Several were acceding countries, not yet WTO members. The chair of MC11, Minister Susana Malcorra of Argentina, delivered keynote remarks at the launch, which included the participation of the Ministers of Commerce of Afghanistan, Liberia, Somalia, Timor-Leste, and Yemen, as well as the Ambassadors of Comoros, Sierra Leone, and South Sudan. Representatives of

Actions to Empower Women." World Trade Organization. December 12, 2017. www.wto.org/english/news_e/news17_e/mc11_12dec17_e.htm

141 "The g7+ WTO Accessions Group Launched to Help Post-Conflict and Fragile Economies." World Trade Organization. December 10, 2017. www.wto.org/english/news_e/news17_e/minis_10dec17_e.htm; "Launch of the g7+ WTO Accessions Group." World Trade Organization. www.wto.org/english/thewto_e/acc_e/mc11g7group_e.htm; "Launch of the g7+ Accessions Group: Welcoming Development for Post-Conflict and Fragile Economies through WTO Accessions. Public Dialogue Session – Statement by Ambassador Alan Wm. Wolff." World Trade Organization. December 10, 2017. www.wto.org/english/thewto_e/acc_e/g7_plus_wolff.pdf

Afghanistan, Comoros, Liberia, Somalia, South Sudan, Timor-Leste, and Yemen issued a declaration on December 10, 2017, which read in part:

> *We call on WTO Members and development partners to continue and strengthen technical assistance and support for the trade capacity building efforts of fragile and conflict affected states, during WTO accession and post-accession. We commit to coordinate our efforts to support WTO accessions and maximize the benefits of WTO membership for the g7+ Members, including through experience sharing and peer learning, and – we look forward to engaging with the WTO membership and development partners to advance these goals.*[142]

I participated in the meeting of the g7+ that was to grow to be the Trade for Peace (T4P) Program.[143]

There was another event not much noticed at the time that would have later consequences.[144] On December 11, I accepted on behalf of the WTO a joint declaration of Chile; Costa Rica; Iceland; Liechtenstein; Mexico; the Republic of Moldova; New Zealand; Norway; Samoa; Switzerland; the Separate Customs Territory of Taiwan, Penghu, Kinmen and Matsu; and Uruguay, urging disciplines for fossil fuel subsidies:

- *We seek the rationalisation and phase out of inefficient fossil fuel subsidies that encourage wasteful consumption, and encourage the international community to join us in those efforts;*
- *We recognise that reform needs to take fully into account the specific needs and conditions of developing countries and minimize the possible adverse impacts on their development in a manner that protects the poor and the affected communities;*
- *We seek to advance discussion in the World Trade Organization aimed at achieving ambitious and effective disciplines on inefficient fossil fuel subsidies that encourage wasteful consumption, including through enhanced World Trade Organization transparency and reporting that will enable the evaluation of the trade and resource effects of fossil fuel subsidies programmes.*[145]

[142] "Ministerial Declaration Adopted at the First Meeting of Trade Ministers of the g7+ WTO Accessions Group." World Trade Organization. December 12, 2017. https://docs.wto.org/dol2fe/Pages/SS/directdoc.aspx?filename=q:/WT/MIN17/51.pdf&Open=True

[143] "Trade for Peace Programme." World Trade Organization. www.wto.org/english/thewto_e/acc_e/tradeforpeace_e.htm

[144] "Trade and Environmental Sustainability Structured Discussions News Archives." World Trade Organization. www.wto.org/english/news_e/archive_e/tessd_arc_e.htm

[145] "Fossil Fuel Subsidies Reform Ministerial Statement." World Trade Organization. December 12, 2017. https://docs.wto.org/dol2fe/Pages/SS/directdoc.aspx?filename=q:/WT/MIN17/54.pdf&Open=True

MC11 was fruitful, while not resolving the great fractures that plagued multilateral cooperation, whether geopolitical rivalries, the North–South division over which countries would receive preferential treatment in future WTO agreements, the lack of progress on restoring binding dispute settlement, and the continued emphasis on the part of too many to reach bilateral preferential trading agreements that were not clearly a contribution to the multilateral trading system. It laid a foundation for future WTO progress on a variety of key fronts.

THE LEGACY OF MC11: OPEN PLURILATERAL AGREEMENTS

Following MC11, members accounting for most of world trade began to meet to consider four new negotiating initiatives – on e-commerce, domestic regulation of services, investment facilitation, and MSMEs. The initiatives were open to any WTO member that wished to join. Some members strongly opposed them as an illegitimate digression from the Doha Development Agenda. The format is very likely an important part of the future of the WTO.

Plurilateral agreements in various forms have existed in the multilateral trading system since the days of the GATT. One of the most noteworthy was the Government Procurement Code, a result of the 1979 Tokyo Round, which became the Government Procurement Agreement (GPA) in 1994, signed in Marrakesh when the WTO package was concluded.[146] It is open to all who agree to meeting the requirements of the agreement. Its benefits – access to other signatories' government procurement markets – only accrue to those who sign the agreement. As of late 2021, the agreement had twenty-one parties comprising forty-eight WTO members. In addition, thirty-five countries participate in the Committee on Government Procurement as observers. Eleven of these are WTO members that are in the process of acceding to the agreement.[147]

There are other WTO plurilateral agreements that not all join, but which do not require reciprocity from non-signatories, providing their benefits on a nondiscriminatory basis. The three – the Information Technology Agreement (ITA), the Pharmaceutical Agreement, and the Agreement on Trade in Civil Aircraft – provide duty-free treatment. This was deemed acceptable to the participants because the signatories accounted for a very high percentage of

[146] "Government Procurement Code (1979)." Jus Mundi. www.jusmundi.com/en/document/treaty/en-tokyo-round-code-on-government-procurement-thursday-12th-april-1979

[147] "Agreement on Government Procurement." World Trade Organization. www.wto.org/english/tratop_e/gproc_e/gp_gpa_e.htm. Accession to the GPA can be a very long process, pursued in fits and starts. China applied to join in 2007 and is still in negotiations, with a revised offer submitted in 2019.

world trade in the products covered, and as a result, the amount of "free-riding" by non-signatories was limited.

The ITA was concluded by twenty-nine participants at the Singapore Ministerial Conference in December 1996. By 2021, the number of participants reached eighty-two, representing about 97 percent of world trade in IT products. At the Nairobi Ministerial Conference in December 2015, over fifty members concluded an agreement for the expansion of the agreement, which covered an additional 201 products valued at over $1.3 trillion per year, according to the WTO.[148] The product coverage of the ITA was due to be reviewed in 2018 but still had not been revisited as of MC12.

The 1994 Agreement on Trade in Pharmaceutical Products (also known as the Pharma Agreement) eliminates tariffs and other duties and charges on a large number of pharmaceutical products and the substances used to produce them, permanently binding the tariffs on these products at duty-free levels. Concluded during the Uruguay Round of trade negotiations, the agreement was signed by and commits only a small group of participants. Its benefits are nevertheless applied on a nondiscriminatory basis. As of 2021, Canada, the European Union, Japan, Macao (China), Norway, Switzerland, the United Kingdom, and the United States participated in the agreement. When it was entered into, the agreement covered about 90 percent of world trade. However, China and India have become major producers of pharmaceuticals and their ingredients since the original agreement was negotiated, and they are not members. Therefore, the coverage of the agreement has dropped to approximately 66 percent of world trade in listed products.[149]

A third and last example of duty-free sectoral agreements in the WTO is the Agreement on Trade in Civil Aircraft. It was negotiated in the Tokyo Round and entered into force on January 1, 1980. The agreement has thirty-three signatories, nineteen of which are EU member states, making it another of the plurilateral agreements signed by a relatively small number of WTO members. The agreement applies to all aircraft, other than military aircraft, as well as civil aircraft engines and their parts and components, all components and subassemblies of civil aircraft, and flight simulators and their parts and components.[150]

148 "Information Technology Agreement." World Trade Organization. www.wto.org/english/tratop_e/inftec_e/inftec_e.htm

149 "The WTO's Pharma Agreement." World Trade Organization. www.wto.org/english/tratop_e/pharma_ag_e/pharma_agreement_e.htm

150 "Map of Signatories to the Agreement on Trade in Civil Aircraft." World Trade Organization. www.wto.org/english/tratop_e/civair_e/civair_map_e.htm

These agreements were each approved by all members as belonging to the WTO *acquis*. They are therefore included as agreements in the WTO canon. None of these are clear forerunners of the more recent Joint Statement Initiatives (JSIs). These earlier open plurilateral agreements (OPAs) were designed primarily to provide trade liberalization. The MC11 crop of plurilaterals, and those that are following, are about rules, even if the reforms they mandate will cause markets to be more open as a result of procedural reforms.

The JSI plurilateral negotiations have in common that they are open and transparent. They are also all criticized as being illegitimate as WTO activities by a number of Doha-Agenda-first (or perhaps Doha-only) members. Since the WTO operates on the basis of consensus of the whole membership, the legitimacy of these plurilateral negotiations has not yet been acknowledged as of this writing (2022). They were "born on the wrong side of the blanket," as malicious gossips of earlier generations would have put it. The groups of like-minded were undeterred by these objections at MC11 and forged ahead.

DOMESTIC REGULATION OF SERVICES

In Buenos Aires at MC11, fifty-nine members launched negotiations with respect to domestic regulation of services aimed at regularizing the process by which parties to the agreement would go about dealing with qualification requirements and procedures, technical standards, and licensing requirements to avoid creating unnecessary barriers to trade in services. The participants had a clear WTO mandate upon which to proceed: the General Agreement on Trade in Services (GATS) Article VI.4 required the negotiation to take place, and a General Council decision of April 28, 1999 had set up a working party to recommend disciplines by services sector.[151]

The Working Party's record over the years was inconsistent with respect to these kinds of services. Disciplines for the Accounting Sector were proposed in the 1990s; members tabled some further proposals in 2011. The effort faltered again until 2016 and failed to reach an outcome at Buenos Aires at MC11 in 2017. At this point, those members that wanted to move forward created the JSI on Services Domestic Regulation, with a view to concluding the negotiations at MC12 (which it was first anticipated would be held in 2019 and then in December 2021 but was delayed by the pandemic to June 2022). This JSI had the benefit of having a foundation of existing rules under the GATS upon which to proceed. The rules already promised nondiscrimination (MFN).

[151] "Decision on Domestic Regulation S/L/70." World Trade Organization. April 28, 1999. https://docs.wto.org/dol2fe/Pages/SS/directdoc.aspx?filename=q:/S/L/70.pdf

Participating WTO members also had existing schedules of concessions under which they had granted some market access. Where market access was granted, this of necessity – for those services and within the limits specified in a member's schedule – would also confer national treatment.

Proponents of the services JSI recognized that the existing rules and commitments still did not guarantee unencumbered market access. Red tape could effectively deny in practice what was being granted in form with respect to the liberalization of services. The remaining procedural hurdles were significant. The JSI participants found that "excessively lengthy, complex and opaque licensing procedures may discourage foreign services providers from doing business in the market of another WTO Member. By the same token, lack of objective and transparent criteria, on the basis of which authorities would grant a qualification, may disguise protectionist intentions."

The domestic regulation of services negotiations finally did deliver results in early December 2021 just before the delayed twelfth Ministerial Conference was once again scheduled to be held. Participants in the negotiations stated that their agreement would result in a dramatic reduction in administrative costs, creating a more transparent operating environment for service providers seeking to do business in foreign markets.[152]

The agreement, in the form of a reference paper,[153] represented a number of firsts for the WTO. It was the first JSI to be concluded. It was the first trade agreement to be produced by the WTO since the Nairobi Ministerial in 2015. It was the first open plurilateral agreement that could be implemented without the possibility of a veto by nonparticipants. (The way around the consensus requirement was for participants to include their commitments in their individual GATS schedules.) It also was the first WTO agreement to explicitly provide that the benefits would be equally available to both men and women. Participants agreed to submit their draft schedules "incorporating the disciplines" for certification by the end of 2022, subject to the completion of any required domestic procedures.[154]

While completion of the agreement, this reference paper, is laudable, it should be noted that the bulk of the obligations are written with limiting terms, such as "to the extent practicable." It is also implicitly recognized that domestic regulation of services may not be within the control of the

[152] "Declaration on the Conclusion of Negotiations on Services Domestic Regulation WT/L/1129." World Trade Organization. December 2, 2021. https://docs.wto.org/dol2fe/Pages/SS/directdoc.aspx?filename=q:/WT/L/1129.pdf&Open=True

[153] Ibid.

[154] "Joint Initiative on Services Domestic Regulation." World Trade Organization. www.wto.org/english/tratop_e/serv_e/jsdomreg_e.htm

signatories' national governments. A regulator may be independent by law or accountable solely to a political subdivision and not to the national government. However, some of the obligations are unqualified, and even those that are conditioned on being mandatory only "to the extent practicable" can be of significant value. Services domestic regulation is infinitely more diverse than the application of tariffs and other border measures, the primary objects of multilateral disciplines when the trading system was constructed. This agreement is reaching deep into members' domestic economies, albeit often with a relatively light touch. Members acting in good faith to implement the agreement fully will potentially begin to change a world that is now carved into regulatory fiefdoms, making them part of a more open global marketplace.

E-COMMERCE

The Joint Statement on Electronic Commerce was issued on December 13, 2017, by seventy-one WTO members, including the United States, China, the European Union, and a wide range of developed and developing countries.[155] It was not, however, the largest members that were providing the lead in creating this negotiation, but the mid-sized countries. The effort was spearheaded by Australia, Japan, and Singapore. This was another indication of change at the WTO. By its terms, the declaration indicated that the initiative was open to all, was cognizant of the particular challenges of developing countries, would be nondiscriminatory, and was without prejudice to existing mandates (i.e., Doha). The joint initiative was declared to be a parallel endeavor to the consideration of the same subject within the WTO's committee structure. The WTO's regular work, however, was always a discussion, not a negotiation, and did not promise to result in an agreement.

The WTO's preexisting Work Program on Electronic Commerce was inaugurated on September 25, 1998, and its continuation was endorsed by a consensus decision at MC11.[156] The work program was to be comprehensive and "examine all trade-related issues relating to global electronic commerce."[157] The term "electronic commerce" was "understood to mean the production, distribution, marketing, sale or delivery of goods and services by

[155] "Joint Statement on Electronic Commerce WT/MIN(17)/60." World Trade Organization. December 13, 2017. www.docs.wto.org/dol2fe/Pages/SS/directdoc.aspx?filename=q:/WT/MIN17/60.pdf&Open=True

[156] "Work Programme on E-Commerce." World Trade Organization. www.wto.org/english/tratop_e/ecom_e/ecom_work_programme_e.htm

[157] "The Geneva Ministerial Declaration on Global Electronic Commerce." World Trade Organization. May 25, 1998. www.wto.org/english/tratop_e/ecom_e/mindec1_e.htm

electronic means."[158] The standing bodies of the WTO were directed to consider how to deal with electronic commerce with respect to transparency, nondiscrimination, national treatment, standards, privacy, public morals, market access, use of telecom networks, customs duties, intellectual property rights, and development (including the financial impact on developing countries and small and medium-sized enterprises). The Work Program did not resolve basic issues over its two-decade existence. Much of the focus during successive Ministerial Conferences concerned extensions of a moratorium on the imposition of customs duties on "electronic transmissions."[159] Major questions as to whether the GATT or GATS applied, with implications for whether national treatment as well as nondiscrimination were required, went unanswered. Other contentious issues, such as freedom of cross-border data flows, forced server location, and privacy also found no resolution.

The mandate of the regular work program was as comprehensive as any that could possibly be drafted at the time. It injected consideration of e-commerce into all the relevant bodies of the WTO and called out every conceivable aspect of e-commerce related to committee and council work, from market access to intellectual property protection. E-commerce was required to be a standing item on the agenda of each General Council meeting. What this 1998 declaration indicates more than anything else is that a comprehensive work program among 164 members spread across numerous standing bodies may simply stall due to its diffuse treatment.

Distributing pieces of the e-commerce discussions around the WTO standing bodies, each given the task of exploring e-commerce issues but not negotiating resolution to them, resulting in no progress, no doubt contributed to the sense of stasis in the WTO. A number of countries strenuously opposed international rule-making before they had put into place a domestic legal regime for the digital economy for the same subjects that were under international discussion. For them, the objective was preserving "policy space," meaning preventing any international action that might narrow future regulatory choices. For others, this was not enough. Japan's Prime Minister Shinzo Abe in particular made global rules for e-commerce a high priority.

It was in this context that the JSI on electronic commerce was initiated in December 2017. After a year of discussions, on January 25, 2019, a group of

[158] "Electronic Commerce." World Trade Organization. www.wto.org/english/thewto_e/minist_e/mc11_e/briefing_notes_e/bfecom_e.htm

[159] "Addendum-3: E-Commerce." Ministry of Economy, Trade and Industry of Japan (METI). 2017. www.meti.go.jp/english/report/data/2017WTO/pdf/02_23.pdf. This is a briefing paper prepared in 2017 by METI, summarizing the history of the efforts up until that time to craft international rules for e-commerce.

seventy-six ministers, including Japan, the United States, China, and the EU, agreed to move the e-commerce JSI to a negotiating phase.[160] On December 14, 2021, coincident with the planned MC12, the three co-convenors of the e-commerce JSI – Japan, Singapore, and Australia – on behalf of what had now become an eighty-six-member group, announced that the group would intensify its efforts to forge convergence on major issues by the end of 2022. They recorded that there was already convergence resulting in clean draft articles on spam, electronic signatures and authentication, e-contracts, online consumer protection, and open government data. They announced that the JSI was close to having an agreed text on transparency.

While the e-commerce talks had not yet resolved the most sensitive issues, such as freedom of cross-border data flow, they had made very substantial progress over the four years since the initiative was established to create broad agreement on negotiated texts. Open questions would remain as to how to bring negotiated results into the WTO as a formal matter and whether the benefits would be extended to non-signatories, able to pay but choosing to free ride.

How does this JSI in its current form compare with the e-commerce chapter of the Comprehensive and Progressive Trans-Pacific Partnership Agreement (CPTPP),[161] committing eleven WTO members, and to which the United Kingdom, China, Chinese Taipei, South Korea, and others, are applying? CPTPP has the following additional elements that are either not included in the JSI or not yet agreed:

- A binding permanent commitment not to apply customs duties to cross-border electronic transmissions among parties.
- A binding commitment to allow the cross-border transfer of information by electronic means, including personal information, when this activity is for the conduct of the business of a covered person. This does not prevent a party from adopting or maintaining measures to achieve a legitimate public policy objective, provided that the measure is not applied in a manner which would constitute a means of arbitrary or unjustifiable discrimination or a disguised restriction on trade.

[160] "Joint Statement on Electronic Commerce WT/L/1056." World Trade Organization. January 25, 2019. https://trade.ec.europa.eu/doclib/docs/2019/january/tradoc_157643.pdf

[161] "WTO Electronic Commerce Negotiations: Updated Consolidated Negotiating Text – September 2021. INF/ECOM/62/Rev.2." World Trade Organization. September 8, 2021. www.bilaterals.org/IMG/pdf/wto_plurilateral_ecommerce_draft_consolidated_text_september_2021.pdf

- A binding commitment not to require the use or location of servers (computing facilities) in a party's territory as a condition for conducting business in that territory.
- A binding commitment not to require the transfer of, or access to, source code of software owned by a person of another party, as a condition for the import, distribution, sale, or use of such software, or of products containing such software, in its territory.[162]
- The parties will endeavor to promote the adoption of ethical and governance frameworks that support the trusted, safe, and responsible use of AI technologies.

The CPTPP parties also agree to collaborate on cybersecurity matters to identify and mitigate malicious intrusions or dissemination of malicious code that affect the electronic networks of the parties.

Other agreements for purposes of comparison with the JSI are the Digital Economy Partnership Agreement (DEPA), the USMCA (the free trade agreement among the United States, Mexico, and Canada), and the US–Japan Digital Trade Agreement. These agreements point ways forward for agreement in the WTO's JSI for e-commerce.[163]

INVESTMENT FACILITATION FOR DEVELOPMENT

At Buenos Aires, on December 13, 2017, seventy WTO members announced the formation of a structured discussion (aka a JSI) on trade and the facilitation of investment for development. The original participants accounted for around 73 percent of trade and 66 percent of inward foreign direct investment (FDI). The initiative featured prominently as participants China, the EU, the mid-sized more active WTO members, and others ranging from Benin to Brazil. The United States did not choose to join. The objective of the initiative was to "identify and develop the elements of a framework for facilitating foreign direct investments in developing countries that would: improve the transparency and predictability of investment measures; streamline and speed

[162] "Chapter 14 Electronic Commerce." New Zealand Foreign Affairs and Trade. www.mfat.govt.nz/assets/Trade-agreements/TPP/Text-ENGLISH/14.-Electronic-Commerce-Chapter.pdf

[163] For two interesting discussions of the way forward in addressing e-commerce in the WTO, see: Arindrajit Basu. "Can the WTO Build Consensus on Digital Trade?" Hinrich Foundation. October 5, 2021. www.hinrichfoundation.com/research/article/wto/can-the-wto-build-consensus-on-digital-trade/; James Bacchus. "The Digital Decide How to Agree on WTO Rules for Digital Trade." Centre for International Governance Innovation. August 16, 2021. www.cigionline.org/static/documents/TheDigitalDecide-Bacchus.pdf

up administrative procedures and requirements; and enhance international cooperation, information sharing, the exchange of best practices, and relations with relevant stakeholders, including dispute prevention."

As the participants intend that the agreement be formally a part of the WTO, as in the current draft, commitments under the agreement (where they go beyond best efforts) are to be enforceable under the WTO's dispute settlement provisions. The agreement preserves policy space for signatories, as it is "without prejudice to Members' rights to regulate in the public interest." It is not about liberalization for investment in that it does not provide for any additional commitments to allow inward flows of investment into any signatory's economy. It regulates process, not access. It also does not provide investor–state dispute settlement.

Interestingly, it applies not only to central governments, but to regional and local governments and authorities as well as nongovernmental bodies in the exercise of powers delegated by any level of government. It requires non-discrimination (most favored nation treatment) with the exception of provisions included in free trade agreements, which may allow discrimination based on the nationality of the investor. It mandates transparency through the publication of laws, regulations and procedures, judicial decisions and administrative rulings of general application. It requires information to be available via electronic means such as on a website and, where possible, through a single portal. The investment agreement goes into substantial detail on what information should be available, with advance publication and an opportunity to comment. Changes in measures would need to be notified to a WTO committee set up under the agreement.

The administration of investment clearance processes is required to be reasonable, objective, and impartial, based on objective and transparent criteria, with a reasonable timeframe for decision. Reasons for rejection are to be given. Fees are to be reasonable. Members pledge to grant impartial and independent review of decisions. They are to facilitate the movement of natural persons for investment purposes. There are to be three categories of commitments, mirroring the structure of the Trade Facilitation Agreement – those to be implemented upon the entry into force of the Investment Facilitation Agreement, those listed for implementation at a later date, and those dependent upon assistance and support for capacity-building. There are also provisions for special and differential treatment and the prevention of corruption.[164]

[164] "WTO Structured Discussions on Investment Facilitation for Development INF/IFD/RF/50/Rev.8." World Trade Organization. February 4, 2021. www.bilaterals.org/IMG/pdf/wto_plurilateral_investment_facilitation_draft_consolidated_text.pdf

A noteworthy aspect of this JSI is that it would extend the scope of the WTO to setting rules for investment, which the WTO currently provides solely for cross-border trade in services, to now apply to investments relating to the production of goods.

This JSI is an example of moving from a regional initiative to a multilateral one, as the launch at the WTO followed a meeting in Abuja, Nigeria, one month earlier, where development partners met with regional leaders of ECOWAS (Economic Commission of West African States) to address the need for building infrastructure – roads, rail, and air – "to aid the free movement of goods, persons and capital in the area with a market of more than 340 million inhabitants."[165] The meeting in November 2017 emphasized the linkages between economic integration, peace, stability, and the reduction of nontariff trade barriers.

The members of the investment facilitation JSI agreed on September 25, 2020, to move from discussions to negotiation. On November 30, 2021, the chair of the JSI announced an agreed date of the end of 2022 to conclude an agreement. At that point, the number of formal participants in the negotiations had grown to 110 WTO members.

The WTO Investment JSI is dramatically different from the Comprehensive Investment Agreement (CAI) negotiated between China and the European Union. That agreement is primarily about market access. Commitments under that agreement include the elimination of quantitative restrictions, equity caps, or joint venture requirements in a number of sectors. Featured sectors for liberalization include: automotive, financial services, private hospitals, R&D in biological resources, telecommunications, cloud computing services, cargo handling, container depots and stations, maritime agencies, airline computer reservation systems, ground handling, selling and marketing services, real estate services, rental and leasing services, repair and maintenance for transport, advertising, market research, management consulting and translation services, environmental and construction services, among others.[166] In manufacturing, the EU claims "China has not made such far-reaching market access

[165] "ECOWAS Seeks the Cooperation of Development Partners in Addressing Infrastructural Deficits." Economic Community of West African States (ECOWAS). November 8, 2017. www.blueprint.ng/ecowas-seeks-devt-partners-support-on-infrastructure-gaps/. The fifteen member countries making up the ECOWAS are Benin, Burkina Faso, Cape Verde, Cote d' Ivoire, The Gambia, Ghana, Guinea, Guinea Bissau, Liberia, Mali, Niger, Nigeria, Sierra Leone, Senegal, and Togo.

[166] "Key Elements of the EU–China Comprehensive Agreement on Investment." European Commission. December 30, 2020. www.ec.europa.eu/commission/presscorner/detail/en/IP_20_2542

commitments with any other partner."[167] This may well be true, but as is often the case, agreements often cement existing market access rather than provide additional access, and this agreement has still not been ratified.

China also commits to provide, upon request, specific information to allow for the assessment of whether the behavior of a specific state-owned enterprise complies with the agreed CAI obligations, and dispute resolution is provided for in the agreement. Services subsidies are to be transparent. Forced technology transfer is banned. Equal access to standard-setting bodies for EU companies would be provided. Labor standards are required. Investment screening for security reasons is still permitted.[168] There is a broad range of commitments with respect to process, and in many respects are similar to those contained in the JSI on investment.

What is crystal clear from a comparison with the CAI, if it needed to be spelled out further, is that the investment facilitation JSI is aimed at process, not market access.

MICRO, SMALL, AND MEDIUM-SIZED ENTERPRISES (MSMES)

At MC11, eighty-seven WTO members, accounting for around 78 percent of world exports, created an Informal Working Group on MSMEs (Micro, Small, and Medium-Sized Enterprises). The rationale for this JSI was that MSMEs form an important part of global trade, particularly in developing and least developed countries, and the smaller the enterprise, the harder the costs of trade are to bear. The participants committed themselves to putting into place a work program for the benefit of MSMEs: to improve their access to information on trade requirements, regulations, and markets; to consider ways to promote a more predictable regulatory environment for them; to identify measures that contribute to reducing their trade costs in areas such as trade facilitation, shipping, and logistics, and procedures and requirements related to origin; to promote, including through cooperation with other multilateral institutions, their access to trade finance; to further identify issues of particular interest to MSMEs that could be addressed in WTO Trade Policy reports; and to consider how technical assistance and capacity-building initiatives could take into account their trade needs and challenges.[169]

[167] Ibid.

[168] "Wins and Losses in the EU–China Investment Agreement (CAI)." Institut Montaigne. January 2021. www.institutmontaigne.org/en/publications/wins-and-losses-eu-china-investment-agreement-cai

[169] "Draft Ministerial Decision on Establishing a Work Programme for Micro, Small and Medium Enterprises (MSMEs) in the WTO. WT/MIN(17)/24/Rev.1." World Trade

In December 2020, the Informal Working Group on MSMEs, with ninety-one WTO members participating, issued a declaration with six recommendations: (1) inclusion of MSME information in trade policy reviews, with the Secretariat maintaining a database of the information provided; (2) making useful information for participating in trade available through utilization of the Global Trade Helpdesk,[170] a joint project of the WTO, ITC, and UNCTAD; (3) supporting trade facilitation for the benefit of MSMEs; (4) assessing the impact of possible new regulatory measures on MSMEs and, as appropriate, consideration of potential steps to identify and mitigate potential economic impacts on MSMEs; (5) improving the data in the integrated database; and (6) "encourag[ing] all WTO Members, in cooperation with other multilateral institutions, to consider the trade-related aspects of MSMEs' access to finance and cross-border payments, taking into account the context of the economic recovery during and post-COVID-19, particularly, in the most affected developing countries and LDCs."[171]

The Informal Working Group prepared a declaration for adoption at MC12 and is engaged in a continuing process to produce outcomes without obtaining a consensus of the entire WTO membership. The work product is similar to a "reference paper." In this case, there are no enforceable obligations. China and the EU are participants; the United States is not.

TRADE AND WOMEN

On December 12, 2017, at MC11, 127 WTO members and observers put forward a "Joint Declaration on Trade and Women's Economic Empowerment on the Occasion of the WTO Ministerial Conference in Buenos Aires in December 2017."[172] Among the key points they listed were:

Organization. December 10, 2017. https://docs.wto.org/dol2fe/Pages/SS/directdoc.aspx?filename=q:/WT/MIN17/24R1.pdf&Open=True

[170] "Trade4MSMEs: The Gateway to MSME Trade Information." www.trade4msmes.org/

[171] "Informal Working Group on MSMEs: Declaration on Micro, Small and Medium-Sized Enterprises (MSMEs). INF/MSME/4." World Trade Organization. December 14, 2020. https://docs.wto.org/dol2fe/Pages/SS/directdoc.aspx?filename=q:/INF/MSME/4.pdf&Open=True

[172] "Joint Declaration on Trade and Women's Economic Empowerment." International Gender Champions. December 2017. http://s3.eu-west-2.amazonaws.com/igc-production/iPyzh5a2Xb7g3R_sCkJ2LBtgOKpyieYa.pdf. The list of member states and observers that joined the Declaration can be found at "Impact: Trade – Trade Impact Working Group." International Gender Champions. www.genderchampions.com/impact/trade. The list does not include the United States. The United States Trade Representative in the Biden administration announced that the United States will join an updated declaration at MC12.

- *the key role that gender-responsive policies can play in achieving sustainable socioeconomic development;*
- *that inclusive trade policies can contribute to advancing gender equality and women's economic empowerment, which has a positive impact on economic growth and helps to reduce poverty;*
- *that international trade and investment are engines of economic growth for both developing and developed countries.*

They agreed:

- *to collaborate on making our trade and development policies more gender responsive, including by:*

1. *Sharing our respective experiences relating to policies and programs to encourage women's participation in national and international economies through World Trade Organization (WTO) information exchanges, ...*
2. *Sharing best practices for conducting gender-based analysis of trade policies and for the monitoring of their effects;*
3. *Sharing methods and procedures for the collection of gender-disaggregated data, the use of indicators, monitoring and evaluation methodologies, and the analysis of gender-focused statistics related to trade;*
4. *Working together in the WTO to remove barriers for women's economic empowerment and increase their participation in trade; and*
5. *Ensuring that Aid for Trade supports tools and know-how for analysing, designing and implementing more gender-responsive trade policies.*[173]

The Declaration went on to list specific activities planned to foster these objectives. In September 2020, the participants established an Informal Working Group on Trade and Gender. It is chaired by Botswana, Iceland, and El Salvador.

The documents generated by this JSI call for international cooperation, but there are no specific commitments that require domestic implementation within the jurisdictions of the individual member signatories. This stands in mild contrast to the Canada–Chile Free Trade Agreement, which, for example, provides that:

6. *The Parties affirm their commitment to adopt, maintain and implement effectively their gender equality laws, regulations, policies and best practices.*

[173] "Joint Declaration on Trade and Women's Economic Empowerment." International Gender Champions. December 2017. http://s3.eu-west-2.amazonaws.com/igc-production/iPyzh5a2Xb7g3R_sGkJ2LBtgOKpyieYa.pdf

7. *Each Party shall domestically promote public knowledge of its gender equality laws, regulations, policies and practices.*[174]

These are commitments mutually exchanged, even if not by the terms of the agreement subject to dispute settlement and therefore unenforceable.

In preparation for MC12, a group of nineteen members together with international institutions prepared a draft declaration on trade and gender.[175] It calls for the improvement of gender-disaggregated data to provide the basis for informed gender-responsive policies, utilizing research to support women's economic empowerment and increase their participation and leadership in international trade, analyzing from a gender perspective women's economic empowerment issues in the work of the WTO, and promoting and highlighting the collaboration on trade and gender between international and regional organizations, and respective development and other relevant authorities with the aim of mainstreaming a gender equality perspective into Aid for Trade.

Comment. The GATT and the WTO were founded to arrive at contractual commitments as to how trade was to be conducted. This was largely creating a legal regime, supported by transparency, to facilitate the flow of international trade on a fair basis, with fairness defined, for example, as consisting of providing national treatment and nondiscrimination. The negotiations were to deliver greater welfare for the peoples of the system's members, but this was to occur through the expansion of rules-based trade. There were no provisions with respect to social responsibility. Forbidding trade in prison-made goods may have been agreed to, not as a prison welfare measure, which it may well not be, but primarily due to a concern over the utilization of this labor as an unfair trade practice from the perspective of those competing with such goods. There was nothing in the GATT or WTO Agreements seeking to remedy inequitable treatment of groups of individuals within countries, other than with respect to national treatment and nondiscrimination vis-à-vis foreign goods and foreign service providers when it came to scheduled services. That this was the history of the world trading system does not exclude a further evolution with respect to social responsibility. The WTO is and will be what its members wish it to be. Treatment of women has strong support, and work will continue on this file.

[174] "Appendix II – Chapter N bis–Trade and Gender." Government of Canada. 2017. www.international.gc.ca/trade-commerce/trade-agreements-accords-commerciaux/agr-acc/chile-chili/fta-ale/2017_Amend_Modif-App2-Chap-N.aspx?lang=eng

[175] "Joint Ministerial Declaration on the Advancement of Gender Equality and Women's Economic Empowerment within Trade, 12th WTO Ministerial Conference, Draft. WT/MIN (21)/4." World Trade Organization. 2021. https://docs.wto.org/dol2fe/Pages/FE_Search/FE_S_S009-DP.aspx?language=E&CatalogueIdList=278631,278632,278621&CurrentCatalogueIdIndex=1&FullTextHash=371857150&HasEnglishRecord=True&HasFrenchRecord=True&HasSpanishRecord=False

The social consciousness of governments evolves over time. Bismarck introduced social welfare policies a century and a half ago. Women were given the right to vote in federal elections in Switzerland just fifty years ago. There is no clear, shared understanding yet of where the effort to focus on women in trade will lead. The approach has been incremental. There are no legally enforceable commitments under active consideration at present. There is exploration of the topic. The Working Group is kept informal, perhaps so as not to arouse concerns on the part of some developing countries that gender equality provisions would lead to trade restrictions on those not conforming to a new international standard. Another reason for taking the informal route is not to get into the division between two camps – those that find Joint Initiatives are an important way to make progress and those that find plurilateral agreements either threatening or a diversion from the reinstatement of the Doha Development Agenda in full.

THE GREENING OF THE MULTILATERAL TRADING SYSTEM

There is a long history in the multilateral trading system of considering the interrelationship of the global environment and international trade. The discussion dates back to 1971. At that time and for many years thereafter, the GATT was concerned with whether environmental regulations might become misused as barriers to trade. Trade negotiators approached environmental issues defensively. The formal expression of this was in the standards code (the Agreement on Technical Barriers to Trade) negotiated as part of the Tokyo Round agreements. During the ensuing GATT years, if there was any reference to the environment in connection with the trading system, the discussion centered on cases that were litigated about whether an environmental measure was really a disguised restriction on trade.

In the period leading up to the creation of the WTO, international attention began to be focused on "sustainable development." Consciousness-raising about the environment came largely from outside the trade community. Even though the references to trade in the Rio Declaration of 1992 of the UN Conference on Environment and Development (UNCED) were still defensive in nature,[176] the narrative was beginning to change – international cooperation would be needed to protect the earth's environment. The opening words of the Marrakesh Agreement Establishing the World Trade Organization are not

[176] "Report of the United Nations Conference on Environment and Development – Annex I: Rio Declaration on Environment and Development. A/CONF.151/26 (Vol. I)." United Nations General Assembly. August 12, 1992. www.un.org/en/development/desa/population/migration/generalassembly/docs/globalcompact/A_CONF.151_26_Vol.I_Declaration.pdf

about eliminating barriers to trade. That comes a bit later in the Preamble. Pride of place is given to serving the environment: "allowing for the optimal use of the world's resources in accordance with the objective of sustainable development, seeking both to protect and preserve the environment and to enhance the means for doing so in a manner consistent with their respective needs and concerns at different levels of economic development."[177]

A dramatic shift in emphasis for the multilateral trading system was solidified in a Ministerial Decision on Trade and Environment, adopted in Marrakesh on April 15, 1994, which called for the establishment of a Committee on Trade and Environment (CTE).[178] The new committee was "to identify the relationship between trade measures and environmental measures, in order to promote sustainable development ... with the aim of making international trade and environmental policies mutually supportive."[179]

The Doha Development Agenda (DDA) adopted in 2001 contained a substantial negotiating mandate for trade and the environment. It sought, among other things, to examine the relationship between WTO rules and obligations contained in multilateral environmental agreements, eliminate tariffs and nontariff barriers on environmental goods and services, and clarify the rules on labeling requirements. Although the DDA collapsed in 2008, the objective of zero tariffs for environmental goods was revived. In July 2014, forty-six WTO members launched negotiations to eliminate duties on environmental goods through an Environmental Goods Agreement (EGA). It was to function much like the ITA, eliminating tariffs on listed products. The effort failed to conclude two years later in disagreements over product coverage. Some WTO members have indicated an interest in restarting the negotiations.

In December 2017, at MC11, as noted earlier, twelve WTO members issued a declaration on creating disciplines over fossil fuel subsidies. They sought "the rationalisation and phase-out of inefficient fossil fuel subsidies that encourage wasteful consumption, and encourage the international community to join us in those efforts." They called for a "discussion in the World Trade Organization aimed at achieving ambitious and effective disciplines on inefficient fossil fuel subsidies that encourage wasteful consumption, including through enhanced World Trade Organization transparency and reporting

177 "Marrakesh Agreement Establishing the World Trade Organization." World Trade Organization. www.wto.org/english/docs_e/legal_e/04-wto_e.htm

178 "Relevant WTO Provisions: Text of 1994 Decision." World Trade Organization. www.wto.org/english/tratop_e/envir_e/issu5_e.htm

179 Ibid.

that will enable the evaluation of the trade and resource effects of fossil fuel subsidies programmes."[180]

The potential breakthrough among members to a more intensive and systematic work program for the environment came during the week that would have seen the convening of MC12 in Geneva but was postponed due to the COVID-19 pandemic. Three "structured discussions" were announced. They were on trade and sustainable development, plastics pollution, and fossil fuel subsidies. On December 15, 2021, Jean-Marie Paugam, WTO Deputy Director-General and a longtime champion of green issues for the Organization, welcomed the launch of the environmental initiatives, stating "the fact that more than 80 co-sponsors across the three statements represent 86 percent of global trade demonstrates that the WTO can and must play a role on environmental issues."[181] He saw in the formation of these initiatives formal recognition of the shift in the trading system when it came to discussion of environmental issues: "Questions have already changed from 'how to derogate from trade rules to pursue environmental objectives?' to 'how can trade make a positive contribution to the environment?'"

A caveat is that the degree of consensus to move forward represents less than one-half of the WTO membership and varies depending on how sensitive the stated objectives are of each initiative – from seventy members accounting for 82 percent of world trade on sustainability, to sixty-seven members accounting for 68 percent of world trade (around 75 percent of plastics trade) for plastics, and only forty-four members accounting for 38 percent of world trade for fossil fuel subsidies.

TRADE AND SUSTAINABLE DEVELOPMENT

The first of the structured discussions (SDs) on the subject of trade and sustainable development is the broadest in scope and in initial participation. The Ministerial Statement launching this initiative recognizes "environmental sustainability as a central issue for the WTO agenda."[182] This, in and of itself, is a

[180] "Fossil Fuel Subsidies Reform Ministerial Statement WT/MIN(17)/54." World Trade Organization. December 12, 2017. https://docs.wto.org/dol2fe/Pages/SS/directdoc.aspx?filename=q:/WT/MIN17/54.pdf&Open=True

[181] The number eighty is derived from different members signing onto each of the initiatives. As shown above, none of the initiatives at the outset had eighty committed participants. "Launch Event of Ministerial Statements on Trade, Environment and Sustainable Development." World Trade Organization. December 15, 2021. www.wto.org/english/news_e/news21_e/ddgjp_15dec21_e.htm

[182] "Trade and Environmental Sustainability Structured Discussions (TESSD) WT/MIN(21)/6/Rev.2." World Trade Organization. December 14, 2021. https://docs.wto.org/dol2fe/Pages/SS/directdoc.aspx?filename=q:/WT/MIN21/6R2.pdf&Open=True

new identification of how the WTO is to proceed and what its orientation is to be. It has substantial credibility in that the Declaration is co-sponsored by the largest trading members: the EU, the United States, and China; as well as the mid-sized active members, including Australia, Canada, Japan, Korea, New Zealand, Norway, Russia, Singapore, Switzerland, Chinese Taipei, and the United Kingdom; a number of Latin American countries, Chile, Colombia, Costa Rica, Ecuador, Honduras, Panama, and Uruguay; and a few African countries including Chad, The Gambia, and Senegal. Notably absent was Brazil. Always absent from JSIs are India and South Africa.

The participants pledged themselves to:

- Identify concrete actions for environmentally sustainable trade;
- Launch dedicated discussions on how trade-related climate measures and policies can best contribute to climate and environmental goals and commitments;
- Explore opportunities and possible approaches for promoting and facilitating trade in environmental goods and services;
- Identify and compile best practices to contribute to: (i) achieving a more resource-efficient circular economy, (ii) promoting sustainable supply chains and addressing the challenges and opportunities arising from the use of sustainability standards, and (iii) promoting and facilitating access to environmental goods and services, including encouraging the global uptake of new and emerging low-emissions and other climate-friendly technologies;
- Strengthen capacity-building and technical assistance on trade and environmental sustainability;
- Support continued discussions on the environmental effects and trade impacts of relevant subsidies and the role of the WTO; and
- Adopt an agreed roadmap, take steps to advance work, and commit to review progress after one year, to take stock with a view to adapting the work plan.

PLASTICS POLLUTION

This initiative began in November 2020,[183] at the instance of China and Fiji.[184] It was the first initiative of China to gain adherents. The updated

[183] "DDG Wolff Remarks on the Structured Discussions on Trade and Environmental Sustainability." World Trade Organization. November 17, 2020. www.wto.org/english/news_e/news20_e/ddgaw_17nov20_e.htm

[184] "WTO Informal Dialogue on Plastics Pollution and Environmentally Sustainable Plastics Trade WT/CTE/W/250/Rev.1." World Trade Organization. July 26, 2021. https://docs.wto.org/dol2fe/Pages/SS/directdoc.aspx?filename=q:/WT/CTE/W250R1.pdf&Open=True

version of it, launched in December 2021, is labeled as an "Informal Dialogue on Plastics Pollution and Environmentally Sustainable Plastics Trade."[185] The United States is not among the signatories. This is the second of the three green initiatives prepared for the pandemic-delayed MC12. The signatories "Recall . . . the need for further commitment and actions across the life cycle of plastics to address marine litter and microplastics, including through a circular economy approach," and acknowledge

> *the impact that plastics pollution (including microplastics pollution) has on economies and the environment, including on oceans, coastal and terrestrial environments, particularly on Small Island Developing States (SIDS) which are especially vulnerable to environmental impacts, and recognize the challenges that developing Members and least developed Members face in addressing trade-related aspects of plastics pollution.*

The statement notes that "trade in plastics accounts for as much as 5 percent of global trade – or more than 1 trillion US dollars in 2019."[186] The statement further provides that its proponents decide to:

- *Identify ways to improve the understanding of global trade in plastics, including flows of plastics embedded in internationally traded goods or associated with them (such as plastic packaging), and enhance transparency regarding trade policies relevant to reducing plastic pollution and more environmentally sustainable plastics trade.*
- *Share experiences of effective approaches to move toward more circular, resource-efficient and environmentally sustainable plastics trade, and*
- *Address trade-related capacity-building and technical assistance needs of developing Members, in particular least developed Members and vulnerable small island developing states (SIDS), to support their efforts.*

The signatories agreed to work together in other organizations such as standard-making bodies, and to identify best practices to reduce unnecessary or harmful plastics and plastic products. The signatories further state that they "will look for concrete, pragmatic, and effective outcomes on these actions and understandings at the latest by MC13."

[185] "Informal Dialogue on Plastic Pollution and Environmentally Sustainable Plastics Trade (IDP)." World Trade Organization. December 10, 2021. https://docs.wto.org/dol2fe/Pages/FE_Search/FE_S_S009-DP.aspx?language=E&CatalogueIdList=279742,279475,279424,279410,279247,279277,279275,279078,278892,278942&CurrentCatalogueIdIndex=3&FullTextHash=&HasEnglishRecord=True&HasFrenchRecord=True&HasSpanishRecord=True

[186] Ibid.

FOSSIL FUEL SUBSIDIES

This is a New Zealand-led initiative,[187] which has attracted the support of the EU. The United States, China, Australia, and Canada are not among the original signatories. It is a second start for an initiative, heralded by New Zealand at MC11 in December 2017 on behalf of itself and twelve other members.[188] David Walker, New Zealand's Ambassador to the WTO and a champion of the cause of bringing fossil fuel subsidies under WTO discipline, said that in 2019, estimated annual government outlays for these subsidies amounted to $500 billion. New Zealand noted that these payments make it harder for renewable energy alternatives to compete. New Zealand hosted the APEC (Asia-Pacific Economic Cooperation) Trade Ministers Meeting in June 2021. The APEC ministers had in 2015 committed "to rationalise and phase out inefficient fossil fuel subsidies that encourage wasteful consumption, while recognising the importance of providing those in need with essential energy services."[189] The APEC ministers tasked their officials to explore options for a voluntary standstill on the subsidies.[190]

In September 2019, a smaller group of like-minded countries decided to explore the possibilities for faster movement toward agreement outside the WTO. New Zealand with Costa Rica, Fiji, Iceland, Norway, and Switzerland also launched a new initiative, the Agreement on Climate Change, Trade and Sustainability (ACCTS), which is to address fossil fuel subsidies.[191]

[187] "New Zealand Relaunches Campaign to Deliver Joint Ministerial Statement on Fossil Fuel Subsidy Reform (FFSR) at WTO MC12." New Zealand Foreign Affairs and Trade. November 19, 2021. www.mfat.govt.nz/en/media-and-resources/new-zealand-relaunches-campaign-to-deliver-joint-ministerial-statement-on-fossil-fuel-subsidy-reform-ffsr-at-the-twelfth-wto-ministerial-conference/

[188] "Ministerial Statement on Fossil Fuel Subsidies WT/MIN(21)/9/Rev.1." World Trade Organization. December 14, 2021. https://docs.wto.org/dol2fe/Pages/SS/directdoc.aspx?filename=q:/WT/MIN21/9R1.pdf&Open=True; www.norway.no/en/missions/wto-un/our-priorities/trade/wto-world-trade-organization/mc11-ministerial-declaration-on-fossil-fuel-subsidy-reform/; "Report by Session Organizer – Fossil Fuel Subsidies Reform: International Collaboration and the Link Between Sustainability Objectives and Global Trade." World Trade Organization. October 10, 2019. www.wto.org/english/forums_e/public_forum19_e/pf19_84_rpt_e.pdf

[189] "APEC Ministers Responsible for Trade Meeting Joint Statement 2021." Asia-Pacific Economic Cooperation. June 5, 2021. www.apec.org/Meeting-Papers/Sectoral-Ministerial-Meetings/Trade/2021_MRT

[190] Ibid.

[191] "Agreement on Climate Change, Trade and Sustainability (ACCTS) Negotiations." New Zealand Foreign Affairs and Trade. September 25, 2019. www.mfat.govt.nz/en/trade/free-trade-agreements/trade-and-climate/agreement-on-climate-change-trade-and-sustainability-accts-negotiations

The participants in the WTO structured discussion are seeking to support the fulfillment of the commitments individual WTO members made in the context of the Paris Agreement on Climate Change. In that forum, each country was to contribute to the goal of limiting the global temperature increase to 1.5°C above pre-industrial levels to deliver lower climate-related global risks, as outlined by the 2018 Intergovernmental Panel on Climate Change Special Report on Global Warming. WTO members in the structured discussion recognized that it would be a slow and arduous process to obtain agreement with meaningful commitments: "The Statement proposes a gradual approach for achieving ambitious and effective disciplines on inefficient fossil fuel subsidies through capacity-building, and exchange of information and experience. It also acknowledges the importance of considering the needs of vulnerable groups to ensure the transition from government fossil fuel support is equitable and 'just'."[192]

How to move forward? The group agreed that it "will share information and experiences aimed at achieving ambitious and effective disciplines on inefficient fossil fuel subsidies that encourage wasteful consumption, including through enhanced World Trade Organization transparency and reporting that will enable the evaluation of the trade, economic, and environment effects of fossil fuel subsidy programmes." The group also agreed to "elaborate concrete options to advance this issue at the World Trade Organization in advance of MC13."[193]

Comment. What is one to make of this pace? Change has to start somewhere. New Zealand has evidenced leadership over an extended period. In 2010, New Zealand's Trade and Environment Minister, Tim Groser, convened a meeting on this subject at the Cancún Ministerial Conference.[194] In 2017, on behalf of the WTO membership, the first declaration of a group of

[192] "New Zealand Relaunches Campaign to Deliver Joint Ministerial Statement on Fossil Fuel Subsidy Reform (FFSR) at WTO MC12." New Zealand Foreign Affairs and Trade. November 19, 2021. www.mfat.govt.nz/en/media-and-resources/new-zealand-relaunches-campaign-to-deliver-joint-ministerial-statement-on-fossil-fuel-subsidy-reform-ffsr-at-the-twelfth-wto-ministerial-conference/

[193] "Ministerial Statement on Fossil Fuel Subsidies WT/MIN(21)/9/Rev.1." World Trade Organization. December 14, 2021. https://docs.wto.org/dol2fe/Pages/SS/directdoc.aspx?filename=q:/WT/MIN21/9R1.pdf&Open=True; "MC11 Ministerial Declaration on Fossil Fuel Subsidy Reform." Norway in Geneva – Permanent Missions to the UN and WTO/EFTA. December 19, 2017. www.norway.no/en/missions/wto-un/our-priorities/trade/wto-world-trade-organization/mc11-ministerial-declaration-on-fossil-fuel-subsidy-reform/

[194] "New Zealand Coordinates Action on Fossil Fuel Subsidy Reform." Government of New Zealand. December 16, 2010. www.beehive.govt.nz/release/new-zealand-coordinates-action-fossil-fuel-subsidy-reform

WTO members was made at MC11 in Buenos Aires. Interested members in early 2022 stated that they would convene a more "structured" discussion with a report back sometime in the next two or more years. Global warming will continue to overtake the Earth's inhabitants at an increasing rate, and to date trade disciplines are not making a meaningful contribution. Government policies and the market do not need to await an agreement on relevant subsidies disciplines. For example, a perhaps optimistic assessment from the Union Bank of Switzerland (UBS) estimates that electric cars will account for 20 percent of new car sales in 2025, 40 percent in 2030, and almost 100 percent in 2040, reducing this source of demand for fossil fuels.[195]

As for the timescale for concluding far-reaching WTO agreements, discussion of the subject matter of the WTO's one truly multilateral trade agreement, the Trade Facilitation Agreement, was initiated in 1996, with the agreement signed in 2013 and its entry into force occurring in 2017. There is much greater urgency for successful action on fossil fuel subsidies and the other green structured discussions. There is now reason to believe that a new beginning has been made in earnest and that it can see fruition in a meaningful timeframe.

RESISTANCE TO THE WTO'S MOVE TOWARD OPEN PLURILATERAL AGREEMENTS

At the first General Council meeting attended by a new Director-General, Ngozi Okonjo-Iweala, India and South Africa tabled an eight-page memorandum entitled "The Legal Status of 'Joint Statement Initiatives' and Their Negotiated Outcomes."[196] It explained their view that the Joint Statement Initiatives, Structured Discussions – all Open Plurilateral Agreements – convened by WTO members were illegitimate unless endorsed by consensus of all of the WTO's members. They maintained that this legal conclusion would be valid, that no agreement could be added to the WTO family of agreements absent consensus, even if the benefits of any plurilateral agreement were made available to all WTO members on a nondiscriminatory basis.

The memorandum seeks to close off all avenues of adoption of commitments at the WTO, including amending individual members' schedules,

[195] "Tesla: Elon Musk Reveals How Long It Will Take All Cars to Go Electric." Inverse. October 14, 2021. www.inverse.com/innovation/tesla-when-will-all-cars-go-electric

[196] "The Legal Status of 'Joint Statement Initiatives' and Their Negotiated Outcomes WT/GC/W/819." World Trade Organization. February 19, 2021. https://docs.wto.org/dol2fe/Pages/SS/directdoc.aspx?filename=q:/WT/GC/W819.pdf&Open=True

except through consensus. The argument is made that WTO agreement schedules cannot include commitments to new rules. The harm to the multilateral trading system of departing from consensus decision making is seen by the two members as multifaceted: that it would erode the integrity of the rules-based multilateral trading system, allow any group of members to bring any issue into the WTO without the required consensus, bypass collective oversight, usurp limited WTO resources, lead to the marginalization or exclusion of issues which are difficult but remain critical for the multilateral trading system, leave members with no option other than to choose between remaining outside the discussions or participating on matters that are inconsistent with their economic development priorities, needs, concerns, and levels of economic development, and fragment the multilateral trading system and undermine the multilateral character of the WTO.

India and South Africa state that JSI participants have three options:

1. Obtain consensus to bring an agreement into the WTO;
2. Negotiate somewhere else, outside the WTO; or
3. Amend the Marrakesh Agreement to provide for the JSIs or otherwise change the procedures that are currently applicable.

The participants in the JSI on the domestic regulation of services nevertheless decided to amend their schedules to implement their agreement. The JSI on micro, small, and medium-sized enterprises may not require any change in any WTO rules. Questions of implementation for the remaining JSIs and structured discussions are not yet ripe, as those talks have not yet reached the stage of resulting in agreements.

Comment. Experienced observers of the trading system have commented on the India–South Africa position and considered the legal analysis correct.[197] Why do India and South Africa oppose the inclusion of open plurilateral agreements within the WTO? Apparently, they fear losing the control any individual member has over the multilateral negotiating agenda through the exercise of a veto, through blocking consensus. What do they gain if the result is driving open plurilateral agreements (OPAs, or calling them JSIs) out of the WTO, given that any benefit imbedded in a preferential trade agreement might not be of benefit to them, and might not even be very transparent?

[197] "A Historical Perspective on India's and South Africa's Threat to Block the Implementation of the Joint Statement Initiatives in the WTO, and a Potential Way Forward." International Economic Law and Policy Blog. February 26, 2021. https://ielp.worldtradelaw.net/2021/02/a-historical-perspective-on-indias-and-south-africas-threat-to-block-the-implementation-of-the-joint.html

There is a flaw in their reasoning. As a practical matter, were a Director-General to decide that the WTO Secretariat will administer an agreement, it would take a consensus to block the decision. If these OPAs require dispute settlement, they can follow the path demonstrated to exist by the EU in the creation of the Multi-Party Interim Arrangement (MPIA) and attach an agreement-specific or generic MPIA to each OPA. In short, OPAs, JSIs, can be attached *de facto*, if not *de jure*, to the WTO *acquis*. The GATT itself existed only *de facto* as an international organization for a half-century. Pragmatism can reliably trump legalism to overcome obstacles, if a sufficient number and weight of WTO ministers wish to proceed.

The twenty-first century issues are real and pressing. Making rules for the global digital economy before it fragments further, dealing with pandemics and climate change, these are essential. Insufficient haste on the part of proponents and excessive obstruction by those opposed to JSI/OPAs can lead to a breakdown of international cooperation for matters that can only be dealt with successfully by the multilateral trading system.

THE TWELFTH WTO MINISTERIAL CONFERENCE

Not much was expected of MC12.[198] *On the agenda were fisheries subsidies disciplines (in their twenty-second year of negotiations), a small but contentious package of elements of a COVID pandemic response, the unlikely extension of the moratorium on customs duties on electronic transmissions, and a potential work program for agriculture. A complication was the fact that there was a split among members as to how to react to Russia's invasion of Ukraine. MC12 surprised everyone.*

In the most famous horse race in the United States, the Kentucky Derby, in the year 2022, Rich Strike, a young, untried horse, coming from the back of the pack, finished first. It had never run in the premiere races. It paid out on 80 to 1 odds, that is $163.20 on a $2 bet.

I had said before MC12 that it would be a mistake to bet against Ngozi Okonjo-Iweala, but I would not have bet that MC12 could deliver all that it did. As far as I know, exactly no one predicted this outcome. DDG Anabel Gonzalez said that the participants hoped for perhaps two results, but not six or seven. No one had the winning lottery ticket except perhaps Ngozi, and

[198] There are a number of good overviews of MC12. One is an FMG-hosted symposium recorded on July 1, 2022. "FMG Brainstorming Session on MC12 and Beyond." Friends of Multilateralism Group – YouTube. www.youtube.com/watch?v=NWy5Xk5uOCo

perhaps not even she did. Even so, the prize in the lottery consisted more of promissory notes than ready money.

It was the maximum that could be obtained and yet it fell short on substance on all points covered. The members of the WTO, an organization reputed to be an epicenter of impotence, delivered. Was it a success? Yes. It was, given expectations, magnificent. So say the Trade Ministers of China, the United States, India, and the EU among others. All, in the end, contributed. Ngozi Okonjo-Iweala did what she was brought in to do; she drove the process.

What was achieved?

THE OUTCOME DOCUMENT

First, there was an "Outcome Document," the equivalent of a ministerial declaration, something that only half the prior ministerial meetings had achieved, signifying that the ministers could agree to something or some things.[199] This was the equivalent of white smoke emanating from St. Peter's to signify that the cardinals had reached a consensus.

Besides a usual recommitment to the principles of the WTO and to special and differential treatment, the Outcome Document called for WTO reform. This task was to be carried out by the General Council and its subsidiary bodies for decisions to be submitted to the next Ministerial Conference. At this point, the members inserted a potentially important footnote stating: "this does not prevent groupings of WTO Members from meeting to discuss relevant matters or making submissions for consideration by the General Council or its subsidiary bodies." Flexibility was to be exercised in allowing different configurations of members to come up with proposals.

Potentially groundbreaking, the ministers acknowledged "the challenges and concerns with respect to the dispute settlement system including those related to the Appellate Body" and committed "to conduct discussions with the view to having a fully and well-functioning dispute settlement system accessible to all Members by 2024." This was a dramatic step. Members were not reiterating for over the 100th time that the United States should just unblock the process, and the United States was committing to work with the others to find a solution to restore binding dispute settlement.

199 "MC12 Outcome Document WT/MIN(22)/24 WT/L/1135." World Trade Organization. June 22, 2022. https://docs.wto.org/dol2fe/Pages/SS/directdoc.aspx?filename=q:/WT/MIN22/24.pdf&Open=True

The outcome document further recognized various concerns and grievances – from LDCs on the pain of automatic graduation from special treatment, from the acceding countries having deeper obligations in many cases than original members, on the need for women's economic empowerment and for greater participation of MSMEs in trade, and on challenges to the environment, among other topics. These points were catalogued but did not present solutions or work programs for these items.

On Fisheries Subsidies

After more than two decades of negotiation, an agreement was reached. It had been a long and tortuous path to reach a negotiated outcome. This was a new area being added to the WTO rulebook. It was about delivering on a sustainable development goal, where it was highly questionable whether trade was the central issue. The oceans were being despoiled, and the members of the WTO chose it to be the venue to negotiate an agreement. Milestones were reached. The following prohibitions were agreed:

> 3.1 *No Member shall grant or maintain any subsidy to a vessel or operator engaged in illegal, unreported and unregulated (IUU) fishing or fishing related activities in support of IUU fishing.*[200]
>
> 4.1 *No Member shall grant or maintain subsidies for fishing or fishing related activities regarding an overfished stock.*

However, in order to reach agreement, what was dropped from the text during the MC12 negotiations was equally if not more important:

> 5.1 *No Member shall grant or maintain subsidies to fishing or fishing related activities that contribute to overcapacity or overfishing. For the purpose of this paragraph, subsidies that contribute to overcapacity or overfishing include:*
>
> (a) *subsidies to construction, acquisition, modernisation, renovation or upgrading of vessels;*
>
> (b) *subsidies to the purchase of machines and equipment for vessels (including fishing gear and engine, fish-processing machinery, fish-finding technology, refrigerators, or machinery for sorting or cleaning fish);*
>
> (c) *subsidies to the purchase/costs of fuel, ice, or bait;*

200 "For a period of 2 years from the date of entry into force of this Agreement, subsidies granted or maintained by developing country Members, including least-developed country (LDC) Members, up to and within the exclusive economic zone (EEZ) shall be exempt from actions based on Articles 3.1 and 10 [dispute settlement] of this Agreement."

(d) *subsidies to costs of personnel, social charges, or insurance;*
(e) *income support of vessels or operators or the workers they employ;*
(f) *price support of fish caught;*
(g) *subsidies to at-sea support;*
(h) *subsidies covering operating losses of vessels or fishing or fishing related activities; and*
(i) *subsidies contingent upon, or tied to, actual or anticipated fishing or fishing related activities in areas beyond the subsidizing Member's jurisdiction (whether solely or as one of several other conditions). A subsidy is not inconsistent with Article 5.1 if the subsidizing Member demonstrates that measures are implemented to maintain the stock or stocks in the relevant fishery or fisheries at a biologically sustainable level.*

Members also agreed to ban subsidies for fishing and fishing-related activities in international waters, threatened by unsustainable fishing practices.[201]

As there were key points that could not be resolved, not least of which was the loss of the subsidies' disciplines contained in paragraph 5 quoted above, and provisions for special and differential treatment, a new procedural twist was added. The agreement was to terminate four years after entry into force unless the period for the agreement was extended by the General Council (meaning in effect by unanimous support for an extension). In addition, developing countries would not be subject to the disciplines for the first two years after entry into force of the agreement. (Entry into force of a WTO agreement, unless otherwise provided, takes the ratification of three-quarters of the members, and this can be time-consuming.)

For an evaluation of the Fisheries Subsidies Agreement, see the interview with Alice Tipping of the International Institute for Sustainable Development, one of a series of interviews conducted by the Friends of Multilateralism Group (FMG).[202] To compare what was hoped for, and what was achieved, one can look at various sources available on the eve of MC12,[203] including most importantly, the chair's text.[204] Although reaching

[201] "Agreement on Fisheries Subsidies. Ministerial Decision of June 17, 2022. WT/MIN(22)/33 WT/L/1144." World Trade Organization. June 22, 2022. https://docs.wto.org/dol2fe/Pages/SS/directdoc.aspx?filename=q:/WT/MIN22/33.pdf&Open=True

[202] "FMG MC12 Interview with Alice Tipping." Friends of Multilateralism. June 23, 2022. www.fmg-geneva.org/fmg-post-mc12-interview-with-alice-tipping/

[203] "A Draft World Trade Organization Agreement on Fisheries Subsidies: What's on the Table?" International Institute for Sustainable Development – Global Subsidies Initiative. May 2022. www.iisd.org/system/files/2022-05/world-trade-organization-agreement-fisheries-subsidies.pdf

[204] Explanatory material and the link to the text is available at: "Draft Agreement on Fisheries Subsidies Submitted for Ministers' Attention Ahead of MC12." World Trade Organization. November 25, 2021. www.wto.org/english/news_e/news21_e/fish_25nov21_e.htm

the fisheries agreement is vitally important, the agreement is incomplete, and whether it works will depend heavily on both the implementation of agreed disciplines and adding back the disciplines that were dropped to reach agreement.

On Food Security

Due to the Russian war in Ukraine, with shipments from the Black Sea ports blocked, food prices soared and export restrictions again began to be put into place. Since the beginning of the pandemic, Singapore had been working to get the WTO members to agree not to apply export restrictions to purchases by the World Food Programme. At MC12, this was agreed, but again in diluted form:

> 1. *Members shall not impose export prohibitions or restrictions on foodstuffs purchased for noncommercial humanitarian purposes by the World Food Programme.*

This would have been good by itself, but added to it was an exclusion, for taking care of one's own needs before sharing with others:

> 2. *This Decision shall not be construed to prevent the adoption by any Member of measures to ensure its domestic food security in accordance with the relevant provisions of the WTO agreements.*[205]

On the Pandemic

There were two agreements reached, one with respect to intellectual property and the other on cooperative measures.

With respect to TRIPS, the members decided that developing countries could authorize the use of the substance of a patent "without the consent of the right holder to the extent necessary to address the COVID-19 pandemic" with respect to vaccines. Flexibilities were added to make this access less cumbersome. The taking of IP could occur "through any instrument available in the law of the Member such as executive orders, emergency decrees, government use authorizations, and judicial or administrative orders, whether or not a Member has a compulsory license regime in place." There would be no need "to make efforts to obtain an authorization from the right holder" as the TRIPS Agreement would otherwise require. In addition, the product made as a result need not be limited to domestic use, but a portion could be exported.

[205] "Ministerial Decision on World Food Programme Food Purchases Exemption from Export Prohibitions or Restrictions WT/MIN(22)/29 WT/L/1140." World Trade Organization. June 22, 2022. https://docs.wto.org/dol2fe/Pages/SS/directdoc.aspx?filename=q:/WT/MIN22/29.pdf&Open=True

A key part of the solution was that China would not avail itself of the right to obtain compulsory licenses under the provision. The members added that "developing country Members with existing capacity to manufacture COVID-19 vaccines are encouraged to make a binding commitment not to avail themselves of this Decision. Such binding commitments include statements made by eligible Members to the General Council," and China stated in the General Council that it would not avail itself of the new flexibility. This was a contentious point, and the earlier proposal had singled out China specifically, not by name, but by describing its export performance in a carve-out that was subsequently deleted.

While the "TRIPS waiver would extend to ingredients and processes necessary for the manufacture of the COVID-19 vaccine," it would not apply beyond vaccines to other pandemic-related pharmaceuticals and products. As for adequate remuneration to the rights holder, those availing themselves of the waiver, if there were any, could "take account of the humanitarian and not-for-profit purpose of specific vaccine distribution programs aimed at providing equitable access to COVID-19 vaccines in order to support manufacturers in eligible Members to produce and supply these vaccines at affordable prices for eligible Members." A five-year limit was provided for use of this waiver provision, and "no later than six months from the date of this Decision, Members will decide on its extension to cover the production and supply of COVID-19 diagnostics and therapeutics."[206]

With respect to the non-TRIPS aspects of dealing with the pandemic, in a "Ministerial Declaration on the WTO Response to the Covid-19 Pandemic and Preparedness for Future Pandemics," adopted on June 17, 2022, the members expressed awareness of a series of practices that are useful to deal with a pandemic from a WTO perspective. They make no binding commitments, do not alter the WTO rules in any respect, and do not include even political commitments other than to try to take into account others' needs and work further on the problems of responding to a pandemic. The word "shall" is not employed, and the word "will" is softened. The members state that they:

- recognize the role of the multilateral trading system in supporting the expansion and diversification of production of essential goods and related services needed in the fight against COVID-19 and future pandemics, including through identifying opportunities and addressing barriers;

[206] "Ministerial Declaration on the TRIPS Agreement WT/MIN(22)/30 WT/L/1141." World Trade Organization. June 22, 2022. https://docs.wto.org/dol2fe/Pages/SS/directdoc.aspx?filename=q:/WT/MIN22/30.pdf&Open=True

- underscore the critical role the WTO can play in promoting inclusive growth;
- commit to transparency, including that notifications of trade-related measures with respect to COVID-19 and future pandemics are submitted in a timely and comprehensive manner in accordance with WTO rules;
- recognize the importance of ensuring that any emergency trade measures designed to tackle COVID-19, if deemed necessary, are targeted, proportionate, transparent, temporary, and do not create unnecessary barriers to trade or unnecessary disruptions in supply chains;
- state that they *will endeavor* to take into account members' diverse circumstances, and their needs for emergency supplies and humanitarian assistance;
- recognize that members may apply export restrictions and otherwise take measures necessary to protect life and health in accordance with WTO rules, and intend to exercise due restraint in the imposition of export restrictions on such goods, including their inputs;
- with a view to expediting access to COVID-19 vaccines, therapeutics, diagnostics, and other essential medical goods, during COVID-19 and future pandemics, encourage regulatory cooperation, as appropriate, and the sharing of regulatory information on a voluntary basis;
- reaffirm that the TRIPS Agreement can and should be interpreted and implemented in a manner supportive of WTO members' right to protect public health and, in particular, to promote access to medicines for all;
- underscore the importance of promoting technology transfer that contributes to building capacity in related sectors;
- acknowledge the importance of facilitating the international operations of service suppliers involved in production and distribution of COVID-19 vaccines, therapeutics, diagnostics, and other essential medical goods, such as logistics and freight transport services;
- recognize that enhanced cooperation and dialogue among members, especially those whose economies are dependent on tourism, can be important in facilitating better understanding of how to potentially mitigate adverse economic effects of a pandemic;
- acknowledge the relevance of further cooperation within the mandate of the WTO and its rules to boost post-pandemic recovery and trade flows, including on testing requirements and results, recognition of vaccination certificates and interoperability and mutual recognition of digital health applications, while continuing to protect public health and ensuring privacy and personal data protection; and

- recognize the particularly negative impact of the COVID-19 pandemic on the food security of developing country members, especially for net food-importing developing country members and LDCs.

The pledge, such as it is, applies to further work within the WTO on obtaining an agreed pandemic response through the following procedures:

- Relevant WTO bodies (the councils and committees) will, within their fields of competence, and on the basis of proposals by members, continue or initiate work as soon as possible, to analyze lessons that have been learned and challenges experienced during the COVID-19 pandemic.
- A stocktaking exercise will be taken of the work by WTO bodies under this declaration yearly at the General Council until the end of 2024, based on the reports of those relevant bodies.

Some credit is given to the Secretariat. In effect, the decision gives the Secretariat a soft mandate to continue to do what it did during the pandemic:

- *We also note the work undertaken by the WTO Secretariat, including in collaboration with other international organizations. That includes analysis, including the mapping of supply and demand, regarding trade in vaccines, therapeutics, diagnostics, and other essential medical goods and services as related to the COVID-19 pandemic.*
- *We further note the importance of the WTO working, along with the World Health Organization and other international organizations, on an international pandemic response, including activities such as expeditious matching of supply to demand, mapping manufacturing capacities and demands, matchmaking to cater to such demands, and mutual recognition norms, related to goods and services that are essential to respond effectively to COVID-19 and future pandemics.*

The bottom line was that the members recognize that collective analysis is useful. They do not, however, commit to having agreed ways of meeting the challenge of this or future pandemics.

On the Moratorium on Placing Duties on E-Commerce

The members agreed "to maintain the current practice of not imposing customs duties on electronic transmissions until MC13, which should ordinarily be held by 31 December 2023. Should MC13 be delayed beyond 31 March 2024, the moratorium will expire on that date unless Ministers or the General

Council take a decision to extend."[207] The extension, which had occurred biennially at Ministerial Conferences, was this year in doubt. Developing countries, particularly India and South Africa, but also Indonesia and others, were intent on gaining tariff revenue by taxing e-commerce.

The moratorium extension, like the TRIPS waiver provision, was essential if there were to be agreed outcomes at MC12.

Why Judge MC12 a Success?

It was clearly a positive outcome compared with expectations. The absolutely key takeaway, easy to overlook when delving into the details, is that the members were negotiating multilaterally, actually negotiating! This is the first time since Bali in 2013 that this occurred with any agreed result.

On substance, I am with Alice Tipping (in Alejandro Jara's interview at the Friends of Multilateralism Group): the members extracted the most that could be obtained at this time. The ministers, and the ambassadors acting under their instruction, slimmed the results down to what was possible until it could pass like a camel through the eye of a needle. It was a small camel.

Observers should recognize that it took courage to accept less than what was optimal, as long as it came in above what was clearly risible. Obstacles were overcome to get to agreed results:

- Strains over Russia–Ukraine were not allowed to be an impediment.
- The United States was active in a positive way (it claimed a leadership role).
- This time, China and the United States cooperated (on the TRIPS vaccine provision).
- India did not, in the end, block positive outcomes for the Ministerial. This may have been situational, in that it had concurrent negotiations with the EU on a bilateral trade agreement and with the USA on the Indo-Pacific Economic Framework which might have been jeopardized.

The Bottom Line

There was both goodwill and pragmatism.

Another good omen was that China led on the WFP, suggesting dissenters take opt-outs rather than blocking a consensus. This could be a new way for

207 "Work Programme on Electronic Commerce." World Trade Organization. June 22, 2022. https://docs.wto.org/dol2fe/Pages/SS/directdoc.aspx?filename=q:/WT/MIN22/32.pdf&Open=True

plurilaterals to coexist at the WTO. (Similarly, China agreeing not to opt in to the TRIPS waiver provision provided a means for getting to solutions that are not equally applicable to all.)

Small groups, whether Green Room meetings or the TRIPS quad, indicate a way forward.

There is growing recognition for an enhanced role of the Secretariat with respect to transparency.

MUCH REMAINS TO BE DONE POST-MC12

There are some deadlines that are either just alarm clocks, or an alarm clock connected to an improvised explosive device.

- The moratorium on electronic transmissions expires in March 2024 or by an earlier Ministerial.
- The fisheries subsidies agreement expires in four years from entry into force unless completed with respect to comprehensive disciplines contributing to overfishing and overcapacity.
- The 2024 deadline on restoring binding dispute settlement – but this does not actually require a solution to be found.

There are some built-in weaknesses:

- Some members may read the result as reiterating the absolute need for consensus meaning unanimity, which can be disastrous.
- There was no mention of the legitimacy of JSIs/OPAs; no solution to bringing JSIs formally into the WTO. They are still considered by some to have been born on the wrong side of the blanket, and they are the principal hope for the future of the WTO.[208]

[208] "G7 Leaders' Communiqué." G7 Germany 2022. June 28, 2022. www.bundesregierung.de/resource/blob/974430/2057828/77d5804dd1ab3047bf0f5f74c1139066/2022-06-28-abschlusserklaerung-eng-web-data.pdf?download=1.

The G7 three days ago called for WTO reform by MC13, and applauded "plurilateral" initiatives at the WTO.

"We underscore the importance of plurilateral initiatives to negotiating meaningful and relevant outcomes at the WTO, including by fostering creative and practical approaches. To this end, we applaud the outcome of the 12th WTO Ministerial Conference in response to major global issues such as fisheries subsidies, the emerging food security crisis and equitable access to vaccines and the commitment to work to towards necessary reform of the WTO."

What is still needed?

- A roadmap for an agriculture negotiation.
- A mandate for a broad services negotiation.
- A clear path to a high-ambition digital commerce agreement.
- A binding set of rules to deal with the next pandemic.
- A clear path to agreements for the environment, for climate change.
- A roadmap for WTO reform: to strengthen all of the WTO's basic functions – negotiation (consensus, OPAs), executive functions including trade intelligence, and binding dispute settlement. (The contours of what will be included in WTO reform are still unclear.)
- A promise to continue the project of trade liberalization.

Unsung Heroes: Individuals matter. Besides Ngozi, the chairs of the negotiating committees, particularly Santiago Wills and his predecessors, individual ministers and ambassadors, such as George Mina and Tan Hung Seng, and, behind the screen, members of the WTO Secretariat. WTO ministerial outcomes are a massive, time-consuming endeavor.

In conclusion, there is a follow-up to the story of the horse Rich Strike. There are three races for the triple crown of American racing. This horse was not entered at the Preakness, the second race, and it finished sixth in a field of eight in the third race, the Belmont. The racing metaphor does not predict what will happen at the WTO, at MC13 and beyond. But it is a cautionary note. Past triumphs do not guarantee future success.

The bottom line as I see it is that we will probably hear more good news from the horseracing and WTO realms, but this will take real effort. It would be a mistake to write off MC13 and beyond, but it is a very steep hill to climb.

PART III

The Regular Operations of the WTO

6

A Week at the WTO

The preceding chapters captured the activities of the WTO that generate headlines – the biennial meetings of trade ministers. Those events are graded by whether the ministers are able to reach agreement or fail to do so. There is much more to the WTO – much that is important but not well-known other than to officials from member countries. This chapter is designed to show what the WTO does on a regular basis, by putting the reader into WTO meetings, vicariously.

INSIDE THE WTO

The level of activity throughout the year at the Centre William Rappard, 154 rue de Lausanne in Geneva, outside of ministerial meetings is immense. These activities receive little public notice, other than when a dispute settlement panel issues a finding. Daily, representatives of members meet in a variety of formats: standing committees (some styled for regular work and others nominally for negotiating), or caucuses of members by region, by level of development, or in a group of members that joined the WTO after it was founded. Members meet to negotiate texts as outcomes from Joint Statement Initiatives and in the equivalent, in "structured discussions." Working Parties meet to consider the applications of countries seeking to accede to the WTO. Panels meet at the request of members to settle disputes as to whether WTO obligations have been breached, with some members participating as interested third parties.

The best way to experience what the WTO is all about is to consider yourself a virtual visitor to the WTO for a hypothetical week, which the following invites you to do. You may be an official from a capital, arriving to attend a dispute settlement panel meeting, but also decide to drop in on a product standards committee, an agriculture committee, or an environmental committee meeting. Perhaps you have just joined the staff of a trade minister from a member country and your assignment is to familiarize yourself with the

WTO during your visit, to sit in on various meetings to get a sense of the place. My first visit to the GATT for the US Treasury was to explain how a proposed US tax measure was consistent with the United States' international obligations (most countries believed that it was not). While I was there, my boss suggested (a suggestion taken as an assignment) that I remain for a three-week drafting session of what became the GATT Product Standards Code.

You have been given a briefing book. I was not, neither in that first visit to the GATT nor later when I was Acting Head of the US Delegation to the Multilateral Trade Negotiations (the Tokyo Round). This shortcoming was not remedied with respect to matters that were not within my list of specific responsibilities when I arrived in 2017 to assume my duties as a WTO Deputy Director-General. This chapter is designed to begin to fill in that gap, to give you some sense of the Organization's daily work, so that you can get a feel for the Organization by being transported constructively, to the extent possible, into actual meetings that have taken place. You are all Connecticut Yankees in King Arthur's court.[1]

BACKGROUND BRIEFING MATERIALS

At the WTO, the highest-level meetings that regularly take place in the General Council are held at the level of Heads of Mission, holding the rank of Ambassador. Trade ministers have delegated their powers to this body. Decisions are taken by consensus or not at all. Although there are provisions in the Marrakesh Agreement for voting, voting does not take place. The meetings are presided over by a chair chosen by the members from among their number. The term of the chair is for one year, and the position is filled on a rotating basis, alternating between developing and developed members. The chair is to act with neutrality with respect to positions taken by members. For this reason, the chair, although an ambassador of a member, does not speak for her country in the meeting she chairs. Someone else from her mission does so.

There are two other senior committees of the whole: the Dispute Settlement Body (DSB) and the Trade Policy Review Body, both subordinate to the General Council. The succession to fill the position of chair of the General Council is traditionally determined in advance by the choice of the chairs, respectively, of the DSB and the Trade Policy Review Body, each of whom is expected to move up to become General Council chair.

[1] Mark Twain, the nineteenth-century American humorist, had the idea of telling a story about a denizen of his era dropping into a mythical time many centuries earlier. The time travel here is less distant, and perhaps a bit less exotic.

Reporting to the Council are a large number of committees, all of which are open to the participation of all members. These committees monitor the implementation of WTO Agreements and provide a forum for WTO members to discuss issues of concern relevant to the subject matter jurisdiction of the committee. The standing committees include:

- Goods Council,
- Committee on Agriculture,
- Market Access Committee (Goods),
- Sanitary and Phytosanitary Measures Committee,
- Subsidies and Countervailing Measures Committee,
- Anti-Dumping Committee,
- Customs Valuation Committee,
- Rules of Origin Committee,
- Import Licensing Committee,
- Investment Working Group,
- Committee on Safeguards,
- State Trading Enterprises Working Party,
- Information Technology Agreement Committee,
- Committee on Technical Barriers to Trade,
- Services Council,
- Intellectual Property Council,
- Trade and Environment Committee,
- Trade and Development Committee,
- Trade Debt and Finance Committee,
- Trade and Transfer of Technology Committee,
- Government Procurement Committee,
- Civil Aircraft Committee,
- Information Technology Committee,
- Regional Trade Agreement Committee, and
- Budget Committee.

A separate, often parallel structure was set up by the Doha Development Agenda to deal with negotiations. A Trade Negotiating Committee (TNC), chaired by the Director-General of the WTO, meets at the level of permanent representatives (Heads of Delegation, HODS) to hear reports from negotiating committee chairs. The TNC reports to the General Council. The TNC has nine bodies reporting to it. These are:

- Negotiating Group on Market Access,
- Negotiating Group on Rules,

- Council for Trade and Services, Special Session,
- Council for Trade-Related Aspects of Intellectual Property Rights, Special Session,
- Dispute Settlement Body, Special Session,
- Committee on Agriculture, Special Session,
- Subcommittee on Cotton,
- Committee on Trade and Environment, Special Session, and
- Committee on Trade and Development, Special Session.

Preparation for General Council meetings takes place in a meeting of Heads of Delegation held a day or two before the formal Council meeting. In the HODS meeting, where delegations can state views with less formality, there is more of a chance for discussion. Due to the quantity of those wishing to take the floor in these meetings, time limits have been set usually at five minutes for an intervention on any given topic, with speakers taking the floor generally in the order in which they raise their "flags" (a placard with the member's name), unless they are the sponsors of a proposal under discussion, in which case they may speak first. The representatives of the twenty-seven members of the European Union only take the floor if something very specific to their country is being discussed, which is rare. Otherwise, the EU representative speaks for all of the member states in all meetings at the WTO. An exception to the EU speaking for its member states is the Budget Committee: as EU member states contribute to the WTO's finances individually, as do all other members on the basis of their shares of world trade, EU member states have their own voice in that committee. In recent years, the EU member states (including the United Kingdom) collectively accounted for close to 31 percent of the WTO budget, with the United States at about 12 percent, China at about 11 percent, and Japan at about 4 percent.

There are twenty-four Accession Working Parties. These meet as needed to consider the progress being made in the accession process, respectively, of Algeria, Andorra, Azerbaijan, The Bahamas, Belarus, Bhutan, Bosnia and Herzegovina, Comoros, Curaçao, Equatorial Guinea, Ethiopia, Iran, Iraq, Lebanese Republic, Libya, Sao Tomé and Principe, Serbia, Somalia, South Sudan, Sudan, Syrian Arab Republic, Timor-Leste, Turkmenistan, and Uzbekistan. The chairs of the Working Parties are usually permanent representatives or deputy permanent representatives resident in Geneva.

The members are served by a Secretariat composed of international civil servants, drawn from around the world, headed by the Director-General chosen by consensus of the members. Four Deputy Directors-General are appointed by the Director-General (with the consent of the country or region from which they are drawn). Currently, the DDGs are drawn from the United States, the EU, China, and Latin America. When the Director-General was from Latin America, a DDG was from Africa.

There are within the Secretariat eighteen divisions, each led by a career-level director. The Secretariat numbers about 650 individuals. Most of their work is devoted to staffing regular member activities. The divisions and currently established offices are:

- Accessions Division,
- Administration and General Services Division,
- Agriculture and Commodities Division,
- Council and Trade Negotiations Committee Division,
- Delivery Unit (new),[2]
- Development Division,
- Division for Knowledge and Information Management, Academic Outreach and the WTO Chairs Program (KMD),
- Economic Research and Statistics Division,
- Human Resources Division,
- Information and External Relations Division,
- Information Technology Solutions Division,
- Institute for Training and Technical Cooperation,
- Intellectual Property, Government Procurement and Competition Division,
- Language and Documentation Services Division,
- Legal Affairs Division,
- Market Access Division,
- Office of Internal Oversight,
- Rules Division,
- Technical Cooperation Audit Division,
- Trade and Environment Division,
- Trade in Services and Investment Division,
- Trade Policies Review Division, and
- Appellate Body Secretariat (currently not staffed).

[2] The Delivery Unit works closely with the Director-General and with divisions across the Secretariat to better support members in their efforts to reach concrete outcomes at the twelfth Ministerial Conference and beyond. Key areas of activity include working with relevant divisions in developing an effective WTO response to the COVID-19 pandemic, fisheries subsidies negotiations, dispute settlement, agriculture, development – including least developed countries (LDCs) issues – and a more coordinated approach to discussing WTO reform issues as well as the Joint Statement Initiatives.

All Secretariat positions are staffed through a competitive process, much as civil servants are chosen in most countries. Staffing as of December 31, 2020 had the following composition: 336 women and 288 men. There were 58 each from North America and Latin America (32 from the United States), 65 from Asia (16 from China), 39 from Africa, 12 from Oceania, and 392 from Europe (165 from France and 18 from Switzerland). As the WTO has no other offices but the location in Geneva, Switzerland, a city bordered on two sides by France, it is not surprising that more than half the staff are drawn from the two local nationalities (some staff no doubt are dual nationals who have settled in the area to be near work). The Directors-General of the WTO and the GATT have been more often European than from other regions. The current DG is the first woman and first African to hold the position. She took office on March 1, 2021.

The committees and similar bodies are each chaired by a WTO member, usually at the Head of Delegation level, with attention paid to diversity by geographic region, assisted by a secretary supplied by the Secretariat. The participants in meetings are composed of representatives from all members wishing to attend. Most of the 164 member delegations have offices (termed "missions") near the WTO campus, which consists of three buildings bordered on one side by the rue de Lausanne and on the other by Lac Léman. Ambassadors (permanent representatives) of small and medium-sized countries may also be accredited to other governments or authorities, headquartered in Bern or Brussels. Many missions will also cover meetings at other UN agencies, such as the World Health Organization (WHO), the International Labor Organization (ILO), the UN Human Rights Council (UNHRC), the World Intellectual Property Organization (WIPO), and the International Telecommunications Union (ITU), among others.

In contrast to committee chairs, who are chosen by the members from among their number and often serve for one year, Working Parties (such as for accessions) can be chaired for more than one year and not necessarily at the Head of Delegation level. As diplomats usually have a tour of duty of three or four years, continuity comes through local mission staff or perhaps through there being less turnover of portfolios back in capitals (although this may not always be the case), and to a very large extent through the staffing provided by the Secretariat, where turnover is relatively low. During my three and a half years as Deputy Director-General (2017–21), there were two Director-level vacancies filled in the Secretariat and very few senior-level appointments, while there was a very substantial turnover of permanent and deputy permanent representatives of the members. The Organization at its policy-making level is impermanent. Country representatives come and go with regularity and, less frequently, the DG and DDGs depart and are replaced. The WTO is now on its seventh Director-General during its twenty-six-year history and has been served by over two dozen DDGs. The GATT, which was in place for the period 1947 through 1994, had four DGs, the last one serving for two years before becoming the first WTO Director-General.

All in-person meetings take place on-site. Some meetings are in hybrid format (both in-person and virtual as online attendance has during the pandemic been made possible), and during the pandemic some meetings were wholly virtual (online only). A separate building houses the Council Room that can accommodate all delegations seated at once, with a relatively small visitor's gallery (meetings are not open to the public). The main building, the Centre William Rappard, was constructed in 1927 for the ILO. The new *extra muros* building has four meeting rooms – three of them below ground level – that seat over 100 delegates each. The original building has several medium-sized and smaller meeting rooms. All the large meeting rooms have booths for simultaneous interpretation into the three official languages of the WTO (English, French, and Spanish), with microphones at each member's place for taking the floor. The large meeting rooms are now equipped for "virtual" (remote) meetings due to the COVID-19 pandemic.

A ONE WEEK (VIRTUAL) VISIT TO THE WTO

The experience of attending in-person a variety of meetings at the WTO can be constructed through minutes and documents where they are publicly available, assisted by personal recollections.

DAY ONE

At 9:30 am, you enter the reception and security building on rue de Lausanne, opposite Geneva's Jardin Botanique and a sculpted group of four workers,[3] each looking somewhat miserable.[4]

3 "Botanical Gardens and Conservatory." Geneva Switzerland Travel Information. www.geneva.info/botanical-gardens/

4 The group of four sculptures opposite the WTO represents workers from four continents – Africa, America, Asia, and Europe – and is called "The Four Races." It was inaugurated in 1937 in honor of Albert Thomas (of France), the first Director-General of the ILO, who had died a few years before, in 1932. On the four sides of the monument, there are phrases of a speech by Albert Thomas:

> *C'est d'audace et de foi que les organisations humaines ont besoin à leur naissance.*
>
> *Le travail doit être placé au-dessus de toutes les luttes de concurrence – Il n'est pas une marchandise. Les hommes de mon temps ont un devoir sacré de faire la paix.*

You cross the few steps to the main WTO building, the Centre William Rappard, and climb the five stairs of the main entrance flanked by the statues of "Peace" (left) and "Justice" (right).[5] In the lobby to your left is the original reception desk from when this was the home of the ILO. Behind the desk is a Delft ceramic panel by the Dutch illustrator Albert Hahn Jr., quoting the preamble of the ILO Charter in several languages. To your right is a television screen showing the day's events. Among these is the EU's Trade Policy Review, a central purpose of your visit. Ahead, through wood and glass doors, Lake Geneva (or Lac Léman) is visible, past a patio where you can take your espresso from the canteen and go outside in good weather and sit at round tables with umbrellas to protect against the sun. Across the lake are villas in a verdant landscape and, beyond them, the snow-covered Alps.

Today, you have time for an espresso at the café of the atrium, so you proceed up the few stairs to your right and emerge into a large sunlit space with a full-grown tree in the middle. The espresso is necessary not just for the caffeine, but for the fact that you will come across delegates from other countries as well as Secretariat members and have a chance to exchange a few words. Among the most valuable aspects of diplomacy and your visit is interaction with others. This and lunch are prime working times. As one American once said about how he spent his lunch break: "I am eating for my country." He was in fact a very able and effective representative of his government.

The EU Trade Policy Review is being held in Room W, formally designated the Salle Eric Wyndham White, after the first GATT Director-General. You take your place in a seat along the wall, unless your delegation has an extra place for you at one of a half-dozen long tables for delegations stretching the length of the room from the dais to the interpreters' booths.

The Trade Policy Review Body

The week starts with a visit with the Trade Policy Review Body. It is examining the trade policies of the European Union, the largest trading member of the WTO.

> *On ne me vole pas ma vie, je la donne.*
>
> (It is audacity and faith that human organizations need at their birth. Labor must be placed above all competitive struggles – It is not a commodity. The men of my time have a sacred duty to make peace. They don't steal my life, I give it.)

The sculptor, Paul Landowski, is the same who created the Reformer's Wall in Geneva/Parc des Bastions, and the statue of Christ the Redeemer in Rio de Janeiro. Source of information: Victor do Prado.

5 "Works of Art." World Trade Organization. www.wto.org/english/thewto_e/cwr_e/cwr_art_e.htm

One of the positive innovations for the WTO era, instituted in 1989,[6] six years before the WTO was founded, was the creation of the Trade Policy Review Mechanism (TPRM). The conduct of a review could be compared to the defense of a doctoral dissertation at a university, requiring encyclopedic knowledge of all manner of information about your WTO member's trade and economic policies. In part it is an open-book exam, because no amount of expertise could supply the answers to the range of questions asked. Every two years, large countries get their trade policy performance reviewed, and smaller and developing countries somewhat less often. The Secretariat works with the subject country to prepare an extensive description of the member's policy measures that affect trade, with emphasis on current developments. The proceeding is largely handled with diplomatic politeness but the questioning by interested trading partners is intensive. The TPR is not designed to be a prelude to litigation or negotiation, so it is less confrontational than in those settings. It is designed to promote a greater degree of openness, or, as it is labeled at the WTO, transparency. Providing transparency is one of the central purposes of the WTO.

There were eighteen trade policy reviews conducted during 2021, and seven during 2020, when activities were curtailed by the pandemic before the world had adjusted more fully to the use of internet platforms for holding meetings. The review conducted on February 18, 2019 was of the largest trading member of the WTO, the European Union. Your timing is good. You are lucky to be able to sit in on these sessions.

The TPR of the European Union. The chair of this TPR, Ambassador Manuel Teehankee of the Philippines, opens the proceeding. For his overview,[7] the chair starts with some compliments, acknowledging positive contributions. He notes that the EU has helped to bring about the successful expansion of the Information Technology Agreement, pursued trade liberalization through bilateral free trade agreements, and ratified the Trade Facilitation Agreement. He goes on to state that in the questions presented for this meeting, "several concerns raised in previous Trade Policy Reviews that had been expressed again in 2017, such as agricultural policies, SPS and TBT measures, and the use of trade remedies" were being raised again now, as

6 A product of the Mid-Term Review of the Uruguay Round in Montreal in December 1988, confirmed on April 12, 1989.

7 "Trade Policy Review – European Union: Minutes of the Meeting WT/TPR/M/395." World Trade Organization. May 6, 2020. https://docs.wto.org/dol2fe/Pages/SS/directdoc.aspx?filename=q:/WT/TPR/M395.pdf&Open=True. The WTO has preserved the audio of Ambassador Terhankee's opening remarks at www.wto.org/audio/tp495.mp3

well as questions regarding the impact of Brexit on the trade interests of other members.

The EU Director-General for Trade, Sabine Weyand, arriving from Brussels, makes the presentation for the trading bloc. Weyand notes that 39 WTO members had put forward 1,600 questions covering not just trade policy but "any economic policy issue of interest to our trading partners such as agriculture, competition policy, foreign direct investment, environment and climate and digital issues."[8] As expected, her statement then supports multilateralism, with a jab at the two largest trading countries, including a condemnation of "unilateralism." Weyand lays out the trade profile of the EU: average tariffs applied at 5.2 percent (which is low compared to most WTO members other than Japan, the United States, and a few others). She states that the EU is the largest importer of agricultural products from developing and least developed countries. She highlights the need for WTO reform as a priority, particularly to restore the functioning of the dispute settlement system and arrive at disciplines for industrial subsidies. In calling for reform, she alludes to a comprehensive reform paper that the EU had authored in September 2018, which in fact had not been shared at that point with the WTO members.

Points of specific interest revolve around Brexit, which was still in the process of being worked out at the time, with the most sensitive issue for third countries being the renegotiation of tariff-rate quotas for agricultural products and governing access to the EU, which Weyand promises would be dealt with in good faith by the EU under existing WTO procedures.

The EU is proud to state that it "continued to expand our FTA network" of non-multilateral trading arrangements. The EU regards as among its recent "noteworthy achievements" a Comprehensive Economic and Trade Partnership Agreement with Canada (CETA), an EU–Japan Economic Partnership Agreement, an FTA and Investment Protection Agreement with Viet Nam, and the conclusion of negotiations with Mercosur. During this period, the EU had forty-one FTAs in force with seventy-two countries. Weyand states that 13 percent of its imports entered at preferential rates under FTAs. Taking pride in preferential arrangements is one of the curiosities of the multilateral trading system, in that its central concept is nondiscrimination. However, the FTAs are seen as making progress toward greater liberalization, and thus, in the eyes of perhaps most observers, a positive contribution to the world trading order.

[8] Ibid. Weyand noted that the EU was the third most scrutinized WTO member, with more questions being asked of China and the United States.

One week prior to the review, the WTO Secretariat circulated a 308-page report on the EU's participation in the world trading system, which you may have skimmed.[9] The report provides much additional information about the EU since its last review two years earlier, including items such as:

- The EU launched negotiations on the modernization of the existing agreement with Chile, and on comprehensive FTAs with Australia and New Zealand.
- In 2019, the EU adopted new legislation for the screening of FDI from third countries due to its growing concerns regarding the impact on the strategic interests of the EU or of its member states of certain types of FDI, especially in cases involving state-owned enterprises and strategic sectors. The EU states that the scheme provides for a framework for the screening by member states but does not create a centralized mechanism at the EU level for the screening of FDI.
- Imports of agricultural products bear significantly higher tariffs (14.2 percent on average) than the average of all EU tariffs, and some sectors stand out with higher rates – fish and fishery products (11.8 percent on simple average) and clothing (11.6 percent) are among the sectors having the highest tariff protection.
- The simple average MFN tariff rate is given as 6.3 percent.[10]
- 712 preferential tariff-rate quotas (TRQs) are in place pursuant to FTAs with 26 trading partners, and 257 conventional TRQs.
- During the review period, the EU put into place one safeguard measure, which pertained to steel imports.

The Secretariat also circulated a 617-page volume encompassing all the questions asked and the answers supplied by the EU, which it has made public.[11] The questions, listed by each member asking them, are very wide-ranging, from "we have been concerned about Chinese financing of infrastructure investments in Europe, and whether Chinese companies domiciled in the EU have access to EU investment bank vehicles," put forward by the United States, to a question about import policy with respect to global deforestation caused by the expansion of land used for agriculture, which focuses

[9] "Trade Policy Review: Report by the Secretariat – European Union WT/TPR/S/395." World Trade Organization. December 10, 2019. www.wto.org/english/tratop_e/tpr_e/s395_e.pdf

[10] Ibid., para. 14.

[11] "Trade Policy Review – European Union: Minutes of the Meeting WT/TPR/M/395." World Trade Organization. May 6, 2020. https://docs.wto.org/dol2fe/Pages/SS/directdoc.aspx?filename=q:/WT/TPR/M395.pdf&Open=True

on countries supplying certain products (food, feed, biofuels, wood, and other basic products) to the EU, posed by Argentina.

The discussant, Ambassador Alexandre Guido Lopes Parola of Brazil, highlights the positive contributions made by the EU, especially on reform and the subjects addressed by the Joint Statement Initiatives. He also briefly lists the primary concerns raised by others centered on the EU's application of sanitary and phytosanitary measures and product standards, its use of trade defense instruments (introduction of a new antidumping methodology), the impact on others of the creation of a Digital Single Market, and the EU's increased screening of inward FDI. The representative of China states that "China cannot agree with the EU's assessment that the current crisis of the WTO roots in the lack of rules to address distortions caused by so called 'non-market policies and practice.'" He says that China is concerned that "the EU's trade policy is moving towards a 'defensive' path" through the use of trade remedies, some of which were discriminatory. He further states that investment screening risked the abuse of national security review, and that the EU strengthening its "toolbox" to have an enhanced means to use sanctions against others' measures that it deems illegal would unduly legitimize sanctions.

This meeting is taking place during the Trump administration, and the US statement takes a hard line. The US delegate complains of America's goods trade deficit with the EU, the EU's barriers to US agricultural exports, and the EU's pesticide policies, "which restrict trade without scientific justification or benefit to human health" and constitute "unjustified non-tariff barriers that impede the use of modern agricultural tools and technologies such as biotechnology, veterinary drugs and pathogen reduction treatments, all of which help to ensure a safe, sustainable food supply." The US representative states that the EU is "foisting its misguided domestic policy on other countries through regional trade agreements and development assistance initiatives," and that EU standards policies "result in a closed, regional approach that discriminates against US – and other foreign – manufacturers by relying on regional, instead of international standards, and by requiring local testing of products." The US expresses concern regarding the reintroduction of subsidies for fishing vessel construction, and "so-called 'green' policy initiatives [that] create a strong risk of additional trade restrictions in the EU market." The US threatens that "in the event a country moves outside the OECD process and unilaterally imposes a DST [digital services tax], the United States will take all appropriate action to defend our interests."[12]

[12] "Trade Policy Review – European Union: Minutes of the Meeting, Addendum WT/TPR/M/395/Add.1." World Trade Organization. May 8, 2020. www.docs.wto.org/dol2fe/Pages/SS/directdoc.aspx?filename=q:/WT/TPR/M395A1.pdf&Open=True

You decide to take in some other meetings and do not stay for all of the interventions, knowing that most statements will be circulated later in writing. However, you do come back for the end of the meeting, when the chair, Ambassador Terhankee, summarizes the themes struck in the exchanges. He notes, interestingly, that "while many Members recognised the importance of trade with the EU under the multilateral trading system, they noted with appreciation the advantageous trade regimes in place between them and the EU to further liberalize trade, such as Free Trade Agreements and Economic Partnership Agreements and other regional arrangements."

In reflecting on the two-day event, you conclude that the TPRM makes a very large amount of information available to WTO members on the trade policies and measures of subject countries. You see that there are often useful citations to regulations that would allow interested officials and those engaged in trade to find and read the text of the regulation itself. It is obvious that the process results in much more transparency. You may ask a fair question: whether there is as a result much more accountability and compliance with WTO obligations? (As one ambassador said of another country's measures a few years earlier, with amazement, "they know no shame!") Is the conduct of the largest players altered by undergoing this process of explanation and justification?

The answer is mixed. Clearly, the trading system is better off for having this opportunity for members to learn more about the trade regimes of particularly the largest trading countries. The opinion of those who deal extensively with the system is that the impact on these large members is minimal, that they do not change their behavior by virtue of the TPR process. For smaller delegations, there is more likely to be a positive impact on their compliance through engagement in the process. Trade ministries in all WTO members are confronted with the necessity of preparing input for the Secretariat report and responding to wide-ranging questions. This can lead to greater coherence within governments with respect to policies and measures that affect trade. Those with responsibility for WTO affairs pull together answers, increasing the ability of commerce ministries to know what their sister bureaucracies are doing that affects international trade and seeking to bring them into greater conformity with their nation's international obligations. It might make more of a difference to all countries subject to TPRs if criticisms were more widely circulated to domestic audiences, holding a mirror up to their country's trade policies for all to see.

Lunch break – a not unimportant time. Between the morning and afternoon sessions, there is a rigidly observed two-hour break (1:00 pm to 3:00 pm). This is essential for those who have to go back to their missions to take care of other tasks. It is also possible to schedule a meeting with another delegate or

Secretariat member to cover some detail that needs attention or just to catch up. The break gives the teams of interpreters the time to be changed to others or to refresh themselves for the next session, which may run longer than the usual 6:00 pm stop time. There is also time to circulate and skim documents that were tabled in the morning session.

For your part, you can have a quickly served lunch in the WTO's "restaurant," what most would call a cafeteria (with food a cut above what the rest of the world would view as cafeteria fare), where you can come across delegates and staff (usually not ambassadors, as their drivers will take them to any one of a host of fine restaurants accessible during the time allowed, for a meeting, or work at their mission). In good weather, an excursion for a lunch of filets de perches from the lake, with frites, eaten beside the lake could not be more pleasant, perhaps at Restaurant du Creux-de-Genthod.[13] Or go much closer to Perle du Lac, a half hour's walk along the lakeside paths to end up along the quay, which provides a welcome respite from an otherwise seemingly interminable meeting that may run for a full day or day and a half. On a fine day there is a view of snow-covered Mt. Blanc, the highest peak in Europe and one of the great attractions of Geneva. Another place nearby for a very fine meal is the Restaurant Vieux Bois,[14] the hotel school on the other side of the United Nations Office at Geneva, where the food is exceptionally good and the service decidedly ambitious. If there is time and transportation, a quiet meal can be had at the Auberge des Trois Coqs,[15] where a husband-and-wife team has turned their home into a very amiable and good restaurant. There are easily some two or three dozen choices, and your host will make the selection as you are a visitor. It is during lunch that you may find some insights leading to possible ways through impasses in negotiating sessions. There follows a quick visit to the Consultative Framework Mechanism for Cotton dealing with the serious needs of some of the world's poorest countries.

Cotton development assistance. Picking up again with sampling WTO activities through sitting in on meetings, you find that the Consultative Forum on Cotton Development Assistance is in session and decide to join it.

There are two fora in which cotton is regularly discussed at the WTO. The Committee on Agriculture in Special Session is the place where members hold a dedicated discussion on cotton trade issues for potential negotiation.

[13] "Restaurant du Creux-de-Genthod." Creux de Genthod. www.creuxdegenthod.com

[14] "Students Cater for and Serve Guests at the Restaurant Vieux-Bois in Geneva." Ecole Hôtelière de Genève. www.ehg.ch/en/food-and-beverage-concept-in-geneva/restaurant-vieux-bois-in-geneva

[15] "Auberge des Trois Coqs à Chambésy (Genève)." Auberge des Trois Coqs. www.3coqs.ch/

For cotton, like the rest of agriculture, the WTO's members have difficulty finding ways to move forward. There is particular attention paid to cotton because a number of the producing countries are exceedingly poor and the effects of subsidies and import restrictions of others are hard for them to bear.

The atmosphere is dramatically different in the meetings of the Director-General's Consultative Framework Mechanism on Cotton.[16] To sit in on these meetings, which occur twice a year, is to find a proceeding that is anything but confrontational or defensive. The Consultative Framework dates back to a General Council decision of August 1, 2004,[17] further endorsed by the Ministerial Conference held in Hong Kong in December 2005.[18] The idea was that the WTO Secretariat would coordinate the efforts of both WTO members and international financial institutions "to direct effectively existing programmes and any additional resources towards development of the economies where cotton has vital importance." The motivating force behind the initiative was and is the Cotton Four, or C4, four African countries – Benin, Burkina Faso, Chad, and Mali – whose economies are heavily dependent on cotton. Per capita GDP in Burkina Faso was only $831 per year in 2020 (compared with China, the world's largest cotton exporter with a per capita GDP of $10,511 that year).

The meeting of the Consultative Framework starts with introductory remarks from the chair, a Deputy Director-General.[19] This in itself sets the meeting apart from other WTO activities. (Other than the Trade Negotiating Committee, or small gatherings in the DG's conference room, Secretariat members do not chair any meetings of members at the WTO, with the exception of the Consultative Framework for Cotton.) A report is then

[16] "Director-General's Consultative Framework Mechanism on Cotton 36th Round of Consultations on Cotton Development Assistance." World Trade Organization. November 3, 2021. www.wto.org/english/tratop_e/agric_e/dg_cons_1121_e.htm; "Cotton-4 Reports on By-Products Initiative, Cotton Trade and Development Issues Discussed." World Trade Organization. November 13, 2020. www.wto.org/english/news_e/news20_e/cott_13nov20_e.htm; "Cotton Sub-Committee News Archive." World Trade Organization. www.wto.org/english/news_e/archive_e/cott_arc_e.htm

[17] "Cotton: Ministerial Decision of 7 December 2013 WT/MIN(13)/41, WT/L/916." World Trade Organization. December 11, 2013. www.wto.org/english/thewto_e/minist_e/mc9_e/desci41_e.htm

[18] "Text of the 'July Package' – The General Council's Post-Cancún Decision." World Trade Organization. August 1, 2004. www.wto.org/english/thewto_e/minist_e/min05_e/final_text_e.htm#cotton

[19] I served as chair from October 2017 through March 2021. The current chair is Jean-Marie Paugam. "Director-General's Consultative Framework Mechanism on Cotton 33rd Round of Consultations on Cotton Development Assistance." World Trade Organization. July 30, 2020. www.wto.org/english/tratop_e/agric_e/dg_cons_30720_e.htm

presented by the WTO cotton staff concerning current developments relevant to cotton development assistance, such as the launch of a World Cotton Day to celebrate the importance of cotton to a wide swath of economies.[20]

Next, the coordinator of the C-4 speaks, Mr. Dieudonné Sougouri, Ambassador and Permanent Representative of Burkina Faso to the WTO, setting out the progress that has been made since the last meeting and the challenges that remain.

The fourth presentation is from Kai Hughes, the Executive Director of the International Cotton Advisory Committee.[21] Kai Hughes' presentation focuses on the economics of cotton production, the state of the current market for cotton, the continuing failure to increase cotton yields in Africa, the need to integrate further with downstream users, the possibilities to mitigate the adverse effects of climate change, and the need to obtain more value from cotton by-products. All parts of the cotton plant can be utilized to increase farmer income. The seeds when treated can be pressed for oil and used for feed. The stems can be processed into a form of fiberboard as a building material. In the prior session of the Framework several months earlier, Mr. Hughes had given a presentation on the first World Cotton Day.[22]

After these scene-setting presentations, the discussion turns to the current state of development assistance projects notified to the Secretariat.[23] This is followed by interventions from donors on their current development assistance activities.

What is remarkable about the meeting is the degree of focus and absence of contentiousness. The C-4 representatives are pragmatic and detailed in their requests, for example, asking for assistance for projects to aid in the production and use of cotton by-products to increase the income of poor farmers. The numerous projects to assist cotton production in the poorest of countries are

[20] "WTO Launch of World Cotton Day (WCD) – 7 October 2019: Report TN/AG/SCC/W/33 WT/CFMC/61." World Trade Organization. July 20, 2020. www.wto.org/english/tratop_e/agric_e/wcd_report_e.pdf

[21] "World Cotton Day – Kai Hughes, ICAC Executive Director." World Trade Organization. October 7, 2020. www.wto.org/english/tratop_e/agric_e/dg_cons_30720_e/i1_hughes_e.pdf; "African Cotton Sustainability Programme 2030 – Kai Hughes, Executive Director, International Cotton Advisory Committee." World Trade Organization. www.wto.org/english/tratop_e/agric_e/item_3_icac_presentation_on_acsp_2030.pdf

[22] "World Cotton Day – Kai Hughes, ICAC Executive Director." World Trade Organization. October 7, 2020. www.wto.org/english/tratop_e/agric_e/dg_cons_30720_e/i1_hughes_e.pdf; "Celebrating World Cotton Day: An Opportunity to Recognize the Global Importance of Cotton." World Trade Organization. www.wto.org/english/tratop_e/agric_e/wcd2021_e.htm

[23] "Evolving Table on Cotton Development Assistance – Update by the Secretariat: 36th Round of Consultations of DGCFMC." World Trade Organization. November 3, 2021. www.wto.org/english/tratop_e/agric_e/item_4_wto_on_evolving_table_update.pdf

then presented one after another by the wide variety of donors. All demonstrate a strong motivation to be helpful, with assistance from both cotton-producing and cotton-consuming countries – for example, India, Pakistan, Brazil, the European Union, China, Japan, the United States, and Germany.[24]

Being in the room is a positive experience. Cataloging good works and stimulating more of them is a fine and satisfying endeavor.

A WEEK AT THE WTO

DAY 2: PRODUCT STANDARDS

Governments adopt standards for a variety of reasons. The primary reason for the creation of most standards is the protection of human safety and health. There are also standards adopted to protect animals and plant life and health, and increasingly standards to protect the environment, such as through recycling. Increased pollution of air and water, increased soil degradation – all drive further standards-making activities. Governments provide consumers and farmers with benefits by specifying quality controls for fruit, vegetables, and meat, as well as through labeling requirements. For telecommunications and other electronics, interoperability is vitally important. Communication among first responders at times of natural disasters is essential. International trade requires the standardization of containers.

Administrative authorities seek compliance with standards through testing, certification, and inspections. This creates a whole additional layer of responsibilities for those engaged in commerce, domestic and international.

Most of us do not think very much about product standards in daily life. When we buy a can of vegetables, it is safe to assume that the rim is going to fit into an electric can opener. Medicines are going to be what they are labeled as. A size 10 shoe is going to be pretty much a size 10. A car will operate on gasoline or diesel or electricity according to the buyer's expectations and what the manufacturer says it will do. An AAA battery is going to fit into toys or an electronic thermometer stating that is what is required. Interchangeability of parts is essential in many circumstances, whether for flashlight batteries or threaded screws, or parts of ventilators during a pandemic.

[24] "Sustainable Cotton and Textile Supply Chain Uzbekistan – Challenges and Opportunities." World Trade Organization. November 3, 2021. www.wto.org/english/tratop_e/agric_e/item_6_a_giz_cotton_project_in_uzbekistan.pdf

Anyone who has traveled abroad knows that a car made to European standards cannot be registered in the United States and vice versa. The ubiquitous electric appliances in one country are likely to have a plug that does not fit into another country's sockets, and the type of current they require may make them unusable.

The individual adapts. She travels with a set of adapters. Charts convert milliliters into ounces. A shopper can select from a table a European size for clothes or shoes equivalent to the American size and vice versa. No great problem. However, for manufacturers, it may be too costly to adapt a product. The maker of small wind turbines may find that a minimum threshold has been set for the size of output that excludes a major product line from being sold in a foreign market. A producer of cars decides that it is uneconomic to adapt all of its models to a foreign market. A ban on growth hormones or the use of antibiotics may make some agricultural commodities unmarketable abroad. For a producer in a developing country, proving that it has met another country's standard, that its conformity assessment procedures are acceptable, may prove impossible.

From the perspective of moving goods in international trade, while tariffs may be an additional burden, meeting a foreign standard may be an unsurmountable barrier.[25] The WTO rules deal with this problem under its Agreement on Technical Barriers to Trade (TBT),[26] governing product standards. The golden rules of the WTO apply: do not discriminate among countries based on where the product comes from (MFN), and do not discriminate in favor of domestic products over foreign products (national treatment). The specific rules applicable to standards are also rather straightforward:

- Do not create unnecessary obstacles to international trade;
- Use international standards if possible;
- Participate in the setting of those standards if possible;
- Remove outdated requirements;
- Be prepared to justify a standard if requested by another member to do so;
- Give positive consideration to accepting equivalent standards of others if they fulfill your country's objectives;

[25] "DDG Wolff: International Regulatory Co-Operation One Key to Managing Trade Frictions." World Trade Organization. March 19, 2018. www.wto.org/english/news_e/news18_e/ddgra_19mar18_e.htm

[26] "Agreement on Technical Barriers to Trade." World Trade Organization. www.wto.org/english/docs_e/legal_e/17-tbt_e.htm

- Prefer the use of standards that specify performance rather than design;
- When proposing to adopt a standard that is not in accordance with international standards, if there will be a significant effect on trade, give other members an opportunity to comment, by publishing it and notifying other members, and before it is adopted, unless prompt adoption of the standard is essential;
- Try to negotiate mutual recognition agreements to accept the test results of other members' institutions and agencies to facilitate conformity assessment; and
- Provide significant transparency with respect to the local government and nongovernmental bodies within their territories.

While the rules are straightforward enough, upon a moment's reflection, one can see that there will be a high probability of adoption of standards in hundreds of jurisdictions at the central and subcentral levels that inadvertently create barriers to trade. There will also be occasional instances where a conscious effort is being made to favor domestic producers. To meet this challenge, the WTO has created a place for deliberation, a Committee on Technical Barriers to Trade (TBT), and a process that is widely seen as among its most successful endeavors.

A WTO TBT "thematic" session. You decide to sit in on a TBT Thematic Session on Transparency.[27] The chair, Mr. Laurence Sandral (Australia), opens the meeting called in part to discuss the progress made on transparency.[28] He calls on the Secretariat to give a status report. The highlights are:

- Since 1995, the Committee has received and circulated almost 40,000 notifications from 142 members related to new or changed technical regulations and conformity assessment procedures.
- While the notifications are of regulations in draft to facilitate comment by interested members, the Committee had adopted recommendations to facilitate access to final texts of regulations as well.
- To supplement the Committee's process, 159 members had designated enquiry points for answering queries related to TBT measures in place or under development.
- Twenty-three members had submitted a total of 156 notifications with respect to agreements they had reached with one or more members

[27] This section describing a TBT Committee meeting is a composite of TBT events in 2020–21.

[28] "As this week's Technical Barriers to Trade Committee meeting #WTOTBT comes to an end, Chair Laurence Sandral (Australia) highlights why these debates matter for our everyday lives." Twitter. February 26, 2021. www.twitter.com/wto/status/1365262997346807810

regarding technical regulations, standards, and conformity assessment procedures.

The Secretariat also gives an update on the online features that facilitate the implementation of the work of the TBT Committee, including how the ePing platform is working. ePing is an ingenious interactive tool that informs members and the public of subjects in accordance with their indicated interests. It enables prompt access to evolving product requirements and facilitates dialogue among the public and private sectors in addressing potential trade problems at an early stage. A great feature of ePing is that the system provides, without charge, email alerts on new SPS (sanitary and phytosanitary) and TBT (product standards) notifications.[29] Registering on your iPad, you see for example that the United States Environmental Protection Agency (EPA) has announced the Agency's receipt of initial filings of petitions requesting the establishment or modification of regulations for residues of pesticide chemicals in or on various commodities, with a link to the actual agency notice.

There follows a discussion by representatives of individual members on how to make good use of the ePing platform. While you are listening to those who take the floor, you log onto the ePing platform to see how it works at https://epingalert.org/. The European Union representative raises the EU's flag (name card) to suggest to the attendees

> *using ePing as a single notification platform to include all Members' notifications, from the initial notification drafts to the notification of final texts. ePing could also have a public face allowing the general public to see how TBT works and where comments on notifications can be published. In addition, ePing could have a restricted access area to be used by officials to communicate comments and replies, to request clarification on a measure and facilitate exchanges in general between Members.*

In addition, ePing can be used to collect current and historic information on Specific Trade Concerns (STCs are notifications by members of issues that they have with a proposed or actual standard of another member).[30]

The Swiss delegate sees in ePing the possibility of earlier disclosure of problems and possible solutions. The United States, Trinidad and Tobago,

[29] "DDG Wolff Underlines Central Role of SPS Agreement in Facilitating Trade in Safe Food." World Trade Organization. November 2, 2020. www.wto.org/english/news_e/news20_e/ddgaw_02nov20_e.htm

[30] "DDG Wolff: Regular Discussion of Specific Trade Concerns Helps to Reduce Trade Friction." World Trade Organization. September 2, 2020. www.wto.org/english/news_e/news20_e/ddgaw_02sep20_e.htm

and Australia note privacy concerns, but on the whole state that the issues could be dealt with successfully.

The United States, the European Union, and China make detailed presentations on how they gather comments to give input to the TBT Committee processes. In the give-and-take discussion that follows, the EU expresses concern that not all notices are filed with translations into the three working languages of the WTO, that not all notifications are filed promptly, and sometimes there is insufficient time for making comments. Some developing country members ask whether there is a deadline for EU stakeholders to provide comments. The US delegate indicates that the process of providing notifications to the WTO spurs inter-agency coordination, creating awareness of the unintended consequences of regulations while they are still in draft. The process, the United States says, also improves US notification performance and connects both WTO members and American stakeholders to US government trade agencies. The representative of China indicates that translation is costly, that it is necessary to get responses to requests for the extension of a comment period, that small and medium-sized enterprises have a challenge in filing comments, and that enquiry points need to train industries to make better use of the tools available to comment on a member's standards.

The final topic for the session consists of presentations by Chinese Taipei (the common name for Taiwan in WTO settings), the United Kingdom, Ecuador, and the United States on how they each deal with domestic coordination.

The chair concludes that ultimately what they have been discussing is how best to provide "regulatory cooperation, predictability and facilitating safe trade."

The thematic session is adjourned.

Lunch break. During the break, you review the Report on the Ninth Triennial Review of the TBT Agreement.[31]

Attending a session of a TBT Committee. In the afternoon, you decide to learn more about TBT by sitting in on an actual TBT Committee meeting.[32] Much of the meeting is taken up with a new specific trade concern (STC)

[31] "Ninth Triennial Review of the Operation and Implementation of the Agreement on Technical Barriers to Trade Under Article 15.4 G/TBT/46." World Trade Organization. November 17, 2021. https://docs.wto.org/dol2fe/Pages/SS/directdoc.aspx?filename=q:/G/TBT/46.pdf&Open=True

[32] "Committee on Technical Barriers to Trade – Minutes of the Meeting of 2–4 June and 9 June 2021 – Note by the Secretariat G/TBT/M/84." World Trade Organization. August 24, 2021. https://docs.wto.org/dol2fe/Pages/SS/directdoc.aspx?filename=q:/G/TBT/M84.pdf&Open=True. This meeting took place on a different day than the thematic discussion on transparency.

submitted by the Russian Federation involving a draft EU Batteries Regulation (implementing the European Green Deal), G/TBT/N/EU/775 (ID 6852). Filing STCs are a nonlitigative means of raising an issue with another WTO member over a standard.[33] In a written statement, the Russian Federation acknowledges the right of all WTO members to regulate to achieve legitimate environmental objectives. However, Russia is concerned with specific requirements on the maximum level of carbon footprint over the life cycle of batteries and the minimum level required of recycled materials such as cobalt, lithium, and nickel.

The Russian Federation believes that the provision discriminates against imported primary materials vis-à-vis domestically remanufactured batteries. It also believes that the regulation is likely to be more trade-restrictive than necessary to fulfill legitimate objectives and would be likely to create unnecessary obstacles to international trade. In this regard, Russia states that it wonders if the European Union considered less trade-restrictive measures to stimulate the recycling of nickel, lithium, cobalt, and lead, rather than administrative measures such as a minimum level of recycled materials in the battery. Russia also states that it believes there is no comprehensive methodology to calculate the maximum level of carbon footprint over the life cycle of batteries. It is concerned that its stakeholders have no specified way to submit its data and that an additional burden would be placed by significantly increasing the number of audits and reporting requirements for the upstream parts of supply chains, diverting resources from proper and efficient risk management.

The representative of China asks that the EU cancel at present the "minimum share of recycled content" and consider it after the methodology of calculation and verification is established. He also considers that the recycled proportion of cobalt is relatively high and recommends that the energy (Wh) information be added to the information on the label of batteries. The representative further expresses concern that core secrets – such as the content of cobalt, nickel, lithium contained in batteries, and data about the carbon emissions of materials in the process of production – would be at risk of disclosure. The delegate proceeds to give further detailed comments. India states that it shares the concerns raised.

Canada states that it finds "common ground with the EU's desire to contribute to sustainable development, green mobility, and clean energy. On that basis, Canada signals its intention to monitor the development of the proposed regulation, and its possible relationship with other Members'

[33] "Trade Concerns Database." World Trade Organization. https://tradeconcerns.wto.org/en

domestic initiatives on sustainability. Canada looks forward to continuing to engage and collaborate with the EU on its Batteries Regulation as its Implementing and Delegated Acts are developed."

In response, the representative of the European Union states that batteries are one of "the key enablers for sustainable development, green mobility, clean energy, and climate neutrality. In order for the EU's product policies to contribute to these objectives, it needs to be ensured that batteries marketed and sold in the EU are sourced and manufactured in a sustainable manner." He proceeds to say that "batteries that are more sustainable throughout their life cycle are key for the goals of the European Green Deal . . . The EU would like to reassure that there will be sufficient time to consider the feedback on the Batteries Regulation proposal." There will be consultations with stakeholders and a notification to the TBT Committee, but there is then also a need to get the proposal adopted by the Council and the European Parliament in 2022.

The "EU considers that the notified proposal is not more trade-restrictive than necessary to fulfill its legitimate policy objectives, also taking account of the risks that non-fulfillment would create. It therefore fully complies with the provisions of the TBT Agreement."

The above exchanges are largely in the form of written statements circulated to all Committee members. The meeting has on its agenda nineteen new STCs, sixty-seven STCs of continuing concern, and five removed from the agenda at the request of the concerned member. With respect to the new STCs, as well as those put on the agenda as being of continuing concern, statements by the member submitting the concern and responses made are filed.

The scope of subjects is breathtaking – some examples:

- Egypt – regulatory guidelines for the circulation of cosmetic products in Egypt, presented by the EU;
- Russian Federation – on the safety of wheeled vehicles, submitted by Korea;
- Viet Nam – concerning the safety of lithium batteries used for laptops, notebooks, mobile phones, and tablets, submitted by Korea;
- Ecuador – sanitary technical regulations for processed foods and processing plants as well as establishments for the distribution, marketing, and transportation of processed foods, submitted by the United States;
- European Union – chemical strategy for sustainability, implementation of the European Green Deal, submitted by the Russian Federation;
- Korea – requirements for appliances such as rice cookers, submitted by China;

- Chile – systems for livestock classification and grading, marking, and marketing of beef, submitted by Brazil;
- EU – withdrawal of approval of an insecticide, submitted by Brazil;
- Colombia – Biofuels Decree, submitted by the EU.

Concern: The measure was not notified and nevertheless was adopted. It specifies maximum content of ethanol in the mixture with regular and extra gasoline. The EU asks Colombia to suspend the measure and notify it. The requirement will result in increasing the actual emissions from vehicles because more efficient fuels do not qualify and would result in banning certain vehicles from sale in Colombia. What, the EU asks, were the tests and studies used to support this measure?

Response: Colombia explained the steps it took to finalize this regulation and suggested a path forward that could lead to a possible resolution: "[In] order to address the concerns raised by the EU, a meeting between our technical authorities and the EU technical authorities would be facilitated from our capital."

- European Union – test procedures and technical requirements for the type-approval of motor vehicles regarding driver drowsiness and attention warning systems, submitted by China.

Concern: The definition of "facial recognition" is too broad. For example, are blinking and yawning included in facial recognition? The activation speed is to be at least 70km/h. However, some commercial vehicles driving on non-highway roads usually cannot reach this speed. Hence, China suggests lowering the activation speed to make sure the monitoring can be realized in most driving courses. The control strategies of each manufacturer will lead to a large difference in the time to determine fatigue.

Suggested remedy: Based on safety considerations, requirements such as a driver's eyes being closed for more than two seconds and head deflection exceeding the normal forward vision range for more than three seconds are given; when the driver's sight deflection exceeds the above threshold, an alarm should sound. However, the requirement of "as soon as possible" is too subjective. The regulation shall clearly define that the alert be presented within a specified number of seconds after the drowsiness occurs, since sounding the alert in time is a key indicator to assure the safety of the system.

The "reference sleepiness scale for the driver drowsiness and attention warning system" is too subjective and has no objective evaluation indicator or content of the scale of distraction. The distraction of attention involves fatigue. But drivers can be distracted for a long time (for example, they look left and right for a long time) without fatigue, which is also a greater risk.

The use of human participants in real road tests is very dangerous since people might be injured. China suggests that highly dangerous tests on real roads be done in a closed testing area with relatively long tracks and a controllable environment.

> *Response*: The EU notes that China has also submitted detailed written comments to the EU TBT Enquiry Point on March 16, 2021. (The TBT Enquiry Point is often the main entity for overseeing the transparency process, but there are many other actors and stakeholders involved, including regulators, standardizing bodies, trade officials, international bodies, sectoral associations, companies, academia, etc.)

In this regard, the EU would like to reassure China that a reply will be sent in due course. Since the EU has not received any additional comments ahead of the committee meeting, the EU hopes that its future written reply will sufficiently clarify China's comments.

Note: There followed a similar exchange between the same parties with respect to uniform procedures and technical specifications for the type-approval of motor vehicles regarding their emergency lane keeping system (ELKS).

- United Arab Emirates – requirement of G-mark for every toy, submitted by India.

> *Concern*: This G-mark requirement makes Indian products uncompetitive in the UAE as no agency is authorized to issue a G-mark in India. To get G-mark-certified products, Indian exporters must send the entire consignment to the place where it can be G-mark certified. As per the extant regulation, the G-mark needs to be obtained for each and every toy. Further, the G-mark notified bodies (NBs) during the conformity assessment frequently request physical samples of all products in a group, and not only of the representative item.

Response: We have already forwarded the concerns of India to the capital. We will get back to you with a response.

This is just part of the list of specific trade concerns to be considered at this one meeting. In addition, there were submissions at this meeting of additional STCs by Paraguay, Colombia, Argentina, India, Saudi Arabia, United Arab Emirates, Costa Rica, Columbia, Uruguay, Chinese Taipei, Singapore, Indonesia, Mexico, Australia, Thailand, New Zealand, Japan, Panama, Guatemala, El Salvador, Philippines, Switzerland, the United Kingdom, Turkey, Qatar, Hong Kong, and Turkey. In a number of cases, a single member filed several STCs or joined in the consideration of more than one STC.

Comment. It is not surprising that WTO members with greater ability to promulgate regulations and greater transparency due to their own procedures are more often the target of STCs. The EU perhaps attracts the most. Likewise, the members with greater capability to collect information from their stakeholders are more likely to file STCs. However, the degree of participation is remarkable. China checks a number of these boxes – it is the world's largest exporter of goods, but it does not file as many STCs as the EU or the United States. This might change over time, as China may invest more in this capability.

It is fair to ask whether more was achieved through this process than providing increased transparency, as important as transparency is. Did the recipient of the comments modify its measure? In asking the WTO Secretariat, the answer is they do not know for sure. What is known is that not that many STCs become formal dispute settlement complaints. There are some standards cases from time to time submitted to dispute settlement, but the measures notified are in the tens of thousands, the STCs are in the hundreds, and the standards issues submitted for formal dispute settlement are far, far fewer, numbering fifty-seven.[34] That the European Union and the United States are the major targets of TBT dispute settlement cases is revealed by the data. The EU was the target of a dispute in twenty cases, and the United States in twelve. The two together account for over half of the TBT disputes that have been brought during the history of the WTO.

Looking forward. Having attended this meeting of the TBT Committee, you learn later that at the next meeting, a new TBT Committee chair, Ms. Elisa Olmeda (Mexico), was elected and installed.[35] The Committee moved toward the adoption of a three-year workplan that is to include a focus on pandemic preparedness, climate change, and plastics pollution, as well as a review of an additional eighty-nine Specific Trade Concerns, twenty-five of which are being raised for the first time, covering issues related to labeling, testing, and safety of products.

Assisting developing countries. In the Ninth Triennial Review of the Operation and Implementation of the Agreement on Technical Barriers to Trade,[36] a number of developing countries addressed the need for assistance

[34] "Disputes by Agreement – Technical Barriers to Trade (TBT)." World Trade Organization. www.wto.org/english/tratop_e/dispu_e/dispu_agreements_index_e.htm?id=A22

[35] "Members Agree on Workplan for Standards and Regulations Committee for Next Three Years." World Trade Organization. November 12, 2021. www.wto.org/english/news_e/news21_e/tbt_12nov21_e.htm

[36] "Ninth Triennial Review of the Operation and Implementation of the Agreement on Technical Barriers to Trade Under Article 15.4 G/TBT/46." World Trade Organization.

to meet their needs for National Quality Infrastructure (NQI – the capability to test and assure conformity). If small and medium-sized enterprises, which account for much of the trade of developing and least developed countries, do not have access to adequate conformity assessment, standardization, and metrology infrastructure, they cannot engage successfully in trade. This risks further isolating those at the margins of the multilateral trading system, prompting further backlash against globalization and integration.

NQI has important trade-facilitating benefits. Coordination between regulators and different parts of the NQI can help reduce barriers to trade, including the imposed conformity assessment procedures. The alternative is often duplicative or overly burdensome testing and certification requirements, which increase trade costs. In this respect, international guides and systems for conformity assessment are of great benefit.

The WTO is part of a successful partnership with four other organizations (FAO, World Bank, World Organization for Animal Health formerly known as OIE, and the WHO), working together in the Standards and Trade Development Facility (STDF), which seeks to enhance the capacity of developing countries to meet sanitary and phytosanitary standards. The STDF promotes coherence in donor activities on SPS by serving as a global coordination and knowledge hub. The STDF also supports specific projects to build SPS capacity (more than seventy-five since 2004). Some examples:

- Enhancing phytosanitary controls to drive growth in Uganda's flower exports;
- Improving Belize's SPS regime and animal health controls to facilitate live cattle exports; and
- Boosting safe fruit and vegetable exports from Thailand and Viet Nam.

There is no parallel mechanism for TBT and quality infrastructure. Given the positive contribution of the STDF as an example, a common TBT data collection hub could help identify and prioritize NQI capacity gaps. This could also be presented as a system for rating the level of development of NQI in different countries.

TBT, STCs, and NQI are often highly technical areas of the work of the WTO. Governments uniformly give the institution high marks for this collaborative effort. Without it, international trade would flow far less freely, needlessly restricted by inconsistent or otherwise ill-considered national regulations.

November 17, 2021. https://docs.wto.org/dol2fe/Pages/SS/directdoc.aspx?filename=q:/G/TBT/46.pdf&Open=True

A VISIT WITH THE DISPUTE SETTLEMENT BODY

Understanding the structure of the DSU, observing a DSB meeting in progress can convey a good sense of the operation of this body.

The DSB provides a window into compliance with WTO Agreements. For this reason, in your virtual tour of the WTO, you decide to sit in on a meeting. It is August 2021.[37]

Ambassador Didier Chambovey (Switzerland) calls the meeting to order.[38] The first item on the agenda covers "surveillance of implementation or recommendations adopted by the DSB in prior meetings." Six cases are on the agenda, and in each case the losing party has filed a brief status report preceding the meeting. The written updates range from announcing that the complained of measure was repealed, to a limited statement that consultations are continuing in one case where it seems obvious that no resolution has yet been achieved. For most of the cases, the statements filed seem to indicate that a satisfactory arrangement was agreed to between or among the parties, or that some form of (unspecified) *modus vivendi* has been worked out. But in the room, as the complainants take the floor and are responded to by the member that lost the case in question, the situation gets much clearer.

Under the item "European Communities – Measures Affecting the Approval and Marketing of Biotech Products," the representative of the EU states that seven authorizations for genetically modified organisms (GMOs) for food and feed use were adopted. The representative refers to the EU's "comitology procedure," a term you think might refer to basing judgments on science, as your biology class some decades earlier referred to cellular division as "mitosis." But upon consulting the web through your smartphone, you discover that "comitology" in EU Brussels-speak refers to the system of member state committee review. The EU representative states that the decisions are science-based, transparent (under a new regulation), and in compliance with the EU's WTO obligations.[39] (Background: Three cases, DS291, 292, and 293, were brought by the United States, Canada, and Argentina in

[37] "Minutes of Meeting – Dispute Settlement Body 30 August 2021 WT/DSB/M/455." World Trade Organization. October 27, 2021. https://docs.wto.org/dol2fe/Pages/SS/directdoc.aspx?filename=q:/WT/DSB/M455.pdf&Open=True

[38] Ambassador Chambovey was to become the next chair of the General Council.

[39] "European Communities – Measures Affecting the Approval and Marketing of Biotech Products: Status Report by the European Union WT/DS291/37/Add.156." World Trade Organization. August 20, 2021. https://docs.wto.org/dol2fe/Pages/SS/directdoc.aspx?filename=q:/WT/DS/291-37A156.pdf&Open=True; "Proposed Agenda – Dispute Settlement Body

2003 claiming that the EU had, *de facto*, unreasonably delayed the approval of twenty-seven agricultural commodities requiring regulatory clearance. The panel found in favor of the complainants.[40])

In response, the US representative notes that the European Union had approved seven biotech crops (three for corn, two for soybeans, one for canola, and one for cotton) and issued three renewals for previously authorized crops (two for corn and one for canola). The United States says that there are still approximately eight products pending, and that the delays are continuing.

As with most items on the agenda, the DSB takes note of the statements. Compliance matters not resolved in this meeting will, under the rules, stay on the agenda until the issues are resolved. A formal record of the status and degree of resolution of the dispute has been created by the exchanges.

In discussion of another case, "United States – Anti-dumping and Countervailing Measures on Large Residential Washers from Korea," the United States reports that it revoked the antidumping order that was the subject of the case. The representative of Canada, however, takes the floor to state that the US antidumping methodology that it employed in this case against Korean washing machines was found by the Appellate Body to be inconsistent with its obligations. What is required, the representative states, is compliance, that the period for doing so expired three years earlier, and that this "failure seriously undermined the security and predictability of the multilateral trading system." (Background: The issue at hand was whether the use of zeroing methodology was consistent with US obligations. The case, DS464, was brought in January 2014. The panel and AB found against the United States.[41])

With respect to "Indonesia – Importation of Horticultural Products, Animals and Animal Products," the representative of Indonesia reports that Indonesia had removed all articles in the relevant laws that were found to be inconsistent with WTO rules. The United States and New Zealand ask specific questions on new regulations that would again affect import licensing regimes. The item will be on the next month's DSB agenda with the answers requested being the focus of that meeting's discussion. (Background: In 2015,

20 December 2021 WT/DSB/W/691." World Trade Organization. December 16, 2021. https://docs.wto.org/dol2fe/Pages/SS/directdoc.aspx?filename=q:/WT/DSB/W691.pdf&Open=True

40 "DS291: European Communities – Measures Affecting the Approval and Marketing of Biotech Products." World Trade Organization. www.wto.org/english/tratop_e/dispu_e/cases_e/ds291_e.htm

41 "DS464: United States – Anti-Dumping and Countervailing Measures on Large Residential Washers from Korea." World Trade Organization. www.wto.org/english/tratop_e/dispu_e/cases_e/ds464_e.htm

the United States and New Zealand had each brought cases, DS477 and DS478, against Indonesia's import licensing scheme, and prevailed.[42])

Again, for anyone attending the meeting or reading the minutes of past meetings, the live exchanges among interested parties in the DSB bring much greater clarity to the remaining issues to be resolved in any dispute than could readily be gleaned from the written statements on compliance status that are filed before the meeting.

In this meeting,[43] there follow two old, repetitive items between the United States and the European Union. With respect to one of these, the EU notes that a measure that the United States repealed fourteen years earlier still has some residual effect, but that the United States had failed to file a status report. In agenda item 3, the United States returns the favor by pointing out that the EU had not filed a status report on compliance on a matter that the two had settled. The exchange is highly technical and of no great significance.

The fourth item on the agenda is more interesting. It concerns new requests for the establishment of panels.

China has asked for a compliance panel to be formed on a case it lost with respect to the administration of unfilled portions of tariff-rate quotas (TRQs) for wheat, rice, and corn. This is unusual; it is the equivalent of asking for a court-martial of oneself for purposes of exoneration. China notes that the United States declared China to be in non-compliance with its obligations in this matter without itself asking for a compliance panel to make that determination, and then proceeded to ask for a panel to set an amount by which it could retaliate against Chinese trade. The US representative responds that there is insufficient transparency in China to determine compliance. The Chinese request is automatically granted, with the matter referred back to the original panel. There is substantial interest in the matter, and Australia, Brazil, Canada, the European Union, Guatemala, India, Japan, the Russian Federation, Chinese Taipei, and the United Kingdom state that they reserve their third-party rights to participate in the panel's proceedings.

The next matter on the agenda involves two neighbors. Costa Rica asks that a panel be formed to review recent trade restrictions imposed by Panama. The Costa Rican representative says, "there had been no changes in the phytosanitary status nor any increase in associated risks for Costa Rican products, yet

42 "DS477. Indonesia – Importation of Horticultural Products, Animals and Animal Products." World Trade Organization. www.wto.org/english/tratop_e/dispu_e/cases_e/ds477_e.htm

43 "Minutes of Meeting – Dispute Settlement Body 30 August 2011 WT/DSB/M/455." World Trade Organization. October 27, 2021. https://docs.wto.org/dol2fe/Pages/SS/directdoc.aspx?filename=q:/WT/DSB/M455.pdf&Open=True

Panama's limitations on Costa Rican exports had affected milk products, beef products, pork, cured beef, poultry, aquatic animal food, pet food, and so on since June last year." Panama retorts that litigation is costly, and it is willing to meet with Costa Rica to talk through the questions it has raised. The Dispute Settlement Understanding provides that unless a request for the formation of a panel is unopposed, it will not be formed at the meeting at which the request is made, but will be reverted to at the next meeting, which is a month away. Requests are automatically approved upon a second request.

It is perhaps noteworthy that Panama and Costa Rica have a bilateral free trade agreement.[44] Presumably, they could have chosen to use the dispute settlement provision of their treaty but preferred to take their dispute to Geneva. This indicates a level of trust in the WTO dispute settlement system. By transferring the litigation to Geneva, they may take the heat of the dispute out of the region. The DSU can serve in a serious way to reduce or prevent conflicts between neighbors. It is likely often the case that the WTO has been chosen as a forum in which to settle disputes, rather than resorting to bilateral or regional trading arrangements.

Japan takes the floor to request the formation of a panel to review "China – Anti-dumping Measures on Stainless Steel" imported from Japan. The representative of Japan states that consultations had not been productive and asks for the formation of a panel. The representative of China states that China is willing to consult further but does not agree to a panel being formed. The DSB takes note and will revert to the matter upon the request of either party.

In the last intervention of the day regarding issues for consideration by a panel, Tunisia addresses a recent panel report on "Morocco – Anti-dumping Measures against School Exercise Books." Morocco had decided to appeal. However, according to the Tunisian representative, Morocco failed to submit a statement with the notice of appeal that would indicate on what grounds the appeal was being made. Therefore, it states, the panel report could be deemed to be final. However, Tunisia is willing to suspend its request for DSB approval of the panel report by negative consensus if Morocco complies with the appropriate procedures. (The Tunisian view is that the suspension of the right to have a final decision from the dispute settlement process can be extended for only ninety days, a period which has expired, and then only if there is an appeal.) This said, however, Tunisia states that it would still like to work out its differences and asks the chair to bring the two parties together to

[44] "Treaty on Free Trade and Preferential Trade Practices Between the Republics of Panama and Costa Rica." World Integrated Trade Solution. 1993. https://wits.worldbank.org/GPTAD/PDF/archive/CostaRica-Panama.pdf

discuss either the merits of the case or to agree on an ad hoc appeal procedure, since there is not an Appellate Body in place.

Morocco states that it remains open to continuing consultations "with the mediation of the Secretariat and the DSB chair in order to reach an agreement or understanding on this matter in the light of the paralysis of the Appellate Body." The chair says that he will contact the parties to this dispute as soon as possible. The DSB takes note of the statements.

There ensues a discussion of the broader issue of the practice whereby a party files an appeal but there is no functioning Appellate Body to hear the appeal. There is no body within the WTO that has ruled on whether the panel report is thus stayed by an "appeal" in these circumstances. All members act on the assumption that the appeal will be warehoused for the time when an AB might be reconstituted and could render a final determination in a case. This practice, known to all informally as an "appeal into the void," is criticized but has been largely accepted by members.

The representative of the Russian Federation takes the floor to state Russia's continuing opposition to the practice of appealing into the void, where WTO members continue to file appeals, although there was no Appellate Body functioning, which leaves cases unresolved. (Russia has however utilized this off-ramp into limbo.)

The representative of Canada observes that "since 11 December 2019, the Appellate Body had no longer operated in practice. ... No Member should seek to derive an unfair advantage from the current impasse ... the absence of an operational Appellate Body." Canada therefore suggests that the parties might make use of the Multi-Party Interim Appeal Arbitration Arrangement (MPIA) to complete the appeal process.[45]

The last item on the agenda, at the request of Mexico, is a proposal by 121 members to launch the selection process for filling the vacancies on the Appellate Body. The proposal lists the vacancies and the dates on which they occurred. The Mexican representative notes that when two of the last three AB members' terms expired on December 10, 2019, the AB ceased to function (although the last AB member Ms. Hong Zhao's term continued notionally until November 30, 2020).

Twenty delegations take the floor to make statements in support of the proposal to launch the AB member selection process.

[45] MPIA is a separate agreement among some twenty parties, including the EU and China, providing for a mechanism among signatories that resembles the AB, and to which they have agreed that any case in which two MPIA signatories are the disputants, the MPIA roster of arbitrators will render an appellate verdict.

This is not a new proposal. The representative of the European Union states that it has consistently noted its position that "WTO Members had a shared responsibility to resolve this issue as soon as possible, and to fill the outstanding vacancies." The European Union agrees "that meaningful reforms were needed in order to achieve that objective."

The representative of Canada states that it would appreciate it if the United States would commit "to discussions aimed at finding solutions regarding the functioning of the Appellate Body," and in the meantime reiterates an invitation to those who have not yet joined the twenty-six-member MPIA to do so. China joins Canada in suggesting that members join the MPIA.

The representative of Turkey underlines the importance "to safeguard the two-stage character and the binding nature of the dispute settlement system."

The representative of the United States takes the floor to state that the United States is not in a position to support the proposed decision. The effect of this statement under the positive consensus rule is that the proposal presented by the 121 countries cannot be adopted. The US representative states that "the United States had raised and explained its systemic concerns for more than 16 years and across multiple US Administrations. The United States believed that Members had to undertake fundamental reform if the system was to remain viable and credible."

Concluding the discussion on this item, the representative of Mexico, speaking on behalf of the 121 co-sponsors, regrets "that for the forty-fifth occasion, Members had still not been able to start the selection processes for the vacancies in the Appellate Body." He states that the United States has "no legal justification for the current blocking of the selection processes and had thus continuously failed to fulfil [its] duties" as a member of the WTO.

In closing the session, the chair states that this matter requires political engagement on the part of all WTO members, and he hopes that members would be able to find a solution and common ground on this matter as soon as possible. He further says that all statements made are noted.

EVALUATION OF THE DSB

This meeting highlights the attempts of sovereign nations to resolve their disputes using panels composed of three individuals chosen for their trade expertise, and when it was functioning, an appeal to an independent division of three Appellate Body members. It comes at a time when one major member, in the absence of significant reforms, remains at odds with perhaps all of the other members on preserving the structure put into place by the Dispute Settlement Understanding that was agreed to in the 1990s in the

Uruguay Round. It is unlikely that any member other than the United States, and perhaps even the United States only with the particular administration that was in office in Washington in 2019, would have deployed its veto to this extent. Members had used their ability to block consensus to limit what agreements could be struck. The EU used its veto to try to link timing and the selection of AB members. No other member had used the veto to end one of the major pieces of the institutional structure of the WTO.

This was resort to a nuclear option, exercising a procedural right that causes institutional damage. The United States could, in its defense, say that the institutional damage was caused by the Appellate Body exceeding its mandate through overreach, altering the rights and obligations of the members, and that it, not the United States, was at fault for the systemic failure of dispute settlement.

What is apparent from sitting in on this DSB meeting, one of the hundreds that have been held since the WTO was founded, is that the DSB, as constructed, with its so-called negative consensus veto in place, has almost no function with respect to shaping the jurisprudence of WTO dispute settlement. It allows some airing of views but can take no decisions that would affect substantive outcomes. The negative consensus is in the views of many distinguished commentators an essential element of the WTO dispute settlement system.[46] It makes decisions binding, a step-function above what the GATT provided. No one has come up with a satisfactory alternative way of making dispute settlement binding. They are generally content, it appears, to leave in place the fiction that the DSB is making the ultimate decision as to whether a panel report stands or fails to be adopted.

The WTO was, as it turned out, an unintended experiment in having a system of governance that had no executive and no effective legislative function, combined with an unrestrained and active judicial function. The flaws built into the system have not been overcome to date.

For those critical of WTO dispute settlement, the fault does not lie so much with the DSB but with the institutional framework as a whole. In this context, one of no effective checks and balances, the Appellate Body never found a case that it could not address, and never found a gap in the rules it could not fill. All of this was done without admitting, perhaps even to itself, that this was what was occurring.[47] Although the AB never admitted that it was creating

46 Bernard Hoekman and Petros C. Mavroidis. 2020. "To AB or Not to AB? Dispute Settlement in WTO Reform." *Journal of International Economic Law* 23(3): 1–20.

47 John H. Jackson. 2000. "The Role and Effectiveness of the WTO Dispute Settlement Mechanism." *Brookings Trade Forum*: 179–236. "The dispute settlement system cannot and

rules, it never referred a matter back to the members to decide. The self-restraint, if there was to be any, had to come from members, from parties to the litigation. For example, in 1996, the United States and the European Union withdrew a national security matter from decision through litigation and decided to work out the matter bilaterally.[48] They realized that it would be unacceptable and a dangerous intrusion affecting their sovereignty to have a quasi-judicial panel define what was in their essential security interests and when that exception to the rules could be invoked.

That degree of self-restraint that the AB needed to apply was not shown as repeated interpretations were made by the AB that one major member, the United States, went beyond the WTO's substantive rules when it came to imposing measures to protect injured domestic industries. A delicate balance in the rules – the price for broad trade liberalization being a degree of freedom to accord selective relief in carefully defined circumstances – was disturbed and could not be put right in recent years. A steam engine has a governor that vents excess pressure to keep the boiler intact. There was no governing device, no escape clause (as the permission to use safeguards was once called) to reduce the pressure on the system of more open trade. The apolitical, independent "quasi-judicial" (only "quasi" because panels were just notionally advisors to the DSB composed of the members) glued the governor down in a largely closed position. And when populism gained ground in the founding member, the system gave out. The following US administration, which centers its trade policy on worker welfare – workers defined first and foremost as producers and not consumers – will not readily allow a return to the old regime as it was. That is why the calls for getting the AB nomination process back underway without other reforms are wholly unrealistic.

The DSB provides transparency and an opportunity for interested parties to learn about matters in which they may wish to choose to intervene. It allows focus, through litigants' statements, on what is taking place in all disputes where parties have been unable to agree to an outcome. It puts pressure through sunshine – through discussion in a committee of the whole – on parties to adhere to their obligations, at least when there was a fully operating dispute settlement system. The practice of "appealing into the void" deprives the operation of the DSB of having that effect because any member losing a

should not bear the weight of formulating new rules either by filling gaps in the existing agreements."

48 "DS38: United States – The Cuban Liberty and Democratic Solidarity Act." World Trade Organization. www.wto.org/english/tratop_e/dispu_e/cases_e/ds38_e.htm. Under the Helms–Burton Act, the United States applied sanctions to firms from its other trading partners that dealt with Cuba.

panel can choose to answer that it is appealing the matter, although no appeal is possible.

Sitting in on one DSB meeting gives a snapshot, a view into the flow of international trade relations in a multilateral setting, to the same degree as sitting in on a Ministerial Conference or a General Council meeting. It gives a view of what will always be a work in progress, of international trade relations at a moment in time. There is no way of telling whether a given dispute will be settled in the future, or whether the start of a negotiation will result in a successful conclusion. What we know is that the mechanisms are imperfect, but they are a major improvement on what existed previously or the conditions for world trade that would exist in their absence. Perfecting them is a permanent challenge.

ACCESSIONS

Countries accounting for over one-fifth of the world's population and over one-seventh of world trade (measured by exports) joined the WTO after it was founded. These acceding countries negotiated their entry in each case with those who were already members. This is the story of their accession process.

Accessions is one of the most interesting parts of the WTO. It is at the cutting edge of countries' integration into the world economy. It is also a vibrant area of negotiation of new commitments. It is where reform takes place in the trading system and is not just talked about. The domestic policy and trade reforms undertaken by acceding members are designed to be virtually irreversible. It is like having a series of interviews for graduate school and the defense of a doctoral dissertation combined. New members are welcomed into the system following a negotiation with every interested existing member, answering hundreds of questions, and getting through an arduous and detailed working party process. This is a one-time series of hurdles to be cleared. There is no provision in the WTO for expulsion, annulment, or divorce. Outside of dispute settlement cases, each of which is focused narrowly on the particular measure that is being examined, there is no effective second look as to whether a member has undertaken obligations equal to its capacity, or beyond it. Trade Policy Reviews (TPRs) do not make this type of evaluation. TPRs describe a country's trade regime and performance. As a result, absent new agreements or a major new round of trade-liberalizing negotiations (and none is being contemplated), the commitments undertaken by a WTO member, the market access it accords, are what they were on the day of their accession, or for those original members which were GATT contracting parties, the state of their obligations as of the end of the Uruguay Round.

Thirty-six countries have joined since the WTO was founded in 1995, and another two dozen are in the queue seeking entry. For each acceding country, the process is momentous, and in some cases for the trading system itself. Countries choose to join for a variety of reasons. In all cases, it is to integrate further into the global economy to promote domestic economic growth. For the conflict-affected, it is to have greater stability and through this means, a better chance of living at peace. Integration into the global economy is not a guarantee of peace – there are too many examples to the contrary, the most recent being between Russia and Ukraine. Accession is also not a complete safeguard against domestic unrest – such as in Ethiopia or Afghanistan. But for Sudan, South Sudan, Timor-Leste, and a not inconsiderable number of others, WTO accession holds out the hope for undergirding nascent peace.[49] Among the benefits of accession for all are institution-building, broad economic reforms, and marketization (for post-Soviet countries such as Uzbekistan and Turkmenistan).

The legal port of entry into the WTO is Article XII of the WTO Marrakech Agreement. It is a very brief and unrevealing provision, merely stating that "any State or separate customs territory possessing full autonomy in the conduct of its external commercial relations and of the other matters provided for in this Agreement and the Multilateral Trade Agreements may accede to this Agreement, on terms to be agreed between it and the WTO." The deciding body for accessions is the Ministerial Conference consisting of all 164 members, which is to approve the terms as agreed by a two-thirds majority vote. This provision is deceptive in that, as a matter of deeply imbedded practice, all decisions are taken by consensus. Voting does not take place at the WTO. Given consensus decision making, a single member can prevent the entry into the WTO of any applicant. For this reason, a country engaging in hostilities or having internal strife that is the subject of criticism by any other member(s) will not move forward toward being permitted, or even to begin to negotiate its accession. Currently Belarus and Iran, for example, are in this position.

An unwritten principle of the WTO is universality.[50] The WTO is about having a single set of global rules. All trade flows under its rules, even under preferential trade agreements. The multilateral trading system was built to accommodate and foster globalization, a term not much in vogue in the 1940s

[49] "DDG Wolff: Trade and Peace are Intimately Related." World Trade Organization, June 16, 2020. www.wto.org/english/news_e/news20_e/ddgaw_16jun20_e.htm

[50] This is not a contradiction of the fact that circumstances may delay an individual country's entry into the WTO. There is no permanence to exclusion.

when the post-Second World War organization of the world economy was being considered, but was implicit, at least in an incipient form, in the Atlantic Charter, with equal trading opportunities promised to all who eschew aggression. In 2014, Chiedu Osakwe, then-Director in charge of the Accessions Division, writing with Uri Dadush, saw accessions as supporting "the increased prevalence, complexity, and capillarity of international exchange" which "increased the need for a universal system of trade rules."[51] At that time, members accounting for 20 percent of world trade were "Article XII" members, new entrants that had paid a price for entry into the WTO after the Organization was founded in 1995. In many cases, these applicant countries transformed their economies through far-reaching economic reforms in order to qualify for membership. In 2014, the average time to accede, from the formation of a working party to the vote on accession, was twenty years. In the intervening years since Osakwe wrote, seeing only another four countries join the WTO through the time of this book (2022), that the average time for negotiating entry into the WTO has remained lengthy.

To be clear, the length of accessions is all too often prolonged by domestic political events, such as the election of a pro-isolationist, anti-trade regime or domestic unrest. National priorities change over time. These events, having nothing to do with the requirements for accession, can and often do stall the accession process for years, even decades. Completing the process heavily depends on domestic political will in the applicant country.

For an organization aimed at universality, there are aspects of it that resemble joining an exclusive social club. Any of the WTO's 164 members can show up at a working party meeting and ask a question about the applicant's laws, policies, measures, and intentions. Each question needs to be answered, often requiring the applicant to substantiate its response with specific domestic legislation and/or trade data. I have been in a working party meeting where a representative of a small African country asked of a Latin American applicant's delegation from an even smaller economy an abstruse question about one of its investment laws. No one questioned the right to ask the question or the need for a response. For the most part, the guardians of the accession process are the United States and the European Union. They each have the resources to review all the materials submitted and the capability to ask penetrating questions. They are investing in the global trading system through preparations they make for each meeting. Other than their participation, it is often the case that neighboring countries join a meeting to make

[51] Uri Dadush and Chiedu Osakwe eds. 2015. *WTO Accessions and Trade Multilateralism, Case Studies and Lessons from the WTO at Twenty*. Cambridge: Cambridge University Press.

positive statements in favor of accession, or nail down a point or two that they would know about from their extensive trade with the acceding country.

Accession negotiations address questions about practices that were of little or no concern when the WTO was created. Each negotiation builds on the last, ratcheting up expectations for the accession commitments that will be adopted by future candidates. In addition, members' economic interests evolve as the world of commerce changes. Article XII members therefore have obligations that original members do not have. Dadush and Osakwe state that the average bound rate for original members is 45.5 percent, compared with 13.8 percent for new members (although average applied rates for both new and old members are much closer). New members have bound twice as many service sectors as the original WTO members.

Article XII members are well aware that they bear more in the way of obligations than the original members. They complain of it. However, there is no prospect for a renewal of vows on the part of prior members. There is no renegotiation for the terms of membership for existing members that would restore balance to the system. Absent a major new round of negotiations, and that is not even a remote gleam in members' eyes at present, there is no truing up in prospect, no equalization of rights and obligations, except with respect to any new agreements reached. Absent new agreements, for the original members, relationships are frozen in whatever state they were during the 1980s, as in the story of the Sleeping Beauty, where every member of the court was frozen in position. This is the case at the WTO for existing members, at least insofar as their obligations are concerned. Measured by trade, trading relationships have altered dramatically since that time. It is the trading obligations that have not evolved.

The chief negotiators for acceding countries are of necessity more conversant with the WTO's rules than the best of scholars. It is said that one of the lead negotiators for China's accession can recite the entire GATT by memory. The chief negotiators also get to know their own economy in much greater detail. In my visits to capitals I saw first-hand that national accession negotiating teams had to bridge the silos that existed among the different departments of their own governments – finance ministries, customs ministries, tax authorities, customs officials, and industrial and agricultural bureaucratic fiefdoms. The process of accession causes interministerial coordination to a greater degree than had previously been the case.

The negotiators of acceding and recently acceded countries are very often the best advertisements for the importance of the WTO to the world economy. Dadush and Osakwe quote the negotiators for the accession of Cambodia and Lao PDR, who point to trade-led economic development and movement toward a market economy as essential if the full advantages of trade are to be obtained from the trading system. WTO accession is a means by which the vision of Roosevelt and Churchill at Argentia Bay in 1941 is being realized – "to further the enjoyment by all states, great or small, victor or vanquished, of access, on equal terms, to the trade and to the raw materials of the world which are needed for their economic prosperity." To see how the accession negotiations anticipate issues that may arise in world trade, one need not look beyond the accession protocols of Ukraine and Russia, the first confirming guaranteed freedom for energy and the latter bringing into the WTO obligations on the pricing of energy in accordance with normal commercial considerations. Issues of strategic and geopolitical importance are addressed in the accession process. They cannot, however, overcome later exigencies.

The first step on the road to accession is often to request observer status (Turkmenistan most recently), providing the applicant with a wide range of experiences of what is entailed in being a member.

> *Governments wishing to request observer status in the General Council shall address to that body a communication expressing the intent to initiate negotiations for accession to the WTO Agreement within a maximum period of five years, and provide a description of their current economic and trade policies, as well as any intended future reforms of these policies.*

The next step after an observer application is filed is the formation of a working party which will meet to examine the applicant's submission of a Memorandum of Foreign Trade Regime (MFTR).[52] This document consists of a snapshot of the country's domestic economic regime, as well as statistical data on its economy, including its trade. It forms one important basis for Q&As that will kickstart the negotiations. The MFTR for the Russian Federation was originally submitted based on 1993 data. The document runs to forty pages of text with a like number of annexes consisting of tables. The first sentences set out the context for the desire for accession:

> *The transition of the Russian economy from central planning to market principles has been a significant historic event in the final decade of the twentieth century. Starting in November 1991, radical reforms have been made to the economic structure of the Russian Federation with the aim of transforming the economy into a market economy and promoting the full integration of Russia into the international trading system.*

[52] "Accession to the World Trade Organization: Procedures for Negotiations Under Article XII – Note by the Secretariat WT/ACC/22/Rev.1." World Trade Organization. April 5, 2016. https://docs.wto.org/dol2fe/Pages/SS/directdoc.aspx?filename=q:/WT/ACC/22R1.pdf&Open=True

The submission from the Russian Federation goes on to explain the importance of the development of the foreign trade sector, based upon integration into the international trading system, listing Russia's tariffs and import and export regulations.[53]

The next phase of the accession process is for the Secretariat to prepare a written summary of points raised, together with the answers supplied by the applicant country. The Working Party continues its discussions with the applicant and, more or less in parallel, interested WTO members engage in negotiations with the applicant on trade matters of particular commercial interest to them, including bilateral market access commitments with respect to goods and services.

The WTO Handbook on Accessions describes the negotiating procedures in the following terms:

> *Negotiations on terms of accession take place in four main parts: multilateral negotiations in the Working Party on the rules to be accepted; plurilateral negotiations among interested parties on agricultural domestic support and export subsidies (which sometimes also deal with SPS and TBT); bilateral negotiations between interested parties on concessions on goods; and bilateral negotiations between interested parties on specific commitments on services.*[54]

The series of negotiations allows the existing members to make the price of entry sufficiently high to compensate for the fact that the applicant is to benefit from all prior concessions granted by and to members on an MFN basis.

Perhaps the most important part of accession consists of the domestic policy reforms put into place by the applicant. A flavor of this dramatic and important process is captured in the remarks of Ethiopia's chief negotiator, Mamu Mihretu, to the fourth session of the Working Party for Ethiopia's accession:

> *Ethiopia has now embarked on a wide-ranging home-grown economic reform agenda. Among the key priorities of this economic reform agenda are:*

- *First, strengthening public-sector finance and reform of state-owned enterprises,*
- *Second, addressing foreign exchange shortages,*
- *Third, improving financial sector stability,*

[53] "Accession of the Russian Federation: Memorandum on the Foreign Trade Regime L/7410." General Agreement on Tariffs and Trade. March 1, 1994. https://docs.wto.org/dol2fe/Pages/SS/directdoc.aspx?filename=Q:/GG/L7599/7410.pdf&Open=True

[54] "The Accession Process – The Procedures and How They Have Been Applied." World Trade Organization. www.wto.org/english/thewto_e/acc_e/cbt_course_e/c4s6p1_e.htm

- *Fourth, structural reforms including improving the investment climate, and*
- *Fifth, sectoral reforms including in mining, agriculture, manufacturing and services.*[55]

For the world trading system, due to the size of its population and territory, no accession has been more important than that of China in 2001. It could not have happened without far-reaching domestic economic reforms. Chinese scholars have observed in an article about reducing the role of state-owned enterprises in the Chinese economy that "the major incentive for the Chinese government to join the WTO is to promote economic reforms through overcoming domestic obstacles."[56] The relationship between domestic reforms and the application of WTO rules was emphasized by Lu Xiankun, counselor to the Chinese Mission in Geneva: "Since 2001 [the year of the accession of China to the WTO], China's reform and opening-up process has entered a new era of continuously locking in reforms and pursuing further negotiations."

The best way to understand the accession process is to be present for the give and take in the Working Party, as recorded in the report that it issues. The Working Party on China's accession to the WTO met twenty times over a period of fourteen and a half years in order to arrive at the point where members could decide favorably on China's application for membership. In July 2000, China's chief negotiator, Long Yongtu, noted in a press interview that China had by then concluded bilateral agreements with thirty-five out of the thirty-seven WTO members that had expressed an interest in having a bilateral solution to issues upon entry, with only the Mexico and Switzerland talks to be concluded.[57] The bilateral negotiations may have been the easier part. The results of the multilateral accession talks with respect to how China would apply the WTO's rules were complicated. They are contained in two documents: a draft Working Party Report and a draft Protocol of Accession.

55 "Working Party on the Accession of Ethiopia, 4th Meeting: Statement by Mr. Mamo Mihretu, Chief Trade Negotiator for the Federal Democratic Republic of Ethiopia." World Trade Organization. January 30, 2020. www.wto.org/english/news_e/news20_e/acc_eth_31jan20_e.pdf; "Ethiopia's Homegrown Economic Reform Plan: Mamo E. Mihretu." Graduate Institute of International and Development Studies. January 29, 2020. www.graduateinstitute.ch/communications/events/ethiopias-homegrown-economic-reform-plan; "WTO Accessions Newsletter No. 98." World Trade Organization. January/February 2020. www.wto.org/english/thewto_e/acc_e/nl_e/2020_01_acc_newsletter_e.pdf

56 Ye Tian and Min Xia. 2017. "WTO, Credible Commitments, and China's Reform of State-Owned Enterprises." *Economic and Political Studies* 5(2): 158–178.

57 "China's Accession to the WTO in the Last Lap." Third World Network. July 28, 2000. www.twn.my/title/lap.htm

The final Working Party Report captures the interests of the parties without naming the ones raising a question, using diplomatic indirection by referring to "some Members."[58] The introduction states China's basic premise for joining: "China's consistent efforts to resume its status as a Contracting Party to GATT and accession to the WTO Agreement were in line with its objective of economic reform to establish a socialist market economy as well as its basic national policy of opening to the outside world." What this "socialist market economy" would become, no one at the time could fully grasp. China at the time was far from being the world's largest manufacturer and exporter of goods, accounting for only 3.4 percent of world exports of goods in 1998, achieving two decades later a global share of 14.7 percent (in 2020).[59]

The report reads as if it were describing a long volley in a game of tennis, or a celebrant and congregation in a religious service. It consists of an important choreographed series of exchanges that span 164 pages of text – a statement of members' concerns followed by the formal recording of the commitments made by China. The first of these sounds like a secular catechism in the temple of the multilateral trading system. It is about non-discrimination:

> *The representative of China confirmed that, consistent with China's rights and obligations under the WTO Agreement and the Draft Protocol, China would provide non-discriminatory treatment to all WTO Members, including Members of the WTO that were separate customs territories.*
>
> - *The Working Party took note of this commitment.*

There follows a recorded exchange on the second founding principle of the multilateral trading system, national treatment. This reads in part:

- *Some members of the Working Party drew China's attention to the variety of types of requirements which could contravene Article III of the GATT 1994. Specific reference was made to the procedures, charges and conditions for granting of business licences, whether to import, distribute, re-sell or retail goods of non-Chinese origin. Reference was also made to taxes and fiscal provisions whose impact depended, directly or indirectly, upon the Chinese or non-Chinese origin of the goods*

58 "Report of the Working Party on the Accession of China WT/ACC/CHN/49." World Trade Organization. October 1, 2001. https://docs.wto.org/dol2fe/Pages/SS/directdoc.aspx?filename=Q:/WT/ACC/CHN49.pdf&Open=True

59 Alessandro Nicita and Carlos Razo. 2021. "China: The Rise of a Trade Titan." United Nations Conference on Trade and Development. April 27. www.unctad.org/news/china-rise-trade-titan; "Report of the Working Party on the Accession of China WT/ACC/CHN/49." World Trade Organization. October 1, 2001. https://docs.wto.org/dol2fe/Pages/SS/directdoc.aspx?filename=Q:/WT/ACC/CHN49.pdf&Open=True. Para. 7.

imported or traded. Those members drew the attention of China to its obligation to ensure that product testing and certification requirements, including procedures for in situ inspections, posed no greater burden – whether financial or practical – on goods of non-Chinese origin than on domestic goods. Those members underlined that conformity assessment procedures and standards, including safety and other compliance requirements, had to respect the terms of the WTO Agreement on Technical Barriers to Trade ("TBT Agreement") as well as Article III of the GATT 1994.

- *The representative of China confirmed that the full respect of all laws, regulations and administrative requirements with the principle of non-discrimination between domestically produced and imported products would be ensured and enforced by the date of China's accession unless otherwise provided in the Draft Protocol or Report. The representative of China declared that, by accession, China would repeal and cease to apply all such existing laws, regulations and other measures whose effect was inconsistent with WTO rules on national treatment. This commitment was made in relation to final or interim laws, administrative measures, rules and notices, or any other form of stipulation or guideline.*
    - *The Working Party took note of these commitments.*

The text continues through balance of payments measures and investment regimes, until the report arrives at the equally important subject of state-owned and state-invested enterprises.

- *In light of the role that state-owned and state-invested enterprises played in China's economy, some members of the Working Party expressed concerns about the continuing governmental influence and guidance of the decisions and activities of such enterprises relating to the purchase and sale of goods and services.*
- *The representative of China further confirmed that China would ensure that all state-owned and state-invested enterprises would make purchases and sales based solely on commercial considerations, e.g., price, quality, marketability and availability, and that the enterprises of other WTO Members would have an adequate opportunity to compete for sales to and purchases from these enterprises on non-discriminatory terms and conditions. In addition, the Government of China would not influence, directly or indirectly, commercial decisions on the part of state-owned or state-invested enterprises, including on the quantity, value or country of origin of any goods purchased or sold, except in a manner consistent with the WTO Agreement.*
    - *The Working Party took note of these commitments.*

The Working Party Report sounds very current in places, as the concerns twenty years after China's accession are still being voiced:

- *Certain members of the Working Party expressed concern about laws, regulations and measures in China affecting the transfer of technology, in particular in the context of investment decisions. Moreover, these members expressed concern about measures conditioning the receipt of benefits, including investment approvals, upon technology transfer. In their view, the terms and conditions of technology transfer, particularly in the context of an investment, should be agreed between the parties to the investment without government interference. The government should not, for example, condition investment approval upon technology transfer.*
- *The representative of China confirmed that China would only impose, apply or enforce laws, regulations or measures relating to the transfer of technology, production processes, or other proprietary knowledge to an individual or enterprise in its territory that were not inconsistent with the WTO Agreement on Trade-Related Aspects of Intellectual Property Rights ("TRIPS Agreement") and the Agreement on Trade-Related Investment Measures ("TRIMs Agreement"). He confirmed that the terms and conditions of technology transfer, production processes or other proprietary knowledge, particularly in the context of an investment, would only require agreement between the parties to the investment.*
    - *The Working Party took note of these commitments.*

The Working Party continues in this manner through almost innumerable subjects in great detail, with China making approximately 100 specific commitments, until it gets to the end, at paragraph 342. It then states that the Working Party "took note of the explanations and statements of China concerning its foreign trade regime, as reflected in this Report" and "took note of the commitments given by China in relation to certain specific matters which are reproduced in [listed] paragraphs." These commitments were then incorporated in the Draft Protocol of Accession. Then comes the conclusion: "[I]n the light of the explanations, commitments and concessions made by China, the Working Party reached the conclusion that China should be invited to accede to the Marrakesh Agreement Establishing the WTO under the provisions of Article XII." This is perhaps the single most important sentence in the relatively short history of the WTO.

China joined the WTO as a self-designated developing country and has vigorously maintained its position up to and including the present that it has a right to do so. That being said, in its accession, China took on more obligations than developing countries generally do. It bound its maximum level of aggregate measure of support for agricultural products at a more restrictive level than do developing countries generally, with a *de minimis* level (which excludes domestic support from disciplines under the Agreement on Agriculture) set at 8.5 percent instead of 10 percent. It did not claim a transition period to put into effect its TRIPS obligations. It bound its tariffs at close to applied rates, and it accepted for a transitional period additional trade remedy mechanisms that could be deployed against its exports, for twelve years with respect to safeguard actions and fifteen years with respect to antidumping measures. In 2020, its weighted average applied tariff, according to the World Bank, was 2.47 percent, a fraction of its bound tariff rates.[60]

The accession of China was one of the most important milestones of the WTO in its twenty-six-year history. For China, accession helped lift hundreds of millions of its people out of poverty. Accession contributed to the transformation of its domestic economy – not in every respect, not complete, but nevertheless very extensive. Xiankun Lu notes that China modified over 3,000 domestic laws and regulations at the central government level and reviewed many tens of thousands at the regional level in order to put China in a position to join the WTO.

All accessions are highly intensive processes. The amount of time taken to accede varies from country to country, but all take years. The pace is most often determined by the willingness of the acceding country to make the necessary changes to assure that market forces will determine competitive outcomes, that trade and investment will not be determined by government fiat. Accessions are a bright spot in international trade relations. Integration into the global economy through WTO accession and accompanying domestic economic reforms invariably leads to faster economic growth, improving the lives of individuals – the people of the acceding country – and contributes to global economic growth.

60 "Tariff Rate, Applied, Weighted Mean, All Products (%) – China." The World Bank – Data. https://data.worldbank.org/indicator/TM.TAX.MRCH.WM.AR.ZS?locations=CN

PART IV

Major Substantive Topics

7

Dispute Settlement at the WTO

The Dispute Settlement Understanding (DSU) was one of the chief results of the Uruguay Round. Dispute settlement under the GATT had not been binding. Adoption of panel reports could be, and too often was, blocked by the losing party. All of the major trading members wanted dispute settlement to be binding, that is to have definitive results. They carefully constructed a complex system to remedy past defects. It had internal inconsistencies that only became apparent over time.

THE INSTITUTIONAL SETTING

There are three basic functions of a global trade organization: negotiation, administration of the rules, and dispute settlement. In putting together the WTO, little attention was paid to providing a structure for the negotiation of future rules, although there were a few specific mandates of continuing negotiations – such as under the Agreement on Agriculture (AoA) and the General Agreement on Trade in Services (GATS). Presumably rule-making would proceed as it always had, with momentum gathering until a new round was called into being. Still less attention was paid to administrative support to be provided by the new WTO Secretariat. Serious attention was paid, however, to the institutional structure for making dispute settlement binding, through the adoption of the Dispute Settlement Understanding.

In the DSU, the negotiators created three main elements for the resolution of disputes: the Dispute Settlement Body (DSB), the panel process (similar to the role of GATT panels), and a new Appellate Body (AB). Through these means, the rules of the multilateral trading system were to be made enforceable. If a case were brought by one WTO member against another, it would definitely be heard, and a report would definitely be issued by a panel. It would indicate whether the measure in question was inconsistent with that member's obligations. A newly constituted seven-person Appellate Body would be available to correct panel errors on appeal, and if voluntary corrective action was not taken by a party found to have violated the rules, there would ultimately be consequences designed to bring about compliance with panel and AB determinations. A detailed timeline was established to bring a matter from its inception, from the moment of asking for consultations, to obtaining a result.

THE NEED FOR BINDING DISPUTE SETTLEMENT

The rule of law was to substitute for the rule of unconstrained national power. Absent rules being applied, restrictive trade measures would be answered by restrictive trade measures, in what could become a downward spiral for the welfare of nations and their peoples. Binding dispute settlement does not always deliver the most just or correct result, although on average it is likely to do so if it is well-administered. What it is designed to deliver is finality. It is a means for moving on, past a dispute.

The DSU states that "the dispute settlement system of the WTO is a central element in providing security and predictability to the multilateral trading system."[1] Knowing the rules, having the rules enforced, nation-states would find a means of cooperating with each other to provide a stable framework for the international exchange of goods and services among them. For a quarter-century, the system provided that agreed framework.

Binding dispute settlement was deemed by many participants in the Uruguay Round negotiations, and by commentators ever since, to be one of the Round's most noteworthy achievements. One of the least satisfactory characteristics of the GATT had been that dispute settlement could not reliably deliver results. GATT panels could be blocked by the losing party, leaving a panel's determination in a legal limbo, not requiring further action to repair the alleged breach. This is not to say that panel reports were largely ignored in the prior GATT era. Countries generally keep their word and live up to their undertakings in international agreements. But often enough in important cases where a losing party found the result not to its liking, it felt no urgency to bring its measures into compliance, or perhaps it simply was not in a domestic political setting where it was able to do so.

Binding WTO dispute settlement was sought by Japan, the EU, and many others to curb unilateralism (during the Uruguay Round seen to be very much

[1] DSU Art. 3.2.

a US practice), to be assured that members would comply with the rules. The United States shared the same goal for different reasons: It thought that obtaining binding WTO dispute settlement could be an important tool to rein in the adverse effects of the EU's Common Agricultural Policy (CAP).

By being binding, the results of dispute settlement would be definitive in determining the rights and obligations of the parties. It also meant that there would be consequences for acting contrary to the rules. What it did not mean is that a panel or AB decision would, like the decisions of the European Court of Justice for EU member states, have direct effect within the territories of WTO members. Decisions of panels and the Appellate Body would never, in most if not all countries, be implemented automatically. A member would have a period of time to implement the decision that was rendered, often requiring legislative or regulatory changes, or face the need to pay trade compensation, or face trade retaliation.

The importance of dispute settlement as it was envisaged to work in the DSU was that it would deliver enforceability of the WTO's agreements, a hallmark of the new trade organization, distinguishing it from other international organizations and agreements.

THE STRUCTURE OF WTO DISPUTE SETTLEMENT

The members retained for themselves the authority for making official interpretations of the rules. There was to be no Supreme Court, or for that matter, subsidiary courts. Article IX.2 of the Marrakesh Agreement provides that: "The Ministerial Conference and the General Council shall have the exclusive authority to adopt interpretations of this Agreement and of the Multilateral Trade Agreements." Despite this provision, neither the Ministerial Conference nor the General Council performed this role. This has been due to the fact that WTO members would need to be able to form a consensus in order to engage in rule-making. As the WTO's legislative function did not operate, the default became litigation. Absent ministers and the Council acting, the DSU sought to transfer the authority for making interpretations of the rules to the Dispute Settlement Body through its notional power to approve or disapprove the results of litigation. The members would not have given up their responsibilities as the DSB was still a meeting of members. This second default option, however, the transfer of the job of interpreting WTO Agreements, also failed. In the end, the panels, and where there was an appeal (which became commonplace), the AB would make the final determinations of what the rules meant.

To understand why this happened, a closer look at the DSB is in order.

THE DISPUTE SETTLEMENT BODY (DSB)

The central organ for administering the DSU was to be the DSB. On paper, it was given the power to make all final decisions on the consistency of measures with the WTO Agreements and whether compliance was being achieved. The DSB was to be at the pinnacle of the WTO dispute settlement system.

The DSB was to be the sun in a Copernican solar system.

> *The Dispute Settlement Body is hereby established to administer these rules and procedures and, except as otherwise provided in a covered agreement, the consultation and dispute settlement provisions of the covered agreements. Accordingly, the DSB shall have the authority to establish panels, adopt panel and Appellate Body reports, maintain surveillance of implementation of rulings and recommendations, and authorize suspension of concessions and other obligations under the covered agreements.*[2]

The Dispute Settlement Body is ranked just below the General Council in its importance within the WTO. It has, in fact, the same composition as the General Council, but meets in an alternative format with its own chair and set of procedures. It is composed of the entire membership, although because of the narrower focus of its institutional responsibilities and its more limited authority, the DSB does not attract a full turnout of the members at the Head of Delegation level at every meeting. It is a standing assumption of the WTO's members that the DSB chair, after one year of service in that role, will become the chair of the General Council.

The DSB was to be the final authority on what the rules meant (unless the members meeting as the Council or in a Ministerial Conference decided otherwise) and what the consequences would be for noncompliance. It was to be the final arbiter of the balance to be maintained under the negotiated agreements that formed the body of international trade law.

The role of the panels and the Appellate Body was, under the terms of the DSU, to be advisory to the DSB. Neither the panels nor the AB were expected to function fully as courts; they were not to make final judgments. That was the function of the DSB:

> *The function of panels is to assist the DSB in discharging its responsibilities under this Understanding and the covered agreements. Accordingly, a panel should … make such other findings as will assist the DSB in making the recommendations or in giving the rulings provided for in the covered*

[2] DSU Art. 2.1.

> *agreements. Panels should consult regularly with the parties to the dispute and give them adequate opportunity to develop a mutually satisfactory solution.*[3]

Two things stand out in this quoted language: that the purpose of the panels was supportive of the DSB and that their mission was to compose differences, to help settle disputes, not to make law. As for the Appellate Body, it was there to correct errors. It was to "uphold, modify or reverse the legal findings and conclusions of the panel."[4] The institutional framework in the DSU gives the DSB the final decision as to whether there is a violation of an agreement and what is to be done about it. Panel and AB decisions would have no effect at all unless adopted by the DSB, that is, by the members.

Why this did not happen can be attributed to an internal inconsistency in the DSU arising from the recognized need to avoid a repeat of the GATT era when disagreeable findings might be blocked by a recalcitrant member, unwilling to join a consensus to condemn itself. The system had to ensure that the dispute settlement process was not only binding, but independent. It was not enough to stipulate that "panel members should be selected with a view to ensuring the independence" and that the AB was to be comprised of "persons of recognized authority, with demonstrated expertise in law, international trade and the subject matter of the covered agreements generally... unaffiliated with any government."[5] However careful the process was in ensuring independent panel and AB members, if, as in the GATT, matters would be decided by a positive consensus when they were put to the WTO's members for decision, a recalcitrant party to a dispute could block its adoption. The noncompliant would then be determining the shape of the trading system. The answer found by the drafters of the DSU to prevent this was to have the DSB operate by "negative consensus," a somewhat counter-intuitive term.

> *Within 60 days after the date of circulation of a panel report to the Members, <u>the report shall be adopted at a DSB meeting unless</u> a party to the dispute formally notifies the DSB of its decision to appeal or <u>the DSB decides by consensus not to adopt the report</u>. If a party has notified its decision to appeal, the report by the panel shall not be considered for adoption by the DSB until after completion of the appeal. This adoption procedure is without prejudice to the right of Members to express their views on a panel report.*[6] (Emphasis added)

3 DSU Art. 11.
4 DSU Art. 17.13.
5 DSU Art. 8.2.
6 DSU Art. 16.4.

This provision in practice completely nullifies the supposed role of the DSB. Decisions of the panels and the AB would as a practical matter always be final. Furthermore, panel and AB reports were on a fast track to adoption from which there was to be no deviation:

> *Within 60 days after the date of circulation of a panel report to the Members, the report shall be adopted at a DSB meeting unless a party to the dispute formally notifies the DSB of its decision to appeal or the DSB decides by consensus not to adopt the report.*[7]
>
> *An Appellate Body report shall be adopted by the DSB and unconditionally accepted by the parties to the dispute unless the DSB decides by consensus not to adopt the Appellate Body report within 30 days following its circulation to the Members. This adoption procedure is without prejudice to the right of Members to express their views on an Appellate Body report.*[8]

To stop the automatic adoption of a report, all members present would have to agree to prevent its adoption. Because attendees at a DSB meeting would always include the winning party, as well as incidental beneficiaries or third parties that rather liked the litigative outcome, and they could not be expected to set aside a victory that they had spent time and energy to achieve, the exact number of times that disapproval would occur would be approximately zero, a null set.

This DSB procedure for the adoption of reports is one bookend of the use of consensus in the WTO. To reach agreement on new rules (or anything else in the DSB, in the General Council, or in a negotiating committee), all have to agree by a positive consensus that has in practice become unanimity of all those expressing an opinion. Picture having a train notionally headed toward a destination, in this case the conclusion of new trade agreements, where each passenger has at hand an emergency brake of its own that will control the entire train, with nothing but self-restraint preventing any passenger from halting forward progress. That is what has happened to WTO rule-making.

Now assume that the train instead operates in the same way as the DSB. To prevent the train from reaching its assigned destination (i.e., prevent the adoption of a dispute settlement panel or AB finding from becoming final), all 164 passengers (or at least all those present) would have to pull the emergency brake at the same time, including those who very much wanted to get to their destination, and in the DSB, those who wished the panel or AB

[7] DSU Art. 16.14.

[8] DSU Art. 17.4.

result to stand. The passengers, the DSB attendees, would never form a consensus to nullify a dispute settlement report, and in fact have not done so.

Decision making by positive consensus (all too rare) and negative consensus (nonexistent) are a large part of the explanation for the WTO's various predicaments. The bottom line: with respect to the approval of dispute settlement results, the DSB has a rubber stamp marked "adopted," which it applies in robotic fashion. If there is a rubber stamp marked "not adopted," it has not been found. Could a proactive chairperson change the dynamic, convince the parties to settle, or to agree that a report would not be adopted? One would suppose so. There have been times when the parties have agreed to take an item off the agenda, through action or inaction. One example is the US and EU dispute on the Helms–Burton extraterritorial application of sanctions, a case in which the parties decided to allow the panel to lapse.[9] Neither party, it appears, wished panels to define for them what the scope was for the invocation of the national security exception to the WTO/GATT's rules.

The DSB has no effective authority over whether a finding or recommendation is reasonable or correct. With no practical ability to reject errant opinions, when these occur, the DSB cannot have direct influence over the panels or the AB. Unless the parties welcome the intervention of the DSB chair, the DSB does not have any real role in shaping the outcome of a dispute, in short, in helping to settle it.

Is this an oversimplification? Perhaps. Were there a serious discussion in the DSB on the legal or factual aspects of a panel decision, or on a point of law addressed by the AB, and a preponderance of members made persuasive points in commenting on the case, this might make an impression on AB members, and thereby affect future results. Criticisms voiced could forewarn the AB of future institutional difficulties if it was politically attuned to popular opinion (meaning strong sentiment among the WTO's members). To preserve their legitimacy in a democratic environment, all courts need to pay attention to public (in this case, member) sentiment. This is not a matter of losing independence but of preserving the institution. But there is no guarantee that the AB members would find the discussion at the DSB persuasive, that

[9] "DS38: United States – The Cuban Liberty and Democratic Solidarity Act." World Trade Organization. www.wto.org/english/tratop_e/dispu_e/cases_e/ds38_e.htm. The DSB established a panel at its meeting on November 20, 1996. On April 25, 1997, the chair of the panel informed the DSB that, at the request of the European Communities, the panel had suspended its work. The panel's authority lapsed on April 22, 1998, pursuant to DSU Art. 12.12.

they would be institutionalists, or that it would be more than an occasion for airing opposing views and canceling each other out.

Before leaving consideration of the DSB, it is worth noting that besides the adoption of panel and AB reports, the DSB has other duties, most of them largely ministerial. The DSB is to establish panels upon request. This is automatic. It is not so much an authority as it is a requirement. So also is the provision that it is within the DSB's authority to authorize "the suspension of concessions and other obligations under covered agreements."[10] This is another automatic function, determined by negative consensus.[11]

The establishment of panels may appear to be a substantial authority, but in fact members choose their own panelists unless they cannot agree, in which case the Director-General chooses them in consultation with the chairperson of the DSB and the chairperson of the relevant Council or Committee. The ministerial act of the chair being consulted by the Director-General on the selection of panel members may not be very real either. It is the Secretariat that keeps a roster of available panelists.

The Appellate Body, not the DSB, makes its own decision as to which of its seven members will sit as a division of three AB members to hear and decide a case (after consulting with the AB members not sitting on that appeal). The AB is wholly independent of the DSB. As for compliance and retaliation, that is the job of compliance panels pursuant to Article 21.5 of the DSU. Again, the recommendations of compliance panels are rubber-stamped by the DSB. Thus, it is not clear how or when the following guidance contained in the Dispute Settlement Understanding to the DSB could come into play: "Recommendations or rulings made by the DSB shall be aimed at achieving a satisfactory settlement of the matter in accordance with the rights and obligations under this Understanding and under the covered agreements."[12] In a practice from which it cannot depart, the DSB is not in fact making recommendations or rulings so much as acknowledging them.

There are other responsibilities of the DSB which are clearly real. When there are vacancies in the AB, the DSB is to make the appointment. The

[10] DSU Art. 3.7: "The last resort which this Understanding provides to the Member invoking the dispute settlement procedures is the possibility of suspending the application of concessions or other obligations under the covered agreements on a discriminatory basis vis-à-vis the other Member, subject to authorization by the DSB of such measures."

[11] Where the DSB administers the dispute settlement provisions of a plurilateral trade agreement that is officially part of the WTO set of agreements, only those members that are parties to the Agreement said to have been breached may participate in decisions or actions taken by the DSB with respect to that dispute.

[12] DSU Art. 3.4.

practice is for the three senior WTO chairs (of the General Council, the DSB, and the Trade Policy Review Body) to interview the candidates proposed by members. The DSB is then to make a selection, and the decision to appoint a new AB member is determined by positive consensus of the members. The European Union and the United States have shown that this is a real decision for the DSB to make. The EU insisted that filling one vacancy (expected to be a Latin American seat) should be linked to the filling of another (that had been and was expected to be filled by an EU nominee). The United States, far more dramatically and devastatingly, blocked all nominations to the Appellate Body, effectively, in the words of a former AB member, asphyxiating (a fancy way of saying "killing") the institution on December 10, 2019.

The fact that consensus, both positive and negative, plays through the operations of the DSB does not mean that the meetings are without substance – very much to the contrary. Its meetings are a platform for discussion by interested members of the state of implementation of panel rulings and recommendations. Members are required to file with the DSB requests and notifications that easily fill a meeting agenda. The notifications serve a variety of purposes, not the least of which is to inform members of various stages of a dispute, allowing each to look after its own interests.

- Requests for consultations being notified, members believing that their interests will be affected can request to join.
- Requests to establish a panel, likewise, present an opportunity to a member which believes its trade will be affected to join as a third party.

Members share a common interest in assuring that the dispute settlement processes are working. Notices and filings allow members to assess for themselves (without affecting the outcome of cases being litigated):

- Whether the panels and appeals (when they exist) are adhering to timelines;
- Whether the agreements are being interpreted in line with their understanding of the requirements of the agreements;
- Whether compliance is taking place with panel and AB rulings; and
- The appropriateness of the level of compensation or retaliation set by a compliance panel.

For these reasons, all members who have an interest in current or potential litigation pay close attention to what takes place in the DSB, often not at the level of ambassadors, unless their member is a party to a case, but especially at the level of dispute settlement experts.

IS JUSTICE DELAYED JUSTICE DENIED?

In the case of the Boeing–Airbus subsidy dispute between the United States and the European Union, if finality has been achieved, it was only after about a decade and a half of various stages of litigation, of cases and counter-cases. To make a judgment as to whether WTO dispute settlement was a useful, the best, or even an effective avenue leading toward resolution of the bilateral dispute, one would need to solicit the views of the parties, as well as the firms and workers with interest in the outcome.

At the other end of the spectrum, compliance can be relatively swift. A case that was filed and did get resolved relatively quickly involved a rebate by China of a large part of the value-added tax on semiconductors manufactured at home as compared with imports which did not receive the rebate. After a formal request for consultations was filed, followed by interested members joining as third parties to the dispute and a round of consultations taking place, China repealed the measure. This was the first case brought against China after it joined the WTO.[13] Members always have the option, when confronted with a claim that one of its measures is palpably inconsistent with its WTO obligations, to terminate the measure without the need to have lengthy panel proceedings before it does so.

In cases where the panel and appellate process run their course, most compliance should take place within the fifteen-month period allotted following the DSB's *pro forma* adoption of the final report in the litigation. Although not anything like the Boeing–Airbus timeframe, there is nothing prompt about obtaining results in the usual case once WTO litigation has begun.

PANEL PROCEEDINGS AND CASE LAW

One of the most active parts of the multilateral trading system is litigation, and this remains the case even in the absence of a functioning Appellate Body.

[13] "DS309: China – Value Added Tax on Integrated Circuits." World Trade Organization. www.wto.org/english/tratop_e/dispu_e/cases_e/ds309_e.htm. Consultations were initiated on March 18, 2004, and settlement was notified on October 5, 2005. This demonstrates that even with lightning speed, a fair amount of goodwill, and the capacity to litigate and meet bilaterally, the time involved in getting from action to positive resolution can easily be over one year, even with no panel being convened. The reason for the delay from complaint to resolution may be the time needed to complete domestic procedures to repeal the measure. As only measures in place – as opposed to those being contemplated – can be subject to formal dispute settlement, this case may well be on the very positive and low side of a range of time needed to resolve a dispute.

When compliance with the WTO rules is not voluntary, the obligations of the WTO Agreements remain enforceable through adjudication for all those members making interim arrangements, which can include accepting panel decisions as final or joining the Multi-Party Interim Arrangement (MPIA). The following briefly lays out the panel process and then examines key substantive areas of enforcement of trade agreements by dispute settlement panels and on appeal. Cases tell much about the nature and scope of the trading system.

Process. The first stage of dispute settlement is for a member concerned with a measure imposed by another member to give notice to that party and seek consultations. The consultations are to take place during the next sixty days. The consultation phase in all too many instances will be *pro forma*, as in most instances the respondent often does not wish to change its practice. At the same time, the complainant, which has very likely already tried to get the offending member to mend its ways, at this stage often decides that it is not wise to outline in detail its legal arguments that it plans to lay before a panel. After the consultation period, the complaining party has the right to ask for the establishment of a panel. The Dispute Settlement Body automatically decides that a panel will be established only at the second DSB meeting at which a request is made, since the first request for a panel can (and often will) be blocked by the responding party. Panelists are trade experts chosen by the parties, often from a roster maintained by the Secretariat. Panelists may not be a national of either of the parties. If there is no agreement between the parties on panel composition, the Director-General will choose the panelists.

When there was an Appellate Body, appeals could be taken within sixty days of a panel report being circulated. Under the Dispute Settlement Understanding, upon receiving the appeal, the AB would have sixty days to issue its report, or ninety days in more complex cases. At present, with no AB in place, members of the Multi-Party Interim Arrangement can appeal to its roster of appellate panelists. Otherwise, parties have a choice: they can decide that the panel report is final, come to an alternative arrangement, or file a *pro forma* appeal to the AB. In this last option, since the appellant knows that there is no AB, appealing is simply putting the result from the panel in what may be permanent limbo. When a case is final, once the DSB has adopted the report,[14] the respondent is expected to remove the measure found to be illegitimate. A timeframe for compliance is stipulated, which should not exceed fifteen months. The complainant can request compensation if the

[14] Ibid.

measure is not withdrawn or can request authority to retaliate in an amount that is determined by an arbitral panel.

The numbers. Since the WTO was founded in 1995, 612 disputes have been filed at the WTO. Panels were established in 365 disputes (as of December 31, 2021), and 277 panel reports have been issued. An appeal was notified in 189 disputes.[15] In only 19 cases from 1995 through 2020 was retaliation sanctioned.[16] PIIE Senior Fellow Chad Bown has tabulated the number of cases during the first twenty-five years of the WTO (1995–2019) that involve trade remedies. With respect to those against G20 members, the tally is 168 anti-dumping (AD) cases, 66 cases regarding countervailing measures, and 16 safeguards cases. The cases against non-G20 countries in these categories are 20, 3, and 7 respectively. Trade remedies account for a very substantial proportion of WTO cases.[17]

Timeliness of outcomes. Under the DSU, panelists are generally to have six months in which to issue their report, with an interim report issued three weeks before the final report. But panels can take up to nine months to issue their final report. The parties have sixty days within which they can appeal. And notionally, the AB would make its decision within sixty to ninety days.

This is not what occurs. The WTO website's description of the process indicates that panel proceedings take an average of twelve months. According to one academic study, the average time between panel establishment and DSB consideration of the report is 539 days.[18] During one relatively recent period, from September 2015 to August 2017, in fourteen cases, the AB took between 131 and 579 days from the notice of appeal to issue its report.

As an illustration of a case where no appeal is taken, in *Ukraine* v. *Russia* (DS512, otherwise known as *Russia – Transit*), consultations were requested on September 14, 2016, and the panel report was circulated to members on April 5, 2019, after two and a half years (933 days). Where an appeal is taken and the parties are deeply entrenched, resolution can be long in coming. In the *Beef Hormones* case, the United States brought a complaint against the EU

15 "Dispute settlement Activity – Some Figures." World Trade Organization. www.wto.org/english/tratop_e/dispu_e/dispustats_e.htm

16 Ibid.

17 Chad P. Bown. 2022. "Trump Ended WTO Dispute Settlement. Trade Remedies Are Needed to Fix It." Peterson Institute for International Economics, Washington, DC. www.piie.com/sites/default/files/documents/wp22-1.pdf

18 Markus Wagner. 2020. "Panel: Dispute Settlement System of the World Trade Organization (WTO)." *Max Planck Encyclopedia of International Procedural Law* – Oxford University Press. August 3. www.academia.edu/43536090/Panel_Dispute_Settlement_System_of_the_World_Trade_Organization_WTO

in January 1996. The panel report in this case was circulated in August 1997. The AB report was circulated in January 1998. US retaliation was authorized in July 1999, 1,276 days from the request for consultations, and a solution was announced jointly ten years later in September 2009.

The dispute settlement process yields results at a far slower rate than the drafters of the DSU contemplated and provided for in their agreement. This is a source of major frustration to WTO members when they are complainants. A number of suggestions have been made over time to increase the pace of decision making. At the panel stage, one interesting suggestion to speed up the process is to have panel chairs be permanent rather than ad hoc – in other words, more like a judiciary with a first-instance judge.[19] Adopting this change would not find favor with those that wish proceedings to be more like arbitration and less judicial.

There is a second WTO website statement that is incontrovertibly misleading: "First rulings are made by a panel and endorsed (or rejected) by the WTO's full membership." As discussed in Chapter 6 in the section on the Dispute Settlement Body, under the negative consensus rule (i.e., all members must agree to overturn a panel finding or it stands), there is approximately a zero possibility for the members to reject a panel or AB outcome, as they effectively have no voice in the matter.

THE APPELLATE BODY

As there is no Appellate Body at present and little likelihood from this point in time (2022) that it will be reconstituted as it was, the discussion of the role of the AB is left to Chapter 14, where reform of the WTO dispute settlement system is addressed.

HOW WTO DISPUTE SETTLEMENT SHAPES THE RULES OF THE SYSTEM

The purpose of this section is primarily to indicate the kind of cases that are dealt with by WTO dispute settlement, not to re-argue the correctness of the results delivered. There is rich literature on this subject, with some useful analyses cited in footnotes following these case descriptions.

[19] James Bacchus and Simon Lester. 2019. "Trade Justice Delayed Is Trade Justice Denied: How to Make WTO Dispute Settlement Faster and More Effective." Cato Institute. November 20. www.cato.org/free-trade-bulletin/trade-justice-delayed-trade-justice-denied-how-make-wto-dispute-settlement

WITH RESPECT TO THE ENVIRONMENT

Shrimp–Turtle. The United States required shrimp fishermen to utilize devices to exclude sea turtles from their nets. The AB found that the United States acted inconsistently with its obligation to avoid imposing measures that constitute arbitrary and unjustifiable discrimination against imports, but the United States could and should "act together bilaterally, plurilaterally or multilaterally, either within the WTO or in other international fora, to protect endangered species or to otherwise protect the environment."

Tuna–Dolphin. The United States required imported tuna to be certified to show that adequate care was taken to avoid killing dolphins which swim above the tuna. A GATT panel found against the United States for seeking to regulate process rather than product, and for applying its regulations to activities outside US territory. Mexico, the complainant, withdrew the case after reaching a settlement with the United States (during the GATT era, panel reports could not be adopted unless all agreed to do so). The EU then brought its own case, but the GATT expired and the WTO came into effect, and the panel report was never adopted.[20] This was not to be the end of the tuna–dolphin saga as further WTO litigation ensued over the next two decades, leading to an indication that the aim or effect, the object and purpose of a regulation, may lead to permissibility, taking into account differences in process or production-based measures (PPMs – process and production methods).[21]

Gasoline mixing regulation. California's regulations treated substitutable gasoline imports differently and less favorably, the panel held, than it treated like domestic products. The measure was found to be inconsistent with the national treatment requirement of the GATT and not excused by any exception.[22]

[20] "Mexico etc. versus US: 'Tuna–Dolphin'." World Trade Organization. www.wto.org/english/tratop_e/envir_e/edis04_e.htm; Christopher C. Joyner and Zachary Tyle. 2010. "Marine Conservation versus International Free Trade: Reconciling Dolphins with Tuna and Sea Turtles with Shrimp." *Ocean Development & International Law* 31(1–2): 127–150.

[21] Joel P. Trachtman. 2017. "WTO Trade and Environment Jurisprudence: Avoiding Environmental Catastrophe." *Harvard International Law Journal* 58(2): 273–309; Elisa Baroncini and Claire Brunel. 2020. "A WTO Safe Harbour for the Dolphins: The Second Compliance Proceedings in the US – Tuna II (Mexico) Case." *World Trade Review* 19(2): 196-215. www.cambridge.org/core/journals/world-trade-review/article/abs/wto-safe-harbour-for-the-dolphins-the-second-compliance-proceedings-in-the-ustuna-ii-mexico-case/CE39F27166290781F5C7458318625EBB

[22] "United States – Standards for Reformulated and Conventional Gasoline: Report of the Panel WT/DS2/R." World Trade Organization. January 29, 1996. https://docs.wto.org/dol2fe/Pages/

Asbestos and asbestos-containing products. France could prohibit imports of these products from Canada as measures necessary to protect human health.[23]

WITH RESPECT TO TRADE REMEDIES

Antidumping. The AB found that the zeroing methodology, as applied by the United States in the administrative reviews at issue, was inconsistent with the Anti-dumping Agreement. In the AB's view, this practice resulted in amounts of antidumping duties that exceeded the foreign producers' or exporters' margins of dumping. The AB upheld the panel's finding that the United States' zeroing methodology (the "zeroing" methodology, generally speaking, involves treating specific price comparisons which do not show dumping as zero values in the calculation of a weighted average dumping margin). The AB further found that zeroing is a "norm" that is inconsistent with US obligations. An "as such" challenge refers to considering the WTO consistency of the methodology itself, even if it has not been applied.[24]

The Byrd amendment. The AB found that the US Continued Dumping and Subsidy Act of 2000 – under which antidumping and countervailing duties assessed on or after October 1, 2000 were to be distributed to the affected domestic producers for qualifying expenditures – was an additional antidumping duty inconsistent with the obligations under the Subsidies and Countervailing Measures (SCM) and Anti-dumping Agreements.[25]

SS/directdoc.aspx?filename=Q:/WT/DS/2R.pdf&Open=True; Martin A. McCrory and Eric L. Richards. 1998. "Clearing the Air: The Clean Air Act, GATT and the WTO's Reformulated Gasoline Decision." *UCLA Journal of Environmental Law and Policy* 17(1): 1–42.

[23] "DS135: European Communities – Measures Affecting Asbestos and Products Containing Asbestos." World Trade Organization. www.wto.org/english/tratop_e/dispu_e/cases_e/ds135_e.htm

[24] "DS294: United States – Laws, Regulations and Methodology for Calculating Dumping Margins (Zeroing)." World Trade Organization. www.wto.org/english/tratop_e/dispu_e/cases_e/ds294_e.htm; Dukgeun Ahn and Patrick Messerlin. 2014. "United States – Anti-Dumping Measures on Certain Shrimp and Diamond Sawblades from China: Never Ending Zeroing in the WTO?" *World Trade Review* 13(2): 267–279; Thomas J. Prusa and Edwin Vermulst. 2011. "United States – Continued Existence and Application of Zeroing Methodology: The End of Zeroing?" *World Trade Review* 10(1): 45–61.

[25] "DS217: United States – Continued Dumping and Subsidy Offset Act of 2000." World Trade Organization. www.wto.org/english/tratop_e/dispu_e/cases_e/ds217_e.htm; Henrik Horn and Petros C. Mavroidis. 2005. "United States-Continued Dumping and Subsidy Offset Act of 2000." *World Trade Review* 4(3): 525–550.

Subsidies. To be a subsidy covered by the SCM, there must be a financial contribution from the government. An entity that is a "public body" is considered as being in the shoes of the government for the purpose of finding a financial contribution by a government, which would allow the imposition of countervailing measures. The AB found that the United States Department of Commerce (USDOC) acted inconsistently with the SCM because it determined that certain Chinese state-owned enterprises (SOEs) were "public bodies" based solely on the grounds that the SOEs were majority owned, or otherwise controlled, by the government of China. The AB found that a "public body" is an entity that possesses, exercises, or is vested with governmental authority. Government ownership was not enough to find that a "public body" exists. Not very many SOEs, other than certain state-owned banks, would qualify under this definition.[26]

Safeguards. These measures are found to be inconsistent with GATT Article XIX:1(a), unless the member imposing the measure establishes that the increase in imports was "as a result of" the unforeseen developments it relied upon in making an original trade concession and identifies the obligations whose effect resulted in the injurious increase in imports.[27] The Safeguards Agreement does not have these requirements. This ruling makes it very difficult to utilize the agreement.

WITH RESPECT TO NATIONAL SECURITY

Ukraine–Russia, 2016, transit measures. For the first time, the panel interpreted Article XXI(b) as vesting in panels the power to review whether the requirements of a claim of essential security interests are met, rather than leaving it to the unfettered discretion of the invoking member. The panel interpreted "emergency in international relations" as including a situation of armed conflict, latent armed conflict, heightened tension or crisis, or general

[26] "DS379: United States – Definitive Anti-Dumping and Countervailing Duties on Certain Products from China." World Trade Organization. www.wto.org/english/tratop_e/dispu_e/cases_e/ds379_e.htm; Mark Wu. 2016. "The 'China, Inc.' Challenge to Global Trade Governance." *Harvard International Law Journal* 57(2). 260–324; Ru Ding. 2014. "'Public Body' or Not: Chinese State-Owned Enterprise." *Journal of World Trade* 48(1): 167–189; Michel Cartland, Gerard Depayre, and Jan Woznowski. 2012. "Is Something Going Wrong in the WTO Dispute Settlement?" *Journal of World Trade* 46(5): 979–1015; Weihuan Zhou, Henry S. Gao, and Xue Bai. 2019. "Building a Market Economy through WTO-Inspired Reform of State-Owned Enterprises in China." *International and Comparative Law Quarterly* 68(4): 977–1022.

[27] "WTO Dispute Panel Issues Report Regarding EU Safeguard Measures on Steel Imports." World Trade Organization. April 29, 2022. www.wto.org/english/news_e/news22_e/595r_e.htm

instability engulfing and surrounding a state. The panel found that as of 2014, there existed a situation in the Russian Federation's relations with Ukraine that constitutes an emergency in international relations and that each of the measures at issue was "taken in time of" an emergency in international relations.[28]

WITH RESPECT TO "AS SUCH" CLAIMS

US Section 301. The panel found that the existence of authority in a statute to make unilateral determinations of the WTO consistency of other members' measures was not inconsistent with US obligations. While the statutory language of Section 301 in itself constituted a serious threat that unilateral determinations contrary to US obligations might be made, the United States had (i) lawfully removed this threat by the "aggregate effect of the Statement of Administrative Action ('SAA')" and (ii) made a statement before the panel that it would render determinations under the statute in conformity with its WTO obligations. In this regard, the panel added the caveat that should the United States repudiate or remove in any way its undertakings contained in the SAA and confirmed in statements before the panel, then the finding of conformity would no longer be warranted.[29]

WITH RESPECT TO PRODUCT STANDARDS

Beef hormones. The AB found that the EU's (formerly EC) measures violated the Sanitary and Phytosanitary Agreement (SPS) because it was not based on a risk assessment, although there need not be a "rational relationship" between the measure at issue and the risk assessment. It did not find that the measure was arbitrary or unjustifiable resulting in "discrimination or a disguised restriction of international trade" because there were genuine anxieties concerning the safety of the hormones, among other reasons.[30]

COOL: Country of origin labeling. The AB found that the *measure* was inconsistent with Article 2.1 of the Technical Barriers to Trade Agreement

[28] "DS512: Russia – Measures Concerning Traffic in Transit." World Trade Organization. www.wto.org/english/tratop_e/dispu_e/cases_e/ds512_e.htm; Tatiana Lacerda Prazeres. 2020. "Trade and National Security: Rising Risks for the WTO." *World Trade Review* 19: 137–148.

[29] "DS152: United States – Sections 301–310 of the Trade Act 1974." World Trade Organization. www.wto.org/english/tratop_e/dispu_e/cases_e/ds152_e.htm

[30] "DS26: European Communities – Measures Concerning Meat and Meat Products (Hormones)." World Trade Organization. www.wto.org/english/tratop_e/dispu_e/cases_e/ds26_e.htm

(TBT), because the measure accorded less favorable treatment to imported livestock than to the like domestic product. The least costly way of complying with the COOL measure was to rely exclusively on domestic livestock, and the record-keeping and verification requirements imposed a disproportionate burden on upstream producers and processors compared to origin information conveyed to consumers. Thus, it was found to be an illegitimate measure.[31]

WITH RESPECT TO MARKET ACCESS

Japan – Film. The United States claimed that access to the Japanese market was denied through actions by Japan affecting the distribution, offering for sale, and internal sale of imported consumer photographic film and paper, in particular, (i) distribution measures; (ii) restrictions on large retail stores; and (iii) promotion measures, and in addition that government decisions affecting market access had not been published. The panel found against the United States on all counts.

Comment: The WTO dispute settlement system is designed primarily for findings of violations of specific obligations by clearly identifiable measures. A general "nullification and impairment" case is difficult to prosecute. None have succeeded in eight tries. The creation and tolerance of an anticompetitive environment are not readily actionable. WTO panels have little capability to deal with highly fact-intensive matters. The absence of transparency is difficult to prove in the absence of transparency.[32]

CONCLUSION

Dispute settlement is one of the three functions of the WTO, the other two being negotiations and Secretariat activities in administering the trading system. Dispute settlement has assumed even greater importance by virtue of the absence of rule-making and the lack of the Secretariat assuming a

[31] "DS386: United States – Certain Country of Origin Labelling Requirements." World Trade Organization. www.wto.org/english/tratop_e/dispu_e/cases_e/ds386_e.htm

[32] "DS44: Japan – Measures Affecting Consumer Photographic Film and Paper." World Trade Organization. www.wto.org/english/tratop_e/dispu_e/cases_e/ds44_e.htm; Japan – Photographic Film: Kodak was a client of the author. "The Kodak–Fuji Film Case at the WTO and the Openness of Japan's Film Market." Congressional Research Service. May 8, 1998. www.everycrsreport.com/files/19980508_98-442_7284c4a65259ea272c3a1ae7d5e024c93ad3836d.pdf

stronger role. For the least developed, while there may be some derivative benefits from litigation, they neither bring nor defend cases. The preponderance of cases is accounted for, as might be expected, by the countries accounting for most of world trade. The United States holds first place, having brought 124 cases and defended itself in 126. The EU holds second place with 110 cases as complainant and 90 disputes as respondent. The comparable figures for China are 22/49, India 24/32, Japan 28/16, Canada 40/23, Korea 21/19, Mexico 25/15, Russia 8/11, Russian Federation 8/11, Thailand 14/4, New Zealand 9/0, Chinese Taipei 7/0, Norway 5/0, and Viet Nam 5/0.

Dispute settlement has been essential to the smooth working of trade relations. The number of trade measures of concern for which no WTO justification is claimed at all is statistically very small but unfortunately growing. These are largely restrictions imposed for geopolitical and systemic reasons. The figures do not address areas where the WTO rules are largely absent, such as domestic industrial subsidies, measures affecting e-commerce, and failure to administer or biased administration of competition policy.

Some of what can be discerned from the cases, on a technical level:

- Clearly deadlines are no longer deemed binding. There seem to be no consequences for taking whatever time a panel feels is necessary or desirable.
- Given the number of times the AB changed the panel result or the reasoning for it, either the panels are underperforming or the AB is overreaching, or both. Issuing a simple affirmation of a first-instance result appeared not to be present in the AB's culture, nor was making a finding that a rule did not cover a measure (i.e., finding a gap in the rules).

On a policy level:

- *Protecting the institution.* Had there been an institutionalist in place at the AB or in the panels,[33] caring for the survival of binding dispute settlement, that person might have pressed for judicial restraint with greater awareness of the realities of the world. The institutionalist would have been careful not to increasingly narrow the use of trade remedies that serve to dissipate some of the pressures of globalization.
- *Trade remedy erosion.* Why are cases against AD and CVD measures so prevalent?

[33] "John Roberts Is an Institutionalist, Not a Liberal." *Financial Times*. July 1, 2020. www.ft.com/content/2248b2e3-b911-48ec-9eeb-632c0c26ab16

Chad Bown theorizes that they are the perfect storm of factors:[34]

1. Not only is the market access problem easy to identify, but the imposing country provides the evidentiary record for the complainant, including the names of the exporting firms that were hit; and
2. The measures are specific to the exporting country, so there is no free-rider problem of the complainant doing work for other exporting countries, i.e., if it wins, it enjoys all the benefits, unlike a challenge to a safeguard or subsidy, where some of the resulting market access benefits accrue to third parties.

I would add that their popularity also stems from their success rate. The return on investment is relatively high. Not only does a trade remedy dispute end a measure in a particular case, but it may make the trade remedy less useable in the future.

- *Regarding essential security interests*: This is a difficult and institutionally dangerous question for litigation. It will often be the better part of wisdom for the dispute settlement system to avoid making judgments as to what is a national security matter and what is not. Perhaps some litigation is unavoidable, but care is needed. It is an instance in which the Director-General might intervene forcefully to find a non-litigative solution.
- *The least and less developed countries.* Their interests should be taken into account in making reforms to the system, perhaps relying more heavily on mediation, given that winning a case may not provide a useable result in compliance, compensation, or authority to retaliate.
- *Extensive state intervention.* Litigation may not be well-suited to subtle but extensive state intervention that has created an ecosystem in which market-based competition is not allowed to play out.

How important have dispute settlement cases been to shaping the rules of the multilateral trading system?

Whether one believes that one case is precedent for another or not (and they always are), making a decision that an environmental rule was permissible or not, or whether invocation of national security in certain circumstances was justifiable or not, by deciding cases, panels and the AB were making law. It was (too) often said that the AB was the "jewel in the crown"

[34] Conversation between the author and Chad Bown, based on his book, *Self-Enforcing Trade Developing Countries and WTO Dispute Settlement*. Washington, DC: Brookings Institution Press, 2009.

rather than binding dispute settlement. This statement ignored the fact that the crown itself, were one referring to dispute settlement, was to be the DSB, the organ that was to make all final decisions in litigation. (And if one were referring to the WTO as a whole, the "crown" should have been accorded to rule-making, had that proceeded as one could have hoped.)

WITHOUT THE AB IN PLACE, IS THERE STILL DISPUTE SETTLEMENT?

In the twenty-five months since the AB ceased to function, nineteen cases were filed (through March 2022). This is down from the sixty-three cases filed in the prior twenty-five months. However, the most recent period occurred during the pandemic, with the lowest number of cases annually, five, being initiated in 2020. This compares with an average during the period through 2021 of just over twenty-five cases per year. Litigation is continuing. The absence of the DSU-mandated appellate level has not ended WTO dispute settlement.

8

Agriculture

A major difference between the WTO as compared with the World Bank and International Monetary Fund is the domestic political sensitivity of trade. Among trade issues, none are more politically sensitive than agriculture. It took eight rounds of GATT negotiations to achieve the landmark Agreement on Agriculture (AoA) in 1993. There has been little progress toward reforming agricultural trade rules in the ensuing years. Much more needs to be done.

One of the major achievements of the Uruguay Round was the Agreement on Agriculture. It came after years of the world's agricultural consuming and producing nations failing to come to grips with the distortions endemic to this sector. During the GATT years, it was difficult to even discuss the shape of the negotiating table. During the short time that I headed the US delegation to the Tokyo Round of Multilateral Trade Negotiations in 1975, I saw firsthand the refusal of the European Commission Director-General for Agriculture to even talk to Americans. This was not just an individual fit of pique. Driving through rural France, you would see hand-painted signs standing in wheat fields that read "GATT NON!"

A plethora of trade-distorting measures were in place, but the first among these was the European Common Agricultural Policy (CAP). It transferred much of the burden of supporting domestic European agriculture to the rest of the world through the use of variable levies – duties at the border to offset world market fluctuations. For example, if Russia had a bumper grain crop, and prices on the world market were low, the CAP would tighten restrictions on access to the European market. At times of higher world market prices and less global production, the levies would be less restrictive. In both situations, the CAP offloaded much of the burden of adjustment to others. "Industrial" policy nearly always leads to overshooting, to overproduction. For agriculture, the CAP created through massive subsidies a "wine lake" and a "butter mountain." It made the retail price in the United States of a tin of Danish butter cookies – which benefited from subsidies on flour, sugar, and butter – less than the price of an empty tin. A Canadian wine producer trying to create a commercially viable industry told me: "we can put labels on bottles, put corks in the bottles, and put them in cartons ready to ship, and leave out the wine, and we still cannot compete with subsidized Italian wine."

The creation of the European Common Market caused the outbreak of a "chicken war" in the 1960s, with US retaliation for the loss of Europe as a destination for American poultry.[1] When President Kennedy called Chancellor Adenauer shortly after the Berlin Wall went up, at least one particular call was not about the threat to national security of the West but was about access to Germany and the EEC for chickens.[2] Seen in the rearview mirror, these events seem relatively minor, but they loomed large in transatlantic relations at the time. During the 1970s, there were years of hostility between Europe and the United States over agricultural trade issues. The Europeans deeply resented US countervailing duties on Danish canned hams and Dutch dairy products. The consequences of the growth of a unified Europe were felt in the American heartland. Enlargement of the European Community had dried up one of the largest overseas markets for American grain.[3]

Agriculture took a back seat in the GATT Tokyo Round of Multilateral Trade Negotiations (MTN) (1973–79). The reason was simple. The European Communities and the United States had to find a way to work together. The price for getting the Tokyo Round through to a successful conclusion was an informal US pledge not to "attack the CAP" during the Round. The US International Trade Commission summed up the result – the Round was marginal in terms of its impact on American agriculture, with some growth in exports of specialty crops such as almonds, but with subsidies and nontariff barriers left untouched.[4] This left major problems to be solved in the Uruguay Round (1986–94). Nor did all go smoothly there.

1 "The Chicken War: A Battle Guide." *New York Times*. January 10, 1964. www.nytimes.com/1964/01/10/archives/the-chicken-war-a-battle-guide.html

2 A statement made to me in the late 1970s by David W. Brooks, chairman of Gold Kist Inc., which was at the time the largest producer of US poultry.

3 I was the lawyer on the American negotiating team that dealt with EC enlargement from the original Six to the Nine and drafted the provision that was intended to preserve America's grain rights under the GATT. It was a legal instrument that could not have any practical effect.

4 "The Impact of Trade Agreements: Effect of the Tokyo Round, U.S.–Israel FTA, U.S.–Canada FTA, NAFTA, and the Uruguay Round on the US Economy." US International Trade Commission. August 2003. www.usitc.gov/publications/332/pub3621.pdf. Page 182.

The state of world agriculture in the 1980s was described in a Senate Finance testimony in terms that echoed the opening of the chapter Genesis in the Old Testament: "In the beginning, there was a formless void and darkness covered the face of the deep, while a wind swept over the face of the waters."

> *D. Gale Johnson, a prominent University of Chicago economist, referred to it as a "world in disarray." Many markets were highly protected through high tariffs, limited quotas, or outright bans on imports. Variable levies were in place in many countries, which allowed countries to adjust tariff levels to protect domestic markets as world prices fell or rose. Domestic support to agriculture, particularly among the rich developed members such as the US, Japan, and the EU, was large and growing. Producers in those countries made production decisions largely insulated from the world market. Governments propped up domestic prices by storing production in large public stockpiles, by maintaining high tariff barriers, or both. Governments dumped surplus production on export markets, using export subsidies and restitutions. This further distorted markets and harmed other exporters, often developing countries that had little or no means with which to protect their own producers and limited recourse within the General Agreement on Tariffs and Trade (GATT) to redress trade disputes.*[5]

The GATT did little to restrain government interventions in agriculture that caused trade distortions. It permitted the use of export subsidies for agricultural primary products, did not effectively discipline domestic support or import restrictions, and permitted high tariffs and import quotas. It facilitated greater self-sufficiency, inefficiency, and reduced trade. Production decisions were insulated from global market conditions.

A chief objective of the Uruguay Round, launched in 1986 at Punta del Este, was "to achieve greater liberalisation of trade in agriculture and bring all measures affecting import access and export competition under strengthened and more operationally effective GATT rules and disciplines." The main actors at the time had diverse interests, many of which remain the same today. The EC and Switzerland were defensive, not wishing to liberalize markets. Many of the net food importers, largely developing countries, were concerned with food security and wanted more flexibility to promote their own domestic production. Japan and Korea wished to protect their rice farmers. The United

[5] "Statement of Joseph W. Glauber: Senior Research Fellow, International Food Policy Research Institute – Before the Senate Finance Committee." United States Senate Committee on Finance. July 29, 2020. www.finance.senate.gov/imo/media/doc/29JUL2020Glauber~IFPRISTMNT1.pdf

States and the Cairns Group of agricultural exporters (Canada, Australia, New Zealand, Thailand, Indonesia, Malaysia, the Philippines, Argentina, Brazil, Colombia, Chile, Uruguay, Fiji, and Hungary) largely sought market access. China was not yet active as a factor in the trade talks, not joining the WTO until 2001, or in global agricultural markets.[6]

Due to an impasse over agriculture, the Uruguay Round nearly collapsed in Brussels in December 1990 when it had been scheduled to conclude. Progress in the Round came to a standstill. In 1991, the GATT Director-General, in one of the most forward-leaning acts of any GATT or WTO DG, tabled a compromise on major Uruguay Round differences, including a first text on agriculture. This document, known as the Dunkel Draft,[7] paved the way forward. It took two more years to accomplish a breakthrough. This occurred in the Blair House Accord of November 1992, setting a limitation on EU farmland that could be planted with soybeans.[8] The Accord amended the Dunkel Draft with respect to base periods for export subsidies, exempted some domestic support programs with production limitations from support constraints, and created overall limits for domestic support.[9] In parallel, the EC was reforming the CAP. It is less likely that the Uruguay Round drove EC CAP reform than that internal cost pressures gave space for the GATT negotiators to reach an accommodation in agriculture and create the Agreement on Agriculture (AoA).

The following sections address the areas usually listed for future negotiations on agriculture (not all of them having the same degree of general interest), and none of them free of controversy. They are a mixture of issues arising from the application of the Agreement on Agriculture, and subjects that have been given attention during the WTO years.

[6] Colin A. Carter and Scott Rozelle. "Will China's Agricultural Trade Reflect Its Comparative Advantage?" U.S Department of Agriculture – Economic Research Service. www.ers.usda.gov/webdocs/publications/42432/15176_aib775k_1_.pdf?v=0

[7] In multilateral trade negotiating history, the Dunkel Draft is every bit as noteworthy and well-known as "The Belay" is in mountaineering, and is of equal importance. In 1953, an American expedition was climbing down K-2 in the Himalayas, when five climbers lost their footing. They were saved by Pete Schoening, who dug in his ice axe and saved his five colleagues with their ropes tethered to that one ice axe. Arthur Dunkel saved the Uruguay Round from its worst near-death experience. It is not clear that there would have been a WTO had he not taken this initiative.

[8] "Blair House Agreement." OECD Glossary of Statistical Terms. https://stats.oecd.org/glossary/detail.asp?ID=222

[9] "1.2.5 The Blair House Accord" in "The Implications of the Uruguay Round Agreement on Agriculture for Developing Countries – A Training Manual." Agricultural Information Modules. 1998. www.nzdl.org/cgi-bin/library?e=d-00000-00—off-0aginfo–00-0— —0-10-0—0—0direct-10—4— — — — —0-1l–11-en-50—20-about—00-0-1-00-0–4— —0-0-11-10-0utfZz-8-00&cl=CL2.13&d=HASH202b615e74ccc00cc6bc93.5.2.3.6&gt=1

MARKET ACCESS

One of the most important changes of the AoA was to convert a plethora of often opaque and byzantine protectionist measures into clear published and bound tariffs. With the conversion, far more certainty was created for cross-border trade. Moreover, once protection was converted to tariffs, it could be bound (creating contractually committed ceilings on import duties). This provided transparency, allowed domestic and international markets to be linked, and allowed outside market forces to have a direct impact on domestic agricultural production and consumption.[10] Once tariffs were bound in schedules, it was feasible to list commitments to tariff reductions phased in over time, with deeper cuts made by developed as compared with developing countries. (Note: the option was given to countries to have ceiling bindings instead of undergoing the tariffication process, which was complex for many developing countries.) Tariff-rate quotas (TRQs) provided assured access within limits. Under the agreement, TRQs could not be made more restrictive and some additional expansion of under-quota amounts was provided. The commitments were calculated on a 1986–88 base period. Quantitative import restrictions, variable import levies, minimum import prices, discretionary import licensing procedures, voluntary export restraint agreements and non-tariff measures maintained through state-trading enterprises, if specific to agriculture, were banned.

SPECIAL AGRICULTURAL SAFEGUARDS (SSG)

Thirty-nine WTO members currently have reserved the right to use a combined total of 6,156 special safeguards on specified agricultural products. These are not distributed evenly by population, agricultural production, or level of development. Switzerland has 961 (53 percent of its tariff lines), Norway 581 (48.7 percent), the EU 539 (31.1 percent), Iceland 462 (36.7 percent), the United States 181 (10.3 percent), Morocco 374 (23 percent), and Botswana 161 (39.5 percent), as examples. They are relics of tariffication and tied to individual tariff lines. SSGs are safeguards that are not dependent upon a showing of injury and are based on imports entering in quantities above or prices below stipulated levels.[11] There are proposals for these

[10] "Market Access." World Trade Organization. www.wto.org/english/tratop_e/agric_e/ag_intro02_access_e.htm

[11] "Market Access: Special Agricultural Safeguards." World Trade Organization. www.wto.org/english/tratop_e/agric_e/negs_bkgrnd11_ssg_e.htm; "Special Agricultural Safeguard – Note by

measures to be abolished in the ongoing negotiations, proposals which are resisted by countries which currently utilize them.

SPECIAL SAFEGUARD MECHANISM (SSM)

At the Nairobi Ministerial Conference in 2015, it was agreed that a special safeguard mechanism (SSM) for developing countries would be negotiated.[12] For a tariffied product, if the volume of imports increased above a trigger level (relating to the 1986–88 base level), or the price of imports declined below a trigger level (referring again to that base level), a temporary additional duty could be levied not to exceed a specified amount of the normal tariff according to a formula in the agreement.

DOMESTIC SUPPORT

The amount of domestic support indicates a very serious problem that is only growing. It is now US$ 817 billion annually according to the OECD. Estimates vary, but the total is likely to be well beyond $1 trillion by 2030. The Cairns Group estimates have it at $2 trillion by 2030. A key element of the AoA consisted in curbing the level of domestic subsidies. The primary components of the new disciplines were (1) the total Aggregate Measurement of Support (AMS, the Amber Box), (2) agreed *de minimis* levels, (3) combined with an area of permitted subsidies, which became known as the Green Box.

What was permitted, what would now be called "policy space," would be contained in the Green Box. These were the subsidies that were presumed not to have much if any distorting effect on trade. Measures that qualified for this category – and thus were exempt from disciplines – included, for example, research, environmental measures, pest and disease control, training, school lunch programs, rural electrification, basic infrastructure, crop insurance, income support for farmers and government advisory services.[13] A borderline measure was public stockholding (PSH) for food security purposes, as PSH might or might not affect world markets directly.

the Secretariat TN/AG/S/29/Rev.1." World Trade Organization. January 11, 2017. docs.wto.org/dol2fe/Pages/SS/directdoc.aspx?filename=q:/TN/AG/S29R1-01.pdf&Open=True

[12] "Special Safeguard Mechanism for Developing Country Members WT/MIN(15)/43 WT/L/978." World Trade Organization. December 19, 2015. www.wto.org/english/thewto_e/minist_e/mc10_e/l978_e.htm

[13] AoA Annex 2.

A further general exception to the agreed disciplines was support that was *de minimis*. Falling into this category were:

> *product-specific domestic support which would otherwise be required to be included in a Member's calculation of its Current AMS where such support does not exceed 5 percent of that Member's total value of production of a basic agricultural product during the relevant year; and*
>
> *non-product-specific domestic support which would otherwise be required to be included in a Member's calculation of its Current AMS where such support does not exceed 5 percent of the value of that Member's total agricultural production.*[14]

For developing country members, the *de minimis* amount is 10 percent.[15] Developing countries do not count development assistance as being subject to AMS disciplines or the *de minimis* exclusion. China and Kazakhstan, upon accession, agreed to a *de minimis* level closer to the developed country level, at 8.5 percent of the total value of production of a basic agricultural product during the relevant year. Due to substantial growth in China's agricultural production in subsequent years, this category, free from subsidy constraints, would grow considerably. It is estimated that the value of China's agricultural production is US$2 trillion. (The *de minimis* level is 5 percent for developed members, including for Chinese Taipei.)

Under AoA Article 6.2, "investment subsidies which are generally available to agriculture in developing country Members and agricultural input subsidies generally available to low-income or resource-poor producers in developing country Members shall be exempt from domestic support reduction commitments that would otherwise be applicable to such measures." For India, this is an enormous exemption, covering about $25 billion annually.

There is a smaller category of exemption, utilized by a few countries, and before *de minimis* is calculated, known as the Blue Box. It "covers payments directly linked to acreage or animal numbers, but under schemes which also limit production by imposing production quotas or requiring farmers to set aside part of their land."[16]

The heart of the AoA, beyond tariffs, consists of requiring the limitation and reduction of domestic support (i.e., government funding), denoted as each member's total AMS. After capping domestic support, the agreement required a

[14] "Agreement on Agriculture." World Trade Organization. www.wto.org/english/docs_e/legal_e/14-ag_01_e.htm#articleVI

[15] AoA Art. 6.

[16] "Domestic Support: Amber, Blue and Green Boxes." World Trade Organization. www.wto.org/english/tratop_e/agric_e/negs_bkgrnd13_boxes_e.htm

phased reduction over six to ten years consisting of a 20 percent reduction for developed countries and a 13 percent reduction for developing countries. It did not require elimination of the support.[17] The formula for calculating AMS involves multiplying the gap between the applied administered price and a specified fixed external reference price ("world market price") by the quantity of production eligible to receive the administered price, by product, and then the sum of support for crops that includes all product-specific support and non-product-specific support. The calculation of the limit ties back to the 1986–88 base period.

EXPORT COMPETITION

The AoA began the process of reduction of export subsidies. Included were direct export subsidies, the dumping of excess non-commercial stocks, levies on production used to promote exports of that product, underwriting freight and handling costs, and subsidies tied to downstream product exports. Members scheduled binding commitments, often by product, with reductions of the export subsidies over a six-year period for developed countries and a ten-year period for developing countries. Fifty-three WTO members (the EU of twenty-eight counted separately) scheduled these commitments. The AoA banned export subsidies that were not compliant with specific rules outlining the cases in which export subsidies were allowed.[18]

In 2015, at the Nairobi Ministerial Conference, developed members agreed to immediately eliminate their remaining scheduled export subsidy entitlements and developing country members agreed to eliminate their export subsidy entitlements by the end of 2018.[19] Outside of direct export subsidies, other forms of export competition of concern include export credits, export credit guarantees, and other forms of financial support including insurance, risk assumption, and foreign exchange hedging. These additional methods of indirect support for exports remain on the agenda for future negotiations.

PUBLIC STOCKHOLDING FOR FOOD SECURITY PURPOSES (PSH)

A major issue leading up to the Bali Ministerial in 2013 was the degree of flexibility that should be available to developing countries for public

[17] "Domestic Support." World Trade Organization. www.wto.org/english/tratop_e/agric_e/ag_intro03_domestic_e.htm

[18] Listed on the WTO website at www.wto.org/english/tratop_e/agric_e/ag_intro04_export_e.htm

[19] "Export Competition WT/MIN(15)/45." World Trade Organization. December 19, 2015. www.wto.org/english/thewto_e/minist_e/mc10_e/l980_e.htm

stockholding programs for food security purposes. The subject is one of the most contentious as it encompasses staple crops in cases where there is a clear risk of breaching AMS (Amber Box) commitments. The argument is made by developing countries that the fixed external price using 1986–88 values is outdated and does not correspond to reality, as prices for most grains and cereals have increased substantially since then. In plain English, the question is whether the disposition of public stocks on world markets would harm agricultural producers in other WTO members' economies.[20] Under the Bali decision, an interim solution was put into place, and it was agreed that a permanent solution should be decided at the Buenos Aires Ministerial Conference in 2017. A member would be free from challenge for breaching its obligations if, in the use of its PSH program, it notified the Committee on Agriculture that it was exceeding or at risk of exceeding its bound AMS or *de minimis* levels, that it was in compliance with its notification and other transparency requirements, and that it ensured that the stocks procured would "not distort trade or adversely affect the food security of other Members."[21] At the Nairobi Ministerial Conference, the members agreed to keep working on finding a permanent solution to public stockholding with a view to agreeing on a permanent solution at the Buenos Aires Ministerial Conference in 2017.[22] This deadline was missed as there was no result on agriculture at the conference. This was still the case after MC12 concluded.

EXPORT PROHIBITIONS OR RESTRICTIONS

The GATT bans export restrictions on commodities – with a prominent exception. The ban does not apply to "prohibitions or restrictions temporarily applied to prevent or relieve critical shortages of foodstuffs or other products essential to the exporting [WTO member]."[23] There is little guidance given as to how this exception is to be applied. However, Article 12.2 of the AoA adds a proviso that "the Member instituting the export prohibition or restriction shall give due consideration to the effects of such prohibition or restriction on

[20] "Report by the Chair, Ambassador John Adank, Informal Meeting of the Committee on Agriculture, Special Session." World Trade Organization. October 11, 2013. www.wto.org/english/news_e/news13_e/agng_11oct13_e.htm

[21] "Public Stockholding for Food Security Purposes." World Trade Organization. December 7, 2013. www.wto.org/english/thewto_e/minist_e/mc9_e/desci38_e.htm

[22] "Public Stockholding for Food Security Purposes WT/MIN(15)/44." World Trade Organization. December 19, 2015. www.wto.org/english/thewto_e/minist_e/mc10_e/l979_e.htm

[23] GATT Art. XI.2.

importing Members' food security," something of a soft law provision. What is important, and not required for export restrictions applied to industrial goods, is the requirement that prior notice be given "as far in advance as practicable, to the Committee on Agriculture comprising such information as the nature and the duration of such measure."[24] A specific consultation requirement is added. An exception to the requirements of AoA Article 12.2 is that it does not apply to "any developing country Member, unless the measure is taken by a developing country Member which is a net-food exporter of the specific foodstuff concerned."

Food scarcity and price spikes have given rise repeatedly in this century to renewed concerns over food export restrictions. Price spikes occurred during the financial crisis in 2008–9. That this situation might recur arose as a concern during the pandemic in 2020, but food stocks globally were robust and a number of countries whose immediate reaction was to impose restrictions on food exports rescinded them. The concerns have returned with the interruption of trade in grain, vegetable oils, and wheat (as well as the curtailment of fertilizer exports), due to the Russian invasion of Ukraine.

During the pandemic, Canada led forty-nine food-exporting countries in pledging not to restrict food exports. Then and during the war in Ukraine, there has been a revival of interest in agreement to a ban on export restrictions with respect to foodstuffs destined for purchase by the World Food Programme (WFP).[25] There have also been suggestions for improving the advance notice provision.

TRANSPARENCY

Throughout the AoA, there are provisions for notifications to illuminate policy measures affecting agriculture. For example, administrative arrangements for TRQs are to be notified in advance, as are changes during their implementation. Similarly, advance notice is required for the use of SSMs and, as noted, export restrictions.

[24] AoA Art. XII.1(b).

[25] "Joint Statement on Agriculture Export Prohibitions or Restrictions Relating to the World Food Programme WT/L/1109." World Trade Organization. January 21, 2021. https://docs.wto.org/dol2fe/Pages/SS/directdoc.aspx?filename=q:/WT/L/1109.pdf&Open=True: "We recognize the critical humanitarian support provided by the World Food Programme, made more urgent in light of the COVID-19 pandemic and other crises. We therefore commit to not impose export prohibitions or restrictions on foodstuffs purchased for non-commercial humanitarian purposes by the World Food Programme." For the version that was ultimately adopted at MC12, see ch.5.

COTTON

In addition to the seven main topics for deliberation outlined above – market access, domestic support, public stockholding, export competition, special safeguard mechanism, export restrictions, and transparency – which are key components of the AoA, there is in each agricultural discussion an item treated as a separate subject: what is to be done about trade measures adversely affecting cotton. Lack of market access and competition from subsidized cotton impair the earnings of some of the poorest farmers on the planet. Four least developed cotton-producing nations of West Africa – Benin, Burkina Faso, Chad, and Mali – have caused additional attention to be paid to this product sector. However, cotton trade issues – subsidies and market access – remain embedded in a stalled vehicle, agriculture negotiations, and particularly domestic support. The most that is on offer, if that, consists of continuing biannual dedicated discussions, monitoring implementation of existing commitments, committing to "intensify discussions on factors negatively impacting cotton trade and markets," and improving data collection.[26]

SANITARY AND PHYTOSANITARY STANDARDS

No discussion of agriculture in the WTO would be complete without addressing the special problems inherent to trade in food and feed products due to sanitary and phytosanitary (SPS) restrictions. Next to food supply, food safety is of paramount concern to governments. While a tariff may slow trade, noncompliance with a standard can prevent trade altogether. This is particularly important for agricultural producers in the least and lesser developed countries, where the infrastructure necessary for conforming to importing country standards may be inadequate. The SPS Agreement provides that "any sanitary or phytosanitary measure is applied only to the extent necessary to protect human, animal or plant life or health, is based on scientific principles and is not maintained without sufficient scientific evidence."[27] Further, SPS measures are not to "arbitrarily or unjustifiably discriminate between Members where identical or similar conditions prevail." Conformity with international

[26] "Committee on Agriculture in Special Session: Draft Chair Text on Agriculture JOB/AG/215." World Trade Organization. July 29, 2021. www.tradebetablog.files.wordpress.com/2021/08/chair-draft-july-2021_rd-ag-215.pdf

[27] "The WTO Agreement on the Application of Sanitary and Phytosanitary Measures (SPS Agreement)." World Trade Organization. www.wto.org/english/tratop_e/sps_e/spsagr_e.htm

standards is sufficient, and members are to base their SPS measures on international standards and guidelines.

At MC12, a declaration was adopted on SPS measures. The ministers instructed

> *the SPS Committee to further enhance the implementation of the SPS Agreement in an effort to better manage issues related to international trade in food, animals and plants by undertaking a work programme, open to all Members and Observers, consisting of new efforts to identify: (1) challenges in the implementation of the SPS Agreement and the mechanisms available to address them; and (2) the impacts of emerging challenges on the application of the SPS Agreement.*[28]

This mandate did not extend to negotiations that would change the rights and obligations of members.

An area of successful cooperation among WTO members, both donors and recipients of assistance, is the Standards Trade Development Facility,[29] which focuses on efforts to build the capacity of least developed and developing countries to meet international standards, which is required to foster their exports.

The Prospects for Negotiations

The drafters of the AoA understood that their Agreement was far from the last word on international rules for agricultural trade. They put in Article 20 of their Agreement a provision for ongoing negotiations. This has not produced new agreements, with the exception of the Nairobi decision to ban export subsidies.

The original divisions among members' interests in agricultural trade persist. Agriculture and food in most countries demand political accountability beyond what the share of economic activity within most countries would suggest. Farmers already facing variability in weather and costs of production are particularly sensitive to fluctuations in prices caused by supply and demand outside of the borders of their own countries. Consumers are concerned with adequate supplies, affordable prices, and quality. It has been very

[28] "Sanitary and Phytosanitary Declaration for the Twelfth WTO Ministerial Conference: Responding to Modern SPS Challenges WT/MIN(22)/27WT/L/1138." World Trade Organization. June 22, 2022. https://docs.wto.org/dol2fe/Pages/SS/directdoc.aspx?filename=q:/WT/MIN22/27.pdf&Open=True

[29] "Welcome to the Standards and Trade Development Facility." Standards and Trade Development Facility. www.standardsfacility.org/

difficult to find common ground. Food-exporting countries' interest in market access is not matched to date by offsetting benefits as perceived by food-importing countries.

The level of disciplines for each WTO member varies. It depends in part on the timing of its having joined the WTO. Those who acceded to the WTO were subjected to more stringent conditions for their agricultural trade than those that apply to original members. While there have been few subsequent generally applicable commitments made in agriculture in the nearly three decades since the WTO was founded, outside of the Nairobi political agreement among developed countries to forgo export subsidies, there have been some intensive negotiations to obtain agricultural commitments as part of the accession process. This had the effect of further liberalization, albeit selectively, with a widening gap between the commitments of original members and acceding members.

Although the categories of countries and the positions taken are, as one would expect, net food exporters differing from food importers, the country shares of world agricultural trade have changed dramatically. "The past three decades have seen East Asia (i.e., mainly China) increase its share of global agricultural production from 25 percent in 1993–95 to 33 percent in 2013/15, that of South and Central America from 9 percent to 11 percent, while Europe's share has fallen from 26 percent to 14 percent and that of North America from 13 percent to 10 percent."[30] The list of countries granting the most domestic support has also dramatically shifted since the AoA was constructed.

The diversity of interests, instead of leading to serious negotiations, has lent itself to a tiresome repetition of positions in Committee on Agriculture in Special Session (CoASS) meetings. The various sides have become entrenched, with no visible movement. This is not due to a lack of effort on the part of the Committee's chairs, who have tried very hard to find areas of compromise. In recent years, both John Deep Ford (Ambassador of Guyana) and his successor Gloria Abraham Peralta (Ambassador of Costa Rica) worked hard on the issues on the table, often ably assisted by friends of the chair in subgroups. I suspect that this was the case for their dedicated and talented forebears as well. Despite their best efforts, there has been no progress.

The need for the trading system to become more responsive is evident in the fact that trade in agriculture is growing in importance. One in six people

[30] "New Pathways for Progress in Multilateral Trade Negotiations in Agriculture." International Food Policy Research Institute. May 24, 2021. www.ifpri.org/publication/new-pathways-progress-multilateral-trade-negotiations-agriculture

around the world depends almost entirely on international trade to be fed. That is 17 percent of humanity, or 1.3 billion people. Currently, over thirty countries rely on imported food, not to increase their food variety, but to avoid starvation. There are many reasons for this situation, including poor agricultural productivity, serious land and water limitations, and climate-related shocks. To the list of calamities affecting world food has now been added Russia's war in Ukraine. Many of the countries most adversely affected are in Africa, and some in the Middle East.

According to the Potsdam Institute for Climate Impact Research, by the year 2050, around 50 percent of humanity could depend on international trade to be fed, up from today's 17 percent.[31] This is because of population growth and changing climate conditions. Using current data on population and food and water consumption in each nation, the Potsdam Institute concludes that countries will find themselves obligated to increase their dependence on each other to feed their peoples. It will also become necessary to dramatically enhance agricultural productivity and make dietary changes. The countries most reliant on imports are to be found in North Africa, the Middle East, and Central America, with over half their populations depending on imported food by 2050.

Status of Negotiations

The CoASS chair, Amb. Gloria Abraham Peralta, summarized the state of play in WTO agriculture discussions in November 2021. The gist of what she conveyed, as I interpret it, is as follows.[32] This is a snapshot of positions that existed, according to the chair seven months before the Ministerial. MC12 did not change the state of play. When negotiations pick up, the starting point is not likely to be where matters stood when Amb. Abraham Peralta prepared this summary, as several members have rejected TN/AG/50 as the basis for the negotiations going forward. Nevertheless, it is instructive as to what the chair saw as the state of play when the document was prepared.

Trade-distorting domestic support. There is no convergence other than on the point that this subject needs to be addressed. Some favor a numerical

[31] Ibid.

[32] "Committee on Agriculture in Special Session: Report by the Chairperson, H.E. Ms. Gloria Abraham Peralta, to the Trade Negotiations Committee TN/AG/50." World Trade Organization, November 23, 2021. https://docs.wto.org/dol2fe/Pages/SS/directdoc.aspx?filename=q:/TN/AG/50.pdf&Open=True; "Agriculture Negotiations." World Trade Organization. www.wto.org/english/thewto_e/minist_e/mc12_e/briefing_notes_e/bfagric_e.htm

target (for example, a 50 percent reduction of members' entitlements). Some would pick a timeframe for implementing an agreed reduction. There is no convergence on the utility of having a *de minimis* exclusion, as this is still trade-distorting support. No agreement exists with respect to what to include, whether the Green Box should be expanded, and its criteria clarified, or what the sequencing of reform should be. Some members are of the view that to level the playing field, there should be elimination of AMS beyond *de minimis* levels before addressing other issues. An attempt to agree on modalities would be made by MC13.

Market access. There is no agreement even on the modest step of increasing transparency by giving *ad valorem* equivalents of specific or complex tariffs. At present, there would be a series of best practices recommended to members regarding goods in transit, giving guidance as to how a tariff might change due to defined factors, permitting the prepayment of customs duties to fix the liability upon shipment, and giving prior notice for changes in tariffs. Needless to say, these steps do not constitute fundamental improvements in market access. A work program is suggested (not agreed) to have deeper cuts in higher tariffs. There have been no focused discussions on tariff reduction formulae for some time.

Export competition. Some convergence exists in increasing transparency, with some resistance based on capacity limitations, to be potentially overcome with assistance from the WTO Secretariat for providing responses to questionnaires. Details to be provided would be spelled out in an annex to the agreement, addressing export credit programs, food aid, and state-trading enterprises, among other issues.

Export prohibitions or restrictions. There is a willingness to continue to work on improving transparency, technical assistance upon request, and a "best endeavor" to provide advance notice. Efforts continue to exempt purchases by the World Food Programme from export restrictions. A compromise text was adopted at MC12.

Cotton. There could be agreement "to continue the negotiations with a view to agreeing on modalities for the reduction of trade-distorting domestic support for cotton, in accordance with the mandate to address cotton ambitiously, expeditiously, and specifically, while also taking into account the overall context of the agriculture negotiations." Despite the upbeat tone of this statement, the linkage to the complete outcome of agriculture negotiations continues. In short, there has been little possibility that progress on cotton could be made outside of broad progress on agriculture negotiations more generally.

Special safeguard mechanism for developing countries. There is no convergence. Negotiations would continue. Some members wish to link talks on SSM and market access negotiations.

Public stockholding. This is an area of sharp divisions. The question is whether and how to approach a permanent solution. Those opposed to doing so are concerned about potential trade distortions from "unlimited market price support beyond the Uruguay Round commitment levels." Parallel progress is sought on domestic support, with more information obtained on the actual use of PSH programs. The suggestion is to continue work, with the adoption of a work program for an attempted resolution at MC13.

Transparency. When there is an outcome on agriculture more generally, there will be elements for enhanced transparency. With the deployment of IT tools, improvements will be made, including online notifications and greater data availability.

* * *

Chairperson Amb. Gloria Abraham Peralta sums up where things stand in the agriculture negotiations as follows:

> *there is still rather a long way left to go – and we have to pick up our pace . . . if we are to make a meaningful difference in people's lives around the world. Markets for food and agriculture still remain highly distorted and protected. All too often, they function poorly and the most vulnerable producers and consumers [are] those that pay their highest price . . . Climate change is creating new challenges for market actors with changing temperature and precipitation patterns and more infrequent and intense extreme weather events compounding existing problems such as food insecurity.*[33]

Current Extreme Circumstances

With agricultural exports not being able to transit the Black Sea due to the Russia–Ukraine war and sanctions being applied to Russia by forty countries, the subject of food security is demanding immediate attention. The resilience of the supply of grains, food oils, and fertilizer, as well as increased costs of natural gas and oil, compounded by shipping constraints, are receiving a fresh focus. The interconnectedness of the world, the necessary flow of trade in both goods and services, an agricultural ecosystem, is forcefully presenting new challenges. The various forms of impact that climate change will have on agricultural trade and food security require a deeper examination, but the demand for doing so with a procrastinating humanity has taken second place to current dire circumstances – the trade distortions caused by war.

[33] Committee on Agriculture in Special Session, Draft Chair Text on agriculture. July 29, 2021. https://tradebetablog.files.wordpress.com/2021/08/chair-draft-july-2021_rd-ag-215.pdf

On April 11, 2022, the WTO Secretariat published a special report entitled the "Crisis in Ukraine: The Impact of War on Trade and Development."[34] It tells us that Russia and Ukraine together "supplied around 25 percent of wheat, 15 percent of barley and 45 percent of sunflower products exports in 2019. Russia alone accounted for 9.4 percent of world trade in fuels, including a 20 percent share in natural gas exports." At least half of the wheat consumption of approximately twenty-five countries depended on Russia and Ukraine. Fifteen countries did so for corn (maize). Twenty-five importing countries relied on Russia and Ukraine for 75–100 percent of their imports of sunflower oil. A number of countries were dependent on imports of fuels from Russia, such as Finland (63 percent) and Turkey (35 percent). Spring and summer 2020 price hikes, 25–30 percent for wheat and 35 percent for soybeans, hurt net food-importing countries, particularly low-income ones. The situation (November 2022) was far worse, another 16 percent price increase for wheat and 19 percent for soybeans above those levels.[35] Shortages of and higher fertilizer prices mean lower yields for crops globally, particularly in poorer countries.

COVID-19 had already caused governments to examine where products originated and where they were needed, first in personal protective equipment, and then vaccines and pharmaceuticals. Agriculture in a time of war and climate change offers some similar challenges. Food needs to move from where it is produced in quantity to where it is relatively scarce. Just as with the pandemic, there needs to be a collective response. Just as with the pandemic, the question remains unanswered as to whether the trading nations of the world can come together with agreed solutions. A meeting of private sector experts and government representatives on April 26, 2022 was convened by the WTO. The meeting failed to identify common ground.

Paths Forward

In a comprehensive paper issued in 2017 on how the AoA has operated and what is needed for the future, Lars Brink and David Orden begin to sum up their findings with the following:[36]

34 "The Crisis in Ukraine: Implications of the War for Global Trade and Development." World Trade Organization. April 11, 2022. www.wto.org/english/res_e/booksp e/imparctukraine422_e .pdf

35 https://tradingeconomics.com/commodity/wheat

36 Lars Brink and David Orden. 2020. "Taking Stock and Looking Forward on Domestic Support under the WTO Agreement on Agriculture." International Agricultural Trade Research

the pandemic has exposed the fragility of the integrated world economy. Stronger international institutions and cooperation will be needed to help counter tendencies in some countries to forgo the benefits of integration. Reinvigorated engagement through the WTO to guide global trade relations may prevail in this setting but cannot be taken for granted.

Before the COVID-19 pandemic was over, the Russian invasion of Ukraine interdicted the supply of wheat, sunflower oil, and fertilizer sourced from those two countries. In the months and years ahead, we do not know the extent to which severe weather events will disrupt agricultural production but can assume that they will be more numerous and severe. Further pandemics are expected, although it is not possible to predict with any accuracy their nature, timing, and impact. Agricultural trade issues will remain of great importance to all nations.

The categories for WTO reform negotiations largely remain what they were when the AoA was being negotiated (although, to be sure, negotiations focused on e-commerce and services, to name two, while not explicitly addressing agriculture, should attract strong interest from agricultural stakeholders). For the purposes of this chapter, the discussion will be confined to the most pressing of the more traditional subjects. Besides the Brink–Orden paper, it is worth consulting "New Pathways,"[37] a coauthored document produced by a pantheon of current experts on trade and agriculture, to look at a range of potential negotiating outcomes.[38]

Domestic support. Of the measures that distort world agricultural trade, outside of abnormal conditions when export restrictions play an immediate and pronounced role, domestic support looms the largest. It is also an area for prospective disciplines where one size clearly does not fit all. Every major agricultural trading nation (counting the EU as one) presents a different profile. This makes easy across-the-board solutions difficult to deploy. Christophe Bellman and Jonathan Hepburn of what was formerly the International Centre for Trade and Sustainable Development (ICTSD) demonstrate this with data from the last two decades. Through a series of charts, they show the impact of a fixed cap on AMS, or a variable ceiling based on the

Consortium. April. www.iatrc.umn.edu/taking-stock-and-looking-forward-on-domestic-support-under-the-wto-agreement-on-agriculture/

37 "New Pathways for Progress in Multilateral Trade Negotiations in Agriculture." International Food Policy Research Institute. May 24, 2021. www.ifpri.org/publication/new-pathways-progress-multilateral-trade-negotiations-agriculture

38 The "New Pathways" paper was coordinated by Carmel Cahill and Stefan Tangermann, with coauthors Lars Brink, Shenggen Fan, Joseph Glauber, Anabel Gonzalez, Tim Groser, Ashok Gulati, Joanna Hewitt, Anwarul Hoda, Alan Matthews, and Guillermo Valles Galmes.

share of agricultural production. Looking at the level of subsidies by country over the period 2001–13, a 5 percent limit fixed on a 2008–10 base would have had no effect on the European Union, the United States, and some cutback of support for Japan and Canada. If the 5 percent cap were based on current production, the discipline for the European Union, the United States, Canada, and China would disappear, with the United States given slightly more room than its current AMS provides.

If product-specific limits are imposed on domestic support, dairy support in the European Union and United States would need to be cut back, as would support for rice in South Korea, wheat in the European Union, corn in the United States, maize in Brazil, and pork, veal, and beef in Japan. The authors also offer another way of looking at trade benefiting from domestic support, examining the size of production by country measured against its share of global exports. This shows that the United States has the potential for being the most disruptive of world maize and soybean markets, Brazil for beef, sugar and soybeans, the EU for wheat, and India for rice. The authors put forward an interesting idea that WTO members consider combining available data on volumes of production, the shares of domestic production being exported, the share of world exports the country accounts for, and the support intensity, probably defined as product-specific support as a share of the value of production (VoP). With this data, an updated AoA could assign to each WTO member a coefficient upon which the required level of commitment would be based.

The system would be complex and need to be recalibrated constantly, as all the data inputs would be both shifting according to trends and showing short-term variations. No country could agree without running a simulation and testing projected estimated variables. The process might at least yield a direction to explore as one of the alternatives, a meat-axe approach (i.e., a 50 percent cut in AMS) produces uneven and for some, unacceptable results, with additional elements needed to obtain balance.

Some of the negotiating challenges show that those with high bound total AMS levels (BTAMS) during the base period of 1986–88, particularly the United States and European Union, were given a lot of additional unintended flexibility in later years as trends developed (with what may be aberrant support behavior by the United States to offset its exchange of China tariff salvos during the Trump presidency). Another variable is that production values have been growing, so *de minimis* headroom has grown as well. Brink and Orden estimate the level could reach $1 trillion by 2030. They recommend that the areas of greatest flexibility for both developed and developing countries be subject to disciplines, and imply that given the growth of Chinese and

Indian production (although these two are not singled out), differential treatment should not be made on the basis of division between developed and developing, but determined based on whose trade-distorting subsidization is the largest (choosing five or ten WTO members for negative differential treatment, that is, imposing more constraint on them). The two authors would meet the needs of the LDC cotton producers by setting lower ceilings on product sectors that benefited from excessive support. The Green Box (chosen as a color suggesting greater freedom for granting support) expands to meet contemporary green (environmental) needs, such as sustainable productivity growth, biosecurity, water management, biodiversity, and climate mitigation.[39]

An International Institute for Sustainable Development (IISD) report making recommendations for MC12 notes that "three quarters of all support classed as trade-distorting by the WTO is concentrated in a handful of Members – China, India, the United States, and the European Union."[40] The report notes that too much flexibility is accorded to the United States and the European Union. Too little discipline exists due to the rapidly increasing production based in China and India. According to the report, using its *de minimis* threshold of 8.5 percent of the VoP, China's allowable *de minimis* support is estimated at over $128 billion in 2016. The approach taken in the IISD report is to cap and then reduce existing limits on total trade-distorting support in the largest producing and trading countries. In so doing, this approach would reduce the inequitable impact of the rules among countries, move the base period to stay current rather than moored in the distant past, tailor special and differential treatment based on need, reduce the flexibility to support individual product categories, and provide a limited exception for publicly held stocks (where the administered price is below an agreed international market price).

Similarly, "New Pathways" would take as one option calculating total domestic support, including Blue Box and all *de minimis* support as a percentage of total agricultural production, cap it and reduce it by tiered groups, the most interventionist to the least. It is a sort of Swiss formula (higher tariffs cut more than low tariffs) applied to AMS. An offered alternative is to calculate total budget support as a percentage of the value of total agricultural

39 Perhaps fifty shades of green.

40 Joseph W. Glauber, Jonathan Hepburn, David Laborde, and Sophia Murphy. 2020. "What National Farm Policy Trends Could Mean for Efforts to Update WTO Rules on Domestic Support." International Institute for Sustainable Development. April. www.iisd.org/system/files/2020-08/farm-policy-trends-en.pdf

production, cap it, and reduce it. Decoupled income support is likewise similarly capped and reduced based on its relationship to total production.

The IISD report highlights the fact that India and China have no effective constraints on domestic support, as they have large and growing *de minimis* levels based on two decades of very rapid and sustained growth in their value of production. The two countries argue that their support levels are minuscule when looked at on a per capita basis given the size of their populations. It is nevertheless impossible to have a global agricultural agreement on domestic support constraints without the full participation of the two largest countries by population which are also major agricultural producers. The report's authors suggest a system that cures the flaws in the AoA by trying to bring greater equity to the system of constraints. This would be accomplished by 1) capping and reducing flexibilities based on a rolling average base period for the value of production, 2) giving added flexibility to the poorest countries through phase-ins and higher permitted levels of support, 3) having individual limits established for specific commodities, 4) exempting public stockholding as long as acquisition prices were below global market prices, and 5) expanding the green category of permitted support.

Market Access

In a paper filed with the WTO in 2014, the United States observed that "tariffs are the only permitted import restriction (other than WTO-consistent non-tariff measures), and all agriculture tariffs are now bound."[41] The paper pointed out how different the level of tariffs was between the United States and emerging-economy countries. In most cases, the extreme being India, the bound level of tariffs was much higher than the applied level of tariffs (the difference between the high bound rate and the low applied rate is referred to by negotiators as the "water" in the tariff schedule, where no commitment is in place to maintain the applied rate). Due to the negotiation for China's entry into the WTO, its bound and applied tariffs are at the same level. The bound level is still a substantial multiple of the level of the average US tariff. The United States and agricultural exporting countries have proceeded to press for examination within the WTO on where tariffs needed to be reduced and

[41] "Tariff Implementation Issues – Communication from the United States of America G/AG/W/132." World Trade Organization. June 4, 2014. docs.wto.org/dol2fe/Pages/FE_Search/FE_S_S009-Html.aspx?Id=125002&BoxNumber=3&DocumentPartNumber=1&Language=E&HasEnglishRecord=True&HasFrenchRecord=True&HasSpanishRecord=True&Window=L&PreviewContext=DP&FullTextHash=371857150#KV_GENERATED_FILE_000004.htm

where their administration could be improved to make them less of a trade barrier.

The Trump administration objected to WTO tariff schedules being frozen in time with some having the trade "advantage" of higher tariffs and not being willing to lower them. At the same time, India and China are unhappy that flexibilities for AMS were frozen in time, with the advantage seen as going to the United States and the European Union.

Another concern of agricultural exporting nations is that some tariffs are not calculated on an *ad valorem* basis (a simple percentage of the value of the import), but are specific (for example, $.05/pound or /kg). Others are even more complex, for example, minimum import prices, price bands, variable levies, and gate price mechanisms. Some tariffs are discretionary within an envelope of high bound rates. Complex tariffs can be deceiving. The United States calculated that the Swiss have tariffs as high as 77 percent *ad valorem* equivalent. Even low average tariffs can mask tariff peaks. For the US tariff schedule, where a third of the agricultural tariffs are bound at zero, peanuts and sugar have maximum rates of over 150 percent, and dairy 140 percent. Some processed products have tariff rates of 100 percent, and one tobacco tariff line has an *ad valorem* equivalent of over 400 percent.

Throughout the tariff discussion, transparency is a problem. There is little that is clear to someone involved in trade when considering whether to ship an agricultural commodity across a border as to what the amount of duty will be when the tariff is not expressed in *ad valorem* terms. Too often it is not. There are similar complexities that exist with respect to the administration of tariff-rate quotas. Special safeguards may be applied with little notice and be lacking in transparency as well. The US papers outlining tariff issues are contained in seven documents, set out in a blog post by Terry Stewart, a leading American trade expert, entitled "Global Agricultural Trade – US Efforts at the WTO to Expand Agricultural Trade," published as part of his series of "Current Thoughts on Trade."[42]

A Greener WTO Agreement on Agriculture

The World Bank and International Food Policy Research Institute collaborated on a paper published in January 2020 that looked at agricultural

[42] Terence P. Stewart. 2011. "Global Agricultural Trade – US Efforts at the WTO to Expand Agricultural Trade." Washington International Trade Association. November 4. www.wita.org/blogs/global-agricultural-trade-us-efforts/. The US submissions are G/AG/W/32, JOB/AG 141, JOB/AG 141, JOB/AG/147, JOB/AG/164, JOB/AG/167, JOB/AG/169, and JOB/AG/192.

policy, including domestic support and trade restrictions, through a green lens.[43] The results are startling. While agriculture contributes very substantially to greenhouse gas (GHG) emissions (about one-third), adjusting the policy mix, the authors find, is anything but straightforward. First, the paper finds that domestic support only benefits farmers in the amount of 35 percent of the cost of the support programs. Then it turns to the effects of the complete elimination of domestic support on green goals: "simply removing all agricultural support, even if a global consensus were achieved to do so, would be insufficient to achieve large enough reductions in global GHG emissions to appreciably reduce agriculture's impact on the climate, and nature."

The paper proceeds to estimate what the impact would be of adjusting other policies as well, such as the removal of all trade barriers. This would reduce the positive GHG impact of the removal of domestic support because it would result in an increase in demand as food prices fall and consumption increases. The removal of protection would also have differential effects by product sector and therefore on diet, as sugar consumption would rise by 14 percent (not splendid for health). The greatest benefits would come from "repurposing a portion of government spending on agriculture each year to develop and disseminate more emission-efficient technologies for crops and livestock." The paper concludes that the gains could be immense from utilizing domestic support expenditures for greener purposes: "a net benefit of over $2 trillion in 20 years."

This is heady stuff and requires serious reflection. It is also not likely to be the kind of negotiation for which the WTO is best suited. Trade negotiators can more readily reflect general policy conclusions reached elsewhere where non-trade issues are more important than trade policy considerations. It is best to avoid the tail wagging the dog. The WTO might nevertheless become the forum chosen by default. This is because the WTO does have jurisdiction over domestic support. Moreover, the WTO cannot proceed to fulfill its mission as the forum for constructing overarching sets of rules for the world trading system without including agriculture. This means that there must eventually be, at the WTO, a multilateral agreement involving all the key providers of domestic support, engaging them in a fair but effective reduction of support

43 Madhur Gautam, David Laborde, Abdullah Mamun, Will Martin, Valeria Pineiro, and Rob Vos. 2022. "Repurposing Agricultural Policies and Support: Options to Transform Agriculture and Food Systems to Better Serve the Health of the People, Economies and the Planet." World Bank. January 24. www.openknowledge.worldbank.org/handle/10986/36875

levels. Unilateral disarmament is highly unlikely to take place – not in any permanent binding form. The United States and the European Union have both reduced domestic support for domestic reasons over the last quarter-century, but as the United States has shown, it was quite willing to increase domestic support very substantially due to the US–China trade conflict. When there were reductions, which was the trend, credit is probably not due primarily to WTO disciplines. The burden of budgetary outlays on national treasuries, not an attempt at a better trade policy through avoiding trade distortions, was no doubt the most important policy driver of domestic support reforms in the European Union and the United States. Since under the AoA, these two major WTO members have the freedom in the future to increase their support levels (once the short-term increase in US support is over), their contribution to the negotiations will be essential. As this is their policy space, they are not likely to give it up without trading it for agricultural concessions from other producers.

CONCLUSION

A failure to converge on agriculture has torpedoed an entire negotiating round, the Doha Development Agenda, the only Round attempted during the WTO era. Agriculture is an extraordinarily politically sensitive subject for a wide range of countries, as well as an essential one for international cooperation. The AoA was a magnificent achievement. It was the first major step toward less distorted, fairer international food trade. It may be that an agreement can be reached for agriculture in isolation, one that is self-balancing. It is reasonably clear how the AoA works and where it currently falls short. It is also reasonably clear which countries must be full participants, and that only a multilateral solution will be effective. All countries have a stake. All need to have a voice, even the poorest. If any point that I made resonated in the 1+6 meetings in which I participated in Beijing, it was that LDCs can contribute to the trading system with their ideas and their understanding of their own needs.

Perhaps climate change will force a global agricultural agreement. A crisis may give rise to sufficient motivation to find negotiated solutions. However, the pandemic has not done so, not in a sufficiently effective way, for trade and health. A single-subject agreement to meet a crisis was not an effective approach. An alternative approach to negotiations is to have more on the table. This could include such disparate matters as an agreement on e-commerce, a restoration of a new arrangement for binding dispute settlement, an environmental goods and services agreement, an expanded services agreement, agreements of special interest for developing countries such as a Standards Trade Development Fund for industrial standards, and the like. All that is needed is ingenuity and commitment. The theory for a future multi-subject negotiation is the same as for the Tokyo Round, which gave the trading system its first nontariff agreements, and the Uruguay Round, which, among other things, gave the world its first world trade organization. It is a process of putting enough chips in the pot so that no country can afford to walk away.

While the single undertaking approach should be seen as impairing forward movement due to its complexity, substantively and politically, the opposite extreme, a single-subject approach, also has marked shortcomings. It is always very difficult to make progress on agriculture. It becomes even more difficult if the subject is dealt with in isolation. There is no incentive for China, India, Nigeria, and other African countries to agree to reduce the support they are providing to their farmers in a standalone agriculture agreement. The argument that it is not economically sound policy for them to pay their farmers as much as they do is not compelling. Wealthier countries such as Switzerland and Japan have ignored sound advice and continue to subsidize their agriculture sectors. The answer as to whether a package broader than an agriculture agreement is needed in order to make progress has to date not been answered. With increased populations and the threat of countries resorting to export restrictions, there is a push for countries to increase domestic production with the assistance of subsidies. The proposal by Egypt in the run-up to MC12 is of interest in this context. Egypt suggested that developing countries be allowed to breach their *de minimis* limits to increase production to address the food security crisis.

A WTO Ministerial Conference should be convened with both members' trade ministers and agricultural ministers in attendance. Agriculture ministers know what their problems are; they are aware of their aspirations as well as their political and factual imperatives. Agriculture ministers have separate and productive meetings at the G20 and the Global Forum for Food and Agriculture (GFFA) in Berlin each year. They are unlikely to delegate responsibility to trade ministers to reach deep inside the domestic programs they administer. The FAO Director-General might be invited to co-chair the sessions at the WTO with the WTO Director-General. As it stands, the trade aspects of agriculture have not been susceptible to negotiation at the WTO and other fora are not places for negotiation. The deadlock must be broken.

In his Senate Finance Committee testimony Joseph Glauber summed up the place reserved for the WTO in agriculture: "The WTO can play an enormous role by reducing trade-distorting support, improving market access, ending distortions caused by export restrictions and subsidies, and perhaps most importantly, continue to provide a forum to which members can bring and hopefully resolve, trade disputes, rather than engaging in unilateral trade actions that can quickly escalate trade tensions."[44] The WTO's members will have to find the will to fulfill that promise.

[44] "Statement of Joseph W. Glauber: Senior Research Fellow, International Food Policy Research Institute – Before the Senate Finance Committee." United States Senate Committee on Finance. July 29, 2020. www.finance.senate.gov/imo/media/doc/29JUL2020Glauber~IFPRISTMNT1.pdf

9

Services

Between a fifth and a quarter of all world trade is accounted for by services, and even this number may be underestimated. Call centers, engineering, creation of software and apps, education, providing content for streaming services for entertainment, not to mention the ancillary services supporting the goods trade – customs brokerage, logistics, air and marine transport, and express delivery. It is a very long list that is constantly growing. A solid start was made with the General Agreement on Trade in Services (GATS) to bring services into the rules of the world trading system. Then little else was agreed but for the Joint Statement Initiative (JSI) on Domestic Regulation of Services. Much remains to be done.

THE WORLD OF SERVICES TRADE

In 2019, the year before the pandemic, world trade in services (measured by global commercial services imports) amounted to just over $6 trillion. In 2020, the first year of the pandemic, the number fell by $1.2 trillion, as quarantines took hold. Still, this was an enormous sum, and one that is growing rapidly over time and projected to continue to do so. In analyzing the data, the WTO and OECD break down services trade into a series of sectors. Telecommunications, computer, and information technology is the largest segment, accounting for 14.5 percent of the total trade in services, followed by transportation (12 percent), travel (11 percent), financial services (11 percent), payments for intellectual property (8 percent), insurance and pension (2.9 percent), construction (1.9 percent), and personal cultural and recreation (1.6 percent). The largest segment shown, however, is undifferentiated and listed as "other business services," which accounts for 27.3 percent of the total.[1]

[1] "WTO Stats." World Trade Organization. https://stats.wto.org/dashboard/services_en.html

On July 10, 1991, years before there was a WTO, the GATT Secretariat circulated an extensive listing of categories of services to allow country representatives in the Uruguay Round to maintain consistency in how they approached their negotiations for what was eventually to become the General Agreement on Trade in Services.[2] Samples from the list indicate the breadth of its coverage: professional services (for specialties ranging from law to medicine to engineering), research and development (R&D), real estate, advertising, printing, postal, courier, email, motion pictures, wholesale and retail, education, sanitation, insurance, banking, securities, tourism, sports, libraries, marine transportation (including pushing and towing), aircraft rental (with crew), trucking, pipelines, and even space transportation. The list gives a sense of the vast scope of the endeavor.

The world of services supply and trade is vastly more complicated than the production and trade of goods. Services are not regulated in a coherent way across different services sectors. Subjecting services trade to negotiations is immeasurably more difficult than trade in goods. It is one thing to regulate how customs officials classify and apply tariffs to goods as they cross borders, whether live horses or computer chips. It is a far more daunting task to address services, each having widely differing characteristics, and not met at the border by a single customs service but dealt with by an immense array of domestic authorities, often not just at the central government level, but lodged with political subdivisions.

THE CREATION OF THE GATS

When faced with a problem of this magnitude, the first question is how to impose some logical order on the subject at hand. This is what the Uruguay Round negotiators did. They determined that services could basically be supplied in four modes:

1. from the territory of one member into the territory of any other member;
2. in the territory of one member to the service consumer of any other member (the consumer travels to the service location);
3. by a service supplier of one member, through commercial presence in the territory of any other member;

[2] "Services Sectoral Classification List – Note by the Secretariat MTN.GNS/W/120 – Multilateral Trade Negotiations: The Uruguay Round." World Trade Organization. July 10, 1997. https://docs.wto.org/dol2fe/Pages/SS/directdoc.aspx?filename=Q:/UR/GNS/W120.PDF&Open=True

4. by a service supplier of one member, through the presence of natural persons of a member in the territory of any other member.

The four modes would be the basis for how trade negotiators constructed their agreement.[3] It is this taxonomy that they were to place in the first article of the GATS.[4]

The next hurdle would be to determine what broad rules would apply. For this, the GATT provided a template. The first rule would be nondiscrimination (MFN), the rock upon which the GATT was built. The second basic rule, one might have thought, would be national treatment. But granting national treatment to a service is tantamount to granting complete market access. Since market access would of necessity be the result of the give and take of negotiations, it would be rationed – accorded only as necessary to provide a degree of market access, ranging from complete openness to access hedged with restrictions, in return for access for one's own service suppliers. As with tariffs, the degree of access would be set out in member schedules of concessions. Listing a service without any conditions – whether specific to the item, to the sector, or applied across the board – would be conferring complete openness. National treatment would be provided pursuant to negotiated schedules indicating the degree of national treatment accorded. While access would be governed by a positive list – that is, no access would be provided unless specified – the schedule would often be hedged with conditions, seeking to define just how much access would be granted.

The third broad element of the GATS would be a requirement of transparency, to "publish promptly and, except in emergency situations, at the latest by the time of their entry into force, all relevant measures of general application which pertain to or affect the operation of this Agreement." Members (and under the single undertaking, this is to be the entire membership) are to notify changes at least annually to the Council for Trade in Services established by the agreement. A provision was also made for counter-notification: any member may notify to the Council for Trade in Services any measure, taken by any other member, which it considers to affect the operation of the agreement.

A fourth general element of GATS calls for specific commitments "by different Members" to strengthen developing country capacity and liberalize

3 The negotiators also recognized that on occasion, more than one mode would be required to supply a service.

4 GATS Art. I.

market access in sectors and modes of supply of export interest to developing countries.

A fifth general element concerns domestic regulations, which are to be "administered in a reasonable, objective and impartial manner." How this provision was to be implemented was left for the Council for Trade in Services to elaborate upon by prescribing disciplines to assure that this mandate was carried out. Within a quarter-century, this objective was fulfilled, but not as expected. It came about in a Joint Statement Initiative, not in the Services Council or in that Council's subordinate bodies.

A sixth general provision applicable to scheduled services commitments requires that members not condition recognition of qualifications of service suppliers of any other member in a manner "which would constitute a means of discrimination between countries in the application of its standards or criteria for the authorization, licensing or certification of services suppliers, or a disguised restriction on trade in services."

As a seventh general provision, members are not allowed to apply restrictions to international transfers and payments for current transactions relating to the member's specific (that is scheduled) commitments, other than where a balance of payments emergency exists.

Once this basic framework was constructed, the agreement could proceed to list exceptions – the first being for preferential trade agreements. This exception was to be in some respects more liberal than that provided for free trade agreements under the GATT. As long as a substantial number of sectors were involved, and substantially all discrimination was removed vis-à-vis the parties for those sectors (as opposed to the GATT FTA provision, which requires that substantially all trade be fully liberalized), discrimination against other WTO members not party to the free trade agreement could be maintained, but not increased. Given that the services of one member's suppliers can be provided from a location within another member's territory (mode 3), the GATS provides that service suppliers of other members having "substantive business operations in the territory of the parties to such agreement" would share in the benefits of the agreement.

Other exceptions allow measures that "are not applied in a manner which would constitute a means of arbitrary or unjustifiable discrimination between countries where like conditions prevail, or a disguised restriction on trade in services" and necessary to protect public morals or to maintain public order; to protect human, animal, or plant life or health; to prevent fraud, protect privacy, promote safety, ensure equitable or effective imposition or collection of direct taxes (including pursuant to an international agreement to avoid double taxation), or take "any action which it considers necessary for the protection of its essential security interests."[5]

Negotiations were envisaged to deal with trade-distorting subsidies. However, no subsidies disciplines have yet been agreed. Unless otherwise specified, scheduled concessions apply also to political subdivisions. If there are to be limits to a concession, the limits must be specified in detail in the schedule if they are to continue to be applied, and, as relevant, must be specific, including the number of suppliers, value of transactions or assets for economic needs tests, number of transactions, number of personnel, type of legal entity through which services may be supplied, and the amount of foreign capital participation.

GATS commitments are enforceable. Mediation, consultations, panel proceedings, and arbitration are available to obtain what was bargained for. GATS Article XIX gamely sets forth that members "shall enter into successive rounds of negotiations … with a view to achieving a progressively higher level of liberalization … promoting the interests of all participants on a mutually advantageous basis and to securing an overall balance of rights and obligations." The envisioned negotiations were to "take place with due respect for national policy objectives and the level of development of individual Members, both overall and in individual sectors." The progressive liberalization was to be achieved "through bilateral, plurilateral or multilateral negotiations."

In the next twenty-seven years, through 2022, no fully multilateral agreement was ever reached with respect to services. The single achievement was the JSI on the domestic regulation of services.

IMPLEMENTATION

The Council for Trade in Services (CTS)

There is perhaps no better way to understand both the subject matter of the WTO and its dynamics than by sitting in on a committee meeting. One can do this efficiently and vicariously for any meeting for which the Secretariat posts minutes. In July 2021, sitting in on a meeting of the Services Council chaired by Amb. Angel Villalobos (Mexico), one would have listened to a series of interventions, summarized below:[6]

5 "General Agreement on Trade in Services." World Trade Organization. www.wto.org/english/docs_e/legal_e/26-gats_01_e.htm

6 "Report of the Meeting Held on 1 July 2021: Note by the Secretariat – Council for Trade in Services S/C/M/146." World Trade Organization. July 22, 2021. https://docs.wto.org/dol2fe/Pages/SS/directdoc.aspx?filename=q:/S/C/M146.pdf&Open=True

- India reiterated that developed countries have fallen behind in notifying measures affecting mode 4 commitments (provision of services through natural persons present in the country consuming the service), a matter of strong and continuing interest for India.
- The United Kingdom and Mexico, and the United Kingdom and Canada, filed notifications with respect to updated FTAs (regional trade agreements, RTAs), and the chair reminded members that the Committee on RTAs was taking up the EU–Viet Nam FTA, the US–Mexico–Canada FTA (USMCA), and the Comprehensive Economic Partnership Agreement (CEPA) between Indonesia and Australia, all of which have a bearing on services.
- A discussion took place on further operationalizing the 2011 waiver for preferential treatment of services of LDCs, with the representative of Chad stating on behalf of the LDC group that a proposal would be made by the group for consideration at MC12 to further improve the exports of services from LDCs.
- India pointed to the need to reinvigorate the work on e-commerce within the Council on Trade in Services. China supported this statement and called for the extension of the moratorium on customs duties on electronic transmissions. India took the floor again to reiterate its position that those wishing extension of the moratorium should present evidence that it was on balance beneficial.
- There was a discussion of the work that the Secretariat should undertake to update data on the various modes of services. The United States suggested that intermodal data needed attention, but this should not consist of simply updating a 2009 data set for all modes of services.
- Japan and the United States each expressed continuing concerns regarding China's data localization requirements included in China's "Data Security Law," "Personal Information Protection Law," and "Regulations for Automobile Data Security Management," as well as Viet Nam's "Draft Decree on the Protection of Personal Information." The United States also raised concerns over Viet Nam's local presence requirements in its Cybersecurity Law and the draft implementing Decree of the Law. The EU, Australia, and Canada took the floor to raise many of the same and similar issues. China stated that it "welcomed Members' comments and suggestions and was willing to work closely with other Members in order to achieve a balance between cybersecurity, data security, protection of personal information and business development in the global digital economy."

- China raised its continuing concerns with Australia's restrictions on its 5G networks. Australia reiterated its prior responses that its measures were WTO-consistent.
- The United States requested a concrete response from the Russian Federation as to how mandating the use of Russian software through pre-installation complied with Russia's WTO obligations not to impose national treatment limitations on email, online information and database retrieval, online information and/or data processing, and computer and related services more generally. The EU took the floor to state that it had similar concerns and added a further concern that Russia intended to give a 50 percent subsidy for the installation of domestic software. Canada and Japan intervened stating similar concerns. Russia responded that there was no prohibition and described how the law was being implemented by the ministry concerned.
- China noted the revocation of relevant Executive Orders of the previous US administration on TikTok, WeChat, and other Chinese applications, which it said was a step in the right direction. But China also noted that the US government required a security risk review of Chinese apps and services and that the investigation of the Committee on Foreign Investment in the United States (CIFIUS) on TikTok was ongoing. These measures, it said, were vague and trade-restrictive, violated the basic principles of the WTO, and undermined the legitimate rights of relevant Chinese companies. The United States thanked China for its intervention and reiterated that the actions had been taken by the United States to protect US national security.
- China said that India had, through invoking national security interests, banned many applications from Chinese companies and discriminated against FDI from China. India said that it was committed to upholding its obligations at the WTO and protecting the democratic rights of its citizens, including access to goods and services, while reserving the right to take measures to ensure the protection of privacy, data security, and national security.
- The United States and European Union raised concerns with the Kingdom of Saudi Arabia regarding the localization of customer services. Saudi Arabia responded that the concern resulted from a misreading of Saudi Labor Law: "Saudization of workforce" had nothing to do with localization, as none of the international firms, whether located in the Kingdom of Saudi Arabia or abroad, were required, either *de jure* or *de facto*, to relocate their operations into the Kingdom in order to provide customer services within the Saudi Arabian market. The

decision specifically regulated the contractual relationship between employers and employees within the Kingdom of Saudi Arabia for "teleworking" in customer services, which was only permissible for Saudi nationals, rather than regulating firms or "customer services" provided by firms.

- A representative of the Secretariat noted that 2020 had witnessed the worst-ever decline in trade in services, not only since the global financial crisis when services trade had decreased by 17 percent in the second quarter of 2009, but also since estimates for world trade in services started being produced in 1980. Global services trade, measured as the average of exports and imports, had fallen by 21 percent in 2020. However, some countries had seen even sharper declines, such as the LDCs, whose exports had decreased by 35 percent in 2020. Consumer demand for services such as leisure, international travel, and recreation had shifted to goods. Travel services had decreased by 81 percent in the second quarter of 2020 and plateaued at –68 percent in the third and fourth quarters of 2020. In the first quarter of 2021, they were still 62 percent below the value of 2020. Transport had recovered substantially, and shipping costs had risen. A major problem was the misallocation of shipping containers, which had, during the pandemic, been left wherever the original shipment had been destined.
- Under the heading "Other Business," Mongolia noted that "since November 2020, the cost of shipping of 40-foot containers from Asia to Europe had risen more than threefold from around US$ 2,200 to US$ 7,900. The price of shipping goods from North America to Asia had doubled." Turkey noted that the lack of prompt coordination among countries had exacerbated the scale of the difficulties experienced. Turkey believed that international cooperation would be critical to finding a common solution, and that the adoption of the JSI on Domestic Services Regulation would contribute to providing a solution. South Africa was interested in working with other members to develop recommendations for preventing and resolving similar situations in the future and exchanging ideas on how members could cooperate or facilitate better circulation of containers.
- The chairman suggested that the Council take note of the statements made. It was so agreed.[7]

7 This is a standard response for chairs, like a responsive refrain in a religious service that through repetition may lose all meaning.

LITIGATION

There has been far less WTO litigation involving services as compared with goods. Thirty-two cases have been brought under the GATS as compared with 507 under GATT 1994. However, the cases that have been brought and decided have had a strong effect on the scope and effect of the GATS.

The object and purpose of the GATS is to provide transparency, "security and predictability of 'the reciprocal and mutually advantageous arrangements directed to the substantial reduction of tariffs and other barriers to trade.'" This recitation of purposes caused a panel to find that the United States' commitment in its GATS Schedule on "Other recreational services, except sporting" extended to internet gambling and betting services, although there was no evidence that this was contemplated by the negotiators.[8] Likewise, the panel in *China – Electronic Payment Services* referred to the principle of transparency expressed in the preamble of the GATS to confirm its interpretation of broad coverage of a new integrated service. The panel went further, stating: "nothing in the GATS suggests that the supply of a service through commercial presence in the territory of a Member does not extend to the 'export' of services from that Member's territory to a recipient in the territory of another Member or to a foreign recipient located in the 'exporting' Member's territory."

Similarly, the objective of "progressive liberalization" has caused panels to take an expansive view of the coverage of the GATS. "In *China – Publications and Audiovisual Products*, the panel found that the scope of China's commitment in its GATS Schedule on 'Sound recording distribution services' extends to sound recordings distributed in non-physical form, through technologies such as the Internet."[9]

In *Argentina – Financial Services*, a panel found that a condition imposed on the withdrawal from a market "affected services." As a result, it found the original concession was within the scope of the GATS and subject to WTO commitments.[10]

[8] "DS285: United States – Measures Affecting the Cross-Border Supply of Gambling and Betting Services." World Trade Organization. www.wto.org/english/tratop_e/dispu_e/cases_e/ds285_e.htm

[9] "WTO Analytical Index – GATS Preamble (Jurisprudence)." World Trade Organization. www.wto.org/english/res_e/publications_e/ai17_e/gats_preamble_jur.pdf

[10] "WTO Analytical Index – GATS Article I (Jurisprudence)." World Trade Organization. www.wto.org/english/res_e/publications_e/ai17_e/gats_art1_jur.pdf: "A measure which, for example, totally prohibits repatriation of invested capital at the time of withdrawal from the market would

In *Mexico – Telecoms*, coverage extended to a hand-off at the border of telecom services to a Mexican company. Physical presence was not required to claim coverage of the GATS. "The GATS creates a wide-ranging agreement covering all services and modes of supply, in order to allow progressive liberalization of trade in services between Members."[11]

In *US – Gambling*, the AB held that the panel would determine for itself whether a measure is "necessary" in the context of qualifying for an exception to the obligations imposed by the GATS. The panel also opined that whether a WTO-consistent alternative measure which the member concerned could "reasonably be expected to employ" is available, or whether a less WTO-inconsistent measure is "reasonably available," is within the bounds of what the panel may address. The burden of proof is on the party claiming the exception. In *Argentina – Financial Services*, the AB ruled that "in an analysis of 'necessity,' a panel's duty is to assess, in a qualitative or quantitative manner, the extent of the measure's contribution to the end pursued."[12] In *Mexico – Telecom*, the panel required complete clarity in the Mexican schedule with respect to carving out any future flexibility to qualify market access. That access was conditioned on the issuance of regulations did not mean that later, "a numerical quota [could] be imposed on the issuance of permits." Rather, it meant that access had to await the issuance of regulations.

In the *Boeing–Airbus* case (*US – Large Civil Aircraft [2nd Complaint]*), the panel made a clear determination that the Agreement on Subsidies and Countervailing Measures (SCM) did not apply to services.[13] There are therefore definitively no disciplines on subsidies to services.

In *US – Gambling*, the AB made clear that restrictions on market access needed to be specified in the imposing member's schedule and "a specific commitment in a given sector or sub-sector is a guarantee that the whole of that sector, i.e., all services included in that sector or sub-sector are covered." The AB also held that a quantitative limitation could not be set at zero. If a member wished to exclude a sector or a particular service, it could simply leave it out of its schedule. Further, the AB stated that inscribing "none,"

most likely influence the supplier's decision as to whether or not to establish a commercial presence in that market."

[11] "DS204: Mexico – Measures Affecting Telecommunications Services." World Trade Organization. www.wto.org/english/tratop_e/dispu_e/cases_e/ds204_e.htm

[12] "DS453: Argentina – Measures Relating to Trade in Goods and Services." World Trade Organization. www.wto.org/english/tratop_e/dispu_e/cases_e/ds453_e.htm

[13] "DS353: United States – Measures Affecting Trade in Large Civil Aircraft – Second Complaint." World Trade Organization. www.wto.org/english/tratop_e/dispu_e/cases_e/ds353_e.htm

meaning no conditions, meant that full market access was granted, just as the word "unbound" meant retaining full freedom to restrict market access. The panels in *China – Publications and Audiovisual Products* and *China – Electronic Payment Services* underlined that "unbound" conferred complete freedom to deny market access, as long as this was done on a nondiscriminatory (MFN) basis.[14]

With respect to both goods and services, there is the possibility that years after a concession has been granted, there will be a disagreement as to whether the concession was intended to cover the good or service under changed market or competitive conditions. This was the situation grappled with in *EU – Computer Equipment* and in several of the GATS cases cited above.[15] Technological change over time makes a backward look at the "legitimate expectations" of the parties at the time of negotiation susceptible to sharp differences of opinion. One gets the sense that with services evolving at a fast rate, perhaps being more difficult to define and contained in categories that were unclear to begin with, concessions covering services may result relatively often in a larger scope for concessions granted than the party granting the concession foresaw. Could the United States have reasonably understood when it filed its GATS Schedule that "other recreational activities" would encompass internet gambling? Or if it did understand, did it later regret having made the concession as broad as it came to be interpreted? This is a reason for exercising caution in making sure that every concession is hedged in with extensive conditions to cover all possible contingencies. That mindset, however, would make trade liberalization difficult to a likely unwarranted degree.

[14] "DS363: China – Measures Affecting Trading Rights and Distribution Services for Certain Publications and Audiovisual Entertainment Products." World Trade Organization. www.wto.org/english/tratop_e/dispu_e/cases_e/ds363_e.htm

[15] "European Communities – Customs Classification of Certain Computer Equipment WT/DS62/AB/R WT/DS67/AB/R WT/DS68/AB/R." World Trade Organization. June 5, 1998. https://docs.wto.org/dol2fe/Pages/FE_Search/FE_S_S009-DP.aspx?language=E&CatalogueIdList=6357,6029,16166,20601,22244,28840,41163,29630,33596,19769&CurrentCatalogueIdIndex=1&FullTextHash=

> *Tariff negotiations are a process of reciprocal demands and concessions, of "give and take." It is only normal that importing Members define their offers (and their ensuing obligations) in terms which suit their needs. On the other hand, exporting Members have to ensure that their corresponding rights are described in such a manner in the Schedules of importing Members that their export interests, as agreed in the negotiations, are guaranteed … We consider that any clarification of the scope of tariff concessions that may be required during the negotiations is a task for all interested parties.*

SERVICES NEGOTIATIONS

As noted above in the description of GATS Article XIX, the GATS negotiators envisaged "successive rounds of negotiations, beginning not later than five years from the date of entry into force of the WTO Agreement and periodically thereafter, with a view to achieving a progressively higher level of liberalization." As a result, in January 2000, five years after the GATS entered into force, negotiations were begun. Progress was made, in line with the lengthening timetables of international cooperation that was experienced in the Uruguay Round, with an increasing number of parties, in the form of adopting the "Guidelines and the Procedures for the Negotiations on Trade in Services" fourteen months later in March 2001. Services negotiations were made a prominent part of the Doha Development Agenda (DDA), which was launched in November 2001. Various midpoints were established, with offers tabled by the Hong Kong Ministerial Conference in December 2005. Failure to agree on agriculture and nonagricultural market access (NAMA) ended any forward motion on the DDA in 2008. Fully multilateral negotiations never resumed.[16]

This is not to say that there were not sporadic attempts at initiating limited negotiations. For example, in May 2017, the European Union circulated a proposal entitled "How Common Principles on Consumer Protection, Unsolicited Messages, Authentication and Trust Services and Electronic Contracts Would Contribute to a Better Integration, Especially of SMEs, in the World Economy and Enhance Trust and Confidence of Consumers Online."[17] On June 6, the Council on Trade in Services in Special Session met to discuss the proposal. Several delegations welcomed the proposal but sought clarifications, or a different approach covering goods as well as intellectual property and services. A number of delegations were opposed to the EU proposal, including the LDC Group, the Africa Group, and India. Some said that there was no negotiating mandate. Some thought that the subject was not appropriate for the WTO at all. Reading the minutes, one can readily determine that the proposal did not have

[16] There is no compelling need to cover negotiations in which the last progress report was issued over a decade ago. "WTO Negotiations on GATS Rules." World Trade Organization. www.wto.org/english/tratop_e/serv_e/gats_rules_negs_e.htm

[17] "Communication from the European Union: An Enabling Environment to Facilitate Online Transactions TN/S/W/64." World Trade Organization. May 23, 2017. https://docs.wto.org/dol2fe/Pages/SS/directdoc.aspx?filename=q:/TN/S/W64.pdf&Open=True

much of a future if any, absent a major effort by the EU to reshape the proposal and gain adherents to it.[18]

In April 2013, twenty-three countries (counting the EU as one) launched negotiations of a Trade in Services Agreement (TISA) to promote “fair and open trade across the full spectrum of service industries.” The participants encompassed most major economies engaged in services trade with the exception of China and India. The only participant from Africa was Mauritius. The European Union and the United States were primary proponents of the negotiations, which were held in Geneva but were not WTO negotiations. Various civil society groups criticized the negotiations as changing the regulation of many public and privatized or commercial services from serving the public interest to serving the profit interests of private, foreign corporations. The anti-globalists preferred the preservation of policy space to a more open international environment for services.

Participating governments describe TISA in the current tense but refer to “the most recent round of negotiations, held from December 6–8, 2016,” which was to take “stock of the good progress achieved this year to advance the negotiations towards conclusion,” referring to “a small number of remaining issues for the more advanced annexes such as Financial Services, Professional Services, Electronic Commerce, Localization, Telecommunications, Movement of Natural Persons and Transportation.” The Government of Canada notes that “parties continue to consult internally until a date is determined among the Parties to reconvene for the next formal round of negotiations.”[19] At the WTO, in Geneva, there has been no indication that TISA is about to be restarted.

At the WTO, the breakthrough for services occurred at MC11, the Ministerial Conference held in Buenos Aires in December 2017. Interested members launched a JSI on the Domestic Regulation of Services, described in Chapter 6 of this book. It was not as fraught with negotiating difficulties as the GATS or subsequent efforts to expand GATS coverage, as no additional market access was being offered. The focus was on providing due process. The negotiation was concluded successfully and the results are being incorporated into members’ schedules.

[18] “Report of the Meeting Held on 6 June 2017 – Note by the Secretariat TN/S/M/47.” World Trade Organization. June 27, 2017. https://docs.wto.org/dol2fe/Pages/SS/directdoc.aspx?filename=q:/TN/S/M47.pdf&Open=True

[19] “Trade in Services Agreement (TISA).” Global Affairs Canada. www.international.gc.ca/trade-agreements-accords-commerciaux/topics-domaines/services/tisa-acs.aspx?lang=eng

10

E-Commerce

The world of digital commerce is relatively new. It is a by-product of an information technology revolution that started with the invention of the integrated circuit, carried forward with advances in computing and unleashed with the creation of the internet. Digital commerce is familiar in some respects and dramatically different in others from the world of trade that preceded it. It poses special problems of privacy, unwanted communication, and new kinds of competition, stemming from the flow of data across borders. It gave rise to the need for devising rules for its nurture and management. It makes the most sense for the rules to be global, as without interference from governments, e-commerce is global. It creates opportunities as never experienced before for innovation and for individual and small business involvement in international commerce. This is the story of the evolution of the process of rule-making in the age of digital commerce.

FIRST STEPS

There is a long history of things sourced in one place being wanted in another. That is the wellspring of long-distance trade. Clay tablets in Sumer and papyrus in Egypt facilitated trade. Eventually, there would be catalogues produced in Venice during the Renaissance and later in England and colonial America in the eighteenth century (including one issued by Benjamin Franklin for books). The invention of the parcel post is credited to Germany with the growth of railroads. The invention of steamships and the telegraph were way stations in the advances made in telecommunications and transportation, creating a new and more interconnected world. Within living memory, at the end of the 1960s, the very first versions of the internet were being tried out in laboratories in California, connecting UCLA with Stanford. A key project that was instrumental in achieving this breakthrough was marvelously titled "Augmentation of the Human Intellect."[1] Its growth was made possible by the invention of the integrated circuit by Robert Noyce and Jack Kilby a dozen years earlier.[2]

It was not long before entrepreneurs found that teleshopping was possible and profitable.[3] Global value chains became enabled to an unprecedented extent. Government regulation lagged – fortunately, in most respects. This meant that e-commerce grew exponentially, due in large part to the fact that national protectionist instincts and restrictive measures had not yet been marshalled. International notice of the growing use of the internet for commerce gave rise to a need for cooperation to avoid a proliferation of national restrictions.

The internet differs from other forms of commerce in its ubiquity and lack of respect for borders. Governments through their customs authorities were accustomed to regulating physical commerce, whether the placing of a tariff on an import or preventing contraband goods from crossing borders, say drugs or elephant ivory. Governments were slow to regulate trade carried out over the internet, which is harder to do when the commerce is taking place, for example, through the downloading of a program or the provision of crop insurance from a foreign source. Governments understood that some form of international understanding would be needed to avoid disparate and counter-productive national regulatory frameworks, but were unclear as to how to approach the subject. Many of them recognized that e-commerce could be a very positive contribution to their economies.

In 1998, member governments adopted the APEC Blueprint for Action for Electronic Commerce,[4] one of the most pro-commerce documents in the history of world trade. It states:

1 Interestingly, that title, "Augmentation of the Human Intellect", has in the current iteration of microelectronics found an echo in "Mission Lucidity," which attempts to marry human tissue to an integrated circuit (neurons grown on top of multi-electrode arrays [MEAs]) at IMEC located at Leuvain to deal with Parkinson's disease. The WTO needs its own "Mission Lucidity," bringing together appropriate new rules to address the issues raised by e-commerce and the measures nations use to deal with it. "Brief History of the Internet." Internet Society. 1997. www.internetsociety.org/internet/history-internet/brief-history-internet/; "How Chip Technology Will Decipher Brain Diseases." Imec R&D Nano Electronics and Digital Technologies. December 21, 2020. www.imec-int.com/en/articles/how-chip-technology-will-decipher-brain-diseases

2 From 1977 until his untimely death in 1990, Bob Noyce was a leader in public policy for the US semiconductor industry in the challenges it faced in international competition.

3 "The History of eCommerce: How Did It All Begin?" IWD Agency. September 23, 2021. www.iwdagency.com/blogs/news/the-history-of-ecommerce-how-did-it-all-begin. This source provides a description and links to some of the steps along the way to today's world of e-commerce.

4 "APEC Blueprint for Action on Electronic Commerce." Asia-Pacific Economic Cooperation. 1998. www.apec.org/meeting-papers/leaders-declarations/1998/1998_aelm/apec_blueprint_for

The role of governments is to promote and facilitate the development and uptake of electronic commerce by:

- *Providing a favorable environment, including the legal and regulatory aspects, which is predictable, transparent and consistent,*
- *Providing an environment which promotes trust and confidence among electronic commerce participants,*
- *Promoting the efficient functioning of electronic commerce internationally by aiming, wherever possible, to develop domestic frameworks which are compatible with evolving international norms and practices, and*
- *Becoming a leading-edge user in order to catalyse and encourage greater use of electronic means.*

The need for the protection of privacy was an early concern. There quickly followed in the same year the adoption of the APEC Privacy Framework,[5] as well as the APEC Cross-Border Privacy Rules (CBPR) System,[6] which were a set of principles to guide domestic legislation, building on the OECD's Guidelines Governing the Protection of Privacy and Transborder Flows of Personal Data.[7]

The WTO took its first formal step into the issues surrounding e-commerce at its second Ministerial Conference in 1998. Internet domains had been licensed only three years earlier. This was still early days in the organization of the web. The forerunners of e-commerce involved only ordering goods via email rather than by means of a phone call or through regular mail. Commerce was now moving online. The WTO ministers gathering in Geneva that year issued a declaration calling on the General Council to set up a work program on trade issues related to global electronic commerce, somewhat bizarrely adding the phrase "including those issues identified by Members."[8] The declaration had the obligatory formula: "taking into account

5 "APEC Privacy Framework." Asia-Pacific Economic Cooperation. August 2017. www.apec.org/publications/2017/08/apec-privacy-framework-(2015)

6 "What Is the Cross-Border Privacy Rules System." Asia-Pacific Economic Cooperation. October 2021. www.apec.org/about-us/about-apec/fact-sheets/what-is-the-cross-border-privacy-rules-system. Developed by all twenty-one APEC economies and endorsed by APEC leaders in 2011, an APEC economy must demonstrate that it can enforce compliance with the APEC Cross-Border Privacy Rules (CBPR) System's requirements before joining.

7 "Recommendation of the Council Concerning Guidelines Governing the Protection of Privacy and Transborder Flows of Personal Data." OECD Legal Instruments. https://legalinstruments.oecd.org/public/doc/114/114.en.pdf

8 "The Geneva Ministerial Declaration on Global Electronic Commerce WT/MIN(98)/DEC/2." World Trade Organization. May 25, 1998. www.wto.org/english/tratop_e/ecom_e/mindec1_e.htm

the needs of developing countries," although what this would mean in a system not yet thought through made it just a placeholder.[9]

Of greatest importance, the ministerial declaration added the pledge: "Members will continue their current practice of not imposing customs duties on electronic transmissions."[10] No one knew exactly what this odd term "electronic transmissions" meant at the time. The customs duties moratorium on e-commerce has since been taken by members to mean that no duties would be imposed on goods or services provided through the internet. Thus, when it became technologically possible to stream a movie or deliver software between computers across borders for the next quarter-century, a pledge was in place that was generally considered to prohibit the application of customs duties, duties that would be applied to the same product imported in physical form.

In July, four months after the 1998 Ministerial Conference, the General Council duly adopted an e-commerce work program,[11] parceling out tasks to four WTO committees – the Councils for Trade in Goods, Services, and Trade-Related Intellectual Property Rights, and the Committee on Trade and Development. The General Council specified a long list of elements of electronic commerce to be examined by these bodies, including:

- modes of supply (relating to trade in services),
- nondiscrimination,
- transparency,
- the participation of developing countries,
- domestic regulation,
- standards,
- competition,
- protection of privacy and public morals and the prevention of fraud,
- market access commitments on electronic supply of services (including commitments on basic and value-added telecommunications services and distribution services),
- national treatment,
- access to and use of public telecommunications transport networks and services (referring to the Annex on Telecommunications),
- customs duties,

[9] Ibid.

[10] Ibid.

[11] "Work Programme on Electronic Commerce WT/L/274." World Trade Organization. September 30, 1998. https://docs.wto.org/dol2fe/Pages/SS/directdoc.aspx?filename=Q:/WT/L/274.pdf&Open=True

- classification issues,
- valuation and rules of origin (for goods),
- protection of IP including new technologies, and
- access to technology.

For developing countries, the elements to be examined included the effects of electronic commerce on their trade and economic prospects, notably on:

- small and medium-sized enterprises (SMEs),
- ways of enhancing developing countries' participation in electronic commerce, in particular as exporters of electronically delivered products,
- achieving improved access to infrastructure and transfer of technology, and the movement of natural persons,
- use of information technology in developing countries' integration into the multilateral trading system,
- implications for developing economies of the possible impact of electronic commerce on the traditional means of distribution of physical goods, and
- financial implications of electronic commerce.

In prospect, this was a vast undertaking. There would be a limit to what could be achieved. But that was in the future. Substantial efforts were made to bring e-commerce into the WTO rulebook in the early years. In November 1998, the way forward was prepared for the Council for Trade in Services by a Secretariat note setting out the interaction of the General Agreement on Trade in Services (GATS) with electronic commerce.[12] It was an example of how the Secretariat can facilitate deliberations on a subject by getting needed information into the hands of members even before being asked for support.

In June 2001, the WTO Secretariat issued a background note providing a list of member concerns.[13] Members could not agree on whether digitized products were services, a step needed to determine if the GATS would apply. No small number of developing country members remained concerned that benefits from e-commerce would not flow through to them. They focused particularly on its fiscal implications, that goods provided over the internet would escape import duties. In the first three years of the grand quest of

[12] "The Work Programme on Electronic Commerce – Note by the Secretariat S/C/W/68." World Trade Organization. November 16, 1998. https://docs.wto.org/dol2fe/Pages/SS/directdoc.aspx?filename=Q:/S/C/w68.pdf&Open=True

[13] "Dedicated Discussion on Electronic Commerce Under the Auspices of the General Council on 15 June 2001 WT/GC/W/436." World Trade Organization. July 6, 2001. https://docs.wto.org/dol2fe/Pages/SS/directdoc.aspx?filename=q:/WT/GC/W436.pdf&Open=True

bringing e-commerce into the WTO, there were more questions than answers. What did e-commerce encompass? What would its impact be?

The conversation as to what should be done in terms of a WTO agreement on e-commerce did not advance very far in the ensuing two decades within the standing committees of the WTO. No new rules were agreed upon within the E-Commerce Work Program. For the years that followed the founding of the Program, most of the action shifted outside the WTO to bilateral and regional trade agreements.

STEPPING STONES ON THE WAY BACK TO GENEVA

A substantial number of bilateral and regional agreements were pioneering efforts in seeking to provide a legal framework for digital commerce. They, like the GATT, are a mix of political commitments and hard law to keep government regulation out of the way of the growth of commerce. These agreements also reserved policy space for their participants, leaving inchoate areas that may be regulated on a national level by omitting some matters from the comprehensive requirements of international agreements. For WTO purposes, for the multilateral trading system, the sub-multilateral agreements can be considered building blocks, and where they did not go far enough or went too far, they can be viewed as local rules to be superseded. (For a survey of common elements in free trade agreements, see a paper by Ines Willemyns, published in September 2021.[14])

Federal and central governments are used to overcoming internal local barriers. In the United States, the commerce clause has allowed the federal government to use the courts to assure that goods flow seamlessly across state borders.[15] There are still some limits. Professional services are licensed by the states, and the right to practice in one state is not necessarily a right to practice in others. States have different indirect (sales) taxes. State phytosanitary certificates are issued for products shipped to other states that require freedom from plant pests. The European Union has a similar continual challenge of perfecting the single market and testing the areas of its competence.

As electronic transmissions know no physical borders, absent national attempts to block them, the relatively comfortable traditional sphere of

[14] Ines Willemyns. 2021. "8 – Evolution of E commerce-Related Provisions in RTAs" in *Digital Services in International Trade Law*. Cambridge: Cambridge University Press.

[15] According to Article 1, Section 8, Clause 3 of the US Constitution, Congress has the power "to regulate commerce with foreign nations, and among the several states, and with the Indian tribes."

domestic law and regulation, subject to the dictates of a federal or central government, would need to adapt to international commercial exchanges via the internet. Where there was enough trust and commercial interest, FTAs provided an incremental way forward.

THE SINGAPORE–AUSTRALIA FREE TRADE AGREEMENT (SAFTA)

Among the earliest efforts to provide rules to promote the use of e-commerce was a 2003 FTA between Singapore and Australia (SAFTA), which included a chapter on the subject.[16] It was a straightforward combination of binding obligations, best efforts, and pledges for coordination. The heart of the agreement was the same provision that the WTO ministers had agreed to in 1998, namely, a commitment not to impose customs duties on electronic transmissions between these two signatories. Added to this was a requirement of transparency, to publish regulations and measures affecting e-commerce. Other commitments that were included: to maintain a domestic legal framework based on the United Nations Commission on International Trade Law (UNCITRAL), to maintain domestic legislation for the authentication of electronic documents, to permit paperless trading (filing trade-related documents with the government electronically), and to work to permit the use of electronic signatures. Other obligations were softer: "to the extent practical and to the extent it considered appropriate," protect data privacy for the persons of the other party in line with the protection of domestic persons, and provide for consumer protection.

Through a series of amendments over much of the next two decades, SAFTA's original chapter with ten articles was expanded to thirty-eight, extending to subjects such as:

- prohibiting forced technology transfer (including protection of source code),
- specifying national treatment including with respect to internal taxation,
- promoting electronic invoicing,
- facilitating electronic payments and express shipments,
- cooperating on enforcement of competition laws,
- protecting against harmful content,
- cooperating to counter spam,
- assuring connectivity to networks,

16 "Singapore–Australia Free Trade Agreement (SAFTA) Consolidated Text." World Integrated Trade Solution. https://wits.worldbank.org/GPTAD/PDF/archive/Singapore-Australia.pdf

- providing for connection charges on a commercial basis,
- facilitating the use of submarine cables,
- barring forced localization of servers (with a special provision for financial information),
- supporting innovation,
- supporting the maintenance of digital identities,
- cooperating on standards and conformity assessment,
- cooperating on artificial intelligence (AI) research including related ethical standards,
- cooperating on fintech,
- sharing approaches to cybersecurity,
- promoting stakeholder engagement,
- working to benefit SMEs and engaging in capacity-building, and
- providing for a review of the agreement if either of the parties enters into an agreement to give better treatment to another country.[17]

CPTPP AND TPP

On October 5, 2015, twelve countries concluded the Trans-Pacific Partnership (TPP). With the United States dropping out, the remaining eleven agreed to the Comprehensive and Progressive TPP (CPTPP), incorporating without change the TPP provisions dealing with e-commerce.[18] On December 30, 2018, the CPTPP entered into force for Australia, Canada, Japan, Mexico, New Zealand, and Singapore.

The heart of the chapter consists of commitments:

- Ensuring free flow of global information and data;
- Pledging not to require localization of data centers as a condition for operating in a TPP market;
- Pledging not to require the transferring of or access to source code of software;
- Prohibiting the imposition of customs duties on electronic transmissions;
- Requiring national treatment;
- Agreeing to adopt and maintain consumer protection and privacy laws;
- Barring spam;
- Maintaining consumer and privacy protections;

[17] "SAFTA Chapter 14 – Digital Economy." Australian Government – Department of Foreign Affairs and Trade. www.dfat.gov.au/sites/default/files/SAFTA-chapter-14.pdf

[18] "Chapter 14 – Electronic Commerce." Australian Government – Department of Foreign Affairs and Trade. www.dfat.gov.au/sites/default/files/14-electronic-commerce.pdf

- Encouraging paperless trading between businesses and the government; and
- Providing for electronic authentication and signatures for commercial transactions.

THE USMCA

In August 2017, the United States pressed Mexico and Canada to renegotiate the North American Free Trade Agreement (NAFTA), updating it in several respects, including the incorporation, with some refinements, of the TPP e-commerce chapter. The resulting US–Canada–Mexico Free Trade Agreement (USMCA), which entered into effect on July 1, 2020, differs in some respects from the TPP e-commerce chapter.[19] The USMCA cites international norms for data privacy, including APEC's cross-border personal data privacy protection. The agreement also narrows the use of restrictions on cross-border data transfers, provides an explicit way of dealing with financial services with respect to forced data localization, creates a safe harbor for interactive computer services shielding them from liability, promotes open government data, and requires that cybersecurity provisions utilize a risk-based approach.[20] PIIE colleague Jeff Schott estimated, however, that the USMCA's e-commerce provisions largely incorporate what Mexico and Canada had committed to in the TPP, providing no further significant gains for US commerce.

JAPAN–US DIGITAL TRADE AGREEMENT

In October 2019, the United States and Japan signed a digital trade agreement that the United States claimed was "the most comprehensive and high-standard trade agreement addressing digital trade barriers ever negotiated."[21]

19 "Comparison of Selected Digital Trade Provisions in the United States–Mexico–Canada Agreement (USMCA) and the Trans-Pacific Partnership (TPP)." BSA – The Software Alliance. April 11, 2019. www.bsa.org/files/policy-filings/04112019tppvusmcacomparison.pdf

20 Jeffrey J. Schott. 2019. "Five Flaws in the USMCA and How to Fix Them." Peterson Institute for International Economics. August 6. www.piie.com/blogs/trade-and-investment-policy-watch/five-flaws-usmca-and-how-fix-them

21 Ines Willemyns. 2021. "8 – Evolution of E-Commerce-Related Provisions in RTAs" in *Digital Services in International Trade Law*. Cambridge: Cambridge University Press; "Agreement between the United States of America and Japan Concerning Digital Trade." United States Trade Representative. October 7, 2019. www.ustr.gov/sites/default/files/files/agreements/japan/Agreement_between_the_United_States_and_Japan_concerning_Digital_Trade.pdf

The agreement contains provisions:

- *Prohibiting application of customs duties to digital products distributed electronically, such as e-books, videos, music, software, and games;*
- *Ensuring nondiscriminatory treatment of digital products, including coverage of tax measures;*
- *Ensuring that data can be transferred across borders, by all suppliers, including financial service suppliers;*
- *Facilitating digital transactions by permitting the use of electronic authentication and electronic signatures, while protecting consumers' and businesses' confidential information and guaranteeing that enforceable consumer protections are applied to the digital marketplace;*
- *Prohibiting data localization measures that restrict where data can be stored and processed, enhancing and protecting the global digital ecosystem, and extending these rules to financial service suppliers in circumstances where a financial regulator has the access to data needed to fulfill its regulatory and supervisory mandate;*
- *Promoting government-to-government collaboration and supplier adherence to common principles in addressing cybersecurity challenges;*
- *Protecting against forced disclosure of proprietary computer source code and algorithms;*
- *Promoting open access to government-generated public data;*
- *Recognizing rules on civil liability with respect to third-party content for internet platforms that depend on interaction with users;*
- *Guaranteeing enforceable consumer protections, including for privacy and unsolicited communication, that apply to the digital marketplace, and promoting the interoperability of enforcement regimes, such as the APEC Cross-Border Privacy Rules system;*
- *Ensuring companies' effective use of encryption technologies and protecting innovation for commercial products that use cryptography, consistent with applicable law.*

DEPA

On June 12, 2020, Chile, New Zealand, and Singapore signed their first Digital Economic Partnership Agreement (DEPA).[22] It has three broad categories of rules with four items under each heading:

[22] "Digital Economy Partnership Agreement (DEPA)." Ministry of Trade and Industry Singapore. www.mti.gov.sg/Trade/Digital-Economy-Agreements/The-Digital-Economy-Partnership-Agreement

- Facilitating digital trade, through
    - Safe mutual recognition of digital identities,
    - E-invoicing,
    - Paperless trade,
    - FinTech and e-payments.
- Enabling trusted data flows, through
    - Protection of personal data,
    - Open government data,
    - Freedom of cross-border data flows for business,
    - Support for data-driven innovation.
- Building trust and facilitating broader opportunities, through
    - Ethical AI governance networks,
    - Capacity-building for SMEs,
    - Online consumer protection,
    - Promotion of digital inclusion.

In contrast with the other FTAs noted in this section, the key modules of the DEPA consist of cross-references to commitments made in other agreements rather than binding rules created in DEPA itself. DEPA Article 4.3 Cross Border Transfer of Information is transposed from TPP/CPTPP Article 14.11:

> *Article 4.3: Cross-Border Transfer of Information by Electronic Means*
>
> *The Parties affirm their level of commitments relating to cross-border transfer of information by electronic means, in particular, but not exclusively:*
>
> 1. *The Parties recognise that each Party may have its own regulatory requirements concerning the transfer of information by electronic means.*
> 2. *Each Party shall allow the cross-border transfer of information by electronic means, including personal information, when this activity is for the conduct of the business of a covered person.*
> 3. *Nothing in this Article shall prevent a Party from adopting or maintaining measures inconsistent with paragraph 2 to achieve a legitimate public policy objective, provided that the measure:*
>   (a) *is not applied in a manner which would constitute a means of arbitrary or unjustifiable discrimination or a disguised restriction on trade; and*
>   (b) *does not impose restrictions on transfers of information greater than are required to achieve the objective.*

The same approach is taken by DEPA, for example, with respect to forced technology transfer and data localization requirements.

E-COMMERCE DIGITAL ECONOMY AGREEMENT: AUSTRALIA AND SINGAPORE

In August 2020, Australia and Singapore entered into an E-Commerce Digital Economy Agreement (ASDEA) that built upon, expanded, and replaced the SAFTA e-commerce chapter.[23] The stated purposes of the two signatories were to accelerate their economies' integration and digital transformation, and establish new benchmarks for cooperation in relation to the digital economy, consciously enhancing their "international and regional leadership roles in the pursuit of ambitious benchmarks, rules and standards for the digital economy" and affirming their undertakings in other agreements, including any at the WTO relating to the digital economy.[24] The new agreement, the governments said, sharpened its provisions to avoid data localization, increased protections of source code, provided new commitments on e-invoicing and e-payment frameworks, improved consumer protection (to protect personal information and discourage spam), added protections against harm from what was on the web, and provided for greater transparency of government regulations pertaining to the digital economy.

COMMON ELEMENTS OF THESE AGREEMENTS

DEPA, SAFTA, ASDEA, the US–Japan Digital Agreement, and USMCA contain five important common obligations:

- No customs duties on content transmitted electronically between parties;
- Grant of national treatment for digital products (except with respect to subsidies);
- Maintaining a legal framework for the protection of personal data (citing international norms);
- Prohibiting forced technology transfer;
- Banning data localization requirements (except for valid public policy reasons).

[23] "Australia–Singapore Digital Economy Agreement." Australian Government – Department of Foreign Affairs and Trade. March 23, 2020. www.dfat.gov.au/sites/default/files/australia-singapore-digital-economy-agreement.pdf

[24] "Australia–Singapore Digital Economy Agreement – Fact Sheet." Australian Government – Department of Foreign Affairs and Trade. December 8, 2020. www.dfat.gov.au/sites/default/files/australia-singapore-digital-economy-agreement-fact-sheet_0.pdf

To these was added a suite of paperless trading provisions (electronic signature etc.).

Often the agreements contain provisions for binding dispute settlement, an exception being, not surprisingly, the US–Japan Agreement.

DEPA and the Australia–Singapore Digital Economy Agreement suggest a path forward. Additional regional or bilateral trade agreements, which the US might join, would give its Indo-Pacific Economic Framework substantive rules with respect to e-commerce. They can serve as a template for WTO Joint Statement Initiative negotiations.

There are numerous additional areas for future work on international rules for digital commerce. Cooperation on competition policy could avert conflicts. AI will require regulation without strangulation. Fintech is already very important and will require further collaboration among regulatory authorities. For the Biden administration, with its emphasis on worker-centric agreements, recognition could be given to the fact that the growth of jobs is increasingly to be found in the digital world, rather than in traditional manufacturing. The digital economy is also not tied to population centers and can restore growth in rural areas. The role of intermediate services is being discovered as a significant source of employment.[25] It would be worker-centric to promote the participation of women and SMEs in digital commerce.

THE WTO JSI ON E-COMMERCE

The 2017 Ministerial Conference (MC11 in Buenos Aires) moved e-commerce into a higher gear at the WTO, creating a separate workstream and calling on members to "reinvigorate" work within the existing WTO structure.[26] Dissatisfied with the absence of sufficient progress in the WTO's regular committees, members accounting for a very large portion of world GDP

[25] "Services Trade." OECD. www.oecd.org/trade/topics/services-trade/

[26] "Work Programme on Electronic Commerce WT/MIN(17)/65 WT/L/1032." World Trade Organization. December 18, 2017. www.mfat.govt.nz/assets/Trade-agreements/WTO-e-commerce-negotiations/WORK-PROGRAMME-ON-ELECTRONIC-COMMERCE-Ministerial-Decision-December-2017.pdf

> *The Ministerial Conference decides as follows: "We agree to continue the work under the Work Programme on Electronic Commerce since our last session, based on the existing mandate as set out in WT/L/274. We will endeavour to reinvigorate our work and instruct the General Council to hold periodic reviews in its sessions of July and December 2018 and July 2019 based on the reports submitted by the relevant WTO bodies and report to the next session of the Ministerial Conference. We agree to maintain the current practice of not imposing customs duties on electronic transmissions until our next session which we have decided to hold in 2019."*

created what they called joint statement initiatives (JSIs), which are groups of like-minded members aiming to work together on open plurilateral agreements (OPAs). There were four JSIs. Arguably the most important, the e-commerce JSI, was brought into being by three co-convenors – Australia, Japan, and Singapore – with a total of seventy-one participants, including the EU, China, and the United States. The creation of the JSIs was met with opposition particularly from India and South Africa. As a result, the JSIs at the outset had something of a twilight existence at the WTO. A mini-negotiation was required even to determine what sort of sequence numbering the documents from the JSIs would have because this might have conferred official recognition on the JSIs. The opponents of JSIs wished to avoid conferring any legitimacy on them. As a result of this opposition, progress within the JSIs would not be reported to the Trade Negotiating Committee (TNC), which, despite its name, thereby excluded four of the five active negotiations at the WTO (the other one being on fisheries subsidies). The TNC remained connected by history to the failed Doha Development Agenda (DDA) and could not readily free itself from this dead weight. The Secretariat could provide quiet support to the JSIs but did not serve as formal secretaries to the JSIs as is done for regular WTO committees and committees in special session that were formed for the purposes of the DDA. The JSIs were initially treated as being born on the wrong side of the blanket,[27] illegitimate as WTO activities.

The JSI phenomenon could not be contained by vocal but limited opposition. Any WTO member or observer can sit in on JSI meetings as an observer as well. Continuing to gain further formal adherents, in January 2019, seventy-six WTO members announced that they would move from deliberations and begin a text-based negotiation. At present, the e-commerce negotiation has eighty-six members as active participants. The text-based negotiations cover six broad subjects: enabling e-commerce, openness and e-commerce, trust and e-commerce, cross-cutting issues, telecommunications, and market access. In December 2021, ministers of the three co-convenors announced the goal of forging convergence on key issues by the end of 2022.[28]

Some of the impetus for the e-commerce talks had come from Japanese Prime Minister Abe (in office 2012–20). Prime Minister Abe made "Data Free

[27] "The Wrong Side of the Blanket." The Wrong Side of the Blanket. www.wrongsideoftheblanket.com/

[28] "E-Commerce Co-Convenors Welcome Substantial Progress in Negotiations." World Trade Organization. December 14, 2021. www.wto.org/english/news_e/news21_e/ecom_14dec21_e.htm

Flow with Trust (DFFT)" a key Japanese objective. With Japan hosting the G20 in 2019, he sponsored the adoption by the group of what became known as the Osaka Track. The DFFT continued to be a Japanese priority in the succeeding administrations of Japanese Prime Ministers Aso and Kishida. In May 2020, Richard Salmans and Sean Doherty at the World Economic Forum (WEF) authored a White Paper[29] giving definition to the aims of the DFFT. Their focus was broader than e-commerce, encompassing data flow governance, but the two are inseparable. The listed recommendations emanated from a forum that the WEF had convened. They covered the following key elements to foster cross-border data flows:

- Protecting security;
- Ensuring data privacy;
- Cooperating for law enforcement;
- Adopting global, market-led, voluntary, and consensus-based standards;
- Prohibiting data localization;
- Protecting source code, algorithms or encryption keys, or other proprietary information relating to cryptography;
- Prohibiting tariffs or customs duties on electronic transmissions;
- Prohibiting forced technology transfer;
- Providing market access;
- Making available technical assistance to developing countries; and
- Giving special consideration to assuring benefits to micro, small and medium-sized enterprises (MSMEs).

Key for trade was the recommended negotiating mandate: "Governments should negotiate trade agreements [including in the WTO JSI] that include robust obligations in respect of data, while ensuring sufficient discretion to regulate in the public interest, and provisions that facilitate data flows across borders." The sentence sums up a key issue and unavoidable tension in considering rules for e-commerce: the balance between robust obligations in respect of data and sufficient national discretion to regulate in the public interest.[30]

The WEF paper enthusiastically endorsed the economic benefits of the freer flow of data across borders. It estimated the contribution of data to a list of

[29] "Data Free Flow with Trust (DFFT): Paths towards Free and Trusted Data Flows." World Economic Forum. May 2020. www3.weforum.org/docs/WEF_Paths_Towards_Free_and_Trusted_Data%20_Flows_2020.pdf

[30] Throughout the book, when nations or countries are referred to, for WTO purposes, this is intended to include the European Union as well as its member states.

industries, ranging from telecommunications at 44 percent to chemicals at 2 percent. The most important finding, however, was not the divergence of the degree of contribution of e-commerce by industrial sector, but that for all industries, the value-added by data is increasing rapidly. According to the US Congressional Research Service, the business-to-consumer (B2C) e-commerce market is considered to reach $4.1 trillion in 2022, and that business-to-business (B2B) e-commerce will grow from $15 trillion in 2020 to over $35 trillion by 2025.[31] The WEF paper cites the European Centre for International Political Economy (ECIPE) as figuring the costs of restrictions on cross-border data flows as just over 2 percent of global GDP, based on data prior to 2015.[32]

IMPLICATIONS FOR THE WTO

The range of provisions of the bilateral and regional agreements demonstrates that the world of electronic commerce is as complicated and idiosyncratic as the GATS was in comparison to the GATT, or the TRIPS Agreement was to any of the other WTO Agreements. E-commerce is both an extension of the world as we knew it before it came along and an alternative universe where some of the problems and opportunities are similar, some have analogs, and some are very different. Freedom of transborder data flow had relevance to goods and services trade before there was an internet, but for e-commerce, it is at the heart of any effective international regime. Interconnectivity presents some similar issues for telecommunications as it does for e-commerce. Encryption has analogs with intellectual property with respect to traditional goods and services, but it is at the heart of e-commerce. Server localization is a *sui generis* issue going beyond local content requirements.

RCEP AND CHINA'S FTAS

In terms of country coverage, the Regional Cooperation Economic Partnership (RCEP) differs from the TPP in that its fifteen participants include China (an applicant to the CPTPP), South Korea, Thailand (also

[31] "International Trade and Commerce." Congressional Research Service. March 14, 2022. www.insidetrade.com/sites/insidetrade.com/files/documents/2022/mar/wto2022_0174.pdf

[32] Hosuk Lee-Makiyama. "The Costs of Data Localization." European Centre for International Political Economy (ECIPE). April 2014. www.ecipe.org/blog/the-costs-of-data-localization/; Matthias Bauer, Hosuk Lee-Makiyama, and Erik van der Marel. 2015. "Data Localisation in Russia: A Self-Imposed Sanction." European Centre for International Political Economy (ECIPE). June. www.ecipe.org/publications/data-localisation-russia-self-imposed-sanction/

interested in CPTPP membership), Laos, Cambodia, Myanmar, Indonesia, and the Philippines.[33] RCEP's e-commerce chapter includes, besides a number of "shall endeavor provisions" (in essence, not hard obligations), several core obligations that are readily recognizable: providing for maintaining domestic laws for consumer protection and the protection of personal information, banning spam, permitting the use of electronic signatures and facilitating electronic authentication and electronic transactions.[34] The ban on the imposition of customs duties on electronic transfers is maintained. Transparency is required for measures of general application.

With respect to the forced localization of servers and free flow of data, there are sizeable carve-outs for "measures [a party] considers necessary to achieve a legitimate public policy objective" or "any measure that it considers necessary for the protection of its essential security interests." Key to understanding the the extent of the commitment to allow cross-border data flow is the proviso that with respect to the transfer of information by electronic means, the "necessity behind the implementation of such legitimate public policy shall be decided by the implementing party." This formulation occurs in both the CPTPP and the Singapore–Australia Agreement with respect to services and investment. In RCEP, this exception is applied to the two central obligations that apply to e-commerce – freedom of cross-border data flows and no forced localization of servers. Further, financial services are not covered, and dispute settlement does not apply to the RCEP e-commerce chapter.

A summary of a comparison of China's FTAs with those of the United States offered by Jia Huang of the University of New South Wales, Sydney, published in 2017, concludes that China's FTAs do not deal with how to classify digital products. They also provide relatively weak protection for consumers and privacy, although Chinese domestic law provides better protection. Not unexpectedly, the paper notes substantial divergence between the United States' and China's FTAs with respect to the free flow of information. The paper concludes that "in the post-TPP era, a polycentric direction will emerge in the regulation of the free flow of information between China and the US."[35]

33 Jeffrey J. Schott. 2022. "Which Countries Are in the CPTPP and RCEP Trade Agreements and Which Want In?" Peterson Institute for International Economics. January 3. www.piie.com/research/piie-charts/which-countries-are-cptpp-and-rcep-trade-agreements-and-which-want

34 "RCEP Chapter 12 – Electronic Commerce." Ministry of Commerce People's Republic of China – Free Trade Agreements. http://fta.mofcom.gov.cn/rcep/rceppdf/d12z_en.pdf

35 Polycentrism is defined in the literature cited in the article as including private parties' contribution to the development of the law: "In a polycentric system, private entities develop informal law that impacts the development of international trade law for digital products.

From the perspective of the multilateral trading system, polycentrism can become another way of describing Balkanization, resembling the city-states of Ancient Greece or Renaissance Italy for purposes of e-commerce governance – unnecessarily harmful to global commerce. It is not clear that any censors, public or private, can successfully weed out private communication (including political opinions) from business-to-business (B2B) or business-to-consumer (B2C) commercial relations. What happens when an order of t-shirts contains a forbidden expression? What sort of self-censorship (filtration system or "content moderation") is desirable or even workable for search engines or chat functions? What if the business involved is providing a communications platform?[36] The world is already somewhat divided through separate legal jurisdictions as to how privacy is to be respected. How is it to deal with censorship? Jurisdictions diverge sharply over internet freedom.[37] If a business is devoted to tracking COVID cases, what is taken as criticism of China can lead to criminal prosecution. And if the business is risk analysis, can it refer to the Russian war in Ukraine without running the risk of the same fate in Russia?

Henry Gao presents a very good discussion of China's somewhat cautious approach to governing e-commerce through international agreements.[38] He cites the evolution of China's approach to its FTAs, Jack Ma's leadership to promote an eWTO, and the interest it generated at the G20. The approach can be summed up in a Chinese submission to the WTO that states: "China proposes that the discussions at the present stage focus on promotion and facilitation of cross-border trade in goods enabled by internet, together with services directly supporting such trade in goods, such as payment and logistics services."[39] While very important and serving the interests of the world's largest

China is one of the largest and most lucrative markets for all e-commerce companies. Private entities are profit-making and may be publicly held. The market power may allow them to promote free flow of information while carving out human rights implications." Jie Huang. 2017. "Comparison of E-Commerce Regulations in Chinese and American FTAs: Converging Approaches, Diverging Contents, and Polycentric Directions?" *Netherlands International Law Review* 64(2): 309–337.

36 Christopher Stevenson. 2007. "Breaching the Great Firewall: China's Internet Censorship and the Quest for Freedom of Expression in a Connected World." *Boston College International and Comparative Law Review* 30(2): 531–558.

37 "Freedom on the Net 2021 – China." Freedom House. 2021. www.freedomhouse.org/country/china/freedom-net/2021

38 Henry Gao. 2018. "Digital or Trade? The Contrasting Approaches of China and US to Digital Trade." *Journal of International Economic Law* 21(2): 297–321.

39 "Work Programme on Electronic Commerce – Aiming at the 11th Ministerial Conference. Communication from the People's Republic of China and Pakistan JOB/GC/110/Rev.1, JOB/CTG/2/Rev.1, JOB/SERV/243/Rev.1, JOB/DEV/39/Rev.1." World Trade Organization.

manufacturing and exporting country, there is more to e-commerce than platforms for the sale of goods and other services promoting goods trade. China emphasizes that one aspect of overriding importance to the world trading system is that SMEs (China uses the full term "micro, small and medium-sized enterprises," or MSMEs) must benefit from the digital world that has become so important to the global economy. Gao sees a trend of convergence among the three largest WTO trading members: the European Union, the United States, and China. One can picture some evolution toward the convergence of regional solutions to common challenges, within limits, but they may still end up in the foreseeable future as being far apart on some of the fundamentals. A *sine qua non* for the United States is the free flow of data across borders. Agreement on that will be difficult. A test of whether there is common ground on that point may come in two places – China's application to join the CPTPP and the e-commerce JSI in Geneva.

One thing is certain. It is in the best interests of the growth of e-commerce and for the health of the world trading system that common ground be found among the largest trading countries, and one would hope that it would include substantial participation by the developing countries.

THE EU

The EU has built upon its goal of a coherent and indivisible internal market to seek to end what it calls "unjustified geo-blocking." This is EU-speak for any measure introduced by a member state that undermines online shopping and cross-border sales in the EU. This term applies both to online sales and purchases of goods, as well as electronically supplied services. It is part of the creation of a Digital Single Market. However, it is not complete, as the current geo-blocking regulation does not extend to streaming content consisting of audiovisual (films), music, books, and similar cultural products.[40] With a draft Digital Market Act and draft Digital Governance Act, the EU aims for "digital sovereignty," within it the oft-cited and undefined term "strategic autonomy."

November 16, 2016. https://docs.wto.org/dol2fe/Pages/SS/directdoc.aspx?filename=q:/Jobs/GC/110R1.pdf&Open=True

40 "Commission Staff Working Document – First Short-Term Review of the Geo-Blocking Regulation Accompanying the document Report from the Commission to the European Parliament, the Council, the European Economic and Social Committee and the Committee of Regions SWD (2020) 294 final." European Commission. November 30, 2020. www.eur-lex.europa.eu/legal-content/EN/TXT/?uri=CELEX:52020SC0294

There is a dual nature to EU policy, a defensiveness – something of a "digital Maginot line" (my own term), which is short of China's "great firewall" – not seeking maximum freedom of cross-border data flow and skittish about full commitments on data localization. It is in line with what Pascal Lamy, former EU Trade Commissioner and WTO Director-General, has termed a movement toward "precautionism" (as occurred in the EU strictly limiting genetically modified organisms in agricultural trade). In line with this approach is mobilizing competition policy to thwart the perceived American threat. The American reaction, here from the National Foreign Trade Council, is one of concern, if not dismay:

> *The EU's focus on discriminatory approaches aimed specifically at innovative American companies threatens to undermine prospects for transatlantic cooperation on trade and technology. By targeting US-based global technology platforms, which serve as bridge-builders rather than gatekeepers, EU regulators also threaten to harm European small businesses and innovators who rely on these services and technologies for visibility, marketing and sales.*[41]

A good summary of American and European approaches is contained in a Congressional Research Study entitled "EU Digital Policy and International Trade." American firms are also concerned that the EU will move ahead and in effect set global standards rather than working them out cooperatively.

It should not be impossible for the European Union and the United States to come closer together on appropriate e-commerce policies. Shared values with respect to the promotion of global digital trade require openness. However, in the near future, with the United States and the European Union not exactly on the same page, and at odds with China on the approach to some fundamentals, the e-commerce JSI will find challenging concluding the hardest part of the WTO e-commerce negotiation.

WHAT ARE THE PROBLEMS THAT NEW RULES WILL HAVE TO DEAL WITH?

Some decades ago, Senator Lloyd Bentsen, then-chairman of the US Senate Finance Committee, had written into US law a requirement that the US Trade Representative (USTR) publish annually a report on foreign barriers to US trade. This annual report is styled the National Trade Estimate (NTE),

[41] "NFTC Statement on EU Digital Markets Act and Digital Services Act." National Foreign Trade Council. December 15, 2020. www.nftc.org/newsflash/newsflash.asp?Mode=View&id=236&articleid=4239&category=All

modeled on the national intelligence estimate issued by the US government. The European Union and Japan publish similar reports from their own perspectives, originally in response to the US initiative in this field. Another source of information on what is taking place in the market is the annual reports of national chambers of commerce located abroad.

The 2022 NTE Report details, by country, e-commerce policies that are or may become a cause for concern.[42] This sample provides an idea of the range of issues arising in the exponential growth of e-commerce, which is drawing behind it an exponential growth of proposed and actual government regulation, some problematic, some not unnecessarily burdensome – but many of them at a minimum posing new challenges. This is a partial list indicating areas of US concern:

- Artificial intelligence: The EU Commission has identified several AI applications as high-risk, including biometric identification, credit scoring, management of critical infrastructure, access to education, job recruitment, essential private and public services, and law enforcement that may interfere with people's fundamental rights. High-risk AI systems would also have to undergo conformity assessment before being placed in the EU market;
- Audiovisual Media Services: EU amendments to the 2007 Audiovisual Media Services Directive (AVMSD) restrictions vary by member states. For example, France: video-on-demand subscription services to contribute at least 20 percent of revenues in France; also regulations in India and Viet Nam:
- Cloud computing: China - service cannot be offered other than through a Chinese company; India, and South Korea;
- Competition policy: EU (Digital Markets Act, or DMA);
- Cybersecurity: China-Cybersecurity Law, NTE: China's approach is to impose severe restrictions on a wide range of foreign ICT products and services with an apparent goal of supporting China's technology localization policies by encouraging the replacement of foreign ICT products and services with domestic ones; also issues in the EU;
- Data localization requirements and restrictions on cross-border data flows in India, Algeria, Bangladesh, India, Indonesia, Kenya, South Korea, Malaysia, Pakistan, and Russia;

[42] Henry Gao. 2022. "E-Commerce Governance: Back to Geneva?" Centre for International Governance Innovation. February 14. www.cigionline.org/articles/e-commerce-governance-back-to-geneva/; "2022 National Trade Estimate Report on Foreign Trade Barriers." United States Trade Representative. March 31, 2022. www.ustr.gov/sites/default/files/2022%20National%20Trade%20Estimate%20Report%20on%20Foreign%20Trade%20Barriers.pdf

- Data privacy: EU (General Data Protection Regulation (GDPR)), also issues in Indonesia, and Nigeria;
- Digital services taxation (DST): EU, India, Indonesia, Kenya, and Nigeria;
- Encryption restrictions: China;
- Export controls: China (rare earths needed for electronic manufacturing);
- Express delivery: Argentina;
- Import barriers for electronic goods: Argentina, Bahrain (proposed), Bangladesh (disposal of hazardous waste), Brazil (high tariffs), India, Indonesia (entry through designated ports, established five Harmonized System (HS) tariff lines at the eight-digit level with import duty rates currently set at zero percent for software and other digital products transmitted electronically, including applications, software, video, and audio); South Korea (hazardous substances in electronic equipment); Malaysia (designated ports), Oman (hazardous waste of electronics products), Qatar (hazardous waste), Russia (reduced *de minimis* duty-free threshold, consumer products that include encryption must include Russian software), Saudi Arabia (hazardous waste), and United Arab Emirates (hazardous waste);
- Internet regulatory regime: China blocking numerous sites, including those necessary for B2B and B2C services;
- Internet access: Cambodia (government-controlled single access point);
- Interoperability: EU (radio equipment);
- Investment barriers (present in many countries and not always listed as applicable separately to e-commerce companies): China (joint venture requirements, foreign equity limitations and various discriminatory regulatory requirements), Kenya, Laos, and Nigeria (forced local partnerships);
- Online payments: Algeria, Bangladesh, Brazil, China (progress noted in NTE), India, Indonesia, South Korea, Laos, Malaysia, Mexico, Singapore, South Africa, Thailand, and Turkey;
- Online platforms and social networks: Australia (mandatory bargaining with content providers, liability for content proposed), Bangladesh, EU (Digital Services Act and antiterrorism regulation), India, Kenya, Singapore (content moderation), Thailand, and UAE;
- Online security: Bangladesh;
- Paperless trading (including customs and sanitary and phytosanitary (SPS) measure filings): Argentina (does not exist for government filings), Colombia, Costa Rica, Indonesia (customs filings), Pakistan, and the Philippines (imported fisheries products);

- Piracy and counterfeiting:
  - Cambodia (e-books),
  - China (the new law introduced provisions that weaken the ability of rights-holders to protect their rights online and lessen the liability of China-based electronic commerce platforms for selling counterfeit and other infringing goods. A draft tort liability chapter in the Civil Code, published in January 2019, contained similar problematic provisions that would weaken the existing notice-and-takedown system; draft regulations have been published to address these concerns);
- Telecommunications: EU;
- Testing and conformity assessment: India (IT products), Indonesia, Mexico (telecommunications products), and South Africa;
- VAT: Bangladesh (streaming), Cambodia (streaming), and Mexico (penalties);
- Voice-over internet: China (restricted);
- E-commerce generally: Ecuador (uncertainties on the state of the law), India (B2C prohibited except through local food retail stores), Indonesia (licensing), and the Philippines (registration).

THE OVERRIDING IMPORTANCE OF THE E-COMMERCE JSI

To have the WTO separate and distinct from the world of e-commerce would be to condemn the Organization to stagnation and steeply declining relevance and undermine global trade governance. The path forward requires serious structural change at the WTO. For a start, those who are like-minded must be able to create at the WTO an international structure that works at least for them and quite possibly for all. There is as of this writing, in November 2022, no certainty that in all respects the benefits of the negotiated outcomes will be accorded on an MFN, nondiscriminatory basis to those not binding themselves to any rules.

There is an urgent need to have domestic regulation evolve within an international framework. Article 4 of China's 2018 e-commerce law provides that: "The State shall accord equal treatment of online and offline commercial activities and promote their integrated development. People's governments of various levels and relevant authorities shall not adopt discriminatory policies or measures or abuse their administrative power to eliminate or restrict market competition."[43] Many countries have no domestic

[43] "E-Commerce Law of the People's Republic of China." IPKEY. August 31, 2018. www.ipkey.eu/sites/default/files/documents/resources/PRC_E-Commerce_Law.pdf

legal provision of the kind. Moreover, while what is in domestic law may smooth the way to achieving international disciplines, it is not an international commitment. It is as likely that domestic laws will make reaching international agreements more difficult. The world of digital commerce is growing fast. Delay in agreeing to international best practices and forging new rules will have increasing costs for the world economy. Policy space can readily be used to impede future international cooperation.

WHAT THE WTO JSI SEEKS TO ACCOMPLISH (A SEPTEMBER 2021 SNAPSHOT)

Many of the eighty-six WTO members participating in the JSI on e-commerce had extensive experience in crafting rules for the subject. They had the texts of relevant provisions from all prior agreements before them. The draft document they created is the most comprehensive set of rules for digital commerce ever collected.[44] It is to some extent a curating of existing rules with refinements introduced by the negotiators. It is by far the most ambitious endeavor in the history of the WTO but for the multi-subject Doha Development Agenda. One has the feeling from reviewing it that for the like-minded, this text holds enormous promise. One way or another, it will be adopted by many of the participants either in an open plurilateral agreement within the WTO or, if the WTO cannot accommodate their agreement and they are forced outside, it is the template for what will be adopted elsewhere.

What follows is a summary of the draft provisions, trying not to leave any out, to give a full flavor of what an e-commerce code should encompass. For those readers who do not wish to get a detailed sense of the subjects being addressed, they can skim the list that follows. Where differences exist among members in their approach to any obligation, the following points seek to reflect the more ambitious of alternatives proposed. The text will change over time. Nothing is agreed until everything is agreed. The provisions are framed in the alternative, as applicable either to all members or just to participants. There is no decision on whether all or some of the benefits will be extended on an MFN basis to non-signatories. At this point, the text does not include provisions for special and differential treatment.

The following are thumbnail summaries of the main potential provisions for a WTO code on e-commerce emerging from the JSI's deliberations, with

[44] "WTO Electronic Commerce Negotiations – Updated Consolidated Negotiating Text INF/ECOM/62/Rev.2." World Trade Organization. September 8, 2021. www.bilaterals.org/IMG/pdf/wto_plurilateral_ecommerce_draft_consolidated_text_september_2021.pdf

headings supplied here for ease of reference. The categories listed are my own. The substance of these provisions is based on my understanding of where the JSI negotiations have been headed. The categories cannot be confirmed as the JSI co-convenors have not released the current text to the public.

SCOPE

- This Agreement shall apply to measures adopted or maintained by a party that affect trade by electronic means;
- "Digital product" means a computer program, text, video, image, sound recording, or other product that is digitally encoded, produced for commercial sale or distribution, and that can be transmitted electronically, but does not include money or broadcasting.

CREATING THE DIGITAL ENVIRONMENT

- Parties shall:
  - Maintain a legal framework consistent with the UNCITRAL Model Law on Electronic Commerce 1996;
  - Endeavor to employ, and encourage enterprises within its jurisdiction to use, risk-based approaches that rely on open and transparent industry or consensus-based standards and risk management best practices to identify and protect against cybersecurity risks and detect, respond to, and recover from cybersecurity events;
  - Avoid unnecessary (or minimize) regulatory burdens on electronic transactions;
  - Agree not to prohibit the use of electronic authentications and electronic signatures;.
  - Encourage interoperability and work toward mutual recognition of electronic signatures;
  - Not deny the validity of electronic contracts because they are electronic;
  - Treat electronic invoices as being equally valid as paper ones.

OPENNESS

- No party shall impose customs duties, fees, or charges on electronic transmissions between a person of one party and a person of another party;
- No party shall restrict the cross-border transfer of information, including personal information, by electronic means, whereby this activity is for the conduct of the business of an investor in the country of that party;

- No party shall adopt a measure requiring data localization or server location, including for data processing (except to protect privacy). This commitment applies to financial services data as long as access to data is available to regulators for prudential purposes;
- Discrimination against digital products created in another participant's jurisdiction as compared to like digital products is prohibited;
- Trade policies are to be transparent, without discrimination as compared with physical goods;
- No party shall require the transfer of, or access to, source code of software owned by a person of another party, as a condition for the import, distribution, sale, or use of that software, or of products containing that software, in its territory;
- No party shall require a manufacturer or supplier of a commercial ICT product that uses cryptography, as a condition of the manufacture, sale, distribution, import, or use of the ICT product, to (a) transfer or provide access to any proprietary information relating to cryptography; (b) partner or otherwise cooperate with a person in the territory of that party in the development, manufacture, sale, distribution, import, or use of the ICT product; or (c) use or integrate a particular cryptographic algorithm or cipher;
- Parties shall:
  - Utilize standards and conformity assessment in a manner that does not create unnecessary barriers to trade;
  - Endeavor to set a *de minimis* value on shipments below which no customs duties or taxes will be collected;
  - Provide national treatment and nondiscrimination for electronic payment services, and full access for their operations;
  - Endeavor to avoid measures that have the effect of treating commerce by electronic means in a more restrictive manner than commerce conducted by other means;
  - Improve the level of commitments for logistics services, including market access and national treatment, including allowing the establishment of commercial presence. Promote the establishment of transport coordination mechanisms, support cooperation with postal services, and cover all modes of transportation;
  - With respect to all measures affecting the production, supply, rental, sale, export, and import of electronic commerce-related network equipment and products, each party shall accord to enterprises and electronic commerce-related network equipment and products of any other member treatment no less favorable than that which it accords to

any other like enterprises or any other like electronic commerce-related network equipment and products, or block the supply chains of electronic commerce-related network equipment and products, unless in a manner that is consistent with the WTO Agreements;

- All parties are to join and implement the Information Technology Agreement (ITA);
- Additional market access is to be provided for computer and business services, communications, distribution, financial services, and transportation. Actual commitments are to be determined;
- Subscribers to an internet access service provider should be able to have access and use services and applications of their choice available on the internet.

TELECOMMUNICATIONS

- Appropriate measures shall be maintained to prevent suppliers of telecommunications networks or services who, alone or together, are a major supplier, from engaging in or continuing anticompetitive practices, such as anticompetitive cross-subsidization;
- The telecommunications regulatory authority shall be separate from, and not accountable to, any supplier of telecommunications networks or services. To this end, the telecommunications regulatory authority shall not hold a financial interest or maintain an operating or management role in any such supplier;
- A major supplier shall make its essential facilities available to suppliers of public telecommunications networks or services on reasonable, transparent, and nondiscriminatory terms and conditions for the purpose of providing public telecommunications services, when this is necessary to achieve effective competition.

TRADE FACILITATION

- Paperless trading: parties shall make any form issued or controlled by customs for import, export, or transit of goods through its territory available to the public in an electronic format, including, for example, e-phytosanitary certificates;

Parties shall:

- Provide a single window at least for customs data, interoperable internally and with those of other countries;

- Provide enhanced trade facilitation, including free zones, improved customs clearance, and providing for returns;
- Use embedded technologies, such as sensors, to perform risk analysis and expedite customs clearance;
- Employ risk management technologies including AI;
- Adopt nonintrusive and remote inspections;
- Allow services suppliers to provide, in a comprehensive and integrated manner, trade-facilitating and supportive services by means of cross-sector operations.

DEVELOPMENT

- Upon request, provide targeted technical assistance and capacity-building to low-income developing countries to improve their digital ecosystems and implement WTO rules on electronic commerce.

CONSUMER PROTECTION/PRIVACY

- Each party shall adopt or maintain a legal framework that provides for the protection of the personal information of the users of electronic commerce;
- To protect consumers engaged in electronic commerce, each party shall endeavor to adopt or maintain measures that aim to ensure that suppliers of goods and services deal fairly and honestly with consumers and promote safety;
- Parties should provide for the minimization of unsolicited commercial electronic messages.

HOLDING PLATFORMS HARMLESS

- Platforms, internet content providers, shall not be liable for the content they did not create;
- Interactive computer service providers shall not be liable for deleting content that they consider harmful.

OPEN GOVERNMENT

- Each party shall promptly publish, or otherwise make publicly available at the latest by the time of their entry into force, all measures of general application pertaining to or affecting electronic commerce;

- Each party shall endeavor to provide, to the extent possible and practicable, on an official website a database that is electronically searchable by tariff nomenclature code and other relevant information.

EXCEPTIONS

- General exception: this Agreement shall not prevent members from adopting or maintaining any measures for the purposes of guaranteeing cybersecurity, safeguarding cyberspace sovereignty, protecting the lawful rights and interests of its citizens, juridical persons, and other organizations, and achieving other legitimate public policy objectives, provided that such measures are not applied in a manner which would constitute a means of arbitrary or unjustifiable discrimination or a disguised restriction on trade, and are no more than necessary to achieve the objectives;
- National security: the national security exceptions of the GATT and GATS are incorporated;
- Prudential measures: nothing in this Agreement shall prevent a [party/member] from adopting or maintaining measures for prudential reasons, including for the protection of investors, depositors, policy-holders or persons to whom a fiduciary duty is owed by a financial service supplier, or to ensure the integrity and stability of the party's financial system. However, such measures shall not be used as a means of avoiding the member's obligations under this Agreement.

INTERNATIONAL COOPERATION

- Parties shall endeavor to cooperate to facilitate and expand public access to and use of government data;
- Parties should strengthen cooperation in order to identify and mitigate anticompetitive practices in digital markets;
- Parties shall maintain cooperation and dialogue on the regulatory issues raised by digital trade;
- Each party shall, within its available resources, establish or maintain one or more enquiry points for notifications, consultation, providing answers, and the facilitation of communications.

ORGANIZATIONAL STRUCTURE

- A Committee on Trade-Related Aspects of Electronic Commerce will be established, open to all parties. The Committee shall elect its own chairperson and vice-chairperson and shall meet not less than once a year and otherwise at the request of any party/member. It will carry out responsibilities assigned to it by the General Council.

DISPUTE SETTLEMENT

- The dispute settlement provisions of the GATT and GATS apply.

PUSH BACK

The concerns of many developing countries over maintaining the moratorium on applying duties to electronic transmissions sharpened over time. On November 5, 2021, India and South Africa circulated a document questioning whether the e-commerce-related moratorium should be renewed and concluding that the pledge should be interpreted as being very limited.[45] The two delegations cited with approval a statement of Indonesia that "the extension of the moratorium applies only to the electronic transmissions and not to products or contents which are submitted electronically." The effect would, however, be a reversal of the moratorium, subjecting e-commerce goods and services to tariffs. The headline issue that India and South Africa highlighted was the loss of tariff revenues. They quoted the United Nations Conference on Trade and Development (UNCTAD) as estimating, based on only "a small number of digitizable goods in five areas, namely, printed matter, music and video downloads, software and video games," "a loss in tariff revenue of more than US$10 billion per annum globally ... 95 percent of which is borne by developing countries."

The implications of this argument go far beyond video downloads. UNCTAD has also looked into the impact on developing countries of 3D printing. UNCTAD calculated that while 3D printing was "currently at a nascent stage in developing countries, its market has grown annually by 22 percent in the period 2014–2018 and it is estimated that if investment in 3D printing is doubled, it could potentially replace almost 40 percent of cross-border physical global trade by 2040." While the case is stated as a concern largely about tariff revenues forgone, the negative implications for e-commerce in terms of creating additional barriers to trade are extremely broad. As 3D printing gains more general use, if tariffs were applied at, say, the average bound rate on

[45] "Work Programme on Electronic Commerce – The Moratorium on Customs Duties on Electronic Transmissions: Need for Clarity on Its Scope and Impacts WT/GC/W/833." World Trade Organization. November 8, 2021. https://docs.wto.org/dol2fe/Pages/SS/directdoc.aspx?filename=q:/WT/GC/W833.pdf&Open=True

industrial products in India, which is 48.5 percent, on the product that emerges from the printer, not just perhaps on the IP and programs used to transmit instructions to the printer, this could drive up the cost of the goods produced by 3D printing to prohibitive levels.[46] The fear of 3D printing finds an echo in history of the effect on local manufacturing that the introduction of the power loom two centuries earlier had on cottage weavers.

Twin concerns are expressed. Not only would local producers of "textiles and clothing, footwear, auto-components, toys, mechanical appliances, and hand tools," largely SMEs, be at a disadvantage, it is claimed, but customs revenues to support the development of non-3D printed domestic production by these companies would be drained.

The potential benefits to local production of 3D printing are not outlined in the India–South Africa submission. The balance between the costs and benefits is not clear, as the technology is not widely in evidence yet in developing countries. The proposed solution by India and South Africa is to preserve "policy space," by freeing WTO members to do as they wish without the moratorium in place, allowing them to apply customs duties to whatever the term "electronic transmissions" might have encompassed. This is at odds with the *raison d'être* of the WTO. If one were to sum up the entire purpose of the WTO in one sentence: it is to limit policy space – that is, to arrive at agreed rules for the benefit of all to reduce any given individual member's freedom to restrict trade.

At MC12, the ministers decided on a further limited extension of the moratorium on customs duties on electronic transmissions:

> *We agree to reinvigorate the work under the Work Programme on Electronic Commerce, based on the mandate as set out in WT/L/274 and particularly in line with its development dimension.*
>
> *We shall intensify discussions on the moratorium and instruct the General Council to hold periodic reviews based on the reports that may be submitted by relevant WTO bodies, including on scope, definition, and impact of the moratorium on customs duties on electronic transmissions.*
>
> *We agree to maintain the current practice of not imposing customs duties on electronic transmissions until MC13, which should ordinarily be held by 31 December 2023. Should MC13 be delayed beyond 31 March 2024, the moratorium will expire on that date unless Ministers or the General Council take a decision to extend.*

[46] "India – Import Tariffs." Privacy Shield Framework. www.privacyshield.gov/article?id=India-Import-Tariffs

A question is whether the opposition to the spread of digital commerce, even if it cannot fully succeed, will create a self-imposed digital divide, further retarding the progress of developing countries.

CONCLUSION

The risks of fracture lines within the WTO becoming breaks are not negligible. China, the European Union, and the United States share some common interests, but they also are not taking compatible approaches on major issues. The JSI is promising, as is China's application to join the CPTPP with its forward-looking provisions on e-commerce. For there to be broad multilateral agreement, WTO members must work to find more common ground. It is essential for the future of the WTO that it be relevant to the world of digital commerce. For global economic well-being, there is no substitute for global rules for this subject. Not all can proceed at the same speed and they need not, as long as convergence is the goal and the goal is kept in sight. For the trading system, it is essential that e-commerce rules be adopted within the WTO and that all members have the option to join. There are still hard issues to face. At a point close to the end of the day, when there is an agreed text for the rest of the provisions of the e-commerce agreement, there will be a question of whether to extend the benefits to non-signatories, whether the agreement applies on an MFN basis (as does the ITA) or is based on reciprocity.

11

Development at the WTO

UN Secretary-General António Guterres in opening the United Nations General Assembly in September 2019 warned of great fractures, calling on the members to "reconnect with the Organization's values, uphold human rights and restore trust."[1] *Those words might equally have been applied to one of the historic fracture lines of the multilateral trading system. One of the most contentious topics within the system since its founding has been how best to include developing countries in its benefits and obligations. No solution has been found that has gained universal support.*

The gains from trade must be shared to ensure progress and nurture development. That is a responsibility to be owned by the entire trading community. An inward-looking repudiation of the well understood economic gains from specialization will inevitably result in shrinking opportunity, lower incomes in growth, and significant risks of heightened conflict.[2]

THE PRIMARY OBJECTIVE OF THE FOUNDERS: POSTWAR RECONSTRUCTION

While one might like to claim otherwise, the issue of how to promote the economic development of what in many cases were countries emerging or on the cusp of emerging from a colonial existence was not the focus of the postwar planners. There were enormous economic and political challenges

1 "Warning against 'Great Fracture', Secretary-General Calls on General Assembly to Reconnect with Organization's Values, Uphold Human Rights, Restore Trust." United Nations – Meeting Coverage and Press Releases. September 24, 2019.

2 Patrick Low, Hamid Mamdouh, and Evan Rogerson. 2018. "Balancing Rights and Obligations in The WTO – A Shared Responsibility." Government Offices of Sweden. www.swedenabroad.se/globalassets/ambassader/fn-geneve/documents/balancing-rights-and-obligations-in-the-wto.pdf. This important paper also contains a good bibliography on the GATT, WTO, and development.

brought about by the destruction caused by the Second World War. Reconstruction dominated the planners' thinking and programs, with development a distinctly secondary concern. It was natural for the industrialized countries to focus on creating conditions that would avoid a return to the warfare and economic ruin that dominated the period beginning with the First World War and extending through the Second World War. The devastation was extensive. In terms of 1938 prices, global trade of fourteen European countries in 1947 was well below prewar levels, about 79 percent of imports and about 64 percent of exports as compared with 1938 volumes. Intra-European trade in 1947 was only 56 percent of 1938 levels. German exports were only 9 percent of prewar levels.[3]

The 1948 United Nations World Economic Report, published in June 1949, viewed the economies of developing countries largely through this lens, and assumed that the fortunes of these countries would primarily be derived from the economic health of the industrialized world:

> *The problems of industrial and under-developed countries are closely interrelated and impinge upon one another in the field of international trade. High levels of world economic activity would permit industrial countries to continue importing a large volume of goods from under-developed countries, thereby enabling the latter to finance imports of capital goods and other essential commodities.*[4]

There was even an element of defensiveness with respect to development, as a challenge to the formerly most industrialized in need of reconstruction:

> *Naturally, economic expansion in under-developed countries will require adjustments elsewhere. These adjustments are likely to prove difficult for some time, particularly in western Europe, where they will have to be superimposed on others necessitated by a decade and a half of economic depression and devastating war. But trade arising from economic development should prove beneficial to all the parties concerned and should eventually help Europe to overcome its trading difficulties rather than increase them.*[5]

Economic recovery in the northern hemisphere was increasing demand for ores, other raw materials, and agricultural commodities from former and

3 "European Recovery, 1945–47." 1948. *European Recovery and United States Aid* 12(3): 293–299. www.jstor.org/stable/40399901

4 "World Economic Report 1948." United Nations Department of Economic Affairs. June 1949. www.un.org/en/development/desa/policy/wess/wess_archive/searchable_archive/1948_WESS_Full.pdf

5 Ibid.

current colonial areas.[6] Wasn't this what the developing world really needed? For the industrialized countries, this was perhaps all that could be managed at the time.

This view put forward by the industrialized countries, particularly the United States, setting out their priorities for the postwar era, was met with pushback from developing countries. India, in the negotiations for the Charter for the International Trade Organization, was critical of the idea that "the attainment of approximately full employment by the major industrial and trading nations ... [is] essential to the expansion of international trade on which the full prosperity of these and other nations depends," or that India's prosperity "must necessarily depend on the expansion of international trade."[7] Brazil urged that development be given pride of place as the key objective of the ITO.[8] The United States, dominating the proceedings, with the United Kingdom as its partner, had no use for anything of the sort.

The concept of concentrating trade negotiations on bringing about economic development was simply not within the frame of reference of the prime mover for the creation of the multilateral trading system – the United States. Robert Hudec, one of the most important scholars of the GATT, reminds us that the negotiating authority granted by Congress that shaped what the United States could do in trade relations with other countries was called the Reciprocal Trade Agreements Act of 1934,[9] with emphasis on the word "reciprocal." Congress would not have allowed the US government to lower American tariffs in bilateral agreements without getting in return market access abroad, and indeed this is what was obtained in the sixteen agreements signed between the United States and developing countries from 1934 to 1942.[10] There was no mention of preferences. This was also true, Hudec reminds us, in the economic postwar aim listed in the Atlantic Charter, agreed to by Roosevelt and Churchill in 1941.[11] Their vision was of *equal* access to markets and to raw materials. The great multilateral economic charters that the US–UK authors initiated in the 1940s contained nothing to require

6 Population growth in the developing world was, however, limiting the level of its agricultural exports. The central problem of developing countries was a serious shortage of capital and foreign exchange.

7 James Scott. "Developing Countries in the ITO and GATT Negotiations." Brooks World Poverty Institute. May 2009. https://hummedia.manchester.ac.uk/institutes/gdi/publications/workingpapers/bwpi/bwpi-wp-9509.pdf

8 Ibid.

9 Robert Hudec. 2010. *Developing Countries in the GATT Legal System*. Cambridge: Cambridge University Press.

10 Ibid.

11 Ibid.

preferential treatment for development – not in the ITO, not in the IMF Articles of Agreement, and not in the GATT. Development as a specific cause was relegated to be the concern of the UN and the World Bank. Preferential trade was left to the colonial powers in their relations with current and former colonies. Although it was not called that at the time, what the developing countries got in the GATT was "policy space" specifically limited to additional freedom to apply restrictions for balance of payments purposes and for infant industry protection – in GATT Article XVIII.

AWAKENING TO THE NEED FOR ECONOMIC DEVELOPMENT AND THE EUROPEAN SOLUTION

In 1958, the GATT contracting parties asked three experts to review the world economy and advise on what conclusions they reached. This became known as the Haberler Report.[12]

Commenting on the perspective of the developing world, the Report's authors concluded: "We think that there is some substance in the feeling of disquiet among primary producing countries that the present rules and conventions about commercial policy is relatively unfavorable to them."[13]

The panel pointed additionally to the problem of the adverse effects of discriminatory treatment of these countries. Some "under-industrialized countries," as they were being called at the time, received better treatment from developed countries than did others. The foremost instance of this form of trade distortion was to be found in the Rome Treaty establishing the European Economic Community (EEC), giving preferential treatment to French and Belgian dependent territories in Africa.[14] The Report states:

> **335.** *The problem of discrimination is, for two reasons, especially serious in the case of overseas territories: first the countries … excluded and discriminated against (Latin American countries, Ghana and others) are relatively poor tropical countries; second, their exports consist largely of tropical products which compete only little with products produced in the highly developed economies of the Six [the member states of the European Community] …*

[12] Roberto de Oliveira Campos, Gottfried Haberler, James Meade, and Jan Tinbergen. 1958. "Trends in International Trade: A Report by a Panel of Experts." Contracting Parties to the General Agreement on Tariffs and Trade. October. www.wto.org/english/res_e/booksp_e/gatt_trends_in_international_trade.pdf. Trivia: Gottfried Haberler was on the Board of Advisors to the Harvard Radcliff International Relations Council when I served as Secretary in 1961–62 and President in 1962–63.

[13] Ibid., para. 62.

[14] Ibid., para. 334.

> 337. *The implication ... is that the preferential elimination of these duties [by the EC] will be predominantly trade diverting and not trade creating. This follows from the fact that larger imports of coffee, cocoa, tea and bananas from the French and Belgian overseas territories into the EC cannot displace high cost of production of these commodities there since these countries do not grow coffee, cocoa, tea or bananas ... [A] preferential reduction in revenue duties can ... not lead to a more efficient reshuffling of productive resources.*

These were the halcyon days of the trading system when economists could point out certain basic facts and be listened to – in this case that unless care was taken as to how they are applied, preferences are more likely to lead to trade diversion than trade creation.

Worse from the perspective of the global trading system, the EEC received "reverse preferences" from its members' colonies, and later, after independence, their former colonies. EEC exports to these markets also received preferential treatment, and those of other developing trading partners were discriminated against. The EEC entered into a series of agreements with these countries, first in Africa with the Yaoundé Convention (1963) and the Lomé Convention (1975) with seventy-one ACP (Africa, Caribbean, and Pacific) countries.[15] Litigation in the GATT and WTO found the EEC's discrimination among developing countries to be inconsistent with global trading rules. Somewhat bizarrely, the result of the litigation was to make a bad system worse. Rather than scrapping the preferences, it perfected them, with the goal of making them GATT/WTO-legitimate. The means of doing so was to move toward preferential trading arrangements that were reciprocal – that is, the EC got preferences back for preferences given. This occurred because there is an exception from GATT Article I (MFN) for "free trade agreements" under GATT Article XXIV. The agreements the developed countries' former colonies were pressed to accept were termed Economic Partnership Agreements (EPAs). Reverse preferences were said to make these agreements "WTO-consistent" as there was a mutual elimination of tariffs. For nonparticipating developing countries, the discrimination remained largely unremedied. For other developed countries, the tariff discrimination against their products both in the European common/single market and in the ACP/EPA countries was perfected.[16] For these industrialized countries, to

[15] "The Lomé Convention." Organisation of African, Caribbean and Pacific States. www.acp.int/content/lome-convention

[16] "EU–ACP EPAs." bilaterals.org. www.bilaterals.org/?-eu-acp-epas; "Economic Partnerships." European Commission. www.ec.europa.eu/trade/policy/countries-and-regions/development/economic-partnerships/; Matthew McQueen. "After Lomé IV: ACP–EU Trade Preferences in the 21st Century." Intereconomics. September/October 1999. www.intereconomics.eu/pdf-

the extent that they exported competing products, these faced discrimination in both Europe and in the former colonies.

CHANGES MADE TO THE MULTILATERAL TRADING SYSTEM: POLICY SPACE

However important to the subject of nondiscrimination, the European distortion field of ACP/EPAs was not the main story, which is about how the trading system did and should treat developing countries. The GATT and later the WTO needed to focus more concretely on the preferential treatment that developing countries required to assist in their development and the degree of reciprocity that could or should be expected of them.

The first major amendment to the GATT to deal with the specific circumstances of developing countries occurred in the mid-1950s.[17] GATT Article XVIII allowed low-income developing countries to utilize import restrictions in a manner not allowed to industrialized contracting parties:

1. *The contracting parties recognize that the attainment of the objectives of this Agreement will be facilitated by the progressive development of their economies, particularly of those contracting parties the economies of which can only support low standards of living and are in the early stages of development.*
2. *The contracting parties recognize further that it may be necessary for those contracting parties, in order to implement programmes and policies of economic development designed to raise the general standard of living of their people, to take protective or other measures affecting imports, and that such measures are justified in so far as they facilitate the attainment of the objectives of this Agreement.*

They agree, therefore, that those contracting parties should enjoy additional facilities to enable them (a) to maintain sufficient flexibility in their tariff structure to be able to grant the tariff protection required for the establishment of a particular industry and (b) to apply quantitative restrictions for balance of payments purposes in a manner which takes full account of the continued high level of demand for imports likely to be generated by their programmes of economic development.

download/year/1999/number/5/article/after-lome-iv-acp-eu-trade-preferences-in-the-21st-century.html

[17] Gabrielle Marceau. "General Presentation of the WTO Agreement." United Nations Office of Legal Affairs – Audiovisual Library of International Law. https://legal.un.org/avl/pdf/ls/Marceau_RelDoc4.pdf. This source provides a good short summary of the evolution of the GATT and WTO provisions.

Taking the more widely used of these two flexibilities first, the one to be used for balance of payments purposes: resort to trade restrictions for certain developing countries was relaxed as compared with industrialized countries. The text of GATT Article XII was transposed with some qualifying words deleted to create Article XVIII, allowing a balance of payments measure to be put into place by a low-income country. Deletions are shown in brackets as follows: GATT Article XII (para. 2) states that import restrictions "shall not exceed those necessary (i) to forestall the [imminent] threat of, or to stop, a serious decline in its monetary reserves" or "(ii) . . . in the case of a contracting party with [very low] monetary reserves, to achieve a reasonable rate of increase in its reserves." Article XVIII:B (para. 9) refers to an "inadequate" level rather than a "very low" level of reserves, with the term "adequate" defined as "adequate for the implementation of its programme of economic development." There was extensive use of Article XVIII:B in the earlier years of the WTO,[18] but then India lost a case where the IMF had not judged India's import-restricting measures as being justified. Ecuador is the most recent country to invoke this provision.

The second flexibility as contained in GATT Article XVIII:C had more limited use. Infant industry protection was required to be the subject of consultations with countries that deemed their trade to be adversely affected. Korea lost a case in which it sought to defend long-standing beef import restrictions under this provision.

The benefits of Article XVIII were from the outset viewed as inadequate by developing countries. The developing country seeking to invoke the provision to promote the development of a particular industry had to thread its way through a series of procedural obstacles. It would have to explain how aiding a particular industry through protection would raise the living standard of its people. Before suspending a concession, it would need to obtain the concurrence of the exporting country benefiting from the concession, unless production was already underway, but could still be asked for consultations and a review as to whether the measure was really necessary. The GATT participants as a whole (the contracting parties) would need to approve the measure, see no other GATT-consistent alternative, and require that either an agreement was reached with interested parties or that the developing country made "all reasonable efforts to reach an agreement and that the interests of other

[18] Hartley Furtan. 1992. "Moral Hazard and GATT Art. XVIII:B." Center for Agricultural and Rural Development at Iowa State University. GATT Research Paper 90-GATT 12. www.card.iastate.edu/products/publications/pdf/90gatt12.pdf. See also Annual Reports of the WTO Committee on Balance of Payments to the General Council.

contracting parties are adequately safeguarded." The seemingly pro-development provision was mostly a dead letter: "Its unattractiveness is evidenced by the fact that although there are so many under-developed countries who are members of GATT, very few have cared to avail themselves of this article … the restrictions and limitations it places practically destroy the benefits that it professes to confer."[19]

CONCRETE STEPS TO AID DEVELOPMENT THROUGH TRADE

The Haberler Report sparked a continuing process of examination of how the trading system could better foster economic development. Ministers in 1961 adopted a declaration to continue to seek to promote the trade of less-developed countries.[20] A Committee on Legal and Institutional Framework was created which resulted in a new Part IV for GATT specifically devoted to Trade and Development. Part IV was completed in 1965 and entered into force in June 1966. Part IV acknowledged that developing countries would not be required to make the same concessions on tariffs, or the removal of nontariff barriers, as developed countries. Gabrielle Marceau,[21] a highly experienced lawyer with the WTO Secretariat who served as legal advisor to Director-General Pascal Lamy, notes that "Part IV did not, however, provide a specific legal basis for preferential arrangements with or between developing countries."[22] Nor, as Hudec writes, did Part IV contain any definable legal commitments. What was important about this addition to the GATT was contained in its statement of principles, such as: "There is, therefore, need for increased access in the largest possible measure to markets under favourable conditions for processed and manufactured products currently or potentially of particular export interest to less-developed contracting parties." This was another installment in the string of promises made by developed to developing countries that always seemed to the latter to be inadequately fulfilled if fulfilled at all. The former regarded the WTO as a place of

[19] "Statement of Shirley Corea, Minister of Commerce, Trade and Fisheries, Ceylon, 1954" in Gerard Curzon. 1965. *Multilateral Commercial Diplomacy*. London: Michael Joseph Ltd.

[20] "Part IV – Trade and Development." World Trade Organization. www.wto.org/english/res_e/booksp_e/gatt_ai_e/part4_e.pdf

[21] "Prof. Gabrielle Marceau." World Trade Institute. www.wti.org/institute/people/251/marceau-gabrielle/

[22] Gabrielle Marceau. "General Presentation of the WTO Agreement." United Nations Office of Legal Affairs – Audiovisual Library of International Law. https://legal.un.org/avl/pdf/ls/Marceau_RelDoc4.pdf

contractual commitments, and in terms favoring the developing world there were very few and these were mostly temporary.

Development assistance was a largely separate matter from legal commitments, and there was continuing progress here. An important institutional change was made: the GATT spun off a new agency, the International Trade Centre (ITC),[23] in March 1964. Three years later, UNCTAD became jointly responsible for this export promotion agency. The mission of the ITC is to support the "internationalization" of small and medium-sized enterprises (SMEs), specifically in developing countries. In 2020, the ITC was active in 128 countries, half of them least developed, and had over a million subscribers to its online services.[24]

The next step to advance the cause of development in the trading system was to seek to replace specific preferences (largely extended to former colonies) with a Generalized System of Preferences (GSP). GSP is nonreciprocal and very broad in its list of beneficiaries. This program is designed to put most developing countries on an equal footing with each other in developed country markets, with each industrialized country listing the products for which it would provide duty-free treatment. Work had begun on this idea in 1968 at the OECD, and resulted in an UNCTAD resolution in 1968, with the program being inaugurated in 1971. Participation of the United States was authorized by Congress in the Trade Act of 1974 (enacted January 3, 1975). US law makes it clear that the granting of duty-free treatment to developing countries is discretionary, and so-called import-sensitive articles are excluded from the program.

GSP was not legitimized under the GATT until 1979, years after its creation. As part of the Tokyo Round of Multilateral Trade Negotiations, the GATT contracting parties adopted the Enabling Clause, formally known as the "Decision on Differential and More Favorable Treatment, Reciprocity and Fuller Participation of Developing Countries." The operational part of the decision provides:

1. *Notwithstanding the provisions of Article I of the General Agreement, contracting parties may accord differential and more favourable treatment to developing countries, without according such treatment to other contracting parties.*
2. *The provisions of paragraph 1 apply to the following –*
   (a) *Preferential tariff treatment accorded by developed contracting parties to products originating in developing countries in accordance with the Generalized System of Preferences;*

[23] "About ITC." International Trade Centre. www.intracen.org/itc/about/

[24] "Annual Report 2020: Pivoting with Purpose." International Trade Centre. July 2021. https://intracen.org/sites/default/files/inline-files/Annual%20Report%202020_English.pdf

(b) *Differential and more favorable treatment with respect to the provisions of the General Agreement concerning non-tariff measures governed by the provisions of instruments multilaterally negotiated under the auspices of the GATT;*

(c) *Regional or global arrangements entered into amongst less developed contracting parties for the mutual reduction or elimination of tariffs and, in accordance with criteria or conditions which may be prescribed by the CONTRACTING PARTIES, and for the mutual reduction or elimination of non-tariff measures, on products imported from one another;*

(d) *Special treatment of the least developed among the developing countries in the context of any general or specific measures in favor of developing countries.*[25]

The decision was a significant derogation from MFN. However, two forms of discrimination were in effect being phased out – a developed country would not prefer some underdeveloped country to the exclusion of others and it would not receive reverse preferences. In addition, as noted in paragraph 2(c) of the Enabling Clause quoted above, the bar was lowered for developing country members to form FTAs among themselves.

Products from eighty-one countries and seventeen territories are eligible for duty-free treatment upon entering the United States.[26] In participating in the GSP program, a major objective for the United States was to "provide an alternative to the proliferation of preferential trading arrangements created by the European Union and developing countries that generally involved a reverse grant of preferences in favor of the European Union and to the exclusion of products from other countries, including the United States."[27] The EU maintained its special preferences alongside its GSP program, but was said to no longer require reverse preferences. The EU's GSP is

[25] "Differential and More Favourable Treatment Reciprocity and Fuller Participation of Developing Countries L/4903." World Trade Organization. November 28, 1979. www.wto.org/english/docs_e/legal_e/enabling1979_e.htm

[26] "Countries Eligible for GSP." Office of the United States Trade Representative. March 2017. www.ustr.gov/sites/default/files/gsp/Beneficiary%20countries%20March%202017.pdf; "Midterm Evaluation of the GSP Regulation." European Commission. October 8, 2018. https://trade.ec.europa.eu/doclib/docs/2018/august/tradoc_157270.pdf. The EU had seventy-one beneficiaries as of its 2018 mid-term report. "Generalized System of Preferences (GSP): Overview and Issues for Congress." Congressional Research Service. January 7, 2021. https://sgp.fas.org/crs/misc/RL33663.pdf

[27] "Generalized System of Preferences Extension Act." govinfo.gov | US Government Publishing Office. August 4, 1999. www.govinfo.gov/content/pkg/CRPT-106srpt137/html/CRPT-106srpt137.htm

administered in parallel with its deeper program of EPAs.[28] GSP benefits are granted by Armenia, Australia, Belarus, Canada, the European Union, Iceland, Japan, Kazakhstan, New Zealand, Norway, the Russian Federation, Switzerland, Turkey, the United Kingdom, and the United States.

The Uruguay Round added to benefits provided by the trading system to developing countries in a variety of respects (to some extent through transitional measures which have by now expired). These are catalogued in a note by the Secretariat and circulated by the Committee on Trade and Development.[29] Elements that stand out include the following:

- Ability to subsidize agriculture through domestic support to a greater extent than industrialized countries; the *de minimis* level under which there is no requirement to reduce trade-distorting support is 10 percent of the total value of production of the agricultural product in question for developing countries rather than 5 percent as for developed countries;[30]
- The WTO joined with the Food and Agriculture Organization (FAO), WHO, World Organisation for Animal Health (OIE, renamed WOAH), and the World Bank to create the Standards Trade Development Facility (STDF), which acts as a coordination and financing mechanism for SPS capacity development;[31]
- There is no presumption under the Agreement on Subsidies and Countervailing Measures that a subsidy with a value of more than 5 percent *ad valorem* granted by a developing country would cause adverse effects;
- There is an exemption for the lowest income least developed countries from the ban on export subsidies;
- Claims of adverse effects of subsidies on the trade of other members which results in serious prejudice must be demonstrated by positive evidence;

[28] "The EU's New Generalised Scheme of Preferences (GSP)." European Commission. December 2012. https://trade.ec.europa.eu/doclib/docs/2012/december/tradoc_150164.pdf

[29] "Special and Differential Treatment Provisions in WTO Agreements and Decisions: Note by the Secretariat WT/COMTD/W/258." World Trade Organization. March 2, 2021. https://docs.wto.org/dol2fe/Pages/SS/directdoc.aspx?filename=q:/WT/COMTD/W258.pdf&Open=True

[30] China agreed in its accession package to an 8.5 percent *de minimis* level rather than 10 percent.

[31] The STDF grew out of a joint communiqué issued by the Heads of FAO, the World Organization for Animal Health (formerly known as OIE), World Bank Group, WHO, and WTO at the Doha Ministerial Conference in November 2001. While it is not strictly an immediate result of the Uruguay Round, it flows from Article 10.1 of the Agreement on Agriculture, which provides: "In the preparation and application of sanitary or phytosanitary measures, Members shall take account of the special needs of developing country Members, and in particular of the least developed country Members."

- Assistance is to be rendered to developing country members in dispute settlement cases;
- Preferential treatment is granted under the rules with respect to the application of safeguard measures, both in ability to maintain relief and in exemption potentially from others' measures.

AID FOR TRADE

Technical assistance from the GATT Secretariat and members has been a feature of the system since at least 1961,[32] and probably before. The GATT programs operate alongside a collection of developed countries' bilateral aid programs geared to helping build capacity for engaging in international trade.[33] In 2005, at the Hong Kong Ministerial, an Aid for Trade Initiative was adopted at the suggestion of then WTO Director-General Pascal Lamy.[34] The Hong Kong Ministerial Declaration states:

> 57. *We welcome the discussions of Finance and Development Ministers in various fora, including the Development Committee of the World Bank and IMF, that have taken place this year on expanding Aid for Trade. Aid for Trade should aim to help developing countries, particularly LDCs, to build the supply-side capacity and trade-related infrastructure that they need to assist them to implement and benefit from WTO Agreements and more broadly to expand their trade.*[35]

The WTO reports that there is development assistance from all sources in the range of $25–30 billion per year, and almost one-third of all official development assistance (ODA) is trade-related. A modest but important portion of this aid is accounted for by direct WTO activities, through the Enhanced Integrated Framework (EIF; see below), the Standards and Trade Development Facility (SDTF) (see below),[36] the Joint Integrated Technical

[32] Gerard Curzon. 1965. *Multilateral Commercial Diplomacy*. London: Michael Joseph Ltd. On page 251, Curzon cited missions in Uganda, Tanganyika, Kenya, Libya, and Somalia to "assist on matters of commercial policy."

[33] Jean-Jaques Caellert, European University Institute, 2015.

[34] "Aid for Trade Fact Sheet." World Trade Organization. www.wto.org/english/tratop_e/devel_e/a4t_e/a4t_factsheet_e.htm

[35] "Ministerial Declaration: Doha Work Programme WT/MIN(05)/DEC." World Trade Organization. December 18, 2005. www.wto.org/english/thewto e/minist_e/min05_e/final_text_e.htm#aid_for_trade

[36] "Welcome to the Standards and Trade Development Facility." Standards and Trade Development Facility. www.standardsfacility.org/. While Deputy Director-General, I served on the Policy Committee of the STDF.

Assistance Program (JITAP),[37] and the ITC. Another activity of WTO members referenced earlier in Chapter 8 is the Director-General's Consultative Framework for Cotton Development Assistance, which is dedicated to assisting the poorest cotton farmers particularly in West Africa (Chad, Mali, Burkina Faso, and Benin) to improve their incomes from growing cotton.[38] The WTO Secretariat also provides direct training to assist in capacity-building through its Institute for Training and Technical Cooperation (ITTC).[39]

The SDTF is a global partnership that includes the WTO, the SPS standards-setting and capacity-building organizations (FAO, WHO, OIE/WOAH,[40] World Bank Group, WTO), donors (the European Union, United States, France, Netherlands, Germany), and developing country experts. It administers a fund that supports the scoping for projects dedicated to capacity-building to help governments, institutions, and the private sector in developing economies meet food and other agricultural (sanitary and phyto-sanitary [SPS]) standards required to allow trade to take place.

The Enhanced Integrated Framework for least developed countries is part of the wider Aid for Trade initiative. It is a joint effort and fund administered by the WTO Secretariat, with fifty-one member countries and partner agencies, working together to help least developed countries by improving their ability to benefit from trade. The six partner agencies are the IMF, the ITC, the UNCTAD, the UNDP, the World Bank, and the WTO. Thirty-six out of forty-nine least developed countries have become beneficiaries. In 2020, the EIF Trust Fund contributions stood at $141 million.[41]

37 "Donors Pledge Substantial Support to JITAP (II)." World Trade Organization. December 20, 2002. www.wto.org/english/news_e/pres02_e/pr328_e.htm

38 "Director-General's Consultative Framework Mechanism on Cotton 33rd Round of Consultations on Cotton Development Assistance." World Trade Organization. July 30, 2020. www.wto.org/english/tratop_e/agric_e/dg_cons_30720_e.htm

39 "Institute for Training and Technical Cooperation (ITTC)." World Trade Organization. www.wto.org/english/tratop_e/devel_e/teccop_e/ittc_e.htm

40 "The Office International des Epizooties (OIE) was established in Paris, France, in 1924 with the signing of an international agreement by 28 countries. In 2003 the Office became the World Organization for Animal Health, but kept its historical acronym OIE. As of 2011, the OIE has 178 Member Countries and Territories, each of which is represented by a delegate who, in most cases, is the Chief Veterinary Officer of the country." Source: USDA. It has been renamed as the World Organization for Animal Health (WOAH).

41 "EIF Annual Report Highlights Resilience of Poorest Countries Despite COVID-19 Crisis." World Trade Organization. June 25, 2021. www.wto.org/english/news_e/news21_e/if_25jun21_e.htm; "Annual Report 2020: Resilience through Trade at the Dawn of a New Decade." Enhanced Integrated Framework. 2020. www.enhancedif.org/en/system/files/uploads/eif_annual_report_2020.pdf?file=1&type=node&id=6305; "Integrated Framework Fact Sheet." World Trade Organization. www.wto.org/english/tratop_e/devel_e/teccop_e/if_factsheet_e.htm

THE CONTINUING EFFORT TO RESOLVE THE PLACE OF DEVELOPMENT IN THE WTO

At the Nairobi Ministerial, the ministers agreed to the following overarching principle: "We reaffirm the centrality of development in the WTO's work and commit to continuing to make positive efforts designed to ensure that developing country Members, and especially the least developed country Members, secure a share in the growth of world trade commensurate with the needs of their economic development."[42] Much is being done by the WTO members and the Secretariat to fulfill this pledge, but as the language indicates, it is a process that can never end – continuing positive efforts will always be needed, because the needs of the developing world are great.

The main issue of contention is not to be found in the Aid for Trade activities, although there is always room for a greater effort, but in how developing countries are to be treated by the WTO's rules. The debate revolves around a subject called out in paragraph 44 of the Doha Development Agenda (DDA) declaration issued in 2001:

> 44. *We reaffirm that provisions for special and differential treatment are an integral part of the WTO Agreements. We note the concerns expressed regarding their operation in addressing specific constraints faced by developing countries, particularly least developed countries.*[43] *In that connection, we also note that some members have proposed a Framework Agreement on Special and Differential Treatment (WT/GC/W/442). We therefore agree that all special and differential treatment provisions shall be reviewed with a view to strengthening them and making them more precise, effective and operational. In this connection, we endorse the work programme on special and differential treatment set out in the Decision on Implementation-Related Issues and Concerns.*[44]

It is the first sentence of paragraph 44 that requires further definition, and further definition defies consensus. In a multilateral trading system built on the foundation of nondiscrimination and ultimately reciprocity, "on a legal relationship based essentially on parity of obligation,"[45] what exactly is the

[42] "Nairobi Ministerial Declaration WT/MIN(15)/DEC." World Trade Organization. December 19, 2015. www.wto.org/english/thewto_e/minist_e/mc10_e/mindecision_e.htm

[43] Ibid.

[44] "Implementation-Related Issues and Concerns WT/MIN(01)/17." World Trade Organization. November 20, 2001. www.wto.org/english/thewto_e/minist_e/min01_e/mindecl_implementation_e.htm

[45] Robert Hudec. 2010. *Developing Countries in the GATT Legal System*. Cambridge: Cambridge University Press. J. Michael Finger quoting Robert Hudec in his 2010 introduction to Hudec's

nature of "special and differential treatment" (referred to as S&D or SDT) that is declared to be an "integral part of the WTO Agreements"? Who are the beneficiaries to be of this S&D, and when? It is relatively straightforward to catalogue the hundreds of instances in which S&D already exists and, at the direction of the members, the WTO Secretariat has done so.[46] But without further definition, how is this mandate from a declaration from the DDA, a negotiation that never concluded and at best has been suspended, to be applied?

The "some Members" referred to in the Doha declaration paragraph 44 as proposing that all WTO members agree to a framework for special and differential treatment were Cuba, Dominican Republic, Honduras, India, Indonesia, Kenya, Malaysia, Pakistan, Sri Lanka, Tanzania, Uganda, and Zimbabwe. They articulated a continuing grievance of many developing countries about how the WTO came about, as a diktat: "Developing countries did not have the option to sign or otherwise on the various agreements because all of them, excepting four plurilateral agreements, were part of the Single Undertaking."[47] They formulated what they saw as a necessary assumption underlying S&D: "an acceptance of deviation from the general rule of *quid pro quo* or reciprocity for the developing countries" (Emphasis added).[48] It was presumably intentional to describe the beneficiaries as one undifferentiated, indissoluble group. But this language was not accepted by all members in 2001, meaning it was not adopted, and is contained in the preamble for what turned out to be a doomed negotiation. As a result, it has no standing, other than as a banner for a cause.

The authors of the proposed S&D framework outlined "elements which can form part of the Agreement on S&D":

- *Special and Differential treatment shall be mandatory and legally binding through the dispute settlement system of the WTO (including notification requirements and inclusion of these commitments in country schedules).*

1987 work: "It is recognized by all that differentiation on the basis of the level of economic development was introduced informally early in the system, through different levels of tariff and non-tariff concessions, and then more formally recognized by longer phase-in periods of obligations of developing countries, and then with more over special treatment. This chapter traces those developments."

46 "Special and Differential Treatment Provisions in WTO Agreements and Decisions: Note by the Secretariat WT/COMTD/W/258." World Trade Organization. March 2, 2021. https://docs.wto.org/dol2fe/Pages/SS/directdoc.aspx?filename=q:/WT/COMTD/W258.pdf&Open=True

47 "Preparations for the Fourth Session of the Ministerial Conference WT/GC/W/442." World Trade Organization. September 19, 2001. www.wto.org/english/thewto_e/minist_e/min01_e/proposals_e/wt_gc_w442.pdf

48 Ibid.

- *Without an evaluation of the fact whether an Industrial Policy has a demonstrable adverse impact on trade, there shall be no prohibition of policies which promote growth and development in developing countries.*
- *The application of the concept of Single Undertaking for developing countries should not be automatic.*[49]

A debate ensued about "differentiation." Would all who claimed to be "developing countries" be treated identically, *ab initio*, a preordained outcome before any negotiation was even attempted? In trying to find a way to come to an agreement in the Doha Development Agenda negotiations, this issue appeared to require resolution. The basic principle, contained in a paper published by IFRI (Institut Français des Relations Internationales) discussing the challenges of providing S&D, would have seemed to be inarguable: "SDT exemptions from trade rules should primarily benefit the most vulnerable countries deprived from alternatives to trade policy instruments."[50] The same could be said of the potential impact of granting special and differential treatment:

> *Odds are great that the negative externalities from smallest trading powers will be negligible, whatever the importance of SDT rules exemptions. But important negative externalities are anticipated from granting the same SDT treatment to the poorest countries and the emerging trading powers. It is therefore unlikely that ambitious and efficient SDT provisions be agreed upon without further differentiating DCs [developing countries].*[51]

In Buenos Aires, in December 2017, the United States Trade Representative presented the US view, stated more starkly:

> *We need to clarify our understanding of development within the WTO. We cannot sustain a situation in which new rules can only apply to the few, and that others will be given a pass in the name of self-proclaimed development status. There is something wrong, in our view, when five of the six richest countries in the world presently claim developing country status. Indeed, we should all be troubled that so many Members appear to believe that they would be better off with exemptions to the rules. If in the opinion of a vast majority of*

[49] "Preparations for the Fourth Session of the Ministerial Conference WT/GC/W/442." World Trade Organization. September 19, 2001. www.wto.org/english/thewto_e/minist_e/min01_e/proposals_e/wt_gc_w442.pdf

[50] Jean-Marie Paugam and Anne-Sophie Novel. 2005. "Why and How Differentiate Developing Countries in the WTO? Theoretical Options and Negotiating Solutions." IFRI – Institut Français des Relations Internationales. September. www.ifri.org/sites/default/files/atoms/files/novel_paugam_nov_2005.pdf

[51] Ibid.

Members playing by current WTO rules makes it harder to achieve economic growth, then clearly serious reflection is needed.[52]

If a number of developing countries wished to question the assumptions upon which the trading system was founded, so would the United States.

In January 2019, the trilateral trade ministers (representing the European Union, Japan, and the United States) "reiterated their call on advanced WTO Members claiming developing country status to undertake full commitments in ongoing and future WTO negotiations."[53] On February 14, 2019, the United States circulated a forty-five-page memorandum describing the differences it saw in the level of economic development among countries that had declared themselves to be "developing," presumably for the WTO purpose of receiving treatment better than others in any future negotiations. The paper concluded:

Self-declaration and its first-order consequence – an inability to differentiate among Members – puts the WTO on a path to failed negotiations. It is also a path to institutional irrelevance, whereby the WTO remains anchored to the past and unable to negotiate disciplines to address the challenges of today or tomorrow, while other international institutions move forward.[54]

The United States followed up on the next day with a draft General Council decision that, while it agreed that "recognizing that reserving flexibilities for those WTO Members with the greatest difficulty integrating into the multilateral trading system can open new export opportunities for such countries," it was necessary "to strengthen the negotiating function of the WTO to produce high-standard, reciprocal and mutually advantageous arrangements directed to the substantial reduction of tariffs and other barriers to trade and to the elimination of discriminatory treatment in international trade relations." It proposed that the WTO members agree that:

the following categories of Members will not avail themselves of special and differential treatment in current and future WTO negotiations:

[52] "Opening Plenary Statement of USTR Robert Lighthizer at the WTO Ministerial Conference." Office of the United States Trade Representative. December 11, 2017. www.ustr.gov/about-us/policy-offices/press-office/press-releases/2017/december/opening-plenary-statement-ustr

[53] "Joint Statement of the Trilateral Meeting of the Trade Ministers of the European Union, Japan and the United States." Office of the United States Trade Representative. January 9, 2019. www.ustr.gov/about-us/policy-offices/press-office/press-releases/2019/january/joint-statement-trilateral-meeting

[54] "An Undifferentiated WTO: Self-Declared Development Status Risks Institutional Irrelevance – Communication from the United States WT/GC/W/757/Rev.1." World Trade Organization. February 14, 2019.

i. *A WTO Member that is a Member of the Organization for Economic Cooperation and Development (OECD), or a WTO Member that has begun the accession process to the OECD;*
ii. *A WTO Member that is a member of the Group of 20 (G20);*
iii. *A WTO Member that is classified as a "high income" country by the World Bank; or*
iv. *A WTO Member that accounts for no less than 0.5 percent of global merchandise trade (imports and exports).*[55]

Recognizing that a country could be developed in some areas of its economy and lag in others, the proposal added that "nothing in this Decision precludes reaching agreement that in sector-specific negotiations other Members are also ineligible for special and differential treatment."

A few days later, a number of countries – China, India, South Africa, the Bolivarian Republic of Venezuela, Lao People's Democratic Republic, the Plurinational State of Bolivia, Kenya, Cuba, Central African Republic, and Pakistan – all of which are considered developing in the WTO under the doctrine of self-designation, filed their response to the US memorandum:

> *Recent attempts by some Members to selectively employ certain economic and trade data to deny the persistence of the divide between developing and developed Members, and to demand the former to abide by absolute "reciprocity" in the interest of "fairness" are profoundly disingenuous ...*
>
> *As a fundamental right granted to all developing Members, each developing Member shall, based upon its own particular situation, make the decision by itself on whether, when, where and how to use S&DT, and to what extent as well. No other members are entitled to interfere with such a self-declared decision.*[56]

Brazil, Japan, and Australia supported the US proposal. The European Union said that while it shared the concerns raised by the United States (setting out categories of developing countries judged by objective criteria), S&D should be based on a case-by-case examination, agreement by agreement.[57]

[55] "Draft General Council Decision – Procedures to Strengthen the Negotiating Function of the WTO WT/GC/W/764." World Trade Organization. February 15, 2019.

[56] "The Continued Relevance of Special and Differential Treatment in Favour of Developing Members to Promote Development and Ensure Inclusiveness WT/GC/W/765/Rev.2." World Trade Organization. March 4, 2019. https://docs.wto.org/dol2fe/Pages/FE_Search/FE_S_S009-DP.aspx?CatalogueIdList=251793. The South Centre also published its negative reaction to the US proposal.

[57] "Trump Administration Will Raise Tariffs on European Aircraft." www.nytimes.com/2020/02/14/business/economy/trump-airbus-trade-tariffs.html; Terrance Stewart. 2021. "The Folly of Self-Selection as a Developing Country at the WTO." Current Thoughts on Trade.

The European Union firmly believes that if this organisation is to prosper, special and differential treatment must become much more granular, in function of an individual Member's demonstrated needs and capacities. Future differentiation should be designed in terms of specific individual country needs at the sectoral or activity level rather than calling for a block exemption of a large category of Members.

Furthermore, the EU considers that each developing country's need for SDT should be assessed on a case-by-case and evidence-based basis. The notable exception should be the LDCs who deserve particular treatment and who in any case have a graduation mechanism.[58]

In any discussion of blanket S&D treatment, the United States would usually point to the fact that China is claiming S&D as a right when it is the world's largest manufacturing and exporting country.

China's global merchandise exports are 14 times greater than the combined exports of all 49 countries that the UN categorizes as LDCs. Its economy is more than 11 times the economies of all 49 LDCs combined. China's per capita income is more than five times higher than that of the LDC average – a remarkable development since 1995, when China's per capita income was within $900 of the LDC's average …

The failure to differentiate some of this organization's most advanced, wealthy, or influential Members from LDCs and others diminishes the value of special and differential treatment to those who need it most. It also imperils our ability to reach new agreements that could provide greater opportunities for the WTO's poorest Members who are least integrated into the global trading system.[59]

China's response has been that self-declaration is for it a red line, something it will not give up. It states that the US desire to engage in this "debate on criteria to differentiate developing members is totally meaningless, as it is a systematic and directional mistake." But it adds a potentially important nuance:

China standing against the differentiation of developing members does not mean we want to enjoy the same favorable treatment as small economies and LDCs. What we want is only to safeguard our institutional right of S&DT.

November 15. https://currentthoughtsontrade.com/2021/11/15/the-folly-of-self-selection-as-a-developing-country-at-the-wto/

58 "EU Statements by Ambassador João Aguiar Machado at the General Council Meeting, 13 October 2020." Permanent Mission of the European Union to the World Trade Organization. October 14, 2020.

59 "Statement by Ambassador Dennis Shea at the WTO General Council Meeting." US Mission to International Organizations in Geneva. October 13, 2020. https://geneva.usmission.gov/2020/10/13/statement-by-ambassador-shea-at-the-wto-item-7/

In practice, according to our accession agreement, China has 14 specific S&DT provisions among all 155 articles, accounting only for 9 percent. Among the 14, 6 provisions are traditionally "obligations" of the developed members, such as providing translations of documents in WTO official languages upon request, only 8 provisions are so called meaningful "rights," such as relatively higher tariffs for certain goods.

Even in such circumstances, China always shows restraint in invoking S&DT provisions. Obviously, China did not request to have the same S&DT as Benin, Liberia, Kenya or Pakistan, which was proclaimed by the United States. On the contrary, as a large trading nation, we recognize the responsibility China should bear. Our approach is to address different issues according to their specific situations and make contributions within our capability. As we did in the ITA expansion negotiations, China is the largest contributor among all the participants. We will continue to do that in the future.[60]

In July 2015, the G90 submitted a package of twenty-five proposals to the Committee on Trade and Development in Special Session (CTD-SS).[61] The G90, consisting of the African Group, the African, Caribbean, and Pacific Group, and the LDCs, have for several years now pressed the developed country members of the WTO to take up seriously a series of proposals that would in some instances reduce the level of obligation of developing countries and, in others, increase the obligations of the industrialized ones. These proposals included:[62]

- Reducing the impediments to resort to GATT Article XVIII to allow greater access to quantitative restrictions by developing countries for balance of payments, and to tariffs for infant industry protection (expanding the definition to include industries harmed by climate change or hostilities) without risk of retaliation;
- Having developed country members bind all their LDC preferences for agricultural products;

60 "Statement by H. E. Ambassador Zhang Xiangchen of China at the General Council Meeting (Item 6 and 7) October 13, 2020." Ministry of Commerce of the People's Republic of China. October 20, 2020. http://sk.mofcom.gov.cn/article/chinanews/202010/20201003009516.shtml

61 "Trade and Development." World Trade Organization. www.wto.org/english/thewto_e/minist_e/mc11_e/briefing_notes_e/bfdevel_e.htm#fntext-1. The G90 was initiated at the WTO's Ministerial Conference at Cancún in September 2003, taking common positions, with sixty-four of the ninety countries in the G90 being members of the WTO. It is the largest trading body in the WTO.

62 "The WTO's Special and Differential Treatment Negotiations (Paragraph 44)." South Centre. January 2017. www.southcentre.int/wp-content/uploads/2017/01/AN_TDP_2017_3_The-WTO%E2%80%99s-Special-and-Differential-Treatment-Negotiations-Paragraph-44_EN.pdf

- In an interesting application of some of what exists for TBT, but with an S&D twist, requiring only developed countries to notify *all* of their sanitary and phytosanitary (SPS) measures in advance of entry into force to allow time for comment (ninety days or longer upon request by LDCs), providing that if SPS measures are urgent, the market share of developing countries and LDCs should be maintained (there is a parallel suggestion for the TBT Agreement);
- Exempting developing countries from the Agreement on Trade-Related Investment Measures (TRIMs);
- Exempting LDCs also from the Agreement on Trade-Related Intellectual Property Rights (TRIPS);
- Providing in the General Agreement for Trade in Services (GATS) minimum quotas for services and service suppliers from developing countries and LDCs and eliminating horizontal limitations maintained by developed country members on the movement of natural persons from developing countries and LDCs;
- Providing in the Agreement on Subsidies and Countervailing Measures (SCM) that WTO members shall exercise due restraint with respect to challenging subsidies provided by developing countries, in order to achieve development goals and allow developing countries to use subsidies based on local content;
- With respect to the Customs Valuation Agreement, allowing LDCs to use minimum or reference values in cases of insufficient or inadequate technical and financial assistance, lack of customs cooperation or lack of access to international pricing data, plus exemption from the agreement until adequate capacity exists in the LDC;
- Providing an exemption for any LDC from safeguard actions if its share of imports is equal to or under 10 percent;
- Not conditioning loans, grants, and ODA to LDCs on terms that are inconsistent with their rights under the WTO;
- Preference erosion should be guarded against but if it occurs, developed countries would be required to provide compensation and adjustment support;
- Developing country preferences to other developing countries should be recognized as WTO-consistent;
- Recognizing the right of LDCs to adequate food as an objective of current and future WTO negotiations; allow LDCs to adjust their applied tariffs beyond bound levels in order to safeguard this human right;
- Requiring that state trading enterprises (STEs), in the case of developing countries, adhere only to the MFN principle and not to national treatment obligations; and

- In dispute settlement proceedings, giving attention to the particular problems and interests of developing countries and LDCs before the establishment of a panel as well as during panel proceedings.

The G90 list of objectives for S&D has reportedly been shortened, or at least rearranged.[63] Key points reported in the press include:

- *Any COVID-19 invention or other technologies must be temporarily treated as global public goods so that they can be manufactured and distributed with a view to make them accessible to all.*
- *Building resilient economies requires transfer of technology. Members are encouraged to put in place measures to incentivize the transfer of technology to achieve their developmental objectives.*

And in what could be read as a diplomatic concession to developed country members:

- *WTO Members should always undertake commitments commensurate with their level of development in recognition of differences in capabilities, capacities and resources.*
- *Members should adhere to the implementation of commitments under the TRIPS Agreement.*

Other highlights that have been advanced by the G90 include:

- Measures utilizing the exemption from TRIMs would be for a specific broad list of purposes, and notified within six months;
- If there is a right to compensatory action to rebalance concessions due to a measure imposed under Article XVIII, it could be exercised only after a five-year grace period from the introduction of the measures;
- Measures for balance of payments difficulties can be applied freely pursuant to a self-judgment of need;
- The now dormant nonactionable subsidies listed in the Agreement on Subsidies and Countervailing Measures shall be reinstated for developing countries for eight years and for LDCs for ten years;
- Developed countries are to make available to developing country members' enterprises, on demand and on fair and reasonable terms, technologies under their control or whose development was funded by them; and
- Technical assistance shall be provided to LDCs to support their innovation capacities.

[63] As of this writing, the latest formulation of the G90 S&D proposal was circulated in the CTD-SS on March 9, 2020, as JOB/DEV/60 and JOB/TNC/79. "G90 Calls for Outcome on S&DT at MC12." Third World Network. July 30, 2021. https://www.twn.my/title2/unsd/2021/unsd210717.htm

Industrialized members of the WTO, and some developing countries, have not accepted the G90 proposals, both because of the scope and number of deviations that would be allowed from WTO disciplines and the lack of differentiation among developing countries.[64]

PRELIMINARY CONCLUSIONS

Writing in the 1980s, Hudec suggested that developing countries would best be served by adopting two policies: the first was making their long-term objective strengthening the WTO's MFN obligation, as he argued that non-discrimination was in their best interests. Secondly, and as importantly, he felt that developing countries would best be served by having obligations rather than being freed from having them: "to provide a regime of developing country legal obligations that would provide support for governments of developing countries in opposing unwanted protectionist policies at home."[65] He regretted that negotiators had taken the easy way out, the path of least resistance for developed countries in that they did not have to explain to their legislators that they had given additional trade concessions in the form of additional access to their own domestic market, and similarly easier for developing countries' negotiators, who could explain to their constituents that they had given no additional market access to others, and were required to do less and less to comply with their GATT obligations. In his view, this was a negative zero-sum game. It is what Low, Mamdouh, and Rogerson term the minimalist bargain, criticizing it as not being "stable and it satisfied no one."[66]

What has developed in the intervening years is an increasing amount of rhetoric in favor of the centrality of development not matched by action. There has been stasis, a somewhat sterile debate on the one hand about there being a right that is unrecognized and on the other about categories of levels of development that have been rejected as not reflecting realities of both needs and lack of capacity. This divide can be an impediment to progress in negotiations if members take the position that resolving this impasse is a necessary precondition. This is true of most preconditions for negotiations.

64 "Trade and Development." World Trade Organization. www.wto.org/english/thewto_e/minist_e/mc11_e/briefing_notes_e/bfdevel_e.htm#fntext-1

65 Robert E. Hudec. 1987. *Developing Countries in the GATT Legal System.* London: Gower, for the Trade Policy Research Center.

66 Patrick Low, Hamid Mamdouh, and Evan Rogerson. 2018. "Balancing Rights and Obligations in the WTO – A Shared Responsibility." Government Offices of Sweden. www.swedenabroad.se/globalassets/ambassader/fn-geneve/documents/balancing-rights-and-obligations-in-the-wto.pdf. Page 26.

The open question is: are they requirements based on actual need, or a position designed to derail attempts at achieving forward motion?

There are broadly three possible outcomes for S&D for developing countries (with the exception of LDCs):

- Blanket treatment as a right for all developing countries in every agreement (the G90 position);
- Placement of countries into baskets based on levels of development or capacity (the US and Brazil position); and
- A more ad hoc approach, issue by issue, agreement by agreement (the EU position).

Brazil, Singapore, and Korea have renounced benefiting from S&D as developing countries. China has indicated that it will contribute in line with its capacity, but that it will not renounce its developing country status. National economies are not uniform in terms of levels of development by sector. Whether for political or economic reasons or both, the "one size fits all" solution is not likely to be agreed upon. While a vast amount has been written about how to amend the global trade rules system based on equality of treatment, as many have said over the years, "equal treatment of those who are not equal does not yield equal results."

In the early years of the DDA negotiations, Bernard Hoekman wrote a paper for the World Bank posing the problem: "SDT should focus primarily on WTO rules and be limited to those countries that need it most – very small and poor economies. [This] implies that criteria should be adopted to differentiate between countries. Leaving this to self-declaration – the current approach – is not feasible, while reliance on case-by-case, agreement-specific negotiation can generate excessive costs, discretion, and associated uncertainty." The World Bank report did not settle the issue of how S&D should be shaped. It called for dedicated study.[67]

While there is no dispute over according the least developed countries as a group S&D, as collectively their impact on the trading system is very small and their needs are uniformly recognized as being great, there are problems in categorizing larger countries by their level of development, as the South Centre has pointed out. In any country's designation of benefits, there must be flexibility. The United States recognizes this to an extent in its proposal.

[67] Bernard Hoekman, Constantine Michalopoulos, and L. Alan Winters. "More Favorable and Differential Treatment of Developing Countries: Toward a New Approach in the World Trade Organization." World Bank Group. August 2003. https://elibrary.worldbank.org/doi/abs/10.1596/1813-9450-3107

As a rule of thumb, several commentators have held that a degree of categorization by "socio-economic indicators" would hold some promise.[68]

Complicating the issue, it is difficult to find homogeneity within the set of WTO Agreements or even within a single agreement, as to the level of capacity needed to fulfill an obligation. Some agreements have some degree of differentiation built in. The Trade Facilitation Agreement allows members to indicate their level and timing of commitment. Likewise, GATS schedules vary by member and sector, with the possibility of carve-outs from coverage for purposes of granting market access within limits. Differentiation occurs in the accession process, without terming this S&D, because each accession is the result of series of bilateral negotiations specific to the acceding country and reflects a balance of concessions at the time of negotiation. The Agreement on Agriculture differentiates between most developed countries and most developing countries. Starting fresh with a new agreement, even a blanket approach might need to be leavened with flexibilities. Another approach to S&D that is worth exploring is that there are core principles that would need to be adhered to (MFN and national treatment, for example), and other rules that might not. The G90 proposals and GATS for that matter are even able to divide core principles, MFN as compared with national treatment.

Using differentiation based on capacity poses the additional problem, noted by Ukpe and Khorana, that this could require implementation audits. National capacities evolve. Fixing S&D at one moment in time does not take into account that trading relationships are not frozen, so freezing rights and obligations will often cause them to be out of step with current realities in the market. Tariff bindings and agricultural commitments that were appropriate at the end of a negotiation, but remain in place a generation later, cause the trading system to be increasingly imbalanced, where the benefits of rights are no longer matched by the burden of obligations. For LDCs, the trading system provides graduation, although even this is not free from controversy. The

[68] Aniekan Ukpe and Sangeeta Khorana. 2021. "Special and Differential Treatment in the WTO: Framing Differential Treatment to Achieve (Real) Development." *Journal of International Trade Law and Policy* 20(2): 83–100: "Albeit, we earlier questioned the propriety of using socioeconomic indicators to categorise countries at the WTO, using them to determine countries' eligibility for SDT holds huge prospects for successfully reforming SDT in the WTO." This paper has a good bibliography for those interested in exploring more sources on the subject of S&D differentiation. Not discussed here is the paper's suggestion that a composite indicator be employed. Having the example of the failed "Ease of Doing Business" rating by country in the World Bank, I suspect that the indicator might have merit in the abstract but would be exceedingly contentious in its administration. Therefore, it is not included here.

question remains: what is to be done for the rest? The US proposal in effect has built-in graduation but has not gained wide adherence.

Recommendation: No exception should be permanent. Each should have a sunset clause, a finite period of effectiveness, but with the possibility of renewal. Every municipal government has licenses that require renewal, with conditions often to be fulfilled if renewal is to take place. It cannot be that the world trading system would be unequal to the task of making determinations of the same sort for member governments and economies. Having a rules-based system requires more than rule-making. It requires administration. The system can either be broad-based or finely curated by agreement. The US proposal has the benefit of simplicity, without necessarily delivering an objectively fair result in every instance. On the other hand, making excessively fine distinctions will result in a greater administrative burden. A pragmatic answer lies somewhere in between and should be found. **One approach would be to have objective criteria lead to a presumption of how a country would be treated in a particular negotiation**, recognizing that differing agreements might lead to differing results, based on the need for S&D.

A complementary solution, suggested by Ukpe and Khorana, is to increase technical assistance with respect to the implementation of agreements based on need, with the objective that none is left behind. The claim that notifications are too burdensome, for example, could be dealt with by help from the WTO Secretariat. There is a precedent in the Secretariat's role in preparing countries for Trade Policy Reviews. A generation ago, Hudec concluded, and a number of commentators have concurred, that "the basic flaw in the WTO's current approach is that it is founded on seeking exemptions from WTO obligations instead of enabling developing countries to meet these obligations and thus integrate them fully into the multilateral trading system."[69]

69 James Bacchus and Inu Manak. 2020. "The Development Dimension: What to Do about Differential Treatment in Trade." Cato Institute. April 13. www.cato.org/policy-analysis/development-dimension-what-do-about-differential-treatment-trade; Robert Hudec. 2010. *Developing Countries in the GATT Legal System*. Cambridge: Cambridge University Press. *The policy of non-reciprocity as the path of least resistance, required nothing of developing country trade negotiators facing hostile interests at home. at the same time developed country negotiators did not have to grant additional access and explain that to their constituents. the response has not been to focus on developing country behavior, in their own interests and in the interests of the trading system.*

With the advent of China being the world's largest manufacturing and exporting nation, that approach no longer worked, if it ever really did. Hudec noted that developing countries sought to relax the conditions for access to GATT Art. XVIII. They were not looking for additional disciplines to help them make policy choices that were more productive by giving infant industry protection to those industries that could become internationally competitive. Hudec

An EU internal concept paper in 2018 laid out some middle-ground options. As they summarize a number of suggestions, they are included here in some detail:

The EU should propose the following:

(a) *Graduation: Members should be actively encouraged to "graduate" and opt-out of SDT, whether horizontally or agreement by agreement. In the interim, Members should be encouraged to clarify in which areas they actually use existing flexibilities and to present roadmaps detailing when they would expect to be able to assume all the obligations stemming from the WTO agreement. This could form an integral part of a Member's TPR process.*

(b) *Special and Differential Treatment (SDT) in future agreements: while acknowledging the need for particularly flexible treatment of LDCs, flexibilities available to other Members should move away from open-ended block exemptions toward a needs-driven and evidence-based approach that will ensure that SDT will be as targeted as possible. Various approaches can be used, which should satisfy the following principles: – the agreement in question will eventually be universally implemented, so that the core rights and obligations will apply to everyone and any exceptions will be time-bound; – in-built flexibility in the form of additional commitments going beyond a core set of provisions should cater for differences among Members – the flexibilities available in any agreement should be proportional to the number of Members participating and the ambition of the agreement. There are a number of tools that can be used to implement these proposals, for example, differentiation, graduation mechanisms, grace periods and assistance linked to implementation.*

(c) *Additional SDT in existing agreements: Though existing SDT provisions in current agreements should not be contested, when Members request additional SDT this should be done only on the basis of a case-by-case analysis, on the basis of: – a clear identification of the development objective that is being affected by the rule in question; – an economic analysis of the impact of the rule and of the expected benefits of its relaxation; – an analysis of the impact of the requested flexibility on other WTO Members; – a specification of the time period for which flexibility is requested and of its scope of application (one Member, a group of Members or all developing country Members). Depending on the outcome*

found that the approach of developing countries, to limit the disciplines that might affect them, was more harmful than helpful. This is Hudec's analysis of how the GATT system got into an institutional rut.

> *of this analysis, various approaches can be used to consider additional flexibilities.*[70]

There is a gap between what would have made sense at the outset of the WTO or would make good sense now, on the one hand, and what is achievable, what is negotiable, on the other. So flexibilities have to be built in, and the WTO has not proved to be able to accomplish this. Added to this challenge is the fact that it is unlikely there can be a wholesale revision of agreements. Much of the trading system will be difficult to change. The world trading system we have is characterized by incrementalism, evolution – but for two key formative events, its creation and the cancelation of GATT 1947 in favor of the WTO and GATT 1994. In cosmology, there was a big bang that created the universe. For the trading system that occurred in 1948 and in 1995, special circumstances of that sort do not exist and are unlikely to exist in the near future. **The best chance for a more tailored and constructive approach to S&D will be in open plurilateral agreements going forward**. It is important that these plurilaterals either have a thoughtful set of provisions for S&D, have a placeholder for them to be added later, or have a design that addresses the subject in a clear and thoughtful manner. Will they emphasize additional technical assistance rather than exemptions? Will there be phase-ins or sunset provisions? Will there be reviews and new decisions taken? Without the single undertaking, if open plurilateral agreements become part of the WTO, there should be scope for differentiation not just among countries but in degrees of participation in obligations and benefits by a developing country participant by agreement.

The "three WTO wisemen" – Low, Mamdouh, and Rogerson – the authors of the paper from which was drawn the quotation that began this chapter, have some conclusions which deserve broad support. They base their conclusions on the precept that "there is no member of the WTO that wants nothing, nor any that can give nothing." They posit a trade negotiation in which tariff concessions of interest are exchanged, within a structure that recognizes participants' needs and capabilities. While I agree it is possible that balance can be achieved within any given agreement, I think it more likely that balance becomes more possible if there is more on the table at once. This is

[70] "Concept Paper: WTO Modernisation – Introduction to Future EU Proposals." Directorate General for Trade of the European Commission. September 2018. https://trade.ec.europa.eu/doclib/docs/2018/september/tradoc_157331.pdf. The concept paper was never presented to the WTO membership, although reference to its existence was made by Sabine Weyand, Director-General for Trade of the European Commission, at the WTO's 2019 Trade Policy Review of the EU.

not necessarily to call for a new round to replace the DDA or to try to resurrect that round, but at a minimum to have a broader set of negotiations in which there is more room for trade-offs – in short, not a new round but the packaging of agreements to obtain maximum buy-in.[71]

The appetite among WTO members for trade liberalization appears to be at a historic low point, while rule-making is still needed. There is a significant amount of member support for negotiating new rules, as evidenced by the existence of the plurilaterals. While at present the degree of interest is manifested to a greater extent among the developed than the developing country members, there is some current participation by developing countries and the number participating is likely to grow. Echoing Hudec, a key intellectual forebear, Low, Mamdouh, and Rogerson state: "Developing countries stand to gain more by strengthening MFN than they do by continuing to press for MFN exemptions. The more the system moves away from preferentialism as a mechanism for securing better market access and towards MFN liberalization, the more solid becomes the contractual relationship among the membership."[72]

If one believes in the multilateral trading system, then it must move forward. Demands on trade change, whether due to the general movement to a global digital economy, or to meet new challenges, such as pandemics and climate change. As a result, the system of rules has to adapt. This process needs the participation of all – the least developed, the developing, and the developed countries. **There will always be a need for some differentiation, but the end point must be convergence, where all benefit fully and undertake all commitments.** The subject of SDT, in whatever form, is the bridge to that future.

My experience in chairing the Consultative Framework Mechanism for Cotton was that cooperation was forthcoming without contentiousness where what was being requested in terms of development assistance was carefully crafted by the recipients to be effective. Political statements were eschewed in favor of pragmatism. SDT as such was not discussed at all, because the sole subject was necessary assistance for those among the neediest. This approach

[71] The art of trade negotiation is the same as having a poker game. There needs to be enough in the pot so that no one feels that he can leave the table. This is Texas folk wisdom of former USTR Robert S. Strauss.

[72] Patrick Low, Hamid Mamdouh, and Evan Rogerson. 2018. "Balancing Rights and Obligations in the WTO – A Shared Responsibility." Government Offices of Sweden. www.swedenabroad.se/globalassets/ambassader/fn-geneve/documents/balancing-rights-and-obligations-in-the-wto.pdf. Pages 14–15.

worked for cotton development assistance. It did not work for cotton trade issues where subsidies and market access were tied into broader negotiations.

What Nelson Mandela told trade ministers in 1998, to celebrate the fiftieth anniversary of the GATT, at a moment three years into the life of the WTO, is still relevant today:

> *The sections dealing with the developing countries and the least developed countries were not adequately thought through. Nor have they been fully implemented. There are elements of an answer: in the mechanism of extension of time to comply; and in recent improvements in the capacity of the WTO to give technical assistance in co-operation with other multilateral agencies. But they are not the full answer.*
>
> *What exactly can be done? . . .*
>
> *The developing countries must accept that we want to be fully part of the WTO, and that includes improving the management of the world trading system to ensure that our economies do develop.*
>
> *These are complex matters, and in dealing with such matters there are no easy solutions. But where there is a determination to find joint, negotiated solutions then there is a way . . .*
>
> *We are firmly of the belief that the existence of the GATT, and now the World Trade Organisation, as a rules-based system, provides a solid foundation for ensuring that increased flows of both trade and investment bring mutual gain for all.*
>
> *To realise this, however, there is work to be done.*[73]

[73] "Address by President Nelson Mandela at the 50th anniversary of the General Agreement on Tariffs and Trade (GATT), Geneva – Switzerland." Nelson Rolihlahla Mandela – Government of South Africa. May 19, 1998. www.mandela.gov.za/mandela_speeches/1998/980519_gatt.htm; www.wto.org/english/thewto_e/minist_e/min98_e/anniv_e/mandela_e.htm

PART V

World Trade Governance and Systemic Reform

12

The Problem of Governance of the Multilateral Trading System

In this chapter, in broad strokes, we look at the governance of the trading system since its inception – across the GATT and WTO periods – and understand the headwinds that must be overcome to achieve needed systemic reforms.

Every social endeavor requires organization. A corporation has a stockholder's meeting, a board of directors, and a number of executives. Governments have legislative, executive, and judicial branches, and sometimes hold referenda. Some form of governance is a requirement for group activities. An organized religion can have a certain amount of received dogma, a creed that binds its members together, or it can be covenantal, mainly based on what its members concur that they believe. The dogma of the WTO consists of its principles. These were identified by the Group of 20 leaders in the Riyadh Initiative in 2020.[1] They agreed that there must be stability, transparency, and nondiscrimination. To this might be added the requirement of enforceability of obligations. How the dogma is to be applied, what additions might be added to the list of

[1] "G20 Trade and Investment Ministerial Meeting: Communiqué." G20 Information Centre. September 22, 2020. www.g20.utoronto.ca/2020/2020-g20-trade-0922.html

Rule of law –
Transparency
Non-discrimination
Inclusiveness
Fair competition
Market openness
Resistance to protectionism
Reciprocal and mutually advantageous arrangements, acknowledging that agreements provide for differential and more favorable treatment for developing economies, including special attention to the particular situation of least developed countries.

common principles, all these points are covenantal. They are whatever the members agree to.[2]

The covenant of the multilateral trading system evolves over time. It was an article of faith in the GATT years that there would be continuing, progressive trade liberalization. That is not a precept of today's WTO. Likewise, it was an accepted principle that if some participants could move further than others, they could have a GATT Agreement on the subject. This is also not completely accepted by today's WTO members.

Trade is a manifestation of international cooperation. It requires a degree of governance, agreed rules, and institutions to flourish. Governance is always complicated. This was so even when the polity seeking to govern itself was a city-state, such as ancient Athens. Governance is even more challenging at the level of a nation. It is not usually free of controversy, and is a subject being debated today in many, perhaps most nations, not least in the United States. In recent times, when the United Kingdom exited the EU, the governance of trade between the two was and remains a major issue for Europe. Past, current, and future EU member states continue to seek to come to workable arrangements with each other. Brussels working with London, with Kyiv, seeks to define their relationship. It was much more difficult for the 128 nations of the GATT. At present, 164 members of the WTO continuously work to define their relationships, how they will govern their relations.

After the American colonies declared their independence, a considered debate took place as to how the resulting thirteen states would govern themselves as a nation, what institutions they would need. They delved deeply into the question of how the new states and their peoples could work with each other in a republic founded on democratic principles. The American experiment in governance worked reasonably well for over seventy years, until the American Civil War. The bonds of cooperation holding the relatively new nation were being tested and were about to dissolve. On the eve of that conflagration, Abraham Lincoln, in 1858, in the most important speech of his career before becoming President, opened his remarks with the following observation: "If we could first know where we are, and whither we are tending, we could better judge what to do, and how to do it."[3] This kind of thoughtful introspection is

[2] The categories of dogma and covenant are taken from a sermon by the Reverend Kenneth Torquil McClean of Cedar Lane Unitarian Universalist Church. "'Pietism, or Religion Alone' with Rev. Kenneth Torquil MacLean, Minister Emeritus." YouTube. June 23, 2019. www.youtube.com/watch?v=h_5NJwICfjM

[3] "House Divided Speech." National Park Service. June 16, 1858. www.nps.gov/liho/learn/historyculture/housedivided.htm#:~:text=%22A%20house%20divided%20against%20itself,thing%2C%20or%20all%20the%20other

needed now for preserving the process of international cooperation on trade issues to undergird the world economy, at a time when the much remarked upon centrifugal force of deglobalization and fractures in international commercial relations are pulling against the underlying centripetal, gravitational force, the strong attraction of increasing international trade for mutual benefit.

SOME HISTORY

The institutional aspect of the multilateral trading system has an idiosyncratic history. If there was a constitutional convention for consideration of the governance of the world trading system, it would have been for the drafting of the Havana Charter for an International Trade Organization (ITO) that never came into being. There was no complete charter for the surviving agreement, the General Agreement on Tariffs and Trade. It was, as the name implies, a contract among sovereigns, providing rules for their trade. It did not have much in it on the institutions of governance. There was no provision for a Director-General or a Secretariat, no board of governors or executive directors, nor much beyond the barest direction as to how to operate:

1. *Representatives of the contracting parties shall meet from time to time for the purpose of giving effect to those provisions of this Agreement which involve joint action and, generally, with a view to facilitating the operation and furthering the objectives of this Agreement …*
2. *The Secretary-General of the United Nations is requested to convene the first meeting of the* CONTRACTING PARTIES, *which shall take place not later than March 1, 1948.*
3. *Each contracting party shall be entitled to have one vote at all meetings of the* CONTRACTING PARTIES.
4. *Except as otherwise provided for in this Agreement, decisions of the* CONTRACTING PARTIES *shall be taken by a majority of the votes cast.*
5. *In exceptional circumstances not elsewhere provided for in this Agreement, the* CONTRACTING PARTIES *may waive an obligation imposed upon a contracting party by this Agreement; Provided that any such decision shall be approved by a two-thirds majority of the votes cast and that such majority shall comprise more than half of the contracting parties. The* CONTRACTING PARTIES *may also by such a vote*
   (i) *define certain categories of exceptional circumstances to which other voting requirements shall apply for the waiver of obligations, and*
   (ii) *prescribe such criteria as may be necessary for the application of this paragraph.*[4]

[4] GATT Art. XXV.

Even this degree of guidance did not foretell how the new organism would function. Contracting parties were generally not going to vote, but act by consensus. There would be a *de facto* Secretariat, through an ad hoc interim arrangement (one that lasted nearly fifty years).

Even when the WTO was being formed in the early 1990s, only a very limited amount of attention was given to the institutions of governance of the multilateral trading system. There was no constitutional convention to debate the institutional arrangements. Outside of dispute settlement, which did receive substantial scrutiny from the Uruguay Round negotiators, institutions of governance received scant consideration and they are today still inadequate to the tasks at hand. Now, when national leaders are calling for WTO reform, it is time to have a serious discussion of the institutional arrangements of the world trading system.

Humble Institutional Beginnings

While it appeared that the starting gun of trade liberalization had misfired when the International Trade Organization failed to leave the starting gate, its vitally important companion agreement, the General Agreement on Tariffs and Trade survived. The GATT was inaugurated on January 1, 1948, with twenty-three participating countries. The founding document was made up of a few dozen articles providing vitally important rules of the road for international trade and detailed schedules of tariff concessions that were committed to by the GATT contracting parties.

As a physical presence, the GATT had an unprepossessing beginning. It occupied three pleasant but not very grand villas on the grounds of the Palais des Nations, the United Nations headquarters in Geneva. This was a pastoral scene, nestled on the hillside of the right bank of Lake Geneva (known to the rest of Switzerland as Lac Léman). Ambassadors and ministers and counselors for economic affairs from local missions met in one of the villas, La Fenêtre, so named because its conference room had a grand window that framed an idyllic nineteenth-century view of the opposing hills across the lake, dotted with mansions surrounded by stately cypress trees. The Secretariat was housed in the two neighboring villas, one of which was named "le Bocage" (the grove). This was the GATT that I was introduced to in 1970 when I first came over to make a presentation on behalf of the US government to the delegates of the other contracting parties.

In the United Nations family, the GATT was treated somewhat like a poor relative, having little rank or formal status, begging meeting rooms from the well-established and imposing UN organization on whose grounds it lived. The informal staffing arrangement and the bucolic Swiss dwellings that it inhabited masked the great importance to the global economy of this underacknowledged organization.[5] As a trade agreement, the GATT was the fulfillment on a much broader scale of what Franklin Roosevelt and Cordell Hull had been striving to achieve since 1934 through bilateral agreements – nondiscrimination and a reciprocal opening of markets. Now it was one of the international organizations providing for postwar reconstruction of war-ravaged nations and the economic development of former colonies.

Years of Growth and Accomplishment

The GATT made its contribution through progressive trade liberalization and providing an expanding scope for the rule of law for international commerce. Its mission was the creation of order out of chaos, and it succeeded brilliantly. It did not have a very high profile. Most of the daily work of the Organization was technical, legalistic, and lacked the drama of what foreign ministries preferred to deal with – international political relations. For years, economic officers in the US State Department, some of whom were responsible for US representation at the GATT, were viewed as having a far less important role than political officers. But those present at the creation of the GATT knew that they had accomplished something major.

During the GATT years, 1948 through 1994, the number of contracting parties grew from 23 to 128. It was a forum for maintaining and expanding the rules of the system, for continuing the process of trade liberalization, and for seeking to resolve trade disputes. There was a rhythm to the eight rounds of multilateral tariff negotiations held between 1947 and 1994: Geneva (1947), Annecy (1949), Torquay (1950–51), Geneva (1956), the Dillon Round (1960–61), the Kennedy Round (1964–67), the Tokyo Round (1973–79), and the Uruguay Round (1986–94). The time taken to negotiate each successive round was getting longer, and the time between rounds was gradually increasing, but each was delivering more. The Kennedy Round sought to provide rules for antidumping and customs valuation as the trading system expanded its coverage beyond cutting tariffs. The Tokyo Round added plurilateral codes – on government procurement (for signatories) and standards and an agreement on subsidies. All but the Government Procurement Code were nondiscriminatory in their application, as were commitments on tariff levels. The five-decade-history of GATT trade liberalization efforts was capped by the

[5] The US Congress refused to recognize it in US law for the first quarter-century of the GATT's existence, although it did fund the US contribution to it.

Uruguay Round, which also extended the trading system to services, to the protection of intellectual property, bringing agriculture fully into the rules of the system, and not least, creating the WTO.

Progress during the GATT years was continuous, in steps, but always on an upward trajectory. Generation after generation of trade negotiators continued the process of trade liberalization, while adding to the rule book of the multilateral trading system. The GATT was seen by political leaders as more than just a technical exercise. There appeared to be a commonly held belief among the trading nations of the world, the contracting parties to the GATT, that the twin objectives of liberalization and maintaining a rules-based trading system were the only correct policy, that it served them all.

Progress required leadership. Originally, in 1947, this was provided by the United States working with Great Britain. By the 1960s and 1970s, in the Kennedy and Tokyo Rounds, it was the United States and European Communities. And in the Uruguay Round, leadership could be found in the "quad" – the United States, the European Union, Canada, and Japan. Economic progress was undeniable. Europe and Japan had, under the umbrella of the liberal international order, more than recovered from the devastation of war. The countries known as Asian tigers rocketed forward on a steep growth curve fueled by trade. Developing countries on average still lagged behind industrialized countries but were also making substantial material progress as they were beginning to gain more access to developed country markets.

At no time during the GATT era did the contracting parties pause, look at their institutional arrangements in a comprehensive way, to provide a considered governance structure for the trading system going forward. Nor did they compare the institutional arrangements of the WTO that they were creating with the other international economic organizations that had been created in the post-Second World War era, the World Bank, the International Monetary Fund, or the OECD. They did not even replicate the governance arrangements of the ITO. Perhaps there was no need to do so. There would be no board of directors, no set of authorities granted to the Director-General for running the Organization. Progress was made, Round after Round, each increasing the scope of coverage of the system and bringing about greater trade liberalization, without institutional reform.

The Advent of the WTO

The Uruguay Round did not set out to create a new global trade organization. It was a late entrant in the planning of the participants of the Round. While academics might look askance at having a Secretariat with no clear legal foundation, the GATT had operated very well for over four decades without a well-defined system of governance. The negotiators concentrated on expanding the scope of the trading system, providing binding dispute settlement, greater transparency, further disciplines on trade, and further tariff reductions.

The WTO, negotiated by 1993 and put into place on January 1, 1995, was designed to capitalize on the progress made in the GATT era. It consolidated all that had gone before. The GATT 1947 was packaged, encased in the GATT 1994, and made an integral part of the *acquis* of the WTO. The only really necessary institutional change was to make dispute settlement binding, and the provisions for doing so were elaborate. Since the scope of the coverage of the rules was going to go beyond goods, to services and intellectual property protection, it made some sense to think about putting the Secretariat on a firmer legal footing, and to rename the Organization that would now deal with more than tariffs on goods. Panels and an appellate body would provide dispute settlement and standing committees were created to administer the WTO agreements, including a largely powerless Dispute Settlement Body (DSB). The role of the Secretariat was not defined however. It was no doubt presumed that it would continue to support the members of the WTO as it had the contracting parties to the GATT.

Economic Cooperation among Sovereign Nations

The early 1990s was a period of international economic institution-building on a regional basis. In 1993, the same year that the WTO was being created, the Maastricht Treaty was signed, with the European Union replacing the European Communities of which the European Economic Community was a part. There are some parallels between multilateral progress and the European regional evolution – each envisioning an expansion of its membership, each with a broader scope of coverage, and each promoting greater integration.

There are also distinct limits to any parallels. There is no executive in the WTO, nothing like the EU Commission. The administration of the WTO Agreements is largely in the hands of its members acting through their committees and councils. Also, while the WTO rules provide some coverage of its members' internal measures that affect trade, there is no direct effect on the internal workings of the WTO members' economies of any WTO decision, whether by the General Council or the dispute settlement process. The WTO's members remained in all respects sovereign, although recognizing that they would face consequences if they engaged in behavior that failed to align with their obligations.

Apogee or Inflection Point?

In March 1994, in a conference on the GATT held in London, Prime Minister Margaret Thatcher, who was a staunch advocate of open markets, articulated the challenges that were present and those that lay ahead. The Uruguay Round had just concluded two and a half months earlier. Recognizing, as perhaps few did as clearly, how fragile the shared experiment in global open markets was, she outlined the challenge:

> *We are now at one of those watersheds in economic affairs which occur perhaps once in a lifetime. The pressures between open trade and protection are finely balanced ... We have still to convince popular opinion in Europe and the United States that opening markets to foreign goods and services raises living standards and generates jobs. We have still to win the argument that just as economic and political freedom go together, so too do open trade and international harmony.*[6]

Five years later, in May 1998, the leaders of fifteen nations, including Bill Clinton, Nelson Mandela, Tony Blair, Jean Chrétien, and EU Commission President, Jacques Santer, came together in Geneva to celebrate the fiftieth anniversary of the GATT. Viewed from the present, the occasion was a distinct high point for the multilateral trading system (MTS). While not ignoring challenges, the leaders sounded an optimistic note. President Clinton issued a clarion call for continued progress:

> *Think about the opportunity that has been presented to us; the chance to create a new international economy ... in which open markets and open economies spark undreamed of innovation and prosperity ... in which the skills of ordinary citizens power the prosperity of nations ... in which poor people find opportunity, dignity and a decent life and contribute to prosperity ... in which increasing interdependence among nations enhances peace and security for all.*[7]

They sensed that they were at an inflection point in world economic history. The Swiss President Flavio Cotti said:

[6] "Speech to the World Trade after GATT Conference." Margaret Thatcher Foundation. March 3, 1994. www.margaretthatcher.org/document/108329

[7] "UNITED STATES Statement by H.E. Mr. William J. Clinton, President." World Trade Organization. May 18, 1998. www.wto.org/english/thewto_e/minist_e/min98_e/anniv_e/clinton_e.htm

> *Like the fathers of the multilateral system five decades ago, we find ourselves at one of history's crossroads – on the threshold of a new era and a new international landscape. There is nothing predetermined about the world we are entering into. It is a work in progress . . . Like our predecessors, whose vision and determination we are commemorating today, we need to look to the future – and to explain this future to the present. This implies a dialogue marked by confidence at the universal level.*[8]

Prime Minister of Singapore Goh Chok Tong, seeing a need for practical steps to capitalize on what had been achieved, looked forward to a new round of multilateral trade negotiations being launched.[9]

Some were more cautious than others. Romano Prodi, President of the Council of EC Ministers, had lower expectations: "I fully agree with those in the political and academic communities who talk about a timeframe of 20 to 25 years for completing the rules of the global market on the basis of the renewed founding pact."[10] The span of years that Mr. Prodi looked to has now passed. The WTO's members can now judge how best to improve the institutional aspects of the WTO to assist in the project of completing, or at least extending, the rules of the global market. For the last half-dozen years, there have been repeated calls for WTO reform from G20 and G7 leaders. It should be clear that there are serious shortcomings in the institutional structure of the WTO that need to be remedied.

Continuity

Before leaving the history of the multilateral trading system to focus on the challenges that lie ahead, there is one further reflection that is in order. There was a clear psychological change involved in moving from the GATT period to the WTO period. As with the Japanese calendar fixed by the years of an emperor's reign, it is no longer the founding of the GATT, the beginning of the multilateral trading system, that is celebrated, but the founding of the WTO in 1995. This is misleading. There was at least as much, perhaps even

8 "SWITZERLAND Statement by H.E. Mr. Flavio Cotti, President." World Trade Organization. May 19, 1998. www.wto.org/english/thewto_e/minist_e/min98_e/anniv_e/cotti_e.htm

9 "SINGAPORE Statement circulated by H.E. Mr. Goh Chok Tong, Prime Minister." World Trade Organization. May 19, 1998. www.wto.org/english/thewto_e/minist_e/min98_e/anniv_e/sing_e.htm

10 "ITALY Statement by H.E. Mr. Romano Prodi, President of the Council of Ministers." World Trade Organization. May 19, 1998. www.wto.org/english/thewto_e/minist_e/min98_e/anniv_e/prodi_e.htm

more, institutional continuity than there was change in moving from the GATT to the WTO. The WTO Secretariat very much resembles the GATT Secretariat in terms of its functions. The role of the Director-General of the WTO is largely indistinguishable from that of the Director-General of the GATT. The manner in which the members make decisions, through consensus, is the same. The accessions process is largely the same. The WTO inherited the building the GATT occupied since it took over the Centre William Rappard from the ILO in 1977. What differed primarily between the GATT and the WTO eras was that there was binding dispute settlement in the WTO; agreements were to be much more reliably enforceable.

The bottom line is that the multilateral trading system should be viewed as progressing along a continuum, an arc of history, marking increasing cooperation, from 1947/48 through the present and into the future. The Uruguay Round's founding of the WTO marked a new phase, but it is not likely to be the last burst of progress, as the WTO moves to deal with crises of health, climate, food, the digital economy, and inequalities. MC12 was an installment.

Dissatisfaction

While during the last several years there have been repeated calls for WTO reform by members, their leaders, trade ministers, and ambassadors accredited to the WTO, there is no agreement on what reforms should be included.

For the developing countries, reform may mean fulfillment of pledges of more favorable treatment for their trade, relieving them of some obligations and giving them greater support, while asking for improved disciplines on developed countries. The thirty-six countries that acceded to the WTO after the WTO was created will call for greater balance, a truing-up of obligations for original members, to raise their level of commitments to that assumed by the later arrivals. With respect to domestic support for agriculture, there will be opposing calls for those who have flexibilities under their aggregate measurement of support (AMS) versus those that had flexibility under the *de minimis* provisions. All are united in favor of others being subject to greater discipline. India wishes to have sales on world markets of agricultural commodities from its public stocks insulated from attack, while developed countries will seek greater market access through a reduction in India's and other developing countries' tariffs that are often bound at high levels. Few if any members feel that the notifications provided by other members are satisfactory in terms of their timeliness and completeness to provide promised and necessary transparency. This is a partial litany of complaints with the current system and therefore likely to point to improvements to be sought in reforming the system.

What triggered the seriousness and urgency of the calls for reform was none of the grievances listed above. It was the Trump administration's blocking appointments to the Appellate Body (AB) and thereby ending multilaterally agreed binding dispute settlement on December 10, 2019. Added to this cause was general disappointment over the inability of the members to produce multilateral agreements. A total of just one such agreement was reached in the WTO's first twenty-seven years, the Trade Facilitation Agreement (TFA) in 2013. Thereafter, the drought in multilaterally negotiated outcomes continued for over eight years, finally broken by the conclusion of a first-stage Fisheries Subsidies Agreement at MC12 in June 2022.

HEADWINDS

Why is multilateral progress so difficult? To what could the dearth of multilaterally negotiated outcomes be attributed? What challenges exist to there being a bright future for the system?

The Temper of the Times

In 2014, Thomas Piketty's book *Capital in the Twenty-First Century* became a best seller in the United States, having been published a year earlier in France. The book crystallized concerns over income inequality. The phenomenon that he was examining had been growing for years in capitalist countries. Disaffection with income distribution and declining upward mobility had been increasingly in evidence. Largely through advances in technology, in increases in productivity through the application of capital, the middle class, once largely supported by jobs in manufacturing, had seen its relative position eroded. The number of jobs that accounted for much of higher-wage employment plummeted. Trade was also blamed. Well-known economists, including Dani Rodrik and Joseph Stiglitz,[11] were sounding the retreat from globalization, from the liberal international order.

Populism was on the rise in the Western democracies. Anti-immigration movements were gaining strength and they certainly were not in favor of open markets. Marine Le Pen called protectionism "the middle path," rejecting

[11] Dani Rodrik. 2011. *The Globalization Paradox: Democracy and the Future of the World Economy*. New York: W. W. Norton; Joseph Stiglitz. 2003. *Globalization and Its Discontents*. New York: W. W. Norton; Joseph Stiglitz. 2017. *Globalization and Its Discontents Revisited: Anti-Globalization in the Era of Trump*. New York: W. W. Norton.

both autarky and free trade.[12] In Italy, the Five Star movement advanced protectionism along with isolationism as its policy choice. Looking at the record, fifteen socioeconomic (as opposed to cultural) populists were deemed to be in power during the two decades before 2018, according to a report published by the Tony Blair Institute.[13] America, under the Trump presidency, promoted what it called an "America First" trade policy. According to Simon Evenett's Global Trade Alert (GTA), during the period of January 2017 to mid-November 2019, which the GTA calls the "current populist era," 2,723 new trade distortions were introduced with a cumulative effect of distorting 40 percent of world trade by November 2019.[14] Chile's new President, Gabriel Boric, "vowed to bury neoliberalism. 'If Chile was the cradle of neoliberalism, it would also be its grave.'"

A problem with the argument that the temper of the times will prevent forward movement in terms of international trade liberalization and rule-making is that history has contrary examples. In 1934, in the midst of the Great Depression, Franklin Roosevelt received from Congress the authority to cut tariffs by up to 50 percent in reciprocal trade negotiations and proceeded to do so in thirty bilateral trade agreements. Those times, with American unemployment hitting 25 percent, would objectively not seem to have been propitious for negotiating trade agreements providing for liberalization. The global economic outlook then was as grim if not more so than at any point in the nation's history, and yet that did not prevent forward movement toward greater not less international cooperation. Leadership can opt for openness rather than retreat. That said, the path to future trade liberalization is not at this point clear.

Exhaustion of Opportunities

It could be argued that trade liberalization had run its course given that developed country tariffs were already very low. There is more to it than that.

12 "La grande alternance de 2012 se construit en 2011." Nations Presse. November 15. 2010. www.archive.ph/20120906014455/http://www.nationspresse.info/?p=116192#selection-183.71-189.291

> *Entendons-nous bien. Ne laissez pas manipuledr les mots que certains voudraient retourner contre nous comme on retourne une arme. Le protectionnisme n'est pas l'autarcie! Si on imagine que l'économie est un fleuve impétueux, le libre échangisme est de laisser dévaler le torrent, l'autarcie est de dresser un barrage, le protectionnisme est d'installer une écluse. Notre position n'est pas extrême comme voudraient le faire croire nos adversaires, mais médiane.*

13 "Populists in Power around the World." Tony Blair Institute for Global Change. November 7, 2018. www.institute.global/policy/populists-power-around-world. However, it listed Donald Trump as a cultural rather than economic populist, so the count may be conservative.

14 "Trade Policy after Three Years of Populism." Vox EU-CEPR. December 23, 2019. www.voxeu.org/article/trade-policy-after-three-years-populism-global-assessment

There is simply no remaining appetite for reducing tariffs due to concerns about competition from more advanced countries, due to concerns over globalization, due to erosion of the middle class. There may be narrow multilateral trade-liberalizing deals in the future, for example, eliminating tariffs on environmental goods. But a broad tariff-reducing round is not in the offing.

The reluctance with respect to trade liberalization does not apply to the same extent to meeting the need for new rules. Areas for rule-making know no bounds, as there are always additional challenges to be addressed, as demonstrated by the pandemic, by food security, and by climate change.

North/South Divisions

The basic idea of having a global multilateral trading system is that all are in it, that it is universal. There can be and are accommodations made for differing levels of development, taking into account different capabilities to undertake obligations. When a right or a discipline is created, in principle it ought to be ultimately, over time, applicable to all, accessible by all. This fracture line, the North/South divide, is not clean-cut. Not all developing countries have the same set of trade policies, nor are all areas of equal economic interest to them. Brazil is a major agricultural exporter, and currently sees more open trade as being in its interest. Argentina is also a major agricultural exporter and is more defensive with respect to parts of its economy. China has its own profile of vastly different levels of development in industry and agriculture. China states that it is interested in zero tariffs for environmental goods, but also has its own defensive interests. South Africa paid a heavier price in terms of liberalization on entry, under a colonial government, than its successor governments would have paid and it has questioned engaging in further liberalization. Afghanistan, Montenegro, and Seychelles are signatories to the Information Technology Agreement; Mexico and Brazil are not. India joined the ITA, but its representatives say the decision was a mistake, and it did not join the expansion of the ITA.[15]

While the developing world is far from monolithic in its interests, nevertheless, there is within the WTO a North/South fracture line. Many developing countries view the Uruguay Round as having been primarily shaped to promote the interests of developed countries, with its signature agreements

[15] "Twenty Years of the Information Technology Agreement: Boosting Trade, Innovation and Digital Connectivity." World Trade Organization. 2017. www.wto.org/english/res_e/booksp_e/ita20years_2017_full_e.pdf

for intellectual property protection (TRIPS) and liberalization of scheduled services (GATS). Many of them feel that the Doha Development Round would have rebalanced the scale, advancing their interests. The Uruguay Round concluded without a real option for any participant to exclude itself from the single undertaking (being obligated under almost all agreements). The Doha Development Agenda (DDA) did not conclude at all. It was declared dead by 2015 by the developed countries,[16] a position opposed by numbers of developing countries.

This state of affairs has led not only to rhetorical skirmishing in WTO General Council meetings but to claims by a number of DDA adherents that negotiations under Joint Statement Initiatives are illegitimate insofar as the WTO is concerned, because they were not sanctioned by all members as an agreed multilateral endeavor.

East/West Divisions, Differing National Economic Systems, Geopolitical Rivalry

The WTO was conceived during a period characterized by a widespread sense of euphoria as the world emerged from a long dark period living under the long shadow of nuclear extermination threatened by the Cold War. In his famous essay entitled "The End of History," Francis Fukuyama heralded

> *The triumph of the West, of the western idea, evident first of all in the total exhaustion of viable systemic alternatives to western liberalization …*
>
> *What we may be witnessing is not just the end of the Cold War, or the passing of a particular period of post war history, but the end of history as such: that is the endpoint of mankind's ideological evolution, and the universalization of western liberal democracy as the final form of human government.*[17]

We now know that that is not what occurred, not in international political relations, and not in international economic relations.

It was evident in the Riyadh Initiative discussions among the G20 members that there was a division over whether the WTO was about members' economies being "market-oriented." Among many of the developed countries, it is an article of faith that the WTO is based on the market determining what is bought and sold. These countries would ask "if market forces do not

[16] "The Doha Round Finally Dies a Merciful Death." *Financial Times*. December 21, 2015. www.ft.com/content/9cb1ab9e-a7e2-11e5-955c-1e1d6de94879

[17] Francis Fukuyama. 1989. "The End of History?" *The National Interest* 16: 3–18. www.jstor.org/stable/24027184

determine competitive outcomes, if the state makes a judgment as to what is bought and sold, what is the meaning of any of the commitments undertaken in the WTO Agreements, whether one is referring to the application of tariffs, domestic regulations, or *de facto* export controls?"

China has been adamant that the WTO does not rest on any assumption that all WTO members' economies must be "market-oriented." This is not a new subject. The issue was well-known when China was negotiating its accession to the WTO, at a time when there was extensive state intervention in its economy. Paragraph 46 of the Working Party Report for the Accession of China in 2001 contains a commitment made by China that its state-owned enterprises would "buy and sell on the basis of commercial considerations." This refers to the conditions upon which a private business would decide whether to buy or sell, "e.g. price, quality, marketability and availability." The provision requires further:

> *that the enterprises of other WTO Members would have an adequate opportunity to compete for sales to and purchases from these enterprises on non-discriminatory terms and conditions. In addition, the Government of China would not influence, directly or indirectly, commercial decisions on the part of state-owned or state-invested enterprises, including on the quantity, value or country of origin of any goods purchased or sold, except in a manner consistent with the WTO Agreement. The Working Party took note of these commitments.*[18]

A natural corollary, not needing to be explicitly recorded, would be that Chinese enterprises that are not state-owned would also be free of state influence, to buy and sell on the basis of commercial considerations.

The commitment was not a major issue during the early years of China's membership in the WTO. There was undoubtedly an assumption on the part of China's trading partners that China's economy would evolve, much as Japan's economic system had after its accession to the GATT, toward allowing market forces rather than state policy and measures to govern competitive outcomes. For a transition period, special safeguards were put in place with respect to what was anticipated to be China's export prowess in manufactured goods, provisions which by their terms fell away after twelve years for safeguards and fifteen years for antidumping. There is a concern on the part of many WTO members that the degree of state intervention in the Chinese economy has begun to increase again and is not, as had been expected, steadily decreasing.

[18] "Substance of Accession Negotiations." World Trade Organization. www.wto.org/english/thewto_e/acc_e/cbt_course_e/c5s2p3_e.htm

With populism rising, with manufacturing employment declining in most Western countries primarily due to technological change, the domestic politics of opening one's market further in the face of substantial competition from industrializing countries, most prominently China, may well have diminished substantially the appetite of many countries, developed and developing, for further trade liberalization. This is likely another cause of the faltering of multilateral trade liberalization in the WTO period.

Into this mix of anxieties about China's trade practices is added the geopolitical rivalry between the United States and China. It is often claimed this is that one of the causes of paralysis of the WTO. There is, however, little evidence to date to support this conclusion. China's stance that it was indisputably a developing country did not block reaching a first-stage agreement on fisheries subsidies. MC12 proved that there were areas for negotiation at the WTO for which geopolitics was not a decisive factor – with initial agreements reached on health (the response to the COVID pandemic), the availability of food for the poorest countries, the extension of the moratorium on electronic commerce, and WTO reform. In none of these did geopolitical rivalry prevent an outcome. Where China's position did play a role was in the inability in 2016 of the WTO to conclude an Environmental Goods Agreement. In that case, the question was not geopolitical rivalry but bridging very specific differences over product coverage between the EU and China.

There is one other primary effect of the question of differing economic systems on the operations of the WTO. The failure of the Appellate Body to understand how to find a subsidy in an economy with a large amount of state intervention through ownership and influence was one of the causes of the United States blocking appointments of Appellate Body members. This unresolved question is likely to be one of the impediments preventing early restoration of binding dispute settlement, as is the degree of deference given to invocation of national security.

Breakdown of the WTO Dispute Settlement System, the Impact of Nonconforming Conduct, Lack of Trust

It is alleged by some commentators that the absence of binding dispute settlement makes the negotiation of new agreements less likely, prospective parties being unsure as to whether any new agreements can be enforced, and that this creates a reluctance to enter into them in the first place. There is no clear evidence that this proposition is correct or that it drives the conduct or underlies the reluctance of members to negotiate new agreements.

A corollary may be a reluctance to enter into new agreements because it appears that the existing agreements are not being honored. Recent years clearly could have witnessed a breakdown of faith in the efficacy of a rules-based system in some headline-grabbing cases. Prominent examples include the United States and China applying across-the-board tariffs on each other's products, in some cases not citing any WTO rule as the basis for doing so. The United States also applied tariffs to imports from all sources of steel and aluminum, claiming a justification under the national security provisions of the WTO/GATT that other members did not accept. The US measures were countered by the European Union claiming that the United States had in reality imposed a safeguard measure and therefore the EU was entitled to retaliate against US exports, and it did so. The United States contended that the EU had not even a superficial legal justification for its response. That the two later, after a change of US administration, largely eased their relationship – although not fully resolving their differences – did not erase the impression that the largest members were coloring outside the lines, that they were regarding the rules as optional when they did not suit them.

The absence of the largest trading nations clearly living up to the letter of their undertakings in specific instances does not seem to prevent agreements from being reached, such as those that emerged from MC12.

A second reason advanced for the reluctance to enter into new trade agreements at the WTO is stated as a lack of trust. The system in fact still engenders trust. Most of world trade still flows subject to, and abides by, the rules of the trading system. Nations generally live up to their contractual commitments under international agreements. For WTO members this means not breaching tariff bindings, not imposing import quotas, and not denying national treatment with respect to internal regulations and taxes. WTO members generally live by the international law maxim of *pacta sunt servanda* (treaties will be obeyed) whether through belief, inertia, or pragmatism. When there are breaches of the rules, cases continue to be filed and litigated even between parties that have not subscribed to the Multi-Party Interim Appeal Arbitration Arrangement (MPIA) or another alternative means of arriving at a binding outcome from their litigation.

In the multilateral trading system, trust exists when the rules are clear and there is transparency to understand whether they are being obeyed. Where there are no rules or economic transactions are opaque, trust dissipates. During the pandemic, there was little trust in many countries that private companies and governments would adequately take into account their needs for essential goods, medicines, and vaccines.[19] The use of formal and informal export controls increased, driving pressures for onshoring, an anti-trade reaction. It intensified a desire for intellectual property rights to be waived. Without full transparency, WTO members could not be sure whether patent arrangements assuring a fair allocation of scarce supplies were being made.

Trust is eroded where trade seems to be distorted, such as by industrial subsidies which are often poorly tracked, poorly understood, and subject to virtually no international constraints. Subsidization appears to be widespread, an infectious behavior due to commercial competition, geopolitical rivalry, and pandemic-era onshoring for critical products. Erosion of trust leads to the urge to endorse "friend-shoring" or at least diversification of supply chain sourcing.

Trust is eroded where state influence is pervasive and exercised in a haphazard or vindictive way. It occurs where there is intensified and opaque state influence, which is much harder to document than when contained in published regulations. State influence exists particularly where permissions, licenses, or infrastructure are needed. State influence can accompany access to credit or other benefits. Business thrives on certainty. Unpredictability in government decision making undermines a basic requirement for growth in the international exchange of goods and services. Disinvestment occurs where the economic environment is unsettled.

Trust in an age of populism is eroded when the negotiated balance between trade liberalization and permitted defense measures is disturbed, when the scope for deploying trade remedies is constantly narrowed. Any judiciary must take exceptional care not to appear to have a political agenda. This is not to impugn the integrity of Appellate Body members. It is simply to note that any judicial function operates in a political context in a broad sense. It gets its legitimacy from its constituency, not just from any document or treaty. The AB operates in a political environment in the original sense: "political" comes from the Greek *politikos*, of citizens, pertaining to the state and its administration; pertaining to "public life," from *polites*, "citizen," and from *polis*, "city." Successive American administrations over the course of more than a dozen years, regardless of the political party in power, complained about overreach by the WTO dispute settlement system at the expense of availability of trade remedies. The AB members collectively did not adequately understand their institutional interests.

19 "An Expanded Essential Goods Monitoring Initiative: 21st Century Tracking of Pandemic-Era Trade and Investment Policies in Food and Medical Products (November 2022 update)," Global Trade Alert. May 4, 2020. www.globaltradealert.org/reports/54

Trust is a perishable and fragile commodity. It is slow to build and can be destroyed almost instantaneously. But it can be restored. If there were a barometer for trust in the WTO, it moved further into positive territory through MC12. The paths forward for arrangements to deal more effectively with the pandemic, food security, and fisheries subsidies were identified and agreed to.

Sovereignty

There is always in world affairs a tension between sovereignty – the desire on the part of national governments to retain freedom of action – and international cooperation. This has been true since the concept of the nation-state was given force by the Treaty of Westphalia in 1648 which recognized that each state has sovereignty over its own territory. The tension is often in evidence in attempts at cooperative endeavors among nations. It was prominently on display in recent times in negotiations between the United Kingdom and the European Union over Brexit.

There are often statements made in WTO meetings citing a need for "policy space," which is a euphemism for an absence of the rule of law under the WTO Agreements, the absence of constraints. This challenge to international cooperation, and therefore to the WTO, is far more sweeping than the desire for special and differential treatment or additional flexibilities to allow the taking on of obligations to proceed in parallel with development. It is asking for complete freedom to adopt any policy at any point, unconstrained by WTO obligations. It can be used as an argument against any new subject matter being introduced into the WTO's disciplines.

Common cause can occasionally be found in a crisis. Jean Monnet, a French civil servant, saw the salvation of France, under attack from Nazi Germany, as union with Britain, not only with a joint army, which the allies later forged to a degree among themselves, but a joint parliament. On June 16, 1940, Winston Churchill and Charles de Gaulle, over lunch at the Carlton Club in London, discussed the proposition that Britain and France should be united into a single country called the "Franco-British Union."[20] That is not what occurred, perhaps due to a lack of time before France fell on June 22. The Second World War was to cause the deaths of an estimated total of 70–85 million people, about 3 percent of the 1940 world population (est. 2.3 billion). The current pandemic has already caused over 6 million deaths. As the

[20] Dominic Tierney. 2017. "When Britain and France Almost Merged into One Country." *The Atlantic*. August 8. www.theatlantic.com/international/archive/2017/08/dunkirk-brexit/536106/

carnage of the Second World War that gave rise to the creation of international economic organizations including the GATT has faded from memory (less than 2 percent of the current world population would have even a faint recollection of that war), 6 million deaths from COVID ought to be sufficiently attention-getting to cause some degree of international cooperation against a common threat. That has, however, not been sufficiently in evidence. The pandemic has not only not given rise to deeper economic integration, but it has also not yet caused a formal agreement to be struck for the sharing of vaccines or other medical goods.

The history of the multilateral trading system is a continuing story of finding the political will and the trust to enter into binding commitments for international cooperation. Even in the case of dealing with the pandemic, it has been difficult to go far in this direction. The political constraints are evident. Governments are wary of committing to sharing scarce supplies, however compelling the logic of doing so.

Common Purpose

While sovereignty is a very strong headwind against which multilateralism must struggle to make progress, a much more serious threat exists. There must be common purpose. It would be a death knell for multilateralism if common purposes were in short supply. The risk is real.[21] Had the largest trading nations given military support on opposite sides in the Russian invasion of Ukraine, the trading world could have fractured and been replaced by a more dystopian order, with a movement toward trading blocs.

The Riyadh Initiative on the Future of the WTO, launched under the G20 Saudi Presidency, identified currently agreed WTO objectives, at least insofar as this broad group of countries was concerned.[22] It is a picture of the common ground that exists. There is no reference to continuing trade liberalization, or

[21] Yeats in his poem, the *Second Coming*, wrote:

> *Things fall apart; the centre cannot hold;*
> *Mere anarchy is loosed upon the world,*
> *The blood-dimmed tide is loosed, and everywhere*
> *The ceremony of innocence is drowned;*
> *The best lack all conviction, while the worst*
> *Are full of passionate intensity.*

That would describe in slightly hyperbolic terms the fate of the global trading system, were there insufficient common purpose.

[22] "G20 Trade and Investment Ministerial Meeting: Communiqué." G20 Information Centre. September 22, 2020. www.g20.utoronto.ca/2020/2020-g20-trade-0922.html#objectives

any desire expressed for expanding the rules to cover behavior in any area that is currently largely undisciplined (such as industrial subsidies or state-influenced enterprises), but that was not the question posed. It provided a window into fundamental systemic objectives, which taken all together, do not constitute agreed operational guidance, with perhaps two exceptions: providing transparency and living by the precept of nondiscrimination. Were the members to wish to do so, they have it within their power to provide better transparency, by empowering the Secretariat to be more aggressive in monitoring and reporting national trade measures. They can address bringing about less discrimination by examining existing trading arrangements to better understand their effects on non-parties. Believing in "open markets," they can negotiate to liberalize trade further. Believing in a rules-based system, they can negotiate to cover gaps in the rules, extending the rules to new areas as well, such as digital commerce, competition policy as it affects trade, as well as environmental and health-motivated measures that seriously affect trade flows.

None of these common purposes that recommend themselves are currently being fully served by the WTO's existing rules, nor does the WTO's current institutional structure, its governance, provide sufficient support to achieve these objectives.

Leadership

With the cataclysms of the first half of the twentieth century ever more distant, the feeling of shared purpose has diminished over time. In recent years, the United States was no longer playing the role of global hegemon devoted to the multilateral project. The European Union's energies were spent for an extended time on a plethora of bilateral trade agreements. China was not ready or willing to take the lead. Some of the emerging markets did not appear to be dedicated to the goals that animated the trading system. In short, the major trading nations were underinvesting in the system.

At international gatherings, ministers and leaders profess at almost every opportunity their fealty to international cooperation in support of the multilateral trading system. But they seem to have little appetite for making the sacrifices needed to maintain or improve the system. Making speeches is not the same as negotiating agreements. The latter is hard work with what may be political and possibly economic costs. Will they meet at MC13 and put into effect rules that will see their peoples through the next pandemic, that will meet the challenge of climate change? Will they make the WTO more effective, achieving a fully accepted dispute settlement system that is binding? Will they reform the Organization to accept open plurilateral agreements?

Will they make sure that no member exercises a veto other than to protect its own national interest and not as a bargaining chip? Will they create a strong executive? These questions remain to be answered.

The United States, the European Union, and China, as the largest participants in world trade, must take on leadership roles to a greater extent. Progress is being made in their doing so. They must seek the positive collaboration of others, including particularly India and South Africa. It will take a concert of nations to bring about more effective governance of the world trading system.

Alternatives to Multilateralism

WTO members have not seen regional preferential arrangements as draining energy from working out multilateral arrangements, although this must be the case. A bilateral "free trade agreement" can build in preferences that vested interests will wish to preserve. However, bilateral and regional arrangements can also be venues for the exploration of forms of international cooperation that can become templates for multilateral agreements. The provisions on digital commerce found in these arrangements have been drawn upon in preparing texts for the JSI on this subject.

There are limits to sub-multilateral agreements becoming stepping stones to global arrangements. A single market works on a regional basis in Europe and the United States, but it is hard to see this degree of economic integration expanding beyond limited geographic limits in the foreseeable future. No WTO member has expressed the slightest interest in the WTO evolving at all in the direction of becoming a single market and would without doubt denounce the idea if it were raised as a possibility. Increasingly, particularly among developing countries, the opposite view is in evidence, seeking greater flexibilities for national choices, not fewer.

Surely other venues (the Comprehensive and Progressive Agreement for Trans-Pacific Partnership, the Digital Economy Partnership Agreement, etc.) will become more attractive over time if progress is too slow or is impossible in Geneva.

Shortcomings in Governance

There are serious institutional shortcomings that hobble the WTO from achieving the objectives for which it was created. These are: (1) the single undertaking; (2) the use of consensus to block any agreements from being reached, including among groups of like-minded members; (3) the failure to delegate the shaping of negotiations to smaller groups of members to tee-up solutions; (4) the absence of any role for the members and Director-General to make sure that dispute settlement does not simply become a rule by judges; and (5) having a highly circumscribed minimal executive. The primary defect of the system is the convoy system for negotiations, moving forward at the speed of the least interested or adept, resulting in too few successes, rule by consensus, the single-member veto, and the inadequate role for the Organization's executive has more often than not, in WTO history proved to be nearly fatal to the negotiation of multilateral agreements. The lack of more coequal branches of international trade governance (legislative and executive to balance judicial) deprived the WTO crown of its oft-cited "jewel" – binding dispute settlement.

These issues are addressed in the following chapters, which describe options for what the WTO could look like after a few years of coordinated intense effort to become more equal to the tasks at hand.

13

The Need for WTO Reform

Inadequate consideration was given by the founders of the WTO to the institutions that would be needed to govern the rules-based trading system that they were seeking to create. This chapter introduces a WTO Reform Quartet, proposals for WTO reform to make the rulemaking, adjudication, and executive functions of the WTO more effective, together with improvements to be made in the gathering of trade intelligence.

World trade governance must, of necessity, as with all such systems operating under law, consist of three branches – legislative (rule-making), judicial ("dispute settlement"), and executive (administrative). The first of these, the legislative function, despite some not inconsiderable achievements, has underperformed during the WTO era. It did not produce packages of major agreements consisting of both trade liberalization and new rules. It did not approach the level of output of the last two great rounds of GATT negotiations, the Tokyo and Uruguay Rounds.[1] Moreover, it is not demonstrably up to the task, as the WTO is currently constituted, of providing any changes in the rules that the WTO's dispute settlement is supposed to interpret.

Given the inability to continuously improve the rules of the system, the second element of governance, dispute settlement, came to dominate the institution, before becoming severely crippled by the loss of the Appellate Body (AB). This loss is of critical importance because it was dispute settlement that gave the WTO's members the ability to enforce the obligations of their trading partners. Enforceability of trade rules had been the distinguishing

[1] References to the "WTO": Unless the context makes it clear that what is being referred to is the Secretariat or the dispute settlement process, the WTO consists of its members acting collectively. The WTO as such does not succeed or fail at anything; it is its members who do so. This terminology differs from that of the World Bank or the IMF, where the institution extends a line of credit or makes a loan. Thus, the "WTO" did not produce a Trade Facilitation Agreement in 2015. Its members did.

feature of the WTO. The third element, the executive function, never quite existed except in a cramped, self-effacing, subordinate way. Change in this circumstance remains almost completely unaddressed by the members when they recite areas requiring reform. The WTO has no board of executive directors. It operates by committees – committees of the whole and subject matter committees. The Marrakesh Agreement creates a Director-General, who is to head up the Secretariat. No particular attention was given to specifying these roles. The Secretariat, the staff of the WTO, has been expected to provide support functions – with one prominent exception, and that is providing transparency through monitoring.

The WTO as an institution was created largely as a reaction to the GATT, its proponents seeking to remedy the GATT's defects and build upon its accomplishments. It is only natural to move now, after more than a quarter-century of the WTO being in place, to examine the current Organization, ascertain what works well and what works less well, preserve and enhance the former, and consider what improvements might be made. It is time for a fresh look.

In the late eighteenth century, the Founders of the United States spent a significant amount of energy thinking about how to adapt political theory to create a new republican form of government. They explained their reasoning in what came to be known as the Federalist Papers, published over the course of eight months (between October 1787 and May 1788) in eighty-five essays, circulated for consideration by the people and their elected representatives inhabiting the original thirteen American colonies. The Papers provided both a historic amount of transparency and a basis for deliberation in the creation of a new institutional framework for national governance. It was an experiment – no republic had ever existed on the scale that the Founders intended for the United States.

Setting up the liberal international order in the late 1940s, including the multilateral trading system, was also an experiment. Nothing like it had ever existed on a global scale. The problems are not dissimilar. The American states, the thirteen original colonies, were sovereigns, and needed to come together for the common good. The 23 countries forming the GATT and the 164 members now in the WTO face similar challenges as sovereigns in designing global trade governance for the common good.

In setting up the US government, the American Founders were seeking a balance within their new institution. Their primary concern was that the new federal government would re-create rule by a king, albeit an American one rather than one in England. Their solution was to create a tripartite structure designed with offsetting forces among three branches of government so that none could be dominant. The courts and legislature were given powers to offset an executive that could easily become too strong. The colonists also knew that the legislature could get out of hand. Their remedy was that there be no concentration of power.

The WTO emerged from a different process. The Uruguay Round negotiations were not initiated to create a world trade organization. It was a proposal that came along four years later, in 1990. It began as the idea of an eminent GATT expert, John Jackson,[2] picked up energetically by a mid-sized country, Canada, and then carried forward by the European Union. All this apparently occurred within a matter of just a few months. When the concept of the WTO was floated, the substantive talks in the Uruguay Round were well advanced. The substantive agreements – on IP protection, services, and agriculture – were regarded as the most important fruit of the negotiations by both the GATT Director-General at the time, Arthur Dunkel, and the US negotiators. The primary institutional innovation up to that point, the Trade Policy Review Mechanism, had been put into place a few years earlier.[3] The most important institutional innovation by far was the creation of a binding dispute settlement system – a dramatic and conscious departure from the GATT system.

Deep consideration does not appear to have been given to the interrelationships among the institutions that the drafters were creating. All eyes were focused on making sure that the new trade organization had binding dispute settlement, primarily to curb US unilateralism. The rest of the institutional elements remained much the same as that which had existed in the GATT era. The legislature was in effect the body of the whole, consisting of all members meeting at the ministerial level in biennial conferences (with delegation to their ambassadors for interim rule-making). A Director-General continued in place with a Secretariat, with no powers specified for this office in the WTO Agreement. The WTO that its members created

[2] John H. Jackson is the author of the seminal work on the GATT, *World Trade and the Law of GATT*, published in 1969. Originally a professor at the University of Michigan Law School, he moved to the Georgetown University Law School. In 1970–71, I hired Jackson to be a consultant to the US Treasury Department, and in 1973 became Deputy General Counsel at the Office of the Special Representative for Trade Negotiations, when he became General Counsel of that Office.

[3] This state of affairs is captured in the official history of the WTO, entitled *The History and Future of the World Trade Organization*, an elegant work written by Craig VanGrasstek on the basis of not only the GATT and WTO archives but extensive interviews with those present at and involved in the creation of the WTO. Craig VanGrasstek. 2013. *The History and Future of the World Trade Organization*. World Trade Organization. www.wto.org/english/res_e/booksp_e/historywto_e.pdf

inadvertently consisted of primarily a court, no effective legislature, and certainly no executive. With hindsight, we can conclude that the imbalance, judge-made law, was the only likely result.

In some ways, the circumstances of the birth of the WTO were every bit as idiosyncratic as the birth of the GATT. The GATT was not supposed to be an organization, but an interim arrangement, a contract really. The organization for which the rules were created was to have been the International Trade Organization (ITO). When the WTO came along at the end of the Uruguay Round, given that the GATT was about trade in goods, and the Round was ranging further into services and intellectual property, logic suggested that some new institutional arrangements be made. The WTO was an umbrella organization fabricated to bring together bold new substantive agreements. Had Professor John H. Jackson not advanced the idea of a multilateral trade organization at that point, and had Canadian Trade Minister John Crosbie – ably supported by Canadian government lawyer Deborah Steger – not picked up the idea and advanced it, had the European Union negotiators not embraced it, the Uruguay Round would have created separate trade agreements covering intellectual property, services, and investment, accompanied by an agreed trade policy review mechanism and binding dispute settlement (the *sine qua non* for having any agreed results in the Round), but with no WTO.

The United States Congress had a history of being wary of binding dispute settlement. The prior (Republican) US administration had seen potential advantages in having binding dispute settlement in the WTO, hoping for an ability to curb the trade-distorting effects of the EU's Common Agricultural Policy (CAP).[4] The successor Democratic administration was more concerned about getting Congress to approve the implementing legislation that

[4] Robert Lawrence and Nathaniel Stankard. 2003. "Imperfect Practice in the US EU Trading Relationship." Peterson Institute for International Economics. www.piie.com/publications/chapters_preview/372/4iie3594.pdf

> *Changes made to the multilateral dispute resolution process in the Uruguay Round may be as important to agricultural trade as the improvement in the substantive rules governing trade in agricultural goods. Initial evidence indicates that the WTO dispute settlement system is a significant improvement over its GATT predecessor. For example, a single country can no longer block the formation of a dispute resolution panel, or veto an adverse ruling by blocking the adoption of a panel report. These improvements have led to a number of important agricultural trade cases being adjudicated before the WTO.*

"International Agriculture and Trade Reports – Agriculture in the WTO: Situation and Outlook Series WRS-98-4." United States Department of Agriculture. December 1998. www.ers.usda.gov/mediaImport/1774123/wrs98-4.pdf

would allow US participation in the Uruguay Round.[5] The United States had a long track record of failure to get legislative buy-in to what the executive branch negotiated, most prominently resulting in the inability to join the League of Nations and the International Trade Organization, and only a few years earlier, the failure to obtain congressional approval of the "nontariff" agreements of the Kennedy Round.[6]

Now, almost three decades later, it is time to focus on how the trading system can be improved, understanding how well the constituent parts of the WTO work and how they fit together. The principal current challenges are:

- Achieving once again binding dispute settlement seen as fully legitimate by all members who wish to invoke it;
- Restoring the negotiating function of the WTO, overcoming where necessary "single undertaking multilateralism" (where all must join every agreement) to make progress through "open plurilateral agreements"; and
- Acknowledging and spelling out effective executive functions for the WTO Director-General and Secretariat.

Woven into these three overarching institutional issues are a number of specific aspects of governance that will also require attention:

- The creators of the WTO wished to engage trade ministers more directly, and this has not been effectively achieved;
- The use of consensus decisionmaking (misinterpreted as unanimity) needs further thought. Nations have discovered that "direct democracy" involving all is largely unworkable;
- Providing more nearly full transparency requires enhanced monitoring;
- Ensuring that agreements can evolve to reflect changes in current factors affecting world trade, for example:
  - the Agreement on Agriculture has obligations based on a long-outdated 1986–88 base period;

[5] Crucial to the Senate taking up the Uruguay Round Agreements Act was President Clinton's acceptance of the Dole–Moynihan Judicial Review Commission to help assure the Congress that WTO dispute settlement would not infringe on US sovereignty. David E. Sanger. "Dole and Clinton Strike a Deal on World Trade Pact." *New York Times*, November 24, 1994. www.nytimes.com/1994/11/24/us/dole-and-clinton-strike-a-deal-on-world-trade-pact.html

[6] Repeal of American Selling Price failed, and the Senate passed a resolution offered by Sen. Abraham Ribicoff seeking to nullify the antidumping code. In recent times, the cautionary event was the unsuccessful effort by the Obama administration to have Congress approve the Trans-Pacific Partnership. After much delay, the incoming Trump administration canceled US participation.

  - the nature of much of trade has changed in what has become the global digital economy; and
  - the relative importance of countries in the global trading system is vastly different today than it was in 1995.
- A review is needed of the unintended broadening of exceptions (such as deviations from MFN for preferential trade agreements or the use of national security-related trade restrictions);
- A more thorough examination is needed of the effects of state interventions affecting trade flows;
- Consideration is needed of how to achieve a better balance between developed and developing nations, between the application of rules and their absence ("policy space"); and
- It is time to apply strategic foresight to identify future risks and policy planning put in place as part of the necessary mechanisms to deal with them.

The relevance of the system depends increasingly on meeting new challenges, most notably, addressing public health in a time of pandemics and the even more existential threat of climate change. Institutional reform will not in and of itself be the answer to current and future challenges. Adjustments in the substantive rules will be necessary. Nevertheless, strengthening the WTO as an institution is essential to working out and implementing satisfactory solutions.

14

WTO 2025: WTO Reform

GETTING BACK TO THE NEGOTIATING TABLE

Negotiations at the WTO have produced too few results during the more than a quarter-century of the Organization's history. Until some results were reached at MC12, most of the action had been among groups of like-minded members, either regionally outside the WTO or in open plurilateral agreements (OPAs) at the WTO, and these contain much of the promise for the Organization. Additional challenges require multilateral – that is, global – agreements: the pandemic, food security, and climate change among them. A breakthrough is needed to make the WTO a more productive venue for reaching new agreements.

A PLACE CREATED FOR TRADE NEGOTIATIONS

Of the multilateral trading system's three pillars – negotiation, dispute settlement, and administration – negotiation is the one of greatest importance. The WTO is the only place where fully multilateral[1] – that is, global – trade

[1] Throughout this chapter, the term "multilateral agreement" is used to refer to agreements that are formally accepted as part of the WTO body of agreements, and where either all WTO members have signed the agreement or are expected to do so. Thus, the WTO's Trade Facilitation Agreement is multilateral. Open plurilateral agreements (OPAs) in the WTO context are administered by the WTO Secretariat and subject to WTO dispute settlement, but not all WTO members are signatories. The Information Technology Agreement (applied on a most-favored-nation basis) and the Agreement on Government Procurement (benefiting only signatories) are OPAs rather than multilateral agreements in the sense used here. There are a number of multiparty agreements such as the Regional Comprehensive Economic Partnership (RCEP) and the Comprehensive and Progressive Agreement for Trans-Pacific Partnership (CPTPP), which are not considered "multilateral agreements" as that term is used in this chapter. For a more complete discussion of WTO agreements, OPAs, and sub-multilateral agreements, and how they interrelate, see my remarks at Nanyang Technological University

negotiations can take place. The WTO has representatives present from 164 members, accounting for more than 98 percent of world trade. Most of the remaining countries that are not members, some two dozen, are in the process of accession and all of them are observers.

The WTO has unrivalled infrastructure to facilitate negotiations – a skilled Secretariat made up of experienced experts thoroughly versed in the existing rules of the trading system, teams of interpreters and translators on call, numerous meeting rooms with audiovisual equipment for simultaneous interpretation into three languages (and more on special occasions), and connections via the web for remote participation. It is the meeting place for a large number of working committees, a repository of their past proceedings, and, beyond this, it holds the records of over 600 cases litigated among its members. In terms of physical facilities and support staff, everything is ready for negotiations.

Almost all members have resident missions located within a few minutes' drive from the WTO headquarters in Geneva. The missions have a core of staff attending committee meetings. The heads of delegation – the permanent representatives to the WTO who are ambassadors sitting as the General Council of the Organization – have been delegated the full plenary powers of the Ministerial Conference. They are empowered, in the view of their counterparts, to commit their countries to trade agreements. Ever since the International Court of Justice issued its Eastern Greenland Decision,[2] ministers (particularly foreign ministers) have been able to bind their governments even with a verbal declaration, enough so that they can definitively transfer sovereignty to another nation of substantial tracts of their nation's territory. All the physical and legal elements are present for trade negotiations to take place.

While the Doha Development Agenda came to naught as an expansive new round,[3] there are continuing mandates for negotiations and built-in agendas as part of the agreements reached in the Uruguay Round. Article 20 of the Agreement on Agriculture provides: "Recognizing that the long-term objective of substantial progressive reductions in support and protection resulting in fundamental reform is an ongoing process, Members agree that negotiations

Singapore: "Plurilateral Agreements and the Future of the WTO." Peterson Institute for International Economics. November 16, 2021. www.piie.com/commentary/speeches-papers/plurilateral-agreements-and-future-wto

2 "Legal Status of Eastern Greenland–Denmark v. Norway Judgment." International Court of Justice. September 5, 1933. www.worldcourts.com/pcij/eng/decisions/1933.04.05_ greenland .htm

3 What one astute commentator described as the Doha Development Agenda having "lost the will to exist."

for continuing the process will be initiated one year before the end of the implementation period."

Likewise, Article XIX.1 of the General Agreement on Trade in Services provides: "In pursuance of the objectives of this Agreement, Members shall enter into successive rounds of negotiations, beginning not later than five years from the date of entry into force of the WTO Agreement and periodically thereafter, with a view to achieving a progressively higher level of liberalization."

Despite the physical facilities, the expert staff, and these important mandates for negotiations, there have been no active *multilateral* negotiations on these two vitally important topics that show any visible movement. The breakthrough did not come on agriculture or services, but in the form of an initial Fisheries Subsidies Agreement at the WTO's Twelfth Ministerial Conference (MC12) in June 2022 after over two decades of negotiations, and this agreement is still incomplete.

The WTO members also came to interim conclusions at MC12 on how the WTO should deal with the pandemic, after over two years of their peoples suffering from the global scourge. However, no binding obligations were agreed. The collective decision was limited to a statement of intentions and best practices, with the addition of one temporary change in the rules, altering obligations under the Agreement on Trade-Related Aspects of Intellectual Property Rights (TRIPS) with respect to vaccine patents. An agreement not to impose export restrictions on purchases by the World Food Programme had a major exemption for domestic needs. A discussion has only just begun on how to restore binding dispute settlement, with no assured resolution in sight, but with a deadline of 2024 set to obtain one. These multilateral outcomes are not good enough.

Where more progress has been demonstrated in recent years is among groups of like-minded WTO members. Their efforts take the form of negotiations of "Joint Statement Initiatives" (JSIs), in essence, open plurilateral agreements (OPA). There are also structured discussions designed to lead to negotiated outcomes on environmental issues. Of these endeavors, the plurilateral agreements on domestic regulation of services and micro, small, and medium-sized enterprises (MSMEs) are complete. The JSI on investment facilitation is said to be close to conclusion and the negotiation on e-commerce has made very substantial progress on drafting text but has not reached an agreement on the most sensitive and therefore most difficult issues. Before the breakthrough at MC12 on fisheries subsidies, there was only one truly multilateral agreement at the WTO, the Trade Facilitation Agreement reached in 2013 – a coming together of developing and developed country interests that is not clearly replicable for other subjects. Prior to MC12, there have been a few other negotiated outcomes during the time the WTO has been in existence – a 2015 agreement on the part of developed countries to ban agricultural export subsidies (a political commitment), and guidance documents for telecom and financial services.

There need to be two paths forward: the fully multilateral, which only produces results after many years of effort, and OPAs. For the WTO to become a serious negotiating forum for major agreements, the parties that wish to negotiate OPAs must be able to find a way to do so within the framework of the WTO. It is highly unlikely that the e-commerce or environmental talks can result in fully multilateral agreements, that is, with the prospect of all WTO members agreeing even in principle to join them. Some, perhaps most, members will not be ready to join. There are also members that are clearly unwilling to allow like-minded participants to register their agreements as part of the WTO *acquis*.

For the WTO to be a forum in which trade agreements can be reached is an existential question for the institution. If it is not, critical emerging issues will increasingly be taken to other venues for negotiation. It is imperative that OPAs, open agreements of the like-minded, become a normal way of doing business at the WTO and be recognized as being fully legitimate. Two options to achieve this result come to mind:

A Great Power Diktat

Getting OPAs accepted as the new normal is in the first instance a political not a legal question. The WTO was created in its current form, with the simultaneous strength and serious flaw of the "single undertaking" – that all must agree to participate and be bound by all agreements. Over 100 nations did not suddenly agree on everything that was involved in the Uruguay Round (1986–94) negotiations. The mechanism for forcing change was the cancellation of the prior multilateral trade agreement, GATT 1947, and giving no option to any then-GATT contracting party but to join the WTO. This created GATT 1994, an integral part of the WTO Agreements. Not going along with the package risked being cast outside the multilateral trading system altogether. The formation of the WTO was a shotgun marriage. In institutional terms, a metamorphosis took place – the chrysalis of the old was left behind and a new butterfly, the WTO, emerged.

Would the great powers of today be aligned? During the 1990s, the United States, the European Union, Japan, and Canada provided much of the leadership for the negotiation of the Uruguay Round. In today's world,

China, by far the world's largest exporting country,[4] needs to be included. On the question of legitimizing JSIs, China may have divided interests. While championing the interests of developing countries, many of whom regard the JSIs as illegitimate, China has been an active proponent of the two remaining JSIs – investment facilitation and e-commerce. India and South Africa take the view that the WTO cannot accommodate plurilateral agreements unless all WTO members agree to allow them to be part of the WTO. They may be wary of these JSI negotiations taking the spotlight off their needs as articulated in the Doha Development Agenda. The two clearly indicate that they have no desire to see OPAs legitimized in the multilateral trading system. The first two JSI negotiations (on MSMEs and domestic regulation of services) skirted these objections by being implemented without the requirement of adding them officially to the WTO *acquis* – the MSME result does not require rule changes and the domestic regulation of services results are being incorporated into members' schedules of services commitments.

There is no reason to believe that China at this stage would force the issue of formal recognition of the JSIs in the WTO. While Europe has evidenced a more active, newfound interest in multilateralism, it is not clear that Brussels would opt to face the criticism from many quarters if it tried to force all members to accept JSIs as legitimate WTO agreements. At present, the United States, the original architect and guarantor of the trading system, has not demonstrated a willingness to make the necessary investment in the WTO to revive it as a negotiating forum and insist on the formal adoption of JSIs as WTO agreements. The United States might instead choose to look elsewhere, for example, to a sub-multilateral agreement in which to subscribe to e-commerce rules. There is likewise no indication from the mid-sized friends of the multilateral trading system – the middle grounders[5] – of their willingness to join in a showdown to take the WTO's self-preserving step of recognizing the legitimacy of plurilaterals within the Organization despite opposition.

In short, at this time neither the largest and most developed trading nations nor the mid-sized friends of the system are likely in the near future to force the

[4] China accounts for 14.7 percent of world exports, compared with the US share of 8.1 percent and German share of 7.8 percent. "Evolution of the World's 25 Top Trading Nations." United Nations Conference on Trade and Development. April 6, 2021. www.unctad.org/topic/trade-analysis/chart-10-may-2021

[5] There is no precise definition of this term. It encompasses forward-leaning multilateralist members. A reasonable proxy for a list of participants would be those that are in the Ottawa Group working on WTO reform: Australia, Brazil, Canada, Chile, European Union, Japan, Kenya, South Korea, Mexico, New Zealand, Norway, Singapore, Switzerland, and the United Kingdom.

shedding of the old order, an order kept in place by a consensus rule employed by JSI nonparticipants to block their adoption as a formal part of the WTO *acquis*.

A Grand Bargain

Commercial diplomacy is a possible alternative to the use of force to bring about a resolution of this issue. This option is not cost-free. The question comes down to whether JSI proponents feel strongly enough to pay for the privilege of having the agreements acknowledged within the WTO *acquis*. Key benefits of bringing JSIs formally into the WTO would be to have a skilled and experienced ready-made Secretariat in place to support the agreements and, at the same time, reinforce the infrastructure of the liberal international order that JSI proponents consider to be central to their interests.

There are two approaches to cutting deals: (1) a largely self-balancing single object agreement, as was the case of the Trade Facilitation Agreement (TFA), or (2) bundling agreements in a much larger package. Prior to MC12, the TFA was the only truly multilateral deal struck in the WTO. Diminishing red tape at borders was a public good, but that by itself was not sufficient to reach an agreement. The TFA not only was based on a perceived mutuality of interests, developing and developed alike, but also had accommodations and sweeteners in terms of self-selected speeds for implementation, the promise of technical assistance, and a trust fund set up to assure that assistance would be forthcoming. The TFA may be difficult to replicate for other negotiations. The essence of the agreement was to opt in, choosing the degree and timing of the assumption of obligations. The obverse of an opt-in agreement would be providing for an opt-out mechanism, selectively by obligation.

The alternative approach is to engage in much broader negotiation on a package of subjects. There are many GATT precedents, eight rounds of them, for achieving this kind of breakthrough, particularly in the Tokyo and Uruguay Rounds, but these examples are now receding into a distant past. The theory of these rounds, as noted previously, was to find in a large package enough to enable every country's negotiators to claim that there were gains sufficient to offset concessions granted.[6] With the demise of the Doha Development Agenda, there is no WTO precedent for successfully packaging agreements in a new negotiating round, although some point out that the TFA itself required movement on other issues during the Bali Ministerial Conference at which it was agreed.

6 The theory of the success of the Tokyo Round as articulated by then-US trade negotiator Robert S. Strauss.

The first question to determine whether a broader negotiated solution is possible is to consider what trading stock exists. This is something that can be explored. For the least developed and some of the developing countries, this might be in the form of aid and investment – for capacity-building, for infrastructure, for whatever will promise their peoples a better future. Trade-offs must be found, such as on measures supporting food security or curbs on subsidies.

Just Do It

There is a further alternative way to bring JSIs into the WTO *acquis*. The reason JSIs exist is that groups of like-minded members came together and determined that they wished to negotiate at the WTO on topics of mutual interest. They succeeded in doing so, over strong opposition from some nonparticipants, because the Director-General stood his ground, holding that he had the authority to provide meeting space and administrative support to any member activity consistent with the trading system. While these activities, the JSIs, remain other than officially acknowledged, they have yielded results and promise more. If in the future a Director-General was approached with an agreement, whether a JSI or a sub-multilateral agreement outside the WTO (even including dispute settlement based on the arbitration provisions of the Dispute Settlement Understanding), that was not inconsistent with the objectives of the WTO and was asked to administer it, there is no direct way for other members to block this. No vote would be required. Introducing JSIs in this fashion would add *de facto* a new virtual "Annex 5" to the WTO Agreement.

Consensus defined as unanimity became a challenge to the viability of the WTO. Simon Evenett and Richard Baldwin note that:

> *While no WTO member should be shut out of any negotiation, no member should be able to veto others moving forward. A government is entitled to decide that it doesn't want to further integrate some aspect of its economy into global commerce, but that does not give it the right to block other WTO members from integrating further.*[7]

It is essential that JSIs, these open plurilateral agreements, become part of the WTO.

7 Simon Evenett and Richard Baldwin, eds. 2020. *Revitalising Multilateralism: Pragmatic Ideas for the New WTO Director-General*. London: Centre for Economic Policy Research Press. https://cepr.org/voxeu/columns/revitalising-multilateralism-new-ebook; R. Lawrence. 2006. "Rulemaking amidst Growing Diversity: A 'Club of Clubs' Approach to WTO Reform and New Issue Selection." *Journal of International Economic Law* 9(4): 823–835.

If None of the Above

Absent change at the WTO, nature may dictate that those who want to accomplish something through trade agreements will take their efforts elsewhere. Eleven nations have a Comprehensive and Progressive Agreement for Trans-Pacific Partnership (CPTPP).[8] The Regional Comprehensive Economic Partnership (RCEP) has fifteen parties.[9] The Digital Economy Partnership Agreement (DEPA) has three members, Singapore, Chile, and New Zealand. The United States could consider joining. Some trade pundits see DEPA as an agreement that the Biden administration will consider having the United States join as an opening to consider reentry into the TPP, although there is no evidence that the United States wants to revive the TPP.[10] The United States announced on February 11, 2022, its Indo-Pacific Economic Framework (IPEF), with somewhat vague economic content and an emphasis on working with the Asia Pacific Economic Cooperation (APEC) forum.[11] The African Continental Free Trade Area (AfCFTA), comprising fifty-five nations, which has now come into force, is something of a special case,[12] where low intracontinental trade provides a strong case for regional integration.

What these non-Geneva-based agreements have in common is that they are vibrant endeavors covering emerging trade issues of importance to their participants. They assume the existence of the WTO, they rely on the existence of the WTO, but they do not yet contribute directly to the future of the WTO.

There is an added layer of complexity with respect to the CPTPP. China, Ecuador, Taiwan, and the United Kingdom have applied to join the agreement, and South Korea and Thailand have indicated an interest in joining.[13]

[8] Australia, Brunei, Canada, Chile, Japan, Malaysia, Mexico, New Zealand, Peru, Singapore, and Viet Nam.

[9] Australia, Brunei, Cambodia, China, Indonesia, Japan, Laos, Malaysia, Myanmar, New Zealand, the Philippines, Singapore, South Korea, Thailand, and Viet Nam.

[10] Matthew P. Goodman. 2021. “DEPA and the Path Back to TPP.” Center for Strategic and International Studies. July 15. www.csis.org/analysis/depa-and-path-back-tpp

[11] “Indo-Pacific Strategy of the United States.” The White House. February 2022. www.whitehouse.gov/wp-content/uploads/2022/02/US-Indo-Pacific-Strategy.pdf

[12] "The Secretariat." African Continental Free Trade Area. https://au-afcfta.org/secretariat/; Anabel González. 2019. “The African Continental Free Trade Area Is Coming into Force. Is It Really?” Peterson Institute for International Economics. May 31. www.piie.com/blogs/trade-and-investment-policy-watch/african-continental-free-trade-area-coming-force-it-really

[13] Jeffrey J. Schott. 2022. “Which Countries Are in the CPTPP and RCEP Trade Agreements and Which Want In?” Peterson Institute for International Economics. January 3. www.piie.com/research/piie-charts/which-countries-are-cptpp-and-rcep-trade-agreements-and-which-want

One of these applicants is not like the others. The United Kingdom does not border on the Pacific. If it does join, it would make CPTPP seem less like a regional answer to globalization than a prototype for a new and revived global order, built not by the United States as a top-down endeavor, as the creation of the multilateral trading system was in the last half of the 1940s, but as a bottom-up approach necessitated by the United States dropping out of the agreement.

What is one to make of these sub-multilateral agreements other than the fact that they contribute more acronyms to the vocabularies of those interested in trade? They each have merit on their own terms. But they still could serve a broader purpose. A hope for TPP when it was negotiated, and included the United States, was that it would lead to a progression, with the next step being the fruition of US–EU talks in a Trans-Atlantic Trade and Investment Partnership (TTIP). Stepping stones clearly would have been present then: building on the TPP, TTIP would take economic integration even further, potentially on a path back to Geneva, to the WTO and multilateralism. But this did not happen. The TTIP talks failed, and then the Trump administration celebrated US withdrawal from TPP as one of its very first acts in office.[14]

A global set of rules for international trade makes good sense and is the most practical answer to maximizing the benefits of trade for most inhabitants of this planet. Economic efficiency can be ignored only at great cost. One cannot discount the world returning to a common effort to improve world trade governance. Perhaps for trading rules, all roads lead back to Geneva.

The Necessity of Having a Multilateral Option

Because there is one globe, some matters cannot be successfully negotiated, or meaningful results achieved, on less than a global scale. The global digital economy requires nurturing before it fragments. Industrial subsidies need to be disciplined. Domestic support for agriculture and food security must be addressed in a manner responsive to today's needs. Movement of goods should be freer to meet global challenges from pandemics to climate change. These issues cannot be successfully dealt with in sub-multilateral fora. It is not practical for some countries to discipline domestic subsidies while others choose not to do so. Battling a global pandemic with some but not all countries participating is far from fully effective. This is even more true for combating global warming. Collective, multilateral responses will be

[14] "Trump Scuttles Trans-Pacific Trade Pact, Jan. 23, 2017." Politico. January 23, 2019. www.politico.com/story/2019/01/23/trans-pacific-trade-pact-2017-1116638

necessary. For the trading system, Geneva is the only place where all the players can come together. The pursuit of national commercial interests and global public goods will eventually bring them there.

Fragmentation of the trading system is not a sustainable long-term trend. There must be a return to multilateralism. This is not to denigrate regional agreements. They should be viewed as laboratories for making improvements in the world trading system, discovering fruitful ways forward, and pointing to broader agreements negotiated multilaterally. Sub-multilateral agreements should not be used, however, for mercantilist ends, being more trade-distorting than trade-creating.

What is uncertain is the degree of vision and commitment of world leaders that causes them to work together for a common purpose. What causes world leaders – a Xi, a Biden, a Scholz, a Macron, a Modi, a von der Leyen, and their successors – to work together? The gravitational pull of economic theory, of efficiency, may not be enough. Even a global pandemic, which threatened their economies and the health of their peoples, did not cause them to pull together and reform the trading rules promptly to meet that crisis. It may be that the next cataclysm galvanizes them to collective action. It could be climate change that unifies them, when it is self-evident to all, and perhaps irreversible without as yet unanticipated great scientific breakthroughs. Enlightened self-interest must and will at some point come into play. As of the time of this writing, it is too early to tell when.

WHAT IS TO BE DONE?

The rules-based trading system needs a reboot, which can only come from a reawakening and recommitment on the part of at least its leading members. The system is still facing a fundamental, existential crisis, despite the breathing space provided by MC12. In the future, trade policy officials and academic scholars will look back upon this time as an inflection point. Is the universality of the trading system viable, or will it be shattered by divisions? Does there have to be a reconfiguration? Leadership will be required to avoid moving toward fragmentation. There are not only great challenges but great opportunities. To fail to respond is to allow the jungle to grow back.[15] Time is not the friend of the system. MC12 provided some reassurance that progress on a broad front is possible.

[15] Robert Kagan. 2018. *The Jungle Grows Back, America and Our Imperiled World*. New York: Knopf Doubleday.

RECOMMENDATIONS TO CREATE A WTO 2025 TO RENEW THE WTO AS A FORUM FOR NEGOTIATIONS

What is required?

- There needs to be a change in culture, a rededication to multilateralism so that the principal purposes of the gathering of nations at the WTO can be realized – the negotiation of rules, followed by their administration and the resolution of disputes.
- A key to a positive future for the WTO is for it to be a welcoming home for the JSIs, the open plurilateral agreements already being negotiated at the WTO. There can be no veto over their negotiation and inclusion in the WTO through continued abuse of the consensus approach for WTO decision making.
- The WTO cannot be a one-speed system. The GATT was not. There are differences among members in capacity, willingness, and interest. This will always be the case, even if differences should diminish over time. This reality needs to be recognized, and flexibilities provided. There must be an openness to what those in the trade field call "variable geometries." A new ecumenicism is needed for the multilateral trading system to thrive.
- Sub-multilateral agreements, the regional and specific-purpose multi-party agreements as well as bilateral arrangements, should be designed as building blocks for the multilateral trading system.
  - Regional efforts are expanding the range of subjects to be covered by trade agreements. They should be regarded as incubators of ideas and approaches for the multilateral trading system.

Milestones:

- At their summits, the G20 leaders will have an opportunity to seek to create an action program to move beyond general statements issued on WTO reform, by tasking their trade ministers to have an agreed agenda for WTO reform with a six-month deadline for making proposals and engaging in negotiations. These twenty countries, which together account for 85 percent of global GDP, 75 percent of international trade, and two-thirds of the world's population, appear to have a degree of common interest. But the stated commitments at the level of national leaders and ministers dissipate in transit to Geneva and too often do not find more than an echo at the WTO.
  - India will hold the presidency of the G20 from December 1, 2022 to November 30, 2023, followed by Brazil (2024) and South Africa (2025).

The meetings could find concrete areas of agreement among the G20 members for the WTO reform agenda.[16]

  - There is some precedent. Saudi Arabia, in hosting the Leaders' Summit in 2020, launched the Riyadh Initiative for WTO Reform. In doing so, the G20 reached a substantial consensus, agreeing to a list of WTO principles.

- Japan will host the 2023 G7 summit, which should spur serious cooperation on WTO reform, going to fundamental issues of WTO governance, and pressing forward with a Japanese priority, rules for digital commerce.
- The United States will host the APEC Leaders' Meeting in 2023. The United States should use the occasion to reinforce the opening messages of the Biden administration's commitment to multilateralism. APEC should become an alliance for progress in the WTO.
- The United States, China, and the European Union should explore where common ground may exist for forging institutional and substantive progress at the WTO. Reading the statements of President Xi at the China International Import Expo,[17] there would appear to be a possible confluence of interests, also evidenced by China's applications to join the CPTPP and DEPA.
- The Trilateral (US/Japan/EU) should reach a consensus on the reform issues it is seized with (including industrial subsidies, disciplines on state-owned enterprises) and seek to gain additional adherents to its agenda.
- The United States and the European Union should agree to binding dispute settlement between them, potentially joined in by others, as a New Multi-Party Interim Appeal Arbitration Arrangement (NMPIA).
- The middle grounders (Switzerland, Canada, Australia, New Zealand, etc.) should continue to launch initiatives. The record shows that the largest players will often join in. The idea is "build it and they will come."[18]
- Members that do not wish to participate in a spirit of constructive engagement, or lack sufficient domestic support for participating, should

[16] There is little understanding within the WTO diplomatic corps of what India wants from the WTO. It professes dedication to multilateralism, but its daily positions are opposed to what most see as progress. To a somewhat lesser extent, this is how South Africa's participation is viewed as well.

[17] "Full Text: Xi's Keynote Speech at 4th CIIE Opening Ceremony." China International Import Expo. November 4, 2021. www.ciie.org/zbh/en/news/highlights/20211104/30424.html

[18] *Field of Dreams* is an American movie (1989) where a farmer builds a baseball diamond and the players are attracted to it (from a great distance).

step aside and allow others to progress without them, understanding that non-signatories will not be bound by the negotiated outcomes that they did not agree to, nor may they in all cases benefit from them.

- Multilateral agreements may be structured on an opt-in basis (as was true substantively with the TFA) or on an opt-out basis, allowing for members to proceed at varying speeds, discarding the convoy system where the slowest vessel determines progress or lack of it.

Specific elements:

- The G7 and G20 leaders should instruct their trade ministers, with a deadline for making proposals and engaging in negotiations, to address specific priorities, including:
  - Restoring binding dispute settlement on an interim basis, while working on a permanent solution;
  - Obtaining a clear positive outcome on the legitimacy of open plurilateral agreements in the WTO, which are consistent with the values of the WTO;
  - Providing for the development of the executive functions of the WTO, with stated mandates for:
    - enhancing transparency through the gathering of trade intelligence;
    - assuring greater compliance by WTO members with their obligations;
    - providing in-depth analyses of trade conditions;
    - being an important source of negotiating proposals; and
    - engaging in strategic foresight and policy planning.
  - Creating negotiating agendas for key priorities, including rules and procedures to deal with the COVID-19 pandemic, future pandemics, food security, and climate change.
- The Director-General should draft and circulate a proposed negotiating agenda if the members fail to do so within six months.
- The Secretariat should be charged with compiling reports for members on the subjects covered in sub-multilateral agreements (and negotiations) that may be useful in considering future coverage of multilateral agreements and go beyond the current scope of the WTO, such as by covering additional services, the environment, trade and health, trade and labor, etc., and provide models for consideration for formulating multilateral rules.
- The Secretariat should prepare, and the members should approve, model provisions for regional and bilateral trade agreements, including on e-commerce and other cutting-edge issues.

- The Secretariat should provide members with estimates of subjects that may require changes in existing rules or warrant new rules, drawing upon current trends in world trade and issues that are anticipated through foresight exercises, as well as drawing upon its annual *World Trade Report* and the results of its enhanced trade intelligence activities.[19]
- The Director-General should supply suggested negotiating outcomes based in part on consultations with members and on their own responsibility, whenever the Director-General decides it is productive to do so, or upon the request of members.
- The Secretariat should supply the members annually with a list of issues addressed by dispute settlement panels which in the Secretariat's opinion appear to be gaps in the current rules.
- The Secretariat should inform the members of the results of its strategic foresight exercise, indicating where the current rules may need to be modified or supplemented. For example:
  - Having identified future pandemics as likely, the Secretariat would compile a list of steps to be taken to create a sufficient response to future epidemics. This could include:
    - Upon identification of a possible pandemic, the formation of a cross-divisional Secretariat task force to specify possible responses, working closely with a ten-WTO-member Pandemic Response Group under the chairmanship of a facilitator chosen by the chair of the General Council for this purpose.
  - A similar approach could be taken with respect to climate change.
- The Director-General should assure that the Secretariat is mission-oriented to obtain negotiated outcomes and have a training program for all staff designed to support a better understanding of negotiating methods.
- Ambassadors and their staff assigned to WTO missions should come to Geneva with a mission to achieve negotiated outcomes. They should receive an appropriate orientation course that supports this mission.
- Committee chairs should be charged with obtaining negotiated outcomes.
- Members must meet in various configurations to bring about progress. Negotiations do not occur in meetings of 164 members. There will be occasions when smaller groups consisting 12 to 18 members meet in

[19] Alan Wm. Wolff. 2022. "WTO 2025: Enhancing Global Trade Intelligence." Peterson Institute for International Economics Working Paper 22-6. April. www.piie.com/publications/working-papers/wto-2025-enhancing-global-trade-intelligence

"a green room setting" with the Director-General to find a productive way forward. (In reaching a result on the TRIPS waiver for vaccines, four directly interested members formulated a solution for the entire membership to consider.)[20]

- WTO committees should have participation from capitals, as the OECD does, to connect directly those engaged in trade policy formulation with their counterparts in other capitals via their WTO committee work.
- Advances in information technology should be deployed as they were during the pandemic to accelerate the work of committees and deepen engagement, for example, as occurred with respect to the treatment of "specific trade concerns" in the Committee on Technical Barriers to Trade.
- An advisory board of trade experts, former trade negotiators, and former WTO senior staff should be constituted to address improvements to be made to facilitate multilateral trade negotiations.

CONCLUSION

Substantial cultural and institutional changes will be necessary for the WTO to reach its full potential as the place where global rules for trade are negotiated. The world economy cannot afford risking deterioration of the WTO into irrelevancy. There are emerging challenges that require adopting a single set of rules. These include, prominently, managing the trade aspects of climate change, meeting food security needs, supporting health for a world threatened with pandemics, and providing for the continued growth of the worldwide digital economy. It is not enough for the WTO to arbitrate differences through an effective dispute settlement system, as important as this is. Nor is it enough to administer the trading system more effectively with a stronger, more proactive Secretariat. It is essential that the rules-based system continues to evolve. This can occur only through negotiations – reaching single-subject agreements in any of these areas, where feasible, or packages of

[20] A small group consisting of four WTO members – the United States, the European Union, South Africa, and India – reached a tentative agreement among themselves to put before the WTO membership as a whole. The four accomplished this with an iterative process virtually, of ministers talking to ministers, experts to experts in capitals, and Geneva delegations to Geneva delegations. They overcame the obstacles of the convoy system where all participate and the physical limitation of not being able to have in-person meetings of all those necessary to the process. Whether or not the tentative agreement to waive intellectual property rights is the right solution to the real problems inhibiting the delivery of vaccines to places where they are scarce, the four parties met the negotiating problem and at least among themselves overcame it.

agreements where balance cannot be found with a narrower focus. The multilateral trading system was founded seventy-five years ago to formalize international cooperation and open trade among nation-states to maintain peace. To fulfill its promise, the WTO's negotiating function needs to be revitalized.

The long peace was due in no small part to the creation of a liberal international order. The case for this point of view is forcefully made by Robert Kagan in the lead article in the May/June 2022 issue of *Foreign Affairs* with respect to geopolitics.[21] The same logic applies to the United States as a global leader with respect to international economic matters. The last US administration adamantly rejected this role. The current one has not fully embraced it. There are costs to the major trading WTO members not making this a joint endeavor. These countries share a common interest, which is to reinforce the open and rules-based multilateral trading system and to increase its relevancy. The WTO is the primary tool to maintain this order, and within the WTO the primary tool is negotiation.

Was the founding of the multilateral trading system in 1948 an aberration, created in circumstances that no longer pertain so that a multilateral approach is simply now an anachronism? When world leaders came together in 1998 to celebrate the fiftieth anniversary of the GATT, and heralded the beginning of a new World Trade Organization, were they engaged in a celebration of something that was already out-of-date? Were they short-sighted when they expressed their strong support for multilateral trading rules for a liberal world order? I do not think so.

Secretary of State Cordell Hull and President Franklin Roosevelt, and a series of their successors, as well as the creators of the European Union, saw a direct relationship between open trade and peace. Peace was not the only objective, even if for some it was the most important one. Economic well-being, reconstruction, and development were deemed to be essential. Economic efficiency, pursuant to the beliefs and efforts of Adam Smith, David Ricardo, Richard Cobden, and their acolytes, was sought not just for its own sake. It was pursued to better the lives of the world's peoples, and this was in fact the overall result. The system delivered. In current times, economic efficiency has come to be paired with the goals of sustainable development, care for the environment. It is also very likely to increasingly reflect other societal values, rewarding workers with dignity and a fair income. The

[21] Robert Kagan, 2022. "The Price of Hegemony Can America Learn to Use Its Power?" Foreign Affairs. May/June. www.foreignaffairs.com/issues/2022/101/3

world trading system can continue to evolve, to continue to deliver positive results. The way to accomplish this is through a process of continuing negotiation of the system's rules.

CONSTRUCTING AN EXECUTIVE BRANCH

The World Trade Organization as an institution accords less of a role to its chief official and staff, the WTO Director-General and the Secretariat, than do any of its sister international organizations – the World Bank, the International Monetary Fund, or the Organisation for Economic Co-operation and Development (OECD). The WTO Secretariat is much smaller than its peer international organizations and is underfunded. In considering WTO reform, this is a deficiency that needs to be rectified if WTO performance is to meet its members' needs.

INTRODUCTION

When the term "WTO reform" is mentioned, what first comes to mind for most observers is restoring binding dispute settlement, followed by overcoming the lack of negotiation of new multilateral agreements, and, in third place, if it is thought about at all, monitoring – a Secretariat function.[22] This grossly understates the current role of the WTO Secretariat and the role it might usefully perform.

It is a fact universally acknowledged by all students of political science that a proper representative form of governance must consist of three branches of activity – legislative (rule-making in the case of the WTO), judicial (dispute settlement), and administrative or executive. Not every situation in international commercial relations requires a new rule, nor is it the subject of a dispute. However, there is often a steady demand for an administrative element that supports daily the smooth functioning of the world trading system. Here, there is an institutional deficiency that any serious consideration of reform should address. The role of the Secretariat, the staff of the WTO, differs substantially in many respects from those of its sister international economic institutions – the World Bank and the International Monetary Fund (IMF or the Fund). There are also features that distinguish the WTO from the OECD. The differences have had consequences.

[22] Monitoring is encompassed in the section on Enhancing Global Trade Intelligence.

COMPARING THE ROLE OF THE WTO SECRETARIAT WITH THOSE OF ITS SISTER INTERNATIONAL ORGANIZATIONS[23]

The World Bank and the International Monetary Fund

Executive functions in the World Bank and the IMF are lodged in Boards of Executive Directors, who are on-site, full-time representatives of the membership as a whole, working together with the staff of the Bank and the Fund. These Executive Boards act on behalf of the Board of Governors, whose members are usually finance ministers or heads of central banks.

The WTO has a different structure. There is no executive board. The General Council is made up of heads of all 164 delegations, most of whom reside in Geneva. It meets every two or three months. The Council has been delegated the full authority of the Ministerial Conference. Full meetings of ministers are supposed to take place every two years (due to COVID-19, none were held for several years after December 2017). Mini-ministerial meetings do in fact take place more frequently with far fewer members in attendance. They are hosted by a member and are often scheduled to coincide with other events such as OECD Ministerial Meetings or the World Economic Forum at Davos.

Below the level of Ministerial Conferences, meetings of the whole membership occur in three different settings – the General Council, the Dispute Settlement Body (DSB), and the Trade Negotiating Committee (TNC). General Council and TNC meetings take place at the ambassadorial level, attended by the permanent representatives. In addition, there are meetings of both operating and negotiating committees, attended by any member wishing to do so, represented by its ambassador (the member's permanent representative), a deputy permanent representative, or a staff member from the country's mission, or, if very specialized, experts from capitals (for example, for fishery subsidies). In short, almost everything at the WTO takes place in settings open to all members, although some members are far more active than others. The level and degree of participation depend on the subject at hand.[24]

23 I benefited from discussions with PIIE Senior Fellows Sean Hagan and Sherman Robinson in comparing the organization of the Bank and the Fund but take full responsibility for the views expressed herein.

24 For example, in accessions working parties, the United States and the European Union carry most of the burden of asking questions and reviewing documents and answers. They do this because they have the capacity to do it, and they have a strong interest in maintaining a high level of obligations that the WTO membership should strive to meet. In the e-commerce Joint Statement Initiative (JSI), the co-convenors – Japan, Singapore, and Australia – are of course very active, but so are Canada, China, and several others.

While there is no WTO Board of Executive Directors, at various stages smaller groups of permanent representatives do meet with the Director-General in the DG's conference room. For example, during 2017–21 the DG would meet with all of the negotiating committee chairs in preparation for TNC meetings. During the GATT years, there was a Consultative Group of Eighteen, the CG18, established in 1975 on a temporary basis, made permanent in 1979, then suspended in 1989. (At the end of the period it was expanded to twenty-two contracting parties.) During most of the years of its existence, the CG18 met regularly, functioning as something of a steering group for the GATT. It had no formal decision-making authority.[25] There is currently no standing body to serve as a steering group for the WTO.

Another major difference between the WTO and its sister international economic organizations is that in none of these settings does the DG or any Secretariat staff member make concrete policy recommendations, and none are expected from them. In sharp contrast, the World Bank President and the IMF Managing Director (MD) do make policy recommendations and initiate proposals and put them to their Boards for decision. Some of their proposals are very far-reaching, such as recommending the creation of new facilities or programs.

What explains the great divergence in the role of the leadership of the Bank and the Fund, as compared with the WTO? First, it is useful to see where the roles differ in these institutions' founding documents. The Marrakesh Agreement Establishing the WTO could not be more economical in its reference to the DG. Article IV entitled "Structure of the WTO" does not mention the existence of either the Secretariat or the DG. Article VI states that the Ministerial Conference is to appoint a DG and stipulate their term of office. The DG is to appoint members of the staff of the Secretariat and "determine their duties and conditions of service in accordance with regulations adopted by the Ministerial Conference." The agreement then provides for something that in fact did not happen: "The Ministerial Conference shall ... adopt regulations setting out the powers [and] duties of the Director-General." The role of the DG was left without a definition beyond being in effect a chief of staff, with some limited, largely administrative, delegations found in the WTO Agreements.[26] None of these specify a policy role.

[25] "Institutions and Procedure." World Trade Organization. www.wto.org/english/res_e/booksp_e/gatt_ai_e/intitu_proced_e.pdf. Page 1115.

[26] Several provisions of the WTO Agreement refer to the role of the WTO DG in specific contexts, namely:

Article VII:1 of the WTO Agreement in the context of the WTO budget.

Compare this lack of specific role and authority with the Articles of Agreement of the International Monetary Fund. The provision on the structure of the Fund formally includes the Managing Director (MD). That may seem a minor drafting choice, but what follows is not: "the Executive Board [which] shall be responsible for conducting the business of the Fund . . . shall consist of twenty Executive Directors elected by the members, *with the Managing Director as chairman*" (emphasis added).

The MD, as chairman of the Board, sets the agenda for Board meetings and makes proposals. The MD is given a vote if the Executive Directors (EDs) are equally divided on an issue, and explicitly in the Articles of Agreement is given the right to participate in meetings of the Board of Governors. More than being the chief of the operating staff of the Fund, the MD is to "conduct, under the direction of the Executive Board, the ordinary business of the Fund."

Not surprisingly, since both institutions emerged from the Bretton Woods Conference, the President of the World Bank has the same role for the Bank as the MD has for the Fund: "The Executive Directors shall be responsible for the conduct of the general operations of the Bank" and the "President shall be chair of the Executive Directors," casting any tie-breaking vote if one is needed.

The fact that the MD and Bank President each wears two hats constitutes an important difference from the situation of the WTO DG. The Bank President and Fund MD are both chair of the institution's Executive Board and head of the staff. It is the combination of the two roles that makes the position so powerful. Since the staff are responsible for the analytical work that provides the basis for all recommendations to the Board, the chair effectively controls the substance of these recommendations. The chair of the Board both controls the agenda of the Board and guides the meetings, increasing the probability that the recommendations will be adopted.

To some extent, there is a role reversal. The Fund and Bank Executive Boards go about their business under the direction of their chairs, the MD for

Articles X:7, XIV:3–4, and XV:1 of the WTO Agreement, Article 20(1)–(2) of the Agreement on Customs Valuation, Articles 9.1.3, 9.6.1 and 9.10.1 of the Agreement on Trade in Civil Aircraft, and Articles XXII:2, 12 and 17 of the Amended Agreement on Government Procurement on the Director-General's role as WTO depositary.

Article 18.3 of the Agreement on Trade Facilitation in the context of the appointment of an "Expert Group."

Article 8.7 of the DSU on the DG's role in composing WTO dispute panels.

Footnote 12 to Article 21.3(c) of the DSU on the DG's role in appointing arbitrators on the reasonable period of time to comply in WTO disputes.

Article 22.6 of the DSU on the DG's role in appointing arbitrators to assess the level of suspension of concessions or other obligations in the context of WTO disputes.

the Fund and the President for the Bank, rather than the reverse. While ultimate decisions as a formal matter rest with the Board, the issues for decision must be put to the Board by the executive. The staff are to make expert judgments as to what sort of financial arrangements are needed, what projects are to be supported, and only then can a political and policy judgment be made by Board members. This is not to detract from the Executive Board's ultimate decision-making power. The Executive Board is not a rubber stamp by any means. Policy must be derived from or at least approved by the Executive Board. Nevertheless, a strong executive function has been created, entrusted to the MD and the President, respectively, placing each in a position to provide leadership for their organizations.

There is another institutional difference. The Executive Directors are appointed by country members, but they are paid by the Bank and the Fund.[27] In addition, their immunity can only be waived by the IMF. The EDs are expected to serve full-time in their positions, applying themselves to the business of the Fund or the Bank, at the call respectively of the MD and the President. The EDs are imbedded in the international institution. This institutional affinity exerts a force on these individuals even as they are responsible to the governments that they represent. One manifestation of their unique role is to be found in the voting process: all EDs are elected and most of them are elected by "constituencies" (i.e., of countries), who pool their voting power to elect a single ED. However, when the EDs cast a vote on the Board, they cannot split their vote. Each must cast their vote as a block – which further demonstrates the point that the ED is not the representative separately of each of the countries in the constituency. This arrangement dilutes the direct influence of individual constituent countries when they are represented in a group by a single ED, and further enhances the role of the Board chairs.

This is the polar opposite of the WTO, where the ambassadors of the members chair WTO committees and are responsible for their output. Each of these permanent representatives speaks only for the country for which they are accredited, except when serving as a chair, in which case they act in a neutral capacity. Decisions at the WTO are made by consensus, and members' representatives are more closely extensions of their governments. It may be just a nuance, but it is an important one. All individual members in the WTO possess at least theoretically a veto over everything and anything, from agenda setting to concluding an agreement. The Fund and Bank operate, in the final analysis, by weighted voting, whether or not votes are actually taken.

[27] "By-Laws of the International Monetary Fund Section 14. Terms of Service." International Monetary Fund. www.imf.org/external/pubs/ft/bl/bl14.htm. Sec. 14(e)(1).

A comparison of institutional arrangements would not be complete without noting the additional delegations to the WTO DG which can be found in the various WTO agreements. Some of these delegations are not in themselves unimportant, at least conceptually. Members can, if they wish, call upon the DG to provide "good offices" to help mediate a dispute.[28] There have been instances of members calling upon the DG to play this role (usually delegated to a Deputy DG), but due to the confidential nature of the proceedings, the frequency and importance are unknown. There is no evidence that this function has played a key part in settling disputes, qualitatively (how important were the disputes?) or quantitatively (how often has this facility been utilized?). Another potentially important specific delegation to the DG is to be found in the setting up of the Trade Policy Review Mechanism, calling on the DG to issue an annual report "setting out major activities of the WTO and highlighting significant policy issues affecting the trading system."[29] This is an opportunity for the DGs to emphasize the issues they consider to be of greater importance. How effective is this? Each of the heads of the international economic organizations is expected to issue an annual report. Do these reports shape the activities and preferences of their respective organizations or largely reflect current events and members' views? It is not clear that the annual reports are as important for the members as they are for the public to better understand these institutions. The remaining references to the DG are largely ministerial, appointing experts, panelists, being the depository of notifications, and the like. The institutional arrangements for the WTO do not suggest that the DG is to guide what the Organization is to accomplish. This is a fundamental difference from the Bank and the Fund.

Besides looking at specific delegations of authority and institutional arrangements stemming from an analysis of the documents setting up the three institutions, one can logically differentiate the roles of executives of the Fund and Bank versus those of the WTO's officials based on the functions of their organizations. A bank or monetary fund cannot operate without making daily decisions on conditions for extending credit to particular borrowers. These matters cannot be managed by a large group, by a committee of the whole that includes all the members. This suggests the need for a strong executive function. But what of the WTO's DG? Is the utility of having the

[28] Articles 5.6 and 24.2 of the Dispute Settlement Understanding (DSU) on the DG's good offices, conciliation, or mediation with a view to assisting members to settle disputes generally and disputes involving least-developed country members, respectively.

[29] Paragraph G of the Trade Policy Review Mechanism on the annual report to be prepared by the DG "setting out major activities of the WTO and highlighting significant policy issues affecting the trading system" in the context of the annual overview of developments in the international trading environment by the Trade Policy Review Body.

WTO simply to host independent dispute settlement and provide rooms in which negotiations can take place? This view would relegate the DG to being a personnel director for staff and a facilities manager for the WTO buildings, and nothing more. Is that all the world trading system needs? The question is answered by the fact that two major purposes of the WTO – negotiations and dispute settlement – have not been working well at all, and part of the cause may lie in the absence of a stronger executive. It is also answered by the choice of a new DG in 2021 whose selling point was high visibility, reinforced by ministerial service in her country under the most trying of conditions,[30] and very good connections at the highest levels of member governments. In short, the members chose to enter an era of more vigorous leadership from their DG, although some might on occasion experience buyer's remorse.

Another institutional comparison is that the WTO was always going to be a forum in which difficult political decisions would have to be taken. Trade liberalization is often a tough political sell to domestic constituencies, and so is the adoption of new rules. A major purpose of the WTO is to restrain members' freedom of action to restrict trade, although you will generally not see this in any pamphlet on the Organization. The Fund and the Bank may have a similar effect on the countries to which they are extending financial support, but the Boards are dominated by the voting power of the lenders, the sources of finance. That is one more reason why, at the outset, there would be a desire for strong leadership at the Bank and the Fund to protect members' assets and for weaker leadership at the WTO – and the GATT before it – to protect members' freedom of action, known as their "policy space," to regulate and restrict trade (even if doing so would be to their net detriment as other members' trade restrictions are burdens on each exporting country's own commerce).

There is one more international economic organization that should be looked at for purposes of comparison.

The Organisation for Economic Co-operation and Development

The OECD has far fewer members (38 versus the 164 of the WTO). When it was founded in 1961, it had only 20 members.[31] It might have been practical to operate like the WTO, based on a committee of the whole, but its charter

[30] In her autobiography, Ngozi Okonjo-Iweala tells the story of her mother being kidnapped when Ngozi was Nigerian Minister of Commerce to intimidate her in the conduct of her official duties. The effort failed, and her mother was returned.

[31] The official OECD founders are Austria, Belgium, Canada, Denmark, France, (West) Germany, Greece, Iceland, Ireland, Italy, Luxembourg, the Netherlands, Norway, Portugal, Spain, Sweden, Switzerland, Turkey, United Kingdom, and the United States.

gives more of an institutional role to its Secretary-General. The Secretary-General (SG) is appointed by the OECD Council, but also serves as chair of the Council when it meets at sessions of permanent representatives, and it is specifically provided that the SG "may submit proposals to the Council or to any other body of the Organization."[32] Another difference is the effective operation of the OECD's committees (more on this later).

The OECD is in terms of its functions perhaps more comparable to the WTO than to the Bank and the Fund. A large part of its work is in the nature of international economic policy coordination and providing member governments and the public with relevant data. But it diverges in several important respects. Total staff numbers are larger (3,300 at the OECD versus 600–700 at the WTO Secretariat). The OECD staff has, members and staff say, a greater amount of discretion as to the economic research it believes is useful to conduct and for the issuance of reports, albeit within overall member guidance. The OECD staff may sometimes withdraw from an activity or study on a subject upon the objection of a member, but this is relatively rare. With much greater resources and freedom, and with the support of members, OECD studies are produced at a far greater rate than those of the WTO. The depth of expertise in particular areas causes national governments to shy away from directly challenging the OECD, which could prevent it from engaging in the range of analyses that it does. A larger staff, a greater budget (supplemented by individual member contributions to sponsor research on topics of specific interest to the donor, something strongly resisted by a few influential WTO members), and more freedom for the staff to choose what is to be addressed and how research is to be conducted – all make a difference in what can be delivered.

Another source of strength for the OECD, allowing it to be more proactive and directly relevant to current challenges, is the nature of its committees. The OECD Secretariat works closely with the over 300 committees and task forces. The Trade Committee attracts the participation of senior trade policy officials from capitals. Those in attendance are not generally reading instructions drafted by someone else because they have often chaired the process at home that develops the positions taken, and they often have the flexibility to amend their positions as deliberations occur. Given the smaller and more

The Organization for European Economic Cooperation (OEEC) was the forerunner of the OECD, formed in 1960 when Canada and the US joined.

32 "Convention on the Organization for Economic Co-operation and Development." OECD. www.oecd.org/general/conventionontheorganisationforeconomicco-operationanddevelopment.htm

homogeneous membership, there is more of an opportunity for key members to consult with each other and with staff before and during meetings to move the agenda forward. The members' primary interest is policy coordination and sponsoring research, not negotiation of new agreements, which makes the process more open and less guarded. As the conversation does not go to legal obligations, it can be less formal. While the objective may be forming a consensus, there is enough in the way of common interests to avoid the threat of vetoes or hostage-taking. The outcomes are reported to the Council, but since the committee members are experts in their fields, are senior, and are based in capitals, the Council is not usually an obstacle to reaching a unified member view, which can then be transmitted to ministers for ultimate approval as necessary. Select nonmembers are invited to nonconfidential discussions. Invited as observers are Argentina, Brazil, Chile, Hong Kong-China, Singapore, the European Free Trade Association, the IMF, and the WTO.

As with any organization, the fact that a problem engages the attention of the OECD does not mean that it is solved. I was a founder and first chair of the OECD Steel Committee in 1979. Steel had been a source of trade friction during that era, particularly involving trade among the European Commission, Japan, the United States, and the Nordic countries, all OECD members. Cartelization and subsidization leading to excess capacity, dumping, and import-related injury characterized the sector. The idea behind the committee was straightforward – that transparency with respect to production and trade would allow more sensible investment decisions to be taken by both governments and private producers. There was substantial restructuring and consolidation in the United States and Europe, but with China becoming the world's largest steel producer, trade frictions (antidumping cases, national security restrictions) have persisted through to the present times.

It is fair to ask why there are no industry-sector committees at the WTO. WTO discussions are held mostly on a broader basis when the problems that occur are manifested in trade. Talks on subsidies, for example, are not focused solely on steel trade. There are a few areas of focus by sector: they are nonindustrial products, and they are exceptions. One is the negotiations to curb fisheries subsidies. A second prospective negotiation is very different in motivation and provenance: it is for cotton, at the instance of four of the poorest cotton producers, the C-4 (Cotton Four – Benin, Burkina Faso, Chad, and Mali). Fisheries talks have produced partial results as of this writing.

The OECD is a place for launching agreements in a number of substantive areas fostering various aspects of international economic cooperation. These can include political commitments, but they are not enforceable. There is no

OECD dispute settlement facility. Examples of OECD work products: 1) the OECD provides a model tax treaty for allocation of income between host and parent country of cross-border corporate activity; 2) OECD members have agreed to nonbinding guidelines for transfer pricing for the allocation of profits derived from international transactions; and 3) major economies agreed under its auspices to impose a minimum corporate tax. Its members also agreed to guidelines against bid-rigging in government procurement.

As a parallel, the WTO could logically have provided a model for free trade agreements. It has not done so.

The International Trade Organization

One additional institutional comparison is useful, this one historical. Had the International Trade Organization (ITO) come into effect, under its Havana Charter, there would have been an Executive Board consisting of eighteen persons selected by the Conference of the whole membership. As with the WTO, the ITO Charter does not specify any duties for the ITO DG, leaving this to the Conference. It only provides that "the Director-General or his representative shall be entitled to participate, without the right to vote, in all meetings of any organ of the Organization." In short, the authority of the ITO DG came under the heading of "to be determined," much as is the case for the WTO DG.

The WTO Governing Structure

As noted, under the Marrakesh Agreement Establishing the WTO, all authority, except over staff, is vested in the General Council, a committee of the whole composed of 164 members, meeting as itself or for dispute settlement purposes as the Dispute Settlement Body, and in three other councils operating under the General Council's guidance. The three additional councils are the Council for Trade in Goods, the Council for Trade in Services, and the Council for TRIPS. The General Council also meets as the Trade Policy Review (TPR) Body. The Councils are assigned a central role. They are charged with overseeing the functioning of the WTO Agreements. These five committees of the whole operate by consensus.

Under the Marrakesh Agreement, the Ministerial Conference is to establish the powers and duties of the DG, but none have been specified. As the General Council has been delegated the powers of the Ministerial Conference, it could specify further functions of the DG if it wished to do so. It does request on occasion reports from the DG, but it does not delegate further powers to that office.

Overseeing the functioning of the WTO Agreements can be a broad mandate. The Councils could determine whether the agreements are accomplishing what was intended by the signatories, specify how they should be administered, and decide on whether they should be amended. The Marrakesh Agreement in setting up the Councils did not confer a negotiating mandate on them. That was done in, for example, two Uruguay Round Agreements – the Agreement on Agriculture (AOA) and the General Agreement on Trade in Services (GATS). The Committee on Agriculture in Special Session and the Committee on Services in Special Session are charged with fulfilling these ongoing negotiating mandates. Neither of these committees has produced new formal agreements (with the possible exception of the political commitment in Nairobi at the 2015 Ministerial Conference for developed country members to forgo agricultural export subsidies).[33] Several WTO committees meet in special sessions to address Doha Development Agenda (DDA) issues. Again, no agreements have emerged, and there is no consensus as to whether the DDA is alive at all.

At the WTO, there is one exception to the absence of the DG from a formal policy role. In setting up the DDA, the DG was made chair of the TNC, which is responsible to the General Council. The TNC meets back-to-back with General Council meetings on adjacent days, and the DG calls on chairs of the WTO's negotiating committees (for example, the Committee on Agriculture in Special Session, the TRIPS Council in Special Session) to report. To date, the areas where negotiations are most active, in the Joint Statement Initiatives (each of which is an open plurilateral discussion or negotiation), are ignored by the TNC, because they are not DDA activities. The only live negotiations clearly within the purview of the TNC are the fisheries subsidies talks. The JSI reports are presented to the General Council. Any Secretariat involvement in the JSIs is kept low-key as these plurilateral activities are not sanctioned by the membership as a whole.

The role of the WTO DG is often described as that of being an honest broker. Brokers require parties and counterparties. Being a broker in the absence of strong interest on the part of members motivated by a sense of purpose, intent on reaching positive conclusions, is a description of an empty assignment. It is not a recipe for action, unless and until there is momentum developing among the members to add to the WTO rulebook or to open markets.

[33] "Nairobi Package." World Trade Organization. www.wto.org/english/thewto_e/minist_e/mc10_e/nairobipackage_e.htm

Reciting the mantra that the WTO is a "member-driven" organization has become an excuse for not developing any executive functions, preventing the Secretariat from initiating proposals. This might be tolerable if there were universal interest in achieving a result, whatever the subject – food security, e-commerce, or domestic support for agricultural commodities, for example. The hope, if it exists, that the regular committees or those in special session will produce results with no leadership from an active DG would be misplaced optimism. The WTO must make greater use of the skilled and experienced Secretariat. This cannot substitute for members reaching agreements, but it could foster the process of getting to results.

ACTIVITIES OF THE WTO SECRETARIAT

The fact that the DG does not chair the Council is the most visible structural difference between the WTO and its sister international economic organizations.[34] This does not mean that the WTO Secretariat is not playing a vitally important role. Far from it; it is essential for the functioning of the Organization. The question is whether the role that it is currently assigned is sufficient.

At present, WTO Secretariat support is often unseen but critical for all council and committee work. Briefing notes and detailed papers on subjects requested by the committees provide the foundation of the WTO's work. These efforts are well-known to members and particularly committee chairs, and are appreciated. Where the WTO Secretariat is most visible independently is in monitoring and in preparing the DG's annual world trade report, illuminating to a significant degree what is taking place in the world of trade. The report serves as the basis for each TPR. The Secretariat is also active in disseminating information notes and in issuing the world trade barometer and other reports generated by the Economic Research and Statistics Division (ERSD) or requested by the operating committees of the WTO. During the pandemic, the Secretariat decided on its own initiative to issue numerous reports giving useful data to aid members in framing their own policies in response to the health crisis. The Secretariat is also very much engaged in training activities, particularly in the least developed countries, relating to

[34] One exception is that a DDG chairs the Consultative Forum on Cotton Development Assistance, which is another committee open to all who wish to participate. It is a bright spot in the WTO with the goodwill shown to the poorest cotton producers and, in concrete terms, it is beneficial to them. The DDG in charge of agricultural issues chairs this forum. I did so from 2017 to 2021, and Jean-Marie Paugam does so at present.

WTO rules and procedures, and in helping applicant countries work their way through the process of accession.

The DG and Deputy DGs attend meetings with other international organizations and fan out across the globe to build support for the multilateral trading system. The Secretariat otherwise seeks to be largely invisible. In every WTO committee, there is a dedicated committee secretary, who is a senior Secretariat member. The secretary sits next to chairs of committees at meetings and usually does not speak unless asked to address a particular matter. Since chairs come and go, as do most ambassadors accredited to the WTO, who usually serve a three- or four-year term, the institutional knowledge of the trading system is largely contained within the Secretariat. The deciduous nature of the body of permanent representatives is most obvious when, in every General Council meeting, the chair reads out the names of departing permanent representatives and the list of arriving ones. True, some permanent representatives are less impermanent, coming back to the WTO having served in a more junior capacity in missions to the WTO in prior times, or having had responsibility in their capitals for relations with the WTO.

There is a lot of talent in the ambassadorial corps, but without negotiations in progress that demand the attention of capitals, the work is largely in the hands of transients, with continuity provided by largely invisible Secretariat members. The conclusion to be drawn is not that the system cannot work as it is. It is that it could work better if a more proactive role was assumed by the Secretariat.

There is another invisible role that is essential to the workings of the Organization, which is both a strength and a weakness of the functioning of an important part of the trading system administered by the WTO. The Secretariat provides essential support to dispute settlement panels and, when it existed, to the Appellate Body. AB members were to be commuters, not devoted full-time to this assignment, and panel members were selected by the individual litigation. In contrast, Secretariat turnover was limited. Over time, the Secretariat and particularly the AB's Division Director became very influential, having a deep institutional history and expertise. To critics of the dispute settlement system, this was not a positive development.

WHAT IMPROVEMENTS COULD BE MADE?

Secretariat Culture

Starting with basics: the DG must be the chief motivator of staff members, defining their mission and individual roles. This is the essence of leadership.

The Secretariat must be imbued with an *esprit* that is the result of a conscious attempt at an inculcation of common values. Successful national governments have a mandarin class of civil servants, loyal to their political masters, but having the expertise in both substance and process to drive agendas forward. This takes training as well as attitude, and the two are related. There is no specific common training to be a division director at the WTO. This should be remedied. The French civil service has created a cadre of professionals (such as the Inspection Générale des Finances, from whose ranks were drawn one President of France and four French prime ministers[35]) well-equipped to meet the extraordinary challenges that seem to only grow greater and more daunting with time. Most countries pay attention to the career development of their civil services in an organized way. Attention to structured career development for the Secretariat would be of substantial value and appreciated, especially if paired with improved opportunities for promotion. In addition, directors should rotate through management positions, to the extent possible, to have varied sets of experiences. Their purpose is to create a vibrant organization, not spend a career in an administrative fiefdom.

There is a justifiable expectation among members that the Secretariat is to be neutral with respect to substantive positions taken by individual members. A DG can choose to be active, to put a spotlight on the need for trade finance during the financial crisis, to convene private sector and government experts to explore solutions to expediting vaccine distribution. The DG can insert a DDG into the process of finding a solution to impasses (e.g., with respect to the TRIPS waiver issue for MC12).

Where decisions are made by consensus, the members are equally unlikely to agree to circumscribe the role of the Secretariat as it might be defined by a strong leader as DG. This is not a recipe for unwise aggressive steps to be taken by any DG that would not have substantial member support. Going too far with a self-defined mandate could simply cause the Organization to become even more dug in, to remain at an impasse.

[35] "The French General Inspectorate of Finance." Public Financial Management Blog. January 17, 2017. https://blog-pfm.imf.org/en/pfmblog/2017/01/the-french-general-inspectorate-of-finance; An assistant secretary of the US Treasury (John Petty) in an earlier era wished to emulate this but was only partially successful. The Treasury attaché in Tokyo, Tim Geithner, was to become chairman of the Federal Reserve Bank of New York and then Treasury Secretary.

What is needed from a DG is forward-leaning leadership to be exercised with political acumen. Passivity would be deadly, especially given the diversity of interests of the members. They need to be moved forward to find common ground. The Secretariat must work with *ad hoc* coalitions of "willing members" to see what can be accomplished at the WTO. A DG should be an advocate for ensuring that the members fulfill their current obligations but should go beyond this to illuminate the path forward for new rules where they are needed, and for trade liberalization where it would be feasible.

There are too many instances of Secretariat members afraid of being accused of violating their responsibility to be free of bias if they take a position that happens to align with that of one or more members. The Secretariat should be neutral as to member positions from the point of view of not taking instruction from any member(s). It cannot both be effective and remain neutral as to whether there are results, whether in negotiation or dispute settlement. Again, political acumen needs to be applied to gauge the sustainable limits of independence.

Most human progress has been achieved by seeking to move past perceived and self-imposed limits. There is a benefit to failing to perceive that what one is attempting is not likely to succeed. The WTO, as beneficial as its existence is and has been, has been far less productive in many respects than it should have been or that the GATT was. The question is whether there is a role for the Secretariat to help change the current relatively flat trajectory of the WTO – already answered in part by MC12. Earth satellites that do not maintain sufficient velocity find themselves in a decaying orbit and end in extinction. This need not be the case for the WTO. I am not suggesting that members of the Secretariat and delegates to the WTO conduct themselves based on an eschatological philosophy,[36] but the reverse. They should see themselves as being posted at the WTO for a reason – the active good management and improvement of the trading system.

The Culture of the Members

A culture of timidity, of dwelling on inhibitions rather than possibilities, is self-defeating. One forward-leaning ambassador lectured his colleagues: "do not say to the public, to your own governments, that nothing is possible at the

[36] "The part of theology concerned with death, judgment, and the final destiny of the soul and of humankind . . . the science of last things." See *Oxford English Dictionary*.

WTO, because that is a self-fulfilling prophecy." The same is doubly true for trade ministers. Governments must send their representatives to Geneva with the instruction that their job is to reach agreements designed to improve the trading system. Their attitude must be that they are negotiators. The one mark of success for negotiators is to bridge differences and reach agreements.

The WTO's mantra that the institution is "member-driven" must be discarded. It is obvious that final decisions are to be taken by the WTO's members, sometimes collectively, and always individually. Repeating this empty slogan has become an excuse for inaction, not just for the Secretariat, but for those members that do not seek to make progress. It is true that the Secretariat will not be able to instill in unwilling members a thirst for greater international trade liberalization and expansion of the rules of the multilateral trading system. For there to be some assurance of a rebirth of the WTO, those who formulate trade policy in capitals must believe that the institution their governments labored to create and maintain is worth the investment of their efforts. Member governments need not only to pay lip service to the importance of the multilateral trading system when they are in G20 meetings but to demonstrate through positions and actions taken at the WTO that the system is vitally important to them and that its improvement is essential.

Committee chairs should be neutral as to member positions but not neutral as to whether negotiated outcomes are achieved. They cannot accomplish progress without strong Secretariat support, combined with their own untiring efforts.

While positive change needs to emanate from committee work, coordination of member efforts more broadly is needed as well. To manage agreements and improve them, smaller groups of members need to meet to develop positions. Working with a small group of key members was the path forward for the TRIPS vaccines compromise that allowed MC12 to come together. The greatest authority that the DG has, unwritten but nevertheless real, is convening power. This was demonstrated during the financial crisis, bringing international financial institutions and large commercial banks together. During the pandemic, the DG brought producers of vaccines and governments together. During the dramatic loss of food security due to Russia's invasion of Ukraine and making the Black Sea impassible, the DG convened experts, representatives of food-exporting and importing countries, and the World Food Program.

To move the system forward, the DG should meet with different configurations of members depending on the issue at hand. But there is also a need for management of the work of the Organization more generally. A standing group of about eighteen (not much larger), as once existed, should be reconstituted for oversight of the agreements and negotiations. For binding dispute settlement, the DSB should have a small steering group of members, with a DDG as co-chair to oversee the operation of the Dispute Settlement Understanding (DSU).

DGs have risen to the challenge to exercise leadership at crucial times in the history of the multilateral trading system. Some of those that stand out are Arthur Dunkel, who tabled a compromise draft that allowed the Uruguay Round to proceed toward a successful conclusion; Peter Sutherland, who is credited with helping to drive that Round across the finish line, without which there would have been no WTO; and Pascal Lamy, who instituted heightened monitoring of trade restrictions, which helped the world economy weather the financial crisis without that recession becoming a second global economic depression. The current example is Ngozi Okonjo-Iweala, who was instrumental in making MC12 a success, even if objectively even more should be accomplished to deal with the pandemic, food security, and other pressing matters.

Secretariat leadership must be given some space within which to operate. This will require a change in attitude on the part of members. Members must conclude that consensus can no longer mean that every member has a veto over everything, no matter how small, or even for large matters. Each member cannot consider that it controls the agenda if paralysis is to be avoided. As for large decisions, a member blocking a JSI from legitimacy within the WTO cannot be allowed where there is no direct harm to the nonparticipant. Opting out by nonparticipants is a better outcome for the institution than blocking progress that can be made by groups of the willing.

Budget

An important difference between the Bank and the Fund on the one hand and the WTO on the other is funding. The Bank and the Fund operate on earnings – what they make on extending credit, plus other fees and charges.[37] The World Intellectual Property Organization (WIPO) also exists on fees.[38]

[37] "Build Forward Better: IMF Annual Report 2021." International Monetary Fund. www.imf.org/external/pubs/ft/ar/2021/eng/downloads/imf-annual-report-2021.pdf See, for example, pages 54-56 of the 2021 IMF Annual Report. "International Bank for Reconstruction and Development: Management's Discussion & Analysis and Financial Statements." World Bank. June 30, 2021. https://thedocs.worldbank.org/en/doc/9e6e5c7c885899cba176dd6e1409cbeb-0040012021/original/IBRD-Financial-Statements-June-2021.pdf; The World Bank's "business model" is displayed on page 6 of its 2021 Financial Statements.

[38] Fee income annually is over US$1 billion.

The ability of an executive branch of an international organization to function is at least in part linked to its funding. Each must propose a budget and get it approved by the members, but the WTO budget is borne by members as the institution does not have an income stream of its own. The budget of the WTO has not increased for over ten years, and discretionary funding is very limited. Staff promotions are difficult to provide. Although activities can be rearranged, their overall level at the WTO is not going to increase, absent a necessary increase in funding. In recent years, the debate over the budget in the WTO Budget Committee has become a means for individual members to exercise greater control over the activities of the Secretariat, to do less rather than more, coupled with some members resisting permitting the WTO to accept additional donations from members to fund activities.

Expectations of the Members

A distinguishing factor between the WTO and its sister international economic organizations is the composition of their respective memberships and how they exercise control. The Fund and the Bank operate by voting, and votes are weighted by contribution. Thus, the influence of providers of financial resources outweighs by far the consumers of these resources at those institutions. The OECD has greater homogeneity of interests given that it was created to coordinate aid largely, if not almost entirely, provided by the United States for the reconstruction of Europe. It is, for the present, dominated by the major Western economies. Although it has voting provisions, it operates largely by consensus. In addition, its membership is more homogeneous in level of development than that of the other institutions. This may change, as on January 25, 2022, the OECD Council decided to take the first step in accession discussions with six candidate countries to OECD membership – Argentina, Brazil, Bulgaria, Croatia, Peru, and Romania.

The WTO operates by consensus. There are voting provisions (one vote per member, not weighted by its share of world trade), but no votes are ever taken. The members range from least developed, to developing, to industrialized. Interests are diverse: there are groups of small vulnerable economies, conflict-affected countries, land-locked countries, those which acceded after the WTO was created (thus not original members), major agricultural exporters, net food importers, members of free trade areas and customs unions, countries outside of many of these arrangements, those who very much like the status quo, and those who seek change. On many issues, there will be divided views. The salient common denominator is the apparent tacit agreement among all members that there will be no voting. Voting would imply that every member, each of which now has a veto, would lose more control than it would gain. An unfortunate derivative of the diversity of interests can be a desire to have a neutral DG, not only neutral as to positions of individual members, but neutral as to whether anything that the members have not agreed to should be attempted.

The lowest common denominator dominates. It consists of members on average making verbal pledges to the idea of multilateralism without pressing too hard for change in the status quo. This is not the position of all members, but it is the sum of all positions. A strong executive would have to overcome this inertial state.

ELEMENTS OF REFORM FOR CONSIDERATION

If there is to be a plan for a WTO 2.0 or WTO 2025, which is very much needed, a reexamination of the role of the DG and the Secretariat should be an important part of the conversation. The suggestions contained in the following are presented to help stimulate a debate about this important but underdeveloped institutional aspect of the WTO. It is time to have a third branch of global trade governance that goes beyond monitoring, alongside enhancing the monitoring function.

There are three broad categories to examine, after determining the institutional place of the DG:

- The DG's and the Secretariat's role in dispute settlement and trade agreement enforcement.
- The DG's and the Secretariat's role in trade negotiations.
- The DG's and the Secretariat's role in administering the trading system.

Possible elements of basic institutional reform could include:

- **The Ministerial Conference shall entrust the overall operation of the WTO to a newly constituted Consultative Group of Twenty-Four (CG24), working within the guidance of the General Council. The General Council is granted the full powers of the Ministerial Conference (MC) between sessions of the MC.**
- **Consultative Group of Twenty-Four (CG24)**: A standing group of about twenty-four members (and perhaps smaller), chaired by the DG, should be constituted for oversight of the operation of the agreements and negotiations.

- **The General Council shall be chaired by the DG.**
- **The DG shall be responsible for the day-to-day operations of the WTO, including strategic foresight and policy planning.**
  - These steps mirror the organization of the World Bank, the IMF, and the OECD.
- The DG should meet with different configurations of members depending on the subject at hand and appoint working groups of members chaired by DDGs as needed.
- The DG should be an advocate for assuring that the members fulfill their current obligations and should illuminate the path forward for new rules where they are needed and for trade liberalization where it would be feasible.
- The DG and the Secretariat should work with ad hoc coalitions of willing members to explore expanding the scope of the WTO.
- The **Director-General** is to be the chief motivator of the staff, defining their mission and individual roles.
- **Secretariat training**. A conscious attempt at an inculcation of common values is needed, with attention to training for staff to be promoted to the level of director. Attention is to be paid to structured career development for the Secretariat. Directors should rotate through management positions, to the extent possible, to gain varied sets of experiences.

The Secretariat's Role in Trade Agreement Enforcement (Including Dispute Settlement)

Binding dispute settlement, mandated by the DSU, cannot be restored absent change. Change can occur in a variety of ways. One path forward is to make changes to the structure of the AB and provide additional written instructions to that body. Another route is reexamining governance by creating balance within the institution. If there is no active legislative function, a body that serves to a degree as a check or balance to judicial power will have to be lodged somewhere else, in the DSB, in the Secretariat, or both. Judicial restraint can be achieved, for example, by enabling the DSB to have a functioning authoritative role on behalf of the members. The creation of an entirely new independent Office of Legal Counsel (OLC) within the Secretariat will, no doubt, be viewed as being extreme. But it is a possible approach, as outlined below. Absent change, the result is a return to kritarchy, or rule by judges, and that has proved to be unsustainable.

- **An independent OLC should be created within the Secretariat.**[39]
  - The OLC would advise the DG and Secretariat on any legal questions involving the interpretation of WTO Agreements.
  - The OLC would be responsible as an independent guardian of the trading system and would not otherwise take sides in any panel or AB process.
  - The OLC would be responsible for performing its assigned duties both to the DG and the General Council.
  - **Pre-litigation**
    - Upon request, skilled and experienced independent OLC staff would give informal, confidential, nonbinding analytical reports on the merits of a case upon request to prospective parties, helping to narrow issues for decision.
    - Upon request, as is currently provided in the DSU, the DG (or in the usual case a Deputy DG) would provide good offices to potential litigants to seek resolution of differences without resort to litigation.
  - **After a request for consultations is filed, good offices to be utilized**
    - Parties are required to utilize the good offices of the DG and Deputy DGs before a panel would be formed.
  - **Litigation**
    - The OLC would be expected to file amicus briefs on key points of legal interpretation, particularly with respect to negotiating history in order to discern the intention of the parties to the agreement. The OLC would identify areas where there appeared to be no coverage within a WTO Agreement to the practice which is subject to the dispute.
    - Neither the AB nor a panel would be bound by the opinion of the OLC.
    - If no appellate level is reconstituted and there is one-tier dispute settlement, with panel decisions becoming final, some of the lack of uniformity may be overcome if the operation of the panels generally is overseen by the appointment of an OLC reporting to the DSB. In rare cases of serious inconsistency, the OLC would be expected to file an amicus brief pointing out the departure from appropriate process or a wayward ruling.
    - The OLC would have no direct powers to adjudicate matters.

[39] There is an existing OLC, which serves to advise the DG on administrative matters. It gives no opinions on the operation of the substantive Agreements of the WTO and has no role in dispute settlement.

- **Independent investigation**
  - The OLC, on its own motion, or upon information received from one or more members, would investigate suspected serious deviations from the WTO rules on the part of any member that in its view would have significant systemic implications.
    - Where the OLC concludes that significant systematic implications existed, it would:
      - Publish its conclusions, identifying questionable conduct without itself initiating litigation.
      - After consultation with the chairs of the General Council, the DSB, and the Trade Policy Review Body, the OLC would be enabled to bring a case directly to the AB for necessary adjudication.[40]
- **Gaps in the rules**
  - The OLC would inform parties to a dispute and the panel if, in its view, the question cannot be decided under existing rules because the WTO members had not yet negotiated a solution. In that case, the OLC would report on any gap in the rules to the DSB, the General Council and WTO committees having subject matter jurisdiction over the issues being litigated.
- **Watch list**
  - The OLC would regularly publish a watch list of measures that appeared to be on their face unjustified, and had a past, current, or expected substantial negative effect on trade.
- **Relation to the DSB**
  - The OLC would review the decisions of panels and AB panels and advise the DSB through triennial reports whether the intention of the parties, as discerned from negotiating history, was being applied, and include any recommendations as to remedies with respect to deviations from the intent of the parties to the negotiation.
  - The chair of the DSB, supported by the OLC, would be responsible for the DSB becoming, to the extent possible, an effective body. The chair should be active in attempting to resolve conflicts wherever the chair deems that it would be productive to do so, prior to and during litigation. It is the responsibility of the DSB chair to bring political acumen to the goal of settling disputes.

[40] Jeffrey J. Schott and Euijin Jung. 2019. "The WTO's Existential Crisis: How to Salvage Its Ability to Settle Trade Disputes." Peterson Institute for International Economics. December. www.piie.com/publications/policy-briefs/wtos-existential-crisis-how-salvage-its-ability-settle-trade-disputes. Schott and Jung would have the AB, where it found that the rules did not cover, on its own motion choose to refer a matter to the committees having jurisdiction over the subject matter.

    - Where, for example, the result is almost fully for one party at the level of the first-instance panel, and for the other party at the appellate level, this may be a *prima facie* case for the chair to seek to resolve the matter by directly working with the two parties and to suggest to them (in consultation with the OLC) that one or the other of the panels be reconvened to reconsider some elements of the case.
  - Operating procedures shall be adopted by the AB, in consultation with the OLC, covering imposition of strict page limits for written submissions, guidelines for briefs, focused hearings, and questions to the parties, subject to approval by the DSB by positive consensus or, if no consensus, by the DSB chair and the OLC.
  - The OLC is to advise the DSB with respect to the selection of AB members to assure that, to the extent possible, AB panel members should have relevant experience and expertise. The background of candidates should be proportional to the kinds of cases being brought. As many cases are about trade remedies, there should be added to the roster a sufficient number of persons with expertise, and preferably hands-on national administrative experience, to sit on cases having to do with antidumping, subsidization, countervailing duties, safeguards, and balance of payments measures. If there were cases in other specialized areas, the same care should be taken to qualify appointees.[41]
- **A Deputy DG would co-chair the steering committee of the DSB with the DSB chair to oversee the operation of the Dispute Settlement Understanding.**

[41] Jennifer Hillman. 2018. "Three Approaches to Fixing the World Trade Organization, the Good, the Bad and the Ugly?" Institute of International Economic Law. December 10. www.law.georgetown.edu/wp-content/uploads/2018/12/Hillman-Good-Bad-Ugly-Fix-to-WTO-AB.pdf. Jennifer Hillman – Professor at Georgetown University Law Center, Fellow at the Council on Foreign Relations, and a former AB member – has an alternative that should be considered: "One option would be to create a special Appellate Body to hear only appeals of trade remedy decisions. This special appellate institution – call it the Rules Appellate Body – could be made up of members chosen in large part because of a strong background in trade remedy law." This to some extent echoes the US court system, which has specialized courts for consideration of appeals from trade remedy decisions of the US administrators of the applicable laws. Hillman suggests another approach to national trade remedy cases: have initial panel decisions final. She argues persuasively that these cases have already been looked at very carefully in domestic proceedings.

WTO Secretariat Actions to Support Negotiations

- The DG shall draft a proposed negotiating agenda based on consultations with the members. (This executive function is the norm at all levels of domestic governance in many countries. The executive proposes and the legislature is to deliberate and establish the rules.)
- The Secretariat shall compile reports for members on the subjects it believes would foster the mission and objectives of the WTO.
- The Secretariat shall provide to the members its estimates of subjects that may require changes in existing rules or warrant new rules, drawing upon current trends in world trade and issues anticipated, derived from foresight exercises, as well as drawing upon its annual World Trade Report and its new individual trade flow anomaly reports.
- The Secretariat shall review and report on matters covered in sub-multilateral agreements (and negotiations), regional and other preferential trade agreements, that may be useful in considering future coverage of multilateral agreements and go beyond the provisions of the WTO, such as covering additional services, environment, health, labor, etc., and which provide models for consideration for formulating multilateral rules.
- The Secretariat shall, on request, provide model provisions for sub-multilateral agreements, including regional trade agreements and free trade agreements.
- The DG would supply suggested negotiating outcomes based in large part on consultations with members and on the DG's own responsibility, whenever the DG decided it was productive to do so, or upon the request of members, at the discretion of the DG.
- The Secretariat shall supply the members annually with a list of issues where dispute settlement panels had probed what the DG assesses to be gaps in the current rules.
- The WTO Secretariat shall inform the members of the results of its strategic foresight exercise, indicating where the current rules may need to be modified or supplemented.
    - An example would be, having identified future pandemics as likely, the Secretariat would compile a list of steps to be taken to create a sufficient response to future epidemics. For instance, upon identification of a possible pandemic, the DG would form a cross-divisional Secretariat task force to specify possible responses, working closely with a ten-WTO Member Pandemic Response Group under the chairmanship of a facilitator chosen by the chair of the General Council for this purpose.
    - A similar approach would be taken with respect to climate change.

- *Providing Economic Analysis*

  - The **Office of the Chief Economist in the Economic Research and Statistics Division (ERSD)** is to have a wide-ranging mandate to fully understand trade flows, their sources and effects, including global value chains, to support the members in making their own policy decisions, as well as in support of negotiations at the WTO. (An example would be to review carbon pricing to assist in the process of assessing the efficacy and appropriateness of carbon border adjustment mechanisms [CBAMs]).
  - The Office shall assess the economic impact of measures identified by the Trade Intelligence Division. This would include trade-restricting and trade-facilitating measures, to the extent possible. Reports of the ERSD shall not include judgments as to the WTO-consistency of any trade measure, a role reserved for the OLC.
  - The ERSD shall assist developing countries to self-identify as such, based on objective criteria and capacity-building needs, as they do under the Trade Facilitation Agreement, in order to obtain sufficient technical assistance. Self-identification shall be taken into account in noncompliance proceedings. As with other Uruguay Round Agreements, new notification requirements can be phased in for the least developed countries as their economies improve. Every effort should be expended with the help of international financial institutions to assure that there is full technical support to achieve full compliance. Self-designation as a developing country shall not be considered in negotiations of new rules or trade liberalization.
  - The ERSD, in cooperation with the Bank, the Fund, and other international organizations, shall provide insights into the levels of development of members and acceding countries.

    Detection of anomalies in trade flows. Anomalies in trading patterns can indicate the presence of unannounced, unofficial trade measures, whether with respect to exports, imports, or sales in the home market or otherwise, or private conduct in restraint of trade.

    Forensic analysis of significant trade distortions shall be undertaken upon the request of members or on the Office's own motion.

    A watch list shall be constructed jointly by the OLC and ERSD of anomalous trade behavior by product and by member.

- *Providing Strategic Foresight*

  Office of Strategic Foresight. A separate office reporting to the DG shall be responsible for strategic foresight.

The OECD defines "strategic foresight" as "a structured and systematic way of using ideas about the future to anticipate and better prepare for change. It is about exploring different plausible futures that could arise, and the opportunities and challenges they could present.[42] We then use those ideas to make better decisions and act now." The OECD has a unit engaged in this activity.

Given the likelihood of continuing major challenges to the global trading system, the Secretariat shall be required to engage in strategic foresight, reporting its conclusions independently, not subject to advance member review or censorship. Obvious subjects include CBAMs, responses to future pandemics and the effects of climate change on agricultural trade.

- ***Policy Planning***

*An **office of policy planning** shall be created reporting directly to the DG.*

The US experience is informative. "Created in 1947 by George Kennan at the request of Secretary of State George C. Marshall, the Policy Planning Staff (S/P) serves as a source of independent policy analysis and advice for the Secretary of State." Drawing on this model:

The WTO DG and members require this sort of support to take a longer-term, strategic view of global trends and frame recommendations to advance the interests and values inherent in the multilateral trading system, to stimulate deliberation and, when necessary, devise basic policies crucial to the conduct of amicable and positive global trade policies, and to develop long-term, strategic plans. This would be accomplished through analysis and coordination across all of the WTO Secretariat's divisions and committee support functions to integrate policy in line with longer-term objectives.

The Office would work closely and regularly with a select network of experts in local missions and capitals to fulfill these goals, stimulating innovation and creativity in the Secretariat and bringing constructive, dissenting, or alternative views on substantive trade policy issues to the DG and senior Secretariat officials.

- ***Create an Independent Evaluation Office modeled on the IEO of the IMF.***
- ***The Secretariat's Role in Administering the Trading System Providing Trade Intelligence***

[42] "What is Strategic Foresight?" Organization for Economic Co-operation and Development. www.oecd.org/strategic-foresight/

ENHANCING GLOBAL TRADE INTELLIGENCE

Calls for WTO reform highlight improved trade monitoring without specifying what should be accomplished. The most common forms of transparency stem from the filing of notifications, specific trade concerns, and increasingly counter-notifications. More is needed, and with advances in technology more is possible, to put governments in a much better place to make decisions to deal with food security, climate change, and others' industrial policies.

The need for current intelligence about trade has been of importance to international commerce ever since trade began. For millennia trade flows have been monitored with keen interest, watching for the arrivals of caravans, ships, and more recently air cargo. This was brought home to everyone in sharp relief by the pandemic, when supply chains became a focus for obtaining needed supplies. Where goods are produced and where they need to be consumed are never far from current headlines, whether for critical minerals for car batteries or semiconductors for advanced applications.

Intelligence about sources and flows of trade played an essential role in winning the Second World War. When the war concluded, the allies set about establishing a world trading system. One of the key elements of the new order was transparency. Most of what was needed was relatively basic, requiring the contracting parties to the new General Agreement on Tariffs and Trade (GATT) to publish government measures affecting trade. The requirement was clear and the obligation unambiguous:

> *No measure of general application taken by any contracting party effecting an advance in a rate of duty or other charge on imports under an established and uniform practice, or imposing a new or more burdensome requirement, restriction or prohibition on imports, or on the transfer of payments therefor, shall be enforced before such measure has been officially published.*[43]

The requirement applied in a simpler world. At the end of the Second World War, much of the world's productive industrial capacity outside the United States was in smoldering ruins or, in the non-industrialized world, it was still grossly underdeveloped from colonial times. Considering a framework for international trade was in many respects a straightforward matter. At Placentia Bay in the summer of 1941, Franklin D. Roosevelt and Winston Churchill set the goal – equal access to markets and equal access to raw materials. There was so much

[43] "The General Agreement on Tariffs and Trade (GATT 1947) – Article X: Publication and Administration of Trade Regulations." World Trade Organization. www.wto.org/english/docs_e/legal_e/gatt47_01_e.htm#articleX

overt protection, discrimination, and trade-distorting conduct that the priority targets for application of the rules of the new multilateral trading system were relatively clear. Trade negotiators knew that they had to progressively eliminate quantitative restrictions and tariffs, and eliminate discrimination against imports at the border imposed through national regulations or implemented through state trading. The spillover effects of more nuanced, more deeply imbedded national policies were of secondary concern.

Globalization rebounded after the war. This was not obvious at first, as global exports grew by only 50 percent (by value in constant dollars) by 1950 from a depressed level.[44] But by 2014, the gain was close to 5,000 percent. The term "global value chains" was not yet in vogue in the mid-20th century, but the interdependence of economies was in a number of instances obvious. In the 1930s, Japan knew it was dependent on oil imports, which the United States through trade restrictions sought to use as leverage to slow Japan's imperial expansion. The allies in the Second World War were very much aware of being cut off from natural rubber when Malaya was invaded by Japan. The two oil embargoes of the 1970s made energy dependency a key topic for American policy makers and caused a quick review of vulnerabilities to loss of access to other commodities. In more recent years, export restrictions placed on rare earths caused a reexamination of sources of supply and measures that interfered with them. In each of these cases, government intervention was so obvious that any informed reader of the world press could see that it existed and the form that it had taken.

The COVID-19 pandemic presented a very different profile. Suddenly, demand for respirators, personal protective equipment, and pharmaceuticals, and even antiseptics shot up. Where were these products made, and in what quantities? Was the trade free or impeded? It was physically impossible in the short term for all countries to be self-sufficient in all essential products. In the medium term, there could be some diversification of foreign supplies. Trade would still have to play a vital role. When the first vaccines were produced, concerns over access multiplied. Once sources of production were identified, would their output be allowed to leave their home countries, and could the products cross borders? It was more difficult to assess exactly what government measures existed.

Government planning, if it were to have a chance at being well constructed, needed information. Appropriate trade policies, among other policy decisions, could not be formulated without more knowledge about government interventions, about national measures that affected trade.

[44] Esteban Ortiz-Ospina and Diana Beltekian. 2014. "Trade and Globalization." Our World in Data. www.ourworldindata.org/trade-and-globalization

In recent times, international institutions – the OECD, the World Bank, the IMF, and the WTO – as well as the Global Trade Alert,[45] provide data concerning measures affecting trade and investment. All the world's contractually bound tariffs can be found on the WTO's website, along with regular reports to the G20 on government measures, both trade-restricting and trade-facilitating. Much less is known about other measures, such as government subsidies. Some measures are ambiguous in their intent. Is a product standard more trade-restrictive than is necessary for its legitimate purpose?

Government policies that affect trade are also often opaque. The US government concluded that semiconductor sales by non-Japanese companies in the 1970s and 1980s into the Japanese market were depressed by relationships among vertically integrated Japanese electronics manufacturers, an oligopsony. It took about five years of research to document what the causes were of the market not functioning. With respect to steel, the US industry documented cartelization among Japanese and European steel companies during that era (as American steel had been cartelized a century earlier). In these two instances, the problem was not government intervention, but the lack of it, as competition laws were not enforced.

In the first decade of this century, American, European, and Indian wind turbine sales in China dropped precipitously due to nonpublic purchasing practices of state-owned provincial utilities. No overt trade measures would explain the disappearance of the market for foreign producers. In modern times, it has become more difficult to identify the hand of government distorting trade. It is imperative to track and understand anomalies that occur in trade flows. Sellers know when their sales have dried up but may not always know why.

It is also true that sometimes measures are openly acknowledged that dramatically restrict trade but are attributed to otherwise generally acceptable policy objectives. Graduated Japanese taxes based on automobile engine size, imposed ostensibly as environmental regulations, had a heavier impact on American than domestic cars. More recently, WTO members increasingly claim instances of economic coercion imposed under the guise of standards or other regulatory requirements. In 2013, Russia cut off imports of wine, fruit, and vegetables from Moldova, reportedly because Moldova was seeking association with the European Union - not the public reason given.[46]

[45] "Global Trade Alert." Global Trade Alert. www.globaltradealert.org/. This is the publication from the University of St. Gallen, Switzerland, collecting and publishing trade data under the skilled eye of Professor Simon Evenett.

[46] "Rogozin Threatens Moldova with Sanctions over Association Agreement with the European Union." Refworld. September 4, 2013. www.refworld.org/docid/523058ab4.html

Trade sanctions have a long and varied history. It is relatively easy to catalogue sanctions that are published as such with a political justification. Sanctions against Russia for invading Ukraine are summarized on the Peterson Institute for International Economics (PIIE) website as well as by the Global Trade Alert (GTA).[47] The PIIE sanctions timeline has up-to-date information listing the country that is the target (Russia), the reason for the measure (the invasion of Ukraine), the country imposing the measure (G7 countries and a number of others), and a description of its coverage.[48] The GTA has its own sanctions tracker containing information on Russia sanctions (978 against Russia and 13 countermeasures by Russia at this writing),[49] as well as a state intervention monitor that lists sequentially nearly 4,000 measures in a searchable database dating back to 2007, with the most recent entries mostly concerning the growing list of sanctions against Russia.

More insidious and more difficult to collect and categorize are instances where the measure is not officially published, or where it is masquerading as something else. The European Union has asked for consultations with China over threats reportedly made against German firms doing business with Lithuania and for Lithuanian exports more directly.[50] This was not the first instance of reported trade coercion raised with respect to China, often less formally and not necessarily in the WTO. Claims of economic coercion were made with respect to Chinese actions affecting imports of Norwegian salmon, rare earth exports to Japan, imports from Australia of coal, barley, beef, copper, cotton, sugar, timber, wine, lobsters, wheat, wool, and beer, and Canadian canola.[51] South Korea claimed that China had retaliated against its trade due to its deployment of the Terminal High Altitude Area Defense (THAAD) missile defense system.[52] The Philippines complained about retaliation on bananas and other products by China during their dispute over Scarborough

[47] "Latest State Acts." Global Trade Alert. www.globaltradealert.org/latest/state-acts

[48] "Russia's War on Ukraine: A Sanctions Timeline." Peterson Institute of International Economics. April 12, 2022. www.piie.com/blogs/realtime-economic-issues-watch/russias-war-ukraine-sanctions-timeline

[49] "Latest State Acts." Global Trade Alert. www.globaltradealert.org/latest/state-acts/affected-jurisdictions_173/announcement-from_20220222

[50] "Lithuania Tests the EU's Resolve on Chinese Economic Coercion." *Financial Times*. February 12, 2022. www.ft.com/content/77adb343-6196-4d66-af84-995c05db7b6c

[51] Bonnie S. Glaser. 2021. "Time for Collective Pushback against China's Economic Coercion." Center for Strategic and International Studies. January 13. www.csis.org/analysis/time-collective-pushback-against-chinas-economic-coercion

[52] "Chinese Economic Coercion during the THAAD Dispute." The Asan Forum. December 28, 2019. www.theasanforum.org/chinese-economic-coercion-during-the-thaad-dispute/

Shoal in 2012.[53] Countries hosting visits by the Dalai Lama reportedly experience a temporary reduction in exports to China.[54] Retaliatory measures labeled as antidumping cases are cited by my PIIE colleague Chad P. Bown in a January 2022 PIIE paper.[55] Trade coercion as a serious threat to the global trading system is the subject of an Asia Foundation Report released in December 2021.[56] Three recommendations contained in the report are directly relevant to the WTO: share information, bring the issue up in relevant WTO committees, and bring WTO dispute settlement cases. (The last poses difficulties where the motive is what is suspect.)

The GTA has collected a database of over 43,000 "commerce-relevant" policy interventions. The GTA estimates that the WTO has over 10,000 entries and the United Nations has 40,000.[57] These databases have differing criteria for their collection activities with respect to the measures that they track.[58] None of the databases claim that they are all-encompassing. The GTA issued a recent study on the massive and growing presence of subsidies, not all of them necessarily to be condemned as they may serve valid social purposes.[59] It also released a background paper prepared for the World Bank that compares the findings of different monitoring initiatives on trade policy changes affecting medical goods.[60]

These sources form one basis on which to inform the process of trade policy formulation. The aggregation of data can point to where further efforts are needed to obtain information, as well as indicating where reforms may be needed to extend the coverage of global trading rules. That said, nothing short of taking a "core sample," examining in a specific national market how imports fare in competition

53 "PH Slams China for Retaliation Threat." Inquirer.Net. June 29, 2013. https://globalnation.inquirer.net/79041/ph-slams-china-for-counterstrike-threat

54 Andreas Fuchs and Nils-Hendrik Klann. 2013. "Paying a Visit: The Dalai Lama Effect on International Trade." *Journal of International Economics* 91(1): 164–177.

55 Chad P. Bown. 2022. "Trump Ended WTO Dispute Settlement: Trade Remedies Are Needed to Fix It." Peterson Institute for International Economics, Washington DC. www.piie.com/sites/default/files/documents/wp22-1.pdf

56 "Responding to Trade Coercion: A Growing Threat to the Global Trading System." Perth US-Asia Centre. November 25, 2021. www.perthusasia.edu.au/our-work/responding-to-trade-coercion-a-growing-threat-to

57 The Global Trade Alert (GTA) was launched in June 2009 when it was feared that the global financial crisis would lead governments to adopt widespread 1930s-style beggar-thy-neighbor policies. The International Monetary Fund noted in 2016 that the GTA "has the most comprehensive coverage of all types of trade-discriminatory and trade liberalizing measures."

58 "Subsidies and Market Access: Towards an Inventory of Subsidies by China, The EU & The USA: The 28th Global Trade Alert Report." Global Trade Alert. www.globaltradealert.org/reports/gta-28-report

59 Ibid.

60 "Form, Frequency, Duration & Scale: COVID-Era Trade Policy Interventions Affecting Medical Goods." Global Trade Alert. March 23, 2022. www.globaltradealert.org/reports/88

with domestic products, can reveal fully why sales do or do not take place. Deep forensic research is necessary to determine whether competitive outcomes are being determined by market forces, undistorted by government interventions.

TRADE INTELLIGENCE AND WTO REFORM

In each of the last four years, the G20 leaders have committed themselves to WTO reform – to improve the functioning of the Organization. An essential function of the multilateral trading system from its inception has been to provide transparency.[61] International trade thrives on certainty. Without transparency, all that exists is uncertainty. Not knowing a standard or tariff or other regulation that might prevent a good or service from crossing a border would make every export or import a gamble with unknown odds.

Six years before the creation of the WTO itself, the parties negotiating in the Uruguay Round put into place a Trade Policy Review Mechanism (TPRM). The reason, they said,

> *was to contribute to improved adherence by all Members to rules, disciplines and commitments made under the Multilateral Trade Agreements and, where applicable, the Plurilateral Trade Agreements, and hence to the smoother functioning of the multilateral trading system, by achieving greater transparency in, and understanding of, the trade policies and practices of Members.*[62]

Transparency is a first principle of the multilateral trading system. It is also, strikingly, as noted above, a precondition for taking any trade action of general application (GATT Article X.2). On paper, at least, this is a very powerful proviso. In the area of product standards, the WTO Agreement on Technical

[61] See "A Glossary of Terms." Congressional Research Service. "Glossary of Terms." World Trade Organization. www.wto.org/english/thewto_e/minist_e/min99_e/english/about_e/23glos_e.htm: "Transparency: [The] Degree to which trade policies and practices, and the process by which they are established, are open and predictable."

> *Transparency – A World Trade Organization principle stipulating that a country's policies and regulations affecting foreign trade should be clearly communicated to its trading partners. For example, out of recognition that sanitary and phytosanitary measures may (sometimes deliberately) be unclear, arbitrary, or capricious, recent international trading agreements have provisions calling on countries to notify others, in advance, about any measures that could affect trade, to fully explain them, and to provide a means for commenting on them. . . . State trading enterprises with monopoly control over marketing agricultural exports are sometimes alleged to cross subsidize, but lack of transparency in their operations makes it difficult if not impossible to determine if that is the case.*

[62] "Trade Policy Review Mechanism as Amended by the General Council (Revision, Effective as of 1 Jan. 2019)." World Trade Organization. www.wto.org/english/docs_e/legal_e/29-tprm_e.htm.

Barriers to Trade (TBT) has a similar approach. It requires that a member notify the WTO before putting a standards measure in place where either a relevant international standard does not exist, or the technical content of a proposed technical regulation is not in accordance with the technical content of relevant international standards:

> 2.9 . . . *if the technical regulation may have a significant effect on trade of other Members, Members shall:*
>
> 2.9.1 *publish a notice in a publication at an early appropriate stage, in such a manner as to enable interested parties in other Members to become acquainted with it, that they propose to introduce a particular technical regulation;*
>
> 2.9.2 *notify other Members through the Secretariat of the products to be covered by the proposed technical regulation, together with a brief indication of its objective and rationale. Such notifications shall take place at an early appropriate stage, when amendments can still be introduced and comments taken into account.*[63]

Although the net cast by these provisions is not perfect (it is a matter of self-judgment by a government as to whether its measure fits the criteria for notification), this is nevertheless an amazingly creative initiative to promote international cooperation, and it works. Members do notify a vast array of standards in draft, without compulsion, and they benefit from the fact that other members do so as well. How complete is the data thus gathered? It is impossible to tell. But for the filing of "specific trade concerns" by other WTO members, highlighting a measure that might not have been notified, there is no effort to identify what has not been notified.

Broad transparency is also required with respect to the regulation of services in accordance with the General Agreement on Trade in Services (GATS) and of intellectual property under the Agreement on Trade-Related Aspects of Intellectual Property Rights (TRIPS).[64] For services and intellectual property, the notification is to follow, and need not precede, the imposition of a measure.

[63] "Agreement on Technical Barriers to Trade." World Trade Organization. www.wto.org/english/docs_e/legal_e/17-tbt_e.htm

[64] Article III.3 of the General Agreement on Trade in Services provides: "Each Member shall promptly and at least annually inform the Council for Trade in Services of the introduction of any new, or any changes to existing, laws, regulations or administrative guidelines which significantly affect trade in services covered by its specific commitments under this Agreement." Article 63.1 of the Agreement on Trade-Related Aspects of Intellectual Property Rights provides:

> *Laws and regulations, and final judicial decisions and administrative rulings of general application, made effective by a Member pertaining to the subject matter of this Agreement (the availability, scope, acquisition, enforcement and prevention of the abuse*

This is just the topmost layer of the multitude of WTO provisions aimed at providing transparency. Seeded throughout the WTO Agreements are a multiplicity of notification requirements. There are so many that the WTO Secretariat has published a WTO notification handbook divided by twenty-two subject areas of the WTO *acquis* where notification requirements are to be found.[65] The extent of what must be reported is remarkable. For a new preferential trading arrangement, five general areas of information must be supplied, and under each heading there are subparagraphs of detailed data requests.[66]

TRADE INTELLIGENCE IS EVEN MORE IMPORTANT DURING A CRISIS

In the introduction to a book he edited for the World Bank entitled *The Great Recession and Import Protection: The Role of Temporary Trade Barriers*, Chad P. Bown, now at PIIE, traces some of the history of the collection of data on restrictive trade measures. The 2008 financial crisis sparked an immediate interest on the part of governments to understand whether the incidence of protection would be likely to cause the world economy to retreat from openness, sinking to a level resembling the Great Depression of the 1930s. Bown had created a data series, the Temporary Trade Barriers Database,[67] first

of intellectual property rights) shall be published, or where such publication is not practicable made publicly available, in a national language, in such a manner as to enable governments and right holders to become acquainted with them.

65 "Technical Cooperation Handbook on Notification Requirements." World Trade Organization. www.wto.org/english/tratop_e/handbook_on_notifications_complete_e.pdf

66 "Transparency Mechanism for Preferential Trade Arrangements WT/L/806." World Trade Organization. December 16, 2010. docs.wto.org/dol2fe/Pages/SS/directdoc.aspx?filename=Q:/WT/L/806.pdf&Open=True. For example, according to Annex I of the Initial Notification of PTAs by Notifying Members, where there is a new Preferential Trade Arrangement (PTA):

> 2. *The Member notifying a PTA shall submit the following data, at the tariff-line level:*
> *(a) A full listing of preferential duties under the PTA per beneficiary partner.*
> *(b) A full tariff listing of the notifying Member's MFN duty rates applied on the year of the PTA's implementation and on the year preceding it.*
> *(c) Other data, where applicable (e.g., tariff-rate quotas, seasonal restrictions, special safeguards and, if available, ad valorem equivalents for non-ad valorem duties).*
> *(d) Product-specific preferential rules of origin as defined in the PTA.*
> *(e) Import data for the most recent three years preceding the notification from each of the beneficiary partners, in value for total imports, imports entered under MFN and imports entered under PTA benefits.*

This listing just scratches the surface of what must be notified with respect to these agreements.

67 "Temporary Trade Barriers Database." World Bank. www.worldbank.org/en/data/interactive/2021/03/02/temporary-trade-barriers-database/

published in 2005 and still available from the World Bank. It provides historical data for purposes of comparison. Bernard Hoekman, then at the World Bank, secured emergency funding to update that data series and help fund the GTA at St. Gallen University.[68]

In reaction to the financial crisis in 2008, the WTO Secretariat went further than relying solely on the extensive notification requirements that populate the WTO Agreements. Under the leadership of Pascal Lamy, the Director-General at the time, the Secretariat engaged on its own in deeper monitoring of trade measures, based on which it initiated the filing of reports to the G20.[69] This practice has remained in place ever since that time,[70] as has the Global Trade Alert, which has collected a broad set of data on government measures that affect trade. In a study in 2009 Bown described how at that time the WTO illuminated trade restrictions but argued that more was needed for surveillance and ultimately for enforcement of the WTO Agreements and beyond to measures that distort trade but may not be WTO-inconsistent.[71] He noted that WTO members impose political limitations on monitoring efforts. The conclusion is as pertinent today: any public institution needs to guard against political pressures skewing data that is collected.[72]

[68] The GTA was also financed by the UK government, the Canadian government, and the German Marshall Fund of the United States.

[69] "DDG Wolff: I Am Optimistic About Improving Transparency at the WTO." World Trade Organization. October 1, 2020. www.wto.org/english/news_e/news20_e/ddgaw_01oct20_e.htm:

> *The regular monitoring reports covering the entire membership are the only horizontal regular transparency exercise within the multilateral trading system. Every six months, they provide a substantive snapshot of the state of world trade, with comprehensive accounts of activities cutting across the spectrum of issues addressed by WTO rules: tariffs, SPS, TBT and agriculture to trade remedies, services, intellectual property and a host of other areas. I am optimistic about improving transparency at* the WTO.

[70] "Review of Developments in the Trading System: Special Council Meeting on Notification, Consultation, Dispute Settlement and Surveillance–Note by the Secretariat C/W/420/Rev.1." General Agreement on Tariffs and Trade. October 20, 1983. https://docs.wto.org/gattdocs/q/GG/C/W420R1.PDF; "Protective Actions by Developed Countries against Imports from Developing Countries, Note by the Secretariat." GATT Digital Library 1947–1994. June 20, 1980. www.exhibits.stanford.edu/gatt/catalog/fn855rf9468. There were precedents: the GATT Secretariat on its own initiative conducted extensive documentation of trade policy interventions during the sharp global downturn of the early 1980s. The Secretariat reported by country and by measure, notified and unnotified. They are models of conciseness and independent reportage.

[71] Chad P. Bown. 2009. *Self-Enforcing Trade: Developing Countries and WTO Dispute Settlement.* Washington, DC: Brookings Institution Press. www.chadpbown.com/bown-set-2009/

[72] "World Bank Aims to Replace Canceled 'Doing Business' Report in Two Years." Reuters. November 10, 2021. www.reuters.com/business/world-bank-aims-replace-canceled-doing-business-report-two-years-2021-11-10/

The need for reliable information was urgent in the face of the COVID-19 pandemic. The WTO's first practical reaction to the health crisis was a call by then WTO Director-General Roberto Azevêdo for members to provide the Secretariat with information about their COVID-19 policies with trade implications.[73] The pandemic caused immediate shortages of personal protective equipment, pharmaceuticals, and hospital equipment. It became apparent that no country was self-sufficient for its current needs. Trade was essential to meeting the public health crisis. Vitally important global value chains were discovered to exist as governments moved to secure supplies for domestic consumption.

A task force of experts was set up from across the Secretariat "to monitor the impact of COVID-19 on trade flows and the overall global economy." The Secretariat issued information notes. The fear of scarcity of agricultural commodities (which caused hardship during the financial crisis) had given rise to some national export restrictions during the early stages of the pandemic. Due no doubt in part to the availability of current and accurate information about supplies and trade measures, through the Agricultural Market Information System (AMIS) and the WTO Secretariat reports,[74] many of the trade-restrictive agricultural measures were rolled back. An important part of the WTO's reporting also consisted of listing trade facilitation measures.

[73] "DG Azevêdo Requests WTO Members to Share Information on Trade Measures Related to COVID-19." World Trade Organization. March 25, 2020. www.wto.org/english/news_e/news20_e/dgra_24mar20_e.htm. This is the message of the Director-General nine days after the WTO headquarters building entered lockdown due to the pandemic.

[74] The Agricultural Market Information System (AMIS) is an interagency platform to enhance food market transparency and policy response for food security. It was launched in 2011 by the G20 Ministers of Agriculture following the global food price hikes in 2007–08 and 2010. Bringing together the principal trading countries of agricultural commodities, AMIS assesses global food supplies (focusing on wheat, maize, rice, and soybeans) and provides a platform to coordinate policy action in times of market uncertainty. AMIS is composed of G20 members plus Spain and seven additional major exporting and importing countries of agricultural commodities. By enhancing transparency and policy coordination in international food markets, AMIS has helped to prevent unexpected price hikes and strengthen global food security. The AMIS Secretariat is formed by the following international organizations and entities: FAO, GEOGLAM, IFPRI, IFAD, IGC, OECD, UNCTAD, the World Bank Group, WFP, and WTO. See also: "DDG Wolff Stresses Need to Make Progress in WTO Negotiations to Enhance Resilience of Farm Sector." World Trade Organization. January 22, 2021. www.wto.org/english/news_e/news21_e/ddgaw_22jan21_e.htm. In remarks to agricultural ministers gathered at the Global Forum for Food and Agriculture in Berlin on January 22, 2021, I stressed the importance of assuring transparency: "Agricultural markets have shown remarkable resilience, but markets work even better with good quality, timely information including with respect to policy measures adopted by governments around the globe. Initiatives such as the Agricultural Market Information System (AMIS) are crucial for well-informed policy responses."

Information regarding good practices – pledges to avoid export restrictions and the use of import-liberalizing measures – could and did lead to emulation in the form of trade facilitation measures. Aided by transparency, nations were working for the common good. This did not mean that there was no resistance. Initially the members did not wish the Secretariat to report on general support measures to the G20. There was still a gap between measures reported and measures in existence, but on the whole, while compliance with making notifications was still far from perfect during the pandemic, it was better than it had been.

Most recently, there is keen widespread interest, not confined to those engaged in trade but essential to them, in the incidence of trade sanctions against Russia due to its invasion of Ukraine. Understanding what is taking place is fostered by PIIE's and the Global Trade Alert's tracking mechanisms.[75,76]

DAY-TO-DAY, THE WORLD TRADING SYSTEM FUNCTIONS BEST WITH TRANSPARENCY

In the normal course, the extent to which members adhere to the WTO's transparency requirements varies by member and by subject. Even a member with substantial bureaucratic capacity and a desire to be compliant may still miss a deadline, or misfile its data. But the problem is deeper than inattention. At the meeting of the Committee on Subsidies and Countervailing Measures on April 27, 2021, the chair noted that: "despite reminders to members to submit their notifications in time, 80 members have still not submitted their 2019 notifications. In addition, 67 members still have not submitted their 2017 subsidy notifications, and 57 have still failed to submit their 2015 notifications." In reaction to this constant shortcoming, at the Ministerial Conference in Buenos Aires in December 2017, as one of three major complaints about the operation of the WTO, the United States Trade Representative declared:

> *[I]t is impossible to negotiate new rules when many of the current ones are not being followed. This is why the United States is leading a discussion on the need to correct the sad performance of many Members in notifications and*

75 "Russia's War on Ukraine: A Sanctions Timeline." Peterson Institute of International Economics. April 12, 2022. www.piie.com/blogs/realtime-economic-issues-watch/russias-war-ukraine-sanctions-timeline

76 "Latest State Acts." Global Trade Alert. www.globaltradealert.org/latest/state-acts/affected-jurisdictions_173/announcement-from_20220222

transparency. Some Members are intentionally circumventing these obligations, and addressing these lapses will remain a top US priority.[77]

On May 4, 2018, the United States submitted its first "counter-notification" to the WTO Committee on Agriculture. Although provided for in the Agreement on Subsidies and Countervailing Measures,[78] counter-notification is not a common practice outside of that agreement. In this case, the United States was reacting to its belief that India was not officially notifying data on its market price support for wheat and rice. Using publicly available information, the United States asserted that the measure would be of commercial concern to its trading partners.[79]

This was just the beginning of a trend toward pressing for more compliance. On March 29, 2019, a group of major exporting WTO members – Argentina, Australia, Canada, Costa Rica, the European Union, Japan, New Zealand, Chinese Taipei, and the United States – circulated a draft proposal to enforce the WTO's notification requirements.[80] The attention-grabbing element of the proposal was the inclusion of sanctions for a member failing to live up to its obligations. If a member failed to notify and did not request technical assistance for capacity-building after a deadline had elapsed, it would be subject to "administrative measures." These included being barred from chairmanships, its questions of other members in Trade Policy Reviews going unanswered, and being subject to financial penalties (the funds to be applied to technical assistance to obtain compliance). If these steps did not bring about compliance, a year later the non-notifying member would be shamed with a recitation of its noncompliance every time its representative sought to take the floor.

77 "Opening Plenary Statement of USTR Robert Lighthizer at the WTO Ministerial Conference." Office of the United States Trade Representative. December 11, 2017. www.ustr.gov/about-us/policy-offices/press-office/press-releases/2017/december/opening-plenary-statement-ustr

78 Article 25.10 of the Agreement on Subsidies and Countervailing Measures provides:

> *Any Member which considers that any measure of another Member having the effects of a subsidy has not been notified in accordance with the provisions of paragraph 1 of Article XVI of GATT 1994 and this Article may bring the matter to the attention of such other Member. If the alleged subsidy is not thereafter notified promptly, such Member may itself bring the alleged subsidy in question to the notice of the Committee.*

79 "United States Issues First-Ever WTO Counter Notification Against India's Market Price Support." Office of the United States Trade Representative. May 9, 2018. www.ustr.gov/about-us/policy-offices/press-office/press-releases/2018/may/united-states-issues-first-ever-wto

80 "Procedures to Enhance Transparency and Strengthen Notification Requirements Under WTO Agreements JOB/GC/204/Rev.1." World Trade Organization. April 1, 2019. docs.wto.org/dol2fe/Pages/SS/directdoc.aspx?filename=q:/Jobs/GC/204R1.pdf&Open=True

On July 10, 2019, the African Group, Cuba, and India responded to the US-led proposal. They held that due to resource constraints, no additional obligations with respect to transparency would be acceptable to developing countries, nor would they accept the introduction into the rules of any punitive measures. The group suggested exploring simplified notification formats, prolonging timeframes for responses, increasing technical assistance, and giving more flexibility to developing countries. They would also ban counter-notifications and admonished the Secretariat to maintain its "international character" by taking no position on these issues. The proposal went further, pointing out the need for developed countries to remedy deficiencies in their own notifications.[81]

There has been no resolution in the WTO to the opposing positions taken on the issue of more stringent requirements for notification compliance. Where notifications are made, a strength of the WTO monitoring process conducted by the Secretariat is that each measure reported by its committees is individually verified with the member administering a measure. Among the defects of this data-collection system is that the accumulation of information can be slow and incomplete, and the data are not regularly updated when a previously notified measure has been modified. WTO monitoring provides a very large amount of transparency, but the system does not capture everything. The Global Trade Alert produced by St. Gallen University under the watchful and entrepreneurial eye of Professor Simon Evenett collects far more information, using web-scrapers and engaging in cross-checking with official statements and press reports to increase reliability, although the reported measures are not verified with governments.[82] GTA data, being comprehensive, are broadly indicative of trade-distorting measures and their trends. The GTA also seeks to track behind-the-border measures, such as subsidies and domestic regulations, to a greater extent than WTO monitoring. In the pandemic recovery period, a major strength of the GTA was including broad measures of economic support, which the WTO could not do due to member

[81] "An Inclusive Approach to Transparency and Notification Requirements in the WTO." World Trade Organization. July 10, 2019." https://docs.wto.org/dol2fe/Pages/FE_Search/FE_S_S009-DP.aspx?language=E&CatalogueIdList=255238,255234,255240,255239,255258,255263,255243,255221,255224,255228&CurrentCatalogueIdIndex=5&FullTextHash=371857150&HasEnglishRecord=True&HasFrenchRecord=False&HasSpa

[82] According to a discussion with Simon Evenett, founder of the GTA, on February 12, 2022: "The GTA database currently has over 43,000 entries (each relating to a policy intervention). We checked and 97.8% of those entries are supported by either (a) an official document or (b) a legal document issued by a firm that is mandated to report subsidies."

opposition.[83] For a forensic analysis comparing CTA and WTO reporting on pandemic-era trade policy responses, see the charts developed by Bernard Hoekman in a book of recommendations to a new WTO Director-General published on November 10, 2020.[84]

PEER REVIEW: PEOPLE WHO LIVE IN GLASS HOUSES ARE RELUCTANT TO THROW STONES

Peer review is considered the single most prominent tool for obtaining transparency. There are now over three decades of history of the WTO's Trade Policy Reviews. The intention of the process is not to pass judgment on a member's degree of conformity with its WTO obligations, as it is generally felt that this would promote reticence rather than openness to examination. The proceedings are conducted with diplomatic courtesy. One participant told me that "the lions in the arena do not bite because their turn will come to play the part of the martyred" – that is, their turns will come to be the subject of a TPR with its attendant scrutiny. While much is made transparent in a TPR, sometimes the information is diplomatically veiled. For example, to extract from the opening paragraph of the 2018 TPR of the United States what was actually happening, one would have to be very knowledgeable about the highlights of US trade policy at that time. It reads: "Since the last Review in 2016, the focus of US trade policy has shifted to adopting policies that are intended to support its national security and strengthen its economy." It is not until paragraph 20 that the US–China exchanges of high additional tariffs on hundreds of millions of dollars in trade are mentioned.[85] The chair's summation states that "Members were of the view that the trade and investment regime of the United States remained overall open and liberal." Perhaps so, but there were US trade measures that dominated the discussion if not the summation.

In the 2021 TPR of China, while the chair's summary praised China's participation in the WTO, it cited a substantial list of member concerns that

[83] "Report on G-20 Trade Measures (Mid-May 2014 to Mid-October 2014)." World Trade Organization. November 5, 2014. www.wto.org/english/news_e/news14_e/g20_wto_report_oct14_e.pdf

[84] Simon Evenett and Richard Baldwin, eds. 2020. *Revitalising Multilateralism: Pragmatic Ideas for the New WTO Director-General*. London: Centre for Economic Policy Research Press. https://cepr.org/voxeu/columns/revitalising-multilateralism-new-ebook. Page 67.

[85] "Trade Policy Review – Report by the Secretariat: United States WT/TPR/S/382/Rev.1." World Trade Organization. March 27, 2019. docs.wto.org/dol2fe/Pages/SS/directdoc.aspx?filename=q:/WT/TPR/S382R1.pdf&Open=True

were more pointed. Listed were lack of transparency, an opaque subsidy regime, lack of timely notifications, support to state-owned enterprises, sanitary and phytosanitary (SPS) restrictions without scientific justification, non-transparent and discriminatory measures and practices sometimes in response to political disagreements, insufficient protection of intellectual property rights, steel overcapacity, and the use of forced labor.[86]

A valid question is whether the exercise accomplishes as much as it theoretically could. There is no official evaluation of the Trade Policy Review Mechanism's effectiveness. The observation of those who are familiar with the process over time is that there is more likely to be an impact on smaller WTO member countries, which may not have been aware of the common view on the part of WTO members of the shortcomings of some of their governments' measures, than on the largest trading members, which appear more impervious to criticism.

Members should be more enthusiastic about full transparency as it applies to themselves, not just to others. Some members are very good about this. They do not shy away from looking in the mirror. Others, well, not so much. And in this regard, there is not a developed/developing country divide. Publicizing TPR criticisms in the domestic press of the country subject to the TPR would be controversial but might bring about changes in wayward conduct.

IMPROVING GLOBAL TRADE INTELLIGENCE GATHERING

Years ago, I said to my friend, then GATT Director-General Arthur Dunkel, that he should subscribe to the *Financial Times* and then he would know what was going on in the world. He replied, "I do subscribe, but the Members will not let me read it." There is still substantial room for improvement in achieving greater transparency throughout the mechanisms that the WTO employs.

When I was growing up, my father made his living by understanding what was being produced in one place that might find demand in another – the essence of trade. Our vacations were largely spent in plant tours, seeing how things were made, and on his sales trips. One newspaper that was always present in our home was the *Journal of Commerce*. Two-thirds of the front page was taken up by ship arrivals, listing the kinds and quantities of their cargoes. In the rest of the paper, which I would later come to rely on when

[86] "US Statement at the Trade Policy Review of the People's Republic of China." US Mission to International Organizations in Geneva. July 11, 2018. https://geneva.usmission.gov/2018/07/11/u-s-statement-at-the-trade-policy-review-of-the-peoples-republic-of-china/

I became a trade negotiator, was some of the best trade policy reporting of that era, at a time when every major publication had dedicated trade reporting.[87] My father had an insatiable curiosity about where things were made. A visit to a store would see him looking at "items" for their prospective value if they were produced or marketed differently. When he entered a warehouse – his was on the docks in East Boston – he would be interested in what was on hand. If talking to a truck driver he would ask what the truck was carrying, where it came from, and where it was going.

Fabrice Boudou, then Director of the WTO's Information Technology Services Division, who kept us connected to the web and made our work possible in this information technology age, shares the vision that I am suggesting here. He notes that many countries, including developing countries, make bills of lading publicly available, that a growing number of companies have developed the big data and artificial intelligence capability to create a precise view on a current basis of which goods are being shipped from which country to which country, which shipper to which shipper. Private firms can use this information to manage their supply chain risks. Government regulation is designed to assure privacy, and technology exists to keep certain data confidential on a disaggregated basis. His view is of members sharing data with the WTO, which would use its privileges and immunities (and technology) to guarantee that confidential information remains confidential and use its access to technical capability in AI and big data to respect this commitment. He concludes that this would be extremely valuable for members. I agree fully with that sentiment.

Data should be regarded as a public good. Not only should WTO members wish to share trade data for better managing their own economies and trade policies but also the system should tap into all potential sources for trade and production information, enabling a much better understanding of trade for the purpose of crafting and administering the rules of the multilateral trading system. The need is greater than having "transparency" in a traditional sense, a founding purpose of the WTO, and the GATT before it, which concentrated on knowing about trade measures. It is to know about trade itself.

87 "Veteran International Trade Journalist Richard A. Lawrence Dies at 82." Cision – PR Newswire. December 3, 2010. www.prnewswire.com/news-releases/veteran-international-trade-journalist-richard-a-lawrence-dies-at-82-111282919.html. "About The Journal of Commerce – Since 1827, The Journal of Commerce has been the most trusted source of intelligence for international logistics executives, helping them plan global supply chains and better manage day-to-day transportation of goods and commodities in the United States and internationally." Keith Rockwell, later to become the WTO's Director of Public Affairs for the Organization's first 26+ years, was one of the star reporters of the paper, as was Richard Lawrence.

Moving to improve the WTO will be a laborious and time-consuming process, and the will to do so in a fundamental way has not yet manifested itself. WTO 2.0 should emerge by 2025, with every positive incremental step taken in the interim to adopt useful changes as quickly as possible. Not all WTO members will welcome an expansion of WTO data collection, dissemination, and analysis. Complementary data collection efforts of the Global Trade Alert, as well as the efforts of the OECD, IMF, World Bank, and other public international organizations to support transparency will be necessary, should continue, and should be financially supported.

What can be done with respect to WTO reform? Some steps can be taken immediately, while others require more time and more capacity-building to bring about necessary change.

RECOMMENDED REFORMS

Overall Goal

- The WTO should move in the direction of becoming a central access point for global trade information relevant to the WTO *acquis* (as it stands at present and encompassing likely future subjects for negotiation), including to the extent practical all government measures that have a substantial effect on trade. This should be accomplished through access to distributed databases and not generally through itself substituting for or duplicating available sources of information.
- With available technology, a global online system of trade measures ought to be kept current. Summary reports should be updated often, and reflect notifications that come in late and changes in reported measures. Counter-notifications and databases of specific trade concerns should be both utilized and cross-referenced. A major effort should be made to capture data on subsidies, recognizing that these measures are more difficult to identify and classify. Measures of general support should be included. Every effort should be made to make the system useful not just to governments but to all those engaged in commerce.
- It is physically impossible and not even desirable for there to be one central node where all data are stored, but there can be a centrally located gateway that identifies locations of more complete information on the sources and flows of trade and the vulnerabilities that may exist. The gateway would be online and always available for information essential for those engaged in commerce to better understand government interventions, but it would also have an emergency response

capability to identify trade vulnerabilities, tapping into distributed resources when calamities occur, whether wars, threats to global health, natural disasters, geopolitical measures, or slower-moving calamities such as would over time occur with climate change, water scarcity, or soil degradation.
– What is called for is not just access to raw data – numbers of measures – but an evaluation of trends and analysis of impact of measures and events.

An Improved Monitoring System

– A priority for the Director-General should be to create space for the Secretariat to fill policy data gaps and to analyze the magnitude and incidence of policies affecting competitive conditions on markets – including in areas where WTO rules are weak or missing altogether.[88]
– The Secretariat should consult with experts such as Simon Evenett, Bernard Hoekman, and Robert Wolfe, as well as experts within the Secretariat, on an official and public basis, on how to design a comprehensive data collection and reporting system that is state-of-the-art.
– The independence of the process and of the Secretariat must be fully respected. It must be clear that members are prohibited from interfering with the monitoring work product.[89]
– The Secretariat, while striving for objectivity and completeness, should not be deterred by political considerations (member sensitivities) in collecting and reporting on measures affecting trade, including in Trade Policy Reviews.
– Members should cooperate with and support the monitoring process in full accordance with their notification obligations.[90]

[88] Simon Evenett and Richard Baldwin, eds. 2020. *Revitalising Multilateralism: Pragmatic Ideas for the New WTO Director-General*. London: Centre for Economic Policy Research Press. https://cepr.org/voxeu/columns/revitalising-multilateralism-new-ebook. In his contribution to the book, Bernard Hoekman sums up the role that the WTO Secretariat must assume with respect to monitoring, transparency, and analysis in the language quoted above. This is his formulation.

[89] "The 16th Global Trade Alert Report: The Global Trade Disorder." Global Trade Alert. November 12, 2014. www.globaltradealert.org/reports/24

[90] "The 16th Global Trade Alert Report: The Global Trade Disorder." Global Trade Alert. November 12, 2014. www.globaltradealert.org/reports/24. "However, just as turkeys don't vote for Christmas, what is the incentive for the monitored to bolster the monitor?" The final section of this report (pages 87–98) contains a comparison of the methodologies employed by the WTO and the GTA in identifying trade measures following the 2008 financial crisis.

- Members should provide the WTO Secretariat with adequate funding to provide more complete transparency in aid of the above-stated objectives. The efforts of the Monitoring and Economic Research Divisions for these functions should be financially self-supporting and independent of the annual WTO budgeting process.
- A newly created Monitoring Division of the WTO would supply its data to the ERSD for assessments of economic impact.
- Summary reports shall be issued often, including notifications that come in late. Counter-notifications and specific trade concerns databases, among others, should be both utilized and cross-referenced.
- A major effort shall be made to capture data on subsidies, recognizing that these are more difficult to identify and classify. This shall include measures of general support.
- Every effort should be made to make the system useful not just to governments but to those engaged in commerce.

Improving Trade Policy Reviews

- There should be a biennial review in the Trade Policy Review Body with recommendations of any improvements that should be made in the collection and dissemination of information.

For these purposes, the Secretariat should provide a summary of all available relevant information from member reports, Secretariat reporting, and other sources, including the Global Trade Alert, the OECD, the Bank, and the Fund.

- The Trade Policy Review Mechanism itself should adopt a more hard-eyed view to provide a greater degree of qualitative and quantitative analysis. What is the degree of contribution – positive and negative – to the trading system, of each member subject to review? What trends are discerned? What is the likely impact of trade measures currently in effect and those that are planned? The nature of trade developments should come through clearly, not just from a summary of members' views but in the report from the Secretariat.
- There shall be a biennial review in the TPR Mechanism with recommendations for any improvements that should be made in the collection and dissemination of information. For these purposes, the Secretariat shall provide a comparison of all member reporting, Secretariat reporting, and other sources of relevant data, including the Global Trade Alert, the OECD, the Bank, and the Fund.

– Horizontal TPRs: Additional specific subjects could be addressed in horizontal TPRs (beyond the current single-country approach), focusing on topics such as food security, vaccine availability, agricultural support, industrial subsidies, effects on trade of inadequate enforcement of competition policy, the gap between bound and applied tariff rates, etc.

Member Notification Requirements

– Members should, as a new normal practice, provide with respect to any instruction to customs officials who impose or change any trade measure at the border, automatically, simultaneously, and electronically, a copy of the instruction to the WTO, with any necessary explanatory material. (The WTO would be added as a "cc:" to every emailed instruction. Data would be complete and up to date.)
– WTO notification requirements should be designed to the extent feasible to include incentives that make compliance more likely through self-interest on the part of members.

  Comment: The standards notification process works very well because there is mutual benefit to notifying standards in draft for comment by others, as well as a system of filing specific trade concerns. The process diffuses likely conflicts, heads off potential litigation, and is a very useful tool for regulators applying standards. As important, it often gives government agencies with regulatory responsibility a participatory role. Information provided can be more complete and timelier if the agencies with responsibility as administrators are directly engaged in the process.[91]

– Incentives should be provided aimed at reducing noncompliance.
  a. The Secretariat should list by member and by agreement all those in noncompliance.
  b. The noncompliant should not share in all of the benefits of the system, such as access to online refined data provided by the WTO. Other forms of sanctions can be devised for penalizing those with the

[91] Robert Wolfe. 2018. "Is World Trade Organization Information Good Enough? How a Systematic Reflection by Members on Transparency Could Promote Institutional Learning." Bertelsmann Stiftung High-Level Board of Experts on the Future of Global Trade Governance, Gütersloh. http://aei.pitt.edu/102529/1/MT_Is_World_Trade_Organization_Information_Good_Enough.pdf

capacity to comply and who do not apply for technical assistance, but continue to fail to comply.

c. To the extent possible, the Secretariat should make efforts to publish information on measures employed by members that underreport. For members that fail to verify information, the Secretariat should publish the best information available.

d. Where noncompliance is due to a lack of capacity, the country falling short would be excused for a reasonable period of time from any penalties if technical assistance is sought from the Secretariat,

– All WTO Committees responsible for the oversight of compliance should welcome counter-notifications, as well as less confrontational statements of specific trade concerns, as in the TBT Committee. The Secretariat should keep Committees currently informed of relevant information collected in the monitoring process.
– Developing countries should be encouraged to self-identify as such, based on objective criteria and capacity-building needs, somewhat as they do under the Trade Facilitation Agreement, in order to obtain sufficient technical assistance.[92] Self-identification shall be taken into account in noncompliance proceedings. As with other Uruguay Round Agreements, new notification requirements can be phased in for the least developed countries. Every effort should be expended with the help of international financial institutions to assure that there is full technical support to achieve full compliance.
– WTO reports on measures should include a notation indicating information that has been verified by the member imposing a measure as contrasted with a report that has not been verified but in which there is a high degree of confidence as to its accuracy.

Proactive Reporting by the Secretariat

– Watch list: When there is a headline in the press of a "trade war" or other act of trade aggression, or, from whatever source, of a measure very likely to distort international trade substantially, the Secretariat should immediately, after seeking an immediate comment from the

[92] William Alan Reinsch. 2020. "Transparency at the WTO: Why Does Transparency Matter, and Are Members Meeting Their Obligations?" Center for Strategic and International Studies, Washington DC. www.csis.org/analysis/transparency-wto-why-does-transparency-matter-and-are-members-meeting-their-obligations. Reinsch also suggests that counternotification provisions be inserted throughout the WTO Agreements, wherever applicable.

country imposing the measure, publish the measure on a watch list while awaiting verification.

- Detecting and tracking trade anomalies: The Economic Research and Statistics Division should track seismic events (trade flow anomalies), such as acts of economic coercion, and inform the Monitoring Division so that it can research the probable causes if these are not apparent. A special trade monitoring mechanism, similar to that which was established under Article 18 of the Protocol on the Accession of the People's Republic of China, could be established with respect to any problem area that warrants heightened and sustained attention.[93]
- Private sector input: Where there are allegations from the private sector of market distortions preventing market forces from determining competitive outcomes, Secretariat resources should be devoted to forensic analysis. The Monitoring and Economic Research Divisions should pay special attention to opaque practices that have not been notified and that have the equivalent trade-distorting effect of notified and officially reported measures.
- Economic impact assessments: The Monitoring Division of the WTO should supply its data to the Economic Research and Statistics Division, which should assess the economic impact of WTO-reported measures, trade-restricting and trade-facilitating, to the extent possible. Reports of the Economic Research and Statistics Division (ERSD) should not include judgments as to the WTO consistency of any trade measure.
- To the extent possible, the ERSD should publish annual estimates of the impact of changes in the trade policies and measures of members. The purpose is primarily to inform stakeholders within countries of the costs and benefits of their country's trade regime.
- The Monitoring and Economic Research Divisions shall pay special attention to opaque practices which have not been notified and that have the equivalent trade-distorting effect of notified and officially-reported measures. Where there are allegations from the private sector of market distortions, depriving market forces of determining competitive outcomes, Secretariat resources should be devoted to forensic analysis.

[93] "Accession of the People's Republic of China WT/L/432." World Trade Organization. November 23, 2001. docs.wto.otg/dol2fe/Pages/SS/directdoc.aspx?filename=Q:/WT/L/432.pdf&Open=True

- The efforts of the Monitoring and Economic Research Divisions for these functions shall be made financially self-supporting and independent of the annual WTO budgeting process.

Crisis Management

- In response to a crisis, any group of members or committee chairs can ask the Secretariat to recommend all the possible responses – including improvements in monitoring.[94] Cross-divisional Secretariat task forces can be formed to monitor and assess trade measures, as was done in the case of the pandemic.
- Special horizontal Trade Policy Reviews should be conducted for matters of great consequence, such as members' measures to deal with the pandemic, trade-facilitating, trade-restricting, or otherwise trade-distorting measures. Emphasis could be given to heightened monitoring of trade-facilitation efforts in the poorest countries to spur the distribution of vaccines, for example.[95] A horizontal review of climate policies and measures should be undertaken.

CONCLUSION

As with all trade rules, and this applies to requirements for notifications as well, the impetus to comply comes in the first instance not from the threat of sanctions but from a view of enlightened self-interest. Robert Wolfe writes:

> *Providers of information must see how doing so helps them meet their own objectives. Do they believe that the information they provide will be analysed, aggregated and disseminated in a way that is helpful to them or crucial for the trading system? If countries do not think they are learning about themselves in preparing a notification, or responding to a TPR questionnaire, and if they do not see the public good aspect of such information, then notification is indeed merely a burden.*[96]

[94] "DDG Wolff: Q&A on the COVID-19 Pandemic and Trade." World Trade Organization. October 2, 2020. www.wto.org/english/news_e/news20_e/ddgaw_05oct20_e.htm

[95] "DDG Wolff Urges G20 Leaders to Back WTO Action to Support Economic Rebound, Pandemic Response and WTO Reform." World Trade Organization. November 21, 2020. www.wto.org/english/news_e/news20_e/ddgaw_21nov20_e.htm

[96] Robert Wolfe. 2018. "Is World Trade Organization Information Good Enough? How a Systematic Reflection by Members on Transparency Could Promote Institutional Learning." Bertelsmann Stiftung High-Level Board of Experts on the Future of Global Trade

Working together, the WTO's members and the Secretariat can bring much greater clarity to the conditions under which world trade is conducted. For governments, facing policy choices when creating new rules or in administering existing ones, working from inadequate information is an unacceptable risk.[97] Perhaps more important for the multilateral trading system than any other improvement to the system is assuring that the WTO rules are based on solid intelligence that is as complete as possible. A trading system operating even partially in the dark cannot deliver fairness.

ADDENDUM: UNDERSTANDING THE FACTORS SHAPING TRADE

My PIIE colleague, Chad P. Bown, commenting on the foregoing reminded me that missing from the analysis was attention to the factors giving rise to and shaping trade.[98] I should have thought of this myself, as the first chapter in this book is on the history of trade.

Tens of thousands of years before the internet and AI existed, our remote ancestors knew where the obsidian was located that they needed for making some of their first tools, and this, it is theorized, gave rise to trade in the first place. Those living in the Bronze Age had a fair idea of the location of tin deposits. Writing is said to have been generated in part in ancient Sumer to be a means of communication over distance to accompany traded goods. In the Iron Age, the search was for iron ore. In the tenth century BCE, Arab traders waited for the monsoon winds to take their cargoes of frankincense and myrrh from Oman across the Indian Ocean and bring back cargoes of silk. The Ancient Greeks looked to the Black Sea and Egypt for grain. Later, in the dash for colonies, there was a desire bordering on compulsion in Spain to know where gold might be in the Americas, and later in England and France to find and control the best sugar-growing areas in the Caribbean for rum. And where would Britain have been without tea from India? In the nineteenth century, Alexander von Humboldt popularized the use of guano as fertilizer, and ships

Governance, Gütersloh. http://aei.pitt.edu/102529/1/MT_Is_World_Trade_Organization_Information_Good_Enough.pdf

97 Simon J. Evenett. 2019. "Protectionism, State Discrimination, and International Business Since the Onset of the Global Financial Crisis." *Journal of International Business Policy* 2: 9–36.

98 Chad P. Bown. 2022. "How COVID-19 Medical Supply Shortages Led to Extraordinary Trade and Industrial Policy." *Asian Economic Policy Review* 17: 114–135. Bown's paper examines a few factors, including price, domestic consumption at the place of manufacture, as well as domestic and trade-related government measures that led to supply and the dearth of it in meeting the demand generated by the pandemic.

carried to Europe that pungent cargo mined from mountains of the countless years of bird droppings along the coasts of Chile and Peru – until German chemists later in the century developed technology to synthesize nitrogen, allowing the onshoring of fertilizer.

The opening of the plains in the United States during the nineteenth century transformed the location of global agricultural production, with a knock-on effect that helped make possible the Industrial Revolution in Europe through freeing up farm workers. Transfers of technology (sometimes involuntary) such as the Arkwright loom moved textile production from England to America.

In the run-up to the Second World War, Germany concentrated on where its iron ore came from and Japan on where it sourced its oil. During that war, the loss of access to Malaya prompted the US government to send intrepid explorers like my father's friend and neighbor Harvard Professor Dr. Richard Evans Schultes to the Amazon Basin to seek alternative sources of natural rubber, a search later rendered unnecessary through the scientific breakthrough of making synthetic rubber.

During the second oil embargo in 1979, demonstrating for a second time the power of the Organization of the Petroleum Exporting Countries (OPEC), it occurred to me that there might be American vulnerabilities in other basic commodities. Consumers standing in line at gas stations in the United States had no doubt in their minds of the relationship of trade to the location of foreign supplies of fossil fuels, and more recently may connect the price of gas at the pump to the invasion of Ukraine and the effect on supplies of energy from Russia. Farmers will be even more readily aware of the interdiction of sunflower oil and wheat that would have transited the Black Sea. As chair of the Trade Policy Review Group, I had overall responsibility for coordinating US trade policy at the time of the Second Oil Embargo.[99] and I called an interagency meeting to learn if other raw materials might be subject to cartelization. The conclusion of a rapid study led by the US Department of the Interior was that this kind of threat did not exist for other commodities.

A decade ago, when China decided to limit exports of rare earths, tungsten, and molybdenum, for what it said were environmental reasons,[100] dependency

99 I was chairman of the Trade Policy Review Group, a subcabinet committee that functioned under the Trade Policy Committee, which rarely met.

100 "DS431: China – Measures Related to the Exportation of Rare Earths, Tungsten and Molybdenum." World Trade Organization. www.wto.org/english/tratop_e/dispu_e/cases_e/ds431_e.htm

on these basic materials needed for electronics in the information technology age received a renewed focus. Concerns were heightened in February 2022 as China began a new study of limiting exports of key minerals necessary to manufacture F-35 fighter jets and other sophisticated weapons. Reportedly, four-fifths of the refining capacity for rare earths exists in China, and the United States needs to send its own rare earth minerals to China for processing as it has no refining capacity of its own.[101]

The countries of the WTO became aware of South Korea's vulnerability to trade restrictions on high-technology inputs from Japan due to repercussions from the Fukushima fish case.[102] With a seesawing of results in WTO litigation, political differences between the two countries appeared to interfere with the smooth administration of export controls by Japan for critical materials needed to manufacture electronics in Korea.[103]

A high dependency on two locations in Asia (Taiwan and South Korea) for semiconductors (computer chips) has ignited a subsidy race in Europe, the United States, and Japan to build cutting-edge fabs (fabrication facilities), with an eye also on offsetting the effects of the subsidies to China's domestic industry.[104] Other important technologies have shifted the demand for raw materials. Articles began to appear in the press about China seeking to buy up sources of lithium, lying in great and beautiful swaths on the surface in areas of the Altiplano in Latin America and elsewhere, as the global car industry sought batteries for electric vehicles.[105]

The COVID-19 pandemic taught many more people about logistics. Express delivery was hampered when passenger jets were not flying. Factories going offline all at once and then onstream all at once caused backlogs at ports on the US West Coast of 60 to 100 ships waiting to offload, while containerization facilities were under stress and truckers were not

[101] "China Targets Rare Earth Export Curbs to Hobble US Defence Industry." Financial Times. February 15, 2021. www.ft.com/content/d3ed83f4-19bc-4d16-b510-415749c032c1

[102] "DS495: Korea–Import Bans, and Testing and Certification Requirements for Radionuclides." World Trade Organization. www.wto.org/english/tratop_e/dispu_e/cases_e/ds495_e.htm

[103] "Why South Korea is No Longer on Japan's Approved Export List." Aljazeera. August 28, 2019. www.aljazeera.com/economy/2019/8/28/why-south-korea-is-no-longer-on-japans-approved-export-list

[104] "2 Charts Show How Much the World Depends on Taiwan for Semiconductors." CNBC. March 15, 2021. www.cnbc.com/2021/03/16/2-charts-show-how-much-the-world-depends-on-taiwan-for-semiconductors.html

[105] "How the US Is Losing the Lithium Industry to China." Forbes. January 11, 2022. www.forbes.com/sites/rrapier/2022/01/11/the-us-is-losing-the-lithium-industry-to-china/. I don't know how healthy it is to do so, but my wife and I have walked through fields of desiccated lithium brine in Chile. For a stock photo, see www.istockphoto.com/photo/lascar-the-volcano-gm908356948–250238105

present in adequate numbers. The pandemic taught us the difficulties of manufacturing mRNA vaccines in sufficient quantities and getting them to where they are needed.

Then came the Russian invasion of Ukraine, and the same concerns that troubled the Ancient Greeks with respect to their grain supply returned, when the world awakened to the fact that 30 percent of wheat exports came from Russia and Ukraine, and the Black Sea had become a war zone. At the same time, both Russia and the EU member states, for different reasons, began calculating exactly how to redirect flows of natural gas and oil, and the US administration and European governments began scrutinizing the capacity to ship liquified natural gas (LNG) across the Atlantic. Most of us were unaware that Ukraine produces some 50 percent of the global supply of neon used in semiconductor manufacturing. EU fuel cell and hydrogen technology development require important minerals from Russia such as platinum (13 percent of world trade), titanium (23 percent), and vanadium (34 percent).[106] News articles recorded that about a million containers needed to find a way from coastal China to Europe without passing through Russia or Belarus, that route being disrupted by the risk of economic sanctions and the continued hostilities in the region.[107] Containers shipped by rail take half as long but cost twice as much as shipping by sea, and a quarter as much as shipping by air.[108]

There is a story in the *Financial Times* of March 26, 2022[109] about private corporations seeking more secure supply lines, about onshoring, part of the numerous recent pieces written about suspected deglobalization. Adam Smith and David Ricardo ushered in the intellectual construct for specialization that ultimately did not respect borders. Businesses applied their economic logic. Aluminum was produced in Canada because that was where there was an abundance of hydropower, lower-cost energy, with no risk to the product entering international trade – that is until the national security restrictions

[106] "Putin's Critical Raw Materials Are a Threat to EU Economic Security." Egmont Royal Institute for International Relations. March 15, 2022. www.egmontinstitute.be/putins-critical-raw-materials-are-a-threat-to-eu-economic-security/

[107] "Charting the Global Economy: Factory Costs Surge from Russia War." Bloomberg. March 26, 2022. www.bloomberg.com/news/articles/2022-03-26/charting-the-global-economy-factory-costs-surge-from-russia-war

[108] "China–Europe Rail Lines Become Supply Chain's Latest Problem." Bloomberg. March 22, 2022. www.bloomberg.com/news/articles/2022-03-23/china-europe-rail-routes-become-supply-chain-s-latest-problem

[109] Harriet Agnew. 2022. "Investors Bet Ukraine War Will Prompt Companies to Bring Production Onshore." *Financial Times*. March 26. www.ft.com/content/07faf1be-88a5-4133- 92c5-c38f117692e6

imposed by the United States on March 23, 2018.[110] Where governments do not intervene with regulation, economic efficiency is the rule. Software programming gravitated to India and chip design to Romania, places where there was an abundance of relevant engineers.

Much is known but still unknown about the global distribution of natural, manmade, and human resources. Political risk, a less precise field of study, provides an overlay to whatever can be known about the physical world. Other dimensions are time and advances in technology. More information on the location of mineral nodules on the ocean floor needs to be collected. Organizations from seven nations have agreements with the International Seabed Authority (ISA) to explore vast regions of the ocean, all but one in the Clarion-Clipperton Fracture Zone, an area larger than the United States located in the North Pacific Ocean. Economic feasibility depends on technological progress. There was a similar story for the extraction of oil and gas due to fracking, and that investment has paid economic and national security dividends.

What is needed is sophisticated multidimensional mapping, combined with in-depth analysis, including foresight exercises examining contingencies. The problems today are not so very different than those our early ancestors faced traveling a few kilometers to barter for obsidian. Would the streams *en route* be swollen, the saber-tooth tigers or tribes along the way menacing? They worried about logistics, as did Queen Isabella as she awaited news of treasure ships due back from the Americas. Complex logistical problems were dealt with successfully without AI or even computers as recently as the D-day landings at Normandy. Understanding trade to a far greater degree than we do today is not an insuperable challenge.

While we have not advanced from our forebears as far as we should have, there are elements of a solution present. What exists today is distributed knowledge, linkable through blockchain technology but still unlinked. Different agencies have data on various factors influencing trade. Specialized agencies are tracking particular aspects of production – the IAEA (for atomic energy) and the IEA (for energy more generally), the Society of Petroleum Engineers for oil, and AMIS (for crop and agricultural market information), to name a few. The Peterson Institute for International Economics has a very accessible tracker for sanctions related to the Russian

110 "Section 232 Investigations: Overview and Issues for Congress." Congressional Research Service. May 18, 2021. https://sgp.fas.org/crs/misc/R45249.pdf

invasion of Ukraine.[111] The Global Trade Alert has current data on trade measures and more generally has begun to track subsidies in greater detail, as these measures dramatically affect trade flows, plus it has its own Essential Goods Inventory (EGI).[112] The GTA also prepared a study for the World Bank on March 23, 2022, comparing current data collection systems at the WTO, GTA, ITC, and the Bank.[113] Nodes of trade, production, and natural resources intelligence can be part of the blockchain to form a more coherent picture of the whole.

What is the institutional capacity of the WTO or any other organization to generate that picture not only of current trade measures but also the factors that affect and will affect trade? What are the needs of the WTO members? Experts need to explore this topic. The WTO has the ability to convene experts and should do so to better understand international trade and the forces that shape it.

What is needed at the WTO is not duplication of specialized nodes of analysis and data, but the ability to reach into resources quickly, especially when responses need to be immediate. The United States government is in the process of identifying supply chain resilience (another way of saying, identifying vulnerabilities). This can be looked at more globally. Net-food-importing countries may have a clear understanding of their needs, but this information may not be adequately shared with food-exporting countries. The WTO might be a good candidate for identifying potential problem areas, whether disruptions might come from war, climate, natural disasters, or threats to global health. Was the misallocation of containers and supercargo vessels avoidable with strategic foresight and policy planning? Perhaps. Does the WTO Secretariat have adequate resources at present to undertake this task? It does not. Expansion of the Secretariat is a subject that warrants attention and is covered in a separate section preceding this one.

The science of trade is in its infancy in many respects. Trade measures are put into place, whether for freer trade or to restrict trade, without sufficient analysis of likely and actual effects. To this must be added calculations related to health, climate, and geopolitical crises, where other institutions have

[111] "Russia's War on Ukraine: A Sanctions Timeline." Peterson Institute for International Economics. April 12, 2022. www.piie.com/blogs/realtime-economic-issues-watch/russias-war-ukraine-sanctions-timeline

[112] An Expanded Essential Goods Monitoring Initiative: 21st Century Tracking of Pandemic-Era Trade and Investment Policies in Food and Medical Products (November 2022 update), Global Trade Alert. May 4, 2020. www.globaltradealert.org/reports/54

[113] "Form, Frequency, Duration & Scale: COVID-Era Trade Policy Interventions Affecting Medical Goods." Global Trade Alert. March 23, 2022. www.globaltradealert.org/reports/88

capabilities that would not be expected to be found at the WTO nor in a single location. During the pandemic, a WTO crisis team given broader capabilities could have identified sources of supply as well as trade and trade anomalies – looking for trade that should have been taking place but did not, much the way the astronomical bodies that cannot be seen by telescopes and subatomic particles not visible to electron microscopes can be identified by their gravitational effects on what is visible. It should have been possible to look beyond trade measures, those that are trade-restricting and those that are trade-facilitating, to understand the factors affecting the availability of components of ventilators, as well as materials for the production and delivery of vaccines. It may be that the World Health Organization had the information. The trade expertise of the WTO is directly relevant to removing obstacles to cross-border supply. During the pandemic, the WTO Secretariat rallied to provide information notes and far better reporting of trade measures than had been the norm. Further trade intelligence-gathering and analysis would have been very useful. The process needed to be more organized and more supported by the WTO's members. There should be better preparation for the next crisis, whatever the cause. Patterns of consumption as well as production need to be better understood, as well as the effects of physical shortages and price spikes.

How will governments and corporations react to having access to greatly improved global trade intelligence? Will individual decisions be in the direction of self-sufficiency and autarky or aimed at more trade, not less, at diversification leavened with some degree of redundancy, nearshoring, onshoring, or "friend-shoring"? The answers will differ by commodity, by capabilities, by policy preferences, factoring in risks but also costs, and making assessments in line with individual interests.

Ignorance is not an option. Lack of knowledge would pose even greater risks. We have eaten of the fruit of the tree of knowledge, and now need more than a first taste.

RESTORING BINDING DISPUTE SETTLEMENT

Binding dispute settlement, meaning the ability to obtain a final judgment of whether a member has acted inconsistently with its WTO obligations, was the defining attribute of the World Trade Organization created in 1995. Having enforceable rules sets the WTO apart from other international arrangements. Global commerce thrived on the certainty provided by a rules-based system. For well over a decade, the United States had complained that the dispute settlement system was undermining the trade remedies allowed under the WTO's rules. When a populist American president was elected in 2016, an administration for which international opprobrium was regarded as a badge of honor, it snuffed out the WTO's Appellate Body (AB). The AB was a device intended to remove errors from the system but had in reality become a powerful court. This occurred because of bizarre but entrenched WTO voting arrangements whereby all 164 members would have to agree to block (or overrule) an AB decision, but one member acting alone could halt appointments to that body. The institutional framework of the WTO is fundamentally flawed. The question now is what to do about it.

Today, the WTO dispute settlement system has become balkanized. The EU (for itself and its member states), China, Canada, and twenty-four other countries have banded together to put into place an alternative mechanism, the Multi-Party Interim Arrangement (MPIA), largely replicating the WTO appellate system that has ceased to function.[114] Outside this system are the other two-thirds of the WTO members, including the United States, Japan, Russia, and South Korea. What this means is that for most WTO members, for any trade dispute in which they are a party, no definitive result is available on whether WTO obligations were violated – unless they make alternative arrangements. As it is, there are no enforceable WTO obligations for two-thirds of the WTO's members.

Any solution reconstructing a binding dispute settlement system must bridge the gap between the United States and the other members. For this reason, it is necessary to understand US criticisms of the Appellate Body and consider the interests and positions of those who found little fault with the prior system.

Absent major WTO reforms extending far beyond dispute settlement, one or more special ad hoc arrangements will be necessary, or the current unsatisfactory conditions will persist. There are, however, potential means to close the gap between the United States and its trading partners.

THE IMMEDIATE PROBLEM

Although there are many aspects of the WTO that after a quarter-century of experience could usefully be reviewed with an eye to making improvements, the calls for WTO reform from government leaders and their trade ministers were provoked primarily by the fact that the Appellate Body ceased to exist except on paper. The loss of the AB, and with it the loss of binding dispute settlement,[115] while not the only deficiency in the multilateral trading system,

[114] "Multi-Party Interim Appeal Arbitration Arrangement (MPIA)." WTO Plurilateral Initiatives Site – Geneva Trade Platform. www.wtoplurilaterals.info/plural_initiative/the-mpia/

[115] For members not making alternative arrangements for appeals.

is the most visible and understandable shortcoming. As a vital part of the WTO's framework for dispute settlement, with no appeals possible but appeals nevertheless being filed, the WTO rules ceased to be enforceable, unless alternative arrangements were made by litigants committing themselves to abide by outcomes at either the panel stage or a substitute appeal mechanism.

The most recent turn of events was entirely the work of the United States, which blocked appointments to the Appellate Body,[116] although it would state that the AB had produced the situation itself through overreach, creating new obligations and narrowing existing rights. This was not the first use of the power of the veto to affect the appointment process. The European Union had insisted that its candidate be considered at the same time as a Latin American seat became available, as a package to avoid US opposition. Preventing a consensus from being formed to fill all vacant seats was an entirely new level of obstruction, going beyond the composition of AB membership to prevent the dispute settlement system from fully functioning. As the terms ended for two of the three remaining AB members at midnight on December 10, 2019, and three members were needed to hear a case, that body was closed down.

Since that date, the dispute settlement system has deteriorated further. WTO members – including the European Union,[117] the United States, Russia, China, India, Brazil, and Korea – have filed appeals although there is no Appellate Body to hear the case. This growing practice of "appealing into the void" could be seen as simply a preservation of rights were the AB to be reconstituted in the future. Alternatively, it can be viewed as an act of cynicism designed to prevent a prevailing party from having a final judgment, tantamount to a return to the GATT system where panel decisions could be blocked. For any member that did not make an alternative arrangement, the loss of the AB combined with the practice of invoking it for appeals marked the end of enforceability of the rules of the system.

[116] Jens Lehne. 2019. *Crisis at the WTO: Is the Blocking of Appointments to the WTO Appellate Body by the United States Legally Justified?* Bern: Carl Grossmann Verlag. The terms of AB members Ramirez and Van den Bossche expired, and the question was whether the two appointment processes should be combined or separate. The EU pressed to have the two vacancies joined. The US opposed. "US Stands Alone against WTO Appellate Body Member." Politico. May 24, 2016. www.politico.com/tipsheets/morning-trade/2016/05/us-stands-alone-against-wto-appellate-body-member-catfish-drug-snag-with-obama-in-vietnam-dueling-tpp-letters-214457. In blocking all appointments the United States had adopted a far more extreme tactic. The United States had in the past blocked the reappointment of a Korean Appellate Body member to a second term. Blocking all appointments was entirely new, however.

[117] In this list, appealing into the void is limited by MPIA participants to cases not involving another MPIA participant.

THE IMPORTANCE OF OBTAINING BINDING OUTCOMES

Dispute settlement under the WTO's Dispute Settlement Understanding is "binding," in that it is intended to be the final adjudication of whether a member's actions are consistent with its WTO obligations. An adverse finding does not directly compel a member to change the practice found to be nonconforming but provides very strong incentives for it to do so. Either it will have to pay compensation by making other (MFN) trade concessions in order to keep the WTO-inconsistent practice (the sufficiency of which may be challenged by other members) or it will be subject to automatically authorized retaliation on its trade by the prevailing party.

Why did the United States and its trading partners agree to binding dispute settlement? GATT panel decisions on complaints could be blocked from adoption by the losing party. Many GATT contracting parties were frustrated by this state of affairs. In the 1980s, America's trading partners deeply resented the US threats of unilateral measures to defend what it saw as its trading interests – whether or not there was any GATT justification for it doing so. For its part, the United States wished to curb trade distortions caused by the EU's Common Agricultural Policy. To each of these problems, binding dispute settlement seemed to provide an answer. Whatever doubts the United States had about the loss of freedom of action under the new dispute settlement rules, by 1993, in the concluding moments of the Uruguay Round, it was confronted with the new dispute settlement system as part of a package that included a code on intellectual property and an agreement on services, both of which the United States very much wanted. It bought into the deal.

Whether or not at the time either the United States or the European Union saw it clearly, they were engaged in creating a public good – greater certainty for all those engaged in international trade because governments' trade commitments would now be enforceable. World commerce takes place by reason of private contracts. Legal commitments among governments provide the framework within which international commerce flows. Enforceability of commitments is central to the world economy operating within a framework of the rule of law. In the eyes of many learned observers, dispute settlement, underpinning the commitments of sovereigns, was the system's greatest accomplishment. The Appellate Body, overseeing the work of dispute settlement panels, was awarded the appellation "jewel in the crown."[118]

[118] Among the problems with the "jewel in the crown" metaphor is that it says too much and too little about the role of binding dispute settlement in the multilateral trading system. Dispute settlement is not a thing wholly apart from the rest of the WTO. What is most important is the

NOT EVERY WTO MEMBER WAS AN ADMIRER, BUT MOST WERE

There is more than one objective reality. The dominant American view, while not the only view within its shores, is that the most serious problem with WTO dispute settlement is that of judicial activism amounting to overreach – expanding obligations under the agreements and narrowing rights. The US Trade Representative stated this objection in very broad terms in December 2017 at MC11 in Buenos Aires: "Too often members seem to believe they can gain concessions through lawsuits that they could never get at the negotiating table." Up until that point, widely ignored was the fact that the United States had for the prior two decades found serious fault with how the AB had gone about its tasks and the results it reached. In the opinion of US officials in a series of presidential administrations, and in the House and the Senate, regardless of party, there was a uniform opinion: the AB had strayed from its original purpose.

The general European view, more popular by far among the WTO members than the American view, was that the problems of WTO dispute settlement lie elsewhere – not having enough capacity, not being adequately insulated from pressure by large members, and not obtaining sufficient and timely compliance by parties losing a case. In the majority view, the AB members had in the main behaved largely as they were supposed to, coming up with the right answers, and that respect for the rule of law meant that WTO members were to accept the results whether they agreed with them or not.

There are two possible approaches to a major problem among nations: confront it and deal with it or work around it. The starting position for the EU, and for the most part all other WTO members, was that the United States was wholly unjustified in its use of the consensus mechanism to block appointments, and that, therefore, the United States should relent. They expressed frustration not only with the US tactic, but the fact that the United States refused to put on the table proposals that it would find acceptable to fix any shortcomings it saw. Over time, with the hope of a quick retreat by the United States fading, WTO members came around to expressing an interest in engaging with the American government, hoping that this would be sufficient

crown itself, the entire WTO organization and the system it administers, the members' means of governing world trade. At the same time, the WTO dispute settlement process is more than an ornament. Rule-making is arguably the most important part of the WTO, but enforcement of the rules is essential. To lose sight of the whole, to focus on a single part of governance, is to risk the system not working as a whole.

to open the AB nomination process. However, those seeking restoration of the appellate function were to be disappointed. They felt that they could not find any interlocutor on the American side who would work with them to resolve the issue. For its part, the United States wanted, as a precondition of any talks, a recognition on the part of other members that the AB had erred, repeatedly telling others: "Members need to engage in a deeper discussion of *why* the Appellate Body has felt free to depart from what Members agreed to."[119] At MC12, the members agreed without preconditions to the following:

> *We acknowledge the challenges and concerns with respect to the dispute settlement system including those related to the Appellate Body, recognize the importance and urgency of addressing those challenges and concerns, and commit to conduct discussions with the view to having a fully and well-functioning dispute settlement system accessible to all Members by 2024.*[120]

THE EU COMES UP WITH A WORK-AROUND

After a period of stand-off, to fill the vacuum, the EU created a substitute for the AB based on Article 25 of the WTO's Dispute Settlement Understanding, which permits arbitration. In most respects, the mechanism was much like the original. It was called the Multi-Party Interim Arrangement (MPIA).[121] Agreeing to it as a substitute for the AB was voluntary, applicable only to its participants. Twenty-six WTO members (counting the EU as one) joined the substitute appellate mechanism. Participants in the MPIA agreed in advance that in any case between any two of them, any appeals would be made to an appellate panel of three drawn from a group of ten distinguished individuals named in advance. Wishing to replicate the original AB as nearly as possible, Brussels explored whether the WTO budget would underwrite not just the costs of the panel of three arbitrators who would decide an appeal, but the ten MPIA "appeal arbitrators" working in a collegial setting, conferring with each

[119] "United States Continues to Block New Appellate Body Members for the World Trade Organization, Risking the Collapse of the Appellate Process." 2018. *American Journal of International Law* 113(4): 822–831.

[120] "MC12 Outcome Document WT/MIN(22)/24 WT/L/1135." World Trade Organization. June 22, 2022. docs.wto.org/dol2fe/Pages/SS/directdoc.aspx?filename=q:/WT/MIN22/24.pdf&Open=True

[121] The parties at the time of publication of this book are Australia, Benin, Brazil, Canada, China, Chile, Colombia, Costa Rica, Ecuador, European Union, Guatemala, Hong Kong (China), Iceland, Japan, Macao (China), Mexico, Montenegro, New Zealand, Nicaragua, Norway, Pakistan, Peru, Singapore, Switzerland, Ukraine, and Uruguay.

other on every case.[122] This lent further credence to the view in the United States that the MPIA was designed not to settle individual disputes so much as to authoritatively interpret WTO law.

MPIA Article 5 provides:

> *Members of the pool of arbitrators will stay abreast of WTO dispute settlement activities and will receive all documents relating to appeal arbitration proceedings under the MPIA. In order to promote consistency and coherence in decision-making, the members of the pool of arbitrators will discuss amongst themselves matters of interpretation, practice and procedure, to the extent practicable.*

The results of an MPIA appeal were to be notified to the DSB.[123] The interim arrangement was designed to largely replicate the prior AB system that the United States had rejected.

The arrangement had some provisions that might in the end find favor with the Americans. It repeated the DSU's injunction that appeals "shall be limited to issues of law covered by the panel report and legal interpretations developed by the panel."[124] It added additional instructions: that issues not appealed are not to be reviewed, and that MPIA arbitrators "address only those issues that have been raised by the parties."[125] However, the MPIA was greeted by the US government as a rejection of its complaints. More precisely, Washington felt that Brussels did not comprehend the depth and nature of US concerns, even when spelled out. When China joined the MPIA, the Trump administration saw the MPIA as a provocation rather than a well-considered response.

[122] "Multi-Party Interim Appeal Arbitration Arrangement Pursuant to Article 25 of the DSU." Directorate General for Trade of the European Commission. March 27, 2020. https://trade.ec.europa.eu/doclib/docs/2020/march/tradoc_158685.pdf

Article 7 of the MPIA states: "The participating Members envisage that appeal arbitrators will be provided with appropriate administrative and legal support, . . . separate from the WTO Secretariat staff . . . The participating Members request the WTO Director-General to ensure the availability of a support structure meeting these criteria. Multiparty Interim Arrangement for Dispute Settlement Pursuant to DSU Article 25."

[123] "Multi-Party Interim Appeal Arbitration Arrangement Pursuant to Article 25 of the DSU." European Commission – Trade. March 27, 2020. https://trade.ec.europa.eu/doclib/docs/2020/march/tradoc_158685.pdf.

[124] A backdoor that the AB had exploited to review factual determinations was left in place. The MPIA panel was given the discretion to meet its ninety-day timeline by means "such as an exclusion of claims based on the alleged lack of an objective assessment of the facts pursuant to Article 11 of the DSU," subject to the approval of the parties.

[125] In addition, while having only a soft ninety-day limit for reports, some means are suggested of speeding decisions up – including the MPIA making decisions on page limits, time limits, and deadlines as well as on the length and number of hearings required.

TALKING PAST EACH OTHER

A misreading of the depth of US concerns occurred in part because the United States – in pointing out what it viewed as being an Appellate Body that was out of control – cited the most visible instances of noncompliance with the DSU rather than its core concerns. Appellate Body reports, contrary to the terms of the DSU, were often rendered in longer than the ninety-day maximum period allowed. To the United States, this practice indicated that the AB considered it would not limit itself to rare findings of egregious error, but would instead examine every case appealed in detail, and come to its own conclusions. The United States also noted that AB members had created for themselves a rule that they could issue reports after the expiration of their terms when they had not yet finished considering a case. To the United States, this was another demonstration of overreach. These were, however, not really the central concerns from the US perspective, but largely symptoms of the problem.

WTO members sought to meet stated US objections in the hope that this would dislodge the United States from its position of unwillingness to fill vacant seats on the AB and bring about the full restoration of the dispute settlement process. Ambassador David Walker,[126] acting at the request of the chair of the WTO General Council, gathered the opinions of WTO members on various reforms to the AB process that most would find acceptable. The package included a requirement that the AB must, in the usual case:

- Honor the DSU's ninety-day limit on issuing reports;
- Not assign new cases to AB members near the end of their terms;
- Not review the domestic laws of members (as these would be considered factual issues); and
- Not issue advisory opinions (only addressing issues raised by the parties).

In addition,

- AB reports would not become binding precedent but would be consulted by future panels solely to achieve greater consistency and predictability of interpretations of rules of the multilateral trading system.

Further, the Walker Principles:

- Reiterated the language already in the DSU that AB decisions could not add to the rights or diminish the obligations of the members;

[126] David Walker was New Zealand's Ambassador to the WTO through December 2021.

- Instructed AB members to pay heed to the standard of review established in Article 17.6(ii) of the Agreement on Implementation of Article VI GATT, that deference was to be paid to domestic administrators of antidumping proceedings;
- Proposed convening the DSB at least once a year to hear expressions of members' views on issues generally, unrelated to a particular case, with AB members present; and
- Required that a vacancy on the AB would automatically launch the process to fill the position.[127]

This was a sincere attempt to understand and deal with US concerns, despite the initial objection of America's trading partners that in the face of the United States not identifying solutions, they did not wish to "negotiate with themselves." The United States, during the Trump administration, remained intransigent, waiting for others to agree that the AB had fundamentally overstepped its mandate. It did not feel that it had been included in serious engagement to arrive at the Walker Principles and felt that they fell far short of what was needed.

WHAT WAS AMERICA COMPLAINING ABOUT?

What had gone wrong to cause the dispute settlement system to break down in so fundamental a fashion? Why had the United States taken so extreme a measure as rendering inoperative a central feature of the WTO structure?

The United States detailed its objections to the behavior of the Appellate Body in a 174-page document shared with the full membership of the WTO in February 2020.[128] The United States alleged that the AB had usurped the rule-making function of the WTO's members, intruding on their sovereignty and narrowing rights and expanding obligations beyond what the parties had negotiated. The United States pointed to what it saw as undeniable evidence of unwarranted judicial activism: second-guessing panels' findings of facts, which is beyond the remit of the AB, and filling in gaps in rules where the members had perhaps been unable to make a rule cover a particular issue. In

[127] "Informal Process on Matters Related to the Functioning of the Appellate Body – Report by the Facilitator, H.E. Dr. David Walker (New Zealand) JOB/GC/222." World Trade Organization. October 15, 2019. https://docs.wto.org/dol2fe/Pages/FE_Search/FE_S_S009-DP.aspx?language=E&CatalogueIdList=257689

[128] "Report on the Appellate Body of the World Trade Organization." Office of the United States Trade Representative. February 2020. www.ustr.gov/sites/default/files/Report_on_the_Appellate_Body_of_the_World_Trade_Organization.pdf

its view, the AB had engaged in judicial overreach. Compounding these faults, the AB had insisted that its rulings be considered binding precedent (to be adhered to "absent cogent reasons").

In its February 2020 paper, the United States laid out in greater detail its specific charges against the AB:

- *The Appellate Body's erroneous interpretation of the term "public body" threatens the ability of Members to counteract trade-distorting subsidies provided through SOEs, undermining the interests of all market-oriented actors;*
- *The Appellate Body has prevented WTO Members from fully addressing injurious dumping by prohibiting a common-sense method of calculating the extent of dumping that is injuring a domestic industry ("zeroing");*
- *The Appellate Body's stringent and unrealistic test for using out-of-country benchmarks to measure subsidies has weakened the effectiveness of trade remedy laws in addressing distortions caused by state-owned enterprises in non-market economies;*
- *The Appellate Body has limited WTO Members' ability to impose countervailing duties and anti-dumping duties calculated using a non-market economy methodology to address simultaneous dumping and trade-distorting subsidization by non-market economies like China.*
- *The Appellate Body's creation of an "unforeseen developments" test and severe causation analysis prevents the effective use of safeguards by WTO Members to protect their industries from import surges.*[129]

It is worth pausing for a moment to consider the controversy over the practice of "zeroing," a methodology the United States employed to determine whether dumping had occurred, which the AB and panels repeatedly constrained.

Article VI of the GATT states that "dumping, by which products of one country are introduced into the commerce of another country at less than the normal value of the products, is to be condemned if it causes or threatens

[129] To countervail a subsidy, there must be a financial contribution from the government. The question arose as to whether certain state-owned or controlled enterprises funneling money into commercial enterprises (often themselves state-owned) met the test of sufficient government involvement to be considered a "public body," and funds coming from them able to constitute subsidies. The AB required that for a public body to be found and therefore its funds to constitute subsidies, an SOE providing the funds must be carrying out government functions and not simply be owned by the government.

material injury to . . . a domestic industry." This definition does not by itself inform the reader whether the prices at which imports are sold in the market are to be looked at entry-by-entry or on average. US (and, for that matter, EU) practice aggregated individual sales at less than fair value to determine antidumping margins. To critics this created an artificial dumping margin by not giving full weight to sales made above fair value. To defenders of the practice, it should have been glaringly self-evident that law enforcement requires addressing harmful conduct, not averages. They would say "it would be foolhardy to argue with a policeman about to write a ticket to try to make the case that on average, you drove at the speed limit." In the Uruguay Round negotiations, several of America's trading partners pressed the United States to agree to end the practice of weighting above-fair-value transactions as being at zero above normal value. The negotiating history was clear that the United States rejected this attempt to change its practice.[130] The AB went on to decide that the use of zeroing was to be curbed; hence the US claim that its trading partners were trying to obtain through litigation what they could not obtain through negotiation.

The more the United States sought to explain its concerns in detail, the less clear the core issues became to many WTO members. The two most serious US accusations, in terms of their political and substantive importance, got lost. They could, however, be encapsulated in a single sentence, in discourse neither fully articulated nor clearly heard: "These errors [by the Appellate Body] have favored non-market economies at the expense of market economies, rendered trade remedy laws ineffective, and infringed on Members' legitimate policy space."

This was the heart of the matter. In the view of the United States, the Appellate Body had rendered nugatory, had gutted, the trade remedy

[130] Petros C. Mavroidis and Thomas J. Prusa. 2018. "Die Another Day: Zeroing in on Targeted Dumping: Did the AB Hit the Mark in *US–Washing Machines*?" Columbia Law School. January. https://scholarship.law.columbia.edu/cgi/viewcontent.cgi?article=3355&context=faculty_scholarship. Japan and Korea sought to prohibit zeroing in the Uruguay Round negotiations. The United States, the European Union and Canada, which employed the practice, refused to agree. Mavroidis in 2018 pointed out that some thirty panel and AB cases had examined challenges to zeroing. He concludes: "Now the fact that the proposal was thwarted does not mean that zeroing ipso facto was legal. At best, nevertheless, there was a disagreement between trading nations on this issue at the moment when the ADA was concluded."

provisions of the WTO, making antidumping and countervailing duties against subsidies less effective, and had rendered the safeguard provision of the WTO Agreements unusable. In terms of global competition, the most serious damage was in limiting the ability of the United States and other WTO members to deal effectively with competition from China.

There were no apparent quick fixes, no easy solutions to matters this fundamental.

FOR THE US A FUNDAMENTAL POLICY ISSUE WAS INVOLVED: BALANCE

In the US view, the AB, through a series of decisions, had undercut the basic bargain underlying the trading system.[131] Ever since 1934, when the US Congress created a framework for trade negotiations, a fundamental premise of US trade policy was that in entering into agreements that provided for broad trade liberalization, which meant opening the domestic US market for reciprocal market opening abroad in return,[132] if an industry was harmed by trade, there would be tools available to remedy the harm or at least soften temporarily the adverse impact of injurious trade. Generations of US trade negotiators had promised this to Congress, as well as to domestic industries, firms, and workers. This was no minor issue; it went to the core of the commitment made to obtain the authority from Congress to offer trade concessions. Under the US Constitution, Congress has the power over US commerce. Congress cannot negotiate. Only the President can do so using his foreign affairs power. What the President could not do with respect to trade barriers imbedded in US law was implement an agreement without action from Congress, which had the exclusive power to regulate trade. To reflect this delicate political balance between liberalization and the freedom to provide selective remedies, the United States had made sure that its trade agreements, including the GATT and the WTO, allowed it to do so.[133]

[131] Terrance Stewart and Elizabeth Drake. 2017. "How the WTO Undermines US Trade Remedy Enforcement." Sherrod Brown: US Senator for Ohio. February. www.brown.senate.gov/imo/media/doc/WTO_Undermines_US_Trade_Report.pdf

[132] It should be noted that the United States did win many, perhaps most, of the challenges that it brought against market closure by other WTO members.

[133] Chad P. Bown. 2022. "Trump Ended WTO Dispute Settlement. Trade Remedies Are Needed to Fix It." Peterson Institute for International Economics, Washington DC. www.piie.com/sites/default/files/documents/wp22-1.pdf. In a January 2022 paper Chad Bown details the close interrelationship between the scope for employing trade remedies with the hope for achieving dispute settlement reform, particularly with respect to the United States.

WORKING PAST THE STAND-OFF: A START, BUT NO BREAKTHROUGH

Over time, intransigence in both Washington and Brussels started to give way to small steps toward engagement with respect to the AB impasse. The EU could agree that the DSU as written did explicitly require that AB reports were to be issued no later than ninety days after the AB received an appeal (even if observers might believe that in complex cases or with a heavy caseload, this deadline could and should be extended with the consent of the parties). In addition, Brussels could agree that issues of fact were not to be addressed by the AB, that the AB should address only issues put before it, and that its decisions would not be binding as precedent, although they should be taken into account to promote consistency in interpretations of WTO rules.[134] The Biden administration in turn promised to engage on the subject of WTO dispute settlement.[135]

Since the primary protagonists over the AB issue were the United States and the European Union, that is where the process needs to begin, and it has to a degree begun quietly already. The central challenge is finding what it would take to close the gap between Washington and Brussels, in a manner that would be acceptable to China, India, and the rest of a very diverse membership.

A NEW CONTEXT IN WHICH THE ISSUES WILL BE FRAMED

What would have worked as a solution in 2017 or 2018 is unlikely to work now. The conditions are different. The status quo from which a negotiation will proceed is not necessarily the DSU as it was, with the AB still functioning. The US position, informally stated in 2017 and in the period immediately following, was "we want what we negotiated [in 1994]." That statement of position also may no longer be operative. Given the higher profile of the US–China rivalry, the existing extra-WTO-justified tariffs exchanged by the two, and US national security restrictions on steel and aluminum imports, it is

[134] "Annex to the Communication from the Commission to the European Parliament, The Council, The European Economic and Social Committee and the Committee of the Regions; Trade Policy Review – An Open, Sustainable and Assertive Trade Policy." European Commission. February 18, 2021. https://trade.ec.europa.eu/doclib/docs/2021/february/tradoc_159439.pdf

[135] "Katherine Tai on WTO Dispute Settlement Reform." International Economic Law and Policy Blog. January 12, 2022. https://ielp.worldtradelaw.net/2022/01/katherine-tai-on-wto-dispute-settlement-reform.html

hard to see a solution as simple as adopting the Walker Principles and restoring the AB.

There has been a paradigm shift in US trade policy since President Obama left office.[136] The Biden administration's trade policy is driven by two lodestars: being "worker-centered" and "creating new standards to combat the harmful industrial policies of China and other countries that undermine our ability to compete."[137] It is extraordinarily unlikely that a restoration of the AB as it was – a return to the *status quo ante* – fits well by itself with those two objectives, both of which may require, in current parlance, "policy space," namely freedom of action to remedy harms to workers and counter Chinese economic policies which the administration sees as damaging to its interests. If there is a WTO component to this strategy, it will not start with a simple restoration of the AB.

DOES THE TRADING SYSTEM NEED AN APPELLATE BODY, AND IF SO, WHAT KIND?

Why Have an AB?

The idea of having an appellate level came late in the Uruguay Round negotiations, after the key requirement that panel decisions be binding had already been agreed upon in principle. It made eminently good sense to add a second stage to the dispute settlement process. Disputes were going to be heard by a variety of panels comprising panelists of widely differing backgrounds and experience. Panels' application of the rules (findings of law) would likely be disparate, given that there would be little or no cross-membership of panels at any one time. Consistency would be beneficial. Even more important, there was a felt need to correct egregious errors. This logically called for the addition of an appellate level. After all, appeals are possible even in the case of minor crimes in most countries, and those cases involve only individuals. It would seem sensible to have at least the same protection for the interests of sovereign nations. Those intimately involved

[136] While the United States is no longer likely to shake the trading system with the President threatening US withdrawal from the WTO or a White House aide calling for line-by-line tariff reciprocity at the WTO, there is a distinctly more domestic orientation, and national security has become a paramount US concern.

[137] "Remarks of Ambassador Katherine Tai Outlining the Biden–Harris Administration's 'Worker-Centered Trade Policy.'" Office of the United States Trade Representative. June 10, 2021. www.ustr.gov/about-us/policy-offices/press-office/speeches-and-remarks/2021/june/remarks-ambassador-katherine-tai-outlining-biden-harris-administrations-worker-centered-trade-policy

with the establishment and use of WTO dispute settlement did not anticipate that there would be a large number of appeals. After all, how often would there be egregious errors? Providing that normally the AB would review a panel report and give it a thumbs up or thumbs down within sixty days, and in more complex cases ninety days, having a time-limited, nonresident appellate mechanism no doubt seemed eminently sensible.

But that is not the way that things worked out. The AB was sensitive to criticism from members that it had not responded to all the issues they raised. The AB appears to have assumed that it had no right to refuse to hear a case or view an issue as beyond its purview, although this is, for example, common US Supreme Court practice. Moreover, litigants had plenty of incentives to appeal. It demonstrated to domestic constituents that their government would go the last mile in trying to defend their interests. At the same time, filing an appeal put off the need for compliance for a while longer, eventually a long while longer – possibly calculated in years. The appellant in the meantime would be benefiting from the putatively noncompliant practice. A less knavish motivation was that a longer period before compliance was required would give often necessary time to obtain passage of legislation to amend or withdraw the measure. Filing an appeal would also allow further arguments to be developed. For a country believing sincerely that it was correct, and that the panel decision was erroneous, the option of an appeal gave a country a desired second bite at the apple.

Since the AB never saw a case that it could not resolve or an issue it could not address and was in effect considering cases on the merits *de novo*, taking into account arguments that had not been made before a panel, completing the analysis for claims not adjudicated by the panel, and in effect issuing advisory opinions, the chances were improved that there could be a reversal of the panel decision. Even better, from the viewpoint of a litigant, the AB report might create a new general rule condemning practices that the member bringing the case considered odious, ending them not just for itself in this one case but for all WTO members for ever more. Filing an appeal could also be useful from the viewpoint of domestic politics.

Cases became not only more numerous but more complex, because the more theories and arguments that were raised, the higher the probability of success on appeal. Briefs filed with the AB and AB reports began to grow like kudzu.[138] Reading the reports and understanding them was itself a time-consuming and mind-numbing task.

[138] Kudzu is an invasive weed in the form of a vine that covers bushes and trees and kills them by blocking the sunlight.

The objective of the calls for dispute settlement reform now is generally described as obtaining a process that is "two-stage, independent and binding." Having two stages may seem obvious, but it is not the only choice. Countries resolve major disputes using arbitration which is final. Article 26.8 of the London Court of International Arbitration (LCIA) requires that parties waive their right to appeal. The Havana Charter of the International Trade Organization provided that ITO members were to settle their differences through arbitration.[139] There being an informal current WTO consensus that having two stages makes eminently good sense, the discussion here is aimed primarily at how to construct an appellate level that could be acceptable to all, although it is recognized that the US will be reluctant to have one.

IS THE APPELLATE BODY A COURT?

The United States contends that the AB is not, or at least was not intended to be, a court.[140] The US argument is as follows: the DSU never calls the AB a "court." AB members are not called "judges." They do not issue "opinions," but instead file reports to "assist" the DSB in making decisions (through the adoption of the reports). AB reports are not issued by the seven members as a formal matter but by a division of three AB members. Under the Marrakesh Agreement, the AB has no role in making authoritative interpretations of the WTO agreements:

> *The Ministerial Conference and the General Council shall have the exclusive authority to adopt interpretations of this Agreement and of the Multilateral Trade Agreements. In the case of an interpretation of a Multilateral Trade Agreement in Annex 1, they shall exercise their authority on the basis of a recommendation by the Council overseeing the functioning of that Agreement. The decision to adopt an interpretation shall be taken by a three-fourths majority of the Members.*[141]

The DSU went further. It gives DSB and not the dispute settlement panels (including the AB) the final authority over dispute settlement:

[139] Article 93.2 of the Havana Charter provided that "the decision of the arbitrator shall not be binding for any purpose upon the Organization or upon any Member other than the Members participating in the arbitration." The only obligation of the members was (1) not to act unilaterally and (2) "the Members concerned shall inform the Organization generally of the progress and outcome of any discussion, consultation or arbitration undertaken under this Charter," pursuant to Art. 93.3.

[140] "Report on the Appellate Body of the World Trade Organization." United States Trade Representative. February 2020. www.ustr.gov/sites/default/files/Report_on_the_Appellate_Body_of_the_World_Trade_Organization.pdf

[141] Marrakesh Agreement Art. IX.2.

> **2.1.** *The Dispute Settlement Body is hereby established to administer these rules and procedures and . . . the consultation and dispute settlement provisions of the covered agreements. Accordingly, the DSB shall have the authority to establish panels, adopt panel and Appellate Body reports, maintain surveillance of implementation of rulings and recommendations, and authorize suspension of concessions and other obligations under the covered agreements.*

The panels are limited in their function: "11. The function of panels is to assist the DSB in discharging its responsibilities under this Understanding and the covered agreements."

The DSB and the panels, including the AB, operate within another stricture. They are only to clarify what was already present in the agreements:

> 3. *The dispute settlement system of the WTO . . . serves to preserve the rights and obligations of Members under the covered agreements, and to clarify the existing provisions of those agreements in accordance with customary rules of interpretation of public international law. Recommendations and rulings of the DSB cannot add to or diminish the rights and obligations provided in the covered agreements.*[142]

In a semantic concession to the United States, the European Union has now stated that the AB is not a court.[143] The problem with this conclusion is that functions matter more than words. *Si anas ut ambulat, et tetrissitare ut anas, anas est*[144] (If it walks like a duck, if it quacks like a duck, it is a duck). The presence or absence in the name of any body of the word "court" is not determinative of whether it is a court. The General Court of Massachusetts is not a court; it is the state's legislature. France has a Constitutional Council (Conseil Constitutionnel) to determine the constitutionality of laws. It is a court, but not in name. In Britain, until 2005, the appellate function was supplied by the House of Lords, which functioned as a court. Reports of the WTO's AB were in fact final judicial decisions, given the inability of the DSB to prevent a report from taking effect.

142 DSU Art. 3.2.

143 "Thoughts on the Geneva Trade Week Session Entitled 'WTO Dispute Settlement – Where Do We Stand?'" Current Thoughts on Trade – Terence P. Stewart. October 1, 2020. www.currentthoughtsontrade.com/2020/10/01/thoughts-on-the-geneva-trade-week-session-entitled-wto-dispute-settlement-where-do-we-stand/. EU Ambassador to the WTO Joao Machado speaking at the Graduate Institute of International and Development Studies in Geneva, Switzerland, quoted by Terence Stewart.

144 *"S'il marche comme un canard, s'il cancane comme un canard, c'est un canard. – Si camina como un pato, si grazna como un pato, es un pato."*

The bottom line, despite the textual evidence, despite applying textual interpretation through application of the Vienna Convention of the Law of Treaties (VCLT), and ignoring the plain written intentions of its founders, the WTO found itself with a court. It is the task of negotiators now seeking to restore binding dispute settlement to the WTO to find ways of dealing with that reality. This is no easy task, as saying that the AB is not a court does not keep it from being one.

The majority of members expressing themselves on the subject felt that the AB was not making law but interpreting existing WTO rules to fit evolving circumstances. Objectively, this is all too often a distinction without a difference. Resolving the degree of allowable elasticity of plain meanings of words to cover new situations is a difficult challenge for reform of the dispute settlement system. The US view is that the AB was engaged in "gap-filling," making law where there was none, contrary to its appropriate role.

This is not the first time in history that the role of the judiciary has been closely examined for overreach. The French Revolution was fought in no small part to prevent a *gouvernement des juges.*

> *It was an old fear ... seeing magistrates set themselves up as creators of law, when they should only be "the mouth of the law." This fear has found a new foundation with the promotion of constitutional courts and other supreme jurisdictions ... It never ceases to fuel fears of seeing it silently set itself up as a post-democratic power.*[145]

France's Civil Code attempted to bar judges from making law, to prevent authority that the Revolution had excised from growing back. Article 12 of the Civil Code with respect to the responsibilities of judges states: "The courts will not be able to make rules and regulations, but they will address the legislature whenever they think it necessary, either to interpret a law or to make a new one ... The courts may not directly or indirectly take any part in the exercise of the legislative power."[146] But they do.

[145] "Gouvernement des Juges." La Toupie. February 13, 2013. www.toupie.org/Dictionnaire/Gouvernement_juges.htm

[146] Article 12 of the Law of 16-24 August 1790, Code de L'organization Judiciare, states: "*Ils ne pourront point faire de règlements, mais ils s'adresseront au corps législatif toutes les fois qu'ils croiront nécessaire, soit d'interpréter une loi, soit d'en faire une nouvelle.*" Article 10: "*Les tribunaux ne pourront prendre directement ou indirectement aucune part à l'exercice du pouvoir législatif, ni empêcher ou suspendre l'exécution des décrets du Corps législatif, sanctionnés par le Roi, à peine de forfaiture.*" See also Article 1351 of the Civil Code: "The courts may not directly or indirectly take any part in the exercise of the legislative power, nor prevent or suspend the execution of the decrees of the Legislative Body, sanctioned by the King, on pain of forfeiture."

ARE AB DECISIONS BINDING PRECEDENT?

The AB had adopted a doctrine that "absent cogent reasons" its rulings would control future legal interpretations of the rules in future cases heard by panels. The United States, holding that the AB was not a court, argued that the dead hand of the past should not control future panel decisions, as the AB was not to make law.[147]

As noted, while the French Civil Code proscribed judges from making law, it is hard (actually close to impossible) to differentiate making law from expanding the reach of a law through legal interpretation. While, as a formal matter, the interpretation of law in a given case would be binding only upon the parties before the tribunal, judges would be aware of what other French judges, including in superior courts, had concluded as to what a statute meant. Judges would be unlikely to come to a different conclusion in a case that presented similar issues. In the British tradition, this is the concept of *stare decisis* (let the decision stand), which means "precedent is to be followed."[148] Commentators on the French courts state that judges will often indicate that they are not following precedent when in fact they are doing so, because they accept the reasoning, perhaps because of a desire for consistency, but also the ever-present wish of all judges not to be reversed on appeal.

The EU came around to agreeing that AB decisions would not be overtly binding precedent, knowing that for the sake of consistency in making interpretations, prior rulings would continue to be very persuasive. It is not easy, or desired by all, to drive a stake through the heart of the natural tendency to bow to precedent; some members really like the precedent, but others do not.

These points are taken from a talk I gave in the fall of 2019 to members of the French Senate to explain what the AB controversy was about. They all understood the reference.

[147] Simon Lester and James Bacchus. "Of Precedent and Persuasion: The Crucial Role of an Appeals Court in WTO Disputes." Cato Institute. September 12, 2019. www.cato.org/free-trade-bulletin/precedent-persuasion-crucial-role-appeals-court-wto-disputes#the-creation-of-the-appellate-body. Lester and Bacchus point out that the gap between the AB's use of "absent cogent reasons" and the "persuasiveness" of prior case reasoning in a future case, the US preference is not that great, so that compromise should be possible. That is true only if the US purpose is not to overturn the precedent that it wishes to see consigned to the dustbin of WTO history.

[148] "Dobbs, State Health Officer of the Mississippi Department of Health, et al. v. Jackson Women's Health Organization et al." Supreme Court of the United States. June 24, 2022. www.supremecourt.gov/opinions/21pdf/19-1392_6j37.pdf, made famous, most recently, in the United States by the Supreme Court, overturning settled jurisprudence of *Roe* v. *Wade*.

GETTING TO THE RIGHT ANSWER: IS FAR-REACHING STRUCTURAL CHANGE NECESSARY TO FINDING A SOLUTION?

We have learned during the last several years that the bounds of what we thought was normal in international trade relations can readily be breached. The United States had been the prime defender of the multilateral trading system. The world was informed that this was no longer the case when the US President in office in August 2018 called the WTO "the single worst trade deal ever made" and talked of leaving the Organization. His administration took down what had become a central feature of the system, the Appellate Body.

Taking a longer view, US administrations come and go and, with patience, perhaps building on the consensus position (of all but the United States) that Ambassador David Walker put together would be sufficient to get the Appellate Body back, would it not?

It will likely not be sufficient, but it is a start. Sometimes in the practice of medicine, treating symptoms is what is done while seeking a cure. Thus, with regard to the ninety-day limit and the ability to continue to decide on a case after an AB member's term has ended, the Walker Principles might readily fix these issues. In some matters, the divisions among WTO members go deeper and are far more difficult to deal with, particularly in assuring that the problems that the United States was primarily concerned with will not recur. How, for example, can one assure deference to domestic decision makers in antidumping cases, to applications of methodologies that are either difficult to understand or repugnant to many when understood? And how quickly can state-influenced enterprise issues be resolved given the geopolitical rivalry? How can the national security exception be dealt with given its new prominence?

Several years ago, when a US official and I were discussing how to meet US concerns, he told me: "words are not sufficient; we had words and they didn't work." This is a reference to, for example, Article 17.6 of the Anti-Dumping Agreement, which requires a degree of deference to national administrative bodies because of their expertise and careful examination of detailed facts. The amount of deference that a court may give is like a rheostat: it can be dialed up or down depending on whether judges reviewing an agency's action agree with the result or not. US Supreme Court Justice Neil Gorsuch, court observers think, believes that too much deference has been paid under the *Chevron* doctrine,[149] so the attitude of that court could change to giving less deference.

[149] In US domestic law, deference to administrators in the interpretation of law when the statute is ambiguous was considered required by the courts, according to *Chevron USA. Inc.* v. *Natural Resources Defense Council, Inc. et al.*, a US Supreme Court case from 1984.

When at the WTO, I tried to get the United States to remedy its problems with the AB by naming persons who had experience in administering trade remedies to vacancies on the body. This would have been one answer to the AB failing to understand what antidumping and countervailing duties were designed to remedy. The response was considered inadequate: "people come and go, and in any event cannot be fully relied upon." This was evidenced by the US government not renewing for a second term even some Americans who were serving as AB members.

The fundamental problem, I was told, was "cultural." A problem with this observation is that "culture" – in this case a culture of judicial restraint, of paying more attention to negotiating history, of the bargains struck and what importance they had – is hard to mandate. Culture changes over time. The US view is that the culture of WTO dispute settlement became that of the boosters of the multilateral trading system: economists, political scientists, and business interests that favor free trade. A "pro-free market" stance also favored countries whose products were on the receiving end of trade remedies complaining in WTO dispute settlement against those remedies. In the eyes of American critics of WTO dispute settlement, the prevailing current in AB decisions regarding trade remedies distinctly favored more open markets, a Humboldt current bringing warming breezes of more trade not less, and therefore sweeping away obstacles to free trade, namely trade remedies. It is hard to change a current. Supporters of the AB deny that this is the case. But the road to solutions leads through Washington, and that is where there is an abundant lack of trust in the appropriateness of outcomes from the prior appellate system. It is necessary, for the purpose of finding a solution, for those offended by US tactics, to accept that the liberal trade policy bias that the United States feels exists in prior Appellate Body jurisprudence is, at least for the Americans, real.

WHAT IS TO BE DONE?

In constructing their new government, a primary concern of the American Founders was that a strong executive would grow back, that the new country would once again be subject to a king, even if this time he was home-grown and not based in London. They did not try to cure this by inserting a plethora of restrictions on presidential authority into the United States Constitution, because, one suspects, they knew that this would be ineffective. Instead, the Founders created a series of checks and balances in the form of coequal branches of government, the legislature and the courts offsetting the executive, and reserving the rest of the authority to the states and the people through the bill of rights. In the case of reconsidering a WTO, a constitutional convention would run into some difficulties. The point of the WTO and the GATT before it is not so much to reserve freedom of action for its nation-state members, but to impose on nations agreed limits for the benefit of the trade interests of all, for the common good. They are not predisposed to create a more perfect form of governance. Nevertheless, given the clear deficiencies in the current institutional framework of the WTO, it is worth considering how the use of checks and balances could result in recreating a stronger world trade organization and a fully functioning dispute settlement system.

Hoekman and Mavroidis in the first of their joint 2020 publications,[150] Payasova, Hufbauer, and Schott,[151] and MacDougal[152] provide brilliant synopses and analyses of what ails the WTO, reviewing much of the literature on the subject and coming up with a range of recommendations both for dispute settlement reform and rule-making. I am in full agreement with many of the recommendations. At points, we diverge. Given their expertise, and that we see many of the system's problems in the same light, this deserves some explanation.

A few years ago, when at the WTO, I thought that it would be a good idea for AB members to be full-time, chosen for their relevant skill sets, with their own clerks, and more independent of a strong-willed entrenched Appellate Body Secretariat staff (a source of the "stubbornness" that Hoekman and Mavroidis appear to attribute solely to the AB members, and in some cases they are certainly right). In a more perfect WTO, it would make sense to have

[150] Bernard Hoekman, Petros C. Mavroidis, and Maarja Saluste. 2021. "Informing WTO Reform: Dispute Settlement Performance, 1995–2020." *Journal of World Trade* 55(1): 1–50; Bernard Hoekman and Petros C. Mavroidis. 2020. "Preventing the Bad from Getting Worse: The End of the World (Trade Organization) As We Know It?" European University Institute, Robert Schuman Centre for Advanced Studies, Global Governance Programme Working Paper No. RSCAS 2020/06. https://scholarship.law.columbia.edu/cgi/viewcontent.cgi?article=3610&context=faculty_scholarship; Bernard Hoekman and Petros C. Mavroidis. 2020. "To AB or Not to AB? Dispute Settlement in WTO Reform." *Journal of International Economic Law* 23(3): 1–20; Bernard Hoekman and Petros C. Mavroidis. 2020. "Burning Down the House." in *21st Century Trade Policy: Back to the Past?*, edited by Bernard Hoekman and Ernesto Zedillo. Washington, DC: Brookings Institution Press.

[151] Tetyana Payosova, Gary Clyde Hufbauer, and Jeffrey J. Schott. 2018. "The Dispute Settlement Crisis in the World Trade Organization: Causes and Cures." Peterson Institute for International Economics. March. www.piie.com/publications/policy-briefs/dispute-settlement-crisis-world-trade-organization-causes-and-cures

[152] Robert McDougall. 2018. "Crisis in the WTO: Restoring the WTO Dispute Settlement Function." Centre for International Governance Innovation. October. www.cigionline.org/sites/default/files/documents/Paper%20no.194.pdf

longer fixed terms for AB members. This would provide consistency to rulings. Hoekman and Mavroidis, like me and others, would have the AB refer matters that have not been negotiated, gaps in the rules, to the members.

I place emphasis on building up the strength of the rule-making and executive and administrative functions of the WTO as a necessary precondition before perfecting the AB. If AB-strengthening changes are adopted before there is greater institutional balance, the problem of AB overreach will likely return and increase over time. Not only is the sequencing of institutional reforms important, but I cannot picture the current or a near future US government signing on to changes perfecting the AB absent more effective legislative and executive branches. More radical changes would be needed in the organization of dispute settlement, in the AB and its constitution, in order to obtain the prize – the restoration of the binding nature of WTO dispute settlement.

Politics is the art of the possible, and it is rarely pretty in its process and too often not in result. It requires a compromise of what is preferred for what might be on offer. I may misjudge the US Congress that torpedoed the ITO. The Congress accepted the WTO and the DSU on the basis of a promise that there would be a domestic review process for WTO case outcomes adverse to the United States.[153] That was never put into place. The only trade agreement of major consequence that Congress has approved since the WTO Agreement in 1994 is the US–Mexico–Canada replacement (and to a large extent, a continuation) of NAFTA, and a political price was paid to obtain that.[154] The history of congressional review of trade agreements provides a caution as to what will be politically feasible to enable the United States to join a reconstructed binding WTO dispute settlement system.

ALTERNATIVE PATHS FORWARD

It is widely recognized that reforms are needed to the DSU. Many of the suggestions for reform can be grouped under one of three headings: (a)

[153] "World Trade Organization (WTO) Dispute Settlement Review Commission Act, Hearings before the Senate Committee on Finance, Testimony of Alan Wolff." United States Senate Committee on Finance. May 10, 1995. www.finance.senate.gov/imo/media/doc/Hrg104-124.pdf; "Remarks by President Clinton, Sen. Dole, Sen. Moynihan, Sen. Packwood and Ambassador Kantor on the GATT." Clinton Presidential Materials Project. November 23, 1994. https://clintonwhitehouse6.archives.gov/1994/11/1994-11-23-remarks-by-president-sen-dole-and-others-on-gatt.html

[154] The United States also provided Permanent Normal Trade Relations to China, allowing China into the WTO.

perfecting the existing dispute settlement structure; (b) assuming that the United States will not accept a return to the system as it existed previously and that it will not accept reform limited to only cosmetic changes, view this as a negotiation and consider what elements might be deployed to restore binding two-stage dispute settlement; and (c) a third path, by default, a single stage of dispute settlement, consisting of independent arbitration panels. The second and third paths move further away from a court structure.

Whatever path is chosen for reconstituting binding dispute settlement, the emphasis throughout should be on bringing about the settlement of individual disputes as a higher priority than clarifying WTO obligations, as important as the latter is. The use of good offices of the Secretariat and mediation should be emphasized as favored parts of the dispute settlement process. Other alternatives, such as the filing of specific trade concerns (STCs), having a forum for providing reactions to the STCs, providing for the filing of notifications and counter-notifications, valuing serious deliberation within committees with respect to the issues raised and crafting lists of best practices more generally – all should be preferred to adjudication. First and foremost, of course, members are expected to live up to their obligations without the threat of compulsion, and this they largely do. Dispute settlement is for instances where they arguably fall short.

(a) *Creating a More Perfect Judicial System*

Putting aside how the current impasse was created and overcoming therefore the counterintuitive nature of the exercise, there are a number of ways in which to strengthen and improve dispute settlement at the WTO with a focus on making the Appellate Body more of a court. This is the path of greatest affinity for most of those who are devoted to the multilateral trading system. It was my first reaction before the reality of the divided WTO membership forced consideration of alternatives.

In broad strokes, this is what would be involved: improve the panel process, then pay more attention to the selection process for prospective AB members, have each serve for only a single but longer term of office of seven to nine years,[155] give each AB member one or more clerks, and, in the case of a

[155] Giorgio Sacerdoti. 2017. "The Future of the WTO Dispute Settlement System: Confronting Challenges to Consolidate a Success Story." in *Future of the Global Trade Order*, edited by Carlos A. Primo Braga and Bernard Hoekman. Florence: European University Institute. Changes designed largely to increase the capacity and the independence of the AB: going from seven to nine members, giving them longer fixed terms, making the AB members full-time (rather than commuters with other interests), and improving compliance. "WTO – EU's

vacancy in the AB, begin the nomination process automatically. AB members would be full-time with no other work, paid or unpaid, that could detract from their dispute settlement duties. Decisions by an AB panel member would not be valid after that member's term, but the remaining two panel members could still issue a decision in consultation with the other AB members. A 90/120-day limit should only be breached in extraordinary cases, and be subject to a specified upper limit, at which point the case would be referred to the General Council. To improve caseload capacity, the AB can be expanded to nine members.

One can add more than a touch of pragmatism to this option (with the hope that this might narrow the gap with the United States). In its decision restoring the Appellate Body, the General Council would provide language reinforcing the deference to be given to domestic authorities in antidumping cases (and countervailing duty cases). It would require the AB to clearly state its reasoning in opinions, make all hearings public, have decisions made only on the issues raised by the parties, and call for an annual meeting with the General Council for the AB members to hear views on the operation of the dispute settlement system. Precedents contrary to General Council guidance would be given no persuasive weight. As an additional option, a statement would be included that trade remedies would be recognized as having equal validity with other provisions of the WTO Agreements. (Although correct, it is hard to imagine this being adopted by consensus.)

One can supplement AB reforms by aiming for higher quality in the first-instance panel process, with a specialized roster of arbitrators. Technical assistance from the ICC, LCIA, and others – including not least the WTO Legal and Rules Divisions – would be sought for considering improvements to be made in first-stage adjudication. Incentives could be provided to settlement, having the losing party at the panel stage owe compensation from the date of the adverse panel decision, unless it prevails on appeal. Emphasis can be given to alternative means of resolving disputes, such as the good offices of the Director-General and Deputy Directors-General, or the filing of specific trade concerns in committees of jurisdiction. Costs can be awarded to the

Proposals on WTO Modernisation." Council of the European Union General Secretariat. July 5, 2018. www.perma.cc/CQ4S-3N2N. The Commission suggested to its member states that a single and nonrenewable six- to eight-year term might be a useful reform for the sake of independence and efficiency. This suggestion would solve the problem of renewals getting conditioned or blocked, which the European Union and the United States had each engaged in. The Commission added that once the United States unblocked the appointment process, the EU would be willing to engage in discussions on the substantive concerns of the United States.

winning party for any appeal (other than against a least developed country, or other criteria).

It is possible to comb through the extensive writings of Hoekman, Mavroidis, Simon Lester, Hufbauer, and Schott, and the sources that they cite, to compile suggestions as to how to improve the system. What should not be included in a recommended list is to move to voting in the Dispute Settlement Body. Resort to voting is a much larger issue of governance for the WTO than trying to get dispute settlement back on track. However, the fiction of DSB adoption of "reports" from panels or the AB can be retained if this is desired, for as constructed it has no meaning.

Caveat: It is unlikely that the United States would agree to binding dispute settlement without a carve-out for dealing with nonmarket competition from and in China, for self-determined national security measures including what John Jackson called "interface" mechanisms,[156] as well as having policy space for trade remedies. This caveat applies to all options.

(b) *Reconstituting an Appellate Body for Two-Tier Dispute Settlement*

AN OVERVIEW

Where to begin? Negotiations would best start with a few basic concepts – that the shared objective is literally the settlement of disputes. The WTO consists of sovereign nations joined together for the purpose of cooperation on matters affecting international trade. They have made rules and they wish them to be effective. Where there are differences, they wish them to be settled amicably, without retaliation. Dispute settlement must be backed up by a judicial process, but that should not be the first option. It should be the default when other attempts at resolution fail. Heading off disputes by sharing measures in draft works well for product standards, along with filing specific trade concerns. While rule-making in the WTO has become rare, consensus has been reached, for example, in the Committee on Technical Barriers to Trade on best practices. The DSU provides for consultations, but those have become all too often a mere formality in a headlong flight toward adjudication. Good offices of the Director-General are available but are not often sought. Too much emphasis has been placed on adjudication as a first rather than a last resort.

[156] David Kennedy. 1995. "The International Style in Postwar Law and Policy: John Jackson and the Field of International Economic Law." *American University International Law Review* 10 (2): 671–716.

A fresh look should be given to the WTO's institutional framework. Attention needs to be given to the roles of all the main institutional elements of the WTO – the Dispute Settlement Body, the General Council, and the Secretariat. As long as the other institutions of governance are inactive, there will be a problem of expecting too much from adjudication. The framework of the WTO lacks checks and balances. The AB is subject to criticism when the DSB and General Council do not perform their assigned functions. In a domestic national setting, if the courts exceeded their mandate, the legislature, often on the initiative of the executive branch, can change or clarify the law. In the WTO, rule-making has proved to be nearly impossible. The Secretariat, the WTO's executive, has no role other than supporting panelists and AB members. The solutions supplied in the current DSU, assigning a role to the General Council and Dispute Settlement Body, have been wholly ineffective.

Confining WTO reform to changes in the Appellate Body will require more far-reaching change than if a broader approach is taken. While a holistic approach is needed, that is not the most likely point where talks would begin, as indicated by the Walker Principles. Members are most likely to concentrate immediately on how the Appellate Body should operate.

THE PARAMETERS FOR NEGOTIATION

The basis for negotiation should be clearly stated at the outset: the effort is aimed at restoring binding dispute settlement. Almost all WTO members who have expressed an opinion on what WTO dispute settlement should encompass have subscribed to restoring the Appellate Body, with some changes to meet current and past criticisms. The MPIA moved in this direction. The US view was that it did not go far enough. It is an open question whether the US can accept having binding, independent, two-stage (panel and appellate level) dispute settlement.

The WTO has forcefully demonstrated that it is nearly impossible to make progress in negotiations in a meeting of the whole. To start the process, it is necessary to have the United States and the European Union intimately involved. They have been the primary antagonists but share a number of common interests. The two have already cooperated on a number of WTO reform initiatives in a trilateral format, with the inclusion of Japan. It is not essential that there be a trilateral base from which to build a broader consensus, but it is one way in which to proceed. The process could also include at the outset Brazil or Canada or another one or two active members. Their work product would be an interim arrangement for disputes between any two of the parties to the talks, designating it as a "New MPIA (NMPIA)." The circle could then be broadened to other MPIA parties and a number of non-MPIA parties. If all WTO members were comfortable with the outcome, this could become an updated DSU.

One can assume that the European Union would wish the outcome to be as close as possible to the current MPIA, and that the United States would wish policy space with respect to worker-centered trade remedies and include flexibilities to deal with non-market-oriented competition and US national security concerns.

The negotiating choices for restoring an Appellate Body may start with giving it further instructions as to what its role is to be, what its limits are. There are also questions about the structure of the AB – a single term, a shorter or longer term, how many AB members there should be (the MPIA has ten), what sort of expertise should be included, making reappointment as automatic as possible, etc. Were the DSB to have a real role in oversight of the AB, then the specifications for the AB could be less constraining. Were there to be a role for the Secretariat, the same may hold true. The parts of the system are interrelated.

Table 14.1 contains a menu of elements of a possible negotiation leading to restoring an appellate stage to which all WTO members might ultimately agree. It is designed to stimulate a more detailed discussion on AB reform. Some of the elements listed are from the Walker Principles, resulting from his consultations with WTO member delegations. More than a few of the ideas in the following grew out of my own discussions with colleagues at the WTO while I was serving there from 2017 to 2021, as the AB crisis grew. In particular, there were long talks with DDG Karl Brauner and AB staff member Kaarlo Castren, both of whom have intimate knowledge of the workings of WTO dispute settlement. The ideas also evolved from discussions with WTO members, including ambassadors, members of their delegations, officials in capitals, past AB members and staff, and expert observers who are students of the process. A number of the elements are also contained in the rich trove of current literature on this subject. I am indebted to all but take full responsibility for the clearly personal menu of elements that follow. There are some innovations that I have not seen elsewhere that would certainly benefit from debate. Again, the way to read the table is as a menu from which choices can be made, not a prescription. The more that is done systemically, in terms of checks and balances, improving the functioning of the legislative and executive functions of the WTO, the less radical need be the changes made in the AB (for example, having two-year terms). An international organization must be responsive to its members, and at the same time have independent dispute settlement. This dual requirement is easier to state than to achieve.

TABLE 14.1 *Reconstituting an Appellate Body for Two Tier Dispute Settlement*

The Authority of the Appellate Body

- It cannot expand or limit the rights or obligations of the members.
- Issues that cannot be resolved based on explicit existing obligations shall be referred to the Dispute Settlement Body and the WTO members for resolution.
- Appeals may only be brought for issues of law, not fact.
- AB decisions are to be confined to issues raised by the parties.
- AB panels shall not issue advisory opinions.
- Where an AB panel finds it necessary due to shortcomings in a panel report, the AB panel can (within sixty days of taking on a case) remand it for further consideration to the panel.
- Decisions are applicable only to the case being heard. There is no presumption of precedential value. However, a searchable compendium of interpretations by the AB and first-instance panels will be maintained by the Office of Legal Counsel (a new OLC, explained below) of the WTO Secretariat and supplied to panels.
- Special terms of reference could be mutually agreed by the parties to specific disputes, including stipulation to certain facts and limitations on the scope of issues submitted for adjudication.
- Matters of national security are political in nature and a rebuttable presumption of deference will be provided to members. This deference shall not be used to allow the provision of disguised protection to an industry, where the claim of an essential security interest is found to be frivolous.
- Major issues of systemic importance, such as export restrictions on vaccines, would be referred to a special working party to foster a systemic response.
- The dispute settlement system could be made available for settlement of disputes under regional and bilateral free trade agreements (RTAs and FTAs).
  - This would contribute to the centrality of a single world trading system.
  - If this practice grew, it could require separate expert staffing from the Secretariat.

Expansion of the Roster of AB Members, AB Panel Composition

- The Appellate Body shall be composed of highly qualified persons of recognized authority with demonstrated expertise in law,[157] international trade, and the subject matter of the covered agreements generally. AB members should each to the extent possible combine the skills of being a lawyer and a trade negotiator. It is optimal to have both of these kinds of experience.
- AB members shall not be affiliated with any government.

(continued)

[157] This is not to say that each AB member needs to be a lawyer as a formal matter, but it helps. There are many subtleties of litigation: when an argument is germane, when a statement in a report is dictum, where burdens of proof lie. Equally, the subject at hand is commerce, and to promote fair commerce, trade negotiators created rules. Understanding what the original negotiators intended, and when they reached a compromise or an impasse, is assisted if one has had relevant trade negotiating experience.

TABLE 14.1 (*continued*)

- The number of AB members is increased from seven to twenty-five.[158]
  - A major complaint concerning current WTO dispute settlement is the seemingly interminable delays in getting an answer. One way of getting back to speedier dispute settlement results is to increase the number of AB members. The MPIA representing twenty-five WTO participants and already has ten MPIA appeal arbitrators. It issued its first opinion in December 2022.
  - How extreme is expanding the number of AB members? A complaint of the old AB (the one the WTO had until December 2019) was overwork. A few years ago, the WTO Director-General congratulated the dispute settlement system for hearing its 500th case over the course of the first twenty years of the WTO. The ICC in recent years typically handles about twice that volume of cases in a single year. International commercial arbitration is considered highly reliable, which we know because it continues to be relied upon in cases involving very large commercial and financial stakes. There seems to be a sufficient number of skilled arbitrators to meet the demand, through the ICC, LCIA, and like bodies.[159] An AB of twenty-five members is hardly a large number compared with the vast demand for adjudication worldwide. There are cost-savings to be achieved as well: it is usual for arbitrators to, in the main, write their own opinions, rather than involving Secretariat staff.
  - A larger roster of AB members would allow for diversity by geographic representation and gender. It would also allow for specialization.
- To the extent possible, AB panel members should have relevant experience. (As many cases are about trade remedies, there should be added to the roster a sufficient number of persons with expertise, and preferably hands-on national administrative experience, to sit on cases having to do with antidumping, subsidization, countervailing duties, safeguards, and balance of payments measures. If there were cases on other specialized areas, the same care should be taken with appointments.)[160]

[158] Expansion of the number of AB members and having, for that matter, panelists who were more like stand-alone arbitrators, might also make the WTO dispute settlement more accessible to developing countries. Increasing the supply might drive down cost.

[159] The International Chamber of Commerce (ICC), the London Court of International Arbitration (LCIA), the International Centre for Dispute Resolutions (ICDR), the Swiss Chamber's Arbitration Institution (SCAI), the Vienna International Arbitral Centre (VIAC), the Hong Kong International Arbitration Centre (HKIAC), the China International Economic and Trade Arbitration Commission (CIETAC), the Cairo Regional Centre for International Commercial Arbitration (CRCICA), the Stockholm Chamber of Commerce Arbitration Institute (SCC), and the International Institute for Conflict Prevention and Resolution (CPR).

[160] Jennifer Hillman. "Three Approaches to Fixing the World Trade Organization, the Good, the Bad and the Ugly?" Institute of International Economic Law. December 10, 2018. www.law.georgetown.edu/wp-content/uploads/2018/12/Hillman-Good-Bad-Ugly-Fix-to-WTO-AB.pdf. Jennifer Hillman, Professor at Georgetown University Law Center, Fellow at the Council on Foreign Relations, and a former AB Member, has an alternative that equally recommends itself: "One option would be to create a special Appellate Body to hear only appeals of trade remedy decisions. This special appellate institution – call it the Rules Appellate Body – could be made up of members chosen in large part because of a strong background in trade remedy law." This to some extent echoes the US court system, which has specialized courts for consideration of appeals from trade remedy decisions of the US administrators of the applicable laws. Hillman suggests

- The DSB, on the advice of the Office of Legal Counsel (OLC), would be tasked with assuring that this mandate is adhered to.
- The dispute settlement system could be made available for settlement of disputes under regional and bilateral free trade agreements (RTAs and FTAs).
  - This would contribute to the centrality of a single world trading system.
  - If this practice grew, it could require separate expert staffing from the Secretariat.

Term of Office of AB Members, Operation of AB Panels

- AB members would serve for two- or three-year terms. Reappointment for a second term is presumed to be automatic absent objection by positive consensus in the DSB for compelling reasons which must be stated. Non-reappointment is to be considered extraordinary.
- An AB member shall serve a maximum of two terms on the roster.
- The terms would be staggered so that one-third of the serving AB members' terms would come to an end every two years.
- An allegation of expansion of rights or obligations by an AB member or members will be heard as an extraordinary challenge by the Dispute Settlement Review Committee (see DSB discussion below), which shall make its recommendation to the DSB for disposition. Decisions of the DSB on this matter would be taken by positive consensus.
- No case is to be assigned to an AB member within the last ninety days of that member's term.
- Decisions can be rendered after the term of office of an AB member by agreement of the parties for up to sixty days, unless a longer period is approved by the DSB (by positive consensus) in extraordinary circumstances.
- No report from an AB panel will be valid if issued after ninety days from the date of referral to the AB, unless the period of validity is extended by the DSB for an additional period not to exceed an additional ninety days for good cause shown, on application of the parties to the dispute.
- An interim AB panel report containing the dispositive findings of the AB panel will be given to the parties and the OLC ten days before the issuance of a final report. Upon motion for reconsideration by a complainant or a respondent, the AB panel will have thirty days to issue a final report.
- As a general rule, hearings conducted by first-instance and AB panels shall be open to the public.
  - AB members are to be remunerated only for work on appeals to which they have been assigned – and on the same basis as panelists.

(*continued*)

another approach to national trade remedy cases: make initial panel decisions final. She argues persuasively that these cases have already been looked at very carefully in domestic proceedings. I would add that an extraordinary challenge might be brought to an AB trade remedy expert panel if the allegation was supported by evidence that the consideration was arbitrary, capricious, and not up to a minimum standard of fairness and objectivity.

TABLE 14.1 (*continued*)

Standards of Review
◦ The primary guide for settling a dispute is traditional contract interpretation, requiring panels to discern the intention of those drafting the rules, relying wherever possible on negotiating history. There is no "plain meaning" of language that is not obvious on its face. The original intent of the parties to the negotiation is controlling. ◦ WTO Agreements are to be viewed as contractual arrangements. Negotiating history is to be a primary source for interpretation as to the scope of the rules. The rules cannot be expanded by the AB to fit later circumstances to the extent that an interpretation could not have been within the clear intention of the negotiators,[161] particularly when the negotiating history was crystal clear that a given point (zeroing) had been the subject of attempts at negotiation which were rebuffed. ◦ The WTO provisions for trade remedies are deemed to have coequal importance with other WTO provisions. They are not to be deemed exceptions to be narrowly construed. ◦ Deference is to be given to domestic tribunals that have detailed, reliable processes with respect to findings of fact.[162] The standard of review that is applicable in Art. 17.6 of the Anti-Dumping Agreement is to be regarded as definitive guidance: ◦ i) in its assessment of the facts of the matter, the panel shall determine whether the authorities' establishment of the facts was proper and whether their evaluation of those facts was unbiased and objective. If the establishment of the facts was proper and the evaluation was unbiased and objective, even though the panel might have reached a different conclusion, the evaluation shall not be overturned. ◦ (ii) the panel shall interpret the relevant provisions of the agreement in accordance with customary rules of interpretation of public international law. Where the panel finds that a relevant provision of the agreement admits of more than one permissible interpretation, the panel shall find the authorities' measure to be in conformity with the agreement if it rests upon one of those permissible interpretations.[163] • (The first sentence of this subparagraph is not to be read to take precedence over the second sentence, nor is resort to the Vienna Convention on the Law of Treaties (VCLT) to be used to nullify the quest for identifying more than one permissible interpretation).[164]

[161] Trade measures evolve in kind. There is room for interpretation as to what a rule is to cover when technology or other factors bringing about change undermine the value of a trade concession or a rule. All that can be done is to give guidance with respect to how the process of interpretation is to take place.

[162] In US domestic law, deference to administrators in the interpretation of law when the statute is ambiguous was considered required by the courts, according to *Chevron USA. Inc.* v. *Natural Resources Defense Council, Inc. et al.*, a US Supreme Court case from 1984.

[163] Anti-Dumping Agreement Art. 17.6.

[164] Isabelle Van Damme. 2009. *Treaty Interpretation by the WTO Appellate Body*. Oxford: Oxford University Press. Van Damme discusses the interpretation taken by various AB divisions on the interplay of interpretation under the VCLT and the Anti-Dumping Code sections quoted above on pages 68–72 of her book.

The WTO Secretariat's Role

- A new Independent Office of Legal Counsel (OLC) would be created within the Secretariat.[165]
  - The OLC would advise the Director-General and Secretariat on any legal questions involving interpretation of WTO Agreements.
  - The OLC would be responsible as an independent guardian of the system and would not otherwise take sides in any panel or AB process.
- Pre-litigation
  - Upon request, skilled and experienced independent OLC staff would give informal, confidential nonbinding analytical reports on the merits of a case, helping to narrow issues for decision.
  - Upon request, Deputy Directors-General would provide good offices to potential litigants to seek resolution of differences without resorting to litigation.
- After a request for consultations is filed, good offices to be utilized
  - Parties are required to utilize good offices of the Director-General and Deputies Director-General before a panel would be formed.
- Litigation
  - The Office of Legal Counsel (OLC) would be expected to file amicus briefs on key points of legal interpretation, confined to the negotiating history, to discern the intention of the parties to the agreement. The OLC would identify areas where there appeared to be no coverage within a WTO agreement of the practice which is subject to the dispute.
  - The OLC, if it found that a matter was not covered by the rules as negotiated, and the panel or AB panel had not declared itself unable to resolve a dispute as a result of the absence of an applicable rule, would refer the matter to the DSB for action, with copies to the WTO committees with subject matter jurisdiction.
- Independent investigation
  - The OLC would investigate suspected serious deviations from the WTO rules on the part of any member that would have significant systemic implications.
  - The OLC would publish its conclusions, identifying "questionable conduct" without itself initiating litigation, unless the systemic implications were deemed extremely serious, and then only after consultation with the chairs of the General Council, the DSB, and the Trade Policy Review Body, in which instance, OLC would bring a case directly to the AB for necessary adjudication,[166] and where existing rules were insufficient, refer the matter to the General Council.

(*continued*)

[165] Not to be confused with the existing WTO OLC, which is a very small office of two lawyers dealing with legal issues involving personnel and other administrative matters.

[166] Jeffrey J. Schott and Euijin Jung. 2019. "The WTO's Existential Crisis: How to Salvage Its Ability to Settle Trade Disputes." Peterson Institute for International Economics. December. www.piie.com/publications/policy-briefs/wtos-existential-crisis-how-salvage-its-ability-settle-trade-disputes. Schott

TABLE 14.1 (*continued*)

- ◦ The OLC would regularly publish a watch list of measures that appeared to be on their face unjustified, and had a past, current, or expected substantial negative effect on trade.
- ◦ Relation to the DSB
  - ◦ The OLC would review the decisions of panels and AB panels and advise the DSB through triennial reports whether the intention of the parties, as discerned from negotiating history, was being applied, and include any recommendations as to remedies for deviations from the intent of the parties to the negotiation.

Role of the DSB

- ◦ A major cause of allegations of AB overreach is that there are no checks and balances built into the system to avoid judicial activism. The DSB, to all intents and purposes, has no role in the administration of the dispute settlement system other than the power of appointment.
- ◦ Going forward, gaps in rules would be identified by AB panels and/or the OLC and referred to the DSB and the appropriate WTO committees with subject matter interest for potential resolution.
- ◦ The chair of the DSB would convene a Dispute Settlement Review Committee consisting of five chairs of WTO Committees and five Secretariat Directors to issue a triennial report on the operation of the AB, including monitoring for areas where potential overreach may have occurred. This DS Review Committee would accept submissions from members suggesting areas where overreach may have occurred. Expert opinions would be sought on cases wherever additional expertise would be needed or would otherwise be beneficial.[167] Relevant WTO Committees (such as Anti-Dumping, Subsidies, TBT, Services, TRIPS, etc.) and staff would be invited to attend. DSR Committee sessions would be open to the public.
- ◦ Any group of no fewer than ten WTO members could identify a particular finding for an in-depth analysis by a special apolitical expert group constituted by the DSB, so as to provide a "measured report of constructive criticism for the information of the WTO

and Jung would have the AB, where it found that the rules did not cover, on its own motion choose to refer a matter to the committees having jurisdiction over the subject matter.

[167] "WTO Dispute Settlement Misunderstandings: How to Bridge the Gap Between the United States and the Rest of the World." International Economic Law and Policy Blog. April 19, 2020. https://ielp.worldtradelaw.net/2020/04/wto-dispute-settlement-misunderstandings-how-to-bridge-the-gap-between-the-united-states-and-the-res.html. Simon Lester suggested an alternative to the DSB addressing overreach. He would have the General Council or a Ministerial Conference vote (three-quarters of members required to carry an issue) on whether the reasoning (not the result of an individual report) was in error, thus making law. The problem with voting is the difficulty or ease of getting enough votes – that is, an unpopular position might not carry, while a popular but erroneous position might do so. Nevertheless, this is a recognition that the members have to rediscover their legislative (rule-making) power and reassert it. The question is how best to do it. This approach could be combined with the Dispute Settlement Review Committee recommended above.

system, including the Appellate Body and panels." Such a report could be provided to the DSB for information, and adopted by the DSB.[168]

- The DSB has the responsibility to fill AB vacancies as they arise. The nominating process is to be automatically begun six months before the expiration of any term.
- The chairman of the DSB is responsible for the DSB becoming, to the extent possible, an effective body. The chair should be active in attempting to resolve conflicts among members wherever the chair deems it would be productive, prior to and during litigation. It is the responsibility of the chair to bring political acumen to the goal of settling disputes. Where, for example, the result is almost fully for one party at the level of the first-instance panel, and for the other party at the appellate level, this may be a *prima facie* case for the chair to seek to resolve the matter directly working with the two parties, and to suggest to them (in consultation with the OLC) that one or the other of the panels be reconvened to reconsider some elements of the case.
- DSB chairs would serve for two year terms rather than one.

Ancillary Changes

- Reports of the AB panels are to be readable, to contain clear findings together with a full justification of reasoning that allowed each finding to be made, with only brief summaries of submissions and arguments, and with reference to online documents submitted by the parties and any amicus briefs for greater detail.
- Operating procedures shall be adopted, covering imposition of strict page limits for written submissions, guidelines for briefs, focused hearings, and questions to the parties, subject to approval by the DSB by positive consensus or, if no consensus, by the DSB chair and the OLC.
- Any official meetings among AB members other than those serving on an AB panel will be open for virtual attendance by WTO members and the Secretariat.
- The roster is not a collegium and is not to gather to discuss cases, except in open meetings. Pending cases are not to be discussed by AB members collectively outside of the AB panel seized with the case.
- The parties can, by mutual agreement, suspend temporarily or terminate an AB consideration of a case, in order to promote settlement.[169]

First-Instance Panel

- Emphasis is placed on experience, with the appointment of highly qualified individuals.
- Part of WTO reform is to review and include suggestions on improvements to the panel process. There have been many useful suggestions in this regard. Addressing

(*continued*)

[168] "The Future of the WTO: Addressing Institutional Challenges in the New Millennium: Report by the Consultative Board to the Director-General." World Trade Organization. 2004. www.wto.org/english/thewto_e/10anniv_e/future_wto_e.pdf

[169] One element is the use of experts, which, while desirable in complex cases, should not unduly delay reaching a result.

TABLE 14.1 (*continued*)

these is beyond the scope of the present analysis, which focuses on the most serious issue with respect to WTO dispute settlement, restoring binding dispute settlement.[170] With the restoration of binding dispute settlement, panel quality and efficiency should also be addressed, as well as more effective means to assure compliance with dispute settlement decisions, including collective action.

Effective Date for Compliance

- The obligation for compensation/removal or adjustment of the nonconforming measure dates from the first-instance panel report if that report is not reversed on appeal. The incentive for delay is removed, and the burden for delay falls on the party losing at the first instance.

Decisions To Be Final

- Appeals into the void are disallowed.[171] The Secretariat has no authority to accept appeals when there is no AB in place (when there are no AB members serving).
- Panel decisions are final if no other arrangement for an appeal is made between the parties.

Voluntary Nature of the Dispute Settlement System

- Opt-in/opt-out
  - No WTO member would be compelled to join the newly revised dispute settlement system.
    - Any member not agreeing to be subject to the DSU would have no access to it and would not have any enforceable rights under the WTO Agreements. It would in effect be reduced to observer status.

[170] Giorgio Sacerdoti. 2017. "The Future of the WTO Dispute Settlement System: Confronting Challenges to Consolidate a Success Story." in *Future of the Global Trade Order*, edited by Carlos A. Primo Braga and Bernard Hoekman. Florence: European University Institute.

[171] Bernard M. Hoekman and Petros C. Mavroidis. "Preventing the Bad from Getting Worse: The End of the World (Trade Organization) As We Know it?" European University Institute, Robert Schuman Centre for Advanced Studies Global Governance Programme Working Paper No. RSCAS 2020/06. https://scholarship.law.columbia.edu/cgi/viewcontent.cgi?article=3610&context=faculty_scholarship. Bernard Hoekman and Petros Mavroidis note in their important essay: "The WTO has taken no official position regarding the question whether the correct interpretation of Article 16.4 of the DSU entails that an appeal to a nonexistent AB is possible or not." This sentence is accurate but has a lot more packed into it than what is on the surface. How can the WTO take a position? No member has decided to take the question to a panel. The rule-making function of the WTO can be cranked up every now and then for a huge effort, such as the Trade Facilitation Agreement or the ban on agricultural export subsidies, but these took years in the making, a concentrated effort. The Dispute Settlement Body has never taken a position. The General Council has not interpreted the DSU. There is no General Counsel of the WTO Secretariat that renders opinions on the meaning of WTO Agreements.

- No WTO member would be compelled to have disputes adjudicated by a reconstituted AB panel but would then be required to abide by first-instance panel decisions or those of an MPIA for a period of five years (before being allowed to opt back in) for any cases in which it is a party, as either complainant or respondent.
- An opt-out of the system would be possible by category – for example, limited to trade remedy cases (AD, CVD, safeguards, national security), with the consequence that it could neither bring nor be subject to a case involving measures of the kind specified. Opt-outs would have a sunset at five years, renewable for additional periods.[172]
- To prevent gaming the system with respect to individual cases, a member deciding to opt in would be obligated to stay in for the next four cases brought against it. Not appearing would result in a default judgment.
- Nonapplication, either complete or by category of case, between two members would also be an option but it should not affect the rights of third members (MFN). This provision would allow two members engaged in a strategic competition to make special arrangements for achieving maximum coverage of WTO dispute settlement between them, without blocking change in the system as a whole or having complete nonapplication of the DSU between them.
  - Domestic means to invoke an opt-out (United States).
    - Congress approved the Uruguay Round Agreements, and therefore the creation of the WTO, because of an agreement between then-President Bill Clinton and the coauthors of a Senate proposal, Robert Dole and Daniel Patrick Moynihan.[173] Their proposal was to have a US panel of retired federal judges review WTO rulings that were adverse to the United States to determine whether the decisions were correctly reached. The legislation did not become law,

(*continued*)

[172] Tetyana Payosova, Gary Clyde Hufbauer, and Jeffrey J. Schott. 2018. "The Dispute Settlement Crisis in the World Trade Organization: Causes and Cures." Peterson Institute for International Economics. March. www.piie.com/publications/policy-briefs/dispute-settlement-crisis-world-trade-organization-causes-and-cures.

Jennifer Hillman. "Three Approaches to Fixing the World Trade Organization, the Good, the Bad and the Ugly?" Institute of International Economic Law. December 10, 2018. www.law.georgetown.edu/wp-content/uploads/2018/12/Hillman-Good-Bad-Ugly-Fix-to-WTO-AB.pdf. Hillman suggests a (temporary) moratorium on appeals of panel decisions involving trade remedy disputes. Jeffrey J. Schott and Euijin Jung. 2019. "The WTO's Existential Crisis: How to Salvage Its Ability to Settle Trade Disputes." Peterson Institute for International Economics, Washington, DC. www.piie.com/publications/policy-briefs/wtos-existential-crisis-how-salvage-its-ability-settle-trade-disputes) The authors suggest that the moratorium on appeals should be permanent and limited to AD/CVD cases (as opposed to all trade remedies such as safeguards). AD/CVD cases would still be subject to binding dispute panel decisions. My suggested variant avoids completely removing trade remedy cases from appellate jurisdiction.

[173] "General Agreement on Tariffs and Trade." C-SPAN. November 23, 1994. www.c-span.org/video/?61755-1/general-agreement-tariffs-trade. There would be no WTO without President Clinton's commitment to a domestic judicial review commission and domestic US procedures for withdrawal from the WTO triggered by WTO dispute settlement engaging in overreach.

TABLE 14.1 (*continued*)

despite the endorsement of the President and the chair and ranking minority member of the Senate Finance Committee. ▪ The Dispute Settlement Review Commission Act can be reconsidered,[174] revised to implement rights under the amended DSU, as a means to determine if the President should decide whether or not to opt out of AB review (not an opt-out from the WTO). ▪ Putting into place an independent review of AB decisions and requiring that the opt-out be invoked only upon a Commission decision, and with congressional approval expressed in a joint resolution, would reduce the likelihood of an ill-considered US opt-out. ◦ Testing a reformed two-stage system. ▪ One of the last sitting AB members, Thomas Graham, recommended in 2019 that the AB be given another chance, with some changes made in staffing to demonstrate that it would be able to meet US objections without changes in the DSU. That option was not tried. ▪ The only way to determine if a new system would work is with another try, after making changes that are broadly acceptable to WTO members. The trial period could be five or ten years, with a sunset clause requiring consideration of renewal of, or making permanent, the system at the end of that period.

An initial problem for dispute settlement is that the rules of the system do not cover every contingency, and they often pose questions of motive. Examples of other areas where there is inadequate coverage by the rules are domestic industrial subsidies, some internet services, and other services more broadly. Trade measures designed for coercion are hard to be judged in terms of their WTO consistency if they also take on the guise of a standards or antidumping measure.

There is a problem posed by the asymmetry of coverage. How is dispute settlement to address practices that are harmful but not covered by the rules when, at the same time, responses in a rules-based system are likely to be covered by the rules?

A new (NMPIA) would offer a convenient path to a solution within the WTO framework, a flexible means to allow for experimentation with different elements of dispute settlement. What it cannot do is restore the AB in any form unless it becomes acceptable to all.

[174] "World Trade Organization (WTO) Dispute Settlement Review Commission Act, Hearings before the Senate Committee on Finance, Testimony of Alan Wolff." United States Senate Committee on Finance. May 10, 1995. www.finance.senate.gov/imo/media/doc/Hrg104-124.pdf; "S.16 – WTO Dispute Settlement Review Commission Act." Library of Congress. January 4, 1995. www.congress.gov/bill/104th-congress/senate-bill/16/text

(c) *Single-Stage Dispute Settlement*

ONE TIER: PANEL DECISIONS ARE FINAL

- Pro: This option has the benefit of simplicity. It is the path perhaps least likely to establish precedent, although this cannot be assured. With a highest-quality roster of arbitrators, as with the LCIA and like bodies, the mechanism can earn the trust of WTO members.
- Con: This is not what the WTO members who have expressed themselves say that they are seeking. Moreover, single-stage dispute settlement can create unappealable but incorrect and inconsistent results for cases with similar fact patterns.
- Comment: Some of the lack of uniformity can be overcome if the operation of the panels is overseen by the appointment of an OLC reporting to the DSB.[175] In the case of serious inconsistency, the OLC can be entrusted with certain powers to intervene. The OLC would inform a panel if, in its view, the question cannot be decided under existing rules because the WTO members had not yet negotiated a rule covering the conduct complained of. The OLC would notify the members of the gap in the rules and recommend appropriate action. Prior to a panel being formed, it could issue on request, after briefing, an analytical report which could obviate the need for litigation.

Given the massive global network of arbitration (often as with the LCIA) without appeal possible, would not single-stage, initial panel only, dispute settlement suffice for the WTO? The answer is, perhaps.[176] That depends on whether the sole objective is settling a given dispute before a given panel or maintaining a single set of rules for the global trading system. As both are desirable, a premium needs to be placed on consistency and predictability. Some guardrails will be required.

THE SPECIAL CASE OF NATIONAL SECURITY

Given the recent increase in the invocation of the national security exception to the WTO's rules, it appears clear that there can be no return to binding dispute settlement acceptable by all without agreement as to how claims of national security are to be dealt with. WTO dispute settlement panels, at the request of individual members, have intruded into this most sensitive of all subjects despite decades of GATT and WTO participants seeking to avoid

[175] This office has, so far as I know, not been suggested elsewhere.

[176] Bernard Hoekman and Petros C. Mavroidis. 2020. "To AB or Not to AB? Dispute Settlement in WTO Reform." *Journal of International Economic Law* 23(3): 1–20.

panels seeking to determine what a country judged was in its own national security interest. (One of the ironies of the existing WTO provision is that a measure is on its face justifiable if the country imposing a national security measure invades the territory of the complainant).

One way in which the national security exception cases could be dealt with is by shifting the burden of proof to the complainant to show that the conditions of Article XXI have not been met or by providing an opt out for members claiming nonjusticiability of this issue from this class of cases. Both of these methods are listed above as possible options, but these will probably not prove to be acceptable solutions to all parties. The suggestion made to me by former USTR General Counsel Warren Maruyama and planned to be the subject of a joint article by the two of us, is one that we would suggest be favorably considered by the WTO's members: The judgment of a country invoking the national security exception under Article XXI would be nonjusticiable, but members adversely affected would be authorized to suspend substantially equivalent concessions (WTO-speak for authorized retaliation). This would have little or no impact in the case of geopolitical rivals, the United States and China, who now act (in the view of most observers) outside the rules to apply broadly reciprocal measures as if they were allowed to do so. It might have a greater impact where a country invokes the national security exception to impose a measure against many countries. The potential adverse effects on its trade would impose much larger costs as all members affected could retaliate against its trade. The proposal would thus bring within the system measures such as the increased US tariffs on steel and aluminum as well as bypassing the need for responding countries (the EU in this instance) to stretch to categorize the US measure as a legitimate safeguard in order to cover their retaliatory response.

This change in the rules could largely be achieved on a *de facto* basis by countries by indicating their acceptance in advance of this outcome. It is within their power to adopt this manner of proceeding unilaterally. There would be little incentive for another member to bring a case when approval of its retaliation was already granted in principle in advance. The level of retaliatory response would be justiciable. The proposal would preserve what the GATT and WTO set out to do – to maintain a balance of concessions. Without this change, the trading system would be seen as increasingly irrelevant. This fix is worth considering as a compromise that may prove to be broadly acceptable where otherwise an impasse may persist.

WHICH OF THE THREE OPTIONS TO START TALKS WITH?

On balance, preserving an appellate function in dispute settlement is desirable, for consistency of decisions and to correct panel errors. A tactical question is how to begin the discussion. It may make sense to start where the system is, on paper, if no longer in reality – that is, start with the current DSU and decide how to repair it.

The problem at this point is not primarily technical; it is political. In the end, balance will have to be restored to the system to obtain US acceptance. Pragmatism, creativity, and agility, if applied to this issue, can provide WTO dispute settlement with an appellate function having a legitimacy that will find general support or otherwise restoring its binding nature.[177]

NEGOTIATING STRATEGIES

To solve the crisis of WTO dispute settlement, part of a larger WTO crisis, there needs to be heightened engagement of members dedicated to making improvements in the global trading system. Binding dispute settlement must be restored, but it is unlikely to be what it was, and it will very likely need to be part of a package. It is unrealistic to assume that dispute settlement can be solved solely on the basis of small adjustments made to the DSU. Either there would have to be exclusions from dispute settlement that would be very large – for use of trade remedies and measures to counter forms of state intervention in commerce that the current substantive rules cannot adequately address – or parallel negotiations will need to provide those rules.

An interim solution can take the form of a New MPIA (NMPIA), applicable only to signatories. This would avoid the need for a negotiation in which 164 members are sufficiently satisfied with the result that none would block its adoption. In effect, the United States and the European Union would agree to a modified MPIA and invite others to join. It would be applicable to those who chose to join it. If the NMPIA (a US–EU + MPIA) was less desirable to MPIA participants than their current arrangement, the two MPIAs could coexist as readily as if the United States and European Union agreed to be bound by any first-instance panel decision.

[177] "DDG Wolff: 'There is Reason for Optimism About the Future of the Multilateral Trading System'." World Trade Organization. October 15, 2018. www.wto.org/english/news_e/news18_e/ddgra_15oct18_e.htm; "WTO Dispute Settlement Misunderstandings: How to Bridge the Gap Between the United States and the Rest of the World." International Economic Law and Policy Blog. April 19, 2020. https://ielp.worldtradelaw.net/2020/04/wto-dispute-settlement-misunderstandings-how-to-bridge-the-gap-between-the-united-states-and-the-res.html

For most economists, anti-dumping and safeguards are, in practice, simply forms of permitted protectionism, whereas countervailing duties try to address a real problem (trade-distorting subsidies). As a policy matter, it is important to continue to make the case against protectionism. However, as a matter of politics, preserving a system with broad benefits requires compromise. The practice of trade remedies needs to be accommodated.

Another approach to negotiations of a permanent solution to dispute settlement might be to include it as part of a broader package with substantively unrelated agreements, such as for e-commerce, trade, and health, environmental issues related to climate change, improved access in various service sectors, dealing with industrial subsidies, and even issues in agriculture. The art of negotiation needs to be rediscovered, as it was at MC12, if difficult problems are to be addressed, with members stretching to reach more ambitious results based on closer international cooperation. It may help to have enough on the table for trade-offs to take place. After Doha, many officials came to the conclusion that rounds are impossible as a means to reach an agreement and one-off deals might work. That conclusion is worth revisiting after years of stasis on services, agriculture, industrial subsidies, and other major issue areas that are not being addressed successfully.

Any new package of agreements should not be limited to dispute settlement, but complementary to it. Institutional reform will be needed to support rule-making and the administration of the global trading system at the WTO, or trade issues will increasingly be dealt with in other settings: regionally (although CPTPP is ceasing to be even notionally regional), by subject matter (for example, digital trade), and sometimes bilaterally. Where new rules arise in other, non-multilateral settings, disputes will migrate to resolution in other fora under sub-multilateral agreements if they are dealt with effectively at all.

What happens with disputes in Geneva before there is agreed reform? Some WTO members will opt for the panel stage being final. More countries will likely join the MPIA or perhaps there might be an NMPIA.[178] Those not choosing one of these alternatives will seek to continue to warehouse appeals on the basis of the fiction that the AB exists. This default position for the conduct of international trade relations will continue to impose systemic costs. There may be an acceleration of the move to the negotiation of regional trade agreements and single-subject preferential trade agreements.

Inertia, persisting with the *status quo* will not be kind toward the future of the multilateral trading system, and it should not be accepted with resignation. Investment is needed, by business, by NGOs, by labor, by the governments that are the stewards of the system to improve it, to make it more relevant to current needs, and to meet future challenges.

[178] Most members joining an alternative dispute settlement system, an MPIA, creates for nonparticipants the same effect as if they had invoked an opt-out but it occurs through the action of others, rather than any decision taken by those left outside.

PART VI

Conclusion

15

Conclusion

The Future of the WTO

There is an increasing need for international cooperation with respect to trade – to meet the challenges to human health, food security, and to deal with climate change, to provide for the greater well-being of the world's peoples. For conflict-affected countries, integration into the trading system is a path to attaining and then maintaining peace. To be successful in meeting these challenges, much will depend on the external environment – conditions that enable and others that obstruct collaboration. But there is also an environment internal to the trading system, making its institution, the WTO, more fit for purpose by putting into place the necessary reforms.

At the beginning, when the ITO, the GATT, the Fund, and the Bank were being created by members of what in the United States is often called "the greatest generation," there was a shared vision. It was to create a world better structured to obtain and maintain peace. The path forward consisted of nations becoming more closely integrated economically for their mutual benefit. They would engage in progressive trade liberalization, proceeding under a set of rules that would bring about greater fairness. Within this structure, trade negotiators would enter the arena and, in a process of give and take, obtain benefits for their country's firms and workers to produce and export more. The interaction of individual countries, each pursuing its own self-interest by exchanging trade concessions, would bring about a result that would be better for all. In eight successive rounds of GATT negotiations, trade negotiators were creating a world in which all nations would benefit.

The multilateral trading system was, for its first fifty years, a story of progressive achievement.[1] Then, for a time, much of the forward momentum

[1] "Progressive" is used here not in its current US domestic political sense, which has little positive to say about international trade, but is used here in terms of a progression toward the goals articulated by the founders of the system.

was lost, although there would still be sporadic breakthroughs. There was only one truly multilateral agreement during the first quarter-century of the WTO's existence: the Trade Facilitation Agreement (TFA). It is not clear that the TFA is replicable as a model. The Information Technology Agreement (ITA) and the Pharmaceutical Agreement, in which not all WTO members participate, bought their way into acceptability by fully sharing their duty-free benefits with nonparticipants. The WTO experience differs from the Uruguay Round, the last and greatest of the GATT rounds which created the WTO, in which all participated, all gave and received substantive trade benefits, and many far-reaching agreements were concluded.

In June 2022, the drought in agreed outcomes was ended by the Twelfth Ministerial Conference, which produced a truly multilateral, if incomplete, agreement to curb fisheries subsidies, and a package of other results addressing food security, a pandemic response, and a commitment to WTO reform. The WTO members had saved the institution by showing that agreement among a diverse group of 164 countries was possible.

However, the founding of the WTO can be seen as the apogee of the multilateral trading system to date. Why didn't the arc of progress, the forward momentum, continue? What went wrong? In part, stasis was due to weaknesses inherent in the structure that was put in place in 1995. Perhaps it was a fundamental error to dragoon the countries of the developing world into a one-size-fits-all system, even with phase-in periods and lighter requirements for contributions from the less and least developed. Perhaps it should have been anticipated that operating by consensus would come to be interpreted as an all-purpose veto over anything and everything, a recipe for "all for one and none for all." Perhaps banking on a transition from nonmarket to fully market-oriented organization of domestic economies by key members was a flaw that could not be cured with twelve and fifteen-year transition periods.

Whatever mistakes were made, inclusion was not wrong. Universality is a necessary and laudable goal for a global trading system. It must, however, not be allowed to come at the expense of progress.

It is easy to see defects in the current WTO, but harder to see cures. The former WTO Director-General, Roberto Azevêdo, who was to preside over the waning of common purpose,[2] now in the private sector, two years after leaving office "categorized members into three broad categories with goals that are not only very different but also frequently at odds":

[2] Roberto Azevêdo held office during most of the second decade of the second millennium (2013–20).

> *You have one group of members who don't like the WTO or the multilateral trading system. They don't want it. It's as simple as that. It's very difficult to get consensus and a positive outcome when you have members who are actually hoping that the system will not progress because they feel that it's overtaking their ability to do things, that the system is taking away their sovereignty.*
>
> *The second group ... consists of countries that are largely happy with the status quo and thus resist changes to the organization.*
>
> *The third ... also wants the WTO but is pushing for significant changes or reforms to the system.*[3]
>
> *Having consensus today, all 164, everyone on board with the same decision – no matter how small or trivial that decision is – I find it very difficult, if not impossible ... even when you have issues where you can discern the consensus – or you can discern the area where the members may converge – even then it's impossible to get consensus.*

Prior to MC12, few if any could convincingly argue with this dark assessment. But the story of the WTO was not over.

FINDING LEADERSHIP

The preceding four chapters of this book – a WTO Reform Quartet – point to a number of changes that can be considered to improve the governance of the Organization within its existing framework. These are aimed at repairing the Organization's judiciary, restoring its negotiating function, and giving it a fully acknowledged executive with the ability to provide its members with comprehensive trade intelligence as well as thought leadership.

The series of recommended changes, even were they to be adopted, would still not be sufficient. The primary solutions for the WTO are not to be found in how it is organized, but in an animating spirit on the part of its members in pursuit of a well-defined common mission. The countries that founded the international economic organizations at Bretton Woods and Havana, and those that brought about European integration, creating institutions for cooperation at a level above nation-states, had a mission. In the 1940s, the members of this founding generation were trying to avoid repeating the catastrophes of two world wars, separated by the Great Depression. They desired to rebuild the world economy from that devastation. Incidentally, as

3 Hannah Monicken. 2022. "Former WTO Director-General: Finding Consensus Largely 'Impossible.'" Inside US Trade. May 13. www.insidetrade.com/daily-news/former-wto-director-general-finding-consensus-largely-%E2%80%98impossible%E2%80%99

it turned out, for this was not their initial purpose, they would also come to recognize and adopt the goal of bringing former colonies and other developing countries more fully into the world economy. Without the leaders showing the way, all might have been lost. They vouchsafed to us institutions that can keep alive the prospects for continued international economic cooperation. Sabine Weyand, EU Director-General for Trade, quoted Jean Monnet, a founder of the European project as saying: "nothing can be done without people; nothing will endure without institutions." It is up to the succeeding generations to restore a life force to the institutions that we have inherited.

At present, the United States, the aging (some say declining) hegemon, has not demonstrated a primary interest in maintaining the world trading system. Its focus turned substantially inward but has been forced by events to engage internationally due to the Russian invasion of Ukraine and the geopolitical competition with China, causing it to see again the value of having allies. While the United States still projects unrivaled military power abroad, it no longer claims the role of the guarantor of the liberal international economic order. This does not mean that the system will not survive, but it does have implications for the system moving forward.

The search for new leadership for the multilateral trading system would logically turn toward Brussels, to the European Union, the world's largest trading entity. The EU should see itself as an inheritor of the British role from the Bretton Woods era. However, here too, the dominant strain of policy after the failure of the Doha Round was not to embrace systemic leadership. Concerns stemming from a greater appreciation of the nature of the competition from China, and to some extent a reaction to competition from giant US digital technology companies, the EU was seen as moving toward a more defensive posture manifested in new measures to protect European businesses. Pascal Lamy expressed concern about a move toward "precautionism," seeing and reacting to challenges defensively rather than seeing opportunities.[4] This is how a respected European think tank viewed the development of EU trade policy:

> *There was a period – quite a long period, in fact – when the debate on trade policy centered around the question of multilateralism versus bilateralism. The objective, however, was always the same – to increase market access – and the debate was only over the best means to advance the free trade.*

4 "'Precautionism' Is Risking Open Trade More than Protectionism: Pascal Lamy." *The Economic Times*. November 18, 2021. www.economictimes.indiatimes.com/news/economy/foreign-trade/precautionism-is-risking-open-trade-more-than-protectionism-pascal-lamy/articleshow/87783291.cms

> *Those days are gone. Now, the debate has little to do with market access or simplifying trade; in the European Union, the focus lies on identifying various ways to reduce access to the European market. Many legislative initiatives are being developed – or have already been implemented – to regulate or close down trading opportunities. Most of these are not traditional protectionism as we know it – although there is certainly an element of that – but rather their aims are security, sustainability and level playing fields.*[5]

This is perhaps too pessimistic, painting too dark a picture of European priorities, but it has elements of truth in it as well. Europe risked becoming too Euro-centric. There has been a change in recent times to include a more outward-looking posture, beyond engaging in a long string of somewhat mercantilist bilateral trade agreements to considering its role in Asia, Africa, and in the WTO, and providing thought leadership and political muscle to bring about the beginning of what could be a turnabout at MC12.

China as the rising economic power has a vital stake in the existing multilateral system. It has not evidenced an interest in leading it. Nor is there a chorus of voices from other nations urging it to do so. There appear to be divisions within Beijing as to whether the liberal international economic order from which China has benefited so dramatically should be fully embraced, a precondition for providing leadership in the Organization. In a world where leadership has always depended upon the great powers, the energy and capabilities of China are needed. It is still an open question whether it will be interested in expending the time and energy to provide leadership for the multilateral trading system.

While the mid-level countries, the "middle-grounders," have done much that is positive for the trading system during the WTO era, particularly providing thought leadership, they do not see themselves as collectively capable of filling the leadership vacuum, other than selectively, aiming at specific and more limited negotiating goals, such as in the Joint Statement Initiatives (JSIs).

THE OBJECTS AND PURPOSES OF THE WTO

On a strictly utilitarian basis, the WTO is to be a place for negotiation of trade agreements providing a global set of trading rules, a venue for settlement of disputes, and a mechanism (notifications and monitoring) for assuring transparency with respect to government measures that affect trade. All of these

5 "The New Wave of Defensive Trade Policy Measures in the European Union: Design, Structure, and Trade Effects." European Centre for International Political Economy. May 11, 2022. www.ecipe.org/wp-content/uploads/2022/05/PR-OP-42022.pdf

functions are supported by a professional secretariat. These institutional arrangements serve a lofty set of purposes, as evidenced in the opening words of the Marrakesh Agreement Establishing the WTO:

> *Recognizing that their relations in the field of trade and economic endeavour should be conducted with a view to raising standards of living, ensuring full employment and a large and steadily growing volume of real income and effective demand, and expanding the production of and trade in goods and services, while allowing for the optimal use of the world's resources in accordance with the objective of sustainable development, seeking both to protect and preserve the environment and to enhance the means for doing so in a manner consistent with their respective needs and concerns at different levels of economic development.*
>
> *Recognizing further that there is need for positive efforts designed to ensure that developing countries, and especially the least developed among them, secure a share in the growth in international trade commensurate with the needs of their economic development.*

Results are delivered through more liberal trade under a set of agreed rules. There is, however, little public enthusiasm for the economic case for the current trading system. No elected official on the world stage is pressing for greater global economic efficiency. Nowhere is there the self-confidence to say that this would in general be a good thing. No foreign minister from any major country is pressing the case for the global trading system as a force for peace, even though it most assuredly is. The cause of peace remains closely connected to trade, particularly among fragile and conflict-affected countries. Recall that in October 2018, the first President of Timor-Leste came to the WTO to testify to his country's vital interest in integration into the world economy through accession to the WTO, saying: "where there is trade, there is peace." He is not alone, as testimonials from officials from Sudan, South Sudan, Afghanistan, and Liberia, the acceding and the recently acceded, attest to the importance of trade for peace.

The linkage of trade to peace is not confined to the least developed. According to Martin Wolf of the *Financial Times*, at the time of the Brexit referendum, the then-Irish foreign minister told him that the EU was "a peace project" and its making borders irrelevant had "facilitated the peace process and might even be what made it possible."[6] In all of these places where

6 Martin Wolf. 2022. "Martin Wolf: Boris Johnson Must Embrace the Brexit He Made." *Irish Times*. May 18. www.irishtimes.com/business/economy/martin-wolf-boris-johnson-must-embrace-the-brexit-he-made-1.4881777

conflict is not distant, including Northern Ireland, the relationship of trade to peace remains anything but a remote concern. But it is not a current motivation for the three largest trading partners, the European Union, the United States, and China, for upgrading the WTO (although for the EU, the inclusion of Ukraine in the Union is a peace project).

Other purposes can be suggested for the world trading system. Worker-centrism is certainly a usable standard for ordering domestic policy goals. But it is more challenging to seek to transpose that standard to a multilateral setting. Generations of American trade negotiators (and their counterparts from other countries) believed that they were serving the interests of their countries' workers, seeking to open markets for exports of agriculture and advanced industrial products and being wary of causing harm to import-sensitive industries. They sought to preserve trade remedies where harm was caused to these industries. One repair to be made to the WTO is to return to having trade remedies available when needed. This is the price for maintaining general trade liberalization.

But, beyond trade remedies, in a global organization, what does it mean to maximize the benefits for workers? The purpose of a rules-based system is to deliver fairness. Whether farmers are located in Iowa or Nigeria, their exports should not face phytosanitary trade standards that are not based on science. It means that entrepreneurs, individuals, wherever located, will have a global market via the internet. It means that product standards will be accessible, understandable, and workable for small and medium-sized enterprises (SMEs) and not discriminatory based on gender.[7] Intellectual property is to benefit the individual innovator as much as a biotech or software company. Workers engaged in large numbers in manufacturing or services are not to have their efforts to gain access to international markets frustrated by discrimination against their collective output through trade barriers. A balanced trading system is by its nature worker-centric.

It is likely that, as the trading system evolves, additional positive objectives will be highlighted. Were the Organization to be founded today, with an e-commerce agreement as part of its sets of rules, the list of objectives could, for example, reflect the objectives cited in the May 12, 2022, Joint Declaration of Japan and the European Union Announcing a Digital Partnership: safe and ethical applications of technology (in this case, artificial intelligence), resilience of global supply chains, secure international connectivity, green infrastructures, protection of privacy, promotion of innovation, development of

7 For example, coffee being traded in sacks whose weight inadvertently disadvantages women.

digital skills for workers, transformation of businesses, including SMEs and of public services in the digital environment, and facilitation of digital trade to the benefit of our workers and businesses.[8]

What the system cannot accommodate is further discrimination that is more trade-restrictive than baseline MFN treatment.[9] Seeking to introduce resilience in supply chains through "friend-shoring" would need to have a strong, objective, and factual basis to justify it under current rules to avoid a successful WTO challenge, as well as being economically costly to those that employ it. If worker-centric means being more defensive in general with respect to open trade, moving toward greater autarky, that would be a recipe for less economic growth, a decline in which all would share. Turning the clock backward is neither desirable nor possible.

Conditioning trade on nontrade factors should be approached very warily. Any number of value judgments can be made when it comes to relations among nations. There are numerous indices that rank countries, from ease of doing business to human rights.[10] US tariff schedules, in a simpler but no less dangerous world characterized by the Cold War, had two columns: one for dealing with friends at relatively low rates and one for dealing with enemies at Smoot–Hawley rates. It was a stable arrangement that involved high tariffs on a relatively small amount of world trade. To seek to have the tariff shift with changes in foreign governments (more or less autocratic or democratic), changes in the openness of a society, their degree of corruption, or other values, would create a variable levy at the border that would strangle trade and global economic growth. It would be capricious and destroy economic freedom for those engaged in trade.

There will always be occasions when noncommercial considerations are brought into trade policy decisions. Targeted sanctions will be applied in times of war or other national emergencies, or to counter forced labor or

8 "Joint Statement EU–Japan Summit 2022." European Council – Council of the European Union. May 12, 2022. www.consilium.europa.eu/en/press/press-releases/2022/05/12/joint-statement-eu-japan-summit-2022/

9 I would argue that the provision for free trade agreements (which discriminate by giving better than MFN treatment) has been an exception to nondiscrimination that has grown beyond what could possibly have been intended and requires serious review.

10 "World Bank Group to Discontinue Doing Business Report." World Bank. September 16, 2021. www.worldbank.org/en/news/statement/2021/09/16/world-bank-group-to-discontinue-doing-business-report. The United Nations Development Programme created the Human Development Index (HDI), the Human Rights Index, the Bertelsmann Transformation Index, the indices ranking global competitiveness, corruption perceptions, press freedom, political rights, civil liberties, international property rights, prosperity, knowledge economy, fragile states, global gender gap, global hunger, global innovation, global peace, global terrorism, and social progress.

promote other social goals. This must be done selectively and with restraint. The global trading system can tolerate some deviations from nondiscrimination, but not a disintegration into trading blocs. It is divided enough by regional trading arrangements that offer better than MFN treatment and are mainly tolerable because they may contribute to further progress for the multilateral trading system.

International trade takes place, before governments intervene, based on a willing buyer in one country acquiring goods and services from a willing seller in another country. The conditions under which traded goods and services are created vary markedly. Into this variegated world the WTO is designed to introduce some basic order. Its primary purpose is to restrain ill-advised government interventions in trade. What the current system cannot accommodate is having competitive outcomes determined by state intervention rather than market forces.[11] Where government intervention exists, there must be strong and broadly accepted public policy reasons for it taking place. If the rule is that government policy is to determine in blanket fashion whether goods are bought and sold, to and from what source, the world trading system will need to be fundamentally altered, with what an early scholar of the trading system called "interface mechanisms."[12] That would require a different trading system than the one we have now.

CURATING THE WTO'S RELEVANCE

Before turning to the future, it is necessary to come to grips with the present. Circumstances over the last four years have forcefully held out example after example of the dependency of the world on the smooth operation of international trade.

- When the pandemic first spread in early 2019, it became strikingly evident that the production of essential medical supplies, equipment, and personal protective equipment was far from evenly distributed among the countries of the planet.
- This was followed by the even more unequal availability of vaccines.
- There then followed the economic consequences of measures dealing with the pandemic, the lockdowns curtailing production, suspension of

[11] There are instances where lack of state intervention causes distortions, such as where competition laws are not being enforced.

[12] John H. Jackson, a law professor who was one of the fathers of the idea of the WTO, referred to the need for interface mechanisms between countries whose domestic practices differ substantially.

international airline passenger travel severely limiting package delivery, and merchant marine crews stranded by quarantines.

- The sharpness of the recovery and its unevenness found supplies of shipping containers severely limited in some areas and piled up in others, making the restoration of trade more difficult.
- Ports became unequal to the task of offloading ships.
- Automobile production lines suffered from insufficient supplies of semi-conductors, mostly sourced outside the countries of final automobile assembly.
- The geopolitical rivalry across the Pacific between the United States and China failed to slow the bilateral exchange of goods but promoted a political reaction in the United States to look toward "friend-shoring" and in China toward "dual circulation."
- Russia's invasion of Ukraine severely limited the transit of wheat, sun-flower oil, and fertilizer from the Black Sea ports to countries heavily dependent on imports of these commodities.
- Sanctions against Russia caused a greater public awareness of Russia as an important source of supply of gas, oil, fertilizer, and critical minerals.
- India's announcement of export restrictions on wheat threatened to exacerbate global shortages, adding to a price spike seriously harming net food-importing poor countries.
- A shortage of baby formula in the United States caused a reexamination of the regulations impeding imports.

These were just some of the recent headline events forcing every farmer, manufacturer, and consumer to learn about supply chains, and for the public to learn more about the trade that they took for granted.

We have also seen examples of trade used for economic coercion, and not just in the form of sanctions during war. In Korea, officials learned of their country's dependence on trade to bring in needed supplies of chemicals and other necessary materials from Japan for semiconductor manufacturing. Australian officials learned that they could not depend on a market in China for wine and a host of other products. European officials found that Lithuanian and German exporters could not rely on their access to China's market. Trade could, it turned out, be easily and not too subtly weaponized. "Trade coercion" entered the vocabulary of officials.

There have been positive responses as well. During the pandemic, the WTO Secretariat, within the limits of its resources, responded as well as it could to providing information to its members to allow them to make better-informed – if not always wiser – decisions. Groups of members did, at that time and during the war in Ukraine, take collective action, such as pledging not to impose restrictions on exports of food. What was painfully evident is that when it came to collective action on the part of the Organization as a whole, WTO members were painfully unequal to the challenges posed. A primary example is the two-and-a-half-year gap between the appearance of COVID-19 and the WTO membership agreeing on an effective response. Nor was there a decision at MC12 that would provide an effective response to future pandemics. All 164 members could not even agree unconditionally that they would not restrict exports of food destined for purchases by the World Food Programme.

In a series of emergencies, the WTO has not been a factor. It did not anticipate challenges, nor did it meet them. At the WTO firehouse, despite multiple major conflagrations, too often the initial response of the firemen was to share papers expressing individual views on how to fight fires, without taking timely and effective action.

In capitals, politicians are focused on greater security of supplies – not an unnatural reaction. However, there are physical as well as economic limits to self-sufficiency. Fertile soil, mineral deposits, capital, labor, resources, as well as calamities – drought, floods, and other extreme weather events, severe poverty and famine – are not distributed evenly across the planet. Trade is more essential than it ever was, and it will always be indispensable to providing supplies where they are needed.

A caveat: The fact that the WTO needs to be more responsive, that it needs reform, should not be a cause for anyone to undervalue what exists at present. Disputes continue to be settled, and results are binding on all those who have chosen, or will choose, to accept them. Almost all of world trade flows under the WTO's rules. Product standards are notified in draft. Most trade takes place within the bounds of the tariffs committed through the WTO. The services covered in WTO schedules can flow across borders in accordance with the commitments made. None of the 164 members of the Organization seek to leave it, and twenty-four countries are seeking to join it. But it still falls short of all that it could and should be. The WTO needs to up its game. It can demonstrate its relevance by reaching agreements, by meeting challenges. MC12 gave it some breathing space, but not much, to become more responsive, more relevant.

The organic parts of the WTO's architecture need to be improved, bringing back the ability to conclude negotiations, restoring binding dispute settlement in whatever form will be acceptable to all, and having an actual executive to manage the negotiating process, engaging in policy planning and strategic foresight, assuing transparency through intelligence gathering, and actively engaging in settling disputes.

THE CHALLENGE AHEAD

The multilateral system can be eroded by

- An incompatibility of economic systems of major trading nations;
- An upsurge in unilateral trade measures;
- Differences over what is needed to promote development;
- An upsurge in populism, nationalism, income inequality, and the absence of political will to liberalize trade further through new trade agreements;
- A lessening of trust;
- Increasing concern that existing trading arrangements are not mutually beneficial;
- Resort to self-serving bilateral trading arrangements;
- The absence of consensus on the part of all WTO members on the way forward; and
- The loss of a sense of common purpose.

There are innumerable reasons for nations to fail to cooperate – due to the temper of the times, due to a desire for strategic autonomy, due to a desire to achieve onshoring, due to application of what Pascal Lamy calls "precautionism" as a new form of protectionism,[13] due to self-interest narrowly defined, due to blaming trade for societal ills such as income inequality where the problem often consists of displacements caused by technological change. The WTO cannot succeed if there is underinvestment by the major trading countries. The default is for competing "regional" fora to displace multilateral approaches, with fragmentation of the trading system or a fall back to "my country first" nationalism.

It may be that the era of the Cold War had greater purpose, greater clarity of vision, when there was a sharp division between communism and the free market. It may be that crafting a global economic strategy built around multilateralism required a slate made clean by world wars and the emergence of an idealistic global hegemon, with leaders who saw more clearly what they needed to do, and who had the means to accomplish their objectives. It was perhaps more obvious in the mid-twentieth century that standing still, accepting the status quo, was not an option. It may be that domestic priorities

[13] "Pascal Lamy's Recent Comments on the Challenges Facing the WTO." Washington International Trade Association. July 27, 2020. www.wita.org/blogs/pascal-lamys-recent-comments-on-the-challenges-facing-the-wto/

simply outweigh international ones. It may be that this is an end of history very different from the one heralded by Francis Fukuyama – this one, the end of international trade cooperation.

A culture of inaction breeds a belief that nothing is possible; that progress is impossible. It can be a self-fulfilling prophecy. MC12 fortunately began the counternarrative.

There are some basic truths, unavoidable facts that make a positive outcome inevitable. Efficiency drives most of global trade. Autarky cannot be achieved. The King Canute approach to international trade, calling for the tide of trade to cease to flow, will always fail. There can be no decoupling of major economies except at unacceptably high costs. Moreover, nations will be compelled to learn that there is only one planet. A lesson of both the pandemic and climate change is that national strategies in isolation are not effective. There needs to be international cooperation. The WTO must adapt to current challenges, and become a central place for trade cooperation. The way must, and I believe will, be found, because for trade there is ultimately no better venue. This will require a change in attitude – in capitals, in the institution itself – changes that will occur because they must.

For all the defects in relations among nations, there is in our species an ability to transcend the present and work for a better future. It is easy to conclude that international cooperation is a goal beyond reach. Sixty years ago, President John F. Kennedy called for travel to the moon, a thoroughly aspirational goal. He created the remarkable national self-confidence to overcome domestic and international challenges, saying:

> *We choose to go to the moon in this decade and do the other things, not because they are easy, but because they are hard, because that goal will serve to organize and measure the best of our energies and skills, because that challenge is one that we are willing to accept, one we are unwilling to postpone, and one which we intend to win, and the others, too.*[14]

In what way, exactly, is the human endeavor of multilateral cooperation more daunting, its attainment more distant, than reaching another part of the cosmos 240,000 miles away? Kennedy cited George Mallory, who, when asked why he wanted to climb Mt. Everest, answered "because it is there." International cooperation for trade is a far more practical goal, if less

[14] "Address at Rice University on the Nation's Space Effort." John F. Kennedy Presidential Library and Museum. September 12, 1962. www.jfklibrary.org/archives/other-resources/john-f-kennedy-speeches/rice-university-19620912

glamorous. Its importance was understood by Woodrow Wilson and Franklin Roosevelt, and the planners who dreamed of the multilateral trading system.

Most choices look clearer and simpler in retrospect than they were at the time. At the end of the Second World War, the United States could have pursued its own imperial preference scheme to replace the one that Great Britain had maintained. If lend–lease and the Marshall Plan were in part self-interested, they were in greater part among the "most unsordid acts of history."[15] So was the founding of the multilateral trading system. Leadership does emerge even when unexpected.

The WTO is no more than the physical embodiment of its members' willingness to cooperate globally on trade. Its problems are its members' problems, and they are largely self-created, its limitations largely self-imposed. There are no insuperable obstacles to international cooperation. There are worse global policy options than cooperation, and many of them have already been tried.

WTO 2050

In Adelaide, in 2019, I outlined my vision for the WTO as it would likely exist in the year 2050.[16] I noted that we already knew something about the world that would likely exist then and could surmise how the system would have to adapt and would have adapted. These were some of the key points that I made:

By 2050, the world's population will have increased by 2.2 billion, causing the demand for food to rise dramatically, and at the same time providing a vastly expanded pool of human talent and labor. Demographics will change the relative influence of countries. India, Indonesia, Nigeria, and Pakistan will have greater influence as both markets and sources of supply. The United States will also gain in population and remain influential.[17]

Due to shifts in weather patterns, as harvests become less reliable, world agricultural trade will have to be more open and agile to move supplies from

[15] "Marshall Myths: The Most Unsordid Act in History." The George C. Marshall Foundation. March 11, 2016. www.marshallfoundation.org/blog/marshall-myths-the-most-unsordid-act-in-history/

[16] While the gist is the same, some of what follows in the text is elaborated to reflect my view of the world in 2022.

[17] "The World's Most Populous Nations In 2050 [Infographic]." Forbes. June 22, 2017. www.forbes.com/sites/niallmccarthy/2017/06/22/the-worlds-most-populous-nations-in-2050-infographic/#1e182d8139f6

areas of surplus to those of deficit.[18] Global commerce will be, for the most increasingly digital. The further expansion of 3D printing and other technological advances will change the nature of trade. Advances in transportation will shrink geographies even further. Drone and other autonomous airborne deliveries will likely be able to move greater quantities of goods from one area to another using less energy.[19] The use of artificial intelligence will transform the administration of the world trading system. The world will have progressed much further toward achieving artificial general intelligence (AGI) or singularity (equivalence in reasoning capability to the human brain, but much faster and with far greater capacity).

Transparency will be commonplace. With the application of AI, the amount of data available on government measures will be immensely greater. Trade measures will be instantly known to all and will be published and analyzed by the WTO, without requiring the intervention of members to make notifications. Proposed changes in national tariffs and other measures affecting trade will be evaluated by AI in draft, for both their impact and consistency with WTO obligations. Every proposed national measure will be vetted in advance, and an immediate right to specified trade compensation will exist whenever AI determines that agreements have been breached (subject to rare appeals).

Trade negotiations will be greatly assisted through analyses supported by AI, but in the end, human judgment will determine what is feasible and desirable politically as well as economically.[20] The exception is that trade negotiations will always be a political process domestically and internationally. AI will never be able to impose obligations on members but will still require a sovereign decision of each member. Open plurilateral agreements will be commonplace, becoming part of the *acquis* of the WTO. Most of the developing countries in 2050 will have progressed dramatically, and attention will be focused on the remaining least developed. For them, economic development will be spurred by tailored programs of assistance based on close consultations with the recipient countries.

[18] "Opinion: Farmers Don't Need to Read the Science. We Are Living It." *New York Times*. August 9, 2019. www.nytimes.com/2019/08/09/opinion/climate-change-food-report.html

[19] "The Future of Transportation World Conference." The Future of Transportation World Conference. www.thefutureoftransportconference.com/en/

[20] Pierre Wack, the Chief Strategist for Shell Oil, was well-known for his decision tree analysis, which predicted each of the two oil crises of the 1970s. Artificial intelligence brings this talent to both negotiation and dispute settlement. It builds on human experience and is extended by the application of Bayes' Theorem of applying probabilities to multiple different but related issues to determine probable outcomes.

AI will have reviewed all cases of infant industry protection and will have gamed out outcomes, as Alpha-GO did,[21] including what happens when protection (through restrictions or subsidies) is applied and when it is removed, whether other countries would also support their industries providing matching subsidized foreign competition, what the likelihood is of a beneficiary industry becoming internationally competitive, what the costs are to foreign competitors and domestic consumers, and more.[22]

Proposed resolutions of disputes will be identified in a fraction of a second. Appeals from AI-determined outcomes of dispute settlement cases will be allowed but a high burden of proof will be required for a member losing a case to avoid being bound by the AI-suggested outcome (or upon an adverse Office of Legal Counsel opinion). The WTO of the future will depend upon and have an ability to legislate where there are gaps in the rules, or where they need to be changed.

Consumer preferences will play a much greater role in determining trade flows. All goods and services serving the environment will be duty-free. Fish stocks will have been replenished as fisheries subsidies will have been curtailed, and under the Fisheries Subsidies Agreement the degree of unregulated, underreported, and illegal fishing, as well as overfishing and overcapacity, will have become minimal. Fossil fuel subsidies will have been eliminated. Domestic support for agriculture will be much reduced, as much due to budget constraints as to negotiated limits, but also because increases in global demand will reduce the demands for protection and subsidization.

[21] "AlphaGo." Wikipedia. https://en.wikipedia.org/wiki/AlphaGo

[22] I am indebted to Bob Koopman, the WTO's former Chief Economist, for this example:

> *The benefits and costs of infant industry protection will be gamed out using AI, just as in a Go or chess match. For example: if domestic pens are protected, they cost more than they would otherwise. Elementary schools could order fewer of them, pay their teachers less, or order fewer soccer balls. Protection has its costs. What is worst for society is the increase in the costs of basic education. Having import duties on needed cross-border dataflows can become the equivalent of taxing the tools of economic development. If the production of pens, notebook makers, soccer ball producers, backpack makers, clothing makers and many others in the economy demand similar "support/protection." Suddenly, education really does get a lot more expensive with costs adding up, and then there truly is not a lot left over for "other things." And with the protection, firms get a bit lazy – they often do not innovate around production processes or products, but they spend on maintaining their privileged protection in the market. These last two points add up to the main and very valid critique of protection and the notion of infant industry. Of course, some interventions will work. But generally, they will have to involve domestic producers who are granted some transitory protection from competition, and then perform successfully in the global market. At that point, successful industrial policy requires that other countries keep their markets open (success cannot be easily found if foreign competitors are also protected).*

Limits will be established to discipline the granting of domestic subsidies for industry.

There will have been a great convergence of domestic economic systems, removing a major source of past conflicts. Trade-related aspects of competition policy will be incorporated into WTO rules. The adverse reaction to globalization will have passed with the generations that were much concerned with it.

Spheres of trade influence will have evaporated, just as Great Britain's imperial preferences of the 1930s became a historical artifact. The less efficient and unequal world of RTAs and FTAs will no longer be considered a rational choice, as progress could be made on a broader front. Positive regional integration, starting with the formation and enlargement of the European Union, the USMCA, and spurred on by the success of the African Continental Free Trade Agreement, will have led to greater trade liberalization on a global basis. The multilateral trading system will become universal and increasingly supersede other trading arrangements, as efficiency per David Ricardo makes the most sense to most trade officials as an organizing principle. Centripetal forces will prove stronger than centrifugal ones.

The WTO will be the world's trade negotiating forum, the world's trade dispute settlement venue, and the world's premiere source of knowledge, data, and analysis on international trade, which will be readily available to all. The WTO of the future – to deal with the enormous amount of available data, to help members consider alternative paths forward, to provide analyses for members and the public, and to assist in compliance with obligations – will need to have a Secretariat that functions more like those of its sister international organizations, the International Monetary Fund and the World Bank, having a scale proportionate to the tasks with which it is entrusted.

CREATING THE WTO OF THE FUTURE

Of course, one cannot know for certain what the world will be like in the year 2050.[23] But if we envisage what it should look like, we can work toward it.

In reading what I said in Adelaide three years ago, I believe that the WTO 2050 can be reached much earlier. Due to underinvestment from the largest trading countries and opposition from others to progress, the WTO is facing a difficult period. The stars may not be fully aligned for immediate and dramatic breakthroughs on a multilateral basis in the next few years. Important

[23] A sign in the Christ's College School library, Christchurch, New Zealand: "Those interested in time travel, please meet here last Thursday at 8pm."

incremental progress can still be made, however. When faced with an enormous challenge, a vast but necessary task, there is only one way to proceed, and that is to begin.[24]

The European Union showed the way forward. It did not accept the United States exercising a veto over binding dispute settlement. It put into place a substitute mechanism by drawing on one of the provisions of the WTO Agreement, the provision allowing arbitration. It was a bit of a lawyer's trick, but not that much of a stretch to in effect re-establish the Appellate Body in all but name for all countries that would agree to join. At this point, the United States and the European Union should be able to work out a similar NMPIA (new multiparty interim arrangement), restoring binding dispute settlement between the two of them and any who might wish to join. It may take a while, but it should be possible with goodwill, if the two sides have the same objective, to reach a workable result that is completely legitimate under the WTO Agreements.

Similarly, there is a way forward to have the JSIs concluded at the WTO and administered by the WTO Secretariat. There is nothing inconsistent with the Marrakesh Agreement that created the WTO to ask the Director-General to have the Secretariat provide support for any trade agreement, as long as it meets the following two conditions: it is consistent with the implicit mandate that the Director-General has to support the multilateral trading system and it is not substantively adverse to the interests of the WTO members. Open plurilateral agreements now in negotiation at the WTO, the Joint Statement Initiatives, each fit this profile. This has been the basis upon which the WTO Secretariat is currently informally supporting both the MPIA and the negotiation of JSIs.

Any future JSI, as long as it is an open plurilateral agreement not inconsistent with the objects and purposes of the WTO, can take the same path toward belonging to the WTO. The technical legal argument raised by India and South Africa that any of these JSIs cannot become Annex 4 agreements without their approval would be side-stepped. The WTO would become relevant again to the interests of its members. It does not matter whether these agreements are "docked" to the pier labeled as part of Annex 4 or a *de facto* Annex 5 of the Marrakesh Agreement, the article creating the Secretariat and the Director-General. It is a technicality that is of no consequence.

That path could also be used by Chile, New Zealand, and Singapore, asking that the Digital Electronic Partnership Agreement be supported by

[24] Terrance Schwab, Columbia Law, JD 1966.

the Secretariat. If the parties to the CPTPP came to the Director-General and warranted that it was an open plurilateral agreement consistent with the purposes and objectives of the WTO, stated that they would like the WTO Secretariat to administer the agreement, asked that the Secretariat support any disputes that arise under the agreement, and stated that they were willing to pay fully for Secretariat support, the Director-General would likewise have authority to instruct the Secretariat to undertake that role unless it were vetoed by the General Council or the Ministerial Conference. It would be highly unlikely, given the consensus arrangement of the General Council and the Ministerial Conference, that the Director-General could be blocked from authorizing the Secretariat to undertake the role. The lack of an available veto at the WTO can be used to prevent the stifling of initiatives.

In the WTO Reform Quartet, I suggested that it was essential that the WTO become the primary place for the negotiation of trade agreements. Improvisation is necessary to move from current impasses at the WTO to that future. It is not likely at present that a WTO 2.0 will emerge from a new constitutional convention, a new Uruguay Round, where the current 164 members agree to a new Marrakesh Agreement, perhaps one with trade-weighted voting (were that considered desirable). But a new WTO Charter is not necessary. *Pragmatism is the muse of trade negotiators and always has been.* The GATT Secretariat itself had no written legal basis in the GATT text. It was a workaround, a way to avoid a failure of the system when the International Trade Organization (ITO) did not come into being.[25]

The third group in the "Azevedo Triage" – those that want a WTO but require reform – has it within their power to deliver it. These members do not have to abandon the system they created just because the machinery seizes up. Pragmatism and dedication would be needed. It can start with Canada, Singapore, or another middle-grounder, or all of them. But one suspects that this effort must include at least two of the three largest trading members – the United States and the European Union, but they should try to bring along China as well. None of the three are at present at all likely to be predisposed to fully take the course recommended above. It may be years before they decide to sail out of the doldrums and make progress again in the Organization that

[25] John H. Jackson. 1969. *World Trade and the Law of GATT: A Legal Analysis of the General Agreement on Tariffs and Trade.* Indianapolis, IN: Bobbs-Merrill. Pages 145–146. The GATT Secretariat itself had no foundation in any formal international agreement. It was an adjunct to the Interim Committee for the International Trade Organization, and the ITO never came into formal existence.

administers the multilateral trading system. But the way forward is clear. If faced with a *fait accompli*, opponents would see if there were a negotiated way forward that took into account their interests as they see them. Either a negotiation results in agreements, open plurilaterals, being legitimized, or they will be made part of the system without a negotiation.

What is certain is that, however long a pause persists, there will be a return to multilateralism. Prompt and effective substantive responses are necessary to tackle health and food crises, as well as climate change. Responses need to be multilateral, not just regional. Consensus can no longer afford to include a veto for those unaffected by an agreement and not wishing to join it. The Organization will either evolve or be relegated to irrelevance, surviving in a diminished state. Trade negotiators, a species that was near extinction, must be brought back and move out of their comfort zones to revive their institution. The WTO is not to be allowed to become "a relic of a vanished civilization."[26]

There is no practical alternative. At present, the CPTPP is not an alternative for future global rules, nor is some other agreement outgrowing its region. But at some point, the CPTPP may become a viable option as it gains major additional adherents. A problem with the notion of the compact or other basis for governing trade outside the WTO is that, eventually, it runs into the same problems that challenge the WTO. It needs to find ways as it grows to set rules for dissimilar national economies.

I am optimistic about the future of the WTO, about the multilateral trading system, because it makes sense. I believe in the place of Ricardian economics in the economic world to the same extent that Newtonian physics governs the physical world. Moving toward greater efficiency, which rewards those who adapt to it and punishes those who do not, will always create more trade, trade based on more than necessity. Governments can intervene to restrict or channel trade, but there will always be a cost for doing so and, over time, those costs will not be willingly borne.

There are elements of dystopia in the present and they seem to be increasing. UN Secretary-General António Guterres has spoken of the great fractures that threaten the current world, fractures that make the name of the organization he heads too often seem to be an oxymoron, as the "United" part of the title "United Nations" seems to defer to a large extent to the second part of the name, referring to nation-states. For the nation-state, the glue that holds it

[26] An image borrowed from *Shadow of the Wind* by Carlos Ruiz Zafón.

together, the patriotism, will always mean to some extent "my country first." The question is the extent to which there is room for a broader vision of national interest, to include making the world a better place in which one's country can prosper. A fragmented world in which national myopia governs will lead to a world fractured not so much into blocs or camps but atomized to the nation-state level (or subdivided further to smaller tribal affinity groups). That is the natural end point of deglobalization.

The process of deglobalization as it affects the WTO has its limits because it moves against the interests of all those who rely on trade, whether producers or consumers. To the extent that there is deglobalization at the margins, there will be an opposing constant force toward greater globalization, as irresistible as technological progress. Power looms did take over from the hand looms in rural England, and the power looms in a relatively short period moved to places where they could be used at a lower cost. Geopolitical rivalry did not eliminate US–China trade, and the nationalism inherent in Brexit can impair but not extinguish the need for more open UK–EU trade. In fact, Brexit provides a real-world test case for the economic costs of disintegration.

For the same reasons that trade flows continue to demonstrate that deglobalization cannot go very far, international cooperation must ultimately be called upon to respond to current challenges. At the WTO, the convoy system, where all members must agree or none can, will be sloughed off. There are new areas to bring within the ambit of the rules. Industrial subsidies and domestic agricultural support need to be disciplined, populations need to be fed despite climate change, and the means need to be found to accommodate geopolitical and geoeconomic divisions. The global digital economy needs common rules. Strategic foresight needs to be applied and policy planning conducted. Common interests need to be discerned and made the basis for collective action.

The WTO is and will remain a place of hope: for the least developed, for the vulnerable, for the conflict-affected, for the industrialized, for any country seeking economic advancement for its people – and that is a category that must include all.

Afterword

The Art and Science of Negotiation

There is nothing more important to the future of the WTO than negotiation. One senior WTO director lamented after MC11 that it was a lost skill. This proved not to be the case on a number of issues decided at MC12. Nevertheless, attention must be paid to making sure that those serving the WTO and those serving their WTO members understand the centrality of negotiation. It is a skill set that makes international cooperation possible.

One can have a variety of roles in dealing with trade policy issues, or for that matter, in any international negotiation. These include setting policy, being a chief negotiator, a chief advisor to the lead negotiator, or a junior team member. You can be on the outside, not directly part of the negotiation but seeking to influence its outcome or be a cheerleader urging a coalescing of views to bring about progress for the common good. Some results can be very good, some less so, sometimes due to circumstances and sometimes due to pilot error. Making mistakes serves a useful purpose, to mull over what might have been done differently. What makes for a successful negotiator is probably, in most cases, experience. Experience is needed to avoid making mistakes. Making mistakes may be the only way of gaining experience.

My principal mentor in the art of negotiation was the US Trade Representative Robert S. Strauss. He had no intrinsic interest in the substance in detail of what was being negotiated. That sounds harsh, but I can assure you that he was not wedded to one tariff-cutting formula over another for the beauty of the algebra. He wanted to know what the United States needed. He had to figure out what could be sold to the other side, our negotiating partners, and what could be sold at home, to Congress and domestic constituents, industries made up of companies and groups of workers that would benefit from increased trade or feared a burden being imposed on them in the form of heightened foreign competition. He could walk into a room and transform the atmosphere, making the air crackle with electricity. He was often outrageous in a first meeting with negotiators from the other side. (They later became his lifelong friends.) There was always a purpose to the drama, moving a negotiation from being mired, not going anywhere, to one where those present were aligned with getting to a positive outcome. It would not always work, but it worked enough of the time. Strauss would say, perhaps accurately, that he had made a career of turning junk into machinery and sometimes machinery into junk. I only saw the first of these two categories.

Sometimes there was no success at all, such as when he was assigned to solve the Arab–Israeli impasse or to whip domestic inflation. These were tasks that may have been impossible at the time, at least with the tools at hand. He knew enough to move on to other subjects. Where he did not succeed, he left those subjects no worse off. He was Ambassador to the Soviet Union at the moment it was no more, and his remit was suddenly much smaller: Russia. Historians will examine whether he made a difference during that transition, whether more could have been done. Turning points in history are best assessed with enough hindsight to see if any actor changed its course. For most negotiators, the visible results will be apparent immediately. No trade negotiator is judged in the present but on the basis of whether international agreements are reached on their watch and ultimately if these have produced positive results.

What follows is an outline of the elements of negotiating skills based on my own experience, which may not suit all situations or individuals. Over five decades in negotiations in various settings, one would hope to have learned something. But human experience indicates that this is not always the case.

The result I wish to convey succinctly can be summed up in ten points.

FIRST: UNDERSTAND THE FRAMEWORK FOR ANALYSIS

In preparation for an international trade negotiation, there are always three categories of analyses – the facts, the economics, and the rules. In a domestic setting, substitute "law" for "rules" to determine what is feasible. One of the areas requiring major improvement at the WTO is its intelligence gathering and analysis. The world has been fortunate to have personnel at the WTO who rose to the challenge and greatly improved reporting on trade measures being imposed. More resources, as well as enhanced foresight exercises and policy planning, are needed at the WTO, but in member capitals as well.[1] Knowing the rules and having the skills to estimate the economic impact of measures cannot

[1] See Chapter 14 on Improving Trade Intelligence as well as Chapter 14 on Enhancing Secretariat Functions.

provide a sufficient basis for negotiation without having as sound as possible a factual foundation. Knowing the facts is vitally important. Without that knowledge, you are sailing without a working compass or GPS. Government officials may assume from statistics that they are clear on what the facts are. This is usually not the case. It is necessary to go deeper, research is imperative.

SECOND: IDENTIFY YOUR OWN INTERESTS AND NEGOTIATING PARAMETERS

In 1858, in a famous speech made before he was President, Abraham Lincoln said: "If we could first know where we are, and whither we are tending, we could then better judge what to do, and how to do it." In valuing a trade concession to be obtained or granted, it is imperative to know not only how competitive your own industry is, but what the trend is likely to be. You have to be like a successful hedge fund manager. Undervaluing or overvaluing a concession, to be granted or received, is all too easy to do. To do so undermines the value and sustainability of the deal. Prescience is not available. The next best thing is to consult with those who really know the market to be found in the relevant industry and agricultural sector. Those that are engaged in commerce are investing or disinvesting based on their best judgment of where demand is headed. Seek out experts who have devoted their lives to the study of particular parts of the economy.

With a fair amount of knowledge of the facts, you can understand if a concession you are about to give may be highly valued by the other party to the negotiation and therefore better trading stock for you, to be swapped for something with greater potential value from the other side. The United States was able to give up a major form of protection for Scotch whisky in the Tokyo Round because we knew that consumer taste at the time was shifting to white goods – gin and vodka. The United Kingdom may have been as well informed. Removing that perversely creative American trade barrier was a long-term British objective, to which it was very strongly attached. It was worth more to the United Kingdom than it was to the United States.

Setting a value is not just an objective exercise, it is also subjective. One British official told me with respect to Brexit, when I mentioned the UK Treasury estimate of the cost to Britain of future economic growth, that the prime motivation for Brexit was not economic, but to regain a greater measure of sovereignty. Imprecise elements, some psychological, which in this case means political, color any major international negotiation. Negotiations almost always have unquantifiable elements.

When Congress in granting a trade negotiating mandate to the President added a complicated private sector advisory structure made up of no fewer than forty-five committees, we in the US Executive Branch were appalled.[2] We thought it would be an excessive burden. We were wrong. The committees were a source of immense strength not only in helping us know what to give and what not to give at the bargaining table, and what to seek and what was not worth very much in export opportunities, but those who participated as advisors became supporters for the approval and implementation of the negotiated results. The outcome in Congress was a vote of 395–7 in the House of Representatives and 90–4 in the Senate – a result never before achieved and probably one that never will be equaled. This favorable vote was due in no small part to the negotiators understanding US commercial interests and the politics of the negotiated outcome. Acting on this knowledge can and did garner political support. For those who might have been hostile and who might have worked against approval of the trade agreements, engagement in the advisory process was in part responsible for obtaining at least acquiescence in the result. US history is littered with trade agreements signed and not implemented, a failure often if not always caused by miscalculation.[3] Getting the politics wrong is as bad as getting the substance wrong, and the two are often closely related.

It is also imperative to know your negotiating limits. You can lead domestic opinion, but you cannot succeed if you flout it. I got a call from a representative of the Congressional Black Caucus one day during the Tokyo Round. It turned out that the Government Procurement Code was going to eliminate the small business set-aside,[4] something unnoticed up until that point, at least at a political level. What was involved in the set-aside was the ability of largely minority businesses to participate in government contracts. I called my opposite number in the European Communities (the EU's predecessor arrangement) and said, "you don't need this as part of the agreement and we cannot give it, so it is off the table." The reply: "no problem." We each knew the value of the US offer and what could and could not be done.

The bottom line: it was great to receive that call before the cake was baked. Afterwards it could have killed the whole negotiating Round.

THIRD: SET THE OBJECTIVE

Yogi Berra, the famous American baseball player and even more famous phrase-mangling epigrammatist, said: "If you don't know where you are going,

[2] The Trade Act of 1974.

[3] This is possibly the case with the EU–Mercosur FTA as well.

[4] An amount of government contracting reserved through a preference for small, often minority-owned businesses.

you'll end up someplace else." Setting the objective may seem like a straightforward enough requirement, but it is not. To be useful, the objective must actually serve one's interests. It requires an inquiry into what happens if one is successful. A former law partner of mine often said that dogs chase cars but would not know what they would do with one if they caught it.

Also worth asking: what is the cost likely to be in order to achieve success? What opportunities were forgone? What is the cost of failure?

FOURTH: UNDERSTAND THE OTHER SIDE'S INTERESTS AND LIMITATIONS

Knowing the other side's interests should be an obvious requirement for negotiation but it is often ignored. The other side's interests are not necessarily easy to ascertain. It is hard to stand in someone else's shoes. How do they view the trade-offs? What are their economic and political interests? Do they need something as a priority that is not impossible to give them? It would be good to know that to avoid a deadlock later in the process. To get the Tokyo Round concluded, the United States needed to pledge that it was not out to try to destroy the Common Agricultural Policy (CAP). This was a compromise of a key US objective, but a necessity.

Overreach: getting more in an agreement than the other side can deliver leads mostly to default and disappointment. It is imperative to know the other side's actual limits, beyond which no deal is possible as the costs for either side are too great, or a deal reached cannot be implemented. That would be the extreme case. More usually, the cost of failing to know enough about the other side consists of not having a clear picture of where the substance of a possible deal is to be found. Did the United States overestimate what the Chinese government could (or would wish to) deliver in Phase One preferential purchasing?[5]

FIFTH: LEVEL OF AMBITION

The word "ambition" by US negotiators in connection with the Trans-Pacific Partnership (TPP) came to be overused to the point of being positively annoying, but it was worth having as a part of the US negotiating team mission.

[5] Chad Bown. 2022. "US–China Phase One Tracker: China's Purchases of US Goods." Peterson Institute of International Economics. March 11. www.piie.com/research/piie-charts/us-china-phase-one-tracker-chinas-purchases-us-goods. In history, an even larger example was President Taft's negotiations of a US-Canada tariff agreement that was never implemented because it brought down the government of the other negotiator, Canadian Prime Minister Laurier.

At the start of a negotiation, a Venn diagram representing the parties' interests might show very little overlap. If so, no deal would be possible. But with political will, the limits on either side can be stretched (but not broken). It is often necessary for each side to be able to go beyond existing instructions, particularly because those who issue instructions are not usually at the negotiating table. In the military, avoiding this trap is the reason for the doctrine known as "mission command." The invention of the doctrine is attributed to both Prussia and Napoleon.[6] The doctrine combines centralized intent with decentralized execution and promotes freedom of maneuver, speed of action, and initiative, within defined constraints. Subordinates – understanding the commander's intentions, their own missions, and the context of those missions – are told what effect they are to achieve and the reason why it needs to be achieved. They then decide within delegated freedom of action how best to achieve their missions.

It may or may not be useful for the other side to know your limits. Your counterpart's ignorance may facilitate or frustrate reaching an agreement, depending on the circumstances. There will be times when having more on offer than can be delivered may raise the level of where the middle ground is to be found. But this has some obvious risks as well.

An objective set too high can deadlock a negotiation. Set too low, the negotiation may not be worth the effort and may foreclose coming back to the table for a more ambitious outcome. If the perfect is the enemy of the good, so also may be the inadequate. It is hard but not impossible to raise the stakes at each meeting of negotiators, but this can strain trust.

Ambition also raises a question about the shape of a negotiation. There are two schools of thought on this, dealt with a bit later below.

SIXTH: PRAGMATISM AND IDEALISM

When I was in the US government, an assignment that I was given was to negotiate with US trading partners the level of allowable US imports of specialty steels (various types of stainless steel and alloy tool steel). This was a safeguard action in which the President had decided to grant relief. As a matter of principle, the Swedish negotiators would not agree to limit Sweden's exports to the United States. So Swedish exports were put into a basket quota

6 "ADP 6-0 Mission Command – Command and Control of Army Forces." US Department of the Army. 2012. "Mission command is the exercise of authority and direction by the commander using mission orders to enable disciplined initiative within the commander's intent to empower agile and adaptive leaders in the conduct of unified land operations."

with other nonsignatories, which meant that the entry of imports into the United States would be on a first-come, first-served basis. This could not have been good for Swedish specialty steel exports. The Swedish government chose to act on principle, but it may have been tinged with pragmatism. It presumably did not want to establish the precedent of agreeing to export restrictions. Maybe this was the best longer-term policy for Sweden, even though it was not at that moment the best commercial outcome for Swedish industry.

Another example comes to mind. When I was negotiating to try to get access to the Japanese market for a product that was very politically sensitive for Japan, I was offered market access for all of the American product that could be incorporated into products solely for export back to the United States – that is, the American product as an input would not be allowed to stay in Japan. My idealism and ignorance guided me to reject the deal and settle for a (relatively small) Japanese import quota. The principle that nothing that the United States producers sold could remain in Japan was infuriating. At that time, Japan had held that American skis were not suitable for Japanese snow, that American rice could not match Japanese tastes, and that American aluminum baseball bats made the wrong sound, and none of these should be imported. My reaction was in the circumstances understandable. What was unknown to me and perhaps to the Japanese side was that Japanese exports to the United States including the US component were going to skyrocket. Was that foreseeable? I very much doubt it, but I should have consulted experts on the American market for the downstream product imported from Japan. Emotions can cloud judgment and can be especially costly when the principle involved is (with hindsight) not worth defending, not in trade terms in the event.

There is also a danger in negotiation of losing focus on what is most important. It does not matter if the language is not idiomatic if the understanding is clear. This is having an eye for the capillary as opposed to going after the main objective, the jugular. There are many other metaphors, "not seeing the forest for the trees" is another. The lesson to be learned: steer away from the nonessentials; do not get distracted by minutia. In my earliest years, my penchant for correcting syntax in negotiating texts was a frivolous misdirection of energy (a fault that I have not fully overcome). A corollary: avoid annoying counterparties with little purpose.

On the other end of the spectrum is the pursuit of principle that serves core national objectives. Every multilateral negotiation should have an element of sustaining and improving the multilateral trading system itself. It is necessary to nurture the structure for the public good, because the endurance, health, and expansion of the global trading system are vitally important to all WTO members, including very much for the United States, which I at the time represented. Lip service to multilateralism is not enough. Deeds are needed. The whole of the deal, the result of a major international negotiation, is worth much more than the sum of its many parts. It is necessary for all WTO members without exception to make a positive net contribution. Each must do so consistent with its capabilities, even the least developed and the most vulnerable. The world trading system is robust, but only with a common agreement that it must remain so, with actions to match.

SEVENTH: LEVERAGE

Traditionally, leverage in a negotiation is achieved through trading stock, concessions which are in your power to make in return for concessions received, and which are desired by others. Of course, the WTO is not hermetically sealed off from its members' other interests. However, the organization of governments is usually not flexible enough to allow concessions under the control of non-trade ministries to be granted in trade negotiations.

Leverage may also take the form of a legal right. This can be reinforced with WTO litigation and can lead to a negotiated settlement. In a safeguard action or unilateral threat of trade restrictions, the leverage can be the threatened or imposed trade measure. The leverage involved is the power to control the market.

In the WTO, leverage can take the form of a threatened or actual veto (of anything, which amounts to hostage-taking, common in many legislatures around the world). This form of leverage will likely persist as long as the WTO practice is maintained that all decisions must be taken by consensus, interpreted as unanimity. I have not heard any WTO member say that it wanted the Organization to operate on any other basis. However, overuse of the veto may lead to the consensus rule being curtailed or extinguished.

Leverage can take the form of public opinion or peer pressure in some cases. Decades ago, a Swedish claim of national security reasons for protecting footwear imports for military use was met with derision. Derision does not always work to restrain countries from taking trade measures, in which case retaliation may do so. This may have played a role in the case of the rollback of some of the Trump administration's tariffs on steel and aluminum imports. It is also possible that the larger objective of obtaining a renegotiation of NAFTA proved a stronger inducement to remove the tariffs on imports from America's immediate neighbors than maintaining the protective tariffs.

A substitute for leverage is a shared belief that there is a common interest in outcomes that support the global trading system. If there is no or little systemic interest, what is left to drive a negotiation is narrower: the value of concessions to be granted and received, or economic or political power.

EIGHTH: DEMEANOR AND ENGAGEMENT

Being tough may be required by the circumstances. Being obnoxious is likely to be counterproductive. Even if one's leverage is overwhelming, the deal will likely not be as good as if there had been more cooperation. Losing the respect of one's opposite number across the negotiating table or simply being irritating is likely to have costs for you that may not be apparent. In brief, personal relations matter, for better communication, and for building trust, to enable more far-reaching results to be obtained.

Most of the above discussion has concerned dealing with one other negotiating partner. I have also experienced multiparty negotiations in several roles, as an advisor to the US government, as someone seeking to promote specific outcomes in the TPP and in the Uruguay and Tokyo Rounds, as the first chairman of the OECD Steel Committee, by chairing the Trade Policy Review Group (the highest level of the US government for coordinating US trade policy in detail), by being involved in the activities of the World Semiconductor Council as a member of the US delegation, by chairing committees on comparative innovation policy at the US National Academies, by co-chairing meetings for the National Academies with China and with delegations from other countries, and as a draftsman moving a text forward to an agreed conclusion.

Being a scribe and being a chair are roles that have some common characteristics. Holding the pen or holding the gavel is very useful. One has to be neutral among parties but not as to whether there are results. For obtaining results, one has to be a dedicated partisan. One has to be very sensitive to what is taking place in the room and the corridors outside the room. One has to pull back when insuperable obstacles are encountered and find other paths forward. It is at times two steps forward and one step back. There is a premium on having the right attitude, that the effort is worth undertaking and that success with sufficient investment of effort is possible, that you believe it and can convey it.

In a multilateral or bilateral setting, there is no substitute for direct engagement. Masses of background reading or other preparation are not a substitute for talking with the other party or parties. There are nuances that do not appear in formal statements, glimmers of possibilities that may be discerned. The chief skill is, perhaps, the ability to listen very carefully to all the parties to find common ground. One does not have the luxury of researching each party's objectives and limits. Onc is rclying on instinct and what you learn from other parties in the process. Hearing what is said and interpreting it, one can adjust the common draft. This is what took place with a project called "regional support" (a euphemism for subsidies) in the global semiconductor industry.

Semiconductors have been called the crude oil of the information age, oil having given us the use of internal combustion engines and fuel for the prior industrial age. Computer chips provide the basis for communication and computing, the basis for the information age. They are as essential to the global economy today as oil had been in prior times. Annual sales of the global industry amount to about a $600 billion annual rate based on the most recent monthly data (SIA press release of July 2022), with a growth rate of 18 percent year on year. It is truly a global industry, with chips designed in one location, "fabbed" (short for fabricated, manufactured) in another, tested elsewhere, imbedded in some other place, and shipped as part of electronic equipment to every country. It was my good fortune to have been trade counsel to the US semiconductor industry association for almost all of my time in private law practice spanning nearly four decades.

One of the global industry's concerns in recent years has been government-led industrial policies aimed at promoting domestic semiconductor sectors. Two parallel fora have been discussing the issue, one at the level of industry CEOs in the World Semiconductor Council (WSC), and the other at the level of officials in the Government and Authorities Meeting on Semiconductors (GAMS). In October 2017, an agreement was reached at the eighteenth annual GAMS held in Busan, South Korea, from October 30 to November 2, 2020.

What is remarkable about the agreement is that it addresses one of the most difficult current areas of concern in international trade today, and that it was supported by China, the United States, Chinese Taipei, Korea, Japan, and the European Union. This is how the agreement has been described: in its statement in support of the regional support guidelines and practices, the GAMS highlighted that regional support programs should be "guided by the principles of openness, transparency, inclusiveness, non-discrimination, and respect WTO rules." It further noted, "government action should be guided by market-based principles, and that competitiveness of companies and their products, not the intervention of governments and authorities, should be the principal driver of innovation, industrial success, and international trade."[7]

7 "Agreement on Regional Support Guidelines Headlines Meeting of Global Semiconductor Industry, Governments." Semiconductor Industry Association. November 20, 2017.

The existence of the agreement among this set of countries competing vigorously in this sector demonstrates that it is possible to agree on a very sensitive issue. The fact that self-restraint was obtained was laudable. The fact that massive subsidization by all parties followed illustrates that no agreement can stand in the way of forces of nature, the same way that the Kellogg–Briand pact calling for peace could not stand in the way of a world war.[8]

Lesson: success may be fleeting.

NINTH: THE SHAPE OF THE DEAL

Harking back again to a bygone era of negotiating rounds, the driving force during the Tokyo and Uruguay Rounds was the size of what was on offer. It was not an option to walk away, especially from the Uruguay Round, when there was no original GATT left to govern trade for any not joining the Single Undertaking. It is not yet clear whether that dynamic will work again in the multilateral trading system. On a much smaller scale, it did seem to be a driving force at MC12. There were trade-offs on the table, but none so large as to cause a country to walk away. Multiple simultaneous negotiations are burdensome and complex. There can be hostage-taking tying up everything. A convoy system, in which the slowest, most reluctant vessel sets the pace for the entire group of nations means that nothing will take place. However, trade-offs are more possible if more than one area is being negotiated. A net positive balance for any party in one agreement can offset a net negative balance for it in another agreement.

The opposite school of thought is that in an age of self-absorption, nationalism, and populism, the common good may be lost sight of, and a multi-subject negotiation will get bogged down by its sheer weight. The absence of a largely benevolent hegemon makes a larger negotiating package of agreements something of a Rubik's Cube which has been dipped in super-glue.[9]

www.semiconductors.org/agreement-on-regional-support-guidelines-headlines-meeting-of-global-semiconductor-industry-governments/

8 "The Kellogg–Briand Pact, 1928." US Department of State – Office of the Historian. www.history.state.gov/milestones/1921-1936/kellogg. "The Kellogg–Briand Pact was an agreement to outlaw war signed on August 27, 1928 … the pact was one of many international efforts to prevent another World War, but it had little effect in stopping the rising militarism of the 1930s or preventing World War II."

9 A puzzle consisting of a cube with colored faces made of smaller colored blocks attached to a spindle in the center, the object being to rotate the blocks until each face of the cube is a single color.

TENTH: ATTITUDE AND PERSEVERANCE

The belief that no agreement is possible is self-defeating. Realism is needed but only to a measured degree. The status quo is usually not preordained; it just happens. Pessimism is infectious, but so is optimism. I have seen a leader walk into a room and change the dynamic. It is rare but not unknown. People matter, not just the substance of what is being negotiated. Both leadership and trust depend on the individuals involved. Some limits are imposed by the context, at home and internationally, but the worst limits are those that are self-imposed. It would take supernatural luck for pessimism to ever accomplish anything. A full dose of optimism, with a dotted line connection to reality, is needed. Everyone who seeks to be a negotiator should look in the mirror and ask that image: "Why are you here? If not now, when? If not me, who?" Creativity is needed. Negotiations reach apparent impasses for which alternative solutions are needed. Defeatism (being excessively "realistic") is not an approach likely to lead to success.

CONCLUSION

There cannot be 100 percent clarity in making negotiating decisions. Risks need to be taken. Where there is little or no risk-taking, there will likely be limited or no results. Bureaucrats are characterized as being risk averse. Negotiators cannot be. Often a political level needs to be brought in to get through seeming impasses. That is one reason why there is a need for involving the political level.

Those who issue instructions can more easily amend them, go beyond them. There are also times to ignore instructions, if what matters is the result. When I took over the chair of the US delegation to the Tokyo Round negotiations, I was told that I would receive a cable (pre-internet days) confirming that I could accept a particular EU proposal involving agriculture. I went into a meeting and did accept it. The cable with instructions arrived, and it was the opposite of what I expected. I went to see my European Communities counterpart, showed him the instruction, and asked whether he could think of a way that his proposal squared with the cable. He could not. I therefore called the White House and told the President's chief economic advisor what had just taken place. He asked, "Did the talks break down?" I replied that they had not. He said, then it was fine. One lesson: catastrophes that occur during negotiations are usually recoverable. Take a deep breath and soldier on.

Participants need to be taken out of their comfort zones, if they have proved to get them nowhere. Often it is the political level that is needed to close the gap at the end. It is also the field commanders, the negotiators, who need to exceed their instructions to move to a deal. If you are right, you are a hero. If not, well, perhaps the next time. Often enough, it is self-imposed limitations rather than external ones that impair a negotiator's ability to reach desired results.

Select Bibliography

"Chronological List of Disputes Cases." World Trade Organization. www.wto.org/english/tratop_e/dispu_e/dispu_status_e.htm

Bacchus, James and Simon Lester. 2019. "Trade Justice Delayed Is Trade Justice Denied: How to Make WTO Dispute Settlement Faster and More Effective." Cato Institute, Washington, DC. www.cato.org/free-trade-bulletin/trade-justice-delayed-trade-justice-denied-how-make-wto-dispute-settlement

Bhagwati, Jagdish and Arvind Panagariya. 1996. "The Theory of Preferential Trade Agreements: Historical Evolution and Current Trends." *American Economic Review* 86(2): 82–87.

Bown, Chad P. 2009. *Self-Enforcing Trade: Developing Countries and WTO Dispute Settlement*. Washington, DC: Brookings Institution Press.

2022a. "How COVID-19 Medical Supply Shortages Led to Extraordinary Trade and Industrial Policy." *Asian Economic Policy Review* 17: 114–135.

2022b. "Trump Ended WTO Dispute Settlement: Trade Remedies Are Needed to Fix It." Peterson Institute for International Economics, Washington, DC. www.piie.com/sites/default/files/documents/wp22-1.pdf

Cahill, Carmel, Stefan Tangermann, Lars Brink, Shenggen Fan, Joseph W. Glauber, Anabel Gonzalez, et al. 2021. "New Pathways for Progress in Multilateral Trade Negotiations in Agriculture." International Food Policy Research Institute. www.ifpri.org/publication/new-pathways-progress-multilateral-trade-negotiations-agriculture

Curzon, Gerard. 1965. *Multilateral Commercial Diplomacy: The General Agreement on Tariffs and Trade and Its Impact on National Commercial Policies and Techniques*. London: Michael Joseph.

Dadush, Uri and Chiedu Osakwe eds. 2015. *WTO Accessions and Trade Multilateralism: Case Studies and Lessons from the WTO at Twenty*. Cambridge: Cambridge University Press.

Dam, Kenneth W. 2004. "Cordell Hull, The Reciprocal Trade Agreement Act, and the WTO." The Brookings Institution, Washington, DC. www.brookings.edu/wp-content/uploads/2016/06/20041010dam.pdf

Ding, Ru. 2014. "'Public Body' or Not: Chinese State-Owned Enterprise." *Journal of World Trade* 48(1): 167–189.

Drache, Daniel. 2000. "The Short but Significant Life of the International Trade Organization: Lessons for Our Time." Centre for the Study of Globalisation and Regionalisation Working Paper No. 62/00, University of Warwick, Coventry. http://wrap.warwick.ac.uk/2063/1/WRAP_Drache_wp6200.pdf

Eckes, Alfred E. ed. 2000. *Revisiting US Trade Policy: Decisions in Perspective*. Athens: Ohio University Press.

Evenett, Simon J. 2019. "Protectionism, State Discrimination, and International Business Since the Onset of the Global Financial Crisis." *Journal of International Business Policy* 2: 9–36.

Evenett, Simon J. and Richard Baldwin eds. 2020. *Revitalising Multilateralism: Pragmatic Ideas for the New WTO Director-General*. London: Centre for Economic Policy Research Press. https://cepr.org/voxeu/columns/revitalising-multilateralism-new-ebook

Gao, Henry. 2018. "Digital or Trade? The Contrasting Approaches of China and US to Digital Trade." *Journal of International Economic Law* 21(2): 297–321.

2022. "E-Commerce Governance: Back to Geneva?" Centre for International Governance Innovation, Waterloo. www.cigionline.org/articles/e-commerce-governance-back-to-geneva/

Gardner, Richard N. 1969. *Sterling–Dollar Diplomacy: The Origins and the Prospects of Our International Economic Order*. New York: McGraw-Hill Book Company.

Glauber, Joseph W., Jonathan Hepburn, David Laborde, and Sophia Murphy. 2020. "What National Farm Policy Trends Could Mean for Efforts to Update WTO Rules on Domestic Support." International Institute for Sustainable Development, Winnipeg. www.iisd.org/system/files/2020-08/farm-policy-trends-en.pdf

Hillman, Jennifer. 2018. "Three Approaches to Fixing the World Trade Organization: The Good, the Bad and the Ugly?" Institute of International Economic Law, Georgetown University, Washington, DC. www.law.georgetown.edu/wp-content/uploads/2018/12/Hillman-Good-Bad-Ugly-Fix-to-WTO-AB.pdf

Hoekman, Bernard and Petros C. Mavroidis. 2020. "Burning Down the House." In *Twenty-First Century Trade Policy: Back to the Past?*, edited by Bernard Hoekman and Ernesto Zedillo. Washington, DC: Brookings Institution Press.

2020. "Preventing the Bad from Getting Worse: The End of the World (Trade Organization) As We Know It?" Global Governance Programme Working Paper No. RSCAS 2020/06, European University Institute – Robert Schuman Centre for Advanced Studies, Florence. https://scholarship.law.columbia.edu/cgi/viewcontent.cgi?article=3610&context=faculty_scholarship

2020. "To AB or Not to AB? Dispute Settlement in WTO Reform." *Journal of International Economic Law* 23(3): 1–20.

Hoekman, Bernard, Constantine Michalopoulos, and L. Alan Winters. 2003. "More Favorable and Differential Treatment of Developing Countries: Toward a New Approach in the World Trade Organization." World Bank Group, Washington, DC. www.elibrary.worldbank.org/doi/pdf/10.1596/1813-9450-3107

Hoekman, Bernard, Petros C. Mavroidis, and Maarja Saluste. 2021. "Informing WTO Reform: Dispute Settlement Performance, 1995–2020." *Journal of World Trade* 55(1): 1–50.

Hudec, Robert. 2010. *Developing Countries in the GATT Legal System*. Cambridge: Cambridge University Press.

Jackson, John H. 1969. *World Trade and the Law of GATT: A Legal Analysis of the General Agreement on Tariffs and Trade*. Indianapolis, IN: Bobbs-Merrill Company.

2000. "The Role and Effectiveness of the WTO Dispute Settlement Mechanism." Brookings Trade Forum: 179–236.

Lester, Simon and James Bacchus. 2019. "Of Precedent and Persuasion: The Crucial Role of an Appeals Court in WTO Disputes." Cato Institute, Washington, DC. www.cato.org/free-trade-bulletin/precedent-persuasion-crucial-role-appeals-court-wto-disputes#the-creation-of-the-appellate-body

Low, Patrick, Hamid Mamdouh, and Evan Rogerson. 2018. "Balancing Rights and Obligations in The WTO – A Shared Responsibility." Government Offices of Sweden, Stockholm. www.swedenabroad.se/globalassets/ambassader/fn-geneve/documents/balancing-rights-and-obligations-in-the-wto.pdf

McDougall, Robert. 2018. "Crisis in the WTO: Restoring the WTO Dispute Settlement Function." Centre for International Governance Innovation, Waterloo. https://www.cigionline.org/static/documents/documents/Paper%20no.194.pdf

Paugam, Jean-Marie and Anne-Sophie Novel. 2005. "Why and How Differentiate Developing Countries in the WTO? Theoretical Options and Negotiating Solutions." IFRI – Institut Français des Relations Internationales, Paris. www.ifri.org/sites/default/files/atoms/files/novel_paugam_nov_2005.pdf

Payosova, Tetyana, Gary Clyde Hufbauer, and Jeffrey J. Schott. 2018. "The Dispute Settlement Crisis in the World Trade Organization: Causes and Cures." Peterson Institute for International Economics, Washington, DC. www.piie.com/publications/policy-briefs/dispute-settlement-crisis-world-trade-organization-causes-and-cures

Preeg, Earnest H. 1995. *Traders in a Brave New World: The Uruguay Round and the Future of the International Trading System*. Chicago, IL: University of Chicago Press.

Reinsch, William Alan. 2020. "Transparency at the WTO: Why Does Transparency Matter, and Are Members Meeting Their Obligations?" Center for Strategic and International Studies, Washington, DC. www.csis.org/analysis/transparency-wto-why-does-transparency-matter-and-are-members-meeting-their-obligations

Rodrik, Dani. 2011. *The Globalization Paradox: Democracy and the Future of the World Economy*. New York: W. W. Norton.

Schmidt, John. 2015. "How We Created the WTO: A Memoir." *The Wilson Quarterly*, Woodrow Wilson International Center for Scholars, Washington, DC. www.wilsonquarterly.com/quarterly/summer-2015-an-age-of-connectivity/a-world-of-hopes-and-a-world-of-fears-how-we-created-the-wto/

Schott, Jeffrey J. and Euijin Jung. 2019. "The WTO's Existential Crisis: How to Salvage Its Ability to Settle Trade Disputes." Peterson Institute for International Economics, Washington, DC. www.piie.com/publications/policy-briefs/wtos-existential-crisis-how-salvage-its-ability-settle-trade-disputes

Schwob, Claude. 2007. "Keynes, Meade, Robbins and the International Trade Organization." *L'Actualité Économique* 83(2): 255–283.

Silverman, Jared R. 1996. "Multilateral Resolution over Unilateral Retaliation: Adjudicating the Use of Section 301 before the WTO." *University of Pennsylvania Journal of International Law* 17(1): 233–294.

Steger, Debra P. ed. 2010. *Redesigning the World Trade Organization for the Twenty-First Century*. Waterloo: Centre for International Governance Innovation.

Stiglitz, Joseph. 2017. *Globalization and Its Discontents Revisited: Anti-Globalization in the Era of Trump*. New York: W. W. Norton.

Trachtman, Joel P. 2017. "WTO Trade and Environment Jurisprudence: Avoiding Environmental Catastrophe." *Harvard International Law Journal* 58(2): 273–309.

Van Damme, Isabelle. 2009. *Treaty Interpretation by the WTO Appellate Body*. Oxford: Oxford University Press.

VanGrasstek., Craig. 2013. *The History and Future of the World Trade Organization*. Geneva: World Trade Organization.

Wolfe, Robert. 2018. "Is World Trade Organization Information Good Enough? How a Systematic Reflection by Members on Transparency Could Promote Institutional Learning." Bertelsmann Stiftung High-Level Board of Experts on the Future of Global Trade Governance, Gütersloh. http://aei.pitt.edu/102529/1/MT_Is_World_Trade_Organization_Information_Good_Enough.pdf

Wu, Mark. 2016. "The 'China, Inc.' Challenge to Global Trade Governance." *Harvard International Law Journal* 57(2): 260–324.

Zhou, Weihuan, Henry S. Gao, and Xue Bai. 2019. "Building a Market Economy through WTO-Inspired Reform of State-Owned Enterprises in China." *International and Comparative Law Quarterly* 68(4): 977–1022.

Index